HEBREWS

THE NEW TESTAMENT LIBRARY

Luke Timothy Johnson

Hebrews
A Commentary

Westminster John Knox Press
LOUISVILLE • LONDON

Book design by Jennifer K. Cox

First edition
Published by Westminster John Knox Press
Louisville, Kentucky

This book is printed on acid-free paper that meets the American National Standards Institute Z39.48 standard. ♾

PRINTED IN THE UNITED STATES OF AMERICA

09 10 11 12 13 14 15 — 10 9 8 7 6 5 4 3 2

Library of Congress Cataloging-in-Publication Data

Johnson, Luke Timothy.
Hebrews : a commentary / Luke Timothy Johnson.—1st ed.
p. cm. — (The New Testament library)
Includes bibliographical references (p.).
ISBN-13: 978-0-664-22118-8
ISBN-10: 0-664-22118-1
1. Bible. N.T. Hebrews—Commentaries. I. Title. II. Series.

BS2775.53.J64 2006
227'.87077—dc22 2005058568

To Joy, always, everywhere, in all kinds of weather

CONTENTS

Preface ix

Acknowledgments xi

A Note on the Greek Text xiii

Abbreviations xv

Bibliography xvii

Introduction 1

- Hebrews in the Christian Tradition 3
- Hebrews as a First-Century Composition 8
  - Language 8
  - Literary Form 9
  - Symbolic World 15
  - Argument 31
- The Circumstances of Composition 32
  - Rhetorical Situation 33
  - Date 38
  - Author 40
- The Theological Challenge of Hebrews 44
  - Living God, Living Word 45
  - Mature Teaching of the Christ 48
  - The Path of Discipleship 56

COMMENTARY

1:1–4 Prologue 63

1:5–14 Scripture Proves That the Son Is Greater Than the Angels 74

Excursus 1: Why the Angels?		82
2:1–9	We Cannot Neglect So Great a Salvation	84
2:10–18	The Son and His Brothers	93
3:1–6	The Son Is Greater Than Moses	104
3:7–19	Warning against Faithlessness	111
Excursus 2: The Wilderness as Paradigm		119
4:1–13	The Sabbath Rest of God	122
4:14–5:10	Jesus the Great High Priest	137
Excursus 3: Suffering and the Obedience of Faith		149
5:11–6:12	Exhortation to Progress and Perseverance	152
6:13–20	God Secures the Promise with an Oath	167
7:1–10	Abraham and Melchizedek	173
Excursus 4: The Mysterious Melchizedek		181
7:11–19	The Change of Priesthood	183
7:20–28	The Son Is an Eternal High Priest	190
8:1–6	The Son Is Mediator of a New Covenant	196
8:7–13	The Promise of a New Covenant	203
Excursus 5: Old and New Covenants		210
9:1–10	The Worship of the Old Covenant	215
Excursus 6: Sanctuaries Material and Ideal		227
9:11–28	Christ's Worship in Heaven	232
10:1–18	The Efficacy of Christ's Priestly Act	246
10:19–31	Exhortation to Enter and Not Fall Away	254
10:32–39	Memory of the Past as Encouragement for the Future	267
11:1–7	The Faith of the Ancients	274
11:8–22	The Faith of the Patriarchs	286
11:23–31	The Faith of Moses and the Israelites	297
11:32–40	The Faith of Many Witnesses	304
Excursus 7: In Praise of Israel's Heroes		310
12:1–17	Exhortation to Join the Pilgrimage of Faith	312
12:18–29	Approaching the Living God	326
13:1–17	Exhortation to Faithful Living in Community	336
13:18–25	Final Prayers and Greeting	351

Indexes **361**

PREFACE

The closer I get to the end of my scholarly life, the more aware I become of the powerful influence exerted on my endeavors by early reading. The long hours working through the intricacies of Hebrews have afforded many opportunities to remember two authors I read in the hot Louisiana summer of 1964, when I was a young Benedictine monk. During my retreat before making simple profession, I walked the dusty back roads of the abbey reading Ceslaus Spicq's monumental commentary on Hebrews, and grew excited by the world of learning he made available and intrigued by the way in which this composition resisted even his impressive skills in historical sleuthing. Ceslaus Spicq was one of the great pioneers of Catholic critical biblical scholarship, and I am both honored and humbled by the chance to study the same composition to which he gave such extraordinary erudition and energy. During the same period, I was also reading Dom Columba Marmion's *Christ the Ideal of the Priest*, and *Christ the Ideal of the Monk*, and like many other religious of my generation, found in his passionate reading of Scripture, especially of Hebrews, a sense of discipleship as a pilgrimage toward God that is walked through obedient faith.

I have tried in this commentary to honor both early influences, emulating Spicq through a serious examination of Hebrews within its symbolic world and historical circumstances, and imitating Marmion through an engagement with the theological voice of Hebrews, especially in its challenge to contemporary notions. I have also profited by the work of other scholars, above all Harold Attridge, whose commentary proves more valuable the more closely it is interrogated, and David deSilva, whose work on the theme of honor and shame in Hebrews has deeply influenced my reading even where I do not explicitly acknowledge it. Modest footnotes scattered throughout the present commentary indicate some places where my views intersect those of others and provide some leads for further reading. From beginning to end, though, my effort has been to stay closely focused on the language and argument of Hebrews, inviting the reader to think with me as I try to think with the ancient author.

I am delighted to acknowledge as well the many contributions made by others during the two difficult years devoted primarily to this task. Thanks to David Charnon for very early research work, and extravagant thanks for the amazing research, organizational, and editorial abilities of Andrea Tucker, who has put exactly what I needed when I needed it in my hands. Her work and mine was made easier by the remarkable resources and staff of the Pitts Theological Library at Candler School of Theology. For hallway conversations and consultations, thanks to my colleagues Carl Holladay and Steve Kraftchick. Thanks to David Fleer for the invitation to lecture on Hebrews at Rochester College and work out some basic ideas. Thanks to my editor, Clifton Black, who has nudged me, ever so gently, toward completion of a project promised long ago. Most of all, thanks to Joy, who is my own hero of faith, as well as my dearest companion on this sometimes difficult pilgrimage to the city of the Living God.

LUKE TIMOTHY JOHNSON
EMORY UNIVERSITY
JUNE 15, 2005

ACKNOWLEDGMENTS

Biblical citations apart from Hebrews are taken from the Revised Standard Version, the New American Bible, the New Revised Standard Version, or the New International Version; some have been modified in light of the original language. Quotations from Philo and Josephus, as well as all other Greek authors, come from the Loeb Classical Library (Cambridge: Harvard University Press). Citations from the Qumran writings are drawn from F. García Martínez, ed., *The Dead Sea Scrolls Translated: The Qumran Texts in English*, translated by W. G. E. Watson, 2nd ed. (Grand Rapids: Eerdmans, 1996). All other citations from Second Temple Judaism are taken from J. H. Charlesworth, ed., *The Old Testament Pseudepigrapha*, 2 vols. (New York: Doubleday, 1983, 1985). Short titles and abbreviations of nonbiblical works are standard and found in these sources.

A NOTE ON THE GREEK TEXT

The translation of Hebrews in this commentary is based on the Greek text found in the twenty-seventh revised edition of *Novum Testamentum Graece*, edited by Barbara and Kurt Aland, Johannes Karavidopoulos, Carlo M. Martini, and Bruce M. Metzger (Stuttgart: Deutsche Bibelgesellschaft, 1998). I provide fairly extensive notes concerning alternative readings found in important Greek manuscripts, particularly in the great uncials and some papyri. A word on the character of the most frequently cited witnesses may be helpful. P^{46} is known as the second Chester Beatty Papyrus, and dates from about the year 200. It contains all of Hebrews, which it places after Romans in the Pauline letters. P^{13} contains substantial portions of Hebrews, and probably comes from the early fourth century. Among the uncials, most familiar to readers will be Codex Sinaiticus (א), discovered on Mount Sinai, dating from the fourth century, and containing the entire composition, and Codex Vaticanus (B), also from the fourth century, which has all of the letter up to 9:14. Perhaps less familiar are three other uncials, each an important witness. Although it contains an inferior text in the Gospels, Codex Alexandrinus (A), dated in the fifth century, is an excellent witness for the rest of the New Testament. Codex Ephraemi (C) is another fifth-century uncial, with a special character. It is often called *Rescriptus* ("rewritten"), because the manuscript is a palimpsest: the text of the New Testament needed to be recovered from the sermons of St. Ephraem, which had been written over it. Finally, Codex Claromontanus (D, D^p, or D^2) is a sixth-century manuscript containing only the Pauline letters—including Hebrews. It is a bilingual manuscript, with Greek and Latin written in separate columns. Each of these codices also contains scribal corrections and comments, and in the notes I refer to the "first hand" or "second corrector" with reference to certain readings. It might be worth stating, finally, that although one task of the text critic is to get as close as possible to the composition as the author wrote it, the actual scriptural text for Christians throughout the ages consisted in precisely these multiple and fragmentary witnesses.

Readers may find some of the cross-references to the Old Testament (especially the Psalms) confusing, for I consistently refer to the Septuagint (LXX) rather than the Hebrew (MT) text. The reason is simply that this is the version to which the author of Hebrews made references, and my citations have to do with specific Greek diction found in the LXX and not in the MT.

ABBREVIATIONS

AB	Anchor Bible
ABD	*Anchor Bible Dictionary*. Edited by D. N. Freedman. 5 vols. New York: Doubleday, 1992
AnBib	Analecta Biblica
AUSS	*Andrews University Seminary Studies*
BGU	*Ägyptische Urkunden aus den Königlichen Staatlichen Museen zu Berlin, Griechische Urkunden*
Bib	*Biblica*
BJRL	*Bulletin of the John Rylands Library*
BSac	*Bibliotheca sacra*
BTB	*Biblical Theology Bulletin*
BZ	*Biblische Zeitschrift*
BZNW	Beihefte zur Zeitschrift für die neutestamentliche Wissenschaft
CBQ	*Catholic Biblical Quarterly*
CBQMS	Catholic Biblical Quarterly Monograph Series
CBR	*Currents in Biblical Research*
diss.	dissertation
ETR	*Etudes théologiques et religieuses*
EvQ	*Evangelical Quarterly*
ExpT	*Expository Times*
FS	Festschrift
HSS	Harvard Semitic Studies
HTR	*Harvard Theological Review*
Int	*Interpretation*
JBL	*Journal of Biblical Literature*
JETS	*Journal of the Evangelical Theological Society*
JOTT	*Journal of Translation and Textlinguistics*
JSJ	*Journal for the Study of Judaism in the Persian, Hellenistic, and Roman Periods*
JSNT	*Journal for the Study of the New Testament*
JSNTSup	Journal for the Study of the New Testament Supplements

JTS	*Journal of Theological Studies*
KEK	Kritisch-exegetischer Kommentar über das Neue Testament
KJV	King James Version
LXX	Septuagint
MS(s)	manuscript(s)
MT	Masoretic Text
NAB	New American Bible
Neot	*Neotestamentica*
NIV	New International Version
NovT	*Novum Testamentum*
NovTSup	Novum Testamentum Supplements
NRSV	New Revised Standard Version
NRT	*Nouvelle revue théologique*
NTS	*New Testament Studies*
OGIS	*Orientis graeci inscriptiones selectae*
PG	Patrologia graeca
REAug	*Revue des études augustiniennes*
ResQ	*Restoration Quarterly*
RevQ	*Revue de Qumran*
RSR	*Recherches de science religeuse*
RSV	Revised Standard Version
SBLDS	Society of Biblical Literature Dissertation Series
SBLMS	Society of Biblical Literature Monograph Series
SBT	Studies in Biblical Theology
SE	*Studia evangelica*
SJLA	Studies in Judaism in Late Antiquity
SJT	*Scottish Journal of Theology*
SNTSMS	Society for New Testament Study Monograph Series
SR	*Studies in Religion*
ST	*Studia theologica*
TDNT	*Theological Dictionary of the New Testament*. Edited by G. Kittel and G. Friedrich. Translated by G. W. Bromiley. 10 vols. Grand Rapids: Eerdmans, 1965–76
TJ	*Trinity Journal*
TynBul	*Tyndale Bulletin*
WA	Luther's *Werke,* Weimarer Ausgabe
WMANT	Wissenschaftliche Monographien zum Alten und Neuen Testament
WTJ	*Westminster Theological Journal*
WUNT	Wissenschaftliche Untersuchungen zum Neuen Testament
ZAW	*Zeitschrift für die alttestamentliche Wissenschaft*
ZNW	*Zeitschrift für die neutestamentliche Wissenschaft*

BIBLIOGRAPHY

Commentaries

In the commentary that follows, commentaries are cited by author and page number.

Attridge, H. W. *The Epistle to the Hebrews: A Commentary on the Epistle to the Hebrews*. Hermeneia. Philadelphia: Fortress Press, 1989.

Braun, H. *An die Hebräer*. Handbuch zum Neuen Testament 14. Tübingen: Mohr (Siebeck), 1984.

Bruce, F. F. *The Epistle to the Hebrews: The English Text with Introduction, Exposition, and Notes*. New International Commentary on the New Testament. Rev. ed. Grand Rapids: Eerdmans, 1964.

Buchanan, G. W. *To the Hebrews: Translation, Comment and Conclusions*. AB 36. Garden City, NY: Doubleday, 1972.

Craddock, F. B. "The Letter to the Hebrews: Introduction, Commentary, and Reflections." Pages 3–173 in vol. 12 of the *New Interpreter's Bible*. Nashville: Abingdon, 1998.

deSilva, D. A. *Perseverance in Gratitude: A Socio-Rhetorical Commentary on the Epistle "to the Hebrews*." Grand Rapids: Eerdmans, 2000.

Ellingworth, P. *The Epistle to the Hebrews: A Commentary on the Greek Text*. New International Greek Testament Commentary. Grand Rapids: Eerdmans, 1993.

Grässer, E. *An die Hebräer*. 3 vols. Evangelisch-katholischer Kommentar zum Neuen Testament 17. Zurich: Benziger, 1990, 1993, 1997.

Grelot, P. *Une lecture de L'Épître aux Hébreux*. Lire la Bible. Paris: Cerf, 2003.

Guthrie, D. *The Letter to the Hebrews: An Introduction and Commentary*. Tyndale New Testament Commentaries. Grand Rapids: Eerdmans, 1983.

Hagner, D. A. *Hebrews*. New International Commentary 14. Peabody, MA: Hendrickson, 1983.

Hegermann, H. *Der Brief an die Hebräer*. Theologischer Handkommentar zum Neuen Testament XVI. Berlin: Evangelische Verlaganstalt, 1988.

Héring, J. *The Epistle to the Hebrews*. Translated by A. W. Heathcote and P. J. Allcock. London: Epworth, 1970.

Hughes, P. E. *A Commentary on the Epistle to the Hebrews*. Grand Rapids: Eerdmans, 1977.

Jewett, R. *Letter to Pilgrims: A Commentary on the Epistle to the Hebrews*. New York: Pilgrim, 1981.

Koester, C. R. *Hebrews: A New Translation with Introduction and Commentary*. AB 36. New York: Doubleday, 2001.

Lane, W. L. *Hebrews*. 2 vols. Word Biblical Commentary 47, 47b. Dallas: Word, 1991.

Long, T. G. *Hebrews*. Interpretation: A Bible Commentary for Teaching and Preaching. Louisville: John Knox Press, 1997.

März, C. P. *Hebräerbrief*. Neue Echter Bibel. Würzburg: Echter Verlag, 1989.

Michel, O. *Der Brief an die Hebräer*. KEK 13. Göttingen: Vandenhoeck & Ruprecht, 1949.

Moffat, J. *A Critical and Exegetical Commentary on the Epistle to the Hebrews*. International Critical Commentary. New York: Charles Scribner's Sons, 1924.

Montefiore, H. *A Commentary on the Epistle to the Hebrews*. Harper's New Testament Commentaries. New York: Harper & Row, 1964.

Pfitzner, V. C. *Hebrews*. Abingdon New Testament Commentaries. Nashville: Abingdon, 1977.

Royster, D. *The Epistle to the Hebrews: A Commentary*. Crestwood, NY: St. Vladimir's Seminary Press, 2003.

Schunack, G. *Der Hebräerbrief*. Zürcher Bibelkommentar, NT 14. Zurich: Theologischer Verlag Zürich, 2002.

Spicq, C. *L'Épître aux Hébreux*. 2 vols. Études bibliques. Paris: Gabalda, 1952.

Weiss, H. F. *Der Brief an die Hebräer*. KEK 15. Göttingen: Vandenhoeck & Ruprecht, 1991.

Westcott, B. F. *The Epistle to the Hebrews*. 3rd ed. London: MacMillan, 1909.

Wilson, R. McL. *Hebrews*. New Century Bible Commentary. Grand Rapids: Eerdmans, 1987.

Monographs and Important Articles

Allen, D. L. "The Lukan Authorship of Hebrews: A Proposal." *JOTT* 8 (1996): 1–22.

Anderson, C. P. "Hebrews among the Letters of Paul." *SR* 5 (1975–76): 258–66.

———. "Who Are the Heirs of the New Age in the Epistle to the Hebrews?" Pages 255–77 in *Apocalyptic and the New Testament: Essays in Honor of J. Louis Martyn*. Edited by J. Marcus and M. L. Soards. JSNTSup 24. Sheffield: JSOT Press, 1989.

Anderson, G. "Sacrifice and Sacrificial Offerings." *ABD* 5:870–86.

Anderson, H. "The Jewish Antecedents of the Christology of Hebrews." Pages 512–35 in *The Messiah: Developments in Earliest Judaism and Christianity*. Edited by J. H. Charlesworth. Minneapolis: Fortress Press, 1992.

Andriessen, P. "'Renonçant à la joie qui lui revenait.'" *NRT* 97 (1975): 424–38.

Attridge, H. W. "'Heard Because of His Reverence' (Heb 5:7)." *JBL* 98 (1979): 90–93.

———. "'Let Us Strive to Enter That Rest': The Logic of Hebrews 4:1–11." *HTR* 73 (1980): 279–88.

Barrett, C. K. "The Eschatology of the Epistle to the Hebrews." Pages 363–93 in *The Background of the New Testament and Its Eschatology* (FS C. H. Dodd). Edited by W. D. Davies and D. Daube. Cambridge: Cambridge University Press, 1956.

Barth, M. "The Old Testament in Hebrews: An Essay in Biblical Hermeneutics." Pages 53–78 in *Current Issues in New Testament Interpretation* (FS O. A. Piper). Edited by W. Klassen and G. Snyder. New York: Harper, 1962.

Bateman, H. W. *Early Jewish Hermeneutics and Hebrews 1:5–13: The Impact of Early Jewish Exegesis on the Interpretation of a Significant New Testament Passage*. American University Studies 7: Theology and Religion 193. New York: Peter Lang, 1997.

———. "Two First-Century Messianic Uses of the OT: Heb 1:5–13 and 4QFlor 1.1–19." *JETS* 38 (1995): 11–27.

Becker, E. M., "'Gottes Wort' und 'Unser Wort': Bemerkungen 30 Heb 4, 12–13," BZ 44 (2000) 254–62.

Bénétrau, S. "La foi d'Abel: Hébreux 11/4." *ETR* 54 (1979): 623–30.

Betz, O. "Firmness in Faith: Hebrews 11:11 and Isaiah 28:16." Pages 92–113 in *Scripture: Meaning and Method*. Edited by B. P. Thompson. Hull: Hull University Press, 1987.

Bonnard, P.-E. "La traduction de Hébreux 12,2: 'C'est en vue de la joie que Jesus endura la croix.'" *NRT* 97 (1975): 415–23.

Bonnardière, A. M. La. "L'Épître aux Hébreux dans l'oeuvre de Saint Augustin." *REAug* 3 (1957): 137–62.

Brawley, R. L. "Discursive Structure and the Unseen in Hebrews 2:8 and 11:1: A Neglected Aspect of the Context." *CBQ* 55 (1993): 81–98.

Bruce, F. F. "The Kerygma of Hebrews." *Int* 23 (1969): 3–19.

Cockerill, G. E. "'The Better Resurrection (Heb 11:35)': A Key to the Structure and Rhetorical Purpose of Hebrews 11." *TynBul* 51 (2000): 215–34.

Cody, A. *Heavenly Sanctuary and Liturgy in the Epistle to the Hebrews*. Saint Meinrad, IN: Grail, 1960.

———. *A History of Old Testament Priesthood*. AnBib 35. Rome: Pontifical Biblical Institute Press, 1969.

Cosby, M. R. *The Rhetorical Composition and Function of Hebrews 11*. Macon, GA: Mercer University Press, 1988.

Coste, J. "Notion grecque et notion biblique de la 'souffrance éducatrice' (à propos de l'Hébreux V,8)." *RSR* 43 (1955): 481–523.

Croy, N. C. *Endurance in Suffering: Hebrews 12:1–13 in Its Rhetorical, Religious and Philosophical Context.* SNTSMS 98. Cambridge: Cambridge University Press, 1998.

Dahl, N. A. "A New and Living Way: The Approach to God according to Hebrews 10:19–25." *Int* 5 (1951): 401–12.

D'Angelo, M. R. *Moses in the Letter to the Hebrews.* SBLDS 42. Missoula, MT: Scholars Press, 1979.

Darnell, D. R. "Rebellion, Rest, and the Word of God: An Exegetical Study of Hebrews 3:1–4:13." Ph.D. diss., Duke University, 1973.

Davidson, R. M. "Christ's Entry 'Within the Veil' in Hebrews 6:19–20: The Old Testament Background." *AUSS* 39 (2001): 175–90.

Delcor, M. "Melchizedek from Genesis to the Qumran Texts and the Epistle to the Hebrews." *JSJ* 2 (1971): 115–35.

Delling, G. "*Telos*, etc." *TDNT* 8:49–87.

Demarest, B. A. "Hebrews 7:3: A *Crux Interpretum* Historically Considered." *EvQ* 49 (1977): 141–62.

———. *A History of the Interpretation of Hebrews 7:1–10 from the Reformation to the Present Day.* Tübingen: Mohr (Siebeck), 1976.

deSilva, D. A. *Despising Shame: Honor Discourse and Community Maintenance in the Epistle to the Hebrews.* SBLDS 152. Atlanta: Scholars Press, 1995.

———. "Entering God's Rest: Eschatology and the Socio-Rhetorical Strategy of Hebrews." *TJ* 21 (2000): 25–43.

———. "Exchanging Favor for Wrath: Apostasy in Hebrews and Patron-Client Relationships." *JBL* 115 (1996): 91–116.

———. *The Hope of Glory: Honor Discourse and New Testament Interpretation.* Collegeville, MN: Liturgical Press, 1999.

Dey, L. K. K. *The Intermediary World and Patterns of Perfection in Philo and Hebrews.* SBLDS 25. Missoula, MT: Scholars Press, 1975.

Dodd, C. H., *According to the Scripture: The Substructure of New Testament Theology.* Under Nisbet, 1952.

Dolfe, K.-G. E. "Hebrews 2,16 under the Magnifying Glass." *ZNW* 84 (1993): 289–94.

Dunnill, J. *Covenant and Sacrifice in the Letter to the Hebrews.* SNTSMS 75. Cambridge: Cambridge University Press, 1992.

Eisele, W. *Ein unerschütterliches Reich: Die mittelplatonische Umformung des Parusiegedankens im Hebräerbrief.* BZNW 116. Berlin: de Gruyter, 2003.

Eisenbaum, P. M. "Father and Son: The Christology of Hebrews in Patrilineal Perspective." Pages 127–46 in *A Feminist Companion to the Catholic Epistles and Hebrews.* Edited by A.-J. Levine with M. M. Robbins. Feminist Companion to the New Testament and Early Christian Writings 8. London: T&T Clark, 2004.

———. *The Jewish Heroes of Christian History: Hebrews 11 in Literary Context*. SBLDS 156. Atlanta: Scholars Press, 1997.

Ellingworth, P. *A Handbook on the Letter to the Hebrews*. United Bible Society Handbook Series. New York: United Bible Societies, 1983.

Fensham, F. C. "Hebrews and Qumran." *Neot* 5 (1971): 9–21.

Filson, F. V. *'Yesterday': A Study of Hebrews in the Light of Chapter 13*. SBT 2/4. Naperville, IL: Allenson, 1967.

Fitzmyer, J. A. "Melchizedek in the MT, LXX, and the NT." *Bib* 81 (2000): 63–69.

Flusser, D. "'Today if You Will Listen to His Voice': Creative Jewish Exegesis in Hebrews 3–4." Pages 55–62 in *Creative Biblical Exegesis*. Edited by B. Uffenheimer and H. G. Reventlow. JSOTSup 59. Sheffield: Sheffield Academic Press, 1988.

Fritsch, Ch. T. "*To Antitypon*." Pages 100–107 in *Studia Biblica et Semitica* (FS T. C. Vriezen). Edited by W. C. van Unnik and A. S. van der Woude. Wageningen: Veenman, 1966.

Gardiner, E. N. *Athletics of the Ancient World*. Chicago: Ares, 1980.

Gheorghita, R. *The Role of the Septuagint in Hebrews*. WUNT 2/160. Tübingen: Mohr (Siebeck), 2003.

Gleason, R. C. "The Old Testament Background of Rest in Hebrews 3:7–4:11." *BSac* 157 (2000): 281–303.

Goppelt, L. *Typos: The Typological Interpretation of the Old Testament in the New*. Translated by D. H. Madvig. Grand Rapids: Eerdmans, 1982.

Gray, P. "Brotherly Love and the High Priest Christology of Hebrews." *JBL* 122 (2003): 335–51.

———. *Godly Fear: The Epistle to the Hebrews and Greco-Roman Critiques of Superstition*. Academia Biblica 16. Atlanta: Society of Biblical Literature, 2003.

Greenlee, J. H. "Hebrews 11:11—Sarah's Faith or Abraham's?" *Notes on Translation* 4 (1990): 37–42.

Greer, R. A. *The Captain of Our Salvation: A Study in the Patristic Exegesis of Hebrews*. Tübingen: Mohr (Siebeck), 1973.

Gudorf, M. E. "Through a Classical Lens: Hebrews 2:16." *JBL* 119 (2000): 105–8.

Guthrie, G.H. "Hebrews' Use of the Old Testament: Recent Trends in Research." *CBR* 1.2 (2003): 271–94.

———. *The Structure of Hebrews: A Text-Linguistic Analysis*. NovTSup 73. Leiden: Brill, 1994.

Hahneman, G. M. *The Muratorian Fragment and the Development of the Canon*. Oxford: Clarendon, 1992.

Hamm, D. "Faith in the Epistle to the Hebrews: The Jesus Factor." *CBQ* 52 (1990): 270–91.

Hanson, A. T. "The Reproach of the Messiah in the Epistle to the Hebrews." *SE* 7 (1982): 231–40.

Hay, D. M., *Glory at the Right Hand: Psalm 110 in Early Christianity* (SBLMS 18; Nashville: Abingdon, 1973).
Hays, R. B. *Echoes of Scripture in the Letters of Paul* (New Haven: Yale University Press, 1989.
Hengel, M. *Crucifixion in the Ancient World and the Folly of the Message of the Cross*. Translated by J. Bowden. Philadelphia: Fortress Press, 1977.
Hofius, O. *Katapausis: Die Vorstellung vom endzeitlichen Ruheort im Hebräerbrief*. WUNT 11. Tübingen: Mohr (Siebeck), 1970.
———. *Der Vorhang vor dem Thron Gottes: Eine exegetisch-religionsgeschichtliche Untersuchung zu Hebräer 6, 19f. und 10,19f.* WUNT 14. Tübingen: Mohr, 1972.
Hoppin, R. "The Epistle to the Hebrews Is Priscilla's Letter." Pages 147–70 in *A Feminist Companion to the Catholic Epistles and Hebrews*. Edited by A.-J. Levine with M. M. Robbins. Feminist Companion to the New Testament and Early Christian Writings 8. London: T&T Clark, 2004.
———. *Priscilla, Author of the Epistle to the Hebrews, and Other Essays*. New York: Exposition Press, 1969.
Horbury, W. "The Aaronic Priesthood in the Epistle to the Hebrews." *JSNT* 19 (1983): 43–71.
Horst, P. W. van der. "Sarah's Seminal Emission: Hebrews 11:11 in the Light of Ancient Embryology." Pages 287–302 in *Greeks, Romans, and Christians: Essays in Honor of Abraham J. Malherbe*. Edited by D. L. Balch, E. Ferguson, and W. A. Meeks. Minneapolis: Fortress Press, 1990.
Horton, F. L. *Melchizedek Tradition through the First Five Centuries of the Christian Era and in the Epistle to the Hebrews.* SNTSMS 30. Cambridge: Cambridge University Press, 1976.
Hughes, G. *Hebrews and Hermeneutics: The Epistle to the Hebrews as a New Testament Example of Biblical Interpretation*. SNTSMS 36. Cambridge: Cambridge University Press, 1979.
Hughes, J. J. "Hebrews ix 15ff. and Galatians iii 15ff.: A Study in Covenant Practice and Procedure." *NovT* 21 (1979): 27–96.
Hunt, B. P. "The Epistle to the Hebrews: An Anti-Judaic Treatise?" *SE* 2 (1964): 408–10.
Hurst, L. D. "Apollos, Hebrews, and Corinth: Bishop Montefiore's Theory Examined." *SJT* 38 (1985): 503–13.
———. "The Christology of Hebrews 1 and 2." Pages 151–64 in *The Glory of Christ in the New Testament* (FS G. B. Caird). Edited by L. D. Hurst and N. T. Wright. New York: Clarendon, 1987.
———. *The Epistle to the Hebrews: Its Background of Thought*. SNTSMS 65. Cambridge: Cambridge University Press, 1990.
Irwin, J. "The Use of Hebrews 11:11 as Embryological Proof-Text." *HTR* 71 (1978): 312–16.
Isaacs, M. E. "Hebrews 13.9–16 Revisited." *NTS* 43 (1997): 268–84.

———. *Sacred Space: An Approach to the Theology of the Epistle to the Hebrews*. JSNTSup 73. Sheffield: Sheffield Academic Press, 1992.

Jaeger, W. *Paideia: The Ideals of Greek Culture.* Translated by G. Highet. New York: Oxford University Press, 1939–45.

Jobes, K. H. “Rhetorical Achievement in the Hebrews 10 ‘Misquote’ of Psalm 40.” *Bib* 72 (1991): 387–96.

Johnson, L. T. *Faith's Freedom: A Classic Spirituality for Contemporary Christians*. Minneapolis: Fortress Press, 1990.

———. *The First and Second Letters to Timothy: A New Translation with Introduction and Commentary*. AB 35A. New York: Doubleday, 2001.

———. “Hebrews’ Challenge to Christian Christology and Discipleship.” Pages 11–28 in *Preaching Hebrews*. Edited by D. Fleer and D. Bland. Rochester College Lectures on Preaching 4. Abilene, TX: ACU Press, 2003.

———. “Imagining the world that Scripture Imagines” in C. T. Johnson and W. S. Kurz, *The Future of Catholic Biblical Scholarship.* Grand Rapids: Eerdmans, 2002, 119–142.

———. *The Real Jesus: The Misguided Search for the Historical Jesus and the Truth of the Traditional Gospels*. San Francisco: HarperSanFrancisco, 1996.

———. *Religious Experience in Earliest Christianity: A Missing Dimension in New Testament Studies.* Minneapolis: Fortress Press, 1998.

———. “The Revelatory Body: Notes Toward a Somatic Theology.” Pages 69–89 in *The Phenomenology of the Body*. Edited by D. J. Martino. Pittsburgh: Simon Silverman Phenomenology Center at the University of Duquesne, 2003.

———. “Sacrifice Is the Body Language of Love.” Pages 27–36 in L. T. Johnson, *The Living Gospel.* London: Continuum, 2004.

———. “The Scriptural World of Hebrews.” *Int* 57 (2003): 237–50.

———*Septuagintal Midrash in the Speeches of Acts* (Père Marquette Lecture in Theology 33; Milwaukee: Marquette University Press, 2002).

———. *Sharing Possessions: Mandate and Symbol of Faith.* Overtures to Biblical Theology. Philadelphia: Fortress Press, 1981.

———. “Suffering, Sin, and Scripture.” Pages 11–18 in L. T. Johnson, *The Living Gospel.* London: Continuum, 2004.

———. *The Writings of the New Testament: An Interpretation*. 2nd ed., with Todd Penner. Minneapolis: Fortress Press, 1998.

Johnson, R. W. *Going Outside the Camp: The Sociological Function of the Levitical Critique in the Epistle to the Hebrews*. JSNTSup 209. Sheffield: Sheffield Academic Press, 2001.

Johnsson, W. G. “The Cultus of Hebrews in Twentieth-Century Scholarship.” *ExpT* 89 (1977–78): 104–8.

———. “Defilement and Purgation in the Book of Hebrews.” Ph.D. diss., Vanderbilt University, 1973.

———. "The Pilgrimage Motif in the Book of Hebrews." *JBL* 97 (1978): 239–51.

Johnston, G. "Christ as Archegos." *NTS* 27 (1980–81): 381–85.

Käsemann, E. *The Wandering People of God: An Investigation of the Letter to the Hebrews*. Translated by R. A. Harrisville and I. L. Sandberg. Minneapolis: Augsburg, 1984.

Kennedy, G. A. *The Art of Rhetoric in the Roman World*. Princeton: Princeton University Press, 1972.

———. *New Testament Interpretation through Rhetorical Criticism*. Chapel Hill: University of North Carolina Press, 1984.

Kiley, M. "A Note on Hebrews 5:14." *CBQ* 42 (1980): 501–3.

Koester, C. R. "Hebrews, Rhetoric, and the Future of Humanity." *CBQ* 64 (2002): 103–23.

Koester, H. "'Outside the Camp': Hebrews 13:9–14." *HTR* 55 (1963): 299–315.

Lakoff, G. *Women, Fire, and Dangerous Things: What Categories Reveal about the Mind*. Chicago: University of Chicago Press, 1987.

Lakoff, G., and M. Johnson. *Metaphors We Live By*. Chicago: University of Chicago Press, 1980.

Lee, J. A. L. "Hebrews 5:14 and *Hexis*: A History of Misunderstanding." *NovT* 39 (1997): 151–76.

Lehne, S. "The Concept of the New Covenant in Hebrews." Ph.D. diss., Columbia University, 1989.

Leithart, P. J. "Womb of the World: Baptism and the Priesthood of the New Covenant in Hebrews 10:19–22." *JSNT* 78 (2000): 49–65.

Lewis, J. P. *A Study of the Interpretation of Noah and the Flood in Jewish and Christian Literature*. Leiden: Brill, 1968.

Lewis, T. W. "'. . . And if he shrinks back' (Heb X. 38b)." *NTS* 22 (1975–76): 88–94.

Lightfoot, N. R. "The Saving of the Savior: Hebrews 5:7ff." *ResQ* 16 (1973): 166–73.

Lindars, B. "The Rhetorical Structure of Hebrews." *NTS* 35 (1989): 382–406.

———. *The Theology of the Letter to the Hebrews*. New Testament Theology. Cambridge: Cambridge University Press, 1991.

Loader, W. R. G. *Sohn und Hoherpriester: Eine traditionsgeschichtliche Untersuchung zur Christologie des Hebräerbriefes*. WMANT 53. Neukirchen-Vluyn: Neukirchener Verlag, 1981.

Longenecker, R. "The 'Faith of Abraham' Theme in Paul, James and Hebrews: A Study in the Circumstantial Nature of New Testament Teaching." *JETS* 20 (1977): 203–12.

McCown, W. "The Nature and Function of the Hortatory Sections in the Epistle to the Hebrews." Ph.D. diss., Union Theological Seminary, New York, 1970.

McNamara, M. "Melchizedek: Gen 14, 17–20 in the Targums, in Rabbinic and Early Christian Literature." *Bib* 81 (2000): 1–31.

McNicol, L. "The Relationship of the Image of the Highest Angel to the High Priesthood Concept in Hebrews." Ph.D. diss., Vanderbilt University, 1974.

MacRae, G. W. "Heavenly Temple and Eschatology in the Letter to the Hebrews." *Semeia* 12 (1978): 179–99.

Malone, F. A. "A Critical Evaluation of the Use of Jeremiah 31:31–34 in the Letter to the Hebrews." Ph.D. diss., Southwestern Baptist Theological Seminary, 1969.

Manson, T. W. "The Problem of the Epistle to the Hebrews." *BJRL* 32 (1949): 1–17.

Manson, W. *The Epistle to the Hebrews: An Historical and Theological Reconsideration*. London: Hodder & Stoughton, 1951.

Marrou, H. *A History of Education in Antiquity*. Translated by G. Lamb. New York: Mentor, 1964.

Marrow, S. B. "*Parrhēsia* and the New Testament." *CBQ* 44 (1982): 431–46.

Martin, D. B. *Slavery as Salvation: The Metaphor of Slavery in Pauline Christianity*. New Haven: Yale University Press, 1990.

Mathewson, D. "Reading Hebrews 6:4–6 in Light of the Old Testament." *WTJ* 61 (1999): 209–25.

Meier, J. P. "Structure and Theology in Heb 1, 1–14." *Bib* 66 (1985): 168–89.

———. "Symmetry and Theology in the Old Testament Citations of Heb 1, 5–14." *Bib* 66 (1985): 504–33.

Melbourne, B. L. "An Examination of the Historical-Jesus Motif in the Epistle to the Hebrews." *AUSS* 26 (1988): 281–97.

Minear, P. S. "An Early Christian Theopoetic?" *Semeia* 12 (1978): 201–13.

———. "Wanted: An Exegetical Realism." *Theology Today* 59 (2003): 178–89.

Mitchell, A. C. "Holding on to Confidence: *Parrēsia* in Hebrews." Pages 203–26 in *Friendship, Flattery, and Frankness of Speech*. Edited by J. T. Fitzgerald. NovTSup 82. Leiden: Brill, 1996.

———. "The Use of *prepein* and Rhetorical Propriety in Hebrews 2:10." *CBQ* 54 (1992): 681–701.

Nardoni, E. "Partakers in Christ (Hebrews 3:14)." *NTS* 37 (1991): 456–72.

Nash, R. H. "The Notion of Mediator in Alexandrian Judaism and the Epistle to the Hebrews." *WTJ* 40 (1978): 89–115.

Nelson, R. D. "'He Offered Himself': Sacrifice in Hebrews." *Int* 57 (2003): 251–65.

Neusner, J. *The Idea of Purity in Ancient Judaism*. SJLA 1. Leiden: Brill, 1973.

Newsom, C. *Songs of the Sabbath Sacrifice: A Critical Edition*. HSS 27. Atlanta: Scholars Press, 1985.

Neyrey, J. H. "'Without Beginning of Days or End of Life' (Hebrews 7:3): Topos for a True Deity." *CBQ* 53 (1991): 439–55.

Olbricht, T. H. "Hebrews as Amplification." Pages 375–87 in *Rhetoric and the New Testament*. Edited by S. E. Porter and T. H. Olbricht. JSNTSup 90. Sheffield: Sheffield Academic Press, 1993.

Owen, H. P. "The 'Stages of Ascent' in Hebrews v.11–vi.3." *NTS* 3 (1956–57): 243–53.

Peterson, D. *Hebrews and Perfection: An Examination of the Concept of Perfection in the "Epistle to the Hebrews."* SNTSMS 47. Cambridge: Cambridge University Press, 1982.

Pfitzner, V. C. *Paul and the Agon Motif: Traditional Athletic Imagery in the Pauline Literature*. NovTSup 16. Leiden: Brill, 1967.

Rahner, K. *On the Theology of Death*. Translated by C. H. Henkey. 2nd ed. Quaestiones Disputatae 2. Freiburg: Herder, 1965.

Rhee, V. (Sung-Yul). *Faith in Hebrews: Analysis within the Context of Christology, Eschatology, and Ethics*. Studies in Biblical Literature 19. New York: Peter Lang, 2001.

Rose, C. *Die Wolke der Zeugen: Eine exegetisch-traditionsgeschichtliche Untersuchung zur Hebräer 10, 32–12,3*. WUNT 2/60. Tübingen: Mohr (Siebeck), 1994.

Sabourin, L. "'Crucifying Afresh for One's Repentance' (Heb 6:4–6)." *BTB* 6 (1976): 264–71.

Salevao, I. *Legitimation in the Letter to the Hebrews: The Construction and Maintenance of a Symbolic Universe*. JSNTSup 219. Sheffield: Sheffield Academic Press, 2002.

Schein, B. E. "Our Father Abraham." Ph.D. diss., Yale University, 1972.

Schenck, K. L. "A Celebration of the Enthroned Son: The Catena of Hebrews 1." *JBL* 120 (2001): 469–85.

———. "Keeping His Appointment: Creation and Enthronement in Hebrews." *JSNT* 66 (1997): 91–117.

Scholer, J. M. *Proleptic Priests: Priesthood in the Epistle to the Hebrews*. JSNTSup 49. Sheffield: JSOT Press, 1991.

Schröger, F. *Der Verfasser des Hebräerbriefes als Schriftsausleger*. Biblische Untersuchungen 4. Regensburg: Friedrich Pustet, 1968.

Seid, T. W. "The Rhetorical Form of the Melchizedek/Christ Comparison in Hebrews 7." Ph.D. diss., Brown University, 1996.

Silberman, L. H. "Prophets/Angels: LXX and Qumran Psalm 151 and the Epistle to the Hebrews." Pages 91–101 in *Standing before God: Studies on Prayer in Scripture and in Tradition with Essays* (FS J. M. Oesterreicher). Edited by A. Finkel and L. Frizzell. New York: KTAV, 1981.

Solari, J. K. "The Problem of Metanoia in the Epistle to the Hebrews." Ph.D. diss., Catholic University of America, 1970.

Sowers, S. G. *The Hermeneutics of Philo and Hebrews: A Comparison of the Interpretation of the Old Testament in Philo Judaeus and the Epistle to the Hebrews*. Richmond: John Knox, 1965.

Spicq, C. "L'Épître aux Hébreux, Apollos, Jean-Baptiste, les Hellénistes et Qumran," *RevQ* 1 (1959): 365–90.

Stanley, S. "Hebrews 9:6–10: The 'Parable' of the Tabernacle." *NovT* 37 (1995): 385–99.

Sterling, G. "Ontology versus Eschatology: Tensions between Author and Community in Hebrews," *Studia Philonica Annual: Studies in Hellenistic Judaism* 13 (2001): 190–211.

Stevenson, G. *Power and Place: Temple and Identity in the Book of Revelation.* BZNW 107. New York: de Gruyter, 2001.

Stevenson-Moessner, J. "The Road to Perfection: An Interpretation of Suffering in Hebrews." *Int* 57 (2003): 280–90.

Stewart, R. A. "Creation and Matter in the Epistle to the Hebrews." *NTS* 12 (1965–66): 284–93.

Sundberg, A. C. "Canon Muratori: A Fourth-Century List." *HTR* 66 (1973): 1–41.

Swetnam, J. "'The Greater and More Perfect Tent': A Contribution to the Discussion of Hebrews 9,11." *Bib* 47 (1966): 91–106.

———. "Hebrews 10, 30–31: A Suggestion." *Bib* 75 (1994): 388–95.

———. *Jesus and Isaac: A Study of the Epistle to the Hebrews in the Light of the Aqedah.* AnBib 94. Rome: Biblical Institute Press, 1981.

Talbert, C. H. *Learning through Suffering: The Educational Value of Suffering in the New Testament and in Its Milieu.* Collegeville, MN: Liturgical Press, 1991.

Thompson, J. W. *The Beginnings of Christian Philosophy: The Epistle to the Hebrews.* CBQMS 13. Washington, D.C.: Catholic Biblical Association of America, 1982.

Thornton, T. C. G. "The Meaning of *haimatenchysia* in Heb IX. 22." *JTS* 15 (1964): 63–65.

Timo, E. *Messiah and the Throne: Jewish Merkabah Mysticism and Early Christian Exaltation Discourse.* WUNT 2/142. Tübingen: Mohr Siebeck, 2001.

Trompf, G. W. "The Conception of God in Hebrews 4:12–13." *ST* 25 (1971): 123–32.

Vaganay, L. "Le plan de L'Épître aux Hébreux." Pages 269–77 in *Mémorial Lagrange*. Paris: Gabalda, 1940.

Vanhoye, A. *Old Testament Priests and the New Priest According to the New Testament.* Translated by J. B. Orchard. Petersham: St. Bede's Publications, 1986.

———. *Situation du Christ: Épître aux Hébreux 1 et 2*. Lectio Divina 58. Paris: Cerf, 1969.

———. *Structure and Message of the Epistle to the Hebrews*. Subsidia biblica 12. Rome: Biblical Institute Press, 1989.

———. *La structure littéraire de L'épître aux Hébreux*. Studia Neotestamentica 1. Paris. Desclée de Brouwer, 1962.

van Vliet, H. *No Single Testimony: A Study on the Adoption of the Law of Deut. 19:15 Par. into the New Testament*. Utrecht: Kemink en Zoon, 1958.

Weinfeld, M. "Jeremiah and the Spiritual Metamorphosis of Israel." *ZAW* 88 (1976): 17–56.

Westfall, C. L. "Moses and Hebrews 3, 1–6: Approach or Avoidance?" Pages 175–201 in *Christian-Jewish Relations through the Centuries*. Edited by S. E. Porter and B. W. R. Pearson. JSNTSup 192. Sheffield: Sheffield Academic Press, 2000.

Wiid, J. S. "The Testamental Significance of *diathēkē* in Hebrews 9:15–22." *Neot* 26 (1992): 149–56.

Wilcox, M. "'According to the Pattern (*tbnyt*) . . .': Exodus 25,40 in the New Testament and Early Jewish Thought." *RevQ* 13 (1988): 647–56.

Williamson, C. M. "Anti-Judaism in Hebrews?" *Int* 57 (2003): 266–79.

Williamson, R. "The Background to the Epistle to the Hebrews." *ExpT* 87 (1975–76): 232–37.

———. *Philo and the Epistle to the Hebrews*. Arbeiten zur Literatur und Geschichte des hellenistischen Judentums 4. Leiden: Brill, 1970.

Witherington, B. "The Influence of Galatians on Hebrews." *NTS* 37 (1991): 146–52.

Worley, D. R. "God's Faithfulness to Promise: The Hortatory Use of Commissive Language in Hebrews." Ph.D. diss., Yale University, 1981.

Wray, J. H. *Rest as a Theological Metaphor in the Epistle to the Hebrews and the Gospel of Truth: Early Christian Homiletics of Rest*. SBLDS 166. Atlanta: Scholars Press, 1998.

Yadin, Y. "The Dead Sea Scrolls and the Epistle to the Hebrews." *Aspects of the Dead Sea Scrolls: Scripta Hierosolymitana* 4 (1958): 36–55.

Young, F. M. "Christological Ideas in the Greek Commentaries on the Epistle to the Hebrews." *JTS* 20 (1969): 150–63.

———. *The Use of Sacrificial Ideas in Greek Christian Writers from the New Testament to John Chrysostom*. Patristic Monograph Series 5. Cambridge, MA: Philadelphia Patristic Foundation, 1979.

Young, N. H. "'Bearing His Reproach' (Heb 13.9–14)." *NTS* 48 (2002): 243–61.

———. "The Day of Dedication or the Day of Atonement? The Old Testament Background to Hebrews 6:19–20 Revisited." *AUSS* 40 (2002): 61–68.

———. "*Haimatenchysia*: A Comment." *ExpT* 90 (1979): 180.

———. "*Tout' estin tēs sarkos autou* (Heb x.20): Apposition, Dependent or Explicative?" *NTS* 20 (1973–74): 100–114.

INTRODUCTION

Hebrews is one of the most beautifully written, powerfully argued, and theologically profound writings in the New Testament. Its anonymous author summons readers to a vision of reality and a commitment of faith that is at once distinctive, attractive, and disturbing.

For present-day readers, Hebrews is also one of the most difficult and challenging compositions in the New Testament canon. It is difficult because we are unable satisfactorily to place this magnificent display of early Christian rhetoric and theology in its historical setting. Its author, first readers, location, and date—these are all matters of debate among scholars, which is another way of confessing ignorance. And while everyone recognizes in Hebrews a Greek of unusual elegance (for the NT), rhetoric of exceptional polish, and an argument that suggests a powerful mind, few agree even on the precise genre of the composition, its structure, or the origin and elements of its symbolic world.

In short, Hebrews challenges the capacity of the historical-critical approach to do what it does best. It reminds us of how little we really know about the history of earliest Christianity outside the framework established by the Acts of the Apostles and the letters of Paul. If Paul had composed Hebrews, as tradition, despite some early questions, assumed for centuries was the case, then the difficulty, though still real, would be diminished. Once Pauline authorship is abandoned—as it should be—then a range of alternative possibilities emerges. The composition itself is sufficiently complex and allusive to support, more or less plausibly, any number of hypotheses.

Despite the astonishing growth in knowledge of the Greco-Roman and Jewish cultures over recent decades, knowledge that far surpasses that available to any previous generation of scholars, Hebrews remains elusive. We are able to say much more about each hypothesis, but are not able definitively to exclude or prove any of them. The growth in cultural knowledge has enabled a far richer appreciation of Hebrews' distinctive and powerful voice, but has not brought us significantly closer to deciding whose voice it might be.

Hebrews is, however, much more than a historical puzzle. It challenges every reader with a vision of reality, an understanding of Jesus Christ, and a sense of Christian identity that are distinctive within the New Testament and that are difficult for present-day readers either to comprehend or to accept. Grasping the world that produced Hebrews is one thing. Our historical knowledge gives us, as I have suggested, only a partial grip on that world. But as a work of literature, Hebrews also produces a world quite different from the one inhabited by early-twenty-first-century readers.

Hebrews challenges our imagination to enter a universe that is not defined by quantitative measure but by qualitative difference, to ponder a world in which the unseen is more real, more powerful, and more attractive than that which can be seen and touched and counted. In a word, Hebrews proposes as real a world that most of us consider imaginary.[1]

Similarly, Hebrews places before us a Jesus who is in turn compelling and repelling, familiar and alien. No writing in the New Testament pulls together so dynamically the tensions within the early Christian confession of Jesus—his humanity and divinity, his crucifixion as well as his exaltation, his slain body and his obedient faith—in the single dramatic image of Jesus the great high priest. It is a magnificent portrayal. But it is also an image that requires an appreciation of religious sacrifice, and such appreciation is virtually absent from contemporary Christianity.

Finally, Hebrews is remarkably stringent in its demands on readers. It calls for unqualified commitment, unflagging perseverance, and the willingness to suffer as a consequence of faith. Indeed, Hebrews suggests that for Christians to enter into full maturity as God's children, they must be transformed by the suffering that comes from obedience in precisely the same manner as Jesus. For present-day Christians who make moral ambiguity and tolerance for wrongdoing the mark of maturity, and who consider suffering as virtually equivalent to evil, Hebrews is strong medicine, bitter to swallow even if salutary.[2]

It is the way Hebrews challenges our construction of the world, our image of Jesus, and our understanding of discipleship that makes reading it truly difficult. However fascinating, the historical puzzles presented by this composition should not distract from what makes it genuinely difficult and deeply challenging. The task of a responsible commentary is not to explain away the difficulties, but to expose the challenge. This requires more than the gathering of historical information and literary parallels; it demands that the commentator (as a guide to other readers) think through the argument, its premises, and its entailments so that other readers might also consider not only the meaning of the text but its truth as well.

1. For a typically evocative presentation on the alien character of Hebrews, see P. S. Minear, "An Early Christian Theopoetic?" *Semeia* 12 (1978): 201–13; idem, "Wanted: An Exegetical Realism," *Theology Today* 59 (2003): 178–89.

2. See L. T. Johnson, "Hebrews' Challenge to Christian Christology and Discipleship," in *Preaching Hebrews*, ed. D. Fleer and D. Bland (Rochester College Lectures on Preaching 4; Abilene, TX: ACU Press, 2003), 11–28.

The present commentary takes up the challenge of engaging the text of Hebrews incrementally and in some detail. This extended introduction seeks to provide the present-day reader with a framework of understanding that will enable such a vigorous and lively engagement. I begin by sketching the place of Hebrews in the tradition of the church as a way of sharpening my point about Hebrews' present strangeness. I then turn to the configuration of the composition itself: how does it disclose itself to a reader attentive to its language and to the world out of which it emerged? Then I take up the standard questions of introduction, knowing that at best we are here in the realm of guesswork: who wrote it, and when, and to what rhetorical situation? Finally, I sketch some of the distinctive theological dimensions of Hebrews that continue to challenge readers today.

Hebrews in the Christian Tradition

Hebrews was first received and read as a letter of the apostle Paul. This is indicated first by its inclusion among Paul's letters in Greek manuscripts. Later in this introduction, I will discuss some of the reasons why scholars have correctly regarded that as a case of misattribution. Hebrews appears after Romans in the earliest extant text of Paul (P^{46}), which is dated about 200 and contains Heb 1:1–9:16; 9:18–10:20; 10:22–30; 10:32–13:25. Portions of the composition appear also in other papyri from the third through seventh century (P^{12}, P^{13}, P^{17}, P^{79}, P^{89}). The complete text is contained by Codex Sinaiticus (א, fourth century) and Codex Alexandrinus (A, fifth century), while the other major uncials preserve substantial portions of the composition: Codex Vaticanus (B, fourth century) has 1:1–9:13; Codex Ephraemi Rescriptus (C, fifth century) has 2:4–7:26; 9:15–10:24; 12:16–13:25; and Codex Claromontanus (D, sixth century) has 1:1–13:20. Hebrews also appeared in all the early versions, including Old Latin, Coptic (Sahidic and Bohairic), and Syriac (Peshitta and Harclean).[3]

The earliest attested use of Hebrews also suggests a Pauline connection. In the late first or early second century, *1 Clement* was sent from Rome to Corinth to address local disturbances. The letter refers explicitly to Paul's First Letter to the Corinthians (47). Much more subtly, but unmistakably, *1 Clement* also makes use of the ideas and distinctive language of Hebrews (see especially 36:1–5), a use that was noted already by Eusebius (*Hist. eccl.* 3.38.1–3). In Alexandria and other major Greek centers of Christianity, Hebrews found instant favor and was received as a Pauline letter, even though the great Origen expressed doubts concerning its authenticity. Origen found the ideas but not the language to be

3. For a full display, see Ellingworth, 81–85. The original translation in this commentary is based on the twenty-seventh revised edition of Nestle-Aland, *Novum Testamentum Graece*, ed. Barbara and Kurt Aland et al. (Stuttgart: Bibelgesellschaft, 2001).

Pauline, and after suggesting either Clement or Luke as possible authors, confessed that "only God knew" (Eusebius, *Hist. eccl.* 6.25.11–14). Origen's predecessor, Clement of Alexandria, enthusiastically cited Hebrews as from "the apostle" (*Stromata* 1.4; 7.10), and Origen himself makes frequent use of Hebrews, introducing his citations as "Scripture" (*First Principles* 2.6.4), "Paul" (*First Principles* 4.1.24), "the apostle" (*Commentary on John* 20), more elaborately as "Paul says in the Epistle to the Hebrews" (*John* 6), and more cautiously as "the author of the Epistle to the Hebrews" (*Letter to Africanus* 9).

Acceptance in Western churches was less rapid and wholehearted. Tertullian approves of the position of Heb 6:1–6 concerning a second repentance and cites it approvingly in a polemic against the "Shepherd of Adulterers"—the second-century Shepherd of Hermas that held open the possibility of repentance after baptism (*Mand.* 4.3.1–7)—but Tertullian thinks it was written by Barnabas, the associate of Paul (*On Modesty* 20). According to Eusebius, Irenaeus made use of Hebrews in some of his writings (*Hist. eccl.* 5.26), but there are no references to it in any of his extant compositions. Cyprian seems not to have been aware of Hebrews, and it is possible that Hippolytus of Rome rejected it. The Roman presbyter Gaius likewise mentions only thirteen letters of Paul, "not counting that to the Hebrews," in his rebuttal of the Marcionites, who set forth new scriptures (Eusebius, *Hist. eccl.* 6.20.3). If the *Muratorian Canon* is from late-second-century Rome, as traditionally thought, rather than fourth-century Syria, as some have argued, the omission of Hebrews from its list of writings would fit this pattern.[4]

Probably because of the authority of Origen in scriptural matters, and the steady support of Hebrews by Eastern writers, we see that by the late fourth century Hebrews was accepted as fully canonical throughout the church. Among Latin writers, Ambrose of Milan cites Hebrews frequently in his works *On the Holy Spirit* (see 1.4, 47; 2.128; 3.140) and *Of the Christian Faith* (e.g., 1.7.49; and especially the extensive discussion of the priesthood of Christ in 3.2.84–91). Both Hilary of Poitiers (*On the Trinity* 4.11) and Rufinus of Aquila (*Commentary on the Apostles' Creed* 3.5.29, and 30) cite Hebrews as they do other Pauline letters. Jerome has favorite taglines, like 12:6 and 13:4 (see *Letters* 22.39; 46.2; 63.2; 130.12), and tells us that while some in the West doubt its authenticity, the Greek churches have accepted it from the first (*Letters* 129). Augustine also notes that some have doubted its authenticity, but that the Eastern churches place it among the canonical writings (*On Forgiveness of Sins and Baptism* 1.50). Augustine himself uses Hebrews vigorously (e.g., *City of God* 18.50; *On the Trinity* 3.11; *Enchiridion* 58; *On Nature and Grace*

4. The debate was generated by A. C. Sundberg, "Canon Muratori: A Fourth-Century List," *HTR* 66 (1973): 1–41; and is discussed extensively in G. M. Hahneman, *The Muratorian Fragment and the Development of the Canon* (Oxford: Clarendon, 1992).

15).[5] Thus the North African Council of Carthage (397) lists among the canonical Scriptures to be "read in the church under the name of divine scriptures," thirteen letters of Paul, and "of the same, to the Hebrews, one" (art. 39).

Greek writers continued to use Hebrews through the third and early fourth centuries. In Alexandria, Gregory Thaumaturgus (see *Homily on Christ's Baptism*), Dionysius (see *Epistle* 3.2), and Alexander (see *Epistles on the Arian Heresy* 1.12) continued Origen's initiative. But we find Hebrews used as well by an opponent of Origen, Methodius of Olympus (see *Oration on Simeon and Anna* 9; *Banquet of the Ten Virgins* 5.7; 9.5; *Discourse on the Resurrection* 1.5). Around 323, Eusebius of Caesarea records the continuing unstable status of Hebrews. In one place he lists the fourteen letters of Paul as "well-known and undisputed," but adds that some have rejected Hebrews since "it is disputed by the church of Rome on the ground that it is not written by Paul" (*Hist. eccl.* 3.3.5). But in another place he lists "the letters of Paul," without distinguishing Hebrews (3.25.2), and in still another place he himself quotes Heb 10:34 as Scripture (6.41.6).

By the last half of the fourth century, the canonicity of Hebrews is assured. In 403/404 John Chrysostom delivers thirty-four homilies on Hebrews. Chrysostom does not question Pauline authorship and places Hebrews during Paul's period of freedom after his first imprisonment: Hebrews precedes 2 Timothy chronologically, and was addressed to Jewish Christians in Palestine (*Homilies on Hebrews*, Argument 2).[6] Athanasius, for whom Hebrews was a key weapon in the battle against Arianism, listed Hebrews in his *Paschal Letter* 39 of 367 among the letters of Paul—after the Thessalonian letters and before Timothy—that together with other canonical writings form the "springs of salvation."[7] This canonical status is not challenged through the Middle Ages, despite the continuing recognition of doubt concerning authorship (see Hugh of St. Victor, *Didascalion* 4.2–6), and remained steady through the Reformation, despite some debate among Lutheran scholars concerning its precise status.

These few remarks on the reception and use of Hebrews in the early church constitute only a small part of a history of interpretation.[8] The substantial employment of Hebrews by Christian writers was less a matter of seeking the

5. For Augustine's pattern of usage, see A.-M. La Bonnardière, "L'Épître aux Hébreux dans l'oeuvre de Saint Augustin," *REAug* 3 (1957): 137–62.

6. Full references for Chrysostom and other patristic and medieval commentaries are in Koester, 135–36.

7. For the influence of doctrinal disputes on commentaries, see F. M. Young, "Christological Ideas in the Greek Commentaries on the Epistle to the Hebrews," *JTS* 20 (1969): 150–63. For a full analysis of interpretation in the patristic period, see R. A. Greer, *The Captain of Our Salvation: A Study of the Patristic Exegesis of Hebrews* (Beiträge zur Geschichte der biblischen Exegese 15; Tübingen: Mohr [Siebeck], 1973).

8. A fuller history of interpretation from the patristic period through modernity can be found in Koester, 19–63.

meaning of this composition than it was a matter of interpreting the meaning of Christian life with the help of this inspired writing. Yes, we do find sustained examination of specific passages, as when Athanasius provides a full exposition of Heb 2–3 in *Four Discourses against Arius* 2.8–9, or when Cyril of Jerusalem and Ambrose of Milan expound the priesthood of Christ (see Cyril, *Catechetical Lectures* 10.11 and 14; Ambrose, *Of the Christian Faith* 3.12.84–91). But for the most part Hebrews is not a puzzle to be construed, as it has tended to become for present-day interpreters. Hebrews is, rather, a set of inspired statements that help clarify the teaching and practices of the community. Even Chrysostom's *Homilies* are less concerned with clarifying the obscurities of the text of Hebrews than they are with exhorting listeners to a life in conformity with its teaching.

One can argue, indeed, that it was the sheer usefulness—or to put it less reductively, the sheer truthfulness—of Hebrews that ensured its place in the canon of Scripture, despite lingering (and never-resolved) doubts about its authorship. What difference did human authorship really make, after all? As Chrysostom notes, it was not ultimately Paul who generated these thoughts, but "the grace of the Spirit [who] shows forth its strength by whomever it will" (*Homilies on Hebrews* 1.3). On two matters above all Hebrews formed an important and perhaps indispensable witness for its early readers: the truth of Jesus Christ, and the truth of Christian existence.

Hebrews provided a valuable resource for asserting and defending the full divinity of Christ against the Arian heresy. Many passages within the composition were put to use, including Heb 13:8, "Jesus Christ is the same yesterday, and today, and forever" (see Alexander of Alexandria, *Epistles on the Arian Heresy* 2.3; Athanasius, *Four Discourses against Arius* 1.36; 2.48; Gregory of Nazianzus, *Oration* 38.1; Cyril of Jerusalem, *Catechetical Lectures* 12.17). Above all it was the characterization of the Son in the prologue, "he is a radiance of his [God's] glory and an imprint of his very being" (1:3), that served as a decisive scriptural support for the Nicene position (see Alexander, *Epistles on the Arian Heresy* 1.12; Methodius of Olympus, *Oration on Simeon and Anna* 9; Athanasius, *Defense of the Nicene Definition* 12; *Four Discourses against Arius* 1.12; 3.65; Basil the Great, *Hexaemeron* 9.6; *On the Spirit* 6 and 19; Gregory of Nazianzus, *Oration* 29.17; Gregory of Nyssa, *Against Eunomius* 1.39; 2.11; 8.5; Ambrose, *On the Christian Faith* 1.13.79).

Hebrews also supported teaching concerning Christian discipleship. Not surprisingly, Heb 10:32–12:17 provides a basis for discipleship as a life of faith that perseveres in imitation of the saints of old and of Jesus (see Clement of Alexandria, *Stromata* 2.4 and 4.16; Origen, *Against Celsus* 7.7 and 18; Augustine, *Harmony of the Gospels* 2.4; *Epistles of John* 8.7; Athanasius, *Defense of His Flight* 16 and 21; Cyril of Jerusalem, *Catechetical Lectures* 5; John of Damascus, *Exposition of the Orthodox Faith* 10, 11, 15).

Most significantly, Hebrews plays a key role in shaping the metaphorical understanding of Christian existence as a pilgrimage toward a heavenly homeland, whose passage is accomplished internally by the life of prayer and contemplation. This is a complex topic, indeed, but we can detect the line that runs from Philo, who interpreted the story of the exodus in terms of liberation from vice and transformation into virtue, through Hebrews, which pictures the people of God moving into God's rest (3:1–4:6), a heavenly homeland (11:10, 15–16), and the heavenly Jerusalem (12:22–24), through Origen, who, with Hebrews' help, reads the story of the people in the wilderness in terms of a spiritual pilgrimage and transformation (e.g., *Homilies on Numbers* 7.5; 9.7; 12.3; 17.4; 23.11; 27.2–12; *Homilies on Joshua* 1.7–2.3), to Christian authors—especially in the East—who use Hebrews liberally in their exposition of Christian existence in terms of a moral and spiritual pilgrimage (see, e.g., Gregory of Nyssa, *Life of Moses*; and Pseudo-Macarius, *Fifty Spiritual Homilies*, esp. 46.4). So powerful is this metaphorical construction that it continues in Christian spiritual literature through the Middle Ages (see Benedict of Nursia, *Rule for Monks*, Prologue; Thomas à Kempis, *Imitation of Christ* 1.23; 2.1; 4.11).

The self-evident and transparent truthfulness of Hebrews—its capacity to illuminate Christian convictions and practices and the very meaning of Christian existence—is no longer accessible to readers, even Christians, in the early twenty-first century. Whereas all the writers mentioned in this discussion saw themselves as inhabiting precisely the same world as Hebrews, we do not. It would be a form of false consciousness for people living in conditions of modernity, or postmodernity, to claim that they can read Hebrews in the same way as Gregory of Nyssa did. The difference is not simply a function of time. Gregory of Nyssa, after all, wrote four hundred years after the time of Hebrews. It is more a function of a fundamental change in consciousness.

At least three elements contribute to the distance between ancient and contemporary readers of Hebrews. The first is the change in cosmology. The author of Hebrews and Gregory of Nyssa shared a basically Platonic view of reality (more on that later), which has scarcely been in evidence among thinkers even by way of revival since the nineteenth century. The second is the rise of the historical-critical approach to Scripture, which takes as its first premise that the Bible is to be read not as inspired revelation from God but as a literary production of a past writer, and takes as its second premise that the "historical" meaning of the text is primary and of greatest importance. The third is the slow erosion of classical Christian belief and practice itself. For many present-day Christians, the statements of the creed concerning God and Christ simply do not make sense. And the link between spiritual transformation and the practice of prayer and fasting is no longer obvious. The causes of such changes cannot be discussed here, but it is helpful to remember that, as we pursue answers for the sort of questions that arise concerning Hebrews because of modern consciousness, the real challenge of Hebrews might be the questions that it puts to us.

Hebrews as a First-Century Composition

We can begin to acquaint ourselves with Hebrews by considering the composition as it presents itself to us, moving from the elementary aspects of language to the more complex questions of symbolic world, and allowing clues concerning the specific circumstances of Hebrews' composition to emerge gradually from the description.

Language

One of the most impressive characteristics of Hebrews is hidden from those who must read it only in translation, namely its excellent Greek, by far the best Koine to be found among New Testament writings. The vocabulary is rich and varied, with about 154 words not found elsewhere in the New Testament, 90 found in only one other New Testament composition, and 10 found nowhere else in Greek literature before Hebrews.[9] The command of Greek style matches the extensive diction. Hebrews contains long complex periods (see 1:1–4; 2:1–4; 10:19–25) and passages of poetic force (see 4:12–13; 7:1–3; 12:18–24), together with short sentences (see 2:16; 3:19; 13:1, 8), rapid questions (3:16–18), and close argument (4:8–9; 7:11–12; 10:2).

Equally inaccessible in translation are the various rhetorical figures that Hebrews employs: the repetition of initial letters (*alliteration*; see 1:1; 2:1–4; 4:16; 11:17), the repetition of the same word in successive sentences (*anaphora*; see "by faith" running through chap. 11), the repetition of conjunctions (*polysyndeton*; see 4:12–13) or the omission of conjunctions altogether (*asyndeton*; see 11:34–35), the use of internal near rhyme (*assonance*; see 5:8; 6:20), the opposition of contrasts (*antithesis*; see 7:23–24), the balance of opposing elements in successive clauses (*chiasm*; see 2:18; 13:4), subtle plays on words (*paranomasia*; see 5:8; 7:9; 9:16), and others. Taken together with the diction of the composition and its supple sentence construction, the use of such figures points to the thoroughly Greek character of the composition and suggests, even before other factors are considered, that the author was at home in the world of rhetoric and considered his readers to be so as well.[10]

Other aspects of Hebrews' language are available even in translation. Readers quickly become aware of Hebrews' appeal to the senses of readers/auditors.

9. Lists of the vocabulary in each category are provided by Spicq, 1:154, and Ellingworth, 12–13.

10. See Attridge, 19–21, for an excellent description of Hebrews' linguistic features.

The smell of sacrifices is only implied (13:16), touch appears by way of contrast (12:18, 20), and taste is metaphorical (6:5). But the author constantly appeals to the hearing of his listeners (2:1; 3:7; 4:7; 5:11; 12:19). Most of all, the sense of sight is invoked, as the readers are asked to "behold," "consider," and "see" what the author seeks to convey (2:9; 3:1; 7:4; 12:3; 12:21). Using oral discourse to portray visual scenes (in "word-pictures") is a common rhetorical technique (*ekphrasis*), and Hebrews uses it effectively, especially in 9:1–5 and 12:18–24.

Hebrews is unusually rich in its use of metaphors, which are not simply verbal ornaments but ways of structuring thought. Hebrews uses metaphors drawn from the realm of law (2:3–4; 6:16; 7:12) and property (2:14; 3:1; 6:13–18; 7:4–10; 9:16–22; 10:34; 11:1), of agriculture (6:7–8; 12:11) and architecture (6:1; 11:10), of seafaring (6:19) and athletics (5:14; 12:1–3, 11–13), of cult (chaps. 9–10) and education (5:12–14; 12:7–11). With the exception of the cult, which is explicitly Jewish, all these metaphorical fields are familiar in Greco-Roman culture.

Perhaps the most powerful metaphor of Hebrews is one that is never fully expressed, but is conveyed in a number of ways: the metaphor of life as a journey toward a destination, or pilgrimage.[11] Hebrews calls its readers to movement. Their danger is that they will drift away (2:1), fall (4:11), fall away (3:12), apostasize (6:6), be led away (13:9), abandon (10:25), be weighted (12:1), be weary or lame (12:12). Their hope lies in moving forward: they are to enter the rest (4:3, 6, 11), draw near to the throne of grace (4:16; 10:22), run the race after Jesus (12:1), make straight paths (12:12), come to Mount Zion (12:22). Jesus has gone before them as forerunner (6:20) and pioneer (2:10; 12:2). They are to "go to him" (13:13). All of these expressions powerfully support the sense of living life as a journey, a journey in which the here and now must be left in order to gain something greater: "for we do not have a permanent city here. We are seeking the city to come" (13:14; see esp. 11:8–16).

Literary Form

Discussions of literary genre and structure are helpful only insofar as they enable readers to better comprehend the nature of the composition and therefore read it with appropriate expectations. Hebrews is clearly not a letter in the normal sense of the term. The beginning lacks the epistolary elements familiar from Paul's letters (greeting, thanksgiving), and the ending has only a few notes suggesting a letter: reference to the author's hope of being restored to

11. The theme is powerfully argued by E. Käsemann, *The Wandering People of God: An Investigation of the Letter to the Hebrews*, trans. R. A. Harrisville and I. L. Sandberg (Minneapolis: Augsburg, 1984); and is developed by W. G. Johnsson, "The Pilgrimage Motif in the Book of Hebrews," *JBL* 97 (1978): 239–51.

the readers (13:19), news of "our brother Timothy" whom the author hopes to join in a visit to the readers (13:23), a brief exchange of greetings (13:24), and a final prayer (13:25).

The author characterizes his work in 13:22 as a brief "word of consolation/exhortation" (*logos tēs paraklēseōs*), which is best understood as a form of oral discourse or speech (cf. Acts 13:15, where Paul is invited to give a *logos paraklēseōs* at worship). Four stylistic features indicate Hebrews' oral character. The first is the distinctive use throughout of the first person plural ("we/us/our"), a technique that allows the speaker to identify with the hearers while also asserting authority. The second is the way references to speaking and hearing—rather than writing and reading—are used to characterize the author's message: ". . . of which we speak" (2:5); "our discourse concerning him is lengthy and difficult to express, because you have become reluctant listeners" (5:11); ". . . even though we are speaking this way" (6:9); "Now the point of what is being said . . . " (8:1); "And what more should I say?" (11:32). The third is the masterful alternation of exposition and exhortation running through the composition, a pattern that allows an orator to drive home points immediately without losing the hearers' attention. The exposition of 1:1–14, for example, leads directly to the exhortation of 2:1–4; the argument of 2:5–18 is turned directly into application by 3:1; and the discussion of 3:2–6 is driven home by the "therefore" that introduces the exhortation of 3:7–13. Then, more rapidly, the exposition of 3:14–19 is applied in 4:1; that of 4:2–10 in the exhortation of 4:11–16, and so forth through the oration. Such emphasis on the hortatory justifies defining Hebrews more narrowly still as a homily or sermon.[12] The fourth characteristic that suggests a fundamentally oral form of discourse is the manner in which the author puts forth themes that are only later developed more fully, thus creating a wavelike, cumulative effect. Thus Jesus' fellowship with humans (2:14–18) is made thematic in 5:1–10; his faith (3:1–6) is made explicit in 12:1–3; his role as priest (4:14; 5:1–10) is developed more fully in 7:1–9:28; and the pilgrimage of the people to God's rest is stated in 3:7–4:11 and brought to a magnificent climax in 11:1–12:29.

Despite the oral character of the discourse, Hebrews may well have been written from the first, may indeed have functioned as a letter from the first. In antiquity, oral and scribal activities were closely interconnected. Sometimes oral discourses were taken down by listeners and then published as writings, as when the *Discourses* of Epictetus were recorded and published as written compositions by his student Arrian. Other orators carefully prepared their oral discourses in writing, as Dio Chrysostom did with his *Orations*. Hebrews could also have been written for oral delivery.

12. See W. McCown, "The Nature and Function of the Hortatory Sections in the Epistle to the Hebrews" (Ph.D. diss., Union Theological Seminary, New York, 1970).

Someone other than the author could also have made the oral presentation, since the same close connection between writing and orality applies to ancient letter writing as well. We know that Paul dictated some of his letters to an amanuensis (see Rom 16:22), and it is probable that his letters were read aloud in the assembly by the delegate who had delivered them to a specific community (see 1 Thess 5:27; Col 4:16). The epistolary elements that now appear tacked on to Hebrews, therefore, could well have been original and intentional, for the "sermon" could well have been delivered (read aloud) as a "letter." The more important point is that Hebrews is a composition that is meant to be heard as a discourse rather than seen as a text, experienced as a whole in its unfolding rather than studied in separate segments. In this commentary, therefore, I usually refer to the author's "hearers" rather than his "readers."

Nevertheless, since Hebrews comes to present-day readers as a long and complex text, it is natural for interpreters to seek some further signs of structure that might help guide reading. Such efforts are the more legitimate since the Greek manuscripts lack punctuation and often even word divisions, and since chapter and verse divisions were established centuries later. While the decisions of scribes and editors represent responsible and often deeply insightful divisions, they are also acts of interpretation that present-day readers can challenge. For commentaries, structural analyses serve to rationalize the division of a single sermon into textual segments for analysis. Practical considerations, therefore, come into play: how much text and how much comment are feasible within a reader's tolerance for detail or attention span?

Commentators today tend to follow one of three approaches to the structure of Hebrews, and therefore to the outline of their respective commentaries. The simplest is the traditional topical approach, which focuses on the subjects being discussed. A typical example divides the letter into eight major divisions and fifty subdivisions.[13] The major divisions are: the finality of Christianity (1:1–2:18); the true home of the people of God (3:1–4:13); the high priesthood of Christ (4:14–6:20); the order of Melchizedek (7:1–28); covenant, sanctuary, and sacrifice (8:1–10:18); call to worship, faith, and perseverance (10:19–12:29); concluding exhortation and prayer (13:1–21); postscript (13:22–25). The fifty subdivisions are purely descriptive. Thus the section called "the finality of Christianity" is divided into these segments: God's final revelation in his Son (1:1–4); Christ better than the angels (1:5–14); first admonition: the gospel and the law (2:1–4); the humiliation and glory of the Son of Man (2:5–9); the Son of Man the Savior and High Priest of the people (2:10–18); and so on, through the rest of the composition. The advantage of the approach is precisely its descriptive character; the disadvantage is that it provides little sense of the argument, only a listing of topics.

13. See Bruce, *Epistle to the Hebrews,* xliii–xliv.

The second approach focuses on form rather than content. Through "discourse analysis" of the Greek text—without regard to the topics being treated but attentive to lexical and linguistic connections and interconnections—this approach finds Hebrews to unfold according to a basic chiastic structure, so that the composition forms concentric circles around a central point.[14] According to one influential example of this approach, the central point of Hebrews is self-identified: 8:1 reads, "Now the point of what is being said is that we have such a high priest. He has taken a seat at the right hand of the throne of the majesty in the heavens. He is minister of the sanctuary and of the genuine tent, which the Lord, not a human, has built." This line occurs in the middle of the central section of the composition (section III) devoted to the theme of the sacrifice of Christ the high priest (5:11–10:39). On either side of this central section are two other sections. Before it, section I (1:5–2:18) develops the name superior to the angels, and section II (3:1–5:10) expounds Christ's faithfulness and compassion. After 5:11–10:39, section III deals with faith and endurance (11:1–12:13), and section IV with the peaceful fruit of justice (12:14–13:19). Finally, these sections are framed by an introduction (1:1–4) and conclusion (13:20–21).[15] The advantage of this approach is that it pays close attention to the form of the Greek text. The disadvantage is that it vastly overestimates the role of chiasm, and misses completely the linear and cumulative force of Hebrews' argument. Discourse analysis treats the text as a static, visual phenomenon, rather than as a dynamic oral presentation. And, after all the labor spent on detailed and sophisticated examination of the text, its actual breakdown of the composition ends up being rather close to the content analysis.

The third approach results from scholars' rediscovery of ancient rhetoric—as described by theoreticians like Aristotle and Quintilian, and practiced by orators like Dio Chrysostom and Cicero—and its applicability to New Testament writings.[16] This approach has much to commend it in general, and has particular pertinence in analyzing a composition such as Hebrews, which presents itself so clearly as a work of rhetorical art.[17] Aristotle distinguished three basic

14. The approach is described fully and sympathetically by Lane, lxxxv–xcviii.

15. A pioneer in this sort of analysis was L. Vaganay, "Le plan de L'Épître aux Hébreux," in *Mémorial Lagrange* (Paris: Gabalda, 1940), 269–77; its most persistent advocate has been A. Vanhoye, in *La structure litteraire de L'Épître aux Hébreux,* 2nd ed. (Studia Neotestamentica 1; Paris: Desclée de Brouwer, 1976), and many other works. For an even further development along these lines, see G. H. Guthrie, *The Structure of Hebrews: A Text-Linguistic Analysis* (NovTSup 73; Leiden: Brill, 1994).

16. For a helpful introduction, see G. A. Kennedy, *The Art of Rhetoric in the Roman World* (Princeton: Princeton University Press, 1972); and idem, *New Testament Interpretation through Rhetorical Criticism* (Chapel Hill: University of North Carolina Press, 1984).

17. The commentator who most fully embraces rhetorical criticism—especially in the aspect of arrangement—is Koester, esp. 80–96; see also idem, "Hebrews, Rhetoric, and the Future of Humanity," *CBQ* 64 (2002): 103–23; T. H. Olbricht, "Hebrews as Amplification," in *Rhetoric and the New Testament*, ed. S. E. Porter and T. H. Olbricht (JSNTSup 90; Sheffield: Sheffield Academic Press, 1993), 375–87; and B. Lindars, "The Rhetorical Structure of Hebrews," *NTS* 35 (1989): 382–406.

forms of rhetoric: the forensic, which asks of the hearers a judgment concerning past actions; the deliberative, which urges hearers to make a decision concerning future actions; and the epideictic, which asks readers to respond with a judgment of praise or blame for the subject being displayed.[18]

Hebrews is clearly not forensic, since it is neither prosecuting nor defending a case. A decision for deliberative or epideictic is more difficult. In favor of epideictic is the pervasive use of honor and shame language (more on that below), the use of *synkrisis* or comparison, which is a frequent feature of epideictic oratory, and the encomium in praise of the heroes of faith in chapter 11.[19] In favor of deliberative rhetoric, however, is the clear hortatory purpose of the composition as a whole. As we have seen, each exposition turns to exhortation, and the entire last section of the discourse calls for a commitment from the hearers to act in certain ways rather than others. It is perhaps best to think of Hebrews as deliberative rhetoric with epideictic features.[20]

Scholars who analyze New Testament compositions rhetorically tend to focus on rhetorical *arrangement*, which is another name for the structure of the argument, how the points are presented. They seek to align the parts of New Testament compositions with the elements of a typical speech as described by ancient rhetorical handbooks, identifying in turn the exordium, narration, proposition, proofs, and peroration. There are two difficulties with this approach. The first is that actual speeches from antiquity seldom conform to the standards of the handbooks, because good rhetoricians most often sought to convince by means of what seemed a natural presentation of materials rather than by following a predictable outline. The second is related: arrangement was regarded as far less important than *invention*, which was the actual stuff of the argument, the proofs (whether in the form of enthymemes or examples) that would serve to persuade an audience.

A good example of rhetorical analysis that focuses on arrangement suggests five sections of Hebrews: (1) exordium (1:1–2:4); (2) proposition (2:5–9); (3) arguments (2:10–12:27); (4) peroration (12:28–13:21); and (5) epistolary postscript (13:22–25). The arguments (part 3) are subdivided into three series, each of which has an element of exposition and of exhortation. The first series (2:10–6:20) argues that Jesus received glory through faithful suffering, a way that others are called to follow (2:10–5:10), followed by warning and encouragement (5:11–6:20). The second series (7:1–10:39) argues that Jesus' suffering is the sacrifice that enables others to approach God (7:1–10:25), followed by further warning and encouragement (10:26–39). The third series (11:1–12:27) argues that God's people persevere through suffering to glory by faith

18. For the sake of simplicity, the treatment of rhetoric here is based solely on Aristotle's *Rhetoric*, esp. book 1.

19. Attridge, 14, decides that Hebrews is epideictic in character.

20. See the helpful comments on this point in Koester, 82.

(11:1–12:24), followed by additional warning and encouragement (12:25–27).[21] The analysis can be challenged in the way others can: Is 2:5–9 really a proposition that sets the theme for the entire discourse? Do the descriptions of the arguments adequately convey what they are about or what they are doing? But the approach has the advantage of corresponding to the approach actually taken by ancient rhetoricians, and is in general a reasonable account of the arrangement of Hebrews.

The more important aspect of rhetoric, however, is invention: the "finding" or construction of the appropriate arguments to persuade a specific audience. Here Aristotle again proposes a threefold distinction among kinds of arguments. The most familiar to us is the appeal from *logos*, or reason. This is what we ordinarily mean by "argument," and it is so important in Hebrews that I will discuss it separately. But equally important in ancient rhetoric are *ethos* and *pathos* arguments. *Ethos* refers to the character of the rhetorician. If the speaker is reliable, demonstrates virtue, and has a reputation for speaking the truth, his character goes a long way toward moving an audience to hearing and responding favorably to his *logos* argument. *Pathos* refers to the feelings of the hearers; ancient speakers knew as well as we do that people are swayed by their emotions as much as by their minds, and appeal to negative and positive emotions was a prominent feature of ancient rhetoric.

In the case of Hebrews, *ethos* ("character") comes into play at three levels. The most obvious is the character of the speaker, the anonymous author of Hebrews, but little specific attention is given to this, apart from the author's explicit declaration that he has a good conscience and seeks to live honestly in all things (13:18), his association with believers whom they know ("our brother Timothy," 13:23; "those from Italy," 13:24; and the leaders of the community, 13:24), his implied advancement to a state of maturity that enables him to lead his readers on the same path (5:11–6:3), and the close association of his "speaking" with that of God. The second level is the character of the God who is the subject of this discourse: Hebrews makes every effort to show that "the one with whom we have to do" (4:13) is reliable and faithful, so that trust in this God who speaks is "secure" (2:2; 3:6). Likewise with the third level of *ethos*, the character of Jesus, whom the readers are to follow. Hebrews insists that Jesus has truly become perfect, and is therefore the "cause of eternal salvation to all who obey him" (5:9).

Hebrews makes use of *pathos* arguments when it appeals to the feelings of hearers as a way of motivating their actions. Negatively, Hebrews invokes the emotion of fear:[22] "Let us be afraid, therefore, so that none from among you

21. Koester, 84–85.

22. See P. Gray, *Godly Fear: The Epistle to the Hebrews and Greco-Roman Critiques of Superstition* (Academia Biblica 16; Atlanta: Society of Biblical Literature, 2003).

seem to be left behind" (4:1); "how shall we escape if we neglect such a great salvation" (2:3); "falling into the hands of the living God is a fearful thing" (10:31; see also 10:27; 11:23, 27; 12:21; 13:6). Positively, Hebrews appeals to the emotion of hope: "we desire that each one of you demonstrate the same enthusiasm all the way to the end for the completion of your hope" (6:11); "let us hold on to the secure confession of hope. For the one who made the promise is faithful" (10:23; see also 3:6; 6:18; 7:19; 11:1).

In brief, Hebrews presents itself as a work of deliberative rhetoric, careful in language and rich in metaphor, which makes strong appeals to character and emotion as well as to reason, and whose arrangement is dominated by the alternating pattern of exposition and exhortation.

Symbolic World

The writings of the New Testament are shaped by, and in turn help to reshape, the complex and pluralistic culture of the first-century Mediterranean world. In assessing Hebrews' symbolic world, by which I mean the social structures and systems and symbols that constitute culture, we must consider in turn the Greco-Roman and Jewish contexts (which are themselves overlapping), as well as the distinctive Christian experiences and convictions that—in compositions like Hebrews—acted as a catalyst for the reshaping of antiquity.[23] It is appropriate here to touch only on those aspects of the respective dimensions of the symbolic world that are present within Hebrews and are necessary to take into account for an adequate interpretation of its rhetoric. As in the case of Paul, what we find are not cultural elements lying side by side, but thoroughly commingled.

1. Greco-Roman Culture

The influence of Greco-Roman culture on Hebrews is evident not only in its elegant language and elevated rhetoric, but as well in some specific cultural values. When discussing Hebrews' language (above), I noted the range of metaphors that were drawn, for the most part, from Hellenistic culture. Metaphors are important as more than verbal adornment: they have real cognitive content, and help to shape an understanding of the world.[24]

23. For fuller discussion, see L. T. Johnson with T. Penner, *The Writings of the New Testament: An Interpretation*, 2nd ed. (Minneapolis: Fortress Press, 1998), 1–19; and for a survey of evidence with respect to Hebrews, see L. D. Hurst, *The Epistle to the Hebrews: Its Background of Thought* (SNTSMS 65; Cambridge: Cambridge University Press, 1990).

24. See G. Lakoff and M. Johnson, *Metaphors We Live By* (Chicago: University of Chicago Press, 1980); and G. Lakoff, *Women, Fire, and Dangerous Things: What Categories Reveal about the Mind* (Chicago: University of Chicago Press, 1987).

We catch several glimpses of athletic contests—a staple of Greek and Roman rather than Jewish culture—as a metaphor for the moral life, a commonplace in the teaching of Greco-Roman moralists, and used as well by Paul (see, e.g., 1 Cor 9:24–27). In 5:14 Hebrews speaks of faculties that are trained by practice, and in 12:1–3 develops a full picture of ancient games: the crowd of witnesses, the runners casting off weights and following after the leader who runs ahead of them, and the joy that awaits them at the end; in 12:12 the hearers are summoned to lift their drooping hands, strengthen their weak knees, and make straight paths for their feet.[25]

This athletic imagery is mingled with that of learning, a natural merger since the Greek term *paideia* connotes both discipline in the physical sense and education in the cultural sense, and since Greek education demanded the training of the body as well as of the mind.[26] Hebrews plays on the axiom *mathein pathein* ("to learn is to suffer/to suffer is to learn") when Jesus is said to have "learned from the things he suffered" (*emathen aph' hōn epathen*) in 5:8. This imagery continues in 5:11–14: the author complains that his hearers have become "dull of hearing" (5:11), needing instructors even for the elementary knowledge of God's words, even though they should already have become teachers (5:12). They are like babies requiring milk rather than the meat that is fit for the mature (5:13)—people who have had their faculties trained by practice (5:14).

The two metaphorical realms come together in the exhortation of 12:7–12, following the depiction of faith as running in a race after Jesus. The theme of a father's discipline *(paideia)* merges the aspects of "training" and of "learning" that are embedded in the term, so that the "discipline" in 12:10 appears less as a "correcting" from the outside than as a practice of self-improvement. The strong "therefore" (*dio*) in 12:12 that introduces athletic imagery makes sense when it is understood how closely athletics and learning went together in Greek culture, and how axiomatic it was in both realms that, as the present-day slogan has it, "no pain, no gain."

In Greco-Roman culture, honor and shame served as powerful motivators for action. One's reputation before the court of human opinion was important. Even philosophers who challenged conventional norms appealed to notions of honor and shame according to their alternative value systems.[27] Hebrews makes

25. For games imagery in general, see E. N. Gardiner, *Athletics of the Ancient World* (Chicago: Ares, 1980); and V. C. Pfitzner, *Paul and the Agon Motif* (NovTSup 16; Leiden: Brill, 1967).

26. See H. Marrou, *A History of Education in Antiquity*, trans. G. Lamb (New York: Mentor, 1964), 238–42; for suffering as educational, see C. H. Talbert, *Learning through Suffering: The Educational Value of Suffering in the New Testament and in Its Milieu* (Collegeville, MN: Liturgical Press, 1991).

27. For a general introduction, see D. deSilva, *The Hope of Glory: Honor Discourse and New Testament Interpretation* (Collegeville, MN: Liturgical Press, 1999); and on Hebrews in particular, see idem, *Despising Shame: Discourse and Community Maintenance in the Epistle to the Hebrews* (SBLDS 152; Atlanta: Scholars Press, 1995).

liberal use of such language. On one side, Jesus' manner of death was shameful (12:2; 6:5) and those addressed by this sermon have also experienced shame and abuse from others (10:33). On the other side, the hearers are exhorted to "despise the shame" in the way Jesus did (12:2; 13:13; see also 11:26), for the sake of a share in the "glory and honor" (*doxa kai timē*) to be bestowed on them by God (see 1:3; 2:7, 9, 10; 3:3; 5:5; 9:5; 13:21).

The pervasive use of "perfection/maturity" language in Hebrews (2:10; 5:9, 14; 6:1; 7:19, 28; 8:5; 9:6, 9, 11; 10:1, 14; 11:40; 12:2, 23) also points to Hellenistic culture.[28] Although *teleios* and its cognates are used widely in quotidian contexts such as the contrast between childhood and adulthood (e.g., 1 Cor 13:10 and Heb 5:14), they occur also in philosophical discourse to designate those who have reached "perfection" in their way of life, and in religious contexts—especially the Mysteries—to describe those who have completed the full round of initiations.[29] Here is a case in which the language of Greek religion may have a genuine influence on the New Testament, although it is certainly true that the LXX also uses *teleios* language with reference to the Jewish cult as described in the Torah (see, e.g., Ex 29:9–34; Lev 4:5; 8:21–33), so the influence may have been indirect.[30]

Beyond these common tropes of Hellenistic culture, Hebrews shares the "worldview" of a specific stream within Greek philosophy that is associated with Plato.[31] The term "worldview" is appropriate, for by the first century C.E., Plato's classic metaphysical theories, as expressed for example in his *Republic* 509D–521B and *Timaeus* 27C–29D, had been filtered through many schools and permutations and been appropriated by others. It was not so widespread, however, as to be universal; certainly Epicureans and Stoics understood the world in quite different terms than such popular philosophers as Aristobulus, Philo, Cicero, and Plutarch, whose view of reality was fundamentally shaped by Socrates' greatest student. For the purposes of this commentary, it is appropriate simply to outline this view of the world as well as the ways in which Hebrews shares it and deviates from it.

In broad terms, this is a view of reality that draws a sharp distinction, indeed a dividing line, between the *phenomenal* world, which is the realm of materiality, characterized by movement, change, and corruption—always passing

28. See D. Peterson, *Hebrews and Perfection: An Examination of the Concept of Perfection in the "Epistle to the Hebrews"* (SNTSMS 47; Cambridge: Cambridge University Press, 1982), although he pays too little attention to the significance of the cognates of *telein* and *teleioun* in religious contexts; see G. Delling, "*telos*, etc.," *TDNT* 8:49–87.

29. As in Plato, *Phaedrus* 249C.

30. It is in any case certain that Philo made use of such language in his construal of Judaism as a mystery; see L. T. Johnson, *Religious Experience in Earliest Christianity: A Missing Dimension in New Testament Studies* (Minneapolis: Fortress Press, 1998), 89–94.

31. See esp. J. W. Thompson, *The Beginnings of Christian Philosophy: The Epistle to the Hebrews* (CBQMS 13; Washington, D.C.: Catholic Biblical Association, 1982).

away, as Heraclitus declared—a world capable of being known only partially, and the *noumenal* world, characterized by changelessness and incorruptibility because it is spiritual in nature. The latter is the world of pure "forms" or "ideas." Plato solved the long struggle among the sages over the question of the one and the many, of change and permanence, by placing them in separate realms. The distinction is metaphysical: one realm of being is denser and "more real" than the other. In contrast to present-day readers who all more or less share the materialist bias of modernity, Platonists regarded as more real the spiritual world of ideas. The distinction is also epistemological: the material world of change and motion can be known only in part and imperfectly, through "opinions." In contrast, the world of ideas can truly be grasped by the mind; here knowledge and truth are possible. Once more, note the contrast with contemporary thinking, in which things that can be empirically measured and verified are alone granted the status of truth, whereas anything having to do with ideas and spirit is relegated to the realm of "opinion." The distinction, finally, is axiological: for Platonists, the noumenal realm is also "better" than the phenomenal realm. The miseries consequent on materiality are all too obvious: disease, death, and the loss of loved ones simply head the list. If there is a superior existence—and both the capacity of the human mind and the longing of the human heart argue that there is—it must be in a realm in which change and corruption are not possible.

Within this understanding, then, that which we do not see is more real and more worthwhile than that which we can see. As the perceived world (the visual here stands for all senses) is only a "shadow" or "reflection" of the noumenal world, the physical manifestation of a being is much inferior to its ideal essence: the idea of "dog," to put it in crude terms, is finer and more real than any panting, barking canine lurking around our feet. The two realms are distinct, but they are also related by a certain order of formal causality. Noumenal being is primordial; the phenomenal world is derivative. If the ideal world can be imagined as a stamp, the phenomenal is the impression of the seal that it leaves on paper: less crisp, smudged, faint, but still recognizable as the image of the stamp. The spiritual world, then, is one of types, and the material world one of antitypes corresponding more or less adequately to the primordial and ideal model.

The Platonism of Hebrews resembles that found in the writings of Philo Judaeus and the book of Wisdom, a version that would soon be termed "middle Platonism."[32] Elements of this worldview are found also in the Hermetic

32. This is not to argue that Hebrews read Philo but that both authors shared a common worldview and set of Scriptures; the resemblance to Philo has been argued most emphatically by Spicq, 1:91, and, although challenged by R. Williamson, *Philo and the Epistle to the Hebrews* (Arbeiten zur Literatur und Geschichte des hellenistischen Judentums 4; Leiden: Brill, 1970), has recently been well defended by G. Sterling, "Ontology versus Eschatology: Tensions between Author and Community in Hebrews," *Studia Philonica Annual: Studies in Hellenistic Judaism* 13 (2001): 190–211.

literature and in certain Gnostic writings.[33] It is a hybrid of Platonic metaphysics and Semitic cosmology, drawn from the Hebrew Scriptures, especially the Genesis creation accounts. There the heavens (*haššāmayim*) is the place where God dwells, and the earth (*haʾāreṣ*) is the place of human activity. According to Scripture, there is a great gap between these realms: "As far as the heavens are above the earth, so great is his steadfast love for those who fear him" (MT Ps 103:11); "God is in his heaven; you are on the earth; therefore, let your words be few" (Qoh 5:2); "Thus says the LORD, "Heaven is my throne and earth is my footstool" (Isa 66:1). In this construction of the world, the distinction between heaven and earth, between God and humans, is the rough equivalent to the Platonic distinction between the phenomenal and the noumenal, and would invite just that sort of application. Notice, furthermore, that the temple can be regarded as the place of access between the two realms: "The LORD is in his holy temple, the LORD's throne is in heaven" (MT Ps 11:4).

Not a great leap is required, then, to identify the Semitic heaven with the Platonic world of forms, and the Semitic earth with the realm of materiality. Philo, for example, observes that Genesis contains two accounts of God's creation of man (Gen 1:26–27; 2:7). He notices that the first account was "according to the divine image" and that the second was "from the dust of the earth." Quite naturally, he reads the first creation in terms of the ideal "form" of humanity, and the second as its material realization. Thus the ideal human is in God's image and androgynous, both "male and female," whereas a consequence of materiality is the division into man and woman (*Allegorical Interpretation* 1.31; *Questions on Genesis* 1.4). Similarly, when Philo reads Exod 25:40 in the Greek translation (LXX), he finds that Moses is instructed to build the material place of worship in the desert "according to the pattern" that God showed him. But the Greek has *typos*, "the type," which inevitably makes Philo think of Plato's ideal archetypes, so that earthly worship is but a shadow of the worship of the heavenly court (see *Questions and Answers on Exodus* 82; *Allegorical Interpretation* 3.102).

Hebrews shares the Platonic language that we find in Philo and also much of the same outlook. Heaven and earth are not simply cosmological but ontological: the realm in which God dwells is more real and true than the realm of human activity. In language that echoes Wis 7:26, the Son is said to be "a radiance of his glory and an imprint of his very being" (1:3). The worship of Jewish priests in the tent is but a "copy and shadow" of the true worship, with the authority for this being the same text from LXX Exod 25:4 as cited by Philo (Heb 8:5). The law is a shadow (*skia*) rather than the real image (*autēn tēn eikona*)

33. Despite its originality and its grasp of the "pilgrimage" element in Hebrews, the effort by E. Käsemann to interpret Hebrews against the backdrop of Gnosticism is not successful; see *The Wandering People of God: An Investigation of the Letter to the Hebrews*, trans. R. A. Harrisville and I. L. Sandberg (Minneapolis: Augsburg, 1984).

of "the good things to come" (10:1). Scripture provides "examples" that anticipate "the real" (4:11; 9:23). Jesus, for example, enters the "genuine tent" (*tēs skēnēs tēs alēthinēs*) in his resurrection (8:2) and is said to have entered "a sanctuary [not] made by hands, a copy (*antitypa*) of the real things, but into heaven itself" (9:24). In contrast to the repeated offerings of earthly priests through time, Jesus' priestly act is one that is "once for all" because it takes place in the realm of "true being," namely heaven (9:26). This contrast between the temporal and the eternal, between the mortal and the immortal, is critical to Hebrews' argument. "Heaven" encompasses God's eternal existence, and "earth" includes all that is transitory in human existence.[34]

Yet in Hebrews Platonism is also reworked in fundamental ways. For example, in Philo Platonism remains static and ahistorical. The "oracles of God" found in Scripture are like the oracles delivered at Delphi, timeless messages whose original context and meaning are not as critical as their enduring significance for Philo's own time. God's word is spiritual and timeless, but is clothed in human speech, which is temporal and changing. Human interpretation must therefore take several levels of meaning into account. The same words can bear a material (literal) sense, a psychic (moral) sense, and a spiritual (allegorical) meaning, all at the same time. Thus Philo can read the exodus story at once as the literal liberation of Israel from slavery, the moral passage from vice to virtue, and the spiritual ascent of the soul to pure freedom and ecstasy.[35]

Hebrews, in contrast, has an acute sense of history, or perhaps more accurately, of eschatology:[36] God spoke of old and now speaks decisively in his Son (1:1–2). The events of the past serve as types or examples for the present, which is greater and "more real" (see 4:11). In a sense, Hebrews can be said to turn Platonism on its side, so that the contrast between type and antitype is spelled out in terms of the past and the present, with the present being the more perfect expression.

Even more important, Hebrews appreciates rather than deprecates the physical. Only because Jesus had a human body could he be a priest (2:17; 10:5).[37] His body, moreover, is not cast off at death but is exalted: Jesus opens the new and living way to God through the veil that is his flesh (10:20). Thus Hebrews softens the sharpness of Platonic dualism. Although corporeal existence is inferior, it

34. See L. K. K. Dey, *The Intermediary World and Patterns of Perfection in Philo and Hebrews* (SBLDS 25; Missoula, MT: Scholars Press, 1975).

35. See, e.g., S. G. Sowers, *The Hermeneutics of Philo and Hebrews* (Basel Studies in Theology 1; Zurich: EVZ Verlag, 1965).

36. See esp. C. K. Barrett, "The Eschatology of the Epistle to the Hebrews," in *The Background of the New Testament and Its Eschatology*, ed. W. D. Davies and D. Daube (Cambridge: Cambridge University Press, 1956), 363–93; G. W. MacRae, "Heavenly Temple and Eschatology in the Letter to the Hebrews," *Semeia* 12 (1978): 179–99; D. A. deSilva, "Entering God's Rest: Eschatology and the Socio-Rhetorical Strategy of Hebrews," *TJ* 21 (2000): 25–43.

37. See R. H. Nash, "The Notion of Mediator in Alexandrian Judaism and the Epistle to the Hebrews," *WTJ* 40 (1978): 89–115.

plays an essential role in God's work. Connected to this is Hebrews' appreciation for change: Christ came once and will come again (9:28); having been made for a little while lower than the angels, he is now enthroned above them (2:9).

The Platonism of Hebrews is real—and critical to understanding its argument—but it is a Platonism that is stretched and reshaped by engagement with Scripture, and above all, by the experience of a historical human savior whose death and resurrection affected all human bodies and earthly existence as a whole. Hebrews shows us what Philo might have written had he been a Christian, and contributes to the transformation of Hellenism that, with the Christian Platonists Clement, Origen, and Augustine, fundamentally affected the shape of Western philosophy.

2. *Judaism*

The comparison to Philo is not inappropriate. Like the author to the Hebrews, Philo was steeped in Greco-Roman culture, yet paid deepest allegiance to the one God of Israel and found the best expression of philosophy in the Jewish Scriptures, which, again like Hebrews, he read in the Greek translation called the Septuagint (LXX). If missing the Greco-Roman metaphors and the Platonic assumptions of Hebrews means missing the richness of its discourse, ignorance of the symbolic world of Scripture means a complete lack of understanding, for Hebrews lives within the imaginative world constructed by Scripture.[38]

Hebrews reveals an extraordinarily comprehensive and thorough reader of the LXX, whose liberal use of citation and allusion suggests a confidence that the composition's hearers would have shared some degree of the author's own competence as a reader. Apart from the double appeal to Hebrew etymology in 7:2—that by itself requires no real knowledge of Hebrew—the composition is thoroughly and resolutely grounded in the LXX, and its argument plays on the specific choices of diction made by the LXX translators.[39] Yet Hebrews is willing to alter the LXX text: in 10:17 it adds "and their lawless deeds" (*kai tōn anomiōn autōn*) to the citation from Jer 31:34 (LXX 38:34); and in Heb 12:26 it inserts the words "not only" (*ou monon*) and "but" (*alla*) to the citation from Hag 2:6 in order to make it better suit the argument.[40]

38. See L. T. Johnson, "The Scriptural World of Hebrews," *Int* 57 (2003): 237–50.

39. Readers of this commentary should know from the first that in all critical cases, the version of the "Old Testament" quoted by Hebrews—and by this commentary—is that of the LXX, which in a fair number of cases differs from the Hebrew text (MT). I consistently use the numbers of the Psalms given by the LXX. The main place where this may cause readers to pause is in LXX Ps 109, the great resurrection psalm that plays such a key thematic role in this composition. Most readers are used to thinking of it as Ps 110, which is the designation in both MT and English translations.

40. For Hebrews' interaction with the LXX, see esp. R. Gheorghita, *The Role of the Septuagint in Hebrews* (WUNT 2/160; Tübingen: Mohr [Siebeck], 2003).

The explicit citations from Scripture are rich and wide-ranging.[41] In its thirteen chapters, Hebrews has some 41 explicit citations from the LXX: 14 from the Law (Genesis 6, Exodus 2, Deuteronomy 6), 1 from the historical books (1 Samuel/1Chronicles), 7 from the prophets (Isaiah 3, Jeremiah 2, Habakkuk 1, Haggai 1), and 19 from the Writings (only 1 from Proverbs, but 18 from the Psalms). It is, to be sure, not by accident that the Psalms and the prophets are favorite texts for citation, for they are easily read as pointing toward the Christ. Although many of its citations are brief, Hebrews is also fond of quoting fairly extensive passages of four lines (7:1–2; 10:37–38; 12:5–6), five lines (1:7–8; 10:16–17), six lines (10:5–7), ten lines (3:7–11), or even twenty lines (8:8–12) in length.

Hebrews is distinctive among New Testament compositions for the variety of ways in which it introduces its scriptural citations and for their unliterary character. Nowhere does the author introduce quotations as "Scripture," that is, "writing" (*graphē*). The common New Testament expression, "it stands written" (*gegraptai*; see Matt 2:5; Mark 1:2; Luke 2:23; Acts 1:20; Rom 3:4; 1 Cor 1:10; Gal 3:10; 1 Pet 1:16), occurs only *within* the citation from Ps 40:8 (Heb 10:7). Consistent with its opening description that God "spoke (*lalēsas*) in the past to the fathers in the prophets" (1:1), Hebrews' considerable repertoire of introductory expressions is entirely *oral*.

With God as the understood subject, Hebrews introduces citations with expressions such as "he said" (1:5), "he says" (1:6; 2:12; 8:8; 10:15), "by saying" (3:15), "he has said" (4:3), "the one who said" (5:5), "he has promised" (12:26), "he swore by saying" (6:13–14). With Christ (see 9:28) as the implied subject, Hebrews introduces the long citation in 10:5–7 with, "Therefore, as he comes into the world, he says." Similarly in 2:12–13, it is by implication the Son who is not ashamed to call humans brothers, "saying" the three texts from Ps 21:23, Isa 8:17, and 18. In 3:17 Hebrews introduces a citation with "the Holy Spirit says," and in 10:15, "the Holy Spirit also testifies to us." More periphrastically, Hebrews introduces the citation from Ps 8:5–7 with "someone has testified somewhere" (Heb 2:6), and introduces the verse from Ps 109:4 with reference to the Son, "it is testified that" (Heb 7:17).

What are the implications of this manner of citation? To some extent, it is simply appropriate that Scripture be delivered "orally" rather than "textually" in a discourse that so emphasizes its own oral character (e.g., 2:1; 5:11; 6:9; 8:1). But more than stylistic fit seems to be at work. The prologue declares that God spoke through the prophets of old (1:1). But what does Hebrews mean by "the

41. See M. Barth, "The Old Testament in Hebrews: An Essay in Biblical Hermeneutics," in *Current Issues in New Testament Interpretation* (FS O. A. Piper), ed. W. Klassen and G. Snyder (New York: Harper, 1962), 53–78; and G. H. Guthrie, "Hebrews' Use of the Old Testament: Recent Trends in Research," *CBR* 1.2 (2003): 271–94.

prophets"? Although it explicitly mentions the law (10:1) as well as the law of Moses (10:28) and its commandments (7:5, 16, 18; 9:19), it does not do so with reference to any citation. Similarly, it speaks in passing of "David, Samuel, and the prophets" as among those who gave prodigal witness to faith (11:32). But with reference to a citation from Scripture, David is mentioned only in 4:7.

By constantly citing passages from the LXX, and by introducing such passages with verbs of speaking, Hebrews in effect treats *texts* as the voices of the "prophets" through whom God spoke in the past. And because many of his verbs of introduction are in the present tense, the hearer experiences these voices as God's speech to the present and not simply to the past. The Holy Spirit bears witness through the text "to us" (10:15). Hebrews happily exploits the biblical chronology that places David long after the time of Joshua, but does so in order to assert the continuing pertinence of the words, "If you hear his voice today, do not harden your hearts" (4:7).

Scripture, in short, is not a collection of ancient texts that can throw light on the present through analogy. It is the voice of the living God: "the word of God is living and powerful" (4:12). It speaks directly and urgently to people here and now: "therefore, just as the Holy Spirit says, 'If you hear his voice today'" (3:7).[42]

Hebrews' use of Scripture goes well beyond its direct citations. In some places, the diction of the composition is a virtual tissue of allusions to the LXX text. Such a thick web of intertextual connections further serves to construct a scriptural symbolic world. The power of such allusion and echo is arguably even stronger than that of direct citation, precisely because Scripture's language is not bracketed off as something "other" but is appropriated without explanation or apology as the author's own language. Hearers who can catch the allusions and echoes are reinforced in their impression that they and the author share in the same, scripturally shaped, world. Two examples make the point. Casual readers of Hebrews will be surprised to realize that in all of chapter 9 there is only one direct citation from the LXX (Exod 24:8 in Heb 9:20). Their surprise is connected to the sense, given by the language of the passage, that it is entirely scriptural. The effect derives from allusion rather than citation. In the extended contrast between the worship of the first tent and that inaugurated by Christ's exaltation, we can detect more than nineteen distinct allusions to Exodus, Leviticus, and Numbers.

Even more impressive is the collection of allusions in the great encomium to faith in chapter 11.[43] The passage contains two direct citations from the LXX,

42. See G. Hughes, *Hebrews and Hermeneutics: The Epistle to the Hebrews as a New Testament Example of Biblical Interpretation* (SNTSMS 36; Cambridge: Cambridge University Press, 1979).

43. See P. M. Eisenbaum, *The Jewish Heroes of Christian History: Hebrews 11 in Literary Context* (SBLDS 156; Atlanta: Scholars Press, 1997).

one from Gen 21:12 (11:18) and one from Gen 47:31 (11:21). But within 11:3–31, we can catch at least twenty-eight separate allusions to Genesis, Exodus, and Joshua. As the intensity of the encomium increases, so does the density of scriptural allusion. In the seven verses of 11:32–38, there are some thirty-two allusions to Judges, 1 and 2 Samuel, 1 and 2 Kings, Daniel, 2 Maccabees, 2 Chronicles, and possibly even the *Martyrdom of Isaiah*. The encomium thus summons a great "cloud of witnesses" to cheer on those who must now run in the path of the pioneer and perfecter of faith, Jesus (12:1–3). But it also draws its hearers into a world constructed by Scripture. The image of the race, we have seen, is drawn from the Greek culture of competitive games. But because of the marvelous intertwining of textual allusion, the hearers know that this race is one of pilgrimage begun already with Abraham's looking for a lasting city (11:13–16), a pilgrimage that will bring them to "Mount Zion and a city of the living God, a heavenly Jerusalem" (12:22).

How does Hebrews interpret Scripture? Much of the commentary focuses on this subject, since the engagement with Scripture is central to Hebrews' argument. The simplest and most adequate answer is simply that Hebrews interprets Scripture entirely from the perspective of the experience of the death, resurrection, and exaltation of Jesus. That said, one can also note that Hebrews uses a variety of interpretive techniques.[44] Unlike Philo, Hebrews does not engage in allegorical interpretation, apart from the modest etymological exercise on Melchizedek in 7:2. Like other New Testament writings, Hebrews applies texts of Scripture directly to Christ, on the assumption that the person of whom the ancient texts spoke was the Messiah (see the "Messianic Florilegium" in 1:5–2:18), and even places the words of a psalm in the mouth of Christ, "coming into the world" (see Ps 40:7–9 in Heb 10:5–7).

Hebrews also engages in the close reading of specific passages of Scripture, and in these sections we can see the employment of several practices.[45] Familiar to us from Jewish midrash are the careful attention to specific words (such as the open-ended implications of "today," 4:7) and to the sequence of events in the narrative (such as the time between Joshua and David, 4:7), the principle that if something does not occur in Torah it did not happen (7:3), and the principle called *gezerah shawah*: passages in Scripture using the same word or speaking of the same thing can be used to interpret each other—thus Hebrews exploits the use of "rest" (*katapausis*) in Ps 94:11 and Gen 2:2, as well as the appearance of Melchizedek in Ps 109:4 and Gen 14:18.

44. S. G. Sowers, *The Hermeneutics of Philo and Hebrews: A Comparison of the Interpretation of the Old Testament in Philo Judaeus and the Epistle to the Hebrews* (Richmond: John Knox Press, 1965).

45. See the useful survey of Jewish interpretive techniques in H. W. Bateman, *Early Jewish Hermeneutics and Hebrews 1:5–13: The Impact of Early Jewish Exegesis on the Interpretation of a Significant New Testament Passage* (American University Studies 7: Theology and Religion 193; New York: Peter Lang, 1997).

Most impressively, Hebrews finds in Scripture examples and precedents that can be imitated and continued—such are the heroes of faith listed in chapter 11—as well as types that correspond to present realities: Abraham in one reading is part of the pilgrimage of faith (11:8–19) and in the other is the type of the Levitical priesthood as Melchizedek is the type of Christ the great high priest (7:4–10). Similarly, Joshua (whose name in the LXX is *Iēsous*), who brought the people into the land of Canaan, is the type of Jesus (*Iēsous*), who enters into God's true rest (4:8–14). The disbelieving generation of the wilderness serves as a negative type of the present people of God addressed by the author (3:1–4:11). And the entire system of worship as described in Scripture serves as the shadow and type of the true worship offered by Christ (9:1–10:18).

The portrayal of Christ as high priest is elaborated below, but it should be noted here that the designation involves more than the simple ascription of a title. It involves as well the apprehension of Judaism as a religious system. A network of interconnected premises runs through Hebrews' argument, especially in chapters 7–10. Among them are the convictions that God and God's people are bound by covenant (7:22; 8:6–13), that every covenant is explicated by laws (7:11–14), that among these laws are requirements concerning sacrifice (8:3–4), that among such regulations are those concerning the cult site, its furnishings, and its rituals, and the qualifications of its priests (9:1–10). The significance of Hebrews' focus should not be missed. Covenant and law are understood first of all not in terms of the structuring of human behavior but in terms of securing the divine-human relationship, not in moral terms but in terms of ritual. In Hebrews the cult of Israel serves as a sort of synecdoche for the covenant with God.

Concerning sacrifice itself, furthermore, Hebrews focuses not on those offerings of grain and fruit that express thanksgiving and dedication, but on the animal sacrifices that are used, particularly on the Day of Atonement (Yom Kippur) as an act of reconciliation between God and humans, drawing its picture of these not from contemporary temple practice—so far as we can tell—but from the prescriptions found in Scripture (Lev 16:1–34).[46] Reconciliation is necessary as a repair of the covenantal relationship because the sin of the people has damaged that relationship. All of this is rather straightforward, as is the ritual prescribed for the priests. Although ordinary priests sacrifice every day in the holy place, the holy of holies (where the ark of the covenant symbolized the presence of God among the people) was entered only once a year and by one person. On the Day of Atonement, the high priest entered the sanctuary carrying

46. For a broad treatment of the topic, see G. Anderson, "Sacrifice and Sacrificial Offerings," *ABD* 5:870–86; for helpful background in both Greco-Roman and Jewish worlds, see F. M. Young, *The Use of Sacrificial Ideas in Greek Christian Writers from the New Testament to John Chrysostom* (Patristic Monograph Series 5; Cambridge, MA: Philadelphia Patristic Foundation, 1979), 1–73; for the topic in Hebrews, see R. D. Nelson, "'He Offered Himself': Sacrifice in Hebrews," *Int* 57 (2003): 251–65; and W. G Johnsson, "The Cultus of Hebrews in Twentieth-Century Scholarship," *ExpT* 89 (1977–78): 104–8.

the blood of the sacrificed victim, and sprinkled its blood on the ark of the covenant (Lev 16:14–16).

More complex and difficult to understand are the further premises that underlie the ritual and the understanding of sacrifice itself. These, in particular, contemporary readers who have no contact with such religious practices—and often regard them as evidence of undeveloped culture—find it difficult to understand or appreciate.[47] Four of these premises are: (1) the importance of the body as symbol of the self—religion is not a matter of thinking or feeling but of disposing of the body in certain ways; (2) the mysterious character of life as a gift from God rather than a "natural" and autonomous possession; (3) the necessity of exchanging gifts within a relationship—the gift of life demands the gift of life; and (4) the mutual participation in life by all living beings. These premises, in turn, support the assumption that living beings can represent one another, stand in for one another: humans can represent all creatures before God, and one human being can represent other humans before God. This is, for Hebrews, the essence of priesthood.

I stated above that the cult of Israel is a synecdoche for covenant. The term "synecdoche" means "the part for the whole," and this is precisely what takes place within the cult itself. The body stands for the self, and blood stands for life (Lev 17:11). Thus if my blood is poured out, that stands for the pouring out of my life. Similarly, then, an animal's life can stand for one's own life—the goat or ox in one's "possession" is as much a gift of life from God as one's own life, and, in strict fact, one's own continued life often depends on the life of the goat or the ox. It follows, then, given the participation between animals and humans, that the pouring out of an animal's blood can represent my life as well as its own life. Likewise, the priest, who represents other people before God and pours out (or sprinkles) the blood of an animal on the ark representing God's presence among the people, stands for all the people as well as himself and offers the blood of the animal as representing himself and all those for whom he stands.

The intended effect of animal sacrifice, then, is the "perfection" or "consecration" of the victim—its movement through death from the profane life of the herd into the realm of "holiness" or apartness that is God's presence; and with the "finishing" or "sanctification" of the victim—its entering into God's sphere in the holy of holies—comes the consecration or perfecting of the people as well. They also, through this process of vicarious representation—through the life of the animal, through the action of the priests—enter into the space of holiness, are consecrated, perfected. They are at peace with God. The covenant is restored.

47. For two efforts to approach the theme from contemporary perspectives, see J. Stevenson-Moessner, "The Road to Perfection: An Interpretation of Suffering in Hebrews," *Int* 57 (2003): 280–90; and L. T. Johnson, "Sacrifice Is the Body Language of Love," in *Living Gospel* (London: Continuum, 2004), 27–36.

Hebrews understands and to a very great extent shares all these perceptions, so that if there is a change of covenant, there will also automatically be a change of law and a change of sacrifice (7:11–14). Hebrews reinterprets the entire system from the perspective of the new covenant that God has made with humans promised by the prophet Jeremiah, a law written on human hearts (Jer 31:31–32; Heb 8:8–12; 10:16–17), and the life, death, and resurrection of Jesus Christ: he is the mediator of that new covenant (Heb 9:15).

But in order to grasp how Hebrews regards the sacrifice of Jesus as superior to that of the first covenant, we need to understand how Hebrews shares a further set of premises characteristic of other Jewish thinkers, like Philo Judaeus, who used the symbolism of cult, but understood the covenant between God and the people primarily in terms of a moral relationship more than a cultic one. In this understanding, it is the human heart—that is, human interior dispositions—that defines the relationship with God more than external observances. When people sin, their *conscience* is polluted: they have acted in a way that, because of God's law, they know is wrong. In order to be truly reconciled with God, then, there needs to also be an internal change, a "purification of conscience."[48]

The problem with animal sacrifice, in this view, is that it is incapable of fully representing the internal dispositions of the human heart. The consecration of the animal imperfectly accomplishes the consecration of the person. Similarly, the actions of priests in pouring out the blood of the animal inadequately represent the rest of the people before God. The offering is, in a sense, two or three steps removed from the internal human response. Finally, the human temple, or tent of meeting, inadequately represents the presence of God in the world. What is needed is a "more perfect" sacrifice, one that can provide access to the living God, and not merely to that representation of God's presence in the cult. Hebrews' understanding of Jesus as the "perfecter" stands within this set of premises concerning the true nature of the relationship between God and humans, one that reaches beyond the body to the depths of human interiority, and beyond the physical space of the temple into the holiness of God's very being.

I have suggested up to this point that the symbolic world of Hebrews most resembles that of Philo. But is there not another manifestation of first-century Jewish life in which we find a set of convictions remarkably similar to Hebrews? One could argue that Hebrews most resembles the thought world of the Qumran sectarians.[49] At Qumran as in Hebrews, we find a "new covenant" community (1QS 1:16–18), a separation from the official cult of Israel (in the Jerusalem

48. See, e.g., Philo, *Allegorical Interpretation* 3.128–37; *Special Laws* 1.145–50, 167, 188, 202–11; *Let. Aris.* 141–71; see also Thompson, *Beginnings of Christian Philosophy*, 101–15.

49. As in Y. Yadin, "The Dead Sea Scrolls and the Epistle to the Hebrews," *Aspects of the Dead Sea Scrolls: Scripta Hierosolymitana* 4 (1958): 36–55; F. C. Fensham, "Hebrews and Qumran," *Neot* 5 (1971): 9–21.

temple, 1QpHab 8:9; 9:9) together with an appropriation of its symbols, the sense of offering prayer as a "spiritual sacrifice" (4QFLor 1:6; 1QS 8:6–8; 9:3–11)—prayer in which angels participate[50]—and most of all, the expectation of a priestly as well as a kingly messiah (1QSa 2:1–21), together with an interest in the figure of Melchizedek (11QMelch). This is, indeed, a remarkable set of parallel concerns and symbols. There are, however, equally important points of divergence: Hebrews rejects the laws of purity and diet about which the sectarians were obsessively concerned (1QS 1:11–12; 6:17–22); has no mythic explanation for the world's division into good and evil (1QS 3:13–4:26); does not advocate a withdrawal from the godless or an absolute community of possessions (1QS 3:2; 5:2–3). Most of all, Qumran does not really help us to grasp Hebrews' most basic conviction concerning what constitutes "the better." For that reason, and for all the positive reasons already given, despite the intriguing ways in which Hebrews shares elements with Qumran, the sort of Hellenistic Judaism represented by Philo remains the best overall symbolic world within which to read Hebrews.

3. Christian Tradition

Hebrews stands apart from Philo and other Hellenistic Jews who read their Scripture in Greek and sought a deeper meaning to sacrifice, because everything has been fundamentally altered by the experience of Jesus Christ. Hebrews is so distinctive within the New Testament canon that it is helpful to remember how much it also stands within the nascent Christian tradition. Although the author of Hebrews would have understood Philo, it is questionable whether Philo would have understood Hebrews, precisely because of the deeply paradoxical character of the Christian confession, which reshaped both the worldview of Platonism and the world of Scripture.

In two passages Hebrews refers in passing to elements of the shared Christian tradition. In 2:3 he asks rhetorically how they should escape if they neglect "so great a salvation," providing a short summary that resembles the narrative of Luke–Acts: this salvation was declared first by the Lord—an unmistakable allusion to the human ministry of Jesus—and then attested to us by those who heard him (see Luke 1:2), while God bore witness by signs, wonders, and powerful deeds (see Acts 2:43; 5:12; 2 Cor 12:12), and powerful deeds of the Holy Spirit "distributed according to his will" (see Acts 2:1–4; 1 Cor 12:11; Eph

50. See C. Newsom, *Songs of the Sabbath Sacrifice: A Critical Edition* (HSS 27; Atlanta: Scholars Press, 1985), 23–48; for the suggestion that a form of Merkabah practice was part of the background of Hebrews, see R. Williamson, "The Background to the Epistle to the Hebrews," *ExpT* 87 (1975–76): 232–37.

4:2–7). In Heb 6:1 the author speaks of the "basic instruction about the Messiah" that he presupposes as he moves on to more mature teaching. The statement is preceded by the same contrast between "milk for babies" and "solid food for adults" (5:11–14) that Paul had used in writing to the Corinthians (1 Cor 3:1–3). But whereas Paul considered the Corinthians incapable of mature teaching since they were full of rivalry and strife (1 Cor 3:3), the author of Hebrews chides his readers for their dullness: they should by this time themselves be teachers (Heb 5:12). Hebrews does not stay, as did Paul, with the basics. It pushes toward an understanding of Christ that does not in the least conflict with the shared Christian traditions, but rather builds on those traditions for hearers able to move toward greater levels of insight and commitment.

Hebrews lists in 6:1–2 some of those basic elements. It can scarcely be a full list, for the rhetoric demands only a brief summation. In fact, the list of six elements touches on only three moments: conversion, initiation into the community, and the end time. First, then, are "repentance from dead works and faith toward God" (see 1 Thess 1:9); second, and most obscure, are "teaching about ablutions and imposition of hands," which could refer to many things but may indicate the ritual of initiation into the community (see Acts 8:12–17); third are "resurrection of the dead and eternal judgment" (Acts 17:31; Matt 25:31–46). That the middle set of terms refers to initiation may be supported by what follows, when the author declares that a second repentance is impossible to those "who have once been enlightened, who have tasted the heavenly gift and become partakers of the Holy Spirit, and who have tasted the noble word of God and the powers of the coming age" if they commit apostasy (6:4–5; see "after you were enlightened" in 10:32, and for comparable language concerning initiation, see Eph 5:15; 1 Pet 2:3; 1 Cor 12:13; Eph 3:19).

This summary omits any mention of Christ, but the deeper understanding of Christ is precisely the main focus of his argument. Although I will discuss Hebrews' Christology extensively below, I can note here that the composition reveals the full range of the basic Christian tradition concerning Jesus: his preexistence (1:2; 10:5); his incarnation (2:14–18; 10:5–7); his sacrificial death (1:3; 2:9; 6:6; 7:27); his resurrection (1:3)—the enthronement imagery of the classic resurrection psalm, Ps 110, runs throughout the composition; and his return "a second time" for judgment (Heb 9:28; 10:25). Hebrews advocates the classic triad of Christian virtues: love (6:10; 10:24; 13:1), hope (3:6; 6:11, 18; 7:9; 10:23; 11:1), and above all, faith (4:2; 6:1,12; 10:22, 38, 39; 12:2; 13:7, and 23 instances in chap. 11!). Similarly, Hebrews calls for the practices that we recognize as standard in the early Christian movement: prayer (13:15); hospitality (13:2), care for prisoners (10:34; 13:3), chaste sexual life (13:4), sharing possessions (13:16), avoiding love of money (13:5). Hebrews encourages attendance at assemblies (10:25) and respect for leaders of the community (13:7, 17).

Beyond these common elements of the Christian movement, Hebrews reveals points of emphasis that resemble in greater or lesser degree specific Christian writers. The most obvious example is undoubtedly Paul, as in the conviction that Christ has given an "access" to God (Heb 4:16; 10:19–22; see Rom 5:1; Eph 2:18), or in the understanding of Jesus' faith as obedience (Heb 5:1–10; Rom 5:12–21). The attention given to God's promise to Abraham (Heb 6:13–18; Gal 3:16–18) and to Abraham's response of faith (Heb 11:8–12; Rom 4:1–25) is likewise noteworthy.[51] In other respects, Hebrews resembles the Gospel of John: it begins with a preexistent Word and a Son through whom all things are created (Heb 1:2–5; John 1:1–18), and does not regard "the flesh" (Heb 2:14; 5:7; 10:20) as an attitude hostile to God (as in Paul) but as a sign of human weakness and mortality (as in John 1:13–14; 3:6; 8:15).[52]

Perhaps most striking are the parallels between Hebrews and 1 Peter, which also calls itself an "exhortation" (*paraklēsis*), particularly the emphasis in each on the death of Jesus in cultic terms as the sacrifice of an innocent victim (Heb 4:15; 7:26; 1 Pet 1:19; 2:22; 3:18), and the sprinkling of his blood (Heb 10:22; 12:24; 1 Pet 1:2), and his exaltation (Heb 1:3–4, 13; 4:14; 5:6; 8:1; 10:12; 1 Pet 3:21–22), as well as in the implied characterization of the church as a pilgrim people (Heb 11:8–16; 12:22; 13:14; 1 Pet 1:1; 2:11), and the epithet "Chief Shepherd" for Christ (Heb 13:20; see 1 Pet 2:25; 5:4).[53] The point of these observations is not that Hebrews drew from any of these writings, or that they drew from Hebrews. The point, rather, is that Hebrews, for all its distinctive rendering of the Christian mystery, is nevertheless not utterly idiosyncratic, but gives its full attention to the development of elements that play a less central role in other Christian writings.

In summary, the symbolic world of Hebrews is profoundly shaped by Greco-Roman culture, above all in its language, rhetoric, and philosophical perspective, but is equally formed by the world of Judaism, especially through the LXX version of Scripture and the sacrificial cult. Both these cultural realms are, in turn, reshaped by the particular experiences and convictions of the nascent Christian movement within which Hebrews stands. The distinctive vision of reality that emerges from the reading of Hebrews does not result, to be sure, from the mere fact of cultural contact or exchange, but from the passionate conviction and brilliant imagination of a single mind, the anonymous rhetorician who crafted this word of exhortation.

51. The parallels with Paul are developed by Spicq, 1:155–56; see also C. P. Anderson, "Hebrews among the Letters of Paul," *SR* 5 (1975–76): 258–66 (for resemblance to Colossians); and B. Witherington III, "The Influence of Galatians on Hebrews," *NTS* 37 (1991): 146–52; Ellingworth, 3–12, elaborates the differences between Paul and Hebrews, on which see further below.

52. For the parallels between John and Hebrews, see Spicq, 1:109–38.

53. For further parallels between 1 Peter and Hebrews, see Attridge, 30–31.

Argument

Earlier, when discussing the rhetoric of Hebrews, I made the point that although the arrangement of an argument is important, even more important is its invention. Invention can include both the sorts of evidences that an orator brings forward for a position—thinking of *logos* arguments, now, and not appeals to character or emotion—and what we might think of as the logic of the argument, the sort of premises that may not appear explicitly on the surface of the text (i.e., in its arrangement) but that hold the argument together as a whole. It is to that aspect of Hebrews, the longest sustained argument in the New Testament (with only Romans a possible challenger), that I now turn.

A simple form of logic—familiar to us from both Hellenistic rhetoric and rabbinic midrash, with the Jewish usage probably borrowing from the Greek—underlies the sermon as a whole. Grasping it enables the reader to follow the author's argument even when details remain obscure. In Hellenistic logic it is called the argument *a minore ad maius*, "from the lesser to the greater"; in Hebrew it is called *qal weḥomer*, "the light and the heavy." Reduced to its bare bones, the argument looks like this: if such and such is the case with *x*, which is a small matter, then it must be even more the case with *y*, which is a greater matter.

Hebrews is not the only New Testament writing to use the logic. We find in Rom 5:12–21, where Paul's *synkrisis* (comparison) between Adam and the new Adam, Christ, is carried by the phrase *pollō mallon* ("how much the more"), and has as its premise that Christ is the beginning of a new humanity and a new reign of God more powerful than the reign of sin and death initiated by the first human: "the free gift is not like the trespass. For if many died through one man's trespass, much more have the grace of God and the free gift in the grace of that one man Jesus Christ abounded for many" (Rom 5:15).

It is a form of argument used also in rabbinic parables and in the parables of Jesus. The argument involves a form of analogy. As in all analogy, two elements are required: an element of similarity (or continuity) and an element of dissimilarity (or discontinuity). In a typical midrashic application, for instance, we find God's way of dealing with Israel compared to an earthly king's manner of dealing with his people (*Sifre on Numbers* 86). The element of continuity is the relationship of rule and submission. The element of discontinuity is the infinitely greater magnitude of God's rule over the universe. The logic thus runs: if an earthly king acts this way, how much more will the King of the universe do the same?

In Hebrews the element of continuity is the word that God speaks to God's people. God spoke in the past, and continues to speak in the present (1:1–2; 2:1–4; 3:5–7; 4:12–13; 7:28). God's consistency in speaking—through prophets or Son—is what provides the ground for comparison: God's word does not change even though the mode of revelation may change. Likewise continuous is a "people" that is addressed by God's speech. The element of discontinuity, then, is the agent bringing the word to the people. Using the technique of *synkrisis*, Hebrews draws a series of contrasts between, on one hand, the mediation of God's speech by prophets, angels, Moses, and Torah (in the cult of sacrifice), and, on the other hand, Christ.

The critical step in the argument is therefore to establish the greater over the lesser, the "heavy" over the "light." The linchpin of Hebrews is, consequently, the supremacy of the word spoken by God through the agency of his Son, Jesus Christ. The author therefore demonstrates in sequence—using Scripture itself as evidence—that, although the angels are ministering spirits, Jesus is God's Son (1:1–14); that although Moses was a servant in God's house (i.e., the people), Jesus is the Son and builder of the house (3:5–6); that although Joshua (*Iēsous*) brought the people into the land, Jesus Christ is the one who enters God's rest (4:1–10, 14); that the cultic acts of the Aaronic priests had to be repeated through time because of their inefficacy, but through his resurrection and exaltation, Jesus is the eternal Son who offers an enduring sacrifice (chaps. 5–10). That the revelation of God through Christ is "greater/better" and that therefore the salvation he offers is greater/better (see the use of *kreittōn* in 1:4; 6:9; 7:7, 19, 22; 8:6; 9:23; 10:34; 11:16, 35, 40; 12:24) is the heart of the *exposition* of Hebrews.

The same logic, however, also characterizes the *exhortation*, which, as I have noted, alternates regularly with the exposition. The word spoken through the Son holds a greater promise and a more certain fulfillment than the words spoken in the past (12:22–24). The term *bebaios* ("reliable, sure, certain") recurs frequently in characterizing this present word (2:2; 6:19; 9:17; 13:9). Because the present word is more sure and powerful, obedience to it gains a greater reward; conversely, disobedience earns a greater punishment (2:2; 4:1–2; 6:6–8; 12:17).

The contrast here is between the people in the wilderness of old and the people of God today. That desert generation failed to hear and obey, so it did not enter the land of Canaan, which was the lesser "rest" promised them. The present people also have a promised and greater rest: the very life of God into which the resurrected Jesus has entered once for all. This promise also demands a response of obedience, and failure will be more grievous than in the former case. Thus the urgency of 4:11–12: "Therefore let us hurry to enter into that rest, so that none fall into the same type of disobedience. For the word of God is living and powerful, sharper than any two-edged sword, cutting to the division between soul and spirit, joints and marrow, able to discern the thoughts and conceptions of the heart."

The Circumstances of Composition

When we speak of the way in which Hebrews was received and interpreted within the church, and when we describe its language and logic, we can have a certain confidence, for we are simply describing what lies before us. But when we turn to the task of determining the historical circumstances within which Hebrews was composed, we are engaged in a far trickier and more difficult enterprise. We must make informed guesses on the basis of clues in the text, which means that we must at the same time be willing to exercise a certain amount of imagination, while disciplining our imagination by the boundaries established by the actual evidence. In this discussion, I will move from what is least to what is most speculative, from the circumstances and identity of the readers—about which the text at least tells us something—to questions of date and authorship—about which we can identify reasonable possibilities, but nothing more.

Rhetorical Situation

Hebrews was written to be read aloud to an audience. A mark of effective rhetoric is that it addresses the real situation of the hearers. We might expect to find, then, some signs of the rhetorical situation within the composition. We have already seen that Hebrews is a form of deliberative rhetoric that seeks to persuade the hearers to avoid certain actions and perform others, and have gathered hints concerning the author's perception of his readers from the sort of *ethos*, *pathos*, and *logos* arguments he has assembled.

The title "To the Hebrews" (*Pros Hebraious*) is attached to the composition in our earliest manuscripts, but probably represents an early effort to identify (from the themes) an anonymous text with no addressees as one written to the Jews. On one side, the title certainly does not mean, as has been suggested, that it is a tract written "against the Jews," any more than Paul's letter *Pros Rōmaious* means "against the Romans!"[54] Hebrews is deliberative, not forensic. On the other side, we cannot determine with full certainty the ethnic makeup of the intended readers (or hearers). There is certainly more internal evidence to support the position that they were Jewish rather than Gentile.[55] It is of the first importance to note, moreover, that the composition lacks any element of supersessionism in the proper sense of the term, that is, the replacement of Israel by Gentiles as God's people. This position will be argued in detail throughout

54. See B. P. Hunt, "The Epistle to the Hebrews: An Anti-Judaic Treatise?" *SE* 2 (1964): 408–10; R. W. Johnson, *Going Outside the Camp: The Sociological Function of the Levitical Critique in the Epistle to the Hebrews* (JSNTSup 209; Sheffield: Sheffield Academic Press, 2001); I. Salevao, *Legitimation in the Letter to the Hebrews: The Contruction and Maintenance of a Symbolic Universe* (JSNTSup 219; Sheffield: Sheffield Academic Press, 2002). These works suppose a Gentile readership and a late dating, as does M. E. Isaacs, *Sacred Space: An Approach to the Theology of the Epistle to the Hebrews* (JSNTSup 73; Sheffield: Sheffield Academic Press, 1992).

55. See, e.g., B. Lindars, *The Theology of the Letter to the Hebrews* (New Testament Theology; Cambridge: Cambridge University Press, 1991), 4–15; J. Dunnill, *Covenant and Sacrifice in the Letter to the Hebrews* (SNTSMS 75; Cambridge: Cambridge University Press, 1992), 13–39.

the commentary, but it is clear that the composition, from start to finish, regards the promises to Abraham as enduring.[56]

Once we have decided that Hebrews is not by Paul—and that is, as I have suggested, the right decision—we unfortunately lack any external controls, and must rely entirely on clues from the text and our very fragmentary knowledge of available candidates. Not surprisingly, scholars have proposed a long list of possible recipients: the Colossians, the Corinthians, converted Jewish priests in Jerusalem, possibly even converts from the Qumran community, or Diaspora Jews in Jerusalem on pilgrimage.[57] The suggestions all depend on the same internal evidence, and the same data can work within several hypotheses. In such circumstances, the best approach is to proceed cautiously on the basis of what the composition says, and respect the limits beyond which we simply indulge in speculation.

We can say with the highest probability that the author considered his hearers to be people who were Christian for some time (6:1–3), to be capable of understanding Greek of the sort a trained rhetorician would employ, and to be able to follow the intricacies of a complex scriptural argument. One cannot always argue from an author's use of texts to the readers' appreciation of them. Origen and Augustine, to name only two, did things with texts that perhaps few of their congregants could fully appreciate. But in the case of Hebrews, the argument relies so heavily on citations and the ability to recognize their import that if the audience was deficient in this respect, the writer was a poor communicator.

Trying to learn something about the implied audience from the author's choice of themes is hazardous, because apart from cases when a local issue is explicitly identified as such, literary themes may be driven as much by an author's vision as by the preoccupations of hearers. We can observe that the author puts the angels in a place subordinate to Christ (1:5–14; 2:2), much as Paul did in writing to the Galatians (Gal 3:19; 4:9) and to the Colossians (Col 1:16; 2:18). But we cannot conclude that these readers had any particular interest in angels as such, whether as objects of or companions in worship. Likewise, Hebrews puts Moses in his place below Christ (Heb 3:2–6), as Paul did in writing to the Galatians (Gal 3:19) and Corinthians (2 Cor 3:7–18). But we

56. On this see C. P. Anderson, "Who Are the Heirs of the New Age in the Epistle to the Hebrews?" in *Apocalyptic and the New Testament: Essays in Honor of J. Louis Martyn*, ed. J. Marcus and M. L. Soards (JSNTSup 24; Sheffield: JSOT Press, 1989), 255–77; and C. M. Williamson, "Anti-Judaism in Hebrews?" *Int* 57 (2003): 266–79.

57. See, respectively, T. W. Manson, "The Problem of the Epistle to the Hebrews," *BJRL* 32 (1949): 1–17; Montefiore, 1–31; Spicq, 1:220–52; idem, "L'Épître aux Hébreux, Apollos, Jean Baptiste, les Hellénistes et Qumran," *RevQ* 1 (1959): 365–90; Buchanan, 256–63.

cannot conclude that the readers were particular admirers of Moses (and Joshua), or that they were especially preoccupied by matters of law.

Most of all, the Levitical (Aaronic) priesthood is made otiose by comparison with the high priesthood of Christ (chaps. 5–10). This is a concern not otherwise reflected in the New Testament writings, although, as I have noted briefly with reference to Qumran, there were rival claimants to the priesthood and authentic worship within contemporary Judaism. Does this suggest that the readers were former priests or converts from Qumran? It does not exclude that possibility, but neither does it make it more than a possibility. Finally, the author makes disparaging remarks concerning diverse teachings and legislation dealing with food and drink (9:10; 13:9), which remind us of similar remarks in Col 2:20–22, 1 Cor 8:1–13, and Rom 14:1–23. Once more, the comments are made in passing, and are of uncertain value in reconstructing the situation of the readers. Given the concentrated and frequent references to worship, however, and the centrality of the theme of priesthood, it is possible that this last theme leads us closer to the author's perception of a concern with respect to his audience.

Clues that the composition gives concerning the social situation of the hearers are more helpful. They have already experienced some suffering for their commitment to the Messiah Jesus (10:32–35; 12:13) and can look forward to more (13:13–14). They have not yet suffered to the point of being killed (12:4), but they knew and visited some among them who had been imprisoned (10:34). Further, they had either themselves experienced or knew of those who had been "publicly shamed by revilings and affliction" (10:33). Perhaps most striking, both because of its specificity and because it gets taken up thematically, is the comment that the hearers had "accepted the seizure of [their] property with joy, since [they] knew that [they themselves] had a better and permanent possession" (10:34). Like the Qumran sectarians in still another way, then, some of them had experienced despoliation of their property.

That they had lost property helps us appreciate the pertinence and poignancy of the author's exhortation to provide hospitality (13:2), to keep free from love of money (13:5), to be content with what they have (13:5), and to share what possessions they have (13:16). Even more, it provides a context for some of the sermon's most powerful imagery, which involves property. Already in 10:34, we see the contrast drawn between the property taken from them and their conviction (the author hopes) that they had a "better and permanent possession." Throughout the discourse, moreover, property language is used to symbolize relationships and especially hoped-for realities (e.g., 2:14; 3:1; 6:13–18; 7:4–10; 9:16–22), and does so climactically in the passage immediately after this recollection of the community's situation, where the heroes of faith provide an example of those who were willing to leave their property and wander as aliens because they "were expecting the city that has foundations, whose designer and maker is God" (11:10; see also 11:14–16). The hearers' experience of dispossession also sharpens the call to go forth to Jesus outside the camp and bear the abuse he suffered, "for we do not have a permanent city here. We are seeking the city to come" (13:13–14).[58]

The author has also drawn a sketch of the community's experience that suggests a falling away from an earlier enthusiasm. After their enlightenment (initiation), they had formerly, we note, "joyfully" accepted the plundering of their property, shown compassion on prisoners, and endured "a great contest of sufferings" (10:32–34). But the author suggests that they have not made the progress they ought to have: by now they should be mature teachers, but they still need to be fed milk (5:12). Hebrews attributes this lack of progress to their being "reluctant listeners" (5:11). The author is concerned that his hearers will fall short of God's promise (4:11), and that they will be among those who "draw back—to [their] destruction" (10:39). He worries about their "drooping hands and wobbly knees" that might tempt them not to finish the race (12:12). Their discouragement places them in the tempting situation (see 2:18) of turning away from their commitment (12:16–17), as a way, perhaps, of relieving some of the oppressive measures being brought upon them. They are in danger of losing nerve and faith, of losing "confidence" (see 2:3; 3:12–4:1; 4:14; 6:4–8; 10:24–29). The visible sign of their disaffection is the failure to meet in assembly as they had before (10:25).

If apostasy or disaffection from an earlier commitment to the community is the rhetorical situation addressed by Hebrews, then can we determine the causes? Above all, can we determine whether the Christian hearers are being positively drawn to something else, or are reacting negatively to their own experience? The evidence tilts toward disaffection because of negative experience rather than apostasy because of a stronger attraction. Little in the composition suggests powerful positive attraction from another source. The obvious candidate would be the Jewish cult of sacrifice, because of the attention given to it thematically, but as I have noted, the short warning not to be "drawn away by various and strange teachings" (13:9) that seem to be connected to the Jewish cult (see "dietary laws that offer nothing useful to those who practice them" and "those who worship in the tent," 13:11) is neither extensive nor highly specific.

It may well be, however, that the Jewish cult—either as a new attraction or as a return—gains in attraction because of the negative consequences of commitment to Jesus as Messiah. Because they belonged to Jesus, some among them had been publicly afflicted, some had been imprisoned, and some had their property taken away. These are significant sufferings by any measure, and

58. This dimension of Hebrews has been particularly well demonstrated by D. Worley, "God's Faithfulness to Promise: The Hortatory Use of Commissive Language in Hebrews" (Ph.D. diss., Yale University, 1981).

calculated to reduce enthusiasm for belonging to a small and unpopular cult associated with a crucified messiah. Such negative experience would encourage attraction to a form of religion in which oppression or persecution was not an essential feature. We remember that Paul drew the same connection between the cross of Jesus and the experience of persecution, when writing to the Galatians who were tempted to be circumcised: "It is those who want to make a good showing in the flesh that would compel you to be circumcised, and only in order that they may not be persecuted for the cross of Christ" (Gal 5:12). Suffering would suffice to discourage adherence to Christ and encourage attraction to an older and safer cult.

Paul's language about "a good showing in the flesh," however, and his continuing, "they desire to have you circumcised that they may glory in your flesh; but far be it from me to glory except in the cross of our Lord Jesus Christ" (Gal 5:13–14), reminds us of the importance of honor and shame in Greco-Roman culture. In Galatians Paul sees the Judaizers as seeking "glory/honor" in a security free from persecution, and he reverses the standard for measuring true honor/glory: for him it is only "the cross of our Lord Jesus Christ." As I noted in the discussion of Hebrews' language, one of the characteristic features of Greco-Roman culture we find reflected in the composition is the acute appreciation for honor and shame. In this light, we recognize that public affliction, imprisonment, and having one's property taken by others are all forms of suffering that reveal weakness and vulnerability—and shame. Indeed, Hebrews itself links these experiences to shame: they were also "publicly shamed by revilings and affliction" (10:33). Their deepest source of potential shame, however, may be connected to the very figure of Christ, for the experience of crucifixion was, in antiquity, the most shameful form of death. His shame has spilled over onto their shame. Adherence to one who has suffered shamefully appears to lead to a life of equally shameful suffering.[59]

Such an experience of shame connected to real physical suffering can account for the loss of confidence and the temptation to "draw back" from an initial commitment (10:35–39). It also gives precise meaning to the author's claim that apostasy would be crucifying Jesus again and holding in contempt (6:6), to his characterization of Jesus as having "endured a cross, despising its shame" (12:2), and to his call to "go to him outside the camp, bearing his reproach" (13:13). Further, it helps us understand why the composition focuses on the glory that the Christ now possesses because of his exaltation (1:3–4, 9), and the efficacy of his death in establishing a firm and better hope for his followers (2:10; 6:19–20; 8:1–2).[60]

59. See esp. deSilva, *Despising Shame*, passim.

60. See D. deSilva, "Exchanging Favor for Wrath: Apostasy in Hebrews and Patron-Client Relationships," *JBL* 115 (1996): 91–116.

The clues provided by the composition provide a satisfying sense of the rhetorical situation in the strict sense: the identity and circumstances of the hearers as the author perceived them. If we seek to find out more about the intended readers, however, we can only speculate. We must be content to remain ignorant of their geographical location (the reference to "those from Italy" in 13:24 notwithstanding), their precise social standing, and even their ethnic background.

Date

Similarly, the lack of abundant external controls makes the dating of the composition uncertain. We can, to be sure, set a broad frame within which Hebrews was written. A definite terminus a quo is the death of Jesus, which is usually dated around 30 C.E. Internal evidence suggests the lapse of a certain amount of time between the death of Jesus and this writing. There is the reference to having the message confirmed by those who heard the Lord (2:3), the complaint at further progress not being made "by this time" (5:12), the call to remembrance of "the earlier days" following their initiation (10:32), and the request that the hearers remember the leaders who spoke the word of God to them, and "consider the outcome of their manner of life" as they imitate their faith (13:7). It is impossible to determine how much time might be involved, but it is reasonable to conclude that some years had passed since the readers' first initiation, time enough that, in the author's view, they had become "reluctant listeners" and no longer had the same joy and enthusiasm as at the beginning. A date earlier than 45 would seem, in light of this evidence, to be highly unlikely.

An equally firm terminus ad quem is set by the use of Hebrews in *1 Clement* (see esp. 36.1–5), which has traditionally been dated about 96 C.E. Although some doubt has been expressed concerning dating *1 Clement* itself so early[61] (once more, the uncertainty of dating from internal evidence), even a dating in the first decade of the second century makes it certain that Hebrews was written well before it, so that a terminus ad quem of 90 remains a reasonable hypothesis. We can, therefore, place the composition of Hebrews fairly confidently between 45 and 90 C.E.

Can we, however, narrow that time frame further? Once more, internal evidence can guide us toward some degree of probability but not certainty. Three lines of argument support the hypothesis that Hebrews should be dated toward the earlier side of the frame rather than the later. The first is deciding whether Hebrews is written before the fall of the temple in Jerusalem in 70 C.E. To be sure, the composition makes no direct reference to the temple or its worship as such, but carries out an elaborate comparison between the cult as described for the tent in the wilderness and the sacrifice of Jesus. Nevertheless, the compo-

61. For discussion and literature, see Attridge, 6–7.

sition speaks of Jewish worship as though it were still being performed (see 7:27–28; 8:3–5; 9:7–8; 10:1–3; 13:10–11) rather than as something that was only in the past. Caution must be taken, for Josephus is also capable of writing about the Jerusalem temple and the sacrificial cult in the present tense even though he was writing well after the destruction of the temple and the cessation of the sacrificial system (see Josephus, *Ant.* 4.102–150, 224–257).

Still, if the Jerusalem temple had been destroyed, it is difficult to imagine that the argument of Hebrews would have proceeded in exactly the same way (cf. *Barn.* 16.4): one would think that some reference would naturally be made, not to a covenant growing obsolescent and a cult being ineffective, but rather to a covenant proven to be broken and a cult demonstrated by God's action as a thing of the past. The argument from silence, to be sure, must be used carefully, but this is a case in which, given the entire structure of the argument, silence on the point of the actual historical fate of the Jewish cult demands of the author an almost incredible delicacy, if in fact the temple had been destroyed. In this case, the nonbarking dog does support, all other things being equal, a date before 70.

The second line of argument is that Hebrews does not have any of those elements that are ordinarily taken (as in the case of the Pastoral Letters or 2 Peter) as indicators of a late composition.[62] It should be obvious that the "high" Christology of Hebrews does not prove anything with respect to dating, since our earliest Christian writer, Paul, has an equally high Christology. Hebrews lacks any sign of an elaborate ecclesial structure: beyond the simple references to "the leaders" (13:7, 17, 24), there is no suggestion of hierarchy. Nor do we find any trace of concern for the patriarchal household, beyond the simple declaration that marriage should be honored and kept undefiled (13:4). In addition, Hebrews shows no concern for the preservation of a set tradition, and undertakes no rebuttal of or polemical attack on false teachers. Finally, Hebrews shows no sign of a diminished eschatology or a desire to come to terms with society.

The third line of argument supporting an early date consists of several indicators that are, taken separately, scarcely probative, but when taken together, have some significance. We can, for example, consider eschatology from the opposite side. Not only is there no sign of a delay of the parousia, but Hebrews expresses a vivid and urgent sense of expectation: the hearers are told to "exhort each other, and this all the more as you see the day approaching" (10:25). Likewise, the rhetorical situation of the composition—the readers' experiencing harassment but not martyrdom, the engagement with the Jewish cult as a contemporary phenomenon—suggests a time early in the Christian movement. Finally, if the brief

62. I enter these criteria for purposes of discussion, since they are often used in scholarship on, e.g., the letters to Paul's delegates; see the lengthy discussion of these criteria and their intrinsic problems in L. T. Johnson, *The First and Second Letters to Timothy* (AB 35A; New York: Doubleday, 2001), 55–90.

reference that "our brother Timothy has been released" (13:23), and the greeting sent from "those from Italy" (a possible allusion to Priscilla and Aquila; see Acts 18:2) are not considered the effort of a pseudepigrapher—and there is no compelling reason so to consider them—then the date of the composition would fit within the (rather elastic) frame of the Pauline ministry.

Although such arguments provide nothing more than probability, the cumulative effect of the three lines of argument I have proposed lead to the likely date for Hebrews being between 45 and 70, with a date between 50 and 70 quite possible.

Author

The reasons for excluding Paul as the author of Hebrews are real and substantial, beginning with the doubts expressed already among early critics such as Origen. The situation here is distinct from that of the "disputed" letters of Paul, all of which—not least the Pastorals—were firmly considered to be authentic until the beginning of the nineteenth century, and all of which can still command that same conviction among scholars of impeccable critical credentials, despite the majority scholarly position that has challenged the authenticity of six of the thirteen Pauline letters.[63] Readers like Origen were able to detect what is also clear to present-day critics, namely, with respect to language (diction, sentence structure), theme, and mode of argumentation, the several fascinating points of contact with Paul's letters (noted above) are more than balanced by points of dissimilarity sufficiently impressive to conclude that another mind than Paul's was at work in the composition of this magnificent oration.

Here, in brief, are the reasons why I consider Hebrews not to be from Paul, even in the broader sense of "Pauline authorship" that I have espoused elsewhere.[64] First, the letter is not ascribed to Paul, but is anonymous. Second, it contains none of the autobiographical remarks that are so characteristic even of the disputed Pauline letters; instead, the author speaks as one who has received the good news from others. Third, the vocabulary it shares with Paul it shares also with the broader Christian tradition. Fourth, the manner of citing Scripture is markedly different from that found in the Pauline letters. Fifth, the mode of argumentation in Hebrews, though resembling Paul in some points, has as a whole a distinctive character. Sixth, and for me most decisive, a "Platonic worldview" is pervasive throughout Hebrews and is almost without parallel in the letters ascribed to Paul (2 Cor 4–5 being the major exception).

63. See the discussion in ibid., 20–54.

64. See Johnson, *Writings of the New Testament,* 267–73.

Still, the reasons I have noted for dating the composition early, the elements in the sermon that do find parallels in Paul, and the allusions in 13:23–24 suggesting Pauline associations have led readers to suggest as author someone from the wider Pauline circle. For example, before declaring that "only God knew" the writer, Origen proposed the possibility of Clement of Rome or Luke (Eusebius, *Hist. eccl.* 6.25.14).[65] It is certainly possible that Hebrews might be considered "Pauline" in this broadest construal of Pauline authorship, that is, as emerging from within the school around Paul that formed already in his lifetime.

Some such suggestions founder on an element of implausibility or simple lack of evidence. It would be pleasant to have a female author of a New Testament composition, for example, but the suggestion that Priscilla—a recognized and honored member of the Pauline circle (see Acts 18:2–3, 18, 26; Rom 16:3–4; 1 Cor 16:19; 2 Tim 4:19)—was the author of Hebrews must overcome the objections posed by the masculine singular self-reference in Heb 11:32, the rarity of rhetorical training among women in the empire, and the fact that everything supporting her candidacy would apply equally to her male partner, Aquila.[66] Other early Christian missionaries like Silas (see Acts 15:40–18:5; 2 Cor 1:19; 1 Thess 1:1; 2 Thess 1:1; 1 Pet 5:12) and Epaphras (see Phlm 23; Col 1:7; 4:12) were perhaps prominent enough and close enough to Paul, but nothing in what we know of them could move their candidacy beyond sheer possibility. Only two names emerge with any serious degree of appeal: Barnabas and Apollos.

I noted earlier that Tertullian ascribed the composition to Barnabas (*On Modesty* 20), although he provides no reasons for doing so. Some aspects of Barnabas as described in the New Testament could support the hypothesis that he was the author of Hebrews. Acts 4:36 notes that he was a Levite from Cyprus, thus locating him in the Diaspora and within the Jewish priestly tradition. Luke also notes that Barnabas sold property and donated it to the community in Jerusalem, making him someone who could speak firsthand about "joyfully" being dispossessed of property "in earlier days" (Heb 10:32–34). Luke further translates the name Barnabas into Greek as "son of consolation" (*huios paraklēseōs*), which some see as tying into the designation of Hebrews as a "word of consolation" (*logos paraklēseōs*)—not, one must admit, a strong argument—and portrays him both as an emissary of the Jerusalem church and as Paul's

65. For an effort to rehabilitate the Lukan hypothesis, see D. L. Allen, "The Lukan Authorship of Hebrews: A Proposal," *JOTT* 8 (1996): 1–22.

66. The possibility of female authorship, put forward by Harnack, was argued vigorously by R. Hoppins, *Priscilla, Author of the Epistle to the Hebrews, and Other Essays* (New York: Exposition Press, 1969); more recently, see idem, "The Epistle to the Hebrews Is Priscilla's Letter," in *A Feminist Companion to the Catholic Epistles and Hebrews*, ed. A.-J. Levine with M. M. Robbins (Feminist Companion to the New Testament and Early Christian Writings 8; London: T&T Clark, 2004), 147–70.

associate in the mission (Acts 9:27; 11:19–30; 13:1–15:35), an association that Paul's letters confirm (1 Cor 9:6; Gal 2:13). All this incidental detail is fascinating, but does not significantly advance Barnabas as a candidate, particularly if Paul's depiction of him as compromised with respect to table fellowship at Antioch is correct (Gal 2:13), since Hebrews speaks decisively against the validity of regulations concerning foods (9:10; 13:9).

It is perhaps somewhat surprising that a candidate for authorship as attractive as Apollos should have taken so long to be nominated, but Martin Luther appears to be the first to suggest his name (see his *Commentary on Genesis* of 1545 [WA 45:349]). We do not have extensive information concerning Apollos, but what we have is indeed suggestive, making him the strongest of the proposed alternatives to Paul. He is intimately connected with the Pauline ministry (though it is not certain that the Apollos in Titus 3:13 is him), playing a significant enough role in the Corinthian church to be one of the figures around whom groups organized themselves (see 1 Cor 1:11), perhaps even the main rival put up against the apostle (3:4), requiring Paul to emphasize the spirit of cooperation between Apollos and himself (4:1–6) as well as suggest the subsidiary role that was proper to Apollos (3:5–22), and the position of authority that was Paul's: it is likely that he counts Apollos among the several "pedagogues" the Corinthians can claim, whereas Paul is the community's only "father" (4:15).

It is also possible that Paul's contrast between "human eloquence" and the "word of the cross" (1 Cor 1:17–18) may have something to do with the effect that Apollos's rhetoric had in displacing Paul in the Corinthians' affection; Paul remains sensitive on the point that in the eyes of the community he founded, his own "letters are severe and forceful but his bodily presence is weak and his speech contemptible" (2 Cor 10:10). The ending of 1 Corinthians suggests that Paul and Apollos are delicately aligned with regard to their mutual positions; Paul says, "Now in regard to our brother Apollos, I urged him strongly to go to you with the brothers [note that such a delegation would clearly signal his subordination], but it was not at all his will that he go now. He will go when he has an opportunity" (1 Cor 16:12).

Against this backdrop, the description of Apollos in Acts 18:24–28 (see also 19:1) suggests the same combination of extraordinary ability and uneasy position vis-à-vis the rest of the Pauline team; indeed, it sounds almost like a job description for the author of Hebrews:

> Now a Jew named Apollos, a native of Alexandria, came to Ephesus. He was an eloquent man (*anēr logios*), powerful in the scriptures (*dynatos ōn en tais graphais*). He had been instructed in the way of the Lord; and, being fervent in Spirit (*zeōn tō pneumati*), he spoke and taught accurately (*akribōs*) the things concerning Jesus, though he knew only the baptism of John. He began to speak boldly (*parrēsiazesthai*) in the synagogue; but when Priscilla and Aquila heard him, they took him and expounded to him the way of God more accurately. And when he wanted to cross to Achaia [i.e., Corinth], the brothers encouraged him and

> wrote to the disciples there to welcome him. After his arrival he gave great assistance to those who had come to believe through grace. He vigorously refuted the Jews in public, establishing from the scriptures (*dia tōn graphōn*) that the Messiah is Jesus.

We can place this description in the frame of our description of the composition:

1. Apollos is a Jew, and Hebrews shows extensive knowledge of Judaism.
2. Apollos is from Alexandria, the home of Philo, and a center for the sort of Platonic outlook shared by Hebrews and Philo.
3. Apollos is learned in Scripture, and Hebrews is filled with intricate scriptural citations and allusions.
4. Apollos learned the Christian message from others, and Hebrews speaks of the message having been received from others.
5. Apollos proves from Scripture that Jesus is the Messiah, and so does Hebrews.
6. Apollos is eloquent and speaks with boldness over against the Jews; Hebrews is a fine example of rhetoric, is bold, and develops an extensive contrast between Jesus and Jewish figures and practices.
7. Apollos was a follower of John the Baptist, and Hebrews has a level of moral and religious rigor, especially concerning repentance.
8. Hebrews speaks of "teachings about baptisms" in the plural, which might be accounted for if Apollos had multiple initiations together with instruction received from Aquila and Priscilla.
9. Hebrews' reference to "those from Italy" would certainly fit Priscilla and Aquila, with whom Apollos had close contact.

This is a significant list of qualities, which cannot be applied with the same precision to any other early Christian figure.

If the author of Hebrews were Apollos, then several aspects of the composition that previously were obscure are clarified: the similarity and dissimilarity to Paul; the date (within the frame of Paul's ministry, ca. 50–68); and, more speculatively, the recipients (the Corinthians), since Apollos had a definite and powerful association with that community. If Apollos were its author, then several of the connections between Hebrews and 1 Corinthians would become clearer: the question of foods (Heb 9:10; 13:9; 1 Cor 8:1–13), the comparison of the congregation to the people in the wilderness (Heb 3:7–4:13; 1 Cor 10:1–13), and the contrast between infants' food and that of adults, with a different lesson drawn by each author (Heb 5:11–6:4; 1 Cor 3:1–3). Finally, if Apollos had written such a powerful bit of rhetoric to the Corinthian church *before* Paul wrote his first letter to them, and had written in such fashion as to generate enthusiasm for himself as a teacher and to encourage the Corinthians to think of themselves as capable of "more mature" thought, then Paul's deflation of that expectation, warning against arrogance, and concern to associate himself with Apollos even as he distanced himself from a preaching based on rhetoric and suggested Apollos's subordinate state, would take on a sharper edge.[67]

Yet the hypothesis that Apollos wrote Hebrews must be recognized as speculation, with just enough support to make it plausible. Three considerations should caution present-day readers who might be attracted to it. First, other aspects of Hebrews loom even stranger if connected closely to the Corinthian church, such as we know it from Paul. Although Acts supports the picture of a strong Jewish community in Corinth and of conflict between the synagogue and the Pauline foundation (Acts 18:5–17), neither Acts nor 1 Corinthians supports other elements in the rhetorical situation suggested by Hebrews (public humiliation and affliction, imprisonment, expropriation of property, the danger of apostasy) or some of its major themes, above all the sustained *synkrisis* between the sacrifice of Jesus and the Jewish sacrificial system. Second, we must not forget the fragmentary nature of our evidence from the first century. The number of points connecting Apollos to Hebrews is impressive, but we cannot suppose that Apollos uniquely possessed those qualities. The past is not the same as what we know about the past.

Finally, even if it titillates our historical imagination, the hypothesis does not substantially affect the reading of the composition. The author of Hebrews lives within the passion and subtlety of the discourse itself; the life he lived outside the rhetoric is not known to us, and does it truly matter? The most important thing Hebrews tells us about the author, whoever he was, is that in the first decades of the Christian movement, another remarkable mind and heart besides Paul's was at work in interpreting the significance of the crucified and raised Messiah Jesus for the understanding of Scripture, of the world, and of human existence.

The Theological Challenge of Hebrews

The theology of Hebrews consists not of a set of propositions about God that can be drawn from its pages, but of the entire argument that engages the hearer. In the case of Hebrews above all, it is appropriate to speak of a "theological voice," which speaks in its own distinctive manner throughout the composition. Much of this introduction has already been devoted to the manner in which Hebrews speaks and the circumstances it addresses. Now I turn to some dimensions of Hebrews that deserve particular attention, not least because they are

67. For the connections, see Montefiore, 9–11; for a critical appraisal, see L. D. Hurst, "Apollos, Hebrews, and Corinth: Bishop Montefiore's Theory Examined," *SJT* 38 (1985): 505–13.

dimensions that in one way or another are troublesome to present-day readers. Our interest is not simply what Hebrews says, but how it challenges Christians today by what it says.

Living God, Living Word

I have stated that the world imagined by Hebrews is one constructed imaginatively by Scripture and read through Platonic eyes. Because it is a world constructed by Scripture, it is a world that reveals God and through which God reveals. God is the supreme reality, the source of all that is, and the goal of all that lives. God creates all things by a word: "By faith we understand that the ages were fashioned by God's word, so that what we see comes from what we do not see" (11:3). Because this word of God is living and powerful, "there is no creature that is not visible to him. All things lie naked and exposed to his eyes" (4:12–13). Although Scripture says that God rested from all his works on the seventh day (4:4), the very story narrated by Scripture, as well as its prophetic voices, make clear that God's presence and power continue within creation. The angels are God's fiery servants (1:7), spirits sent as messengers for the sake of those who are to inherit salvation (1:14). Humans are created lower than the angels, but God cares for them and will crown them with glory and honor (2:6–8).

Scripture also reveals the world as one in which the creator God enters into personal relation with humans. By faith, humans can approach God, and God rewards those who so seek him (11:6). Hebrews 11 reads Scripture as showing that God was a constant companion of his faithful ones. God approves the sacrifice of Abel (11:4), is pleased with Enoch, and takes him up from the earth (11:5). God warns Noah (11:7), calls Abraham (11:8), gives to Abraham and Sarah the power to beget heirs (11:11), tests Abraham, gives back Isaac as though by resurrection (11:17–20), and prepares a city for his descendants (11:16). And it is God who commends them all (11:4, 39). God's choice to form uneven but lasting partnership with humans is revealed by Scripture in the making of covenant, a first one (9:15–22) and the promise of a new one (8:8–13). So profound is God's commitment to humans that through his Son God involves himself in their very fleshly existence, takes part in every aspect of their lives apart from the rebellion of sin (2:10–18; 4:15), and works a salvation so profound and perfect that it transforms their very hearts (8:1–13). But Scripture makes clear as well that God judges the people (10:30–31).

Above all, Scripture reveals God as one who speaks to humans "many times and in many ways through the prophets" (1:1). The prophets through whom God spoke "in the past to the fathers" included the very texts of Scripture itself. But for Hebrews, Scripture does not speak only to the past. Scripture speaks most truly about the Messiah Jesus, who has "come into the world" (1:6; 10:5), and speaks to the present generation living in the "today" of Ps 94 (Heb 4:7) and the "days that are coming" of Jeremiah (8:8). Scripture is needed in order to perceive in Jesus the Messiah who is a priest according to the order of Melchizedek. But without the experience of Jesus as a Messiah who died shamefully on the cross and then entered into the glory that is God's own life, Scripture also could not properly or profoundly be understood.

Because Hebrews is so deeply shaped by Scripture, it can insist as well that Scripture is not the only source of God's voice. Rather, Scripture itself points to the God who speaks in and through God's creation. It is Abel's *faith* that keeps speaking even though he is dead (11:4); it is his *blood* that speaks (12:24). Most of all, God speaks to us "in these final days" through Jesus Christ his Son (1:2). By this simple turn, Hebrews makes the life, death, resurrection, and royal enthronement of Jesus a form of speech, a word spoken by God. Jesus is mediator of a new covenant through "a sprinkling of blood that is speaking better than Abel" (12:24). This word, in turn, is brought into the lives of hearers by the testimony of God in their lives, a testimony that takes the form not of speech but of the presence of the Holy Spirit. Hebrews asks, if those who neglected the message declared through angels (*di' angelōn lalētheis logos*) were punished, how could his hearers now escape if they neglect "such a great salvation; it took its start from the things spoken by the Lord (*laleisthai dia tou kyriou*). It was secured for us by those who heard him. God has joined his own testimony through signs and wonders and various powerful deeds, and distributions of the Holy Spirit according to his will" (2:1–4). The present experience of transforming power among the hearers of Hebrews is here understood as the continuous speaking of God to the people, an address from God that demands a response: "Watch that you do not reject the one who is speaking. For if those people did not escape when they had rejected the one who warned them on earth, how much less shall we, if we turn away from the one from heaven?" (12:25–26).

When Hebrews speaks of the "word of God" (*logos tou theou*) as "living and powerful, sharper than any two-edged sword, cutting to the division between soul and spirit, joints and marrow, able to discern the thoughts and conceptions of the heart" (4:12), it clearly means more than Scripture. It means God: "there is no creature that is not visible to him. All things lie naked and exposed to his eyes" (4:13).

Nevertheless, that "word of God" does speak powerfully through Scripture, through God's Son, and now powerfully through the work of the Holy Spirit among them. Does it not also make sense, then, to see the author's designation of his composition as a *logos paraklēseōs* (13:22) to mean that his discourse stands in continuity with God's constant speaking to the people? If this is so, perhaps the best way to translate the very difficult phrase occurring at the end of 4:13 (*pros hon hēmin ho logos*) is not as some recent translations prefer (NAB,

NRSV, "to whom we must render an account"; NIV, "to whom we must give account"), but closer to the RSV's "with whom we have to do," understanding it precisely as "to him is our account directed."

Hebrews' understanding of the living God and God's living Word present three difficult and interrelated questions to readers today. The first is whether Christians today share a biblical world in any sense. That Christians no longer "imagine the world that the Bible imagines" in the fashion of earlier generations is clear. The symbols of Scripture are no longer those of a living and familiar city whose ways are so deeply and pervasively known that they need scarcely be made explicit. Scripture is approached more like a buried city that needs to be excavated by means of archaeology.[68] The question, though, is not simply whether Christians today are familiar with biblical symbols. It asks whether Christians today any longer see the world as one created by God at every moment, sustained by God's word, addressed by God's prophets. Do they still perceive the world as mystery, having a depth of being that lies within and beneath that which is observable, measurable, calculable? Such a sense of mystery and magic at the heart of reality is not a function of Hebrews' Platonism—though it is also that—but is even more a function of perceiving the world as Scripture imagines it. If Christians are incapable of experiencing the world in at least some sense as enchanted, can they do more than explain Hebrews as a quaint expression of antique views? Can they, as the first readers were invited to do, live within its world?

The second, related, question is whether Scripture is, for present-day Christians, merely a record of the past—even a past of particular significance to them—or whether it continues to speak as God's word that places a demand on their lives, and indeed places their lives in question. Does Scripture continue to possess prophetic force? It is difficult, after all, to combine convictions concerning the prophetic character of texts and the methods of the historian. The historian's business is to keep the past in the past. The value of the historical study of Scripture is clear (and has been vigorously employed in this introduction) not least because it helps maintain the otherness of the text, and therefore its resistance to manipulation. But if Scripture's meaning is confined to its original context, where is its prophetic force? Contemporary expertise in uncovering the ways in which Hebrews' use of Ps 94 (MT 95) fits within the midrashic practices of Judaism can easily distract and deflect from hearing the point of that use, which is God's call to obedience every day as long as it remains "today."

The third question is whether present-day Christians can, with Hebrews, perceive the living word of God as active not only within Scripture but also and

68. See L. T. Johnson, "Imagining the World That Scripture Imagines," in Johnson and William S. Kurz, S.J., *The Future of Catholic Biblical Scholarship* (Grand Rapids: Eerdmans, 2002), 119–42.

especially within the fabric of the world, in God's powerful work of transforming human lives. Hebrews, like all of Scripture, turns the attention less to itself as revelatory and more toward the bodies of men and women through whom God's Holy Spirit constantly surprises with a new and powerful witness.[69] The cloud of those witnesses is not complete with the roll that Hebrews itself recites. Many continue to run the race, following the pioneer and perfecter of faith. Those whose lives are shaped by obedient faith in the manner of Jesus can also reveal the presence of the resurrected one in the present.

Hebrews closely combines two hortatory statements in its final chapter, inviting them to be read as mutually informing. In 13:7 the hearers are exhorted, "remember your leaders, those *who spoke the word of God to you.* As you consider carefully the outcome of their manner of life, imitate their faith." Then Hebrews says, "Jesus Christ is the same yesterday and today and forever" (13:8). It is when the words of Scripture are connected to the work of God in human lives that present-day Christians can truly enter into the world imagined by Hebrews. The three questions are interrelated and so are the answers to all three. The capacity to hear and see God's work in the world—in the stories of real men and women—is the way in which the world again becomes as Scripture imagines it, as enchanted, as revealing mystery at its heart. Reading Scripture in light of such perception is, in turn, to read it not simply as a historical document but as a prophetic voice.

Mature Teaching of the Christ

It is a deeper understanding of Christ that makes Hebrews a "lengthy discourse that is difficult to express because you have become reluctant listeners" (5:11), and the conception of Christ in this composition is indeed one of the richest in the New Testament canon.[70] We can begin to approach this theme by noting the unusually varied way in which Hebrews speaks of Jesus.

Hebrews uses his simple name "Jesus" frequently, corresponding to the author's interest in his humanity (see 2:9; 3:1; 4:14; 6:20; 7:22; 10:19; 12:24; 13:12, 20). Some of the titles used by Hebrews are common in New Testament writings. The title "Christ" occurs often (3:6, 14; 5:5; 6:1; 9:11, 14, 24, 28). The combination "Jesus Christ," however, appears only three times (10:10; 13:8,

69. See L. T. Johnson, "The Revelatory Body: Notes Toward a Somatic Theology," in *The Phenomenology of the Body*, ed. D. J. Martino (Pittsburgh: Simon Silverman Phenomenology Center at the University of Duquesne, 2003), 69–85.

70. For some of the antecedents and traditions used by Hebrews in its Christology, see H. Anderson, "The Jewish Antecedents of the Christology of Hebrews," in *The Messiah: Developments in Earliest Christianity and Judaism*, ed. J. H. Charlesworth (Minneapolis: Fortress Press, 1992), 512–35; and W. R. G. Loader, *Sohn und Hoherpriester: Eine traditionsgeschichtliche Untersuchung zur Christologie des Hebräerbriefes* (WMANT 53; Neukirchen-Vluyn: Neukirchener Verlag, 1981).

21). Hebrews speaks often of Jesus as "the Son" (1:2, 5, 8; 3:6; 5:5, 8; 7:28) as well as "Son of God" (4:14; 6:6; 7:3; 10:29) and "Lord" (1:10; 2:3; 7:14; 13:20). By implication, Hebrews ascribes the designation "Son of Man" to Jesus (2:6; see Ps 8:4), and its use of Ps 44:7–8 in 1:8 implies as well that Jesus can properly be designated as "God" (*theos*).

Other titles used of Jesus by Hebrews are either unique in the New Testament or rare. Jesus is designated as "heir" (1:2), "the firstborn" (1:6), "the great shepherd of the sheep" (13:20), "the pioneer" (or "captain"; 2:10; 12:2), and the "perfecter" (12:2). He is the "sanctifier" (2:11), the "apostle" (3:1), and the "builder of God's house" (3:3). He is the "cause of salvation" (5:9), the "forerunner" (6:20), the "guarantor" (7:22), the "minister" (8:2), and the "mediator" (8:6; 12:24). We can view these special designations synoptically and see in them the two main emphases of Hebrews' Christology. On one side, Jesus is the one who brings salvation to humanity from God (apostle, cause, sanctifier, shepherd, minister, builder, guarantor). On the other side, Jesus is also a human being who reaches first what all seek (heir, firstborn, pioneer, forerunner, perfecter). As the one who accomplishes both, he is preeminently the "mediator."[71]

These two aspects come together in the titles that Hebrews alone ascribes to Jesus, drawn from the language of the Jewish sacrificial cult. Hebrews is not unique, to be sure, in picturing Jesus' death and resurrection in terms of sacrifice. Paul says that "Christ our Passover lamb (*pascha*) has been sacrificed" (1 Cor 5:7) and speaks of Jesus' death in terms of the sprinkling of blood on the mercy seat on the Day of Atonement (Rom 3:25). Peter speaks of the precious blood of Christ that is like that of a lamb (1 Pet 1:21). John says that the blood of Jesus cleanses us from all sins (1 John 1:7), and Revelation portrays Jesus as the lamb who was slain (Rev 5:12). Furthermore, the Synoptic accounts of Jesus' last meal with his followers speak of the cup as the blood of the covenant poured out for many (see Matt 26:27). The conviction concerning Jesus as sacrificial victim, then, is a shared one; Hebrews' originality among the canonical witnesses is to portray Jesus also as the priest who carries out the sacrifice.

Hebrews alone calls Jesus "priest" (10:21), "high priest" (3:1; 4:14; 5:5, 10; 6:20; 7:26; 8:1; 9:11), and a "merciful and faithful high priest" (2:17). Throughout the composition, the title of priest is mingled with the imagery of royal enthronement, drawn from the language of Ps 109:1–4. Jesus is priest as the Lord who has taken his seat at the right hand of God—he is Priest-King (see 1:3, 8, 13; 2:5, 7, 9; 4:16; 7:1, 2; 8:1; 10:12; 12:2, 28).

71. See F. F. Bruce, "The Kerygma of Hebrews," *Int* 23 (1969): 3–19; L. D. Hurst, "The Christology of Hebrews 1–2," in *The Glory of Christ in the New Testament* (FS G. B. Caird), ed. L. D. Hurst and N. T. Wright (New York: Clarendon, 1987), 151–64; A. Vanhoye, *Situation du Christ: Épître aux Hébreux 1 et 2* (Lectio Divina 58; Paris: Cerf, 1969).

The range of titles applied to Jesus reveals how Hebrews eludes easy categorization of its Christology in terms of "high" and "low" or "early" and "late." Hebrews may well be among our earliest extant Christian writings. Yet, as in Paul, we see a complex apprehension of the figure of Jesus that simultaneously affirms his divine status as well as his human character and work. That both aspects of Jesus be held together is, in fact, critical to Hebrews' argument concerning his priesthood. Chalcedon cannot simply be read off the pages of Hebrews, but the Chalcedonian understanding of the two natures in Christ can certainly be found in Hebrews. Hebrews demands of us some appreciation for the ontological dimensions of the story of Jesus.

On one side, then, Hebrews emphasizes that Jesus is divine, a point made most impressively, as early patristic readers saw, in the prologue: though God spoke in the past through prophets, now God speaks through a Son (1:1–2). Hebrews immediately makes clear that "Son of God" means more than the metaphor that was routinely applied to ancient kings. This Son is the heir of all things, is the one through whom God created the world, and upholds the universe by his word of power (1:1–3). These three expressions place the Son at the origin of all things with God, sustaining all things, and, at the end, receiving all things. Between these "functional" statements, the author applies to the Son two characterizations that echo Wis 7:25–26, and can only be read as statements about "being": he is "a radiance of his glory and an imprint of his very being" (1:3). In these opening statements, Hebrews makes no real distinction among the various stages of Christ's existence: he is the same "being" whether as creator or as making purification for sins or as taking his place at the right hand of the majesty on high (1:1–3).[72]

Creation is again directly ascribed to the Son in 1:10 through the citation of Ps 101:26–28: "From the beginning, O Lord, you have laid the foundation of the earth, and the heavens are the work of your hands." The world that he created is also subject to him (2:5–8). That the Son is greater than the angels is the point of all the citations in 1:5–14: unlike them, he is to be worshiped, and who can be worshiped but God (1:6)? The actual title *theos* is ordinarily reserved for the Father in the New Testament; every application to Christ either carries a weakened meaning or is disputed (see John 1:1, 18; 20:28; Rom 9:5; Titus 2:13). But the designation seems to be intended to bear its full significance in Heb 1:8, where Ps 44:7–8 is applied to Jesus: "Your throne, O God, is forever and ever, and the righteous scepter is the scepter of your kingdom." When Hebrews calls Jesus "Son," then, it means this in the fullest possible sense:

72. For a different angle, see P. M. Eisenbaum, "Father and Son: The Christology of Hebrews in Patrilineal Perspective," in *A Feminist Companion to the Catholic Epistles and Hebrews*, ed. A.-J. Levine with M. M. Robbins (Feminist Companion to the New Testament and Early Christian Writings 8; London: T&T Clark, 2004), 127–46.

Jesus is and does what God is and does. It is because he is divine that he can be the "cause of eternal salvation" to those who obey him (5:9) and can come a second time for the "salvation of those awaiting him" (9:28). Although he was made for a little while lower than the angels, he has been crowned with glory and honor (2:9), and "he is able also to save completely those approaching God through him, since he is alive always to intercede for them" (7:25).

Just as emphatically, Hebrews insists on the full humanity of the Son. The one made "lower than the angels" is the Son of Man of Ps 8:5–6, to whom God subjects the world to come (Heb 2:1–8). The common nature of Jesus and "his brothers" is celebrated in 2:10–18, which rhetorically responds to the emphasis placed on his divinity in the opening sequence. The one who sanctifies (Christ) and the ones who are sanctified "all have the same source," meaning that they share the same ancestry or origin, and therefore have a common identity (2:11). It is appropriate, therefore, to follow Scripture in calling humans his "brothers," as well as his "children" (2:12–13), since these children share flesh and blood and "he himself has likewise taken a share of the same" (2:14).[73] Like all other humans, Christ tastes death (2:14). And like all other humans, Christ belongs to a very specific lineage: he belongs to the family of Abraham (2:16). He is like his brothers in every respect (*kata panta tois adelphois homoiōthēnai*, 2:17), including the experience of temptation (or testing; see 2:18). This last element is qualified in 4:15: Jesus was "tested in every way as we have, apart from sin." Because Jesus shares so fully in the human condition, he has human feelings. He can be a "merciful and faithful" high priest because he has experienced the trials that others have (2:17–18). He can "deal gently with those who are ignorant and go astray because he himself is also clothed in weakness" (5:2).

These human characteristics are all on display in Hebrews' description of Jesus "in the days of his flesh," making prayers and petitions to God. He prayed "with a loud cry and tears" and was heard because of his pious submission to God (5:7). In a moment I will consider the remainder of this remarkable and key passage. For now, notice the steady emphasis on Jesus' full humanity. We cannot be certain that Hebrews refers to a specific scene such as Jesus' prayer before his death (see Matt 26:36–46 par.; John 12:27). But that Jesus experienced the "fear of death" that holds all humans captive (Heb 2:15), and that he had to approach God through deeply felt prayer as other humans do, seem clear enough. He is, indeed, the "finisher" as well as the "starter" of faith (12:2). Also clear is Hebrews' allusion to the manner of Jesus' death, the most shameful imaginable in the Greco-Roman world (6:6). He suffered outside the gate and bore his reviling outside the camp (13:12–13), while despising the shame of the cross because of the joy that was set before him (12:2).

73. See P. Gray, "Brotherly Love and the High Priest Christology of Hebrews," *JBL* 122 (2003): 335–51.

Hebrews develops its portrayal of Jesus as high priest precisely on the basis of this gritty and shameful human experience. Unlike other priests, Jesus is God's own Son. But like other priests, he is "taken from among humans for the sake of humans" (5:1). By its dramatic appropriation of Ps 40:7–9 in 10:5–8, Hebrews can make clear that both Jesus' body and his will are the instruments of his priestly activity. Rather than other sacrifices and offerings, God fitted him with a body, the psalm says, and concludes, "Then I said, in the scroll of the book it stands written of me, 'Behold, I am here to do your will, O God'" (Heb 10:7).[74]

Jesus' eagerness to do God's will is singled out by Hebrews as the effective replacement of the sacrifices external to humans that God no longer seeks (10:9), and concludes, "By this will we have been sanctified through the offering once for all of the body of Jesus Christ" (10:10). By his resurrection and exaltation, Jesus has entered into the true holy place, which is the presence of the eternal God, with his own blood (9:12–14), which he offers for the sins of many (9:28). In a daring appropriation of temple imagery, Hebrews makes Jesus' flesh the curtain through which he has entered into God's presence, thereby opening "a new and living way" of access to God for other humans (10:19). He is thus the pioneer who goes ahead of others (12:2), the forerunner (6:20), and he is so because he finishes or perfects faith (12:2). This last aspect of Jesus' humanity—his faith—draws us into the deepest dimension of the Christology of Hebrews (and the topic most difficult to explore!), which is the role of Christ's suffering.

The theme is announced in 2:10: "It was indeed fitting that the one for whom are all things and through whom are all things, in leading many sons to glory, should bring the pioneer of their salvation to perfection through suffering." Four discrete aspects of the statement deserve attention.

First, Jesus is said to be the first among others. He is a "captain" or "pioneer" (*archēgos*) among "many sons" whom God is bringing to glory. We legitimately infer that what happens to him is available to his brothers as well.

Second, as a human being, Jesus undergoes a process of perfection. It is "when he has been made perfect" (*teleiōtheis*, 5:9) that he can be the cause of salvation to those who obey him. We correctly infer that the human Jesus grows from one stage to another in the direction of perfection. The cognates of *teleioun* ("bring to perfection") that run throughout Hebrews have obvious religious and moral associations in antiquity. One who is *teleios* has finished a course of initiations, is more mature, further along, better, than one who is not. Comparison and progress are essential to the notion of perfection. Thus the tent in which Jesus offers himself is "more perfect" than the tent in the wilderness (9:11), and the Levitical priesthood could not bring "perfection" to worshipers (7:11; 9:9;

74. See D. Hamm, "Faith in the Epistle to the Hebrews: The Jesus Factor," *CBQ* 52 (1990): 270–91.

10:1), just as the law could "perfect" no one (7:19). In contrast, the sacrifice of Jesus has brought "perfection" to those it sanctifies forever (10:14). Those who had faith in previous generations were not "perfected" apart from the present generation (11:40), but the readers of Hebrews approach the place where reside the spirits of the righteous who have been brought to perfection (12:23). These readers must turn from milk to the solid food that is appropriate to the perfect (mature, 5:14), and the author's discourse will lead them to such considerations of perfection (6:1).

Third, we observe in 2:10 that *suffering* is the means by which Jesus reaches the perfection that enables him to save his brethren. It is noteworthy that not the glorification of Jesus but his human suffering is so characterized.

Fourth, Hebrews declares that the path to perfection through suffering is "fitting" (2:10). But why? In order to grasp this "appropriateness," we must consider in turn what Hebrews might mean by suffering, and what role it plays in moral transformation.

Hebrews itself provides some guidance in the second passage where "suffering" and "perfection" appear together, namely 5:7–9, a passage that we have already viewed as an expression of Jesus' humanity, but without attending to the key clauses in 5:8–9: "even though he was a Son, he learned obedience from the things he suffered. And after he was made perfect, he became the cause of eternal salvation for all those who obey him." Hebrews connects suffering, obedience, learning, and perfection. In order to understand the connections, we must first consider the nature of suffering itself.

Suffering can be defined—in as neutral a fashion as possible—as the pain consequent to the disequilibrium of a sentient system. Only sentient beings can suffer, that is, experience pain. But they can suffer in various ways and with both positive and negative results. To speak of "sentient systems" is to identify the physical, emotional, mental, and spiritual dimensions of humans. So long as any of these systems is in equilibrium, it experiences no pain. But pain is an inevitable corollary of disequilibrium. A body experiences pain through injury or disease (and that is negative), but also experiences pain through growth, muscular development, childbirth (all positives). Pain is neither good nor bad in itself, it is simply a signal concerning the state of the system. Similarly, emotional pain can result both from fear and from passionate desire. Mental pain accompanies the enlargement of the universe through new ideas, for cognitive dissonance is a frequent accompaniment.[75]

The conviction that the education of the mind, body, and emotions required pain (suffering) is one of the great insights of ancient philosophy, distilled in the maxim *mathein pathein*, "to learn is to suffer," which can also be reversed, as "to

75. See L. T. Johnson, "Suffering, Sin, and Scripture," in *Living Gospel* (London: Continuum, 2004), 11–18.

suffer is to learn." Contemporaries who might think of this in terms of athletics (as the ancients did as well) might translate idiomatically but accurately as "no pain, no gain." The training of the body and mind and will went together in Greco-Roman culture, which used the same term, *paideia*, for education, culture, and discipline. Note that in this conception, suffering is not something inflicted from the outside (as an injury might be, or a taunt, or a lie) but is rather intrinsic to a certain process of growth or "maturation," that is, "perfection" (*teleiōsis*).

In the case of Jesus, Heb 5:7–9 does not refer explicitly to his bodily suffering in the passion, but to a process of suffering that he experienced before his actual death. The author connects it to his prayers and petitions with loud cries and tears in the days of his flesh (5:7). The suffering is integral to Jesus' response of faith and trust in God, his *eulabeia* (5:7). Hebrews identifies this as "obedience" (*hypakoē*) in 5:8: "he learned obedience from the things he suffered," and connects Jesus' "being made perfect" directly to this process (5:9). Jesus' suffering, therefore, was essential to the process by which he learned to be fully God's Son. His obedience to God was the way through which he became more fully (more perfectly) that which he was, God's Son. This process was brought to completion by his death and exaltation.

If I have understood these passages correctly, then the Christology of Hebrews is far from a mechanical or static juxtaposition of "two natures in one person." Instead, the composition daringly suggests that the human Jesus grew progressively into the full stature of being God's Son. Through his human faith and obedience, he progressively opened himself to the mystery of God. Such opening to infinite mystery stretches the human beyond all measure, and inevitably involves pain and suffering at every level, just as pain and suffering themselves have the capacity to open humans to the mystery of God. A saying attributed to Leon Bloy is that there are places in the heart that do not yet exist but only come into being through suffering. In the heart of the human Jesus, Hebrews leads the reader to imagine, God increasingly took occupation, carving an ever greater space for God's own presence and freedom. To put it another way, the divine within Jesus progressively found more explicit expression through the freedom of the human person Jesus.

Viewed in this fashion, the moment of death, which appears from the outside as the final and ultimate closure, the shutting down of existence, became for Jesus the ultimate opening of his humanity to the presence of God. In that final act of faithful obedience the man Jesus "stepped through the veil of his flesh" and through his death and exaltation opened a new and better way of access to God: a way established not externally through the killing of animals, but internally through the embodied freedom of human response to God.[76] He

76. For the theological implications, see K. Rahner, *On the Theology of Death*, trans. C. H. Henkey, 2nd ed. (Quaestiones Disputatae 2; Freiburg: Herder, 1965).

is the pioneer of faith because he went first. He is the perfecter of faith because he himself was perfected through it.

The Christology of Hebrews is a challenge to present-day adherents of Christianity, for its rich and complex understanding is, among many of them, split asunder. Perhaps because of a distaste for—and ignorance of—ontology, and the flat epistemological monism that shapes modernity, it is difficult for many to hold together the human and divine in Christ, whether in profession or in piety or in politics.

On one side, we find the fervent profession of Jesus as Son of God. Those who emphasize the divinity of Christ, however, sometimes slight the full significance of his humanity. The human Jesus tends to be swallowed up by the Trinity. Jesus is the object of faith and of prayer. His help is sought in every matter. But there is little sense of Jesus as exemplar for life. The slogan "What would Jesus do?" remains external and superficial. But for all its deficiencies, this overemphasis at least maintains continuity with the doctrinal convictions of the church through the ages, and at least comports with the logic of Christian piety.

The other christological extreme is represented by the search for a historical Jesus. Here the humanity of Jesus is so emphasized that any consideration of his divine nature is regarded as a doctrinal imposition that must be resisted if the "real Jesus" is to be discovered through the process of historical reconstruction. The positive effect of this effort has been to recover some sense of Jesus' rootedness in the world of the first century and in particular his Jewishness. But the costs are high. Quite apart from the distortions of historical method that often accompany such endeavors, and the mutually exclusive portraits of Jesus that result (often a "mirror image" of the investigators), the "human Jesus" ends up being more of a sociological stereotype than the robust character depicted by the Gospels. Some insight has been gained into Jesus' Jewish identity and the social and political implications of his activity, but an appreciation for his human character and the religious implications of his presence have been diminished. As simply another human figure of the past, the historical Jesus is significant simply as a critic of the structures of society rather than—as Christian faith has always proclaimed—the one whose life, death, and resurrection have fundamentally altered the structures of human existence itself.[77]

Against this disjunctive and distorted set of Christologies, Hebrews demands taking Jesus both as fully God and as fully human, if our profession is to be adequate to the mystery he reveals. Hebrews asserts as strongly as does the Gospel of John the divinity of Christ, and it asserts as forcefully as the Gospel of Luke the humanity of Christ. Hebrews does not pretend to show how this paradox can be sustained. But it provides a hint when it speaks of the man-

77. See L. T. Johnson, *The Real Jesus: The Misguided Search for the Historical Jesus and the Truth of the Traditional Gospels* (San Francisco: HarperSanFrancisco, 1996).

ner by which Jesus became perfected through his suffering. It allows Christians to imagine, not a grotesque hybrid, but rather a human person who was more and more human as he was opened more and more to the divine, and a Son of God who was perfected as Son precisely through his humanity.

The Path of Discipleship

The main goal of Hebrews as a "word of exhortation" (*logos paraklēseōs*) is transparent: it seeks to maintain and even strengthen the loyalty of believers against the temptation to fall away in the face of shameful trials (2:1–3; 4:1–2, 11–16; 6:4–12; 10:19–39; 12:1–28). The christological argument is in service of the hortatory aim: showing that Christ is the bearer of a greater hope and the high priest of a better covenant provides the motivation for such loyalty. If the promise of life through Christ is greater, so also is the threat of punishment for those who abandon this promise: fear is also a great motivator (see 10:19–31). The roll call of the witnesses in Heb 11 supports the exhortation to fidelity: the author reminds his hearers that the ancient witnesses, like themselves (see 10:32–35), also suffered loss of land and family, experienced hardships, wandered as aliens and strangers, seeking a "city with foundations" (11:8–16), yet remained loyal to the God who called them. They did not sell their birthright for a pot of porridge (12:16). So also, Hebrews says, "we do not draw back—to our destruction. Rather, we have faith—to the saving of our life" (10:39).[78]

In addition to this central hortatory theme, Hebrews encourages its readers to the common virtues of the Christian life in chapter 13.[79] They are to practice brotherly love (13:1; see 6:10) and hospitality (13:2), visit those in prison (13:3; see 10:34), avoid sexual immorality and keep marriage holy (13:4), eschew love of money and cultivate contentment (13:5–6; see 10:34), avoid strange teachings (13:9), imitate the faith of their leaders (13:7) and show them obedience (13:17), share their possessions (13:16), and pray (13:15, 18–19). Each instruction finds its match (often many times) in the other writings of the New Testament. But Hebrews adds two other statements in chapter 13 that catch the eye because of their distinctiveness, inviting a closer look at Hebrews' understanding of discipleship. Does it mean more than holding to the confession and practicing virtue?

At the conclusion of his prayer in 13:20–21, the author asks that the God of peace "equip you to do his will in every good thing, accomplishing among us what is pleasing to him, through Jesus Christ." Just as it was Jesus' obedience to God's will that caused their salvation (10:10), so are they to do the will of

78. For a discussion of the several dimensions of faith in Hebrews, see V. (Sung-Yul) Rhee, *Faith in Hebrews: Analysis within the Context of Christology, Eschatology, and Ethics* (Studies in Biblical Literature 19; New York: Peter Lang, 2001).

79. See above all F. Filson, *'Yesterday': A Study of Hebrews in the Light of Chapter 13* (SBT 2/4; Naperville, IL: Allenson, 1967).

God. But note that they are to do this by "God working in [or among] us," and, further, that God's working and their doing alike is *dia Iēsou Christou*, "through Jesus Christ." Read in this fashion, the prayer closely connects Jesus' obedience toward God and theirs, so much so that it appears as "through Jesus" that God works their obedience.

The second statement occurs in 13:12–13: "For this reason, Jesus also suffered outside the gate in order to sanctify the people through his own blood. Therefore, let us go to him outside the camp, bearing his reproach." Once more we find the closest possible connection between the example of the human Jesus and the behavior of his followers. They are to embrace the suffering he endured as their own. These two statements in chapter 13 propose that we understand Jesus as "pioneer and perfecter of faith" in the sense that what God worked in him is meant to be worked in his followers as well. They cannot literally "go to him outside the camp," for his shameful death is in the past. They can, however, be shaped by the same sort of obedient faith that enables them to "despise the shame of the cross" as it shapes their existence within their own troubled circumstances. Jesus is not only the Son of God who is the cause of salvation; he is the forerunner who shows in his own faith the pattern for his followers.[80]

That Hebrews intends just this understanding is shown by the elaborate athletic imagery of chapter 12. The author masterfully evokes the scene of an athletic contest, specifically a race. There is the "cloud of witnesses" gathered to cheer the contestants (12:1). Jesus is the pacesetter and first finisher (12:2). The readers are urged to join the race, to "run with endurance the race that is set before [them]." They are to throw off whatever weighs them down, just as athletes prepare for action by stripping off their impediments (12:1). They are to avoid the easy distractions of sin (12:1). They are to "keep [their] eyes on Jesus" and "consider the one" running ahead of them (12:2; see 3:1).

The athletic terminology continues in 12:11, where the author notes that all "discipline/education" (*paideia*) seems painful rather than pleasant, but that it eventually yields good results for those "who have been trained in it" (*gegymnasmenois*). This echoes 5:14, where the author stated that solid food is for the "mature people, for those who on account of habit have their faculties trained" (*dia tēn hexin ta aisthētēria gegymnasmena*). Hebrews 12:12 continues the athletic metaphor: "Therefore strengthen your drooping hands and wobbly knees and make straight paths for your feet, so that what is lame may not be dislocated but be healed." This set of exhortations fits those preparing to run a race, or those tempted to fall out of a race because of its difficulties and pains.

It is this athletic imagery that enables us to make sense—and perceive the true depth—of Heb 12:5–11. It seems at first one of the most puzzling passages

80. On this see B. L. Melbourne, "An Examination of the Historical-Jesus Motif in the Epistle to the Hebrews," *AUSS* 26 (1988): 281–97.

in the letter, an apparently extraneous excursus. Properly read, however, it states the real point of Hebrews' teaching on discipleship. The passage takes up the hard experiences of the hearers, the things that tempt them to quit the race (see 10:32–35). They have not yet, the author reminds them, suffered to the point of shedding their blood (12:4)—as had Jesus. How, then, should they view the hard things happening to them?

They should regard them, says the author, as the discipline (*paideia*) imposed by the father on a beloved son (12:5–6, citing Prov 3:11–12). Fathers discipline only the sons they acknowledge as their own, Hebrews asserts; they fail to discipline their bastard children (12:7–8). The logic here may be offensive to some present-day readers who think immediately of the physical abuse of children carried out "because we love you." We must, therefore, place ourselves imaginatively in ancient patriarchal cultures, in which the issue is not physical abuse but training in character, as 12:10–11 makes clear. Ancient moralists like Xenophon and Plutarch were aware of how refractory human nature could be, and how much discipline was required to form good habits. They understood that moral education was a matter of the transformation of the mind and of dispositions as well as the control of the body, and that such transformation involved painful change.

Two important but easily overlooked aspects of 12:5–11 emerge more clearly when placed in this context. The first is that the language of father and son used for God and community is scarcely accidental. Jesus is God's Son preeminently, but we remember that being perfected through what he suffered, he was to lead "many sons" to glory (2:10). Hebrews places the suffering experienced by the community within the framework of the suffering experienced by Jesus as God's Son. They are experiencing what he did. This is why they are told: "consider him who endured from sinners such hostility against himself, so that you may not grow weary or fainthearted" (12:3).

The second thing we notice is that this passage picks up the theme of education through suffering announced first in 5:8: "Even though he was a son, he learned obedience from the things he suffered." Here we must remember the triple nuance of *paideia* in Greco-Roman discourse: discipline, education, culture. The three meanings go together. The suffering now being experienced by the hearers is in fact their education as "sons" just as Jesus as God's Son learned obedience from what he suffered (*emathen aph' hōn epathen*). Thus the best translation of the short sentence in 12:7, *eis paideian hypomenete*, is as an indicative rather than an imperative. Not the RSV's "It is for discipline you have to endure," or even the NRSV's "Endure trials for the sake of discipline," or the NAB's "Endure your trials as discipline." It is, rather, "you are enduring for the sake of an education." Why they should endure is made clear by the next line: "God is treating you as sons!"

The meaning of discipleship in Hebrews, then, is more than a matter of loyalty to the confession or the practice of virtue. It means walking in the path of transformation into true and mature children of God. Like the heroes of faith who lived as strangers and aliens on earth, seeking God's city, so also Christians "have no permanent city but seek a city that is to come." The way to this city, however, is through the same path run by Jesus, being transformed by the experience of suffering as he was, into the maturity of God's beloved children, through the obedience of faith that progressively opens them to God's fearful freedom. It means enduring for the sake of an education (12:7), and it means "going to him outside the camp" and bearing the abuse he endured (13:13).

Hebrews challenges present-day Christian understandings of discipleship, which, corresponding to the disjunctive and distorted Christologies, fall into two opposing emphases. On one side, we find the peculiar phenomenon of the "gospel of success," in which the profession of Jesus as Lord, a personal relationship with him in faith, and a reliance on his assistance in every circumstance is thought to lead to a life free from distress and suffering, one abounding in physical health, emotional calm, and monetary prosperity. Discipleship is understood as right belief and right practice, spelled out in the consistent moral teachings of the church through the ages, each understood in highly individualistic fashion. If Christians are to engage the social or political order, it is to secure the social dominance of these codes and the political security within which it is safe to practice them. In such an understanding of discipleship, change is a threat, and physical, emotional, or mental suffering is taken as a sign of failed faith.

Corresponding to the Christology that focuses exclusively on the humanity of Jesus is a vision of discipleship that is completely ordered to the transformation of social and political structures. Being a follower of the prophet Jesus means living out a vision of the gospel that liberates the marginalized and oppressed from destructive social systems, since sin is more structural than personal: racism, sexism, and capitalism are systems that distort human dignity and must be changed if the good news is to be realized. Hope is not for internal transformation or living in a future life with God; such are forms of alienation that deflect and distract true political action and change. Once more, remarkably, suffering is excluded from discipleship. The suffering of the oppressed must be removed: it has no value to them or anyone else. The continued suffering of the world is a sign of failed faith in the power of the prophetic word to effect real change.

Hebrews challenges both kinds of distorted discipleship. To be sure, it calls for utter loyalty to the profession of faith and the keeping of the most traditional forms of moral rectitude—"let the marriage bed be without defilement!"—but it also calls for hospitality to be shown strangers (a risky business), for sharing possessions, for visiting the imprisoned and ill-treated, "as though you were in their bodies" (13:3). In a word, the intense piety of Hebrews is not individualistic but communal, not a seeking of the self (even the self's salvation) but a care for the community.

Hebrews challenges present-day sensibilities most of all by seeing suffering as the very heart of discipleship. Suffering is not merely a matter of things that come upon people from the outside, although Hebrews would certainly not consider the loss of property or imprisonment as a judgment on inadequate faith. Suffering, rather, is the inevitable concomitant of obedient faith itself. It is the sound of the human spirit opening itself to the presence and power of God. It is the very path by which humans become transformed, as was Jesus, into fully mature children of God.

COMMENTARY

1:1–4 Prologue

Although Hebrews is included among the New Testament letters, and may even have originally functioned as a letter—being composed for oral delivery to a group separated from the author—it lacks any formal epistolary elements, apart from the few closing remarks (13:22–25). In particular, Hebrews lacks the greeting and thanksgiving characteristic of Paul's letters (e.g., Rom 1:1–15; 1 Cor 1:1–9). Instead, this composition begins with a prologue or exordium. In a single complex sentence extending through four verses, the author announces major themes and prepares for the first stage of his argument.

The syntax of the sentence directs the readers to the central point. There is one independent clause, "God has spoken to us in a son," with every other clause and phrase dependent on, and in various ways modifying, that basic assertion, which is also the central claim of the composition. Verses 1 and 2 are made up of four clauses. The first two provide a contrast between God's speaking in the past and in the present. The next two elaborate on the nature of the Son through whom God now speaks. Verse 3 consists of a long and complex relative clause that further describes the identity and role of the Son, and verse 4 asserts the superiority of the Son to the angels, thus preparing for the argument that picks up immediately in 1:5.

The prologue establishes the framework of continuity and discontinuity that is critical to the author's exposition and exhortation, the dignity of the Son and his priestly work (the purification from sins) accomplished by his exaltation to God's presence. Remarkably, the prologue does not actually mention the name Jesus. The author delays that explicit identification—though, to be sure, it is understood throughout—until 2:9.

> 1:1 In the past, God spoke at many times and in many ways to the fathers[a]
> in the prophets. 2 In these final days,[b] he has spoken to us in a son, whom
> he has made heir of all things, through whom also[c] he created the universe. 3 He is a radiance of his glory and an imprint of his very being, and
> he bears[d] all things by the word of his power.[e] Having accomplished
> purification from sins,[f] he has taken a seat at the right hand of the majesty
> on high. 4 He has become as much greater than the angels[g] as the name
> he has inherited is more excellent than them.

a. Some MSS add *hēmōn* ("our") to "fathers." The addition makes explicit what is already implicit in the term. Even without the personal pronoun, "our fathers" would be a legitimate translation.

b. The best MSS read literally, "the last of these days" (*eschatou tōn hēmerōn toutōn*), but others have "at these last days" (*eschatōn tōn hēmerōn toutōn*).

c. *Pace* Lane (5), the *kai* ("also") omitted by P[46] and a few other witnesses is neither adversative nor concessive.

d. The original hand and the second corrector of B have "revealing" (*phanerōn*) rather than "bearing" (*pherōn*).

e. There are substantial disagreements among MSS concerning the presence of the personal pronoun "his" (to be read as in the translation given), or its replacement by some variation of "through himself" (to be read with the following phrase—"having through himself accomplished purification from sins"). The shorter reading is preferable, since the longer may be due to conflation or to the dogmatic preoccupation of scribes.

f. Doctrinal concerns probably account for the addition of "our" to make "purification from our sins," to avoid the impression that Jesus was himself sinful (see Heb 5:3).

g. P[46] and B omit the definite article before "angels."

[1:1–2] Verses 1–2a confirm both the rhetorical polish of the author and the basic framework of his argument. The framework is the continuity and discontinuity of God's speech to humans set out in a clear contrast. The rhetorical self-consciousness is signaled by the use of alliteration in the very first lines: of the first twelve words in Greek, the five most important start with *p*. Translations cannot hope to replicate the style without mangling the meaning. My translation, "at many times and in many ways," for example, is a feeble effort to capture the Greek's *polymerōs kai polytropōs*. Another difficulty that the rhetoric of Hebrews creates for translators—and this, throughout the composition—is its long and complex Greek sentences, which rely heavily on subordinate clauses. My translation uses the more paratactic style of American English, which requires breaking the long clauses into shorter sentences. This represents both gain and loss. The sentences sound more like our speech. But once the splendid syntactical markers of the Greek are abandoned, an inevitable lack of clarity results. In the present passage, for example, all the sentences starting with "he" refer to the Son rather than to God. But in 1:3, the "his" in "his glory" and "his very being" refers to God, whereas "his word of power" refers to the Son. The only solution to this problem is to repeat "God" and "Son," but that distorts the sense of the Greek even more—not to mention that there is some ambiguity in the Greek as well.

The most difficult translation decision in 1:1–2a is which aspect of the initial contrast most requires highlighting. I have emphasized the contrast between the past (*palai*) and the eschatological present (*ep' eschatou tōn hēmerōn toutōn*), since the other contrasts fit within that temporal distinction. The contrast between God's former revelation (especially through the prophetic writings) and the present revelation through Jesus appears in other New Testament writings (see Rom 1:1–5; 16:25–27; 2 Tim 1:9–10; 1 Pet 1:1–10). Corresponding to the distinction between past and present is that between God's audiences: in the past, God spoke to "the fathers." We cannot conclude anything about the ethnicity of either author or audience from this locution, since Paul—writing to a mixed congregation in Corinth—can also speak of the wilderness generation as "our fathers" (1 Cor 10:1; see also Acts 7:11, 39, 44). On the other side, Hebrews does not use the distancing "your fathers" found in Luke 11:47–48 and Acts 7:52. For Hebrews, those who confess Jesus find their ancestors in the story of Israel. The new revelation is superior to the old but also builds upon it: the same God who spoke to the fathers now speaks "to us" (cf. also 1 Cor 10:6). The "us" includes not only those who first heard Jesus and witnessed to him (Heb 2:3), but the author and his hearers as well. As in Luke–Acts, the scope of God's speech and activity *hēmin* ("to us") extends into the present (see Luke 1:1).

The prologue's main contrast is between the agents of God's speaking. In the past, God spoke "in" the prophets and now speaks "in" a Son. The Greek preposition *en* used for both phrases is instrumental, and the translation "through prophets/son" is appropriate. I retain the literal "in" because I think Hebrews retains some of the locative sense of the preposition as well, especially in the case of the Son. The special and superior character of God's speech in and through his Son Jesus is the main point of Hebrews' argument, together with the corollary that it requires a greater and better response of faith than that shown by "the fathers." Indeed, the prologue will move immediately in its next line to assert the special character of the one "in whom" God now speaks.

Before moving forward, however, we can pause over two aspects of the opening verses that point to a contrast between the many and the one, and thus indirectly to the Platonic worldview of the writings (see Introduction, pp. 17–21). In Platonism the choice between the one and the many is always resolved in favor of the one. First, God in the past spoke through prophets (in the plural). As mentioned in the Introduction, Hebrews applies the title *prophētēs* in the discourse proper only as a general designation, "David and Samuel and the prophets" (11:32). As it is used in the prologue, therefore, the term is probably meant to suggest all the agents by whom God's word and will were disclosed to the people, including angels, Moses and Joshua, and the priestly cult, in addition to all the heroes of faith recorded in chapter 11. But the term in the plural may also refer to the very texts of Scripture that report all these acts of revelation, and thereby also reveal them. The key point, though, is that in a Platonic worldview, the sheer multiplicity of revealing acts—to present-day readers a positive thing—would suggest inadequacy (cf. the argument Hebrews makes concerning the priesthood, 7:23–25; 10:1). Second, Hebrews characterizes this earlier speech as *polymerōs kai polytropōs*, which I have translated as "at many times and in many ways." This is the only phrase in the first two verses that lacks a corresponding element, emphasizing this aspect of the earlier revelations. Once more, the "many" (*polys*), which might appear positive to present-day readers, would have been viewed within a Platonic worldview as inferior—necessarily fragmentary and partial—in contrast to the singularity of revelation in God's Son.

Nevertheless, the prophets and the Son also stand in continuity as the agents of God's speaking to humans. With this stroke, Hebrews cuts to the heart of the world imagined by Scripture (another way of saying, the world imagined by the prophets themselves!), which in an odd way fits well with the world of Platonism. We recall that in Platonism there is a relation of cause and effect between the noumenal and phenomenal, so that "what we see comes from what we do not see" (Heb 11:3). In Scripture this relationship between the unseen God and the visible world is expressed in terms of God's creative speech: "By faith we understand that the ages were fashioned by God's word" (11:3). Creation itself, then, is conceived as intrinsically verbal, as articulate, and as revelatory of the God who speaks it into being. As Ps 18:1–2 says, "The heavens proclaim the glory of God, and the firmament proclaims his work; day to day pours forth speech (*rhēma*) and night to night declares knowledge (*gnōsis*)." If speech ("God's word") is an appropriate metaphor for all the forms of divine agency in the world, it is particularly apt when used for forms of human speech and gesture that, moved by God's Spirit, declare themselves as "the word of the Lord" (*logos/rhēma tou kyriou*), as in the words of the prophets of Israel (Hos 1:1; Amos 5:1; Mic 1:1; Zech 1:1; Isa 1:10; 40:8; 66:5; Jer 1:1, 4). Fundamental to the prophetic view of reality running all through Scripture is the premise that some humans look at what others look at but see something more, namely God's vision of reality; and that some humans hear what others hear and yet discern as well another word, namely God's message for humanity. The prophet therefore is essentially one who speaks for God to other humans.

How much of God's vision can be seen by the prophet and how much of reality can be interpreted by the prophet as God's word depends upon the prophet's capacity for bearing both the lot of humanity (the realm of the visible and the audible) and the perspective of God. Of no prophet of old was it thought that the divine Spirit was their own spirit or remained with them permanently; of none of them could it be said that they saw and heard always as much from the side of God as from the side of shared humanity. Through them, then, God's speech was necessarily fragmentary and partial. Hebrews argues that the Son, in contrast to all the other prophets, possessed both elements in the highest degree and could therefore be the perfect mediator between God and humans (Heb 9:15).

The second half of verse 2 addresses both dimensions. The Son is both the one through whom God created the universe (and therefore shares God's vision of all reality), and the one whom God has made heir of all things (and therefore a receiver as well as a shaper of God's vision). We note again the balance in the clauses: the Son plays a role in the making of *tous aiōnas*—the term means literally "ages" but is used for both temporal and spatial realms (e.g., 1 Cor 1:20; 2 Cor 4:4; Heb 9:26; 11:3)—so he will also "inherit" all things. The protological function of the Son points to his eschatological victory.[1] We can consider them in the order Hebrews presents them, the logic for which will become apparent as we proceed.

In a patriarchal society, the notions of "sonship" and "inheritance" (*klēronomia*) are naturally linked. The extent and nature of one's inheritance depends on the wealth and power of one's father, and one's position among the offspring. "But if children, then heirs" (Rom 8:17; Gal 4:7). In the biblical narrative, God's promise to Abraham and to "the fathers" (Heb 6:13–14) is spelled out in terms of an inheritance. They are to "inherit the land" (Gen 15:4; 28:4; Deut 1:8; 4:10; see Rom 4:13). The New Testament takes over the language but gives it new content by dramatically reinterpreting the meaning of inheritance in light of the experience of Jesus. Now, as the unique Son of God, Jesus is simply "the heir" (Matt 21:38; Mark 12:7; Luke 20:14), and his followers become "fellow heirs" through their connection to him (Rom 8:17). The inheritance, furthermore, is not of the material "land" (see only Matt 5:5), but of a participation in God's rule over creation, the *basileia tou theou* (see Matt 25:34; 1 Cor 6:9–10; 15:50; Gal 5:21; Eph 5:5; Jas 2:5), which Peter calls "imperishable, undefiled, unfading" (1 Pet 1:4), and which can also be described in terms of "eternal life" (Matt 19:29; Mark 10:17; Luke 10:25; 18:18; Titus 3:7).

The statement of Heb 1:2 that God has made the Son "heir of all things" (*klēronomon pantōn*) finds an emphatic echo in 1:4, where the author asserts that the Son "has inherited a more excellent name" than the angels. Hebrews here anticipates the theme that Jesus is the forerunner or pioneer who has reached first the goal toward which his brothers struggle. Joshua, we will learn, led the people into "the land," but that was not the real "rest" or "inheritance" (4:8–10). If Jesus is heir not simply of the land but of "all things," then those who follow him as brothers will likewise share in that inheritance which is "eternal" (see 6:12, 17; 9:15; 11:7–8; 12:17).

The Son's capacity to inherit "all things" from God is, in turn, connected to his role in fashioning "all things" in the universe. He is to inherit what he himself participated in bringing into being. Hebrews stands within the stream of scriptural tradition that ascribes a role in creation to God's Wisdom (see Prov 8:22–31; Sir 24:1–12; Wis 8:3–6), a tradition that, in the New Testament, becomes focused on the figure of Jesus. The same prepositional phrase, "through whom,"

1. See K. Schenck, "Keeping His Appointment: Creation and Enthronement in Hebrews," *JSNT* 66 (1997): 91–117.

is used also by Paul in 1 Cor 8:6: "One Lord, Jesus Christ, through whom are all things and through whom we exist," as well as by the prologue to the Fourth Gospel, which declares concerning the Word that was with God in the beginning, that "all things were made through him" (John 1:3), and "the world was made through him" (1:10). In Col 1:16 Paul states flatly that "he is the image of the unseen God, the first-born of all creation, because in him were all things created."

Such statements about a historical human being who died a shameful death by crucifixion, not after centuries of reflection, but within two decades of his execution—ascribing to him a role in the shaping of the world!—are not to be attributed simply to a process of textual study, but above all to the impact of the resurrection experience, by which Jesus' followers experienced him after his death as the powerful and life-giving spirit (1 Cor 15:45). If his resurrection is a "new creation" (2 Cor 5:15; Gal 6:15), and he now shares God's life as "Lord" (1 Cor 12:3), and the result of incorporation into him is "eternal life," that is, an anticipation of God's own glory (Rom 6:5–11, 20–23), it is but an experiential inference to conclude that this same one was also at work in the first creation. If God is eternal, and Jesus is God's Son in an ontological and not simply honorific sense, then no temporal considerations block such a conclusion. The one who "creates the ages" is scarcely to be defined by them! The language used in Scripture of God's Wisdom provided the vehicle for expressing this insight, and it is precisely this ontological understanding of "the Son" that is next elaborated.[2]

[3] Verses 3–4 of the prologue form a chiastic expansion on verse 2b-c, rather than a true development: *a*. the Son inherits all things; *b*. the Son participates in creation; *c*. the Son makes purification for sins and sits at God's right hand; *b′*. the Son is the image of God and sustains all things; *a′*. the Son inherits a name greater than angels. As often in chiasm, the middle term *c* is central both spatially and thematically, pulling together the other affirmations to their salvific point: purification from sins is accomplished by God.

Verse 3a-b amplifies the terse affirmation, "through him he has also created the universe" (1:2c), by stating the Son's relation to God in terms of identity and power. Wisdom 7:26 could well have influenced the language and thought here, in its three affirmations concerning Wisdom: "a reflection (*apaugasma*) of eternal light, a spotless mirror (*esoptron*) of the working of God, and an image (*eikōn*) of his goodness." Hebrews calls the Son a "radiance (*apaugasma*) of his [i.e., God's] glory (*doxa*)," an "imprint (*charaktēr*) of his very being (*hypostaseōs*)," and one who "bears (*pherōn*) all things by the word of his power (*dynamis*)." Before considering the terms individually, it is important to note that in combination they clearly and overwhelmingly assert the divine status of

2. For an argument that the seven designations given to Jesus in 1:2–4 correspond numerically to the seven biblical citations that follow in 1:5–14, see J. P. Meier, "Structure and Theology in Heb 1, 1–14," *Bib* 66 (1985): 168–89.

the Son. It is small wonder that the patristic defenders of Nicene orthodoxy found in Heb 1:3 a powerful scriptural basis for their position that everything God was, the Son was also (see Introduction, pp. 6–7).

Even taken separately, the three characterizations point in the same direction. The term "glory" (*doxa*) is used in Scripture with reference above all to the visible presence of God among the people (see Exod 16:7, 10; 24:16; Lev 9:6; Num 14:10; Deut 5:24; Ps 18:1; Heb 9:5). The association of God's presence with *light*, furthermore, is common (Exod 10:23; Pss 4:6; 35:9; 77:14; 88:15; 118:105). It is natural, then, for "glory" to carry the connotation of "radiant light," as we see elsewhere in the New Testament (John 1:4–14; 2 Cor 3:7–18). Thus Wis 7:26 speaks of wisdom as the radiance of eternal light, and extends the metaphor by designating wisdom a "spotless mirror" of the working of God and "image" of his goodness. In the present case, the noun *apaugasma* could be understood either actively (as "radiance") or passively (as "reflection"): should we consider the Son a reflection of God's glory or an emanation of it? The distinction breaks down, however, when we remember that with light, reflection becomes radiance, and radiance is what is reflected. The complex role of the Son in Hebrews is signaled by this use of "glory." We learn in 2:7 and 9 that he has been crowned "with glory and honor" by his exaltation to God's right hand, and in 2:10 we hear that he will lead many brothers "to glory."[3]

The Son is also an "imprint of the very being" (*charaktēr tēs hypostaseōs*) of God. This is similar to Wis 7:26, which speaks of Wisdom as the "image" (*eikōn*) of God's goodness: just as the mirror reflects the light, so does it show the face of the one gazing into it. But the metaphor here is even stronger. In material terms, the *charaktēr* is the imprint that a seal makes on a surface. What has been engraved on the seal (the cause) appears (as effect) also on that into which the seal has been pressed; thus the close similarity of the terms "image," "type," and "character." The obvious example is a coin (see Philo, *On Planting* 18). Metaphysically, the language is applied to spiritual realities. Thus Philo can speak of the soul as a certain *typon kai charaktēratheias dynameōs* ("a certain type and imprint of divine power," *The Worse Destroys the Better* 83). Such a metaphysical sense is obviously required when speaking of the eternal God, and is suggested as well by the noun *hypostasis*. It is a term that is used in a wide variety of contexts, since its basic etymological sense of "that which stands under" can apply to everything from foundations to down payments (see, e.g., 2 Cor 9:4; 11:17, as well as Heb 3:14 and 11:1), to "the fundamental being" of an existent—especially in contrast to "mere appearance" (see Pseudo-Aristotle, *On the World* 395A). With reference to being an "imprint" of

3. As important as it is to recognize the "honor-shame" dimensions of Hebrews' language, it is equally important to note the ways in which the language of "glory" in particular has been affected by the remarkable uses of it in the biblical texts available to the author.

God, it must here bear its most metaphysical sense, and Attridge (44) captures the meaning well with "fundamental reality." What God is, the Son is: they share the same "imprint of being."

Wisdom 7:26 speaks of Wisdom as a spotless mirror of the "working of God" (*tou theou energeias*), and Hebrews strikes a similar note when it says of the Son that he "bears (*pherōn*) all things by the word of his power (*to rhēmati tēs dynameōs autou*)." The question posed by the statement is whether it has been inserted simply to fill out the chiasm, or whether it adds anything to what has already been stated by "through whom also he created the universe." If the term *pherein* is taken—as it could be—as "produce or bring into being" (see Philo, *Who Is the Heir?* 36; *On the Change of Names* 192), then the present line would repeat the earlier assertion, adding only "by the word of his power." But *pherein* here probably has its common sense of "carrying" or "bearing" (cf. Heb 12:20; 13:13), so that the nuance added to the earlier statement is that the Son *sustains* "all things" as well as participates in creating them. Once more, the book of Wisdom may provide the background. Wisdom 7:27 says of *sophia*: "although she is but one she can also do all things, and while remaining in herself, she renews all things"; and in 8:1 we read, "she reaches from one end of the earth to the other, and she orders all things well." The Son, in short, participates in the ongoing governance of the universe.

But why is this expressed with "by the word (*rhēma*) of his power"? The "his," by the way, refers to the Son himself, although the textual confusion at this point in the manuscripts shows that some scribes felt impelled to clarify the referent. The confusion is understandable, since the biblical story leads readers to think of *God* as "creating by a word" (see Gen 1:3, 6, 9, 11, 14; Wis 9:1; Sir 42:15; Ps 32:6; 2 Pet 3:5). Indeed, Heb 11:3 itself reminds us that "by faith we understand that the ages were fashioned by God's word (*rhēma tou theou*)," and speaks in 6:5 of tasting the "noble word of God (*kalon theou rhēma*)." If, then, the word of his power—or "his powerful word"—belongs to the *Son*, Hebrews is once more dramatically asserting his identity as divine. The affirmation suggests as well that all the times Scripture speaks of the *rhēma kyriou* ("word of the Lord") as addressed to and through the prophets of old (e.g., Gen 15:1; Exod 17:1; 19:6; Deut 5:5; Isa 16:13; 38:7), the Son's "powerful word" is also somehow involved. The "word" that God speaks now through his Son, then, is not utterly discontinuous with the "word of the Son" that was spoken by God in creation and in prophecy. The same "power" (*dynamis*) has been at work from the beginning and continues now in the "last of these days," namely the power of God (see Heb 2:4; 6:5; 7:16; 11:11).

What has been said of the Son up to this point has been expressed passively (God made him heir) or through the timeless present participle (he "is," he "bears all things"). In 1:3c-d Hebrews shifts to the temporal mode (aorist participle and verb) to express the other dimension of the Son, who is the single mediator and priest between God and humans, showing his saving work through his human death and resurrection/exaltation. The reader is therefore to understand that the one carrying out the purification of sins and taking a seat at God's right hand is the very one who shares fully from the beginning in God's being and power.

The clause "having accomplished purification from sins" is more troublesome than it first appears. Two things are clear: first, the use of the aorist participle indicates that this purification was completed and preceded the Son's exaltation; second, the theme of purification (*katharismos*) is central to Hebrews' argument concerning Jesus' priesthood. According to Exod 30:10, the Day of Atonement was to accomplish such purification: "Aaron shall make atonement once a year (*hapax tou eniautou*) upon its horns [i.e., of the altar]; from the blood of the purification from sins (*tou katharismou tōn hamartiōn*) of atonement shall he purify it once a year unto your generations. It is a holy of holies to the Lord." Similarly, Lev 16:30 declares that the Day of Atonement is to make "atonement for you to purify you from all your sins (*katharisai hymas apo pasōn tōn hamartiōn hymōn*) before the Lord." Hebrews argues that Jesus alone has effectively accomplished the purification that earthly priests could not (9:8–14), by purifying them internally in their conscience (9:14, 20, 23), and once for all (10:2). For the understanding of the ritual language of "purification" as a moral or religious cleansing of the person, see also Acts 15:9; 2 Cor 7:1; Titus 2:14; Jas 4:8; 2 Pet 1:9; and above all, 1 John 1:7–9: "The blood of Jesus his son cleanses us from all sin . . . cleanse us from all unrighteousness."[4]

The two textual variants connected to this statement show, however, that some misunderstanding might be possible. Was Jesus required to make purification for his own sins? Hebrews asserts later that Jesus was tested like other humans in every way "apart from sin" (*chōris hamartias*, 4:15). Some scribes felt a need to make that clarification explicit here, and so added the pronoun "our" to the phrase to make it read "purification from/of our sins." Similarly, the confusing combination of personal pronouns immediately preceding the phrase (some MSS have "his," others "through himself," and still others, both!) suggests that some scribes wanted to emphasize that this purification was accomplished by the Son himself, possibly to avoid implications of patripassionism (the early heresy holding that the Father suffered in the death of Jesus).

With the statement that the Son "has taken a seat at the right hand of the majesty on high," Hebrews initiates the theme of Jesus' exaltation, by alluding to Ps 109:1: "The Lord said to my lord, 'Sit at my right hand (*ek dexiōn mou*) until I make your enemies a footstool at your feet.'" This is the classic resurrection proof text of the earliest Christian movement (see Matt 22:44; 26:24;

4. For this theme throughout the composition, see W. G. Johnsson, "Defilement and Purgation in the Book of Hebrews" (Ph.D. diss., Vanderbilt University, 1973).

Mark 12:36; 14:62; 16:19; Luke 20:42; 22:69; Acts 2:34; Rom 8:34; 1 Cor 15:25; Eph 1:20; Col 3:1), demonstrating that the resurrection of Jesus is not a mere resuscitation by which he resumed empirical existence, but an exaltation or enthronement by which he entered fully into the life and rule of God as "Lord" (*kyrios*).

Hebrews alludes repeatedly to this first verse of Ps 109 (see 1:13; 8:1; 10:12), and will appropriate in conjunction with it the psalm's fourth verse, to show that Jesus is also a high priest according to the order of Melchizedek (see Heb 5:6, 10; 6:20; 7:3, 11, 15, 17, 21). Hebrews is, to be sure, much more than a "homiletical midrash based on Psalm 110 [LXX 109]" (Buchanan, xix), but it is surely also that; no other early Christian writing makes such creative use of this psalm in order to make the powerful christological argument that Jesus is at once king and priest.

Hebrews adds phrases in order to emphasize the transcendent, divine character of the Son's session at the right hand. The term "majesty" translates *megalasynē* (lit. "greatness"), which is used in the LXX to render forms of *gdl*, especially as applied to God (see Deut 32:3; 1 Chr 29:11; Pss 78:11; 144:3; 150:2; Prov 18:10; Wis 18:24). Similarly, the phrase "on high" (*en hypsylois*, lit. "in the heights") occurs in the LXX for God's "right hand lifted on high"—a metaphor for God's power (see Ps 135:12; Deut 5:15)—and for the status of God above all creatures: "who is like the Lord our God who dwells on high" (*en hypsylois*; Ps 112:5; see also Pss 88:27; 92:4; 98:2; 137:6). The Greek term will reappear in Heb 7:26, where the Son is declared a priest who is "exalted above the heavens" (*hypsēloteros tōn ouranōn*).

[4] The entire thrust of Heb 1:2–3 has been the dignity and power of the Son in relation to God. The same point is made again now by means of the first of the comparisons that run through the argument of the entire composition: because of his exaltation, the Son is also greater than the angels. This verse therefore both concludes the prologue—it is still part of the single long sentence that begins the composition—and provides a transition to the argument proper. I will take up in the first excursus the question, "Why the angels?" but can observe at once that despite receiving intense concentration in the first two chapters (1:4, 5, 6, 7, 13; 2:2, 5, 7, 9, 16), the term *angelos* (lit. "messenger") occurs later only in 12:22 and 13:2.

The structure of the comparison is provided by the correlative adjectives "so much . . . as" (*tosoutō . . . hosō*) and the comparative adjective *kreittōn* ("better/greater") that is one of Hebrews' characteristic expressions (6:9; 7:7, 19, 22; 8:6; 9:23; 10:34; 11:16, 35, 40; 12:24). At this point, nothing at all is said about the angels; some manuscripts even omit the definite article before the noun. As throughout the prologue, the focus is rather on the status of the Son. Here we observe that he "has become" (*genomenos*) greater than the angels, a phrasing that suggests a prior condition in which he was less than them. This is precisely what is stated in 2:9, where we learn that Jesus was for a little while lower than the angels (*par' angelous ēlattōmenon*) and then was crowned with glory and honor.

How any of this happened is not spelled out by explicit narrative, either here or anywhere else in Hebrews. Both author and hearers clearly share a story of Jesus' death and resurrection/exaltation that can be alluded to without further qualification and without fear of misunderstanding. Nor does Hebrews untangle through analysis the paradox of one who shares fully the status of God becoming lower than angels and then becoming greater than them. Such untangling would in any case be impossible because the affirmations do not arise from the pursuit of logical propositions but from the conviction, arising from experience, that both in the shameful death of Jesus and in his glorious exaltation the one who creates the universe is at work.

The elevation of Jesus above the angels is connected to the "more excellent name" that he has inherited. The notion of inheritance refers back to 1:2: the Son is the one whom God has made (or appointed, *ethēken*) heir of all things. The verse suggests that the Son enters fully into this inheritance following upon his work of purification for sins and as a consequence of his exaltation to the right hand of the majesty on high (1:3). It follows, then, that the "more excellent name" is precisely his designation as "Lord" (*kyrios*). In the biblical tradition, the name (*onoma*) is more than an arbitrary designator; it evokes the identity of the one named (see Gen 2:19–20; Exod 3:13–15; 34:5, 14). And in the LXX, the "name" *kyrios* is used to translate the Tetragrammaton (YHWH), the proper name of Israel's God (see Gen 2:4; Exod 3:15–16; Deut 6:4–5; Ps 148:5). Psalm 109:1 (the verse being troped in Heb 1:3), in turn, has "the Lord" commanding "my lord" to take a place at his right hand. By his enthronement, Jesus enters into full participation in God's being and power.

The widespread use of Ps 109:1 (MT 110:1) among early Christians in connection with the resurrection undoubtedly arises from the perception that Jesus' exaltation gave him the same status as "the Lord God."[5] In Acts 2:36, immediately after citing Ps 109:1, Peter says to the gathered crowd, "Let the whole house of Israel know that God has made him both Lord and Messiah, this Jesus whom you crucified." The same connection of "exaltation," "name," and "Lord" occurs at the climax of Paul's christological hymn in Phil 2:9–11: "God has highly exalted him and has given him a name (*onoma*) that is above every other name, so that at the name of Jesus every knee shall bow, above the heavens and above and beneath the earth, and every tongue confess to the glory of God the father that Jesus Christ is Lord (*kyrios Iēsous Christos*)." Paul probably alludes here to the earliest form of postresurrection confession, "Jesus is Lord" (see 1 Cor 12:3; Rom 10:9).

5. See D. M. Hay, *Glory at the Right Hand: Psalm 110 in Early Christianity* (SBLMS 18; Nashville: Abingdon, 1973).

If the Son has "inherited" the name "Lord," and thereby shares fully in God's dominion over "all things," then indeed his name is "more excellent" (*diaphorōteros* almost suggests "to be distinguished from") than angels. As the argument develops, Hebrews will show that no such "name" has ever been attached to them, but has been to the Son.

The opening sentence of Hebrews is a prologue to the composition that establishes the basic premises of the argument to follow. Above all, it sketches the basic mythic pattern out of which the discourse of Hebrews grows: God's Son has entered the plane of human existence (and sin) and has again been exalted. This pattern of descent and ascent (from God to humans and back to God) also defines the path of pilgrimage for the readers: they are to follow the one who has come to them back to the place that is properly his and, by gift, theirs.

1:5–14 Scripture Proves That the Son Is Greater Than the Angels

Hebrews launches immediately into the *synkrisis* (comparison) between the Son and the angels that was announced at the end of the prologue (1:4). From 1:5–13, the argument is carried entirely by a string of citations from the LXX, leading to a summary rhetorical question in 1:14. In this section, the comparison concerns entirely the "more excellent name" of the Son, his dignity and status as God's Son. With only the briefest of editorial links, the author constructs a catena ("chain") of texts that serve as scriptural warrants for the claims made by the prologue, and that anticipate themes of the later argument as well. Seven passages from the LXX are explicitly cited. The first three (from Ps 2:7; 2 Sam 7:14 par. 1 Chr 17:13; and Deut 32:43 [Ps 96:7]) are addressed to the Son, as are also the last three (Pss 44:7–8; 101:26–28; 109:1). Only the middle citation from Ps 103:4 directly addresses the angels.[1]

With this chain of citations, Hebrews demonstrates immediately how God spoke in the past "in the prophets," but the remarkable feature of the demonstration is that texts usually thought of as prophetic are not employed. Rather, the dominance of the Psalms, read messianically, is clear. Four distinct premises underlie this display of scriptural passages. The first is that, through such words of Scripture, God *speaks* (1:1). Note the way the passages are introduced, not with "where is it written," but with "when did he ever say?" Scripture reports God's speech. Second, these scriptural testimonies are authoritative and true; no effort is expended on defending the proposition that they are trustworthy—

1. See K. L. Schenck, "A Celebration of the Enthroned Son: The Catena of Hebrews 1," *JBL* 120 (2001): 469–85.

they are understood to be reliable witnesses. Third, Scripture speaks about the Son (already in the past!) and even reports how God speaks to the Son. Fourth, it is the experience of Jesus as the exalted "Son of God" that enables these ancient writings to be aligned with their proper subject. Messianic exegesis simply finds, on the basis of this crucified and raised Messiah, what God had wanted to be heard in Scripture all along.[2]

We find the use of scriptural catenae in other Jewish and early Christian writings. Of special interest are two fragmentary compositions from Qumran.[3] The first (*4QFlorilegium*) gathers together a series of texts pertaining to the Messiah. The collection weaves together without comment 2 Sam 7:10; Exod 15:17–18; 2 Sam 7:11–14; Amos 9:11; Isa 8:11; Ezek 44:10; and Ps 2:1. It is noteworthy that Heb 1:5–13 draws from Ps 2:7 and 2 Sam 7:14, and will shortly make use of Isa 8 (Heb 2:13), while Amos 9:11 is employed messianically by Acts 15:16–17. A second Qumran text (*4QTestimonia*) likewise strings together a series of texts (Deut 18:18–19; Num 24:15–17; Deut 33:8–11; Josh 6:26).

Such catenae provided a writer or speaker with a set of scriptural "proofs" for a specific topic. We find similar examples in the New Testament. The catena in Rom 3:10–18 (drawn from the Psalms and Isaiah) demonstrates the sinfulness of all humanity; that in Rom 9–11 forms the basis of an argument concerning the place of Jews and Gentiles in God's plan; that in 1 Pet 2:6–10 is used to support the place of Gentile believers as God's house. Later Christian writers, in turn, gathered both Old and New Testament texts into collections of "testimonies" to demonstrate the truth of Christian beliefs and practices (see, e.g., Cyprian of Carthage, *Treatise 12: Three Books of Testimonies against the Jews*). Such catenae, in short, were used frequently and flexibly as aide-mémoire for the rhetorician's art. It is futile to ask whether a specific form of catena served as a written source for Hebrews in this place. Nothing would be gained by such a determination, even if it were possible, especially since the author of Hebrews is certainly capable of gathering together his own set of "witnesses" (see chap. 11!).

> **1:5** For to which of the angels did he ever say, "You are my son; I have
> begotten you today"? And again, "I will be as a father to him, and he will
> be as a son to me." **6** And, once more, as he leads the firstborn into the
> world, he says, "And let all the angels of God worship him." **7** Also,
> whereas he says to the angels,[a] "He is the one who makes his angels to
> be spirits and his ministers to be a flame of fire," **8** he says in contrast to

2. For the argument that the citations in the catena correspond thelogically to the designations of Jesus in 1:1–4, see J. P. Meier, "Symmetry and Theology in the Old Testament Citations of Heb 1, 5–14," *Bib* 66 (1985): 504–33.

3. See H. W. Bateman, "Two First-Century Messianic Uses of the OT: Heb 1:5–13 and 4QFlor 1.1–19," *JETS* 38 (1995): 11–27.

the Son, "Your throne, O God, is forever and ever[b] and[c] the scepter of integrity is the scepter of your kingdom.[d] **9** You have loved righteousness and hated lawlessness.[e] For this reason, O God, your God[f] has anointed you with the oil of gladness over your companions." **10** And, "From the beginning, O Lord, you have laid the foundation of the earth, and the heavens are the work of your hands. **11** They indeed will disappear, but you remain.[g] And all these will grow old like a garment, **12** and like a cloak that you will roll up,[h] and, like a garment,[i] they will be changed. But you remain yourself and your years will not end." **13** When did he ever say to any of the angels, "Sit at my right hand, until I make your enemies a footstool for your feet"? **14** Are they not all ministering spirits sent out for service[j] in behalf of those who are to inherit salvation?

a. A few MSS add the personal pronoun "his" (*autou*) in anticipation of the one in the citation.

b. B and a few other witnesses omit "and ever" (*tou aiōnos*).

c. A number of MSS omit "and" (*kai*) to bring the citation in line with the LXX.

d. A substantial number of witnesses alter the position of the definite article (*hē*) to make the citation agree with the LXX, and some excellent early MSS—P[46], א, and B—have "his" (*autou*) rather than "your" (*sou*), even though the reading given agrees with the LXX.

e. Some MSS have "injustice" (*adikian*) rather than "lawlessness" (*anomian*).

f. The sequence *ho theos ho theos sou* can be read either as "God, your God," or "O God, your God." See discussion.

g. The liquid verb *diameneis* can be accented so as to yield the present ("you remain") or the future tense ("you will remain").

h. In agreement with the LXX, many MSS have *allaxeis* ("you will change") rather than *helixeis* ("you will roll up").

i. Many MSS, in agreement with the LXX, omit either "as a garment" (*hōs himation*) or "and" (*kai*).

j. B reads *diakonias* ("services").

[1:5–6] The first two citations, linked only by the adverbial phrase "and again" (*kai palin*), are from Ps 2:7 and 2 Sam 7:14 (1 Chr 17:13), without any alteration. The introductory question, "To which of the angels did he ever say?" refers back to God as the speaker in the prologue (1:1) and as the speaker in these texts of Scripture. The passages serve to demonstrate the claim of the prologue that God's Son is also the one who rules.

The question expects the answer, "to none of them." Although in the Hebrew of the Masoretic Text (MT) as well as in the Greek of the LXX, members of God's heavenly court can sometimes be called "sons of God" (*huioi tou theou*; see Gen 6:2, 4; LXX Pss 28:1; 88:7), the LXX also sometimes turns "sons of God" into "angels of God" (see Dan 3:25; Job 1:6; 2:1; 38:7). But as Koester (191) observes, the title "sons of God" in such instances is always collective rather than individual. More significant, no angelic figure is formally declared "son" in connection with the sort of royal enthronement envisaged by these two texts.

The passages are linked in several ways. Both speak of a son who is also a king. They are connected to the figure of David. They are in the form of royal pronouncements (Ps 2 as an enthronement psalm and 2 Sam 7 as a prophetic oracle delivered by Nathan to David). And both texts figure elsewhere in messianic contexts. As noted above, the Qumran composition *4QFlorilegium* contains Ps 2:1 and 2 Sam 7:10–14. In the New Testament, Ps 2:1–2 is interpreted by means of a messianic *pesher* with reference to the passion of Jesus,[4] while 2:7 is cited with reference to the resurrection of Jesus in Acts 13:33. Finally, the declaration of the voice from heaven to Jesus at his baptism can be regarded as an allusion to Ps 2:7 as well (Mark 1:11; Matt 2:17; Luke 3:22). In Heb 5:5 Ps 2:7 will be cited explicitly again, in connection with Ps 109:1. Nathan's oracle in 2 Sam 7:14, in turn, is cited in Rev 21:7 by the one who "sits on the throne" and is part of a mixed citation in 2 Cor 6:18; its imagery also helps shape the language of Acts 13:23 and Luke 1:32–33.

A question of perennial pertinence in the analysis of New Testament citations of scriptural texts is whether readers are expected to understand some aspects of the original literary context of the cited texts, or if the entire meaning is borne by the cited words alone.[5] Each case must be evaluated separately, but it is of the essence of ancient midrash to exploit verbal associations, and present-day readers must be open to connections, especially in the Greek text, that might at first appear far-fetched. The two passages with which Hebrews opens its argument make the case that elements of their original contexts are indeed significant for grasping fully what the author intends by citing them.

With respect to Ps 2:7, we see that it is a pronouncement that accompanies the enthronement of a king (*basileus,* 2:6), who is to have as inheritance (*klēronomia*) all the nations and the bounds of the earth (2:8). Other kings are to serve him with rejoicing (2:11). Most striking, the pronouncement is introduced by "the Lord said to me" (*kyrios eipen pros me*), which echoes Ps 109:1, "The Lord said to my lord." Finally, the "today" (*sēmeron*) of the declaration points ahead to the thematic importance of "today" as found in Ps 94:7, which Hebrews develops in 3:7–4:10.

A similar set of associations are found in 2 Sam 7:9–16, the original context for the statement, "I will be as a father to him and he will be as a son to me." In Nathan's prophecy to David, we learn that the king has been given a

4. L. T. Johnson, *Septuagintal Midrash in the Speeches of Acts* (Pere Marquette Lecture in Theology 33; Milwaukee: Marquette University Press, 2002), 29–35.

5. For this discussion, see C. H. Dodd, *According to the Scripture: The Substructure of New Testament Theology* (London: Nisbet, 1952); and R. B. Hays, *Echoes of Scripture in the Letters of Paul* (New Haven: Yale University Press, 1989).

great name (*onoma*) over other kings (7:9), and that his seed (*sperma*) will be raised up as a king (cf. Heb 2:16; 11:11, 18), and that his kingdom and throne will last forever (2 Sam 7:13, 16). Most intriguing is the statement that he will "build a house for my name" (7:13), an image that will be picked up by Heb 3:3, which calls Jesus the "builder of the house." I am not suggesting that the citations were chosen because of these associations, but once the citations are employed, both author and hearers (depending on their competence as readers of the LXX) may well have noted and appreciated such additional messianic overtones.

The next citation in the catena (1:6) presents two problems: the precise source of the text and the meaning of the introduction. The line, "and let all the angels of God worship him" (*proskynēsatōsan autō pantes angeloi theou*), sounds much like Ps 96:7, although that line lacks mention of God and has the form of an indicative rather than a third person imperative: "All his angels worship him." Closer in form is Deut 32:43, in the final lines of the Song of Moses that appear only in the LXX: "rejoice you heavens with him, and let all the sons of God worship him (*proskynēsatōsan autō pantes huioi theou*)." I discussed above the relative interchangeability of "angels" and "sons of God" in Scripture. In both the psalm and Deuteronomy, the "him" who is to be worshiped is the Lord God. The basic point Hebrews wants to make, then, is clear: if the angels pay the Son homage by the bending of the knee (*proskynein*), they acknowledge his superiority to them.

Both possible source passages, furthermore, contain suggestive associative elements. In Ps 96:1 we learn that it is the "Lord" (*kyrios*) who has "taken rule" (*ebasileusen*, 96:1). Flames of fire (*pyr phlogiei*) are around his throne (*thronos*, 96:2–3). Most fascinating, his lightnings appear "in the world" (*oikoumenē*), and the earth sees them and trembles. See below for the discussion of *oikoumenē* in the introductory clause. Deuteronomy 32:43, in turn, also contains elements that catch the attentive ear. In addition to the worship of the sons of God, "all the angels of God are strengthened in him," and "the Lord will purify (*ekkathariei*) the people's land." In short, either passage would suggest to the author and hearers of Hebrews multiple links to the enthronement of the Son at the right hand of the Majesty on high (Heb 1:3).

The introduction of the citation is obscure in each of its terms and in the situation it envisages. The temporal particle *hotan* plus the aorist subjunctive verb suggests the condition under which the statement is made, along the lines of "on the occasion of." The verb *eisagein* has the simple sense of "leading" someone, but often has the effect of "introducing" something or someone, "bringing it/him/her on." We are to picture God, then, as introducing his Son, who is here designated *prōtotokos*, "firstborn." The term has its obvious meaning in a system of primogeniture (see Gen 25:13; 27:19; 35:23), but in two LXX texts it takes on a special significance: Israel is God's firstborn son (*prōtotokos*) in place of the firstborn sons of the Egyptians (Exod 4:22–23; see Heb 11:28), and in the royal Ps 88:28 David is called God's "firstborn."

In the New Testament, the term is restricted to Jesus. Luke uses it in the obvious sense for Jesus' birth (Luke 2:7). Revelation 1:5 refers to Jesus as "the firstborn from the dead and the ruler of the kings of the earth." In Col 1:15 and 18, Paul speaks of Jesus as "the first-born of all creation," and "the first-born from the dead." Paul also uses the designation of Jesus with reference to those who are baptized as his followers: "Those whom God foreknew he predestined to be conformed to the image of his Son, in order that he might be the first-born (*prōtotokos*) among many brethren" (Rom 8:29). This is a notion that is also clearly important for Hebrews (see 2:1–18), and it may figure into its use here; but of more obvious significance is Jesus as the resurrected and exalted one. Note that in Heb 12:23 believers are to come into the "assembly of the firstborn inscribed in the heavens."

This brings to the last difficult term in the introductory clause, *oikoumenē*. It is often translated as "world" (see KJV, RSV), and can certainly bear the sense of "inhabited world." But for that meaning, Hebrews uses *kosmos* (see 4:3; 9:26; 10:5; 11:7, 38). In only one other place does Hebrews use *oikoumenē* (2:5): "it was not to angels that he subjected the world to come (*tēn oikoumenēn tēn mellousan*)." It is reasonable to conclude, then, that *oikoumenē* here means "world" not in the sense of the empirical cosmos, but in the sense of the realm of the divine presence. If this is the case, then the introduction of the Son refers once more to his enthronement—after he had for a little while been made lower than the angels, he is now crowned with glory and honor (see 2:9). The Son's "coming into the world" refers here not to his incarnation (contrast 10:5) or to his parousia (see 9:28), but to the precise scene envisaged by the prologue itself, the exaltation of the Son to God's right hand.

[7–12] The catena continues with three further citations drawn from the LXX. A passage directed to (or about) the angels (Ps 103:4) is opposed to another directed to (or about) the Son (Ps 44:7–8), which is then expanded by a third passage (Ps 101:26–28). My translation tries to mark the strong contrast intended by the first two citations by pushing the *men . . . de* construction in Greek as far as it will go: "also, whereas he says to the angels . . . he says in contrast to the Son." The use of the preposition *pros* in each introduction is ambiguous. As it is used in 1:8 and 1:13, it is best translated as "to" since it introduces a direct address to the Son. But the *pros* in 1:7 could be rendered as "about" as well. My translation of the actual citation alleviates the situation by making it work as a direct address.

Psalm 103 is unlike the earlier citations in that it contains no explicit royal ideology. Rather, as a hymn to God as creator, it focuses on the might and majesty of "the Lord God" as shown by the works of creation. We note that God is described in the psalm as "clothed in light as with a garment" and as "laying the foundation of the earth" (see Ps 101:26–28, to follow). In the list of God's wonders are the angels: he is the one who makes his angels (messengers) spirits and his ministers a flame of light. We can observe that in its original context, the Greek could equally well be translated as "he makes winds to be his messengers, and flames of fire to be his ministers." In either translation, "angels" are simply among God's creatures sent to do his bidding.

The contrast presented by the next two citations could scarcely be greater. Hebrews adduces another royal psalm (44:7–8) but then joins it (by a simple "and") to a petitionary psalm (101:26–28) in which, once more, the distance between Creator and creature is emphasized.

The choice of Ps 44 is bold and brilliant. Bold, because it is originally an ode for a royal wedding in the Davidic dynasty and is redolent of a royal ideology that is entirely this-worldly—to suggest that this psalm "speaks" of a crucified Messiah requires a courageous interpreter! The choice is also brilliant, because the psalm uniquely offers a combination of thematic elements that fit the powerful yet paradoxical Christology of Hebrews. The king who is the subject of the psalm is thoroughly human, indeed is called comely "over other sons of men" (*huioi tou anthrōpou*, 44:3; see Heb 2:6), and God blessed him "forever" (*eis ton aiōna*, 44:3). Yet, because of his enthronement, this human king can be designated as God (*ho theos*): the first line quoted must be translated as, "your throne, O God, is forever and ever." The shock of this attribution is greater when we appreciate the New Testament's general reluctance to use this title for any but the Father. The title *theos* is ascribed to Jesus only in John 1:1, 18; 20:28; Rom 9:5; Titus 3:4; and 2 Pet 1:1, and most of these are disputed in one way or another. Nowhere outside John is the intention to designate the "son" as *ho theos* so obvious and deliberate.

The ambiguity involved in calling even a great king "God" is suggested by the last line of the citation, which can be translated either as "therefore, O God, your God has anointed you," or "therefore God, your God, has anointed you" (Ps 44:8; Heb 1:9). Given the deliberateness of the attribution in the first line, it is best to render it, as my translation does, as a vocative. An anointing with the "oil of gladness" suggests royal status, which places the king "above his companions (*metochous*)." Hebrews is able to exploit the messianic associations of "anointing" (*echrisen* is the verb from which *Christos* derives), and will later refer to the readers as "companions of the Messiah" (*metochoi tou Christou*, 3:14; see also 3:1; 6:4; 12:8). Rather than explain or reduce the prologue's paradox of the human and divine in one son, this psalm citation reinforces it—and grounds the paradox in the words of Scripture!

The psalm citation also characterizes the rule (*basileia*) of the anointed one in terms of its moral qualities. The scepter (*rhabdos*, the symbol of power and authority) of his kingdom is a scepter of "integrity." The term *euthytēs* occurs only here in the New Testament. In ordinary usage it can mean straight as opposed to crooked, and thus be used to suggest moral integrity. The LXX uses it often for "judging rightly," that is, with integrity (Pss 9:8; 66:4; 74:2; 95:10; 97:9). Strikingly, in all these cases, it is *God* who so judges the people with integrity. Not only is the ruler designated as God, he is to exercise his authority with God's own dispositions.

The one anointed by God is also said by the psalm to "love righteousness" (*dikaiosynē*) and "hate lawlessness" (*anomia*). It is noteworthy that the name Melchizedek will be translated in Heb 7:2 as "king of righteousness," maturity is defined in terms of righteousness (5:13), and righteousness is associated with the "inheritance" of those who are faithful (11:7, 33; 12:9). Perhaps even more pertinent is the way the psalm makes the possession of such moral qualities precisely the reason (*dia touto*) for his being exalted above his companions and enthroned.

In reinforcement of the ascription of the name "God" to the Son, the citation from Ps 101:26–28 ascribes to the Son what was first said of "the Lord," the God of Israel. The petitionary psalm elaborates the distance between the mortal realm ("my days like a shadow [*skia*] have declined and I have withered like the grass," 101:12) and the immortal God ("But you, Lord, remain forever, and the remembrance of you from generation to generation," 101:13). The passage selected for citation focuses on the work of creation: the Lord laid the foundation of the earth from the beginning and the heavens are the work of his hands. The citation works to support the prologue's assertion that it was through "the Son/Lord" that God "created the universe" (Heb 1:2).

Other details in the citation require little comment. The contrast between clothes that are changed and the person who remains unchanged is powerful and nonproblematic. We should observe, though, that the short phrase *sy de ho autos ei* ("But you remain yourself," or "you remain the same") anticipates the majestic declaration in 13:8, "Jesus Christ is the same (*ho autos*) yesterday and today and forever."

[13–14] The climactic citation in the scriptural catena is Ps 109:1, which was already alluded to in the prologue's saying of the Son, "taking his seat at the right hand of the majesty on high" (Heb 1:3). I remarked there on the widespread use of Ps 109:1 (MT 110:1) in early Christianity as a proof text for the exaltation/enthronement of Jesus, and its thematic use throughout Hebrews. Above all, Hebrews will exploit Ps 109:4, which declares of "the Lord" who has been enthroned, "You are a priest forever according to the order of Melchizedek" (Heb 5:6). Other elements in this psalm also make its use appropriate. We note reference to a "scepter of power," which provides a verbal link with Ps 44:7. In addition, the Greek of Ps 109:3 can be read either as "with you is the rule (*archē*) in the day of your power" or "with you is the beginning (*archē*) in the day of your power" (see Heb 1:3). This assignment of "origin" is elaborated—once more, only in the Greek, not in the Hebrew text—by this remarkable phrasing: "out of the womb, before the daystar, I have begotten you (*egennēsa se*)," which forms a clear link to Ps 2:7, the first citation in this catena (the Hebrew reads, "from the womb of the morning like dew your youth will come to you"). The Greek of Ps 109:1, especially when read in its full context, wonderfully confirms from Scripture the assertions made in the prologue.

The final rhetorical question in 1:14 summarizes the impact of these citations, and also adds something new, providing a hinge to the next portion of the argument. That the angels are not divine has been made clear by all the citations. That they are "ministers and spirits" is established by the citation from Ps 103:4. But that they are "sent out for service in behalf of those who are going to inherit salvation" is new. The term "inherit" (*klēronomein*) echoes the double designation of the Son as heir of all things (1:2, 4) and anticipates the theme that others are also to share in his inheritance (see 6:17; 9:15; 11:7–8). By defining what is to be inherited as "salvation" (*sotēria*), Hebrews clarifies the significance of the "purification for sins" in 1:3—it is a salvific act—and establishes a central theme of the letter (see 2:3, 10; 5:9; 6:9; 9:28; 11:7) that we will examine as it unfolds. The status of the angels is therefore reduced even further: their "ministry" (*leitourgia*) is not one of worship around the throne, but one of service (*diakonia*) to humans (see 2:16). The question that remains is, why should so much attention be paid to the angels?

Excursus 1: Why the Angels?

The distance between the world imagined by present-day readers and the world imagined by the author and first readers of Hebrews is marked by the fact that today's readers have little or no sense of why angels need be discussed at all, much less take the prominent place in Hebrews' argument. Those living in post-Enlightenment modernity can scarcely even give serious consideration to "spirit" with reference to the human soul and have no place in their "mental universe" for spirits as agents of God. Those living in technologically sophisticated societies can—apart from the odd glitch and blackout—even pretend that humans are in full control of their destiny, not least because their techniques of manipulation have demystified the world.

Angels are not real in today's worldview because they have no job. Present-day readers are consequently likely to find this section of Hebrews either trivial or quaintly irrelevant, having nothing to do with the serious (i.e., scientific) reality of the world they inhabit. Now, any number of things can be said to the adequacy of modernity as a worldview. It is not quite so compelling as it once was. Most of us, nevertheless, live our everyday lives by its premises, but those premises are far from those found in Hebrews.

In contrast, both Greeks and Jews of the first-century Mediterranean—at least the religiously inclined among them—inhabited a universe far more richly populated by spiritual forces than our own. For Gentiles, the membrane separating the divine from the human was permeable, with traffic moving in both directions: members of the divine family could mingle with and even appear as humans (see Ovid, *Metamorphoses*), and humans of special valor or virtue could find an adopted place among the gods (see Herakles). Some of the gods—above all Hermes—even served the special function of "messengers" between the divine and human realms (see Plato, *Cratylus* 407E). And there were any number of *daimonia*, good and bad, at work in the world. In different ways, both religious and magical practices sought the effective management of all these intelligences and spiritual powers influencing human affairs. Such negotiation was all the more delicate when the cultural presupposition was that an agent fully represented the one who sent him. The appearance of a messenger (*angelos*) of a god was thus an anxiety-provoking phenomenon. Powerful itself, the angel brought with its presence possibly an even more terrifying force for good or evil.

Jews were distinguished from their Mediterranean neighbors by their strict monotheism and the practices that expressed that singular commitment. Their Scripture, however, contained traditions of considerable complexity concerning the multifaceted presences of the Divine through his messengers. Most ancient is the language concerning the "angel of the Lord" (*angelos tou kyriou*), who in many passages appears as God's messenger and agent (e.g., Exod 14:19; 23:20; Num 22:22; Ps 33:7; Judg 6:11; 1 Sam 29:9; 2 Sam 14:17), but in other passages seems virtually equivalent to "the Lord" himself, simply another way of expressing the presence of the Lord among the people (see Gen 16:7; 21:17; 22:11; 31:11; Exod 3:2; Judg 2:1). Equally ambiguous is the language concerning the heavenly court of the Lord, whose members can variously be called "sons of God" or "angels" (see, e.g., Gen 6:2, 4; Job 2:1; Pss 28:1; 81:6; 88:6; Dan 7:10). In the prophetic literature, *angeloi* continue to serve as messengers and mediators between God and humans (see Zech 1:9, 12; 3:1), and as protectors of nations (Dan 4:10, 13, 20).

Jewish literature roughly contemporary with the New Testament gives even more attention to angels, with speculation concerning their creation (*Jub.* 2.2; *2 En.* 29.1), their place in the heavenly court (*T. Levi* 18.5; *1 En.* 9.3; 12.2; 71.1), their function as guardians of the nations generally (Sir 17:17) and—especially Michael—of Israel particularly (*Jub.* 35.17; *1 En.* 20.5; *2 En.* 22.6), and their power to visit humans with blessing (Tob 5:4, 17, 20; 2 Macc 10:29; 11:6; 4 Macc 4:10) or with punishment (Wis 18:25; Sir 48:21; 4 Macc 7:11). At Qumran, the *Songs of the Sabbath Sacrifice* portray angels as present around God's throne, participating in eternal worship.[6]

Philo Judaeus can speak of angels in general as powers and movements in the universe (see *On Giants* 6 and 16), but also can connect the singular "angel of the Lord" to the *logos* or "word" of God that he also considers as a "son" (see *Change of Names* 87). In *On Dreams* 1.239, he refers to the angel as "his word, the image of God." Such characterizations make it understandable why New Testament compositions that seek a way of connecting Jesus to God's identity and power, as well as making him a messenger/mediator between God and humans, would find it necessary to distinguish him from such pervasive and powerful figures within the tradition.[7]

In many of the New Testament compositions we find an assertion of the presence and power of the angels as God's agents combined with an effort to reduce their significance

6. See the texts and discussion in C. A. Newsom, *Songs of the Sabbath Sacrifice: A Critical Edition* (HSS 27; Atlanta: Scholars Press, 1985).

7. See L. K. K. Dey, *The Intermediary World and Patterns of Perfection in Philo and Hebrews* (SBLDS 25; Missoula, MT: Scholars Press, 1975); and esp. L. McNicol, "The Relationship of the Image of the Highest Angel to the High Priesthood Concept in Hebrews" (Ph.D. diss., Vanderbilt University, 1974).

relative to Jesus. In the Gospel narratives, angels appear frequently in their role of messengers (Matt 1:20–24; 28:2; Luke 1:11; 2:9; 22:43; John 5:4; 12:29; 20:12; Acts 5:19; 8:26; 10:3; 12:7; 23:8; 27:23). They will perform eschatological functions (Matt 13:39, 41, 49; 22:30; 24:31; Mark 13:27), but mainly they will be part of the entourage of the Son of Man when he appears in glory (Matt 18:10; 25:31; 26:13; Mark 8:38; Luke 9:26, 52; 15:10). They serve Jesus (Matt 4:6, 11; Luke 4:10; Mark 1:13), and signal that the divine presence is with him (John 1:51). There is a place of punishment prepared for the devil and "his angels," who do not keep their place (Matt 25:41; see *Jub.* 5.5–6). Stephen's speech in Acts 7 is particularly interesting because it carries forward the tradition that it was the "angel of the Lord" who was at work with the patriarchs and Moses (Acts 7:30, 35), and in particular in the giving of the law (7:53).

The same mixture of elements is found in the New Testament letters. Angels are able to see human activity in the present (1 Cor 4:9; 11:10) and will be present at the parousia (2 Thess 1:7); but far from judging humans, the angels will be judged by the elect (1 Cor 6:3)! Paul declares that the law was given through the mediation of angels (Gal 3:19), and recognizes the (limited) good of "the tongues of angels" spoken through the gift of the Spirit (1 Cor 13:1), but he also is concerned to deny the advantage of the "worship of [or: with] angels" in Col 2:18, and associates the angels with those "powers and principalities" over whom Jesus as Lord is triumphant (Rom 8:38; see also Eph 3:10–11; 6:12; Col 1:16). The same note of triumph over angelic powers is struck by 1 Pet 3:22, Jude 6, and 2 Pet 2:4.

The most elaborate angelology of the New Testament is undoubtedly that of the book of Revelation, in which the term occurs some sixty-seven times. Angels stand as guardians or representatives of churches in Asia Minor (1:20; 2:1); they stand in the presence of God in heaven (5:2; 7:1, 11) and move around the heavenly temple and altar (14:17–18). They bear announcements of God's decrees (8:4) and do battle with the devil in behalf of the saints (12:7–9; 20:1). As with the "angel of the LORD" in the Old Testament, some ambiguity is connected to the main angelic figure. God sent his message to the seer by an angel (1:1), but he seems to become one like a Son of Man (the risen Jesus) in 1:13. Similarly, the seer is told not to worship the revealing angel at the end of the book (22:8), for it is Jesus who has sent the angel with his message (22:16).

When Hebrews begins its argument by asserting the superiority of the Son of God to the angels, then, it stands within the same concern that animates other New Testament witnesses: while the reality and power of angels as spiritual messengers and mediators must be acknowledged, they must also be regarded as of less dignity and might than the one who, because of his exaltation to God's right hand, can be called, simply, "Lord."

2:1–9 We Cannot Neglect So Great a Salvation

The intensely pastoral and practical emphasis of Hebrews now becomes evident in this, the first of its hortatory turns. Having established from a catena of scriptural passages in 1:5–13 that the Son is indeed greater than the angels, the author concluded in 1:14 with the statement that the angels were sent to serve those who were to inherit salvation. That the hearers of this discourse are precisely such heirs and that receiving so great a salvation demands an appropriate response is the point of 2:1–4. After the simple declarative statement of 2:1, a long conditional sentence with a rhetorical question as its apodosis ("how shall we escape?") forms the remainder of the hortatory period. Once more, we see the use of comparison in the form of a chiasm: *a*. The message (*logos*) announced by angels was secure (*bebaios*), and *b*. transgression or disobedience of that word received punishment. *b′*. How could those who have heard a greater message escape (punishment) if they neglect so great a salvation *a′*. that has been established (*ebebaiōthē*) in such an impressive fashion? The bulk of the comparison in 2:3b–4 is devoted to showing the impressive establishment of the present word; the nature of the threat for disobedience will be developed later.

Hebrews then moves to another stage in 2:5–9, returning to the exposition of Scripture. This time Ps 8:5–7 demonstrates that "the world to come" of which this discourse deals (Heb 2:5) is not intended for angels but for humans, and has been realized in an anticipatory fashion through the exaltation of Jesus (2:9). In his rapid exposition of the psalm the author opens two questions that will be answered by his subsequent exposition. The first concerns the fact that "all things are not yet subjected," which points to the path of pilgrimage toward God for those who follow Jesus; the second concerns his "tasting death for all," which points to the specific character of the Son's "being made lower than the angels" as well as the specific character of Jesus' priestly act.

2:1 Because of this it is necessary for us to be all the more attentive to the
things that we have heard, so that we do not drift away.[a] **2** For if a word
spoken through angels[b] was sure and every transgression and disobedi-
ence received its proper punishment, **3** how shall we escape, if we neglect
such a great salvation? It took its start from the things spoken by the Lord.
It was secured for us by those who heard him. **4** God has joined his own
testimony[c] through signs and wonders[d] and various powerful deeds, and
distributions of the Holy Spirit according to his will.[e]

5 For he did not subject to angels the world of which we speak—the
one which is to come. **6** Rather, someone has testified somewhere, "What[f]
is man that you should remember him, or the son of man that you should
care for him? **7** Although you have made him a little lower than the angels,
you have crowned him with glory and honor,[g] you have subjected all
things beneath his feet." When he has subjected all things to him,[h] he has
left nothing unsubjected to him. But now we do not yet see all things sub-
jected to him. **9** Instead, we see Jesus, who was made lower than the
angels for a little while because of the suffering of death, crowned with
glory and honor, so that, by the grace of God,[i] he might taste death in
behalf of everyone.

a. A handful of late MSS omit the entire verse, perhaps under the impression that the conditional clause follows well upon 1:14.

b. The eighth-century L has the singular "through an angel" rather than the plural in the translation.

c. B has the simpler form *symmartyrountos* rather than the one found in the majority of MSS, *synepimartyrountos.*

d. A substantial number of witnesses omit the particle *te* as redundant, and it is not, in any case, reflected in the translation.

e. The original hand of D has "according to God's (*tou theou*) will" rather than "his (*autou*) will."

f. Some MSS, including the early P^{46}, have *tis* ("who") rather than *ti* ("what").

g. Many MSS (including א and A and the original hand of D) supply in this place the line from Ps 8:7, "and you have set him over the works of your hands."

[2:1–4] The first short sentence draws a conclusion that is then supported by the next lengthy one that runs from verses 2–4. The connecting phrase "because of this" (*dia touto*) is strong (see 1:9 and 9:15 as well as Rom 1:26; 4:16; 5:12; 1 Cor 4:17). The pertinent question, however, is what the "this" is that grounds the exhortation. The author draws on the entire presentation of 1:1–14: God has spoken "to us" in a single son, in contrast to the many prophetic voices (1:1), and therefore "we" are thus those "who are to inherit salvation" (1:14). The point of the previous exposition, in short, is precisely this exhortation. As the *synkrisis* between past and present is elaborated in the next three verses, the "more" of the present reality will be seen to demand a "more" in the response of those who are being offered "so great a salvation" (2:3). Such a response is "necessary" because the penalties for disobedience correspond to the magnitude of the gift being offered.

The author's fondness for alliteration is observed again in this verse with the repetition of the initial *p*: *perissoterōs prosechein . . . pararyōmen*. The combination *prosechein/pararyōmen* ("be attentive . . . drift away") may bear the hint of a nautical metaphor, since *prosechein* can be used for anchoring a ship at port (Herodotus 9.99) and *parareō* (lit. "flow by") can have the sense of "slipping away" (Xenophon, *Anabasis* 4.4.11). Such wordplay is made more plausible given the characterization of Jesus as "anchor of the soul" in Heb 6:19. Both terms, however, are also used in moral discourse for "paying attention" (Plato, *Symposium* 174D; Luke 17:3; 1 Tim 1:4) and "being careless/inattentive" (Prov 3:21). Here the attention of the readers is demanded "all the more" (*perissoterōs*; see 6:17; 7:15; and especially 13:19). The tone is urgent. To what should they attend? I have changed the passive construction of the Greek into the active: "the things that we have heard." The exhortation carries forward the notion of God's communication through speech that was established in 1:4 (in the next verses also: see "word" in 2:2 and "things spoken by the Lord" in 2:3).

Three preliminary observations concerning the conditional sentence in 2:2–4 may be helpful. First, the form of the simple conditional presumes an assent to the terms of the protasis: we are to take as given the proposition that the word spoken through angels had the entailments here stated. Second, the inferential particle *gar* ("for") with which the sentence begins is deliberate: the sentence as a whole goes to support the need for "greater attention." Third, the apodosis of the conditional sentence is much more elaborately developed than the protasis, to show that the word now spoken is indeed of "such a great salvation."

Although "the word" (*logos*) spoken through angels could refer to all of God's former revelation, the author seems specifically to have in mind the revelation of the law on Mount Sinai (Exod 19–31). As we saw in the first excursus ("Why the Angels?"), traditions in contemporary Judaism connected the ministry of angels to the giving of the law (see *Jub.* 5.1–2, 6, 13; 6.22; 50.1–2; Gal 3:19; Acts 7:30, 38, 53).[1] The combination "transgression and disobedience," furthermore, is appropriate in the context of the revelation of commandments (for "transgression" [*parabasis*], see Rom 2:23; 4:15; 5:14; and esp. Heb 9:15; for "disobedience" [*parakoē*], see Rom 5:19; 2 Cor 10:6).

The author of Hebrews makes two points. The first is that the message delivered by angels was "secure" (*bebaios*). The verb *bebaiō* means to secure something or make it certain, such as a peace (see Thucydides 1.122), and the adjective denotes steadiness and certainty (Plato, *Phaedo* 90C). The term recurs thematically in Hebrews (3:6, 14; 6:19; 9:17; 13:9) and will be repeated by the verbal form immediately in 2:3. The second point is that because of the certainty of this word—its reliability rooted in its divine source—every transgression and disobedience receives "appropriate punishment" (cf. Rom 3:8). It is not simply that the law prescribes punishments, but that the lawgiver knows the hearts of the transgressors and delivers the "right recompense" (*endikos misthapodosia*). The Letter of James states the idea succinctly: "there is one lawgiver and judge, who is able to save and to destroy" (Jas 4:12).

The implication to be drawn is that disobedience to a greater salvation will bring still greater penalties, from which they will not be able to "escape" (*ekpheugein*; cf. Rom 2:3, and the repeated warning in Heb 12:25). The author does not develop this implication here. Indeed, rather than speak here of obedience and disobedience, the author speaks in terms of "attentiveness" (*prosechesin*) and "neglect" (*amelein*), a term that also occurs in Greco-Roman moral discourse (see Epictetus, *Discourses* 3.24.113); and rather than speak of

1. The tradition of angelic involvement in the transmission of Torah is challenged by L. H. Silberman, "Prophets/Angels: LXX and Qumran Psalm 151 and the Epistle to the Hebrews," in *Standing before God: Studies on Prayer in Scriptures and in Tradition with Essays* (FS J. M. Oesterreicher), ed. A. Finkel and L. Frizzell (New York: KTAV, 1981), 91–101. Silberman thinks that the "angels" here are equivalent to the "prophets" in 1:1, but he ignores the powerful evidence offered by Galatians and Acts.

punishments, he focuses on the greater degree of reliability offered by the present word. Nevertheless, it is clear that Heb 2:3a uses the *pathos* argument of fear as a motivation for the desired attitude among the listeners to this discourse.

The phrase "such a great salvation" (*tēlikautē sōtēria*) refers back to the statement concerning "those who are to inherit salvation" in 1:14. Hebrews acknowledges that the people of old could experience "salvation," as when Noah and his family were saved in the flood (11:7), but his readers are caught up in a "better" salvation (6:9; 2:10; 5:9; 9:28), which has to do, as he will say shortly, with "the world to come" (2:5). My English translation of verses 3b–4 breaks into three separate sentences a series of dependent clauses in Greek, each of which marks off distinct aspects of the message of salvation to which they must attend.

The message had its (chronological) "start" and its (essential) "origin" (*archē*) in the things spoken by (or "through," *dia*) the Lord. Since there is a deliberate contrast here to the things said of old, the referent of "Lord" here must be Jesus. We have seen the title *kyrios* applied to him already through the citation of Ps 101:26 in 1:10, and suggested as well by the citation of Ps 109:1 in 1:13. The "things said" by or through him would then logically refer to the preaching and teaching of Jesus during his ministry. We catch here a first glimpse of Hebrews' distinctive emphasis on the humanity of Jesus and the importance of what the human Jesus did. His words—and perhaps also his deeds, since "word" throughout this discourse can include both—are themselves the start and source (*archē*) of the salvation that the readers are to inherit.

The author and readers are not, however, the direct recipients of the things said by Jesus. Those who heard the things said by the Lord "confirmed/secured" them "for us." The author and readers are thus identified as once removed from the human ministry of Jesus and dependent on the witness of others to that ministry. This does not by any means imply that they are living at a significantly later period. Paul's associate Apollos—not to mention Paul himself as well as Priscilla and Aquila—were in much the same relationship to Jesus' first witnesses, within ten or twenty years of Jesus' death (see Acts 18:24–28). The phrase "was secured" (*ebebaiōthē*) echoes the "security" (*bebaios*) of the message delivered by angels. We begin to see the importance for Hebrews of human witnesses (see above all 12:1). Hebrews is one of the New Testament writings that employs the principle in Deut 19:15 that in every matter of life and death, the testimony of two or three witnesses is necessary for a charge to be legally sustained (see Heb 10:28; also Matt 18:16; 2 Cor 13:1; 1 Tim 5:19). He has now cited the witness of the Lord Jesus, and those who heard him.[2]

Most impressive, this great salvation is secured by the third witness offered by "co-testimony" (*synepimartyresthai*) of God. God's witness is not simply

2. See H. van Vliet, *No Single Testimony: A Study on the Adoption of the Law of Deut. 19:15 Par. into the New Testament* (Utrecht: Kemink en Zoon, 1958).

verbal, but manifests itself in works of power in support of the human witnesses. Hebrews' language in verse 4 is strongly reminiscent of that used by Luke–Acts and Paul. For "signs and wonders" (*sēmeia kai terata*) as demonstrating the power of the preached word, see Acts 2:19, 22, 43; 4:30; 5:12; 6:8; 14:13; 15:12; Rom 15:19; 2 Cor 12:12. For "powerful deeds" (*dynameis*) serving precisely the same function, see Acts 2:22; 6:8; 18:13; 19:11; Rom 15:19; 1 Cor 2:4; 4:20; 12:10, 28; 2 Cor 12:12; Gal 3:5; 1 Thess 1:5. The expression "distributions of the Holy Spirit according to his will," in turn, most clearly echoes Paul's language in 1 Cor 12:11. Speaking of the "variety of gifts" (*diaireseis charismatōn*), Paul says, "all these are activated by the one and same Spirit who allots to each one individually just as the Spirit chooses."

Although the author of Hebrews is referring to evidence from his hearers' own experience of God's powerful deeds (though he does not specify what they were), his main point is that such manifestations of power were God's way of bearing witness to the message of salvation received by those hearers. This passage is key to the argument of Hebrews as a whole. If these "confirmations" have not occurred among them, then Hebrews' entire argument is empty and abstract. But if God has acted in this fashion among them, then they are faced with a reality—and a demand—from which they truly cannot "escape."

[5–9] Translators and commentators tend to slight the inferential character of the *gar* ("for") in verse 5, rendering it as "now," as though Hebrews was simply picking up the thread that had been dropped in 1:14 (see NRSV, Attridge, Lane, Koester, Ellingworth). I think it important to note, however, that the resumption of the contrast with the angels is not merely a return to the prior subject but builds on the exhortation in 2:1–4, providing further support for the necessity of paying attention to the great salvation announced to those hearing this discourse. The world to come is for them, and comes to them through the exaltation of the Son. This is precisely the reality to which they must more closely attend. In a word, this is all about them. They, not the angels, have everything at stake in their response.

As in the catena of 1:5–13, Hebrews again argues from Scripture, quoting verbatim from Ps 8:5–7, but leaving out one clause from 8:7. The introduction to the citation is extraordinarily vague: "someone has testified somewhere." Is this just an example of rhetorical litotes—similar expressions can be found in Philo (see *On Planting* 90)—since the readers already know that God is the one who "spoke through the prophets"(1:1) and "bore accompanying witness" (2:4)? Or is the introduction so vague because the psalm seems, despite being a "psalm of David," less messianic, a simple example of wisdom in the form of prayer, with a human speaker rather than God? It is impossible to determine.

More significant is that, in contrast to his earlier practice of simply citing texts with minimal introductory comment, the author here elaborates an interpretation of the passage. Indeed, the interpretation begins even before the citation, when he asserts that "the world to come" of which he speaks was not subjected to angels, since the term *hypetaxen* ("subject") points forward to the psalm citation. As I stated in the discussion of 1:6, the term *oikoumenē*, especially in combination with *mellousa* ("to come"), refers not to the empirical world (*kosmos*) but to that realm into which the Son entered because of his exaltation to God's right hand, and in which those who are to follow him to glory (2:10) are also to enter. This "great salvation" of which Hebrews speaks, then, is not only a matter of being rescued from some negative worldly condition; it means participating in a higher order of reality.

When the psalm speaks of "man" (or "human being" = *anthrōpos*) and "son of man" (*huios tou anthrōpou*), its first meaning is obviously humanity: in accord with the practice of parallelism in Hebrew poetry, the second term is synonymous with the first. Salvation, then, is meant for humans rather than for angels. But there is another consideration: salvation is also accomplished by a "man" and "son of man," namely Jesus. The author's interpretation of the psalm will play on this ambiguity of reference. At one level, the psalm can be read as about God's care for humans generally: although they are created a little lower than angels in the order of being—the phrase *brachy ti* is undoubtedly to be understood within its original context as spatial rather than temporal—God remembers and cares for humans; both terms are used in Scripture for the special attention God bestows on Israel (for "remembering" [*mimnēskesthai*] see Gen 8:1; 9:15; 19:29; Exod 2:24; 6:5; Ps 136:7); for "caring for" [*episkeptesthai*] see Gen 21:1; 50:24; Exod 3:16; 4:31; Ruth 1:16; Ps 105:4). In this setting, the "crowning with glory and honor" can be taken as the special position assigned humans over all the other works of creation (Gen 1:28).

For Hebrews, however, this "psalm of David" is even truer when applied to the "man" and "son of man" who is Jesus. It is not clear that the author is aware that the title "Son of Man" was used for Jesus in the Gospels (see Matt 13:41; 19:28; 24:27); apart from Rev 1:13 and 14:14, the title is not used for Jesus outside the Gospels (including Acts 7:56). But the meaning of the term "son of man" in its ordinary, nontitular usage, with reference to sharing the common fragile lot of humanity (see Matt 8:20; 11:19), would have been known to the author even from the LXX of Ezekiel (e.g., Ezek 1:3; 2:1; 6:2; 12:3), and is essential to this composition's understanding of Jesus. There is the further intriguing possible link between the use of the expression "Son of Man" in contexts of vicarious suffering (see Mark 8:31; 10:45), and Hebrews' understanding of Jesus as "tasting death in behalf of all" (2:9), but since that composition does not actually develop such connections, speculation on the matter is inconclusive.

Hebrews certainly reads the "crowning with glory and honor" in the psalm with reference specifically to the enthronement of Jesus at God's right hand (Heb 1:4), and the "subjecting of all things beneath his feet" with reference to the declaration of Ps 109:1: "The Lord said to my lord, sit at my right hand until

I place your enemies as a footstool for your feet" (Heb 1:13). Indeed, Paul also brings these same two psalms together in 1 Cor 15:25–27 with reference to Jesus' resurrection. When the psalm is read with reference to Jesus, moreover, the phrase *brachy ti* can be taken in the temporal sense of "for a while." The Son who never ceases to bear the world by his powerful word (1:3) has been lowered for a time below the angels, and is now "crowned with glory and honor" by virtue of his exaltation to God's right hand.

This is the first mention of the name of Jesus in the composition. As in 3:1, 6:20, 7:22, 10:19, 12:2, 12:24, and 13:12, the name appears without any title attached. In 4:14 the author combines Jesus with "the Son of God" and uses "Jesus Christ" in 10:10, 13:8, and 21; in 13:20 he uses "our Lord Jesus." The simple and unadorned name here is striking and exultant. This is the Son of whom the author has been speaking. This is the Jesus who as "the human" goes before other humans in pilgrimage to the presence of God (2:10). The use of the verb "we see" is part of the author's rhetorical use of *ekphrasis*: the scriptural texts and their own experience are so vivid as to enable them to "see" this reality. The visual metaphor will continue. The readers will be told to "look to" (*aphorōntes*) Jesus as their pioneer and perfecter in 12:2. Here in 2:8, however, is an important qualification. The author notes, "but now we do not yet see all things subjected to him." Jesus' lordship is actual, but it has not yet been extended to all reality. Indeed, there would be no need for this exhortation, if the obedience of the hearers were itself assured: the roll call of the faithful is not yet complete and "a cloud of witnesses" awaits the perfecting of the present generation for the Lord's rule to be brought to completion (see 11:39–12:1; 12:28). The "now" (*nyn*) is fully realized for Jesus himself (9:24), but is in process for those following him (11:16; 12:26).[3]

In verse 9 Hebrews provides a transition to the next stage of its argument by elucidating the manner in which Jesus was for a short time "made lower than the angels." It is not, as we might expect, due to his incarnation, but rather due to his suffering of death (*dia to pathēma tou thanatou*). There is more to this terse expression than at first appears. Simply taking on a human nature would not, for Hebrews, have "lowered" the Son below the angels, for the Son never ceases being the one who sustains the universe. But the Son has been fitted with a body (10:5) and has therefore so completely entered into the sphere of human existence as to embrace mortality, in contrast to the "ministering spirits" (1:14) who need not face death. But Hebrews adds another note: the "suffering" (*pathēma*) of death. This theme of suffering is key to the author's conception of Jesus' priesthood and to his understanding of discipleship (see the Introduction, pp. 52–54, and 2:10, 18; 5:8; 9:26; 10:32; 13:12). Jesus' death is significant not

3. See R. L. Brawley, "Discursive Structure and the Unseen in Hebrews 2:8 and 11:1: A Neglected Aspect of the Context," *CBQ* 55 (1993): 81–98.

merely because he shares mortality with other humans, but also because he has participated fully in the distinctive experience of death under the reign of sin, namely fear and suffering (see 2:14).

The phrase *dia to pathēma tou thanatou* ("because of the suffering of death") can be read in two ways: as explaining the manner in which Jesus was lowered beneath the angels, or—somewhat more tenuously—as providing the reason why Jesus has been exalted. In the second option, Hebrews would be following the same pattern as Paul's christological hymn in Phil 2:6–11: it was "because" (*dioti*) of Jesus' self-emptying in obedient death on the cross that God highly exalted him. Each understanding gives a slightly different emphasis to the purpose clause (introduced with the conjunction *hopōs*), with which verse 9 concludes.

The main point is clear enough: Jesus tasted death in behalf of all. The verb "taste" (*geuein*) is used by the LXX in its literal sense of tasting food (1 Sam 14:24; Job 34:3), and in the metaphorical sense of "experiencing" (Ps 33:8). It is also used in this sense in Heb 6:4–5. The expression "taste death," however, does not occur in the LXX. We do find it, fascinatingly, in sayings associated with Jesus (Matt 16:28; Mark 9:1; Luke 9:27; John 8:52). The metaphor of "tasting" death is powerful and reminds us of the language, also associated with Jesus, of "drinking the cup" of suffering (Matt 20:22; 26:27, 29; Mark 10:38–39; 14:23–25; John 18:11).

Another possible connection to the primitive Jesus tradition is the phrase *hyper pantos* ("in behalf of everyone"). Jesus is said to give his life as a ransom in exchange for many (*anti pollōn*; Mark 10:45), to give his body "in behalf of you" (*hyper hymōn*, Luke 22:20; 1 Cor 11:24), to pour out his blood "in behalf of many" (*hyper pollōn*, Mark 14:24). His flesh is bread "given in behalf of the world" (*hyper tou kosmou*, John 6:51), and his death is in "behalf of the people" (*hyper tou laou*) and "in behalf of the nation" (*hyper tou ethnous*, John 11:50–51). We find the same language in Paul: Christ died "in behalf of us (*hyper hēmōn*) when we were still sinners" (Rom 5:8); God handed him over "in behalf of us" (*hyper hēmōn*, Rom 8:34), and Christ was crucified "in behalf of you" (*hyper hymōn*, 1 Cor 1:13; see also 1 Cor 15:3; Gal 1:4; 2:20; Titus 2:4; 1 Thess 5:10). In line with this tradition, Hebrews asserts that Jesus' death—while entirely his own experience, what he "tasted"—was undertaken purposefully as an act in behalf of others. Distinctively within this tradition, Hebrews extends "the others," in behalf of whom Jesus died, to "everyone."

The phrase "by the grace of God" (*chariti theou*) in verse 9 is most difficult to construe. It modifies the phrase "that he might taste death for all," but in what manner? I think we can safely leave aside the odd textual variant, "apart from God" (*chōris theou*), since it is both weakly attested and cannot be made meaningful in this context. Hebrews uses the noun *charis* several more times (4:16; 10:29; 12:15, 28; 13:9, 25), playing, as most New Testament compositions do, with the range of nuances offered by the term, from "the showing of favor" to "gift." In the present case, the gift aspect of *charis* seems to be foremost, so that the phrase can be rendered "by the gift of God."

The ambiguity comes in connecting this modifier to the previous clause. Does the author wish to emphasize as God's gift the profound level of Christ's share in humanity, so that we are to understand by it "that *he tasted death* for everyone"? Or does he wish the reader to link this phrase with Christ's "being crowned with glory and honor," so that it is by the gift of God's empowerment of Jesus (cf. Phil 2:9, "God exalted him and gifted him [*echarisato autō*]"), that "he tasted death *for everyone*"? One reading places the emphasis on Jesus' share in humanity. The other emphasizes the power that was his through the resurrection—his singular death was salvific for all. Both readings are possible and each fits within the complex Christology of this composition.

2:10–18 The Son and His Brothers

Hebrews is a sustained argument from beginning to end. In these beginning stages, each section connects closely to the ones before and after it, establishing fundamental points—sometimes a bit obscurely because stated so succinctly—that will be elaborated more fully as the argument proceeds. The present passage (2:10–18) builds immediately on the preceding one: having shown that the world to come is subjected to the Son, who is now crowned with glory and honor, rather than to angels, and that the temporary lowering of the Son was so that he could "taste death in behalf of everyone," the author now develops the specific bonds between Jesus and the ones for whom he dies. In the process, the author reveals something more about the nature of their salvation (it is a liberation from death and its entailments) and the nature of the Son's salvific role (he is a high priest).

The first and last verses in the section (2:10 and 2:18) bracket the passage by addressing the same point from slightly different angles: verse 10 speaks of the fittingness of the Son's suffering from the side of God's purpose in bringing many children to his presence; verse 18 speaks from the side of human experience of the capacity of the Son to be a faithful and merciful priest because he was tested and suffered like other humans. The middle verses (2:11–17) establish the ways in which the Son has "taken hold of" the children of Abraham rather than angels (2:16): they have the same origin (2:11), they have blood and flesh and must face the terrors of death (2:14–15), they have been tested (2:18). As in the earlier comparison of the Son and angels, this association of the Son with his brothers is substantiated by the citation of passages from Scripture (2:12–13).

The passage is carefully constructed, with the use of strong inferential connectives (*di' hēn aitian* in v. 11b, *epei oun* in v. 14a, and *hothen* in v. 17a), and purpose clauses (*hina* in vv. 14b and 17b, *eis to* in v. 17c). These purpose clauses indicate, as did the final clause of 2:9, that the association of the Son and his brothers was purposeful and deliberate. The one who makes holy and those who are made holy are "from one source," to be sure, but the brothers do not share the place with God that is solely the Son's from the beginning (1:3), and that empowers him to sanctify, save, liberate humans, and conquer the cosmic forces of death and the devil.

> **2:10** It was indeed[a] fitting that the one for whom are all things and through whom are all things, in bringing many sons[b] to glory, should bring the pioneer[c] of their salvation to perfection through sufferings. **11** For the one who makes holy and those who are made holy all have the same source.[d] For this reason he is not ashamed to call them brothers. **12** He says, "I will proclaim your name to my brothers, in the midst of the assembly I will sing your praise." **13** And again, "I myself will trust in him," and further, "I and the children whom God has given me." **14** Since therefore the children have shared in blood and flesh, he himself has likewise taken a share of the same,[e] so that he might, through death, destroy the one holding the power of death, that is, the devil, **15** and free those who, in fear of death, were subject to slavery all through their lives. **16** For surely he does not take hold of angels. He takes hold of the descendants[f] of Abraham. **17** Consequently[g] he was obliged to become like his brothers in every way, so that he might become a merciful and faithful high priest in the worship of God,[h] in order to make expiation for the sins[i] of the people. **18** For because he himself, being tested, experienced suffering, he is able to help those who are being tested.

a. Literally "for" (*gar*), making this passage explanatory of the one preceding it.

b. The symbolism of sonship, brotherhood, and inheritance is woven throughout Hebrews; whenever the word "sons" appears in the plural, readers can supply "and daughters"; similarly they can understand "and sisters" when the Greek reads "brothers."

c. The term *archēgos* is impossible to translate, combining elements of "founder," "captain," "author," and "pioneer"; see the discussion below.

d. Literally "from out of one" (*ex henos*).

e. The original hand of D and a few other witnesses supply *pathēmatōn*, making the phrase "the same sufferings."

f. "descendants" translates lit. "seed."

g. The Gk. *hothen* (often translated "whence") draws a strong inference.

h. The phrase "in the worship of God" translates *ta pros ton theon*, lit. "the things toward God."

i. A and a few other MSS have the dative *tais hamartiais* rather than the accusative *tas hamartias*.

[2:10–13] The opening statement in this section is extraordinarily bold and draws us into the heart of Hebrews' distinctive vision. It would have shocked ancient hearers and ought to shock us. How can it be fitting that God perfect his Son through sufferings? The impersonal construction *prepei autō* suggests propriety or appropriateness (see 1 Cor 11:13; Eph 5:3; 1 Tim 2:10). Hebrews will later use the same construction with respect to the readers, "It was fitting to us to have such a high priest . . ." (7:26). Greco-Roman writers could speak about what was "appropriate" to the gods (see Plutarch, *Isis and Osiris* 78 [*Mor.* 383A]). But they would have found it incomprehensible to associate suffering with the Divine. God is, after all, as Hebrews says, the one "for whom and through whom" all things exist (for similar statements, see 1 Cor 8:4–6; Rom 11:36). Precisely such eminence in being should remove God far from the realm of suffering. How can suffering be connected to God as "appropriate"? Once more we find thoroughly Greek sensibilities altered by the paradoxical experience of the crucified and raised Messiah. Only after the death and resurrection of Jesus, and after the experience of transformation among his followers (Heb 2:1–4), could participation in the suffering of humans be stated as fitting to God. This passage struggles to make sense of that conviction, and begins by stating it in stark terms.[1]

Four aspects of the statement need consideration. First, we see that God's purpose is "bringing many sons to glory." The participle *agagonta* can be connected either to God or to the Son, and as a circumstantial participle it can serve several syntactical functions. I attach the phrase to God and translate it as an occasional clause, "in leading," but it could just as legitimately be translated as a purpose clause, "in order to lead." Such, in any case, is the meaning: God's plan is to bring many sons to glory. I will not linger over the phrase "many sons," except to note that although I retain the masculine gender throughout Hebrews in order to maintain the distinctive symbolism of the composition, the term when used in the plural should be understood as inclusively as "children" (as the use of *paidia* in 2:13–14 indicates).

Similarly, the adjective "many" (*polloi*) does not delimit the "for everyone" (*hyper pantos*) in 2:9, since the terms can be used equivalently (see, e.g., Mark 10:45). More significant is the goal toward which God is leading those many sons, namely glory. The noun *doxa* can, to be sure, mean roughly the same as "honor" (see Heb 2:9; 13:21; Rom 11:36; 16:27), but in the present case it surely refers to God's own being and presence (see Heb 1:13; and cf. Luke 21:27; Acts 7:2, 55; Rom 1:23; 1 Cor 15:43; 2 Cor 3:18). The Son, we have learned, has been "crowned with glory and honor" precisely because he has entered that presence "at the right hand of the majesty on high" (Heb 1:3). God's intention, then, is to draw all other humans into that same transcendent sphere, that same

1. For further discussion, see A. C. Mitchell, "The Use of *prepein* and Rhetorical Propriety in Hebrews 2:10," *CBQ* 54 (1992): 681–701.

elevated form of existence. "Glory" here is synonymous with "so great a salvation" (2:3) and "the world to come" (12:5). We learn, therefore, that God's plan is not to elevate only Jesus to his presence and power, but other humans as well, who are his "many sons."

Second, since this is God's plan, it is indeed "fitting" that the primordial Son, namely Jesus, be perfected first. As noted in the Introduction, p. 17, the language of perfection (*teleiōsis*) is widespread in Hellenistic culture. The basic idea is to be complete or whole (Aristotle, *Metaphysics* 1021B). In philosophy the term applies to those who have accomplished full moral maturity (Plato, *Laws* 653A; Diogenes Laertius, *Lives* 7.128). Religiously, such language applies to those who have completed an entire series of initiations, as in the Mysteries (see Plato, *Phaedrus* 249C; Philo, *Life of Moses* 2.149). In the LXX the adjective "perfect" (*teleiōs*) can be used of an unblemished animal (Exod 12:5) as well as for moral achievement (Gen 6:9; 1 Kgs 15:3; Wis 9:6; Sir 44:17). The verb form *teleioun* and the noun *teleiōsis*, however, appear in several important passages concerning the cult, with specific reference to the ordination (consecration) of priests (see esp. Exod 29:9–35; Lev 4:5; 7:27; 8:21–33; 16:32; 21:10; Num 3:3). The idea of "finishing" or "perfecting" the human Jesus here suggests also therefore his priestly role, which will be picked up in the following verse. Since Jesus is the first of "many sons," his perfection must be the perfection of his humanity.[2]

Third, it is fitting to perfect the son as the *archēgos tēs sotērias autōn*. The term *archēgos* is rich in nuance. Any translation can capture only some of its aspects. Etymologically derived from *archē* ("beginning/source") and *agein* ("to lead"), the term combines the sense of originator and leader. Thus the *archēgos* can be the founder of a city (Plato, *Timaeus* 21C) or the originator of something (Plato, *Cratylus* 401D). In this sense, compare Jesus as "the author of life" (*archēgos tēs zōēs*) in Acts 3:15 and as "author and savior" (*archēgos kai sōtēr*) in Acts 5:31. Hebrews clearly includes this sense of the term, for Jesus is named as the "cause of salvation" (*aitios sōtērias*) in 5:9. The term *archēgos* can also emphasize the note of leadership.[3] Herakles leads humans to what is best (Aelius Aristides, *Oration* 40.14) and Moses leads the people (Philo, *Confusion of Tongues* 92–98). Thus I translate as "pioneer," since Jesus leads the other sons as their "forerunner" (*prodromos*, Heb 6:20) to their goal. The combination "pioneer" and "perfecter" (*archēgos, teleiōtēs*) will be applied to Jesus in 12:2. The idea here, then, is that the one who causes and leads must himself be perfected before those who follow him can be. Thus it is "fitting."

2. See Royster, 78–79.

3. G. Johnston, "Christ as Archegos," *NTS* 27 (1980–81): 381–85, suggests the translation "Prince," but not only does that not mean a great deal in today's world, it also misses the sense of "going first" that "pioneer," for all its obvious deficiency, nevertheless conveys.

Fourth, and most startling, this perfecting takes place by means of "sufferings" (in the plural). The construction *dia pathēmatōn* must be understood instrumentally. It is not simply that the Son was perfected by "passing through sufferings," but that "by means of sufferings" he was perfected. Hebrews makes sufferings essential to the process of perfection, here anticipating the fuller statement in 5:8–9. By implication, suffering is also the means by which those whom the Son leads to God's presence will also be perfected. Although the construction in Hebrews is both elegant and distinctive, the "necessity" of the Messiah's first *suffering* and then entering *glory* is stated by other New Testament writers (see Luke 24:26; Acts 17:3; 1 Pet 1:11), as is the conviction that discipleship must follow in the same path of suffering to God's presence (see Rom 8:18; Phil 3:10; 1 Pet 4:13).

If the language of perfection would already suggest for readers of the LXX a connection with priesthood and sacrifice, then the statement in 2:11 follows naturally: the one who makes holy and those who are being made holy share the same source. In the LXX the verb *hagiazein* ("to make holy") is associated particularly with the cult. God is the "Holy One of Israel" (*ho hagios tou Israel*; see Isa 12:6; Ps 70:22; Lev 19:2), as the one who is separate and above all other gods and transcendent over all created reality. To "sanctify" or "make holy" is therefore to render something within the realm of created reality dedicated, or set apart, for this "separate" God. Thus "making holy the sabbath day" (Deut 5:12, 15) means to distinguish it from other days to show that it belongs to God. The Holy One of Israel is most accessible to the people in the sanctuary of his presence, first the tent of the wilderness and then the temple (see Pss 2:6; 5:7; 10:5; 17:6; 19:2; 21:3; 28:2; 46:8; 64:5; 67:5; 78:1; 98:9; 137:2). To approach that presence, however, humans must themselves be "made holy," marked as belonging to God, as were Aaron and his sons who entered into the tent of the wilderness (see Exod 29:1–46; Lev 8:1–34). Just as with the language of "glory," then, the language of "holiness" connotes access to the presence of God.

The "ones being made holy" (*hoi hagiazomenoi*, the present passive participle) are, correspondingly, the ones being offered to the holy God, brought into his presence (Num 5:9–10; 18:8–9, 29). In this case, the "ones being made holy" are not animals or grain offerings, but human beings who are approaching God's glory. This is made plain by the insistence that sanctifier and sanctified are "from one source." It is fundamental to Hebrews that a priest is "taken from among men for worship of God" (5:1), and also that sanctification involves the transformation of humans themselves rather than the exchange of possessions through ritual. The phrase *ex henos* (lit. "out of one") can be taken as referring to a common creation by God—they are all God's creatures—or as referring to a common human ancestor, namely Abraham. Since the point about the Son's "taking hold" of Abraham's descendants will be made explicit in 2:16, that is the most obvious sense intended by the author. Just as the first mention of Jesus himself in 2:9 grounds the language about God's Son in a specific historical person, so does the connection with Abraham connect God's entry into the human fabric with a specific human ancestry and story (see the use of *aph' henos* with respect to Abraham in 11:12).

It is for the very reason (*di' hēn aitian*) that the sanctifier and sanctified share a common source that he can call them "brothers" (*adelphoi*)—the Greek means having the same mother. We are reminded again of Rom 8:29, "Those whom [God] foreknew he also predestined to be conformed to the image of his Son, in order that he might be the first-born of many brothers." Also reminding us of Romans is the phrase "he is not ashamed" (*ouk epaischynetai*), which is the same construction used by Paul in Rom 1:16 with reference to preaching the good news. Like Rom 1:16, this may be an example of litotes, or understatement, meaning in truth, "he is proud to call them brothers." Compare Heb 11:16, "God is not ashamed to be called their God."

The expression may also, however, carry with it an implicit exhortation. The readers are in the position of "being ashamed" of their association with a crucified Messiah and with those who are being reviled because of that association—they are contemplating "drawing back" (see 6:4–8; 10:32–39). The author will exhort them to "bear the reproach" that Jesus bore (13:13), which has as its corollary that they "be mindful of prisoners, as though you also were imprisoned, and of those being afflicted as though you were in their bodies (*hōs kai autoi ontes en sōmati*" (13:3). The boldness and the boast of the Son's association with humans in their distress is the ground not only of their lack of shame in being associated with *him* but also of their glad willingness to bear *one another's* human humiliations.

Hebrews supports the association among the Son and his brothers by two scriptural citations in 2:12–13. I have translated the present participle *legōn* ("saying") as the start of a new sentence, "He says." We are intended to hear the declarations from Ps 21:23 and Isa 8:17–18, therefore, as statements of the Son, the "pioneer of salvation." Even as God spoke through the prophets of old (1:1), he sometimes did so, we learn, in the voice of his Son. The citations are verbatim from the LXX, except that in the first, Hebrews replaces the expression "I will relate" (*diēgēsomai*) with "I will declare" (*apangelō*; see 1 John 1:2, 5; 1 Thess 1:9). Although the main point of both citations is clearly about family—"I will declare your name to my brothers," and "I and the children whom God has given me"—in support of the intimate bond shared by Jesus and other humans, the citations have other aspects that should not be slighted.

Both citations, for example, are drawn from passages that are used extensively in other New Testament writings. Psalm 21:1 is quoted explicitly at the death of Jesus by Matt 27:46 and Mark 15:34. Psalm 21:19 is cited in the passion account by all four Gospels (Matt 27:35; Mark 15:14; Luke 23:34; John 19:24), and Ps 21:14 is quoted by 1 Pet 5:8. Isaiah 8 (together with Isa 28) is also employed in New Testament passages dealing with the Messiah as a stumbling block to the people and as an object of faith (see Rom 9:32–33; 1 Pet 2:8; 3:14–15). Hebrews is therefore using scriptural passages that would be recognized within the Christian community as messianic in the broad sense, and as touching on the paradox that the one rejected by humans is vindicated by God. But as in the case of Ps 109, Hebrews is creative in its use of the shared text, emphasizing an aspect that the other New Testament compositions ignore. In the case of Ps 21:23, the stress is not on the suffering just one—though that is certainly also to be understood—but on the proclaiming of God's name to his brethren. This reminds us that the "start" (*archē*) of this salvation was the things spoken by the Lord (Heb 2:3). His "singing praise" to God "in the assembly," moreover, suggests the presence in the community (see 12:27) of Christ as high priest (2:17).

Likewise in the case of Isa 8:17–18, the emphasis is placed first on Jesus' own faith toward God: "I myself will trust in him" (with the explicit *egō* adding emphasis), and then on "the children God has given me" (his "brothers") sharing in that same response of faith: "I and the children whom God has given me." The distinct stress is enabled by the deliberate separation of the parts of the Isaiah citation by the repeated phrase, *kai palin . . . kai palin*, which I have translated, "and again . . . and further." For a similar linking of the two verses from the same Isaiah passage (8:12–13), see 1 Pet 3:14–15. The point here is that the Son and his brothers are not merely linked ontologically but also morally: as he responds to God with faith, so shall they—or so they should!

[14–18] In verses 14–15 Hebrews makes another statement of how the association of the Son with his brothers is fitting, and thereby reveals more of the author's understanding of the human predicament and what salvation from it means. The section begins by stating the deepest identity between humans and the author of their salvation. Since they share in "blood and flesh," he himself took a share of the same. The phrase "blood and flesh" is found elsewhere in John 1:13 and Eph 6:12, and, like the more common ordering, "flesh and blood" (Sir 14:18; Matt 16:17; 1 Cor 15:50; *1 En.* 15.4), suggests above all the mortal frailty of humans. The children, to be sure, "have blood and flesh in common": the verb *koinōnein* (lit. "to share in common") is here in the perfect, denoting a present and universal condition consequent on birth into the world. The pioneer of their salvation "himself likewise" (the stress on *autos* is emphatic) took a share (*meteschen*) of the same human frailty. In his case, the verb *metechein* is in the aorist: the incarnation is not a universal condition but a particular event in the past.

Although the sentence begins by stating a given condition, "since" (*epei oun*) the Son and brothers share the same condition, the stress in the sentence falls on the way in which the *archēgos tēs sōtērias autōn* ("pioneer/origin of their salvation") transcends their condition even as he shares in it, since he is able to accomplish what other humans are unable to do. Hebrews now fills in the meaning of "tasting death in behalf of all" in 2:9. Through death (*dia thanatou*)—that is, to be sure, through his own death—the Son accomplishes two things (expressed by a purpose clause with two aorist subjunctives). The first is expressed in apocalyptic terms as a victory over cosmic forces; the second is expressed in psychological terms as a transformation of the human spirit.

First, he has died to "destroy the one holding the power of death, that is, the devil." Since Hebrews makes no further mention of the devil (*ho diabolos*), of Satan, or of any other demonic powers, it is safe to suppose that this formulation emerges from the apocalyptic framework widely shared by ancient Jews and Christians, in which the devil stands for the cosmic forces opposed to the righteous (see Matt 4:1; 25:41; Luke 8:12; John 6:70; 13:2; Acts 10:38; Eph 4:27; 6:11; 1 Tim 3:6; 2 Tim 2:26; Jas 4:7; 1 Pet 5:8; 1 John 3:8; Rev 12:9; 20:2), and over whom the Messiah will triumph (see *T. Levi* 18.2; *As. Mos.* 10.1; *1 En.* 10.13; *4 Ezra* 13.1; Matt 12:25–30; Luke 10:18; John 12:31; 14:30; Rev 12:7–10). Because the devil, in turn, can be associated intimately with death (see above all Wis 2:24), victory over him can be expressed in terms of a victory over death (see Hos 13:14; 1 Cor 15:26, 55; 2 Tim 1:10; Rev 20:14; 26:4). Indeed, Paul uses the same verb, *katargein* ("to destroy"), in the same connection: "Then comes the end, when he hands over the kingdom to God the Father after he has destroyed every authority and power. For he must reign until he has put all his enemies under his feet. The last enemy to be destroyed is death" (1 Cor 15:24–26). What is remarkable about Hebrews' statement is the instrumental phrase "through death," which matches the phrase "through sufferings" in 2:10: Jesus does not conquer death by avoiding it or commanding its disappearance, but by *experiencing* it in the manner of other human beings.

Second, Christ has died to transform humans internally and behaviorally. The verb "liberate" (*apallasein*) might tempt us to think in terms of exodus imagery, especially in anticipation of a closely following passage (3:7–4:10). But the verb does not occur in this connection in the LXX. Rather, it is commonly used with reference to being healed. Thus one is "released from" an illness (Plato, *Eryx* 401C; Josephus, *Ant.* 11.270; 13.363; Acts 19:12; and D in Luke 9:40 and Acts 5:15). Here the "brothers" are liberated from an emotion that distorts their existence, a "fear of death" that has made them "subject to slavery" all through their lives. This is a remarkable formulation, with profound spiritual insight. Scripture only occasionally refers to the contemplation of death (Qoh 9:4–5; Sir 41:1–4). But that paralyzing fear is one of the effects of the contemplation of mortality is a commonplace among Greco-Roman moralists (see Seneca, *Moral Epistles* 24; Epictetus, *Discourses* 4.7.15–17; Dio Chrysostom, *Oration* 6.42; Lucretius, *On the Nature of Things* 1.102–26). Philo expresses it forcefully: "Nothing is so calculated to enslave the mind as fearing death through a desire to live" (*Every Good Man Is Free* 22). Among these moralists, fear leads to slavery because it leads people away from courage and boldness: their liberty is turned to craven cowardice because they seek to go on living.

Hebrews uses a particularly powerful expression. The adjective *enochos* itself suggests "being bound" (Aristotle, *Metaphysics* 1009B) or "subject to" (Plato, *Laws* 869B). In combination with the substantive *douleia*, it creates the phrase "being bound to slavery." But we notice that this enslavement is not simply one that occurs when contemplating or facing death in the situations that, for the philosophers, caused the knees to quake and people to abandon their liberty for survival. Hebrews speaks of this slavery as stretching "all through their lives" (*dia pantos tou zēn*). The author suggests that fear of death leads to a slavery that is not acute—arising in moments of crisis—but rather chronic, and therefore more fundamentally shapes human choices.

In terms of existential psychology, Hebrews supports the thought that terror of nonbeing (mortality) itself supports and structures the patterns of compulsion that can be regarded as idolatry. Human self-enslavement through compulsion is, in effect, a response to the awareness of mortality. Whether we can actually attribute this insight to the author of Hebrews is not clear. But it is certain that Hebrews here adds "liberation" to his glossary of terms expressing the Son's work for his fellow humans and "the gift of God" (2:9), a list that already includes "salvation," "sanctification," "bringing to glory," and "the world to come." It is also certain that Hebrews here touches on the theme that will be developed later: the process of human perfection involves a change in one's moral consciousness and moral behavior.

Apart from the quite different references to angels in 12:22 and 13:2, Hebrews concludes in 2:16 its extended *synkrisis* between the Son and the angels. Whereas earlier the comparison had as its point the superiority of the Son over the angels with respect to status and power (i.e., as active agents), the contrast here is between angels and humans as the recipients of the divine favor, as the receivers of salvation or liberation. The adverb *dēpou* ("surely") together with the explanatory conjunction *gar* ("for") express a truth that the author considers obvious: humans rather than angels need liberation from the fear of death, for angels are not, in the tradition, mortal in the first place: they are "ministering spirits" who do not die (1:14).[4]

The point of 2:16, however, is not to repeat what has already been stated; it is to affirm that the Son's participation in humanity is not general or abstract, but specific. It takes place in the single human person, Jesus (2:9), who belongs to a particular family of humans, namely the descendants of Abraham. For the

4. For this reason, M. C. Gudorf, "Through a Classical Lens: Hebrews 2:16," *JBL* 119 (2000): 105–8, argues that the difficult verb *epilambanomai* should refer to the fear of death: it does not apply to angels but does to the children of Abraham. But good sense can be made of the more traditional understanding.

use of the "seed" (*sperma*) of Abraham in the New Testament, see Luke 1:55; John 8:33; Acts 7:5; 13:23; Rom 4:13; 9:7; 2 Cor 11:22; Gal 3:16, 29; in Hebrews see 11:11 and 18. The pioneer of salvation has "grasped" (*epilambanesthai*) this specific historical people. The verb has the same basic meaning as *koinōnein* and *metechein*, used in 2:14. The Son has "taken hold" of this people in the sense that he associates with and participates fully in their being (cf. Matt 14:31; Luke 9:47; 14:4; Acts 9:27; 1 Tim 6:12).[5] The verb can also carry the nuance of "coming to the aid of," when read in light of passages like Jer 31:32, which will be cited in Heb 8:9: "On the day when I took their hand to lead them from the land of Egypt." In his encomium of the heroes of faith, the author of Hebrews will say of Abraham, "Therefore also there were born from one man (*aph' henos*), and him indeed nearly dead, descendants as many as the stars in the sky and as countless as the sand on the seashore" (11:12). It is this particular people (*laos*) that the Son seizes hold of to work out humanity's salvation (2:18).

As a consequence (*hothen*) of this close association of the Son and his brothers, it follows that it was necessary for him (*ōpheilen*) to be like them *kata panta* ("in every respect"). This statement does not simply repeat the foregoing. Beyond an ontological bond with humanity or even a biological connection to the family of Abraham, there is an even deeper level of engagement required of the pioneer of salvation. His likeness to his brothers must extend to the experience of the same testing and suffering that are theirs. For the perception of gods "becoming like men" (*homoiōthentes anthrōpois*), see Acts 14:11, where the natives of Lystra think Barnabas and Paul are Zeus and Hermes (cf. Ovid, *Metamorphoses* 8.611–724). More than appearance is meant here, though: the Son becomes "like" humans in the sense that he fully participates in their somatic condition and emotional sensibilities; see the use of *homoipathēs* ("of like feeling") in Acts 14:15 and Jas 5:17. Similarly, see Paul's language about Christ Jesus, who "emptied himself, . . . being born in the likeness of men" (Phil 2:7). The overall thought in the Hebrews passage—that participation in the human condition is a dimension of making expiation for sins—is likewise paralleled in Rom 8:3: "God has done what the law, weakened by the flesh, could not do; by sending his own Son in the likeness of sinful flesh (*en homoiōmati sarkos hamartias*) and to deal with sin, he condemned sin in the flesh."

In 2:10 Hebrews spoke of salvation in terms of "perfection," which we saw contained a likely allusion to the language of the LXX about Israel's cult; in 2:11 the language of cult became explicit when Hebrews spoke of "the one who makes holy and those who are made holy." Now in 2:17 the author of Hebrews depicts the Son's work as "making expiation for the sins of the people," using the specific term *hilaskesthai*, which in the LXX translates Hebrew *kipper*, "to

5. K.-G. E. Dolfe, "Hebrews 2,16 under the Magnifying Glass," *ZNW* 84 (1993): 289–94, makes an elaborate argument that *epilambanomai* must mean "resist" or "stop," but whatever the linguistic antecedents, such a reading is impossible in this context.

make expiation/atonement" (see Exod 32:14; Pss 24:11; 64:3; 77:38; 78:9). In the LXX such expiation comes about through the sprinkling of blood on the *hilastērion* (*kappōret*, "mercy seat"). See Exod 25:16–22 for the description of the *hilastērion* in the tent of meeting, and Lev 16:2–28 for the ritual of Yom Kippur ("Day of Atonement/Expiation"). The term draws the reader once more into the circle of the descendants of Abraham through allusion to their cult, and makes more specific the programmatic statement in the prologue, "having made purification for sins" (Heb 1:3). Despite the importance of this background for the composition, Hebrews uses *hilaskesthai* only here and *hilastērion* only in 9:5. Paul also speaks of the *hilastērion* with the blood of Jesus in Rom 3:25, and *hilasmos* ("expiation") is used of Jesus in 1 John 2:2 ("he himself is expiation for our sins") and 4:10 ("He sent his son as an expiation for our sins").

The internal and moral understanding of Christ's sacrificial act is revealed in the statement that he needed to become like his brothers in every respect (cf. Heb 4:15), so that he might become (*genētai*) a "merciful and faithful high priest in the worship of God." I translate the phrase *ta pros ton theon* (lit. "the things toward God"; see also 5:1) as the "worship of God" because it is familiar and elegant, and the translation is appropriate so long as worship is understood not as peripheral but at the very heart of religion. The translation "in matters pertaining to God" would be superior, if it reminded us that for Hebrews the essence of Christ's work is to "represent humans" in their movement toward God.

Here is Hebrews' first use of its characteristic title for Jesus, "high priest" (*archiereus*; see 3:1, 14, 15; 5:1, 5, 10; 6:20; 7:26, 27, 28; 8:1, 3; 9:7, 11, 25; 13:11). The designation is unique among the New Testament writings, which otherwise use the title only for Jewish high priests (e.g., Matt 27:1; Mark 14:1; Luke 22:2; John 7:32; Acts 4:1). The designation "high priest" is found frequently for the chief minister in Greco-Roman religions (see Herodotus, *Persian War* 2.37; Plato, *Laws* 947A; and often in inscriptions). The LXX uses *archiereus* to translate the simple *kōhēn* ("priest") in Lev 4:3; Josh 22:13; 24:33; other instances all have textual variants. In other places, *ho hiereus ho megas* ("the priest, the great one") is used to render *kōhēn* (Jdt 4:6, 14; Sir 50:1; Zech 3:1, 9; 6:11), a designation that also occurs in Heb 10:2. In the Maccabean literature, in contrast, *archiereus* appears frequently (e.g., 1 Macc 10:20; 12:3; 2 Macc 3:4; 4:13; 3 Macc 1:11; 4 Macc 4:13, 16). The use of the term appeals to the author of Hebrews first because it asserts the superiority of this one priest, Christ, over all the many priests (*hiereis*) who labor in an ineffectual worship (Heb 7:20, 21, 23; 8:4; 9:6), and second because it matches the sense of "origin/cause" embedded in the designation of Jesus as *archēgos* (2:10).

It is noteworthy that Hebrews' treatment of Christ's priesthood first emphasizes his moral dispositions. His being made like his brothers in every respect enables him to be merciful (*eleēmōn*) and faithful (*pistos*) as a priest. The adjective *pistos* pertains to the theme of the faith of Christ that Hebrews argues is essential to his priestly act (see above at 2:13, and the characterization of Jesus as "pioneer and perfecter *of faith*" in 12:2), and anticipates the statement to follow in 3:2 that Jesus was "faithful (*pistos*) to the one who made him" (deSilva, 120). Jesus' fidelity is turned toward God and also toward his brothers, whom he represents before God. Hebrews, therefore, also speaks of his being "merciful." The adjective *eleēmōn* bears a strong affective element—lenience is shown toward another because of a feeling of "pity" or "compassion," a sense of empathy with their situation (Homer, *Od.* 5.191; Epictetus, *Discourses* 2.21.3). In the New Testament, the adjective otherwise appears only in Matt 5:7, "Blessed are the merciful, for they shall be shown mercy." But in the LXX it is used frequently with reference to God, as the translation of *ḥesed*, God's characteristic disposition of "lovingkindness" (see Exod 22:7; 34:6; Pss 85:15; 102:8; 110:4; 111:4; 114:5; Jonah 4:2; Joel 2:13). Indeed, the combination *pistos kai eleēmōn* might well be read as roughly equivalent to the Lord's own self-designation as full of *ḥesed wĕ'ĕmet,* "steadfast love and faithfulness" (Exod 34:6). Jesus brings the same dispositions to his role as priest, who is turned toward God (*ta pros ton theon*) for the sins of the people (*tas hamartias tou laou*).

We come finally in 2:18 to the deepest way in which it was "fitting" for God to perfect the pioneer of salvation through sufferings: precisely to the degree that (*en hō*) he *himself* (the *autos* is emphatic) has experienced suffering (the verb *peponthen* is the perfect tense of *paschō*, cognate with *pathēmata* in 2:10) through being tested (*peirastheis*) is he able to give assistance (*boēthēsai*) to those who are being tested (*tois peirazomenois*). The alliteration of the initial *p* adds solemnity as it did in the prologue. But something more than style makes this statement striking. The verb *boēthein* means to come to the aid of someone. It is used in the LXX for the help given humans by God (Gen 49:25; 1 Chr 12:18; Pss 36:40; 40:3; 43:26; 45:5; 85:17; Isa 49:8; see also Matt 15:25; Mark 9:24; 2 Cor 6:2). Hebrews here connects Christ's "capacity" (*dynatai*) to provide such help to humans not simply to his divine sonship, but to his experiential knowledge of human testing and temptation.

Hebrews 2:10–18 contains much of the composition's subsequent argument *in nuce*. Compressed in expression and powerfully paradoxical, it invites the reader to examine further this "discourse that is difficult to express" (5:11). But before searching more deeply into the character of Christ's priesthood, still more must be said concerning "the people" with whom the Son has associated himself.

3:1–6 The Son Is Greater Than Moses

Hebrews moves to the next stage of its argument. Having shown the superiority of the Son to the angels in terms of status and power, and that the salvation brought by the Son was for humans—specifically the descendants of Abraham—the composition now turns to a lengthy consideration of this "people" for whose sins the "faithful and merciful high priest" Jesus died (3:1–4:13), before returning to a richer development of Christ's priesthood. The section 3:1–6 provides a transition to the theme of God's people by establishing a comparison between Jesus and a figure who might, in terms of Israel's lore, claim equal or even greater honor.

The theme of faithfulness (*pistos*) is carried over from 2:17, but it is not the point of contrast between Jesus and Moses. As this passage and 11:23–28 show, Moses is one of the heroes of faith for the author of Hebrews. The contrast, rather, concerns the relative status and role of the two figures, and is developed through the elaboration of the metaphor of "house/household" (*oikos*) for God's people that is drawn from Num 12:7: Moses was faithful as a servant within the household, and Jesus is faithful as the Son who is over all the household. Hebrews 3:6 marks the transition to the *hearers* as the Son's household, and the conditional character of that identity. It is dependent on their own fidelity, the point that will be extensively developed in 3:7–4:13.

> **3:1** Therefore, my holy brothers, sharers in a heavenly calling, consider
> Jesus, the apostle and high priest, whom we confess.[a] **2** He was faithful
> to the one who made him,[b] just as Moses was "in all his house."[c] **3** For
> he[d] is worthy of greater glory than Moses, just as the builder has more
> honor than the house.[e] **4** Now,[f] every house is built by someone, but God
> is the one who has built everything.[g] **5** And while Moses was "faithful in
> all his house as a servant"—to give evidence of things yet to be spoken[h]—
> **6** Christ was faithful[i] as a son who is over his house. We are his[j] house, if
> indeed we keep hold of the boldness and the boast that is our hope.[k]

a. "Whom we confess" is lit. "of our confession."

b. From the KJV on, English translations tend to translate *to poiēsanti auton* as "the one who appointed him," rather than "the one who made him." The Vulgate has *qui fecit* ("who made").

c. Some MSS lack "all," and it may have crept into this verse under the influence of the citation of Num 12:7 in Heb 3:5.

d. "He" is "this one" (*houtos*) in Greek; the antecedent is clearly Jesus.

e. The Greek syntax is clear but convoluted; lit. "more honor than the house has the builder of it."

f. The inferential conjunction *gar* ("for") is here softened to "now."

g. Some MSS supply the definite article *ta* to form "all things" (*ta panta*), which I translate as "everything."

h. Here *eis martyrion* is translated as a purpose clause, and "yet" serves to signal the use of the future passive participle "of the things that will be spoken" (*tōn lalēthēsomenōn*).

i. The translation repeats "was faithful" to make the intended contrast as obvious in English as it is in Greek.

j. Some MSS have *hos* ("which") rather than *hou* ("whose"); the translation is literally, "whose house we are."

k. The translation adds "our" to "hope," and makes the genitive *tēs elpidos* epexegetical. Some MSS add "secure until the end," undoubtedly due to the influence of 3:14, where the phrase occurs without any variant.

[3:1–2] This is not really a new start, for the connective adverb *hothen* ("whence/therefore") establishes a strong link with 2:18 and the theme of fidelity is carried forward into this section. Nevertheless, 3:1 marks a sharp turn rhetorically, because the author picks up the language of "brothers" and "ones sanctified" from 2:11 and addresses his hearers directly as "holy brothers." The combined designation occurs nowhere else in Hebrews, and "brothers" in the vocative appears only in 3:12; 10:19; and 13:22. The author thus joins his hearers as those who count themselves as among the seed of Abraham, and as "fellow participants" (*metochoi*) in the salvation brought by the Son.

That salvation is here characterized as a "holy calling" or a "call from heaven." The adjective *epouranios* appears as early as Homer in association with the realm of the gods (*Il.* 6.129; *Od.* 17.784), and in the New Testament likewise refers to a realm superior to visible creation (Matt 18:35; John 3:12; 1 Cor 15:40, 48, 49; Eph 1:3; 2:6; Phil 2:10; 2 Tim 4:18). In Hebrews the adjective appears in 6:4; 8:5; 9:23; 11:16; and climactically in 12:22: "You have come . . . to a city of God, a heavenly Jerusalem." This is the only time *klēsis* is used in Hebrews, but as in Rom 11:29; 1 Cor 1:26; Eph 1:18; and Phil 3:14, it signifies both the "summons" or invitation from God and the reality to which they have been summoned. Note further that a "heavenly call" suggests a pull elsewhere, beyond the dimensions of empirical existence, a theme that the composition will develop later.

At the same time that he establishes commonality with his readers, the author also demarcates his role as an authoritative teacher by his first use of the second person imperative; compare the first person hortatory subjunctive in 2:1–3. He tells his hearers to "consider Jesus." The verb *katanoein* means to "contemplate" in order to learn something from, as well as physically to "look at" (see esp. Luke 12:24, 27; Rom 4:19). Nevertheless, the language of seeing/observing a Jesus who is not physically accessible to their sense of sight continues the imagery established by Heb 2:9 and will be picked up again in 12:2, where readers are told to "look to (*aphorōntes*) Jesus, the pioneer and perfecter of faith."

In this case, Jesus is designated as "high priest" (see 2:17) and as "apostle," titles that are otherwise never used of him in the New Testament. The title *apostolos* is invariably used for one sent on a commission by another, and is given specifically to the representatives of Jesus sent out by him (see Matt 10:2; Mark 3:14; Luke 6:13; Acts 1:2; 14:14; Rom 1:1; 1 Cor 4:9; 12:28; Eph 1:20). There is, nevertheless, a fine symmetry in the combination *apostolos kai archiereus* that goes beyond the obvious alliteration. As the *apostolos* is sent by God to deliver the summons from God to humans through the proclamation of the good news, so the *archiereus* is preeminently the one who responds from the side of humans to God (see Heb 5:1). The two terms combine to form Hebrews' understanding of Jesus as *mesitēs* ("mediator"; see 8:6; 9:15; and especially 12:24).

Jesus is the apostle and high priest, "whom we confess." I have translated the genitive phrase "of our confession" as a relative clause with an active verb, in order to capture the probable emphasis: Hebrews does not mean to say here that Jesus is one element among others in the Christian creed, but that he is the source and substance of their entire commitment (for *homologein* see 11:13; 13:15; for *homologia* see 4:14; 10:23).

What about Jesus are the readers to contemplate or consider? How he is faithful (*pistos*) to "the one who made him." As in 2:17, we see that Hebrews focuses on Jesus' moral dispositions, above all his faith, rather than the specifics of what he might have said or done during his ministry. Jesus' fidelity is turned toward God. The phrase *tō poiēsanti auton* is most naturally translated as "the one who made him," with "making" understood as "creating." Like Moses, Jesus is, as a human being, created by God, the source of all reality. And Hebrews has already used *poiein* in the sense of "create" (see 1:2, 7). Following the KJV, most contemporary English translations have instead, "the one who appointed him," a translation that focuses attention on the office of apostle and high priest, and therefore on the dutiful fulfillment of those roles by Jesus. That translation is certainly legitimate. The point developed by the rest of the passage, however, is that Jesus is faithful not as an officeholder, but as a Son. Is it possible that a certain dogmatic nervousness influenced the standard translation, because "the one who made him" might detract from Jesus' unique status? Yet for Hebrews the human Jesus is surely a creature—this is precisely the point that the author has just been arguing (see 2:10–18)!

If the readers are encouraged to consider Jesus as faithful to the one who made him, then the natural figure with whom to compare him is Moses.[1] In 3:5 Hebrews will explicitly cite Num 12:7, which declares that Moses "is faithful in all my house." In the verse I am now analyzing (3:2), the author anticipates that citation by stating that Jesus was faithful to the one who made him, "just as Moses was 'in all his house.'" Before pursuing the author's argument—not,

1. See C. L. Westfall, "Moses and Hebrews 3, 1–6: Approach or Avoidance?" in *Christian-Jewish Relations through the Centuries*, ed. S. E. Porter and B. W. R. Pearson (JSNTSup 192; Sheffield: Sheffield Academic Press, 2000), 175–201; and M. R. D'Angelo, *Moses in the Letter to the Hebrews* (SBLDS 42; Missoula, MT: Scholars Press, 1979).

in truth, entirely perspicuous—it is helpful to consider the passage from Numbers a bit more fully, for in context it provides us with a sense of why Jesus should be compared to Moses in the first place.

The citation from Numbers comes from the narrative concerning Israel's sojourn in the wilderness (and therefore nicely anticipates the author's argument in 3:7–19). The passage deals with Aaron and Miriam's challenge to Moses. They criticize him for marrying a Cushite woman (Num 12:1). They use this as a means of challenging his authority as a prophet: the Lord spoke through them as well as through Moses (12:2). In response to their challenge, the Lord himself declares that while he speaks to other prophets in dreams, he speaks to Moses "face to face" (in the LXX, *stoma kai stoma*, "mouth to mouth"), clearly rather than in a riddle. Moses, moreover, had seen the glory of the Lord (*doxa kyriou*, 12:6–8). Moses does not defend himself. Indeed, Numbers says that Moses was "very humble [LXX *praus*, 'meek'], more so than anyone else on the face of the earth" (12:3).

No, it was God who heard and responded by vindicating Moses. It is in the middle of this vindicating declaration that God says that "my servant (*therapōn*) Moses is faithful in all my house." As with other passages in Scripture (notably Deut 34:10–12), the supreme authority of Moses as God's prophet is based not only in the "signs and wonders" that were worked through him (34:11), but in his astonishing intimacy with God, with whom he spoke "face to face" (34:10; Num 12:8), and whose *doxa* he saw (Num 12:8; see Exod 33:17–34:7). Among human mediators, then, Moses is surely the main figure to whom Jesus must be compared; Deut 34:10 declares confidently, "Never since has there arisen a prophet in Israel like Moses."

[3–6] Since 3:2 has already made clear that both Moses and Jesus were faithful (*pistos*) to God, the contrast between them must be based on some other factor. Here is where the argument, though transparent enough in its intention, becomes murky in its details. The author wants to assert that Jesus is worthy of more glory (*doxa*) than Moses (3:3), because Jesus is a Son, and Moses is a servant (3:6). From the start, we can note that the point depends on ancient cultural presuppositions. First, in an honor/shame context, the expressions "worthy of" (*axioun*), "glory" (*doxa*), and "honor" (*timē*) stand as markers of comparative status. Second, it is "obvious" that the freeborn son in a great household has more status—and therefore more worth and therefore deserves more honor—than even the most well-situated servant within the same household. Contemporary sensibilities may quail at these cultural premises, but honesty demands the recognition that to a considerable extent our world continues to employ a similar axiological calculus. Third, we can note that the noun *doxa* in this passage is polyvalent. Within the honor/shame framework, it means roughly the same as the honor paid the greater by the lesser in the social scale. But within the symbolic world of Scripture, we have seen, *doxa* also is used to express the presence and power of God. Embedded in the phrase "is worthy of more honor (*doxa*)," then, is a contrast between Moses, who may have seen the Lord's glory (see Exod 33:18), and Jesus, who as Son is the "radiance of [God's] glory" from the beginning (Heb 1:3), and who by his exaltation was "crowned with glory and honor (*doxa kai timē*)" (2:9).

The details of the argument become murky because of the author's metaphorical use of "house/household" (*oikos*). In the scriptural citation, the term is clearly metaphorical: house = house of Israel = the people of Israel (see Exod 19:3; 20:22; Lev 10:6; Judg 1:35; Pss 113:17, 20; 117:2). Moses is said to be a *therapōn* within this house/household. In secular usage, the term ranges in meaning from attendant (Homer, *Od.* 4.23) to companion (*Od.* 16.253) to worshiper (Plato, *Symposium* 203C). In the ancient cultural framework, to be the servant or slave of a great person meant to have considerable status. Moses, as God's *therapōn*, had such status precisely as prophet, God's representative among the people (see Exod 4:10; Deut 3:24; Josh 1:2; Wis 10:16). He was "servant" only in the sense that he was answerable solely to God and not to the people.[2]

But Hebrews reverses the metaphor by playing on the literal sense of "house" as a building. Staying with the theme of honor, the author declares that the builder of a house deserves more glory than the house he builds (3:3). That makes sense: an architectural wonder is evidence for the brilliance of the architect; when the building is praised, the designer is praised by implication. The building is derivative and caused. Its worth is rightly perceived as dependent on its creator. Hebrews then quietly adds that every house has a builder (we are still at the literal level here), and God is the one who has built everything (now we shift from the literal house to house as metaphor for people/world created by God, 3:4). One can scarcely argue with the assertion, particularly in light of 1:1 and 1:10. But what is the point of the assertion here?

Hebrews seems to want to affirm two things simultaneously. First, God is the source of all things, so all honor ultimately goes to God; nothing that is not God is anything more than creature. Second, the Son—as we have learned—is not simply another creature "faithful to the one who made him" (3:2), but is also *as Son* a participant in the creation of all things ("through whom he created the universe," 1:2). The impossibility of stating these apparently contradictory propositions in any coherent fashion accounts, I think, for the confused sequence of statements in this section. But the confusion also points to Hebrews' distinctive understanding of Jesus, which brings together both the "highest" and the "lowest" of Christologies, with equal emphasis. As Son of God, Jesus is "over all the house" as its maker. But as Son, Jesus is also a human being "faithful to the one who made him."

2. See, e.g., D. B. Martin, *Slavery as Salvation: The Metaphor of Slavery in Pauline Christianity* (New Haven: Yale University Press, 1990).

We note that Hebrews has nothing negative to say about Moses, who will later be portrayed as one of the great heroes of faith (11:23–26) in terms that make his response of faith anticipate that of Christ. It is in this light that we are to understand that Moses was faithful "to give evidence of things yet to be spoken" (*eis martyrion tōn lalēthēsomenōn*). Just as in the prologue the contrast was between the things said of old through the prophets and that which is spoken now through the Son, so here the faith of Moses as a servant in the house finds its full expression in the "finisher of faith," Jesus (12:2). In 11:26 Moses "considered the reproach of the Messiah as greater wealth than the treasure of Egypt." He is therefore also a model for Christians, who are exhorted by the author to "go outside the camp bearing his reproach" (13:13).

In this passage, we see the first use of the title *Christos* for Jesus ("Christ/Anointed/Messiah"); see also 3:14; 5:5; 6:1; 9:11, 14, 24, 28; 10:10; 11:26; 13:8, 21). It is one of three instances where the title appears without the definite article (see also 9:11 and 9:24). Here it appears virtually as part of a proper name, corresponding to the unadorned "Jesus" in 3:1, and serves to connect the designation of Jesus as Messiah to that of Son. Moses was faithful as a servant within the house (*en oikō*), Christ as a Son over the house (*epi ton oikon*). The Son's privileged position over the people makes his response of fidelity even more important. We see the return of the link between the Son and his brothers that was argued so vigorously in 2:10–18. The author associates himself once more with his hearers when he observes, "we are his house," or "whose house we are." This is a dramatic claim to continuity with historic Israel. If the author and readers are "God's house" ruled by God's Son, and if the Son has taken "hold of the descendants of Abraham," as we learned in 2:16, then author and readers participate in the story of that people. By being "sharers in a heavenly calling" (3:1), they are therefore those being summoned to fidelity now, just as the people in the wilderness was being summoned. It follows that everything said of old about God's people has pertinence to the readers as well, as we shall see immediately in the citation and midrashic interpretation of Ps 94:7–11 (in Heb 3:7–4:11).

The lesson to be drawn from that citation and interpretation is that although the call is real and continuous, a faithful response is always required every day. Thus the author here follows the assertion that "we are his house" with the strong qualification, "if indeed [*eanper* is used only here and possibly at 6:3 in the NT] we keep hold" (for *katechein* as "hold on," see Xenophon, *Symposium* 8.26; *T. Jud.* 26.1; Heb 3:14; 10:23). Corresponding to the implied plea not to "neglect such a great salvation" in 2:3 and the explicit plea to "be all the more attentive" in 2:1, is this statement of the need to "keep hold" in order to remain "sharers" of this calling. But keep hold to what?

We are certainly to hold fast to the confession of Jesus as apostle and high priest (see 3:1), but Hebrews' language is richly evocative. The term "boldness" (*parrēsia*) suggests the frankness of the philosopher in speech (Dio Chrysostom, *Oration* 32.11; 4 Macc. 4:1) as well as the freedom of action in public (Philo, *Special Laws* 1.321; Mark 8:32; John 7:14; 18:20), and therefore "fearlessness" in the presence of powerful personages (see esp. Acts 4:13, 29). Thus in Eph 3:12 Paul joins *parrēsia* to "access" (*prosagōgē*) to God as the effect of the work of Christ and the gift of the Spirit. Similarly, Hebrews will later exhort readers to "approach with *parrēsia* the throne of grace" (4:16) and will speak of the *parrēsia* with which they can enter the sanctuary by the blood of Jesus (10:19). Such boldness and confidence befits those freed from that fear of death that held them captive to slavery all their lives (2:15). The warning in 10:35 not to "lose your confidence (*parrēsia*)" should be heard in the context of these powerful affirmations.[3]

Similarly, *kauchēma* ("boast") fits within the framework of the honor/shame language throughout this passage. Here "boast" does not mean the act of bragging (see 2 Cor 9:3) but rather the ground for such boasting, namely the reality of which one is proud (see Deut 33:29; Prov 17:6). The usage here is the same as in Rom 4:2; 1 Cor 9:16; Gal 6:4; 2 Cor 1:14; Phil 2:14. Although this is the only occurrence of the term in Hebrews, it is particularly appropriate to the exhortation that readers not be ashamed of the sufferings of Christ. I have translated the genitive *tēs elpidos* epexegetically, "that is our hope." An equally good translation would be "that comes from our hope." If hope is the disposition that enables people to act with confidence rather than out of despair, then having hope be the basis or the substance of their boast and boldness makes good sense. This is the first time *elpis* appears in Hebrews, which will later speak of "keeping the full assurance of hope to the end" (6:11), of "seizing (*kratēsai*) the hope that lies before us" (6:18), of the "introduction of a better hope, through which we approach God" (7:19), and of "holding on to the confession of hope" (10:23). The connection between this hope and the fidelity of Moses and Jesus will be made in 11:1, where *pistis* is defined as "the substance of things hoped for" (*elpizomenōn hypostasis*). The need to "hold to" this hope marks the transition to the lengthy exhortation that follows in 3:7–4:11.

3:7–19 Warning against Faithlessness

Hebrews has asserted that its readers are God's "house," that is, God's people, and also that this status is conditional on fidelity to their calling—they must

3. See S. B. Marrow, "*Parrhēsia* and the New Testament," *CBQ* 44 (1982): 431–46; and A. C. Mitchell, "Holding on to Confidence: *Parrēsia* in Hebrews," in *Friendship, Flattery, and Frankness of Speech*, ed. J. T. Fitzgerald (NovTSup 82; Leiden: Brill, 1996), 203–26.

"keep hold" (3:6). Now the author begins to develop that implied warning, using the experience of the people of old in the wilderness as an example. For a comparison between this and other Jewish and Christian uses of the wilderness narrative as paradigm for the present, see excursus 2 below.

The passage begins with an extended citation from Ps 94:7–11, introduced with a strong "therefore" that makes the citation (ascribed to the Holy Spirit) part of the author's own exhortation (3:7–11). The author will continue to make use of the psalm through this portion of his argument, drawing direct citations from it again in 3:15, 4:3, and 4:7. The warning proper is bracketed by two uses of the verb *blepein*, in 3:12 and 19. The first is in the imperative, used in the sense of moral attentiveness ("watch out"), and the second is in the indicative, used in the ordinary visual sense ("we see"). The warning concerns the danger of "faithlessness" (*apistia*), which the author explicitly identifies as the reason why the ancient generation failed to enter the land of promise (3:19). A second explicit citation from the psalm (3:15) leads to a series of abrupt questions and answers (3:16–18) that drive home the point. The theme of faithfulness/unfaithfulness has thus passed from Moses and Jesus to the people. Jesus' brothers and sisters must be "perfected" in the same way he was, and for Hebrews that way is through the trust, obedience, and loyalty of faith.

3:7 Therefore, just as the Holy Spirit says: "If you hear his voice today,
8 do not harden your hearts as in the rebellion in the day of testing in the
wilderness. **9** Then your fathers tested[a] by putting to the test[b] and they
saw[c] my deeds **10** for forty years.[d] For this reason[e] I grew angry at this
generation[f] and I said, 'They are always wandering of heart and[g] they
have not known my ways. **11** As I swore in my anger, they shall not enter
into my rest.'"[h] **12** Watch out, brothers, that there not be within any one
among you a heart that is evil because of a faithlessness that turns away
from the living God. **13** Instead, admonish yourselves every day, as long
as it is called[i] "today" so that none of you be hardened by the deception
of sin. **14** For we have become sharers in the Christ, if in fact we hold
secure the beginning of this reality[j] all the way to the end. **15** It says,[k] "If
you hear his voice today, do not harden your hearts as in the rebellion."
16 Now, who were those who, even though they heard, rebelled? Was it
not all those who had come out of Egypt with the help of Moses? **17** And
with whom was God angry for forty years? Was it not those who sinned,[l]
whose corpses fell in the wilderness? **18** To whom did he swear, "they will
not enter into my rest," except to those who were disobedient?[m] **19** And
we see that they were not able to enter because of faithlessness.

a. A substantial number of MSS insert the personal pronoun *me* ("me"), which is lacking also in the LXX.

b. "By putting to the test" is an awkward rendering of *en dokimasia*, a noun not elsewhere attested in the NT and found in the LXX only in Sir 6:21. The reading is found in the oldest and most reliable MSS (e.g., P^{13}, P^{46}, א, A, B, D), and is therefore probably original, especially since it is also the hardest reading. Other MSS have *edokimasan* or *edokimasan me*, which are closer to the LXX.

c. The LXX has *eidosan* rather than *eidon,* the difference being simply that between a first and second aorist ending.

d. In the LXX the "forty years" goes with "I was angry with them," rather than with "they saw my deeds." Note that Hebrews itself has this reading in mind in 3:17, when it asks, "With whom was God angry for forty years?"

e. The *dio* ("therefore"/"for this reason") is both strong and absent from the LXX; it represents an interpretive interjection by the author. It is because of their faithlessness that God grew angry.

f. Some MSS (e.g., C and the second hand of D) agree with the LXX in reading "that generation" (*genea ekeinē*) rather than "this generation" (*genea tautē*).

g. Hebrews deviates from the LXX slightly by having *autoi de* rather than *kai autoi*; there is no difference in meaning.

h. "They shall not enter into my rest" simplifies the Semitic oath form followed by the LXX, which begins with the protasis of a conditional sentence, "if they should enter into my rest," with the apodosis left unexpressed, "may such and so happen to me."

i. A few MSS have *kaleite* ("you call") rather than *kaleitai* ("is called").

j. "The beginning of this reality" is an infelicitous translation of *tēn archēn tēs hypostaseōs* (see commentary for discussion). Some scribes also had difficulty with the expression, altering it to "his substance" (*hypostaseōs autou*) or "faith" (*pisteōs*).

k. The translation "It says" simplifies the syntax of the Greek phrase introducing the citation, lit. "by saying" (*en tō legesthai*), which stands in only a loose connection with the clauses before and after it.

l. A anticipates v. 18 by having "those who are disobedient" (*apeithēsasin*) here rather than "those who sinned" (*hamartēsasin*).

m. P^{46} and a substantial part of the Latin text tradition have "those who were faithless" (*apistēsasin*) rather than "those who were disobedient" (*apeithēsasin*).

[3:7–11] The introduction to the scriptural passage itself deserves attention. The words of the psalm are attributed to the Holy Spirit (*to pneuma to hagion*). Similarly, in 10:15 Hebrews introduces a citation from Jer 31:33 with "the Holy Spirit testifies to us." The prologue told us that God spoke in the past through the prophets. We begin to understand two aspects of that declaration. First, "the prophets" very much include the words of Scripture, above all the Psalms. Second, Hebrews understands such texts as "living words" that have "power," because they are inspired by God's own Spirit. Here is a high estimation of Scripture, one that regards the text not only as sacred, but as directly revelatory. Even more striking is that the Spirit's speaking is in the present: "Just as the Holy Spirit says." This is not only a stylistic variant, for the subsequent interpretation of the psalm stresses the contemporaneity of its voice. The author's argument is building to the declaration in 4:12 that "the word of God is living and powerful."

Although Hebrews quotes only Ps 94:7–11, the last half of this brief psalm, the first part of the psalm shows how appropriate was the author's choice. After an initial call to praise, the psalm enumerates the reasons why God should be honored (94:1–3). He is named as God (*theos*), as savior (*sotēr*), as a great Lord (*megas kyrios*), and as king (*basileus*). Directly or by implication, these titles have also been ascribed to God and to Jesus in Hebrews (see 1:1, 8; 2:3). Most of all, the psalm recounts God's creative deeds (94:4–5), and calls Israel "the people of his pasture, the sheep of his hand" (94:7). They are therefore summoned to worship, bow down, and cry out before "the Lord who has made us" (*kyriou tou poiēsantos hēmas*, v. 6). The phrase "who made us" exactly echoes the statement in Heb 3:2 that the Son was faithful "to the one who made him" (*tō poiēsanti auton*). In a word, the first part of the psalm sets up the second part, which summons the people to an obedience not demonstrated by their ancestors (*hoi pateres hymōn*) in the wilderness. Within the argument of the Hebrews, the psalm's exhortation also serves to call the author's hearers to a fidelity *like* that of Jesus, who was "faithful to the one who made him."

The part of the psalm quoted by Hebrews uses the wilderness generation as a foil for those it summons to obedient hearing. The occurrence of *sēmeron* ("today") draws the author's attention (he will cite it again in 3:15 and 4:7) and it is worth pondering. In Scripture the word "today" is used most notably in the speeches of Moses in Deuteronomy, where the people are told repeatedly about the demands of the covenant on them "today" (Deut 4:1, 2, 26; 5:3; 6:2, etc.), and in the covenant-renewal ceremony in Joshua, where the people accept as their own "all that you have spoken to us today" (Josh 24:27). In the Psalms, however, the term occurs only twice: in Ps 2:7 (which Hebrews quoted in 1:5) and in Ps 94:7 (cited here). As we shall see again, the author of Hebrews is fond of such textual consonance. Both uses of *sēmeron* in the Psalms suggest a sense of continuing and open-ended revelation by God: God speaks "today" (cf. Heb 1:1).

The exhortation to "hear" (*akouein*), in turn, fits perfectly within the understanding of "faith" and "obedience" that for Hebrews is the basic positive human stance toward God, a deeply responsive "hearing" of God in the texture of human life (see Exod 19:5, 8; Deut 4:1; 5:1; 6:3–4; 9:1; Matt 13:18; Mark 7:14; Luke 10:16; 18:6; Rom 10:14; Col 1:6). Hebrews has already stated the need for "hearing more attentively" in 2:1, and will continue this emphasis in 3:15, 16; 4:2, 7. Another link to the experience of Hebrews' readers is that the people in the wilderness "saw God's deeds" for forty years, yet still wandered in heart and did not understand his ways (3:10), and the author has reminded his readers that they also experienced "signs and wonders" (2:4) such as those associated with Moses and the wilderness sojourn (see Deut 4:34; 29:3; 34:11; Pss 77:43; 134:9).

The point of the citation, to be sure, is twofold: the people in the earlier generation did not "hear faithfully" (3:8–10), and God swore an oath that they should not enter the land (3:11). The psalm speaks of the people's behavior in terms of "rebellion" and "testing": *parapikrasmos* is used only in Ps 94:8, but the verb form *parapikrainein* is used several times for the uprising of the people against the Lord (Deut 31:24; 1 Kgs 13:21, 26; Ps 5:10), especially in the wilderness (Pss 77:8, 17, 40, 56; 104:28; 105:7, 33, 43). For "testing" Ps 94:8 uses the term *peirasmos* (Deut 6:16; 7:19; 9:22), and Ps 94:9 uses the verb *peirazein*. The "testing" in the wilderness has two aspects. Some texts speak of the Lord "putting the people to the test" (see Deut 4:34; 8:2; 13:3; 29:3), that is, allowing them to go through bad things to see if they would remain faithful. When they rebelled, in turn, they were "putting God to the test" (Exod 17:2, 7; Deut 33:8; Pss 77:41, 56; 105:14), that is, pushing the limits of his tolerance for such a faithless crowd. Psalm 94:9 uses still another term for testing, *dokimazein*, which has the specific sense of "testing for worth" and is used more often for God's probing of humans (see Pss 16:3; 35:2; 65:10; 80:7; 138:1). Psalm 94:9 has "they tested and saw my works" (*edokimasan kai eidosan ta erga mou*). The best manuscripts of Hebrews change this to *en dokimasia*, which is found elsewhere in the LXX only in Sir 6:21, and nowhere else in the New Testament. In ordinary usage, it appears in forensic or review contexts (Plato, *Laws* 759D; Aristotle, *Nicomachean Ethics* 1162A).

According to the psalm, the rebellion of the people revealed certain internal dispositions. First, they had "hardened their hearts" (Heb 3:8). As so often in biblical diction, the heart (*kardia*) is the seat both of knowledge and of choice (see, e.g., Pss 4:4; 5:9; 9:1; 11:2). The term *sklēros* ("hard") can refer to that which is difficult (see Deut 1:17; 15:18; John 6:60), but is also used for a person who is obdurate or stubborn (see Deut 31:27; 1 Sam 25:3; 1 Kgs 12:13; Prov 4:27; Isa 48:4; Matt 25:24). The phrase "hard heart" (*sklērokardia*) appears in Matt 19:8; Mark 10:5; 16:14. For the heart as the source for the human response to God in Hebrews, see especially 10:16–22. For the people in the wilderness, the hardening of the heart meant their refusal to hear and obey God.

The psalm says also that the people were "always wandering in heart" (*aei planōntai tē kardia*, 3:10). This time the internal disposition of the heart is one of wavering or lack of direction, with a tendency toward error (see Gen 37:15; Ps 118:176). In Heb 11:38 the author will say of the heroes of faith that they "wandered over desert places and mountains," but that is a physical rather than, as here, a moral wandering. Note, however, that in 5:2 Hebrews will speak of the priest as one who is able to deal gently with "the ignorant and confused" (*agnoousin kai planōmenois*). Finally, the rebellion of the people shows them "not to know [God's] ways," even though they had seen his works (Heb 3:10; Ps 94:10). The metaphor of "the way" is particularly appropriate for those on a pilgrimage; when they rebelled, the people "wandered" from the way on which and in which God was leading them. The "ways" of God here refers even more, however, to God's directions on how to live (see Deut 11:18–19; Pss 24:4, 10; 26:11; 118:15, 33, 151). Their "not knowing" is not really a form of ignorance, but a form of rebellious disobedience.

God responds to their rebellion with anger: "I was angry (*prosōchthisa*) with this generation." The verb *prosōchthizein* means to be provoked or to become angry. This is the only use in the New Testament, but see Num 22:3; Deut 7:26. The anthropomorphism, "God's wrath" (*orgē theou*), appears repeatedly as a response to human infidelity (see Exod 4:14; Num 11:1; 12:9; Deut 11:17; Pss 2:5; 7:66). Here that anger moves God to take an oath. The verb *omnyein* is used frequently in Scripture for the oath that God swore to Abraham in Gen 22:16: "By myself I have sworn," when God promises him the land, an oath that is constantly recalled (see Gen 50:28; Exod 13:5; 33:1; Num 11:12; Deut 9:5; Josh 1:6; Judg 2:1). But the oath referred to in Ps 94 is the one God swears in Num 14:21–22, in response to the rebellion of the people: "As I live and as my name lives," none of that generation would "see the land, which I swore on oath to their fathers." Hebrews seizes upon three oaths taken by God as reported by Scripture: the oath to Abraham (Gen 22:16; see Heb 6:13), the oath to the people (Num 14:21–22) referred to here, and the oath to the Son that he is a priest according to the order of Melchizedek (Ps 109:4; Heb 7:21). Note the seriousness of this second oath: even though God promised the land to the children of Abraham by oath, he can revoke it for those who have proven themselves to be unfaithful.

In the short textual notes following the translation, I have observed some of Hebrews' alterations to the psalm as it appears in the LXX, and in this comment I have discussed the unusual occurrence of *en dokimasia*. The other emendations are slight, with two exceptions. First, Hebrews inserts the word *dio* ("therefore"), making God's wrath directly connected to their having tested him, though they had seen his works for forty years. Second, Hebrews thereby makes the forty years go with the time of God's wonders in the wilderness, whereas in the LXX it appears that God is angry with the people for forty years. Indeed, Hebrews also uses this reading in 3:17, which states that God was angry with the people for forty years.

Finally, the Scripture passage concludes with the word *katapausis* ("rest"), an unusual term for the promised land, though it could be understood as a place of rest from the time of active and difficult wandering in the wilderness (see this meaning in Deut 12:9 and 1 Kgs 8:56). The term is also used with reference to the "sabbath rest" (Exod 34:21; 35:2; 2 Macc 15:1). The ambiguity will be exploited by Hebrews when this part of the passage is made thematic in 4:1.[1]

1. For this section, see D. R. Darnell, "Rebellion, Rest, and the Word of God: An Exegetical Study of Hebrews 3:1–4:13" (Ph.D. diss., Duke University, 1973); and R. C. Gleason, "The Old Testament Background of Rest in Hebrews 3:7–4:11," *BSac* 157 (2000): 281–303.

[12–15] The exhortation itself is brief, with a negative warning ("watch out") and a positive encouragement ("admonish yourselves"), both connected to the scriptural citation by its introductory adverb, *kathōs*. If we eliminate the actual citation, the sentence in 3:7–12 would run, "Just as the Holy Spirit says . . . watch out . . . admonish." The admonition calls for vigilance among the readers in a manner similar to 2:1, and for mutual and internal upbuilding—the reflexive pronoun *heautous* can be taken either as "yourselves" or as "one another." I translate the imperative *parakaleite* in 3:13 as "admonish" in order to capture the urgent tone; other possibilities are "exhort" and "comfort." The translation "encourage one another" could, to be sure, strengthen the sense of community building (see 1 Thess 5:11, and the key passages in Heb 10:25; 13:19, 22).

The exhortation uses the language of the psalm. Their mutual admonition should be a continuous practice of alertness and attentiveness carried out "every day, as long as it is called 'today'" (3:13). It should be practiced by and for all the readers, "so that there not be any from among you" (*tis ex hymōn*) who falls short. The call, therefore, is for a constant attention to the commitment that the community has made.

Such watchfulness has as its goal the eradication of those dispositions that kept the earlier generation from entering the land of promise. The first is the possession of an "evil heart" (*kardia ponēra*), which is further modified by the genitive *apistias*, and the particular infinitive construction, *en tō apostēnai apo theou zōntos*. I take the genitive and infinitival clause as making the same point in clarifying the meaning of "evil heart." Rather than "unbelief," then, *apistia* here means the "faithlessness" that is the opposite of "faithfulness"; compare especially Paul in Rom 3:3; 4:20; 11:20, 23. It was not the failure of the Israelites to believe in God that prevented their entry, but their failure in loyalty and obedience. This translation is further supported by the infinitival phrase, "that turns away from the living God." Such faithlessness is precisely apostasy (see Acts 5:37–38; 15:38; 1 Tim 1:4). Finally, drawing a lesson from the rebellion of the people as described in the psalm, Hebrews itself states flatly in 3:19 that *apistia* is the reason they did not enter the land.

This is the first of four times that Hebrews uses the expression "the living God" (see 9:14; 10:31; 12:22). The phrase "I live, says the Lord," occurs several times in Scripture (see Num 14:21, 28; Isa 49:18; Jer 22:24; Zech 2:9), as does the designation "living God," applied to the Lord (Deut 4:33, 26; 16:20; Ps 83:2; Hos 1:10; Isa 37:4). The solemn designation appears with some frequency also in the New Testament (Matt 26:63; Acts 14:15; Rom 9:26; 2 Cor 3:3; 6:16; 1 Thess 1:9; 1 Tim 3:15; 4:10). The use of the designation is particularly apt here, since to turn away from the living God is to turn toward death (see Heb 3:17).

The second negative disposition keeping the people from the land is the possession of a "hardened heart" caused by "the deception of sin," which is probably best understood as "the deception that is sin." For *apatē* as deception, see

Col 2:8 and Eph 4:22. In light of this language, it is worth noting that here and in 3:17 "sin" is understood not in terms of an error but in terms of a (self-)deception as well as rebellion. Similar to Paul in Rom 1:18–32, Hebrews suggests that a rebellious disposition that denies God's claim on humans can seduce and deceive the sinner into even deeper levels of alienation.

The "for" (*gar*) in verse 14 provides the basis for the positive admonition/exhortation to be carried out among readers: they are "sharers in the Messiah" (*metochoi tou Christou*). The term *metochos* was used also in 3:1 for "sharers in a heavenly calling." Here it points to the readers' shared participation in the messianic reality: the use of the perfect tense ("we have become," *gegonamen*) indicates they once were not such participants but have entered into it through baptism (see "sharers in the Holy Spirit" in 6:4), and now remain in this reality. Although the translation "partners of the Christ" is a possibility (see Luke 5:7; *T. Benj.* 2.5), the egalitarian tone of "partner" in English makes it less suitable to the point being made by Hebrews. They are not partners of Christ but, rather, have become sharers in him.[2]

However reassuring this status, Hebrews immediately reminds readers that it is nevertheless conditional (see 3:6). Thus there is need for constant vigilance. As in 3:6, the use of *eanper* stresses the seriousness of the condition: they must "hold secure to the end" (*mechri telous bebaian kataschōmen*). We recognize here the phrase that had crept by scribal attraction into variants of 3:6. We also recognize the themes of "secure" (*bebaios*; see 2:2) and "to the end" (*telos* is cognate to "complete/perfect" in 2:10). Likewise, we can see that *archē* ("beginning/origin") corresponds to "the end," just as in 2:10 *archēgos* corresponds with *teleiōsai*. In essence, then, Hebrews is repeating its earlier exhortation: they must hold on from beginning to end. The main puzzle is the meaning of *hypostasis* in the phrase *tēn archēn tēs hypostaseōs* (3:14). The textual variants indicate that some scribes were puzzled as well. As we saw in the discussion of 1:3, the meaning of *hypostasis* ("that which stands under") can range from a down payment on property to the essence of a being. I have chosen to translate simply as "the beginning of this reality"—that is, their having become partakers of the messianic identity. Perhaps an even better translation would be: "the reality that we have begun."

The infinitival phrase in verse 15, *en tō legesthai* (lit. "when it says"), I have translated as "It says," which makes for a more straightforward syntax in English. But it can also obscure the fact that in the Greek, this phrase actually concludes the sentence begun in 3:12, which was interrupted by the interpretation offered by verse 14. The renewed citation in verse 15, "If you hear his voice today, do not harden your hearts as in the rebellion," echoes the use of "hearing," "today," and "hardening" in the previous verses, and the phrase "in the rebellion" also sets up the following set of questions.

2. See E. Nardoni, "Partakers in Christ (Hebrews 3.14)," *NTS* 37 (1991): 456–72.

[16–19] The lesson to be drawn from the wilderness narrative, as recalled by Ps 94:7–11, is now driven home by three short questions and a conclusion. The questions pick up three aspects of the citation from Ps 94, and each question has in effect the same answer, from a slightly different perspective. Who were those who, "even though they heard," nevertheless rebelled against God? The participle *akousantes* adds something to the scriptural citation: it is possible to *hear* and yet not to obey, to *see* and yet not to understand God's ways. Thus there is need for vigilance, even for those who have now heard (see Heb 2:1). The answer to the question is supplied: "all of those who had come out of Egypt with the help of Moses" (see Exod 17:1–7). The phrase *dia Mōyseōs* acknowledges that Moses was indeed not only himself faithful, but also a "leader of salvation" (2:10).

The second question (3:17) again represents a variation on the quotation from Scripture. According to Heb 3:10, the "forty years" was connected to the people's seeing God's deeds. Here, in contrast, Hebrews connects the forty years to the period of God's anger, a feasible reading of the LXX. Toward whom did God exhibit such long-term irritation? Against those who had sinned (*hamartēsasin*)—see the use of *hamartia* in 3:13. That the bodies of those who sinned were to fall in the wilderness is found in Num 14:29 and 32 (see also 1 Cor 10:5).

The third question (Heb 3:18) concerns those to whom God swore an oath (Num 14:22) that they should not enter the land. The answer once more sharpens the sense of the psalm quotation. The biblical text of the psalm does not directly identify the rebellion as a case of disobedience, but the participle *apeithēsasin* must be translated in that sense. Deuteronomy 9:23 has, "When the LORD sent you from Kadesh-barnea, saying, 'Go up and inhabit the land that I am giving you,' you did not obey the word of the LORD your God and did not believe him and did not obey his voice." And Deut 1:26–27 has, "You did not wish to go up and you disobeyed the LORD your God, and you grumbled in your tents" (see also *apeithein* in Rom 2:8; 10:21; 11:32; Eph 2:2; 1 Pet 3:1, 20).

Hebrews draws the conclusion that, by now, seems inevitable: that generation was unable to enter the land because of *apistia*. In light of the identification of the rebellion as *disobedience*, it is clear that *apistia* here as in 3:11 must be translated not as "unbelief" but as "faithlessness." In contrast to Moses, who was *pistos* in every respect, the people he led were faithless. Christ has been presented as the Son over the whole house, who is also perfectly *pistos*. The question is whether the present generation of readers will imitate and learn from their leader, or from their ancestors in the wilderness.

Excursus 2: The Wilderness As Paradigm

When the author of Hebrews makes the experience of the Israelites in the wilderness the basis for his exhortation to faithfulness, he is scarcely being innovative. The adventures following the exodus from Egypt and before the entry into Canaan, narrated a first time in the biblical books of Exodus, Leviticus, and Numbers, become an essential moment in Israel's history, for good and ill. Sometimes the recitation of events serves to remind the people of its past history with God and to bring readers to a point of recommitment to the story of the people and the God who shaped that story: the recitation is prologue to covenant. Already in Deuteronomy, Moses prepares for his call to the obedience of the people (chaps. 4–6) with a recitation of their previous history, including their repeated rebellion against God in the desert (1:26) and the Lord's response of anger and his swearing of an oath (1:32–34). Similar in function are the long recitations in Josh 24:1–15 and Neh 9:8–23.

Some retellings of the tale scarcely touch on the rebellion of the people. In several of the psalms, the focus is entirely on the wonders worked by God for the people (see Pss 104, 134, and 135). For two of the prophets, the time of the wilderness is portrayed in entirely positive terms, as the period when Israel was in most intimate relationship with the Lord. Corruption occurs only after the people entered the land of Canaan (see Hos 3:14–23; Jer 2:1–3:5).

Other retellings of the story acknowledge elements of grumbling or rebellion, but turn them positively, to praise of the hero or to God's pedagogical purpose. Josephus, for example, emphasizes the leadership of Moses (*Ant.* 3.11, 33, 296), although he touches—very gently—on God's anger: 'However God, not long after, chastised the Hebrews for their abusive behavior towards Him; in fact, no small number of them perished" (3.299). In his *Life of Moses*, Philo mentions the grumbling of the people at the manna in order to emphasize the efficacy of Moses' prayer (1.181–85), and alludes to the rebellion against the order to enter the land, but recasts the anger and oath of God into this mild statement: "This roused their ruler's indignation, who, at the same time, feared lest some scourge should descend upon them from God for their senseless disbelief in His utterances. This actually happened" (1.235–36). And in *On the Decalogue* 2–17, Philo speaks of the wilderness experience entirely in terms of God's pedagogical purposes, providing four reasons why it was a good thing for them to wander for forty years: (a) they would be uncorrupted by the pride of city life; (b) they would purify their souls from the licentiousness of city life; (c) they would have the chance to practice the laws; (d) they would learn that it was God and not humans who gave them the laws.

Similarly, Sirach uses the moments of rebellion in order to highlight the heroic actions of Phinehas, Joshua, and Caleb (Sir 45:23; 46:1–10), and in the reformist composition *Jubilees*, the period in the wilderness is mentioned only as a time for learning the commandments of the Lord (*Jub.* 50.4); the corruption of the people will happen when they go into the land (*Jub.* 21.16–23). The Hellenistic Jewish historians merely touch on the forty years in the wilderness, Eupolemus to identify it as the period of time Moses prophesied (*Frag.* 2.1), and Artapanus to comment on the "meal like millet" that God gave the Israelites (*Frag.* 3.27). Pseudo-Philo gives more attention to the wilderness saga, touching on the forty years of manna (*L.A.B.* 10.7), the "bread of angels" (19.5), the incident of the golden calf (12.4), and the rebellion of Korah (16.1–7). But no moral lesson is drawn from the incidents. Indeed, God's preventing Moses from entering the land is interpreted as a merciful intervention, so that Moses will not see the apostasy and punishment of the people when they forget the law once they are in the land (19.6–7).

Other retellings focus on the negative events in the wilderness. In contrast to Hosea and Jeremiah, who idealize the time in the desert, Ezek 20:1–31 emphasizes the "abominations of their fathers" (20:4) all through the wilderness experience: "The house of Israel rebelled against me in the wilderness; they did not observe my statutes but rejected my ordinances, by whose observance everyone shall live" (20:13). In response, God grew angry (20:13), but did not "destroy them or make an end to them in the wilderness" (20:14). But the pattern of disobedience recurred (20:18–26): "In this again your fathers blasphemed me, by dealing treacherously with me" (20:27). The purpose of this recitation is to challenge the present generation: "will you defile yourselves after the manner of your fathers, and go after these detestable things?" (20:30). The wilderness generation is a negative example from which to learn.

The same emphasis appears in some of the Psalms. Hebrews makes full use of Ps 94:7–11 but could also have found support for the theme of Israel's wilderness disobedience in Ps 77:5–67, which alternates sections that praise God's wonders with sections bemoaning the infidelity of the people: "Yet they sinned still more against him, rebelling against the Most High in the desert. They tested God in their heart by demanding the food they craved" (77:17–18; see also 77:33–37). When the pattern of rebellion continues in the land of promise, God responds: "He was full of wrath, and he utterly rejected Israel" (77:59). Similarly, Ps 105, which follows immediately upon the "nothing but goodness" recitation in Ps 104, emphasizes the disobedience of the wilderness generation (105:6–33), leading to God's angry response: "Therefore he raised his hand and swore to them that he would make them fall in the wilderness" (105:26).

The negative assessment of the people appears briefly also in *4 Ezra* 14.29–30: "Our fathers were at the beginning strangers in Egypt, and they were delivered from thence. And they received the law of life, which they kept not, even as you also after them have transgressed it." Particularly striking is the version found in the Qumran composition called the *Damascus Document*, in which the wilderness generation "preferred the desires of the hearts, and did not listen to the voice of their creator . . . and the wrath of God flared up against their congregation. And their sons died through it" (CD 3:7–9). Their rebellion stands in immediate contrast to the members of the Qumran community who had gone into the desert precisely to serve the Lord: "But with those who remained steadfast in God's precepts, with those who were left from among them, God established his covenant with Israel forever" (CD 3:12–13). The Qumran composition juxtaposes the failure of the earlier covenant (3:4) because of the disobedience of the people to an eternal covenant with those committed to obedience (3:13).

Three passages in the New Testament in addition to Hebrews take up the wilderness narrative. The allusion in John 6 is very brief. In response to the crowd's claim that "our ancestors ate the manna in the wilderness, as it is written, 'He gave them bread from heaven to eat'" (John 6:31), Jesus makes clear that it was not Moses who gave them manna, but God (6:32), and that Jesus himself is the true "bread of life" (6:36). The contrast is drawn again in 6:48–50: "I am the bread of life. Your fathers ate the manna in the wilderness, and they died. This is the bread that has come down from heaven, so that one may eat it and not die."

Stephen's speech in Acts 7 contains an extensive recital of biblical history, with particular attention to Moses. The account is structured in three scenes: Moses first visits the people for their salvation, is rejected, and must flee (Acts 7:23–29); then he is empowered by God and sent back to save the people, demonstrating his commission by the working of signs and wonders and the giving of the law (7:30–39). Then the people reject Moses a second time through the incident of the golden calf, with the result that they are rejected by God and sent into exile (7:39–43): "Our ancestors were unwilling to obey him; instead they pushed him aside, and in their hearts they turned back to Egypt" (7:39). Stephen's speech uses this history to castigate the present generation that has rejected Jesus, the prophet like Moses: "You stiff-necked people, uncircumcised in heart and ears, you are forever opposing the Holy Spirit, just as your ancestors used to do" (7:51).

The passage closest to Heb 3:7–19 is 1 Cor 10:1–13. Paul begins not with a citation from Scripture but with an interpretive summary of the exodus story, starting with a catalog of the gifts that "all our fathers" were given (1 Cor 10:1–4), and then stating, "Nevertheless, God was not pleased with most of them, and they were struck down in the wilderness" (10:5). As in Hebrews, Paul makes thematic the continuing significance of the scriptural story for his contemporary readers. The events happened to people in the past, says Paul, but were written down "to instruct us on whom the ends of the ages have come" (10:11; cf. Heb 1:1). Again, "These things occurred as examples for us, so that we might not desire evil as they did" (10:6). Just as Heb 3:16–19 draws specific lessons from the past events, so does Paul: the Corinthians should not become idolators as they did (10:7), or indulge in sexual immorality (10:8), and "we must not put Christ [!] to the test as some of them did and were destroyed by serpents. And do not complain as some of them did, and were destroyed by the destroyer" (10:9–10). Paul, like Hebrews, and like a substantial portion of the tradition, sees in the wilderness generation a paradigm of how not to respond to God's wonderful works for the people.

Hebrews therefore stands within a long—and continuing—tradition of inner-biblical exegesis and inner-Jewish critique, when it rereads the story of the wilderness and uses it for hortatory purposes in the present. A comparison with other such retellings of the story also helps us locate Hebrews in the line of interpretation from Deuteronomy to *4 Ezra*, revealing even more sharply its distinctive emphasis on the theme of faith and faithlessness.

4:1–13 The Sabbath Rest of God

Hebrews continues to develop the argument begun in 3:1, based on the conviction that its readers are "sharers in a heavenly calling." The author has now established, first, that although both Moses and Jesus were faithful to God, Jesus as Son is the real "pioneer/founder" of salvation (3:1–6), and second, that the people in the wilderness did not enter into God's rest because of their faithlessness (3:7–19). Now, the author argues that the "rest" of which God spoke in Ps 94:11 (Heb 3:11) was not the promised land of Canaan but a share in God's own way of existing. God said, after all, "they shall not enter into *my* rest," rather than "they shall not enter into *their* rest."[1]

1. For the passage as a whole, see H. W. Attridge, "'Let Us Strive to Enter That Rest': The Logic of Hebrews 4:1–11," *HTR* 73 (1980): 279–88.

The author begins in 4:1 with the same hortatory tone as he had used in 3:12–13, but shifts quickly to an exposition of the thesis that a rest still remains for those who are, unlike the wilderness generation, faithful (4:2–3). The heart of this exposition is the resolution of the apparent contradiction between two texts of Scripture (Gen 2:2 and Ps 94:11) in Heb 4:4–5, by appeal, in good midrashic fashion, to a third text, Ps 94:7. The author then constructs a tight enthymeme (a syllogism with the middle term implicit) in 4:8–9, and a conclusion in 4:10 that makes clear that the "rest" meant by Scripture is indeed a share in God's own; theirs is, in truth, a "heavenly calling." A final exhortation to "hurry" in entering God's rest (4:11) concludes with a rhetorically polished and powerful—yet also ambiguous—encomium of the word of God (4:12–13).

4:1 Let us be afraid, therefore, so that none from among you seem to be
left behind, so long as a promise[a] of entering into his rest remains. **2** For
we have indeed been given the good news just as they were. But the word
that they heard did them no good, because it was not joined by faith[b] to
the hearers.[c] **3** For[d] we the faithful[e] are entering[f] into the rest, just as he
said, "As I swore in my anger, they shall not enter into my rest," even
though his works have been done from the foundation of the world. **4** For[g]
he said this somewhere concerning the seventh day, "And God rested on
the seventh day from all his works." **5** Yet[h] in this passage again he says,
"they will not enter into my rest."

6 Since therefore it remains for some to enter into it, and those who first
received the good news did not enter because of disobedience,[i] **7** he again
sets aside a day, namely "today," by David, saying after such a considerable length of time, just as was said[j] earlier, "If you hear his voice today,
do not harden your hearts." **8** For if Joshua had given them rest, he would[k]
not have spoken about another day after these. **9** Therefore, a sabbath rest
remains for the people of God. **10** For the one entering into his rest also
rests himself from all his works, just as God did from his own works.

11 Therefore let us hurry to enter into that rest, so that none fall into
the same type of disobedience. **12** For the word of God is living and powerful,[l] sharper than any two-edged sword, cutting to the division between
soul and spirit,[m] joints and marrow, able to discern the thoughts and conceptions of the heart. **13** There is no creature that is not visible to him. All
things lie naked and exposed to his eyes. To him is our account directed.[n]

a. D supplies the definite article, "so long as the promise remains."

b. The participle *synkekerasmenous* here is very difficult, although it is found in P^{13}, P^{46}, and major uncials and versions. ℵ has the nominative singular *synkekerasmos* rather than the accusative plural found in the majority of MSS, and 104 has *syskekerammenoi*, while leaving out *tē pistei* ("faith") altogether.

c. "to the hearers" is replaced by "of the hearers" in the original hand of D, and by "with the things heard" in 1912 (Latin).

d. The connective *gar* ("for") is read by P^{13} and P^{46}, B, and D, but is replaced by *oun* ("therefore") in א, A, and C. Neither connective fully satisfies, and the Syriac Peshitta has "but" (*de*).

e. Literally, "we who have come to have faith," with the aorist participle indicating a starting point to that disposition.

f. Rather than the present indicative ("we are entering"), the codices A and C have the hortatory subjunctive "Let us enter."

g. "For" (*gar*) is omitted by A and apparently by P^{13}.

h. The Greek text reads simply "and" (*kai*). I have translated as "yet" in order to stress the opposition that the author establishes between the two citations.

i. Consistent with the variations found in 3:17–18, P^{46} and the original hand of B have *apistian* ("faithlessness").

j. B and a few other MSS have "just as he said," and still other MSS have simply "was said," without the prefix indicating "earlier."

k. B has "therefore" (*ara*) rather than the particle *an,* which is demanded by the syntax of the contrary-to-fact conditional sentence.

l. B has *enargēs* ("clear, evident") instead of *energēs* ("powerful"), found in all other witnesses.

m. A few MSS have "body" (*sōmatos*) rather than "spirit" (*pneumatos*) as in the majority of witnesses.

n. I use Attridge's (133) translation here since it captures the ambiguity of the Greek; see comments.

[4:1–5] The hortatory subjunctive *phobēthōmen* ("Let us be afraid") links the author to his hearers again (see 3:1 and 3:14); the exhortation begun in 3:12–13 continues, but the verb shifts from the second person plural to the first person plural. Summoning a fear of falling short is a classic example of a *pathos* argument: the author uses emotion as well as reason to persuade his readers (see Introduction, pp. 14–15). Their salvation, we have learned, frees them from a "fear of death" (2:15) and the "fear of rulers" (11:23, 27; 13:6), but the one with whom they have to do must always be feared with a reverential awe (10:27, 31). The prospect of not reaching the presence of God is truly reason to fear. In this instance, fear is a positive impetus. They are not to be "fearful" of someone or something, but rather "fear lest" they fall short of their destination.[2]

For the first time, Hebrews speaks of "promise" (*epangelia*) as equivalent to "entering the rest." Throughout the composition, the author will play—as he does with the "rest" that is both the land of Canaan and God's own glory—with the promise made to Abraham (6:12, 15, 17; 11:9, 13, 17, 33) and the "better

2. On this theme see P. Gray, *Godly Fear: The Epistle to the Hebrews and Greco-Roman Critiques of Superstition* (Society of Biblical Literature Academica Biblica 16; Atlanta: Society of Biblical Literature, 2003).

promise" of entering God's life (8:6; 9:15; 10:36; 11:39). Thus here the promise still remaining to them (*kataleipomenēs*) is that of "his rest" (*katapausin autou*), namely God's own way of existing. They are called to be fearful, "so that none from among you seem to be left behind": their fear is preventative (*mēpote* + subjunctive). The construction *dokē hysterēkenai* is ambiguous, since each term can bear different senses. The verb *dokein* often means to have an opinion concerning something (see Luke 12:51; 19:11; John 5:39), or "to seem to be" (Acts 17:18; Matt 21:18). Similarly, *hysterein* can mean to be in lack of something (Phil 4:12; 1 Cor 1:7; Mark 10:21), or "to fall short of" something (2 Cor 11:5; 12:11). The basic translation options are therefore "think he has come too late" (as though the promise was no longer available), or "seem to fall short" (as through a lack of effort to enter). Since this passage leads in verse 11 to a moral exhortation to "hurry to enter," in order to avoid the example of the disobedient wilderness generation, the moral sense is clearly intended here as well. Note as well the use of *hysterein* in 12:15: "so that no one of you fall short of the gift of God."

The next statement establishes the analogy between the wilderness generation and the readers, and serves as a transition to the assertion that the promise still remains for the readers: "For we have indeed been given the good news just as they were." We are again reminded of the prologue, which connected God's speech in the past to his speech now. But the phrasing is striking. Hebrews uses the verb "proclaim the good news" (*euangelizomai*), a term that is to be expected for the Christian community (see Acts 5:2; 10:36; Rom 1:15; 1 Cor 1:17; 15:1; 2 Cor 10:16; Gal 1:9; 1 Pet 1:12, 25), but that appears at first strange when applied to the people in the wilderness. To be sure, the term appears in the Psalms (39:9; 67:11; 95:2) and in the prophets (Joel 2:32; Nah 1:15; Isa 40:9; 52:7; 60:6; 61:1), and Paul, at least, uses the passage from Isa 52:7 to assert that Israel of old did hear the good news preached to them (Rom 10:15); but here the author reverses the expected order. He does not say that they received the good news as we did, but the opposite: we were evangelized just as they were—the speaking of God to the people was a proclamation of "good news."

The problem in the past, then, was not the character of the message, but the mode of reception of the message. The phrase *ho logos tēs akoēs* has the sense it does in 1 Thess 2:13—the word that is heard—although it is given depth by the use of *logos* in Heb 4:12. Why was this good news, spoken to them by God, of no efficacy? Because it did not profit (*ouk ōphelēsen*) the hearers. The notion of "usefulness" in practice and speech is a commonplace among Greco-Roman (Epictetus, *Discourses* 1.4.16; 3.24.51) and Jewish moralists (Philo, *Migration of Abraham* 55; *Posterity and Exile of Cain* 86), as well as the other New Testament writings (see 1 Cor 15:32; Jas 2:14, 16; Rom 2:25; 1 Cor 13:3; 14:6; Gal 5:2); Hebrews will later use it in connection with the uselessness of dietary regulations (Heb 13:9).

The precise reason for the inefficacy of the word spoken to the desert generation is obscurely expressed although clear in overall meaning, repeating the point that was substantially made earlier in 3:19. The Greek construction found in the best manuscript tradition is difficult, combining the perfect passive participle *synkekerasmenous* ("joined to") in agreement with *ekeinous* ("those"), the noun "faith" in the instrumental dative (*pistei*), and the articular aorist participle *tois akousasin* ("those who heard"). My translation, "because it was not joined by faith to the hearers," is faithful to the Greek, but it has the disadvantage of separating those who were joined and the hearers, as though they were two groups. It is indeed tempting to follow the minority reading of Codex Sinaiticus, which makes the participle nominative singular, enabling it to modify "the word," in this fashion: "It did not meet with faith in the hearers." For "being joined with" in this sense, compare 1 Cor 12:24 and Ignatius, *Ephesians* 5.1. In either reading, the basic idea is that hearing must be accompanied by faith in order to be profitable (cf. the link between "hearing" and "faith" in Rom 10:16–17; Gal 3:2, 5).

In contrast to those whose lack of faith kept them from entering the rest, "we the faithful" are now in position to enter (Heb 4:3). The participle *hoi pisteusantes* is again in the aorist: "we who have come to have faith." Some manuscripts have the subjunctive here, "let us enter," but this would make even less sense of the already difficult connective "for" (*gar*); the Peshitta, indeed, has the conjunction "but," which works well with the indicative, "we are entering." The combination of indicative voice and the explanatory connective "for" makes best sense if we see the statement as referring back to the exhortation not to fall short of entering his rest in 4:1. In any case, Hebrews has now repeatedly linked entering with faith and failure to enter with faithlessness, and has also linked faithlessness to disobedience. The further link between faith and obedience will be made explicit in 5:8.

When discussing the first long citation of Ps 94:7–11 (in Heb 3:7–11), I pointed out the polyvalence of the term *katapausis*. It referred there to the land of Canaan as the people's "rest" from their wandering in the wilderness (Deut 12:9; 1 Kgs 8:56). But it is also used with reference to the people's sabbath rest (Exod 34:21; 35:2; 2 Macc 15:1). With this second citation of Ps 94:11 ("as I swore in my anger, they shall not enter into my rest"), the author of Hebrews exploits this polyvalence to draw a distinction between the temporal, material destination of that wilderness generation, and the eternal, spiritual destination of those who now have faith—God's own power and presence. The distinction fits comfortably within a Platonic worldview, which sees the material realm (the phenomenal) as pointing to a greater reality beyond materiality (the noumenal), but is suggested as well by the ambiguity within Scripture itself. Hebrews here employs the midrashic technique of *gezerah shawah*: where the same term occurs in two different scriptural passages, new insight can be derived from their being placed in conversation.[3]

In this case, the term *katapausis* appears to present a contradiction. The first passage (from the psalm) has God speaking of "my rest" (*katapausin mou*), but the author adds, "even though" (*kaitoi*) his works have been done since the creation of the world (lit. "foundation of the cosmos," *katabolēs kosmou*). It is not itself an easy line to construe. The particle *kaitoi* is found in the New Testament only here and in Acts 14:17, "and yet he has not left himself without a witness in doing good." As with the use of the term also in 4 Macc. 2:6, 5:18, and 7:13, the particle suggests a contrast between the first clause and the second. Here God says in the psalm that he has a rest, *and yet* his works have been done from the start of the world.

To make sense of the implied contrast, then, we must take the aorist passive participle *genēthentōn* not as "done and finished" at the beginning, but as "still done and being done" from the time of the world's foundation. This loose construction is supported by two observations. First, the psalm itself declares that the wilderness generation "saw my works for forty years," which must mean that God has continued to speak and act in the world. Second, the preposition *apo* ("from") extends God's working beyond the days of founding the world described in Genesis; Hebrews does not use *en* ("in" or "by" the foundation of the world). The initial question, then, is how God can speak of "my rest" when he is still at work in the world.

The issue is pressed further in 4:4–5, when the author places two specific verses side by side. He introduces the quotation from Gen 2:2 with the periphrastic clause, "he said this [lit. 'thus,' *houtōs*] somewhere concerning the seventh day." The first question that springs to mind is, Who says thus? When the author used the perfect tense "he said" (*eirēken*) in Heb 4:3, it referred to God speaking in the psalm. But in what sense is God also the one speaking in Gen 2:2, especially when it speaks about God? Or perhaps we are to understand the subject of "he has said" in both places as the Holy Spirit, identified as the source of the psalm passage in Heb 3:7.

The deeper tension is found, however, within the citation itself, drawn from the LXX with no alteration: "and God rested on the seventh day from all his works" (*kai katepausen ho theos en tē hēmera tē hebdomē apo pantōn tōn ergōn autou*). This passage "answers" the verse from the psalm with three shared terms: "rest" (*katapausis/katepausen*), "works" (*erga*), and "day" (*hēmera*), but in 4:5 the

3. For full discussions of the theme of "rest," see O. Hofius, *Katapausis: Die Vorstellung vom endzeitlichen Ruheort im Hebräerbrief* (WUNT 11; Tübingen: Mohr [Siebeck], 1970); and J. H. Wray, *Rest as a Theological Metaphor in the Epistle to the Hebrews and the Gospel of Truth: Early Christian Homiletics of Rest* (SBLDS 166; Atlanta: Scholars Press, 1998).

author focuses particularly on the term "rest" as he quotes again from Ps 94:11, "Yet in this passage again he says, 'They shall not enter into my rest.'"

This juxtaposition of authoritative texts raises questions concerning God's intended meaning and concerning Hebrews' entire argument. If God ceased "working" on the seventh day (*tē hebdomē*)—if creation is not an ongoing activity of the living God revealed in his saving acts—then God is otiose, not truly a living God who continues to "speak" and "act," but a passive retiree. And if God's "rest" is simply the land of Canaan, then God's promise is already exhausted by that material realization, and humans have nothing better for which to hope.

[6–10] The textual tension is resolved by two considerations: an appeal to still a third text, also found in Ps 94:7–11, and an appeal to the experiential fact that God continues to address some as though they had not yet entered, even as some others had already failed to enter. These appeals appear in reverse sequence. That it remains for some to enter the rest (4:6) was implicit already in the exhortation of 3:13–15, as was the fact that "those who first received the good news" (see 3:2) did not enter because of their disobedience (see 3:18–19). Now, to relieve the tension between Gen 2:2 and Ps 94:11, Hebrews follows good midrashic technique by bringing in another text from Ps 94: "he again sets aside a day [*hēmera*]." The conflict between the two meanings of "rest" and the two references for "works" is to be resolved by appeal to another meaning of "day," namely the ever-now, ever-new "today" (*sēmeron*) spoken by Ps 94:7: "just as was said earlier."

The author specifies that this word was spoken "by David" (lit. "in David," *en Dauid*), and "after such a considerable length of time." The point here is that the Holy Spirit spoke through the prophet David long after the words of Genesis and the oath of Numbers had been spoken. If God still speaks to people of a rest that is available on a day, "today," in the time of David, then two things follow: the rest spoken of must be God's own rather than the land of Canaan, and the call to enter that rest continues for those who can hear it every day, for God is the living God and his word is a living word (4:12).

In 4:8–10 the author draws out the implications of this midrashically derived and experientially based conclusion. The typological reading of the wilderness story is made even more plausible because the name of the leader who finally led the survivors into Canaan was Joshua, which in the LXX appears as *Iēsous* (see Josh 1:2; 2:6–7). Hebrews makes a point beyond the one that some of the people who came out of Egypt did not enter the land (3:16–18): the land itself is not the real promise! If the Jesus of the past had been able to provide that, then God would not have spoken about another day "after these" (*meta tauta*), namely the days spoken about in the accounts of the wilderness and conquest. This new day points beyond the "seventh day" of Gen 2:2 and even beyond the *katapausis* ("rest") associated with the ritual observance of the seventh day (i.e.,

Sabbath, Exod 34:21). Hebrews draws the bold conclusion: therefore (*ara*) there remains (*apolepeitai*; see 4:6), a "sabbath rest" (*sabbatismos*) for the people of God (*tō laō tou theou*).

Two aspects of this remarkable conclusion deserve attention. The first is the author's identification of his readers with "the people of God." Although everywhere in Scripture there is a close association between the people of Israel and the Lord God, so that expressions like "my people" and "his people" abound (see, e.g., Exod 3:10; 5:1; 6:7; Deut 7:6; 26:15; 33:29; Hos 1:9–10; Pss 27:8–9; 28:11; 47:9), the actual expression "the people of God" is extremely rare, found only in Judg 20:2, 2 Sam 14:13, and Esth 10:10. Similarly in the New Testament, the designation is assumed more often than it is made explicit (see Acts 7:34; 15:14; Rom 9:25–26; 11:1–2; 2 Cor 6:16; Rev 18:4), finding full expression only in 1 Pet 2:9–10 and in Hebrews. The author employs the term "people" (*laos*) vigorously (2:17; 5:3; 7:5, 11, 27; 8:10; 9:7, 19; 10:30; 11:25; 13:12), and twice—here and in 11:25—uses the full expression "people of God" (*laos tou theou*). What is noteworthy is that Hebrews makes no distinction between a past and present people, makes no suggestion that one people has replaced another; Moses was willing to suffer for "the people of God" in times past (11:25), and Hebrews' readers now can expect a rest offered to "the people of God."

The second aspect of the statement is the choice of the distinctive term *sabbatismos*, which is otherwise unattested in the LXX and New Testament, and its appearance in Plutarch's *On Superstition* 3 (*Mor*. 166A) also finds no parallel in other Greco-Roman and Jewish literature. The Greek term *sabbaton* is distinctively Jewish, transliterating Hebrew *šabbāt*, meaning "rest." The noun is used to designate the seventh day of the Hebrew week, as the day specially devoted to the Lord, who according to Gen 2:2, "rested on the seventh day from all his works that he had accomplished." The command to the people that they observe such a day of rest is, indeed, connected to the divine example: "The seventh day is a sabbath to the LORD your God; you shall not do any work . . . for in six days the LORD made heaven and earth, the sea, and all that is in them, but rested on the seventh day; therefore the LORD blessed the seventh day and made it holy" (Exod 20:10–11). The notion of "rest" is therefore implicit in the very term "sabbath." The verb form *sabbatizein* in the LXX is constructed from the noun, and is occasionally used to mean "keeping the Sabbath" (see Exod 16:30; Lev 23:32; 26:35; 2 Chr 36:21; 2 Macc 6:6). The unusual form *sabbatismos* is related to *sabbatizein* in much the way that *baptismos* (see Heb 6:2; 9:10) is related to *baptizein* and points to the essential element of the Sabbath, namely its being dedicated to rest. The choice of the noun here seems deliberately to evoke the "seventh day" on which *God* rested (Gen 2:2), as the next verse makes explicit. The word choice, at the very least, indicates that the promise offered to God's people now is no longer that of a material possession, but of a participation in the divine life.

The use of the connective *gar* ("for") in verse 10 indicates that this statement explains what is meant by "a sabbath rest remains for the people of God." It means that those who enter into "his rest," that is, God's rest, will enjoy a relief from their labors in exactly the same way that God does. But here we are back at our initial dilemma. How can God be at rest if God continues to speak and act in the world—the central premise of Hebrews? Hebrews does not make this clear. But perhaps we can approach an answer through a conviction that seems to lie beneath the language, an assumption shared by author and hearers. I think that conviction is simply that the goal of human existence is a share in God's own *doxa* ("glory"). It is stated explicitly in 2:10 that God is leading many sons to glory, and we saw in that place that *doxa* must mean a share in God's own way of existing, a participation in God's own presence and power. The promise remaining to the people, their heavenly calling, is literally that, heavenly, beyond the empirical, material realm. It is a life extended to them through the pioneer of their salvation, Jesus, who has gone before them to the place they approach. The "sabbath rest" is therefore to live as God lives.

Can this help us understand how those who enter God's rest can "rest from all their works, just as God did from his own works"? Perhaps it can, but only in a paradoxical fashion. The "rest" that is God's very being (God's glory) is not disturbed by God's "working" in the world because all that God does empirically is an outpouring of infinitely rich life rather than an effort to redress a lack. From the other side, human participation in God's rest comes about entirely by God's gift (the author will shortly speak of approaching the throne of grace), and is not something that can be accomplished by human striving alone. Despite the language of exhortation that encourages "entering" and even "hurrying to enter," Hebrews makes clear that this is a matter of hearing, trusting, and obeying a gift already given through Christ. Humans who accept this gift "cease from their works" not in the sense that they cease human effort, but in the sense that, like God, their works are no longer a striving to fill a need, but share in an outpouring of abundant life.

[11–13] The part of Hebrews' argument that began in 3:1 with the plea to those who shared a heavenly call, and that has centered in the call of God to the people in the wilderness and the people of God today, concludes in 4:11–13 with a final exhortation to make haste in responding to God's invitation to a rest, and a rhetorically complex encomium on the word of God. The join between the two is indicated by the conjunctions with which each begins. Verse 11 starts with *oun* ("Therefore"), picking up the implication of a "sabbath rest remains for God's people" (4:9). Verse 12 begins with *gar* ("For"), indicating that the meditation on the word of God grounds the exhortation in verse 11.

The verb *spoudazein* has the basic sense of eager engagement, whether in a physical "making haste" or "being busy" (see Xenophon, *Oeconomicos* 9.1;

Josephus, *Ant.* 8.202; Titus 3:12; 1 Thess 2:17; 2 Tim 4:9), or in a moral "being seriously committed to" (Plato, *Gorgias* 481B; Josephus, *Ant.* 17.203; Gal 2:10; Eph 4:3; 2 Tim 2:17; 2 Pet 1:10; 3:14). This is the only occurrence of the verb in Hebrews (although see the noun *spoudē* in 6:11), and it is well chosen to express both the sense of urgency demanded by the call of God "every day as long as it can be called today," and the peculiar character of the "entering" to which the readers are being summoned.

So convincingly does Hebrews evoke the imagery of a physical pilgrimage that a reader is constantly tempted to think of "entering" as a physical-spatial reality, when in fact Hebrews speaks of an internal, moral transformation of persons. When the author enjoins them then to enter "that rest" (*ekeinēn tēn katapausin*), he means the sabbath rest for God's people, which requires not a journey through space but a moral and spiritual dedication.

Such eager dedication is demanded of them if they are not to miss out on this rest as the wilderness generation missed out on the rest that was the land of promise. Once more, as in 4:1, we see the *pathos* argument invoking the emotion of fear. Also as in 4:1, the author speaks to all the readers but focuses on a concern that "any one" of them fall short: the concern here is not individual achievement but rather that "the people of God" reach its goal intact. Once more also as in 4:6, the reason why that former generation did not enter the promised rest is identified as disobedience (*apeitheia*), which for our author is equivalent to faithlessness (*apistia*; see 3:19). The image of "falling" (*piptein*) echoes the language of 3:17—their corpses fell (*piptein*) in the wilderness—and fits into the imagery of journeying (see 12:12–13).

The author's use of *hypodeigma* ("pattern/example") here is particularly interesting. Although normally used for a positive model for imitation (see Josephus, *J.W.* 6.103; Philo, *Who Is the Heir?* 256; John 13:15; Jas 5:10), it stands here as a negative warning, as in 2 Pet 2:6. When we note the ways that Hebrews uses the term later, with reference to the cult—the earthly worship is a "type and shadow of the heavenly things" (8:5), and "types of heavenly things" (9:23)—we see that Hebrews is using a sort of Platonism both vertically and horizontally (or spatially and temporally): just as the earthly, material realm is an "example" of the heavenly, so is the past an example (*paradeigma*) for the present. Here is the basis for a "typological" reading of the Old Testament, found also in Paul (see 1 Cor 10:6, 11).

It is important to read Heb 4:12–13, not as a separate discussion, but as part of the author's argument, indicated by the explanatory connective *gar* ("for"): this is the reason why we should be eager and avoid disobedience of the past generation, namely, the word of God that summons us is of such a character. The rhetorical evocation of this "word of God" (*logos tou theou*) is both powerful and ambiguous. It begins with what appears as a straightforward description of

God's word as *speech*. But in verse 13 the use of the personal pronoun *autou*, although hypothetically translatable as "its," seems to demand the translation "his," especially since the penultimate clause speaks of "his eyes."[4]

The Word of God, by this point, appears as personified, so that the subject is not God's speech but God, and perhaps God's Son, who has been the major topic of the first and second chapters of this composition. The final ambiguous element occurs in the final clause, where "the word" (*ho logos*) appears again, but this time in apparently quite a different sense than in verse 11. The best way to deal with this rich yet puzzling passage is to walk through it step by step.

By using the expression *logos tou theou*, Hebrews taps into a deep and vital biblical tradition. Although in the LXX the actual term is seldom used (see only Judg 3:20; 1 Chr 15:5), the concept of God's word as creating (Gen 1:3; Pss 32:9; 55:11; Wis 9:1) and acting in history—above all through the prophetic "word of the LORD" (*logos kyriou*; see 1 Sam 15:24; 2 Sam 12:9; 1 Kgs 12:24; 2 Kgs 9:36; 1 Chr 10:13; 2 Chr 11:2; Amos 5:1; Mic 1:1; Joel 1:1; Hag 2:20; Zech 1:7; Isa 1:10; 28:4; Jer 1:4)—is at the heart of the prophetic understanding of revelation. The connection between God's speech and God's being and identity, furthermore, is close, leading to the sort of personification we find in Ps 146:15 and Prov 8:1–9:6.

In the New Testament, *logos tou theou* is used for Scripture (Matt 15:6; John 10:35), for the preaching of Jesus (Luke 5:1; 8:21; see Heb 2:2), for Christian preaching (Acts 4:31; 6:2, 7; 8:14; 11:1; 13:5, 7; 13:44–48; 18:11; 2 Cor 2:17; 4:2; Phil 1:14; Col 1:28; 1 Thess 2:13; 2 Tim 2:9; Titus 2:5; 1 Pet 1:23; 1 John 2:14), as equivalent to the witness of Jesus (Rev 1:2, 9; 20:4), and even Jesus himself (Rev 19:13; cf. John 1:1–2). Hebrews, in turn, uses the term for the message delivered to its readers by their leaders (13:7). But Hebrews' use of *logos* by itself is even richer in association. The author has already spoken of the *logos* that was brought by angels (2:2) and of the "*logos* that was heard" by the desert generation (4:2); and after this passage, he will speak of those who have partaken of the *logos* of righteousness (5:13), of the *logos* concerning the Messiah (6:1), of the *logos* of God's oath (7:28), and of the *logos* presented at Mount Sinai (12:19). In each of these instances, *logos* refers to a speech or a reality that in some fashion takes its origin in God. Quite another sense of *logos* (found in 5:11; 13:17; and 13:22) will be discussed below in connection with 4:13.

The author begins in verse 12 by calling the word of God "living" (*zōn*), and thereby immediately introduces the ambiguity of reference: is this merely speech, or a living being, or the living being? In Scripture the Lord God of Israel declares himself as the one who preeminently lives: "As I live, says the LORD" (Num 14:21, 28; Zech 2:9; Isa 49:15; Jer 22:24). The Lord is called "the living God" (Deut 4:33; Ps 83:2; Hos 1:10; Isa 37:4, 17). This is also Hebrews'

4. See G. W. Trompf, "The Conception of God in Hebrews 4:12–13," *ST* 25 (1971): 123–32.

favorite designation (see Heb 3:12; 9:14; 10:31; 12:22). But Scripture also connects God's life to the capacity of God's words to give life: the people hear the voice of the living God (Deut 5:26), and the psalmist prays to receive "life by your word" (Ps 118:25, 50, 54). Elsewhere in the New Testament, we find "the living God" (Matt 26:63; Acts 14:15; Rom 9:26; 2 Cor 3:3; 6:16; 1 Thess 1:9; 1 Tim 3:15; 4:10) and Jesus as "the living one" (Luke 24:5), but again, there is also the characterization of the word as "living" in 1 Pet 1:23. The passage in 1 Peter contains the same ambiguity as we find here, since the verse can be read either as "you have been reborn not through a perishable seed but through an imperishable, through the living and enduring word of God," or as "through the enduring word of the living God." In short, Hebrews applies the same quality of *life* that is normally associated with God's being to God's word.

The author also describes God's word as *energēs*. This adjective does not appear in the LXX, but in ordinary Greek usage suggests both strength and effectiveness, as with a medicine (see P.Oxy. 1088.56). The term occurs in the New Testament only here and in Paul (see 1 Cor 16:9; Phlm 6), but the cognates *energein* and *energeia* appear frequently (for *energeia* see Eph 1:19; 3:7; Phil 3:21; Col 2:12; for *energein* see 1 Cor 12:6, 11; Gal 2:8; 3:5; Eph 1:11, 20; 3:2; Phil 2:13; Col 1:29; 1 Thess 2:13), most often with reference to the working of God in the community. The translation "active" (see RSV) is certainly possible, but while it captures well the sense of "energy," it fails to capture the nuance of "power."

Hebrews next speaks of God's word as "sharper than any two-edged sword" (*tomōteros hyper pasan machairan distomon*). The image of the sword as a literal instrument of God's justice is frequent in Scripture, with the LXX using either *rhomphaia* (Gen 3:24; Pss 16:13; 62:10; 77:64; Amos 4:10; 7:9; Hag 1:11) or, as here, *machaira* (Gen 15:9; Num 21:24; Isa 3:25; Jer 4:10). The "mouth of a sword" is its edge (see "mouth of the sword" in Josh 6:20; 8:24; Judg 1:25; 4:15; Sir 28:18), and a "two-edged sword" (*machaira distomos*) is literally "two-mouthed." Such imagery moves easily to the sword as a tongue (with two edges) and the tongue as a sword (see Ps 56:4). In Isa 49:2 the prophet's mission is described in this manner: "and he has placed my mouth as a two-edged sword (*machaira oxeia*)."

In Wis 18:14–16 the divine word (*logos*) is personified as a fierce warrior, "bearing the sharp sword of your inexorable decree." Philo likewise identifies instances of the sword in Scripture with the word of God (see *Cherubim* 28 and 31). This image continues in the New Testament. In Eph 6:17 Paul tells his readers to "take up the helmet of salvation and the sword of the spirit, which is the word of God" (*tēn machairan tou pneumatos ho estin rhēma theou*). Even more dramatically, Rev 1:19 describes the Son of Man in this fashion: "He has seven stars in his right hand, and coming out of his mouth is a sharp two-edged sword" (*rhomphaia distomos oxeia*; see also Rev 2:12).

As a sword, the word is "sharper" (*tomōteros*) than any two-edged sword because of its capacity to cut precisely and deeply to the interior of things. The verb *diikneomai* is relatively rare, used on one side for the way a missile could "penetrate" walls (Thucydides, *Peloponnesian War* 7.79; Josephus, *Ant.* 13.96), or the way a reputation could "reach" hearers (Plutarch, *Demosthenes* 20.4; Dio Chrysostom, *Oration* 12.35). Used with a sword, it must mean to "cut to." The sharpness of the blade is revealed by its ability to cut to "the division between soul and spirit, joints and marrow." The sequence may seem a bit odd: we might expect the progression from the more obviously material to spiritual, unless, in some fashion, the bones of the body are regarded by the author as deeper and less accessible than the soul. Philo similarly interprets Abraham's dividing the animals in Gen 15:10–11 allegorically with reference to "God's word," which is "the severer of all things material and immaterial whose natures appear to us to be knitted together and united. That severing word whetted to an edge of utmost sharpness never ceases to divide. For when it has dealt with all sensible objects down to the atoms and what we call 'indivisibles,' it passes on from them to the realm of reason's observation and proceeds to divide it into a vast and infinite number of parts" (*Who Is the Heir?* 130–31).

The noun *merismos* comes from *merizein*, "to divide," and is used only twice in the New Testament, both times in this composition and each time with a different sense. In Heb 2:4 it refers to the diverse works of the Holy Spirit; here it refers to the distinction between elements in the human person. The distinction between soul (*psychē*) and spirit (*pneuma*) surprises slightly, because otherwise Hebrews speaks of *pneuma* only with regard to supernatural realities (see 1:7, 14; 2:4; 3:7; 6:4; 9:8, 14; 10:15, 29; 12:9, 23), and uses *psychē* by itself for the inner human person (6:19; 10:38, 39; 12:3; 13:17). The usage here seems to reflect the tripartite psychology familiar in Platonism (see *Timaeus* 43A–45E, 69A–90E), and alluded to by Paul in 1 Thess 5:23. The noun *harmos* is not common, appearing mainly with reference to the joining of stones by mortar (Sir 27:2) and to the connection between bones (4 Macc 10:5). The noun *myelos* refers specifically to the inmost part of the bone or even of the self (Euripides, *Hippolytus* 255). In each pair of terms, the contrast suggests that which is interior and difficult to observe or locate precisely with any human instrument. The rhetorical point, then, is that God's word can penetrate precisely to those places where human knowledge cannot—what human can accurately distinguish between soul and spirit?

The next characterization extends the discriminating ability of God's word. It is able to "discern (*kritikos*) the thoughts (*enthymēseōn*) and conceptions (*ennoiōn*) of the heart." Once more Hebrews uses a term that is not found elsewhere in the New Testament or even the LXX, but appears frequently in secular Greek for the capacity to make mental judgments (Plato, *Statesman* 260C; Aristotle, *Parts of Animals* 432A). Here the judgments are directed to the inmost and private movements of human interiority, the heart (*kardia*; see 3:8, 10, 12,

15; 4:7; 8:10; 10:16, 22; 13:9). The difference between "thought" (*enthymēsis;* see Matt 9:4; 12:5; Acts 17:29) and "conception" (*ennoia*; see 1 Pet 4:1) is slight; both terms are used primarily for mental states rather than acts of will; for this reason the translation "intentions" (NRSV) tilts too much in the direction of the volitional. As with "soul and spirit, joints and marrow," the discernment between thought and conception is the more impressive because the difference between them is so slight and unavailable to human perception.

We have seen in the discussion of Heb 1:3 that the outlook and language of the book of Wisdom came close to our author's own. Here again, what that Hellenistic Jewish composition has to say in praise of Wisdom (*sophia*) in 7:22–24 sounds very much like Hebrews' praise of the *logos tou theou*: Wisdom is declared to have within her "a spirit (*pneuma*) most intelligent, holy, unique, manifold, subtle, agile, clear, unstained, certain . . . all-powerful, all-seeing, and pervading all spirits, through they be intelligent, pure, and very subtle. For Wisdom is mobile beyond all motion, and she penetrates and pervades all things (*diēkei de kai chōrei dia pantōn*) by reason of her purity" (NAB).

The implicit personification of the word of God becomes explicit in verse 13, where the personal pronoun *autou* ("his") applies much more naturally to God than to speech, and becomes unavoidable in the prepositional phrase *pros hon* ("to him") in the final clause. When Hebrews declares "there is no creature (*ktisis*) that is not visible (*aphanēs*) to him. All things lie naked (*gymnos*) and exposed (*tetrachēlismena*) to his eyes," it is affirming the common understanding of the relationship of God to creation: God has "maker's knowledge," that is, as the maker, God knows things from within, whereas other creatures can know them only from the outside, from surface appearances.

Even pagan authors assert that God has a knowledge hidden from humans (see Marcus Aurelius, *Meditations* 12.2; Epictetus, *Discourses* 2.14.11; Seneca, *Epistles* 83.1–2), and in Jewish literature the conviction is constant (Jer 11:20; Pss 37:9; 139:1–18; *Let. Aris.* 132–33; Philo, *On Abraham* 104; *On Dreams* 1.90; *1 En.* 9.5). That God is the "knower of the heart" (*kardiognōstēs*) is axiomatic as well for the New Testament writers (Acts 1:24; 15:8; cf. Matt 6:4, 6; 1 Cor 4:5; 8:1–3; 1 Thess 2:4; Gal 4:9; Rom 8:27; Col 3:22–4:1).

The utter visibility of all creation to the Creator (and Judge) is emphasized by the choice of words that explicate "made visible." The state of being naked (*gymnos*) is, from the start of the biblical tradition, an expression of vulnerability to the other (Gen 2:25; 3:7, 10, 11; 1 Sam 19:24; Job 1:21; 26:6; Qoh 5:14; Hos 2:3; Isa 20:2; Ezek 16:7, 22; 23:29). The passive perfect participle *tetrachēlismena* derives from the verb *trachēlizein*, which itself has a range of meanings, all involving the neck (*trachēlos*; see Luke 15:20), and all involving some sort of vulnerability—Paul speaks in Rom 16:4 of those who "put their necks at risk for my sake." Thus one can twist the neck of a sacrificial victim (like an oxen) to bring it down (Theophrastus, *Characters* 27.5; Philo, *Cherubim* 78), or one can pin an opponent in wrestling by seizing the neck (Plutarch, *Antony* 33), or, in the passive, one can be overpowered. If such nuances apply here, then the perfect passive form of the verb suggests "being laid open" and vulnerable to another's gaze and power. It is clear that the author of Hebrews has shifted from the word of God as God's speech to the word of God as God, the one before whom all beings are exposed and to whom all beings are accountable. The passage anticipates 10:31, "Falling into the hands of the living God is a fearful thing."

If the word is personified, is there any reason for thinking that the author intends the reader to regard the word christologically? The application of "word of God" to Jesus is certainly possible, as the passages cited above make clear. In my judgment, however, there is only one reason for thinking that it might be, and stronger reasons for thinking it is not. If the final phrase is taken in a purely rhetorical sense, "our discourse concerns him," one could make the case that Christ is meant, since the discourse turns immediately to Jesus as high priest, and, in fact, Hebrews uses a similar expression in 5:11 with specific reference to Christ/Melchizedek: "concerning whom we have much to say" (*peri hou polys hēmin ho logos*). But nothing else in the passage suggests that the author has Jesus in mind here, and when we understand this to be the conclusion of the argument begun in 3:1 concerning God's ever-renewed call to fidelity among the people, it is more probable that Hebrews is thinking here of the word as a dimension of God's creating and judging power.

This brings us to the final ambiguity of the section. How should we construe the final clause, *pros hon hēmin ho logos*? It is tantalizingly brief and obscure.[5] The phrase *pros hon* must have as its antecedent either *ho logos* (in 4:12) or, more likely, the double *autou*, which, as I have suggested, refers implicitly to God. The dative *hēmin* is here roughly equivalent to a possessive: "to us" or "our." The difficult term is, once more, *logos*. Does it mean the author's own discourse? This is certainly possible, since 13:22 describes this composition as a *logos tēs paraklēseōs*. The phrase could then be translated as "our discourse concerns him/it." The usage has parallels in Philo, *The Worse Attacks the Better* 13: *peri hou nyn ho logos estin* ("about whom is our speech").

Another possibility is that *logos* here means "account" in quite a different sense, namely an accounting that an underling must make to a superior (see Herodotus 8.100; Plutarch, *Sayings of Kings and Commanders: Alcibiades* 4 [*Mor.* 186E]; Josephus, *Ant.* 16.120). Thus in Luke's parable of the unjust steward, the man is told, *apodos ton logon tēs oikonomias sou*, "give an account of your household management" (Luke 16:2; see also Rom 14:12). The problem with this translation is that Hebrews actually uses that idiom in 13:17, in language different from here: he speaks of the leaders of the community keeping watch over the hearers, *hōs logon apodōsontes*, "as those rendering an

5. For discussion see E.-M. Becker, "'Gottes Wort' und 'Unser Wort': Bemerkungen zu Heb 4, 12–13," *BZ* 44 (2000): 254–62.

account"—note the similarity to Luke 16:2. If the author wanted the present phrase to mean simply "render an account," he could have said it more plainly.

It is best to recognize that the same linguistic subtlety that has run through the entire passage is present here as well, so that something of both meanings may well be intended. It is this God/Word of which the author's composition speaks. And it is this Word/God to whom humans must give a reckoning. The RSV captures the ambiguity well, with its "with whom we have to do." My translation borrows from Attridge, who manages to capture both meanings with: "to him our account is directed."

4:14–5:10 Jesus the Great High Priest

In its first mention of a high priest in 2:17, Hebrews spoke of the need to be merciful and faithful in the worship of God in order to make expiation for the sins of the people. In 3:1 Jesus is named as the high priest whom the readers confess, and the argument from 3:1–4:13 served to establish the readers as "the people" whom God continues to call. Having firmly established that connection, the author turns in 4:14 to the great theme that will dominate the composition until 10:31, the manner in which Jesus is the great high priest and the manner in which he carries out his priestly work for the people of God.

This first section begins to develop the points that were made first in 2:17–18, namely the way in which Jesus shares fully in the humanity of those he represents before God, and the way in which his faithfulness was learned through his human experience of suffering. The opening affirmation leads at once to an exhortation to draw near: what gives confidence to approach him is not only his entering heaven and sitting on God's throne, but above all his having shared in every dimension of human existence (4:14–16).

In 5:1–4 the author presents, in a remarkably compressed fashion, a description of "every high priest" (5:1), enumerating twelve qualities that in one way or another will also be ascribed to Christ over the course of the composition. First, the job description: a high priest is (1) taken from among humans, (2) in behalf of humans, (3) in matters pertaining to God, (4) to offer gifts and sacrifices, (5) for sins. Next, the personal dispositions: (6) dealing gently with ignorant and wandering, (7) sharing their weakness, (8) offering gifts for himself (9) as well as for the people. Finally, the matter of vocation: (10) not chosen by oneself, (11) chosen by God, (12) in the manner that Aaron was.

Out of this list, two elements are immediately selected for development: first, Jesus was chosen by God as high priest, demonstrated by the collation of two psalm verses (5:5–6); second, Jesus shared our weakness and learned obedience through what he suffered, demonstrated by a depiction of Jesus' human prayer (5:7–10).

After picking up this great theme and beginning its development, the author will then pause once more in 5:11–6:20 to gather his readers before returning to the grand exposition of Jesus' priestly work that dominates his composition.

4:14 Since, therefore, we have a great high priest, Jesus the Son of God, who has passed through the heavens, let us hold on to our confession. **15** For we do not have a high priest who is incapable of sympathizing with our weaknesses, but one who has been tested in every way we have, apart from sin.
16 With boldness, therefore, let us approach his gracious throne, so that we might receive mercy and might find[a] favor for timely help. **5:1** For
every high priest taken from among humans is appointed for the sake of humans in matters pertaining to God, so that he might offer gifts[b] and sacrifices for sins. **2** He is able to deal gently with those who are ignorant and
go astray because he is himself also clothed in weakness. **3** And he must, because of it,[c] make offering concerning sins[d] for himself[e] also just as for
the people. **4** Also, no one assumes the honor for himself, but when called by God, in the way[f] even Aaron was.

5 Thus even Christ did not glorify himself in becoming a high priest. Rather, it was the one who spoke to him, "You are my Son. Today I have
begotten you." **6** Just as also in another place, he says, "You are[g] a priest
forever in the order of Melchizedek." **7** For in the days of his flesh he offered, with a loud cry and with tears, prayers and supplications to the one able to save him from death. And he was heard because of his rever-
ence. **8** Even though he was a Son, he learned obedience from the things
he suffered. **9** And when he was made perfect, he became a cause of eter-
nal salvation for all those who obey him. **10** He has been designated by God as a high priest in the order of Melchizedek.

a. B omits the verb *heurōmen* ("we might find"), but it is attested by all the other witnesses.

b. The particle *te* is omitted as redundant by P[46], B, D, and a few other witnesses, but Hebrews is capable of combining *te* and *kai,* as 5:7 immediately reveals.

c. The expression *di' autēn* is awkward but is read by the original hand of P[46] and the major uncials. The reading is corrected to *dia tautēn* ("on account of this") by a majority of MSS and to *dia tauta* ("because of these things") by some others.

d. The reading *peri autou* ("concerning him") is correctly perceived as awkward by many MSS, which correct it to *peri heautou* ("concerning himself"), as demanded by the context (and found in this translation).

e. Some MSS have *hyper hamartiōn* ("in behalf of sins") rather than *peri hamartiōn* ("concerning sins"), possibly to harmonize with formulas like that in 1 Cor 15:3.

f. The comparative conjunction *kathōsper* (found in P[46], the original hand of א and D, as well as A and B), splits the difference between the *kathaper* and *kathōs* found in other witnesses. No difference in meaning is involved.

g. P[46] and a few other witnesses add *ei* ("you are"), in conformity to Ps 109:4.

[4:14–16] I have observed before how the rhetoric of Hebrews alternates between exposition and exhortation, with themes appearing and being developed in both. Depending on the division of material, this is now the third or fourth explicit exhortation (see 2:1–4; 3:1; 3:12–4:4; 4:11–13). The plea to "hold to the confession" (*kratōmen tēs homologia*) echoes 3:1 and recapitulates the recurrent concern that readers are "falling away." The exhortation to "approach" (*proserchōmetha*), in turn, echoes 4:1 and evokes the imagery of pilgrimage. Loyalty and perseverance are critical components of faith in this composition.

The earlier part of the discourse is summoned as well by the designation here of "Jesus the Son of God." Although the language about "the Son" occurred frequently in earlier chapters (1:2, 5, 8; 2:6, 10; 3:6), this is the first time that Jesus is explicitly identified as "the Son of God" (*ho huios tou theou*) within the composition. The designation is repeated in 6:6, 7:3, and 10:29. From 2:17 and 3:1, in turn, the author picks up the description of Jesus as high priest (*archiereus*), but in this instance adds the adjective "great" (*megas*). Hebrews thereby combines two distinct ways of speaking about the "chief priest" in Israel. Some texts refer to the "great priest" (*ho hiereus ho megas*; see Lev 21:10; Num 35:25, 28, 32; Hag 1:1, 12, 14; 2:3; Zech 3:1, 9; 6:11). More rarely, "high priest" (*archiereus*) appears, although before the Maccabean period the only certain occurrences are Lev 4:3 and Josh 22:13. In the books of the Maccabees, the designation "high priest" is standard (see 1 Macc 10:20; 2 Macc 3:1; 3 Macc 1:11; 4 Macc 4:13). This is the only time Hebrews brings the two terms together. In 10:21 the author will speak of Jesus as a "great priest" over the house of God, and in 13:20 will call Jesus "the great shepherd." More commonly, Hebrews calls Jesus simply "high priest" (*archiereus*; see 2:17; 3:1; 4:15; 5:10; 6:20; 7:26, 27, 28; 8:1; 9:11).

The description of Jesus as high priest is here meshed with the imagery of enthronement, which we saw earlier in 1:3, 13, and 2:9–10. Jesus is a priest who has "passed through" the heavens. This is the only time Hebrews uses the verb *dierchomai*, and it gives the reader the sense of a spatial journey that penetrates through heavenly realms into God's presence. Later, Hebrews will use a similar spatial image, when it pictures Jesus as priest "entering into the heavenly sanctuary" (6:19–20; 8:1–2; 9:11, 24; 10:20). The "ascent" to God's throne through the heavens is attested in other Jewish writings, especially those associated with Merkabah mysticism (see *1 En.* 14–19; 70–71; *2 En.* 67; *3 En.* 6–7), as well as in the New Testament (2 Cor 12:1–5; Rev 4:1–11).[1]

For Hebrews, however, this is not a mystic's temporary prayer experience that culminates in a vision of the divine presence. It is, rather, the full and ontological entry of the human Jesus, through his resurrection from the dead and his exaltation to the right hand, into the power and glory that are proper to God. It was of the Son that this composition declared, "[he] took a seat at the

1. See E. Timo, *Messiah and the Throne: Jewish Merkabah Mysticism and Early Christian Exaltation Discourse* (WUNT 2/142; Tübingen: Mohr Siebeck, 2001).

right hand of the majesty on high" (1:3), and to this Son that the Scripture was addressed, "Your throne, O God, is forever and ever" (Ps 44:7; Heb 1:8). Likewise in 8:1, Hebrews will report that "he has taken a seat at the right hand of the majesty in the heavens," and in 12:2, "he has taken a seat at the right hand of the throne of God." Hebrews may not simply be a "midrash on Psalm 110" (Buchanan, xix), but the imagery of enthronement in Ps 109:1 is fully as important to the construction of this composition as is the imagery of priesthood in Ps 109:4.

Jesus, therefore, is enthroned as Lord, and because of this, the readers also can approach the presence of God's throne "with boldness." The term *parrēsia* ("boldness, frankness, free speech") was particularly associated with philosophers of the Cynic stripe, who celebrated such an "open-air" style of life (see Dio Chrysostom, *Oration* 32.11; 77/78.45; Lucian of Samosata, *Demonax* 3.11), but it was also used for ordinary folk who exhibited courage and confidence, especially in the presence of the powerful (Philo, *Joseph* 107; *Let. Aris.* 125; see also Acts 4:13, 29, 31). In Heb 3:6 it was used in combination with "boast" to characterize the hope to which readers should cling (see also 10:35). But here, as in 10:19, *parrēsia* expresses the joyful confidence with which they can approach God because of Christ, in the sense of Eph 3:12, "in whom we have confidence (*parrēsia*) and access (*prosagōgē*)."

Their confidence is based on the character of the one who has passed through the heavens and now sits at God's right hand. They recognize him as one of themselves. Hebrews touches again on the shared humanity of Jesus and the "many sons" that he is to lead to God's presence ("glory") as their pioneer (*archēgos*; 2:10–18). In particular, the present passage echoes 2:17: "He was obliged to become like his brothers in every way, so that he might become a merciful and faithful high priest," and elaborates both of the aspects stated by 2:18: "For because he himself, being tested, experienced suffering, he is able to help those who are being tested." So here we find the phrase *kata panta homoiotēta* repeated, and applied specifically to his being tested (*pepereirasmenon*).

It is a commonplace among ancient moralists that virtue was proven or demonstrated by means of testing (see Seneca, *On Providence* 2.1–6; Epictetus, *Frag.* 286; Prov 27:21; Wis 3:5–6; *Sentences of Sextus* 7a). But it was less common for such testing to be seen as an opening to compassion for others. Here as in 5:9, however, we see that the testing of Jesus as a human being disposes him to help others. Christ's experience of being tested makes him capable (*dynamenon*) of "suffering with" the weaknesses of others. The verb here is *sympathēnai*, and while it is perfectly legitimate to translate it as "sympathize," that word in English has been watered down to a sort of vague emotional distress, whereas its use in passages like 4 Macc 13:23 suggests a stronger "common feeling" among those who are suffering. At the very least, the term as used by Hebrews should not bear the slight air of condescension carried by the English "sympathize," for it is precisely this composition's point that Christ entered fully into the human experience of suffering. The term "weaknesses" (*astheneiai*) encompasses every form of physical debility such as those caused by illness (see Xenophon, *Memorabilia* 4.2.32; Gal 4:13; 1 Tim 5:23; Luke 8:2; Jas 5:14), as well as any lack of capacity (see 1 Cor 15:43; Rom 8:26; 2 Cor 11:30), including moral judgment or behavior (Rom 6:19; 1 Cor 8:7–10).

Christ's identification with human weakness and even failure does not, however, extend to a participation in human sin: the phrase *chōris hamartias* is emphatic. That the human Jesus was free from sin is the consistent teaching of the New Testament (see 2 Cor 5:21; John 7:18; 8:46; 1 John 3:5–7; 1 Pet 1:19; 2:22; 3:18), so this affirmation by the author of Hebrews is not, in itself, surprising. But since the work of Christ in this composition is so much connected to his making "purification for sins" of others (1:3; 2:17; 5:1, 3; 7:27; 8:12; 9:26, 28; 10:2, 3, 4, 11, 12, 17, 18, 26; 13:11), and since his capacity to do this for others rests, as the following section will insist, on his being made perfect through the things that he suffered (5:9), it is worth asking what Hebrews understands by "sin" (*hamartia*). It cannot mean simply human weaknesses and temptations, for the author has already identified Christ completely with those human experiences (4:15).

Sin is, rather, a matter of a deliberate disobedience of God's will. We remember that the wilderness generation had "sin" connected to them (3:13, 17) as well as "disobedience" (3:8) and "faithlessness" (3:12, 19). Sin, therefore, is a matter of "hearing" but not responding (3:16). Those who fell in the desert did so because their hearing did not combine with faith (4:2). In contrast, Hebrews will say that Christ, from the moment he entered the world, declared, "Behold, I have come to do your will" (10:9). In 5:8 we will see that he learned obedience from the things he suffered, and in 12:2 he is characterized as the "pioneer and perfecter of faith." On one side, then, we find sin, disobedience, and faithlessness—such as characterized the wilderness generation. On the other side, we find obedience and faith in Jesus. He is, therefore, "without sin": he is completely attuned to the hearing and doing of God's will in his human life.

Because Christ shares all the weaknesses and temptations of humans yet because he has bent his will in obedience toward God, he "was made perfect" (5:9), and it is "through this will" that others are able to be sanctified, that is, also move into the realm of God's own presence and power (10:10). Jesus' obedience was not for his own sake, but so that others might be saved by their obedience to him, by listening and responding to God in the manner that he has (5:9). Those who approach his glorious throne with boldness, therefore, do so because they recognize in him a king utterly concerned for them. The very phrase *thronos tēs charitos* ("gracious throne") can also be rendered "throne of grace"—he is a king who is the source of favor and gift, a king who is the "cause of eternal salvation" (5:9).

As people filled with weaknesses and temptations as well as sins, they appropriately approach the divine throne as petitioners, seeking "mercy" (*eleos*; see Gen 24:12; Pss 6:4; 12:5; 24:6; 30:16) and "favor" (*charis*; see Gen 30:27; 32:5; Exod 3:21; 33:12; 1 Sam 1:18), and as those approaching one like themselves now made Lord, they expect such a response, rather than rejection and punishment. The phrase *eis eukairon boētheian* signifies purpose or result: the mercy and favor leads to or is expressed by "timely help." The substantive *boētheia* picks up from 2:18, which stated that, because Christ also was tested, he was "able to help those who are being tested." The translation of the adjective *eukairos* as "timely" is more accurate than the RSV's "in time of need" (cf. Mark 6:21 and the adverb form *eukairōs* in Mark 14:11 and 2 Tim 4:2), but the RSV certainly gets at the meaning: help is timely when we need it (see Ps 103:27)!

This short exhortation breathes an air of encouragement and confidence. The triumph of Christ over sin and death is a triumph for each one of us as well, and his sharing in the power of God means that humans have a genuine hope of mercy and favor when they approach God's throne, for we have as our advocate one who is like us in every respect and who knows us from the inside.

[5:1–4] After that word of exhortation, the author again returns to exposition, this time developing the theme of the high priest from 4:14. He elaborates first more dimensions of the high priesthood as found in Scripture (5:1–4), and then applies two of them specifically to Jesus (5:5–9). The conjunction *gar* ("for") leads the reader to expect that 5:1 will explicate what preceded it, and it does, by showing that Christ met the criteria for priesthood established by Torah.

Hebrews' selection of those criteria, to be sure, is already determined by the author's understanding of Jesus as priest. The statement that every high priest represents the people *ta pros ton theon* ("in matters pertaining to God"), for example, echoes the words of Moses' father-in-law in Exod 18:19; but in that passage Moses and those appointed by him are to represent the people by teaching them and making judgments (18:19–23), rather than offering sacrifices. Perhaps it would be more accurate to say that Hebrews offers an anthropological definition of all priesthood, or at least what our author considers to be its essence.[2]

First, then, every high priest is drawn from humans for the sake of humans. The priest, in this reading, cannot fully act in behalf of humans unless he is also drawn from among them. Second, the priest represents humans in "matters pertaining to God" (*ta pros ton theon*; see 2:17). Third, this representative function is one to which a human being is "appointed" (*kathistatai*). The verb *kathistanai* is regularly used for the designation of leaders in Scripture (see Exod 18:21; Num 3:10; 31:48; Deut 1:13; 2 Sam 3:39; 15:4; Pss 2:6; 9:20; 2 Kgs 10:3; Luke

2. For the priesthood in general, see A. Cody, *A History of Old Testament Priesthood* (AnBib 35; Rome: Pontifical Biblical Institute Press, 1969); and for Hebrews' knowledge of the priesthood, see W. Horbury, "The Aaronic Priesthood in the Epistle to the Hebrews," *JSNT* 19 (1983): 43–71.

12:42; Titus 1:5; Heb 7:28). The passive voice suggests appointment by another, which is made explicit by 5:4.

Fourth, every high priest is appointed to offer "gifts and sacrifices for sins" (*dōra te kai thysias hyper hamartiōn*). The verb translated as "offering" is *prospherein* ("to bring forward/present"), and focuses not on the preparation of the sacrifice (e.g., the killing of the animal) but on its transference from the realm of the profane to the sacred. Scripture uses the term frequently with both *dōra* and *thysia* (see Lev 1:2; 2:1, 8; 4:23; 7:19; 21:6; Num 9:7; 15:4), and Hebrews uses the verb consistently (e.g., 5:7; 7:27; 8:3; 9:7; 10:1), without intending thereby any specific distinction among types of offering. It is certainly the case that many sacrifices in Israel's cult were not "for sins," but were expressions of thanksgiving and dedication (Lev 2:1–3:7; 23:9–21). Many other sacrifices were performed for sins, whether intended (4:1–5:19) or unintended (6:1–7). The high priest had the specific duty of offering sacrifice for the sins of all the people on Yom Kippur, the Day of Atonement (16:1–34). And it is in such "purification from sins" (Heb 1:3) that Hebrews finds the essence of the priestly role. This opening set of characteristics, then, has focused on the position and the role of the high priest.

In 5:2 Hebrews returns to the capacity of the human priest to identify with those whom he represents, which itself has two dimensions. Since he himself is "clothed in weaknesss"—the verb *perikeitai* means literally "to be clothed" and metaphorically "to be fully covered with" (see Herodotus 1.171; Josephus, *Life* 334; 4 Macc 12:2; Acts 28:20)—the high priest is able to "deal gently" with those who are "ignorant and go astray." The attitude expressed by the verb *metriopathein* (not found in the LXX but familiar from Greek moralists like Plutarch, *On Consolation to Apollonius* 3 [*Mor*. 102d]) is not precisely the same as *sympathenai* in 4:15. It has the sense rather of acting in a measured or moderate manner toward another, instead of an active participation in the experience of another (see Philo, *Abraham* 257; Josephus, *Ant.* 12.128).

The high priest is not in a position to be high-handed or haughty toward those with whom he shares faults. The emphasis here, we note, is on those who sin out of ignorance (*agnoousin*) or error (*planōmenoi*)—as though these were committed "unwittingly" (see Lev 4:1–35). The terms are gentler than those used to characterize the "faithlessness," "apostasy," and "hardening of heart" that the author ascribed to the wilderness generation (Heb 3:12–13). The high priest can deal moderately with those who sin in this way, for he does himself as well.

Another dimension of the high priest's close identification with the weaknesses of others is his need to offer sacrifices not only for them but for himself as well. Hebrews repeats this requirement in 7:17 and 9:7, building on the clear statement of Scripture: in Lev 9:9 Moses tells Aaron, "Draw near to the altar and offer your sin offering, and make atonement for yourself and for the people," and in Lev 16:6 we find that "Aaron shall offer the bull as a sin offering for himself, and shall make atonement for himself and for his house."

Finally, Hebrews makes explicit that no one assumes for oneself "the honor" of the high priesthood, but must be called by God. The allusion to Aaron recalls Exod 28:11, where God orders Moses, "Then bring to you Aaron your brother, and his sons with him, from among the priests of Israel, to serve me as priests." The high priesthood, then, is not simply a matter of lineage, of being born into a certain tribe, but requires a specific call from God. In this respect it is an elevation in status that brings "honor" (*timē*). Josephus calls it "the highest dignity" (*J.W.* 4.149; see also 4.164; Philo, *Special Laws* 1.42; *Life of Moses* 2.225). In antiquity such a status elevation could come only from above.[3]

[5–10] Against the backdrop of these generalizations about "all" high priests, Hebrews takes up two of the qualifications of Jesus: his calling by God, and his intense identification with the weaknesses of those he represents. The nature of his priestly activity will then be developed in chapters 7–10.

The *houtōs* ("Thus") that begins verse 5 clearly responds to the statement that the high priest must be called by God as even Aaron was. The *kai* might be read as "also," but I take it as emphatic: even the Messiah did not glorify himself. The verb for glorification (*doxazein*) occurs for the only time in Hebrews, but in combination with *timē* in the previous verse, distinctly echoes the citation from Ps 8:6 in Heb 2:7 and 9: in his exaltation, Jesus was crowned with glory and honor. With regard to Jesus as exalted Lord, then, the language of glory and honor necessarily has two levels of meaning: that of human status elevation, and that of entering into the divine presence. The main point here, to be sure, is that neither was his own doing, but came from the authority of God, "the one who spoke to him" in the words of the Psalms.

With the phrase "the one who spoke to him," the author reminds his hearers of the sequence of scriptural passages that opened his sermon: the words spoken there to "the anointed" apply above all to Jesus *ho Christos*, whom believers confess as Lord (3:6, 14). The first text now cited, from Ps 2:7, is also the first quoted in that opening sequence, and triggers the hearers' memory of the words of God that certified Jesus as the very Son who had been enthroned at God's right hand (Heb 1:3–4).

The second citation is something of a surprise. Rather than quoting from Ps 109:1 as in the opening sequence—"sit at my right hand until I make your enemies a footstool for your feet"—the author quotes the fourth verse of the same psalm: "You are a priest forever in the order of Melchizedek," and thus initiates the comparison that will dominate this discourse through chapter 7. The phrase *kata taxin* ("according to the order") can mean either that Jesus is in a "fixed succession or order" started by Melchizedek (see Epictetus, *Discourses*

3. See deSilva, *Perseverance in Gratitude*, 186–88.

3.2.2; *T. Naph.* 2.8) or that he is "of the same kind of priest" as Melchizedek (see *Let. Aris.* 69; Ignatius, *Magnesians* 3.1).

The use of Ps 109:4 is unique to Hebrews in the New Testament, and probably derives from the author's own close reading of the entire psalm in light of Jesus' death and resurrection. For the moment, the aspect of the verse that is important is God's declaration to the one enthroned as king: "You are a priest forever." Since the subject addressed in Ps 109:1 is the same as the subject addressed in 109:4, we can conclude that, just as Jesus is king, so is he also priest. Other aspects of this dramatic pronouncement will be developed by the subsequent argument. For now, the author has established that Jesus did not "glorify himself" but was called to be a priest by God.

The subject of verse 5 is *ho Christos* ("the messiah"), and the relative clause beginning with *hos* ("who") in verse 7 refers back to Christ. In my translation I simply start with a fresh sentence, but in the Greek this long relative clause is built on two main verbs, to each of which are connected participles. The first main verb is "he learned" (*emathen*). To it are connected the participles *prosenenkas* ("he offered"), *eisakoustheis* ("he was heard"), and *ōn* ("being"). The second main verb is "he became" (*egeneto*), and to it are connected the participles *teleiōtheis* ("made perfect") and *prosagoreutheis* ("designated"). This long and complex clause sketches in brief much of Hebrews' understanding of Jesus' faithful existence and therefore of his priestly identity.

Within its syntactical complexity, the clause presents a clear reversal. "In the days of his flesh" Jesus cried out to the one *who could save him.* Now, "being made perfect," he is the *cause of salvation* to those who obey him. The reversal hinges on the short clause that occupies all of verse 8: "Even though he was a son, he learned obedience from the things he suffered."

Is Hebrews here alluding to the Gospel accounts of Jesus' prayer in the garden preceding his arrest and death? The phrase "in the days of his flesh" unequivocally points to Jesus' human condition (see esp. 2:14), but does not specify an occasion. Since Jesus is said to pray with "a loud cry and with tears," and since his prayer is to the one who is "able to save him from death," it would be natural to connect this scene to the Synoptic accounts of the passion (Matt 26:36–46; Mark 14:32–42; Luke 22:39–46). However, none of these versions—nor the equivalent account in John 12:27–33—mentions "a loud cry and tears," although they note Jesus' emotional distress in other terms (see Matt 26:38; Mark 14:33–34; John 12:27). The phrase "able to save him from death," on the other hand, echoes the prayer reported by Mark: "All things are possible to you. Take this cup away from me" (Mark 14:36). There is no reason to think that Hebrews is dependent on any canonical account, but good reason to conclude that Hebrews here makes use of an independent tradition concerning Jesus' disposition in the face of death.

Most striking in Hebrews' description is the use of the same verb (*prospherein*, "offering") that was used in 5:3 and throughout the rest of the composition for the offering by the priest of gifts and sacrifices. Here prayers (*deēseis*) and supplications (*hiketērias*) are "offered" by the priest Jesus. Both terms are used only here in Hebrews. We can, however, compare the "sacrifice of praise to God, one that is the fruit of lips confessing his name" (13:15), that Christians offer to God "through him" (i.e., Christ). The priesthood of Jesus begins with the offering of his will to God (10:9). The prayers and supplications are not explicitly said to be "that he might not die," but the phrase "to the one able to save him from death" would seem to imply that this was the substance of Jesus' prayer, as it was in the Gospel accounts. There Jesus added, "but your will be done, not mine." The passion account that follows in the Gospels makes clear that Jesus' prayer for God's will to be done was heard, rather than his prayer for the cup of suffering to be taken away from him.

The interpretation of the phrase *kai eisakoustheis apo tēs eulabeias* in 5:7 is therefore difficult. "He was heard" is easy enough, and because it is in the passive voice, we can add, "he was heard by God." But in what respect was he heard, and why?[4] The difficult phrase is *apo tēs eulabeias*. There are two basic approaches (see Koester, 289–90). The first is to take *eulabeia* in the sense of literal fear (see Sir. 41:3, "Do not fear [*eulabou*] the judgment of death"; Epictetus, *Discourses* 2.1.14), and to understand "was heard" in the sense of "heard and delivered from fear." Thus Jesus would be a moral hero who overcame his "fear of death" that holds humans captive (see Heb 2:15). The second approach is to take *eulabeia* in its more common meaning of "piety" or "reverence" (see Philo, *Cherubim* 29; *Who Is the Heir?* 22; Luke 2:5; Acts 2:5; 22:12), which is the way Hebrews uses it elsewhere in the composition (Heb 11:7; 12:28). In this reading, the preposition *apo* is read as causal ("because of"), as in Luke 19:3; 24:41. Now Jesus is not liberated *from* a fear—of death—but is heard *because* of a fear—his piety, expressed through his prayers and supplications.

The second understanding seems more reasonable, and my translation adopts it. There is, however, a final difficulty. In what sense was Jesus "heard" (*eisakoustheis*) by God? The verb *eisakouein* is stronger than "to hear" in the sense of something registering aurally. It bears the nuance of "obey" when used of humans with respect to God (see Deut 1:43; 9:23; Sir 3:6; 39:13). If used of God with respect to humans, then, it suggests a responsive hearing, whether to the prayer being spoken (Sir 34:26; Acts 10:31) or, as here, to the person who is praying (Matt 6:7). God therefore responds positively to Jesus in prayer "because of his reverence." But how is that positive response manifested? It is not by Jesus' escaping death, or the fear of death, but by his transcending death through his resurrection and exaltation to God's right hand (1:1–4; 2:9; 4:14). Here, as every-

4. For discussion of the difficulties, see H. W. Attridge, "'Heard Because of His Reverence' (Heb 5:7)," *JBL* 98 (1979): 90–93; and N. R. Lightfoot, "The Saving of the Savior: Hebrews 5:7ff.," *ResQ* 16 (1973): 166–73.

where in Hebrews, "saving" (*sōzein*) or "salvation" (*sōtēria*) signifies more than the continuation of temporal existence or human success; it signifies sharing in God's own life and glory (1:14; 2:3, 10; 6:9; 7:25; 9:28; 11:7).

Verse 8 is a key not only to this passage but as well to the understanding of Christology and discipleship in Hebrews. It begins with a concessive phrase, "Even though he was a Son" (*kaiper ōn huios*). The conjunction *kaiper* as usual sets up a contrast (cf. Phil 3:4; 2 Pet 1:12; and Heb 7:5; 12:17) between one situation, that of being a Son, and another, learning from what is suffered. But why is it set up as a contrast? If we read the statement in light of the entire letter, especially 12:4–11, we might be tempted to change it to "*because* he was a Son" (if the Greek would allow such a change, which it does not).

But the point of rhetoric is that it is read (or heard) in sequence. Hearers do not yet have the author's subsequent argument in 12:4–11, but only what has been spoken to them up to this point. We must therefore understand the contrast in terms of what the author of Hebrews has *already* said about "the Son." When we scan those earlier statements, we realize that, apart from 2:10—which anticipates the present passage by speaking of the perfection of the Son through suffering—every other statement concerning the Son focuses on his exalted status (see 1:2, 5 [bis], 8; 3:6; 4:14; 5:5). The reader who has heard of the Son that he made the universe can now hear of his learning through suffering "even though he was a Son" as an appropriate contrast.

The next phrase is a rhetorical flourish on a commonplace of Greek moral discourse, based on the wordplay *mathein pathein* ("to learn is to suffer," or "to suffer is to learn"). Hebrews says, "he learned (*emathen*) from the things he suffered (*epathen*)." The link between suffering/experience and learning is made as early as the Greek tragedians (Aeschylus, *Agamemnon* 177; Sophocles, *Trachiniae* 143), and is widely attested (see Herodotus 1.207; Aesop, *Fables* 134.1–3; 223.2–3; Philo, *Flight and Finding* 138; *Dreams* 2.107; *Special Laws* 4.29; *Who Is the Heir?* 73; *Life of Moses* 2.55, 280). It is a commonplace because discerning people can see that a certain kind of real learning is always experiential, and that the process of learning itself involves a certain kind of suffering (see excursus 3 below). Hebrews thus finds another way of asserting the close and sympathetic relationship of the Son to other humans: he learns from his experience in the way that they do (2:17; 4:15; 5:2). But Hebrews tropes this commonplace by providing a specific attitude or disposition that Jesus learned from the things he experienced/suffered, namely obedience (*hypakoē*). The full significance of this term cannot be gained from observing the frequency of its use in the composition. The noun occurs only here, and the verb *hypakouein* ("to obey") only in the next verse and in 11:8. It is only when we see that Jesus' obedience is an aspect of his faith that we begin to appreciate Hebrews' point.

When discussing the wilderness generation in 3:7–19, we saw that they had applied to them a set of roughly equivalent terms: they rebelled and tested (3:8), they had hard hearts (3:8) and did not understand God's ways (3:10). Hebrews summarized these as faithlessness (*apistia*) and sin (*hamartia*; see 3:12–13, 17, 19) and disobedience (*apeitheia*, 3:19). Rebellion, disobedience, sin, and faithlessness all go together. In contrast, Hebrews has applied a different set of terms to Christ. He is "apart from sin" (4:15), and "faithful" (2:17; 3:2, 6). It is entirely legitimate, therefore, for us to understand "obedience" in 5:8 in light of these sets of opposing characteristics, and to identify the obedience that Christ learned as a learning that is also integral to faith. In short, Hebrews would entirely agree with Paul's phrase, "the obedience that is faith" (*hypakoēn pisteōs*) in Rom 1:5 and 16:26. I develop this aspect of the verse in excursus 3 below.

Verse 9 is virtually an elaboration of 2:10, "It was indeed fitting that the one . . . in leading many sons to glory, should bring the pioneer of their salvation to perfection through suffering." Here we find the aorist participle *teleiōtheis* (lit. "having been made perfect"). If we read this in light of 2:10, we shall not conclude too hastily that Jesus' perfection resulted simply from his exaltation to God's right hand (*pace* Koester, 290), but was rather a result precisely of what he learned through his suffering. If we ask "what sufferings/experiences," the first thing we think of is Christ's passion. But the element of "learning" in this verse suggests that Hebrews has more in mind than Christ's last moments, more even than his experience of external affliction and rejection during his ministry. The author points to the sort of suffering that is consequent upon the way Jesus lived as a human, a corollary of the very faithfulness that was announced from the start, "Behold, I am here to do your will" (10:9).

The relationship of the participle *teleiōtheis* to the verb *egeneto* can be understood in several ways: "by being made perfect he became," or "after being made perfect he became," or "because he was made perfect he became": such is the flexibility of the Greek circumstantial participle. In any reading, the time of the participle precedes that of Jesus' becoming "cause of salvation" (*aitios sōtērias*) to others. The language here again picks up from 2:10, reminding us that the term *archēgos* in the earlier passage has as much the sense of "founder" and "cause" as it does "pioneer" and "leader." Of particular significance is that Christ becomes the cause of "eternal" (*aiōniou*) salvation. This is Hebrews' first use of the term "eternal" (see also 6:2; 9:12, 14, 15; 13:20). As with Paul (Rom 2:7; 5:21; 2 Cor 4:17; 5:1; Gal 6:8), Peter (1 Pet 5:10; 2 Pet 1:11), and John (John 3:15, 16; 5:24; 17:2; 1 John 1:2), the notion of "eternal" does not mean simply "everlasting," but more, a participation in the life that is God's own. Salvation, therefore, is more than possession of the land and success, it is "heavenly" (3:1; 4:14), transtemporal because also transmaterial.

This salvation is available to those who "obey him." The turn is striking, because we might have expected—in view of Christ's depiction as "pioneer of faith"—that Christ would be the source of salvation to those "who obeyed as he did" or "have the faith of Christ." Hebrews does strike this note, as we shall see in our discussion of chapters 10–12, but it is important to note that in this passage, Christ's role as *aitios* of eternal salvation places him as the one who shares God's life and power. For Hebrews, Christ is certainly more than a human hero; he is Son of God. Christians therefore do more than imitate his example—they obey him. They approach him as Lord, seated at the right hand of the throne of majesty.

Jesus has been designated by God as high priest (5:10). We can note three aspects of this brief clause, which concludes the very long sentence beginning in verse 5. First, the verb *prosagoreuein* has the sense of being designated or named by another, therefore "recognized" as something (Xenophon, *Memorabilia* 3.2.1; Wis 14:22; 2 Macc 1:36; Philo, *Abraham* 121). Second, Hebrews specifies that Christ is so designated, not by humans, but *hypo tou theou* ("by God"), thus making clear that Christ fulfills the criterion that a high priest be called by God (Heb 5:4). Finally, the author attaches the title "high priest" (*archiereus*) here to Melchizedek, even though the citation from Ps 109:4 merely designates "the Lord" as "a priest (*hiereus*) forever according to the order of Melchizedek."

Excursus 3: Suffering and the Obedience of Faith

A close reading of 5:5–10, and especially 5:8, has suggested that for Hebrews the suffering endured by Jesus was essential to his education as a Son. Because this theme is critical to the Christology of this composition as well as its understanding of discipleship (see esp. 12:4–11), it is important to examine this provocative pronouncement more closely.

If Hebrews thinks of Jesus as "learning from the things he suffered," then it must have more in mind than the physical sufferings of Jesus' passion, even though the depiction of him pleading with the one "who could save him from death" evokes the Gospel accounts of Jesus' prayer before his arrest. It would be difficult to think how Jesus "learned" from the brutal moments before his death, unless we understood "learned obedience" in the sense of "learned what obedience really involved," or "learned the consequence of obedience." In this case, however, why speak of "learning" at all? Why not simply state, with Paul, that Jesus was "obedient, even unto death" (Phil 2:8)? It may well be, then, that the author of Hebrews is thinking of a learning that took place over the course of Jesus' human existence, and a learning that involved the very process of obedient faith. To explore this possibility, we must begin with careful attention to the phenomenon of suffering and a richer appreciation of the human response of faith.

Suffering is a matter of pain, and pain is the sign of a sentient system in disequilibrium. This fairly bloodless definition enables us to explore suffering in its several dimensions. When the subject of pain arises, we tend to think first of physical pain, and we understand that pain requires a sentient creature. A stone may "suffer blows" from a stick, but the stone—so far as we know—does not experience pain, and therefore does not "suffer from blows." We also tend to think of pain in negative terms: who wants to experience pain? Thus our instinct is to think first in terms of physical injury or disease or a wound inflicted by another.

But physical pain can also result from another form of systemic disequilibrium, such as is caused by growth or childbirth. The adolescent who grows five inches in a summer hurts all over. The athlete who grows muscles through training hurts. Mothers endure the great pain of labor in order to give life. In such cases the pain is no less real (or severe) yet it has a positive meaning. Pain is the corollary of an increase in life rather than the signal of a threat to life. Even physical suffering, then, can be positive as well as negative, at least in its results.

Precisely this realization underlies the Greek proverb *mathein pathein*. What applies in the physical realm applies also in matters of spirit (remember that ancient education closely linked physical, mental, and moral training). Thus, intellectually, the learning of new ideas is a form of growth: our minds expand to include new realities of which we had not previously been aware. The growth is good. But it is also painful, since it implies the disruption and rearrangement—and often the abandonment—of our previous mental furnishings. To enter into new mental territory means at last a partial death to old mental territory. Stretching the mind to encompass new truth means suffering the pain of mental disequilibrium. The same applies also to emotional "learning through experience." Grief at the death of a loved one is terribly painful, and not something we would choose. Yet we understand that the avoidance of affection out of the fear of loss means an emotional truncation, and that the willingness to "learn through emotional suffering" means a deepening of our human capacity to feel and to feel with others that nothing else can teach. Can we not, on analogy with these forms of learning through suffering, suppose that the same sort of pain is integral to spiritual growth in the proper sense, that is, in the learning of God's will as it pulls us beyond our present circumscribed grasp of reality?

To answer this question, we must look more closely at Hebrews' understanding of the human response to God called faith. Faith in Hebrews means more than belief, although it certainly demands belief as its premise: "the one approaching God must believe that he exists and that he is the rewarder of those who seek him" (11:6). Faith in Hebrews also means more than hope concerning the future, although hope is an essential dimension of faith: "Faith is the substance of things hoped for, a proof of things not seen" (11:1). And faith in Hebrews means more than perseverance, although that aspect of faith looms large in this composition: "we do not draw back—to our destruction. Rather, we have faith—to the securing of our life" (10:39). Faith in Hebrews is also a response to God that involves obedience.

The contrast between the people of Israel in the desert and Jesus is revealing in this respect. The wilderness generation that failed to meet its promised goal of the rest committed sin (3:13), was disobedient (3:18), and was faithless (3:12, 19). In contrast, Jesus is characterized as being "apart from sin" (4:15) and "faithful" (2:17; 3:2, 6), but these qualities are spelled out in terms of the obedience through which he was perfected (5:9). It remains, then, to ask how obedience is an essential dimension of faith.

With regard to Jesus, we see in chapter 10 that the Messiah declared on his entrance into the world, "Behold, I am here to do your will!" (10:9). But the will to do God's will requires the overcoming of the internal resistance posed by one's own will, a resistance that had to have been experienced even by the Messiah, who shared all the weaknesses of his brothers and sisters in the flesh (2:14–18; 4:15–16). If he was truly like us in every respect "apart from sin," we can conclude that he always did God's will—and in this he was different from us; but in order to do God's will, he had to overcome his own desires—and in this he was like us. Paradigmatically, when God called on him to die, Jesus had to overcome the most powerful of all human instincts, toward self-preservation, in order to hear that will and do it. We see in contrast that the sin and faithlessness of the wilderness generation consisted in their "testing" of God and "rebellion" against his "voice."

Faith, then, is a deeply responsive hearing of God's voice (will) as it comes to humans in the circumstances of their worldly existence. It is saying yes to a "call" (3:1) that leads them beyond their present world into a larger one defined not by their desire but by God's creative and commanding word. Such faith is "obedience" because it is a hearing that overcomes the human reluctance to move into a larger and more frightening world, and the human preference to live within the comfort zone of the accustomed. It is important to note that for Christ as for other humans, such obedient faith cannot be accomplished once for all.

Such obedient faith, therefore, is itself a form of suffering. It is impossible to answer the call of *any* "other" and enter into the other's project—even the call of spouse, student, child—without experiencing the stress of letting go of the absoluteness of what, until then, had been our own quite legitimate project. But if the call that summons us is God's call, if the space into which we are asked to step is infinitely larger than the one we presently inhabit, then the pain of responding is commensurate with the stretching involved. But no human can step all at once into God's will, for two reasons: the first is that God's call is new every day; the second is that humans can dispose of their freedom only moment by moment. The suffering that is integral to the obedience of faith, therefore, is chronic rather than acute, a constant learning so long as one keeps responding.

Even though Jesus as "Son" came into the world to do God's will, the voice of God was new every day for him also. Like us, Jesus had to respond moment by moment, and therefore "learn obedience" precisely in and through the stress and pain generated by constantly allowing his present understanding of God and of God's will to be challenged and relativized by the voice of God that he heard within the circumstances of his everyday life. Hebrews says that Jesus was "perfected" by this process of experiential learning. In what respect was he perfected, made mature, complete? Hebrews must mean that Jesus grew into his full identity as God's Son. Although he came into the world as Son, he could only "finish" that project moment by moment, in every response of obedient hearing, and could be "perfected" completely only through the final yes to God in the suffering that is death.

Here is the distinctive way in which the author of Hebrews brings together his remarkably high Christology (Jesus is the "preexistent" Son of God) and remarkable emphasis on Jesus' humanity (Jesus is like us in every respect, apart from sin). He understands Jesus precisely as growing into his stature as Son through the process of obedient faith, through a process of creative suffering. As human, Jesus progressively entered into the immensity of God's presence, even within himself, as he responded to the call of God in his temporal existence. The moment of death, which to outward appearance is the ultimate closure to human possibility, was therefore in the case of Jesus the ultimate opening to the presence of God, an exaltation to the right hand of the throne of glory. Since for Hebrews Jesus is the pioneer as well as the perfecter of such obedient faith (12:2), he has shown the path toward maturity also for all those "sons being led to glory" (2:14).[5]

5:11–6:12 Exhortation to Progress and Perseverance

Having announced the theme of the priesthood of Jesus in 2:17–18 and begun its development in 4:14–5:10, the author once more interrupts his exposition to exhort his hearers (cf. 2:1–4; 3:1, 12–14; 4:1, 11, 14–16) in 5:11–6:12, before picking up the thread of exposition once more in 6:13 and pursuing his argument without hortatory interruption until 10:19. Since this is the last exhortation before such a long stretch of argument, it is appropriately lengthy. It is also unusually severe.

The exhortation falls into four parts. The author begins by rebuking his readers for their lethargy and immaturity (5:11–14), and then states his intention to carry them toward maturity (6:1–3). He warns his readers about the dire consequences of apostasy and neglect (6:4–8), and encourages them to zeal rather than laziness (6:9–12). The careful balancing of elements throughout is suggested by the presence of the same adjective (*nōthros*, "lazy, lethargic") in the first and last lines of the passage and points to a chiastic arrangement. Although the section as a whole clearly forms a rhetorical unity, I divide it in the middle for the sake of more focused discussion of its parts.

The section 5:11–6:3, then, unfolds in two balanced stages that are also arranged chiastically: *a.* they are lazy and need to be taught the basics (*tēs archēs tōn logiōn tou theou*); *b.* they should be mature (*teleiōn*); *b′*. the author will move them toward maturity (*epi tēn teleiotēta*), *a′*. which requires getting past the basics (*tēs archēs tou Christou logon*). A further rhetorical feature is the way that the phrase *peri hou polys hēmin ho logos* in 5:11 ("our discourse concerning him is lengthy") echoes the phrase *pros hon hēmin ho logos* in 4:13 ("to him is our account directed"). The section 6:4–12 also has two parts: in the first (6:4–8), the author issues a dire warning about falling away, but then shifts to words of gentle encouragement and reassurance (6:9–12).

> **5:11** Our discourse[a] concerning him is lengthy and it is difficult to express, because you have become reluctant listeners. **12** For even though by this time[b] you ought to be teachers, you again need someone to teach you[c] the

5. For further development of this perspective, see L. T. Johnson, *Faith's Freedom: A Classic Spirituality for Contemporary Christians* (Minneapolis: Fortress Press, 1990).

elementary principles of God's oracles, and you have become in need of
milk rather than[d] solid food. **13** Now[e] everyone who drinks milk is inex-
perienced in reasoning concerning righteousness. He is a child.[f] **14** But
solid food is for mature people, those who on account of habit have their
moral faculties trained to distinguish between a good thing and a bad
thing.[g] **6:1** Let us therefore move on toward maturity, leaving behind the
basic instruction about the Messiah, not laying again the foundation of
repentance from dead works and faith toward God, **2** of a teaching[h] about
ablutions and imposition of hands, of resurrection of the dead and of eter-
nal judgment. **3** And we will do this if God allows.[i]

4 For it is not possible to renew again to repentance those who have
once been enlightened, who have tasted the heavenly gift and become
partakers of the Holy Spirit, **5** and who have tasted the noble word of God
and the powers of the coming age, **6** and who have fallen away, thereby
in their own regard crucifying and mocking the Son of God. **7** For the land
that drinks the rain frequently falling on it and brings forth a suitable plant
for those on whose account it was cultivated shares in a blessing from
God. **8** But the land that produces thorns and thistles is useless and close
to being cursed. Its end is the fire.

9 Even though we are speaking in this way, beloved,[j] we are confident
concerning you of the better things belonging to salvation. **10** For God is
not so unrighteous as to forget your labor and your love[k] for his name that[l]
you have demonstrated, as you provided service and continue to provide
service to the saints. **11** But we desire that each one of you demonstrate
the same enthusiasm all the way to the end for the completion of your
hope,[m] **12** so that you not become sluggards, but rather become imitators
of those who through faith and long-suffering inherit the promises.

a. P^{46} and the original hand of D omit the definite article before *logos* ("discourse").

b. Literally "on account of the time" (*dia ton chronon*), indicating that the hearers had been members of the community for at least long enough to create such an expectation.

c. Some MSS have the passive *didaskesthai* ("to be taught") rather than the active *didaskein* found in the best witnesses. The pronoun *tina* is accented by some witnesses as interrogative and by others as indefinite. The phrase is probably best understood as an indefinite pronoun serving as the subject of the infinitival construction: "someone to teach you."

d. Literally "and not solid food." A number of important MSS (including P^{46} and the original hand of א) have no *kai* ("and").

e. The Greek has the explanatory conjunction *gar* ("for"); to achieve some variety, I have translated with "Now," which can have the same function in English.

f. D inserts the adverbial accusative *akmēn* to create the phrase "still a child." My translation once more omits the conjunction *gar* in order to achieve a more natural English.

g. The translation "a good thing and a bad thing" is a bit wooden, but the common translation "good and evil" tends to be overly abstract. The point is that the prudent person can make appropriate concrete choices.

h. P^{46} and B have the accusative *didachēn* rather than the genitive *didachēs*. The fact that the other constructions are genitives makes the accusative the harder reading, which is often to be preferred, but in this case the genitive is almost certainly right.

i. The MS evidence is split between the hortatory subjunctive *poiēsōmen* ("let us do") and the future *poiēsomen* ("we will do"). The translation follows P^{46}, א, B, and many other witnesses in taking the future as the intended sense.

j. Some ancient witnesses have "brothers" rather than "beloved," and others conflate the two, forming "beloved brothers."

k. Many MSS have the phrase "labor of love," probably under the influence of 1 Thess 1:3.

l. Some scribes apparently did not recognize that the relative pronoun *hēs* (in the genitive case) is correct—by attraction to its antecedent in the same case—and so change it to the grammatically more obvious accusative *hēn.*

m. A small number of MSS have "faith" (*pisteōs*) rather than "hope" (*elpidos*), and a few others have "faith and love." The corrections are accountable by the appearance of "faith" in the next line.

[5:11–14] Like effective communicators today, ancient rhetoricians knew how to alter the rhythm and pace of their discourses. They understood that sheer unrelenting argument is difficult to assimilate, and deliberately shifted readers' attention in order to refresh and refocus them. The author of Hebrews provides just such an attention focusing in 5:11–6:12. He begins mildly enough, by mentioning the length of his discourse (cf. Philo, *Who Is the Heir?* 133, 221). The conventional character of the remark is supported both by the relative brevity of Hebrews compared to many ancient discourses, and by the author's own characterization of his *logos tēs paraklēseōs* in 13:22 as *dia bracheōn* ("briefly"). The Greek phrase *peri hou hēmin ho logos* ("our discourse concerning him") closely resembles 4:13, but unlike that earlier line, which clearly referred to God, the antecedent here is uncertain. Could it refer to Melchizedek, or to the subject of priesthood? Possibly, since the author takes up that subject in 7:1. But it is more likely that the relative pronoun refers back to "the Messiah" (*ho christos*), the subject of the entire lengthy sentence running from 5:5 to 5:10.

The author's discourse is not only lengthy, it is also "difficult to express" (*dysermēneutos legein*). The complaint is not uncommon among ancient speakers (see Philo, *On Dreams* 1.188; Artemidorus, *Oneirocritica* 3.67), and can serve to suggest the author's struggle with difficult subject matter. Hebrews, however, connects the difficulty to the disposition of his hearers. They have become—and the perfect *gegonate* suggests, still are—*nōthroi tais akoais*. The adjective *nōthros* means lethargic or careless (see Prov 22:29; Sir 4:29; 11:2). When combined with the dative of respect *tais akoais* ("in hearing"), it indicates a dullness or even a reluctance to listen (see Heliodorus, *Ethiopians* 5.1.5; Epictetus, *Discourses* 1.7.30). I use the translation "reluctant listeners" in order to stress what I consider the deeper implication of the passage. Jesus has just been portrayed as one who became mature/perfect by "learning obedience" from the things he suffered (5:8). Obedience, as we have seen, is a form of responsive *hearing*. The listeners' reluctance to learn more about such a messiah, therefore, may have much to do with their perception that such learning leads them into the same path of suffering. The difficulty faced by the author is not simply mental laziness, but spiritual resistance.

Hebrews next elaborates the dimensions of their spiritual torpor. They should by this time be teachers—ones who do the speaking—rather than learners—those who listen! The phrase *dia ton chronon* (lit. "on account of the time") indicates that these are not fresh converts (see 2:1–4), and that some advance in understanding and maturity is expected of them. They "ought to be" (*opheilontes einai*) teachers. The author does not mean that they should hold that office in the community (as in Rom 12:7; 1 Cor 12:28–29; Eph 4:11; 1 Tim 1:6). Rather, as in Heb 5:5–10, he continues to work within the metaphorical framework of ancient education. Maturity is marked by progress from student to teacher. They ought by now to be well past the basics and be in the position of leading others by word and example to maturity (cf. Philostratus, *Life of Apollonius* 1.17; Epictetus, *Enchiridion* 51.1). Instead, they not only themselves need teachers, but they require instruction in "the elementary principles of God's oracles." The phrase *tes archēs tōn logiōn tou theou* could scarcely express their immaturity more clearly. The noun *archē* ("beginning") stands in contrast to *telos* ("end/maturity"; see Wis 7:18). The noun *stoicheia* can refer to the basic elements of a subject (as in Xenophon, *Memorabilia* 2.1.1) or even the letters of the alphabet (Diogenes Laertius, *Lives* 7.56; Philo, *Preliminary Studies* 149–50). They are at the beginning of the beginning!

The specific "basic elements" concerning which the hearers need instruction have to do with the "oracles of God" (*logia tou theou*). In the LXX, *logia* ("sayings/oracles") is used for God's declarations through law and prophecy (see Num 24:16; Deut 33:9–10; Ps 118:10–11), a usage that continues in Jewish literature (Philo, *Moses* 2.56; *Decalogue* 36; Acts 7:38; 1 Pet 4:11). It can also refer to Scripture as a whole (Philo, *Moses* 2.188; *Let. Aris.* 176–77; Rom 3:2). We remember, however, that in Hebrews "Scripture" is always a matter of God's living speech, so the translation "oracles of God" is particularly appropriate. But what does the author imply that they need once more (*palin*) to be taught as the elementary principles of these oracles? At the most obvious level, he suggests that their need is even more rudimentary than the "basic instruction about Christ" (6:1). But he also allows the inference that his readers do not yet grasp the meaning of God's word as it points to the Messiah. Thus they cannot comprehend the significance of Jesus as a priest like Melchizedek (5:10) because they do not yet appreciate that God's living word (4:12) is a call every day to obedient hearing (3:12–15).

The author elaborates the rebuke—they should be teachers but remain learners—by employing the common rhetorical contrast between infants (*nēpioi*) and mature (*teleioi*) and the food appropriate to each. Paul used the same contrast in 1 Cor 3:1–2: "I was not able, brothers, to speak to you as spiritual people [i.e., as mature; see 2:6], but as fleshly, as babes (*nēpioi*) in Christ. I gave you milk (*gala*) to drink, not solid food, for you were not yet able." In the case of the Corinthians, immaturity is marked by attitudes of rivalry and envy ("the flesh"). In the case of Hebrews, immaturity means resisting God's call to faithful endurance.

Both Paul and the author of Hebrews make use of a common Hellenistic topos. Epictetus tells his students, "Are you not willing, at this late date, like children, to be weaned (*apogalaktisthēnai*) and to partake of more solid food (*trophēs stereōteras*)?" (*Discourses* 2.16.39; see also Philo, *Noah the Planter* 9; *Every Good Man Is Free* 160; *Preliminary Studies* 19; Seneca, *Letters* 88.20). In Heb 5:13–14, the author makes the obvious connections explicit: milk is for children, solid food is for the mature. We are to grasp that simple, preliminary instruction is for beginners, and advanced learning is for those who have made progress toward maturity.[1]

It is striking, though, that our author applies the metaphor not simply in terms of ideas but in terms of moral capacity. The phrase *apeiros logou dikaiosynēs* is difficult to translate, particularly since all three of its terms are polyvalent. The adjective *apeiros* appears here for the only time in the New Testament. It derives from *peiraomai*, which means "to try, attempt, or experience." The adjective therefore means something like "inexperienced in" or "unaccustomed to." It is appropriately applied to children and beginners (see Philo, *Noah the Planter* 160). What about *logos*? In the rest of the composition, it consistently refers to speech of one sort or another (2:2; 4:2; 7:28; 13:7), and it would be possible here to translate the phrase as "speech concerning righteousness" or even "righteous speech." In the present case, though, the more fundamental meaning of *logos*, namely a form of calculation or reasoning, seems to be meant (see Herodotus 1.209; Plato, *Republic* 529D; Aristotle, *Eudaemonian Ethics* 1149A; Epictetus, *Discourses* 2.2.20), especially since the contrasting ability among the mature involves a mental/moral activity. Finally, the noun *dikaiosynē* should in all likelihood not be taken in the "biblical" sense of divine righteousness (see Gen 18:19; Deut 33:21; Ps 5:8; Rom 1:17; 3:5; Gal 2:21), but in the sense commonly found in Hellenistic moral discourse (Plato, *Republic* 433A; Aristotle, *Politics* 1291A), the virtue that enables precisely the appropriate sorts of decisions concerning right and wrong (see Heb 12:11). The immature, then, are those who are inexperienced in moral reasoning (Koester, 302).

1. See H. P. Owen, "The 'Stages of Ascent' in Heb v.11–vi.3," *NTS* 3 (1956–57): 243–53.

Such an understanding is supported by the author's characterization of the "mature"—those who eat solid food. In contrast to the child's "inexperience in reasoning," they have their moral faculties (*aisthētēria*) trained (*gegymnasmena*) on account of practice or habit (*dia tēn hexin*). The Greek noun *aesthēsis* means a "sense" of perception or feeling (see Josephus, *J.W.* 7.69; *Ag. Ap.* 2.178), and the *aisthētērion*, correspondingly, is the "organ of sense" or capacity to feel or perceive (see 4 Macc 2:22). The passive perfect participle of *gymnazein* points once more to the Greek educational framework of the entire passage (see 5:8). Mental and moral education took place in connection with the training of the body at the gymnasium (see Isocrates, *To Nicocles* 10; Pseudo-Isocrates, *To Demonicus* 21).

More pertinently, the passive perfect participle indicates that the mature stand at the end of that process of education. They have reached that condition because of repetition: the term *hexis* is used in Greek moral writings for the acquired state or skill or "habit" that is the result of practice (see Plato, *Phaedrus* 268E; *Laws* 650B; Aristotle, *Nicomachean Ethics* 1098B; *Let. Aris.* 121; Philo, *Allegorical Laws* 1.10).[2]

In contrast to the immature, who are incapable of reasoning righteously, the mature are able to distinguish (*pros diakrisin*; see Rom 14:1; 1 Cor 12:10) between a good and a bad thing. Once more we see that, for Hebrews, perfection or maturity is understood in terms of human moral transformation. In a manner remarkably similar to Paul, the author locates the difficulty of moving to higher things precisely in the lack of moral development among his hearers. The precise character of their immaturity in regard to discerning "a good thing from a bad thing" will be suggested by 6:6–8: not moving forward is the same as falling backward. Failure to grow is tantamount to regression.

[6:1–3] The emphatic "therefore" (*dio*) that begins 6:1 may seem a bit surprising, given the tone of rebuke in the previous verses, but as 6:9–12 will show, the author is actually confident in his hearers' capacity for the learning toward which he prods them. Note that he now shifts from the accusatory second person plural of 5:11–12 to the hortatory first person plural, "we." With the verbs of "moving toward" (*pherōmetha epi*) and "leaving behind" (*aphentes*), the author once more employs a spatial imagery that enables his hearers to imagine themselves on a journey: at this end is the *archē* ("start"), at that end is the *telos* ("finish"). But the "end" toward which they are "moving" is not actually spatial, but a process of internal growth: they seek "maturity" (*teleiotēta*). The "movement" exactly matches that from infancy to adulthood in the previous verses. The journey is not from one place to another but from one stage of learning to another.

2. For the difficult translation of 5:14, see M. Kiley, "A Note on Hebrews 5:14," *CBQ* 42 (1980): 501–3; and J. A. L. Lee, "Hebrews 5:14 and *Hexis*: A History of Misunderstanding," *NovT* 39 (1997): 151–76.

When he speaks of "leaving behind the basic instruction about the Christ," the author does not mean "abandoning," but rather building on the earlier knowledge—note the image of "laying a foundation again." For similar usage see Plutarch, *Obsolescence of Oracles* 23: "It appears, I said, that we have already discontinued (*aphentas*) our discourse about oracles and are now taking up another topic just as large" (*Mor.* 423C).

Hebrews calls readers to move beyond "basic instruction about the Messiah." The difficulty in translating *ton tēs archēs tōu Christou logon* is similar to that attaching to *ta stoicheia tēs archēs tōn logiōn tou theou* in 5:12. Although the designation *ho Christos* is used in 5:5, and the phrase in 5:11, "our discourse concerning him," again refers to the Messiah, the author here encourages only that they move beyond basic instruction (in wooden literalism, "the word of the beginning of the Messiah"). Such basic instruction is like a foundation on which to build. Once more Paul's language in 1 Corinthians provides a useful comparison: "according to the gift of God given to me, I put down a foundation like a wise builder, and another will build on it. But let each one see how he builds. For there is no other foundation possible to lay apart from the one that has been set down, namely Jesus Christ" (1 Cor 3:10–11).

For Hebrews, "laying a foundation again" is an exercise in futility. The author assumes the basic teaching about Christ and wants to start building on it. This is clear enough. What is less than clear is the nature of the specific items he enumerates, and the manner in which the author (and presumably, his hearers) might attach these to "instruction about the Messiah." There is no implied distinction here between the things spoken and done by Jesus and the practices of the church (see Heb 2:3–4). But neither is there a clear distinction drawn between things broadly practiced in Judaism and those specific to the "messianic movement" centered in Jesus.

Take, for example, "repentance from dead works and faith toward God." The author's precise meaning is impossible to pin down, because the possibilities of reference are multiple. The term "repentance" is standard in Scripture for the human turning to the one God and changing one's life in accordance with that commitment. In the LXX, *epistrephein* is most often used to translate Hebrew *šûb* ("to turn") in this covenantal sense (see Deut 4:30; 30:2; Isa 6:10; 9:13; 46:3), but in the New Testament, the idea is carried by the verb *metanoiein* and (as here) the noun *metanoia* (see Matt 3:8, 11; Luke 5:32; Acts 5:31; Rom 2:4; 2 Tim 2:25). Hebrews uses *metanoia* here, again immediately in 6:6, and for a final time in 12:17. The way the term is used suggests a once-for-all, definitive turning.[3]

The positive pole of this change is expressed by "faith toward God," and is given specificity by the negative pole, "from dead works" (*apo nekrōn ergōn*).

3. For background see J. K. Solari, "The Problem of Metanoia in the Epistle to the Hebrews" (Ph.D. diss., Catholic University of America, 1970).

But this term itself can mean several things. It could refer to "the dead works" of sin—this seems to be the sense of 9:14: "the blood of Christ will cleanse our conscience from dead works (*apo nekrōn ergōn*)." But 9:14 and this passage could also conceivably refer to the "dead works" of the Jewish law (see 9:10), with "dead" in this case meaning "ineffective" (see 10:3–4). A more likely sense, however, is also suggested by 9:14 when it contrasts dead works to worship of the living God. The turn, then, could be from idolatry to the worship of the true God of Israel (cf. Acts 14:15 and 1 Thess 1:9). Still another option is worth considering. If we take "basic instruction about the Messiah" in the strict sense, then, as in 1 Thess 1:9, the turn from dead idols to the living God is mediated by the confession of Christ as the one whom God has raised from the dead as Messiah and Lord. A firm decision among these options is not required, and perhaps is even inappropriate. The author's point, after all, is that such a turning is now in his hearers' past. He will shortly insist that they cannot return to that most fundamental turning (6:6). It is now time to move forward.

The same ambiguity attaches to "a teaching about ablutions and imposition of hands." The term *baptisma* was used for John's baptism for repentance (Mark 1:4; Matt 3:7; Luke 3:3; Acts 19:3) and also for the ritual of initiation practiced by Jesus' followers (Rom 6:4; Eph 4:5; Col 2:12; 1 Pet 3:21). But Hebrews here uses the noun *baptismos*, which is used for ritual Jewish washings (Mark 7:4) and for John's baptism (see Josephus, *Ant.* 18.117). In 9:10 Hebrews speaks of "diverse washings" (*diaphorois baptismois*) together with Jewish practices of eating and drinking (see also Philo, *Special Laws* 1.261; 1QS 3:4–9; 5:13–14). The usage in the present passage suggests the ritual initiation of baptism, but the plural is puzzling. We must remember, however, that a single person could conceivably have undergone, in sequence, a proselyte baptism, circumcision, John's baptism, and baptism into the Jesus movement. An instruction concerning baptisms, therefore, could well involve the distinctions between other washings and baptism into Christ.

The "imposition of hands" (*epitheseōs cheirōn*) similarly could be used in several contexts: blessing (Mark 10:13), healing (Matt 9:18; Mark 5:23; Acts 9:12), and commissioning (Acts 6:6; 13:3; 1 Tim 4:1–4; 2 Tim 1:6). Since the imposition of hands seems here to be closely linked to baptism, and since in Heb 6:14 the author speaks of partaking in the Holy Spirit, the reference here may well be to the laying on of hands through which the Holy Spirit was bestowed (see Acts 8:17–18; 19:6) in connection with the ritual of baptism.

The remaining items also are shared by Jews outside the messianic community. Belief in the resurrection of the dead (*anastaseōs nekrōn*) arises explicitly in the Maccabean period (see Dan 12:2; 2 Macc 7:9, 11, 14, 23) and is a distinguishing conviction of the Pharisees (Josephus, *Ant.* 18.14–17; Mark 12:26; Acts 23:8). It is also a constant affirmation of the first Christians, not only concerning Jesus, but also as a hope for others (Luke 20:35; John 5:29; Acts 4:2;

17:32; 24:21; 1 Cor 15:12–13; Phil 3:11; 2 Tim 2:18; Rev 20:4–15). In Heb 11:35 the author alludes to the Israelite women who "received back their dead by resurrection" and others who did not accept human deliverance in order to "attain a better resurrection." There were, to be sure, variations within this general expectation. Hebrews would undoubtedly have agreed with Paul that Christ was the "firstfruits" (*aparchē*) of the general resurrection (1 Cor 15:20–23), since he has already entered fully into the life and power of God. But it does not use the actual language of "resurrection" with regard to Jesus himself.

Nor is it possible to gain further insight into Hebrews' understanding of the final term of the list, "eternal judgment." That God will judge all humans after death is also a widely shared conviction within the symbolic world of Torah (Dan 7:26–27; *4 Ezra* 7.33–34; Matt 25:31–46; Rev 20:11–15). That this is an "eternal judgment" (*krimatos aiōniou*) might in Hebrews mean one of two things. Given the way the author uses the adjective "eternal" elsewhere (see 5:9; 9:12, 14, 15; 13:20), it can almost mean simply "God's judgment." But it can also bear the sense of a judgment that has eternal, that is, never-ending, consequences (cf. Matt 18:8; 25:41, 46; Luke 16:9; Acts 13:46; Rom 2:7; 2 Thess 1:9; 2 Tim 2:10). Note how the author refers to "the coming age (*aiōnas*)" in Heb 6:5, which in Jewish thought was sometimes associated with the coming of the Messiah and the resurrection of the just (see below).

This second section of the rhetorical pause and exhortation concludes with a resounding statement of the author's resolve: "we will do this (*touto poiēsomen*)!" The future tense is clearly to be preferred here over the subjunctive offered by some witnesses, and the "this" (*touto*) must refer to the movement toward maturity (through consideration of the priesthood of Jesus). But in light of the acknowledged difficulty of the task, the author appropriately also calls on God's help: "if God allows" (*ean perepitrepē ho theos*) is found in Josephus (*Ant.* 20.267) and in the New Testament (1 Cor 16:7). The expression "if God/the Lord wills" is found in 1 Cor 4:19; Jas 4:15; Acts 18:21, but remarkably, not in the Old Testament. It found its way into Judaism (at least in this formulation) from Greek piety (see Plato, *Alcibiades* 135D; *Phaedo* 80D; Epictetus, *Discourses* 1.1.17; 3.21.12).

[4–8] The author now shifts from the personal ("you . . . we") to the impersonal, with two explanatory statements—each beginning with *gar* ("for")—that add even more power to his warning. The first is a flat statement of the impossibility of renewing repentance for those who have fallen away. The impersonal construction *adynaton* ("it is not possible") is stark because of both its primary position in the sentence and its absolute character. My translation alters the sequence of the Greek by shifting "to renew again to repentance" to the front of the sentence. The Greek builds suspense by delaying the infinitival clause: the initial "it is not possible" is followed by a series of clauses describing the ones it is impossible to renew.

The verb *anakainizein* ("make new, restore"; see 2 Chr 15:8; Pss 102:5; 103:30) points back to the *archē* that was their first "repentance (*metanoia*) from dead works" in Heb 6:1. The impossibility of repeating such repentance is located in a hypothetical "falling away" (*parapesontas*). The verb *parapiptein* once more indirectly suggests the pilgrimage motif—they have fallen (*piptein*) by the side (*para*). It occurs only here in the New Testament. In Polybius's *History* it is used literally for missing a road (12.12.2) and metaphorically for missing the truth (8.11.8). In the LXX it is used for faithlessness to the covenant (Ezek 14:13; 15:8; 18:24; 20:27; 2 Chr 20:18; 28:19; 29:6; 30:7; Wis 6:9). This is not a matter of faults and errors, in other words, but of apostasy, of making a deliberate choice not to participate in the gift once given.[4] The author returns to this theme in Heb 12:17. Speaking of Esau, who sold his birthright for a single meal, he declares, "Even though he sought it with tears, he was rejected, for he found no opportunity to repent (*metanoias gar topon ouch heuren*)." We are to understand this apostasy, in short, against the backdrop of 3:7–19, which spelled out the rebellion of the wilderness generation: "falling away" alludes to an entire pattern of disobedience and faithlessness following upon a first deliverance.

This hypothetical apostasy is given further emphasis by two participles, "crucifying and mocking the Son of God." Apostates among the author's hearers are scarcely in a position to crucify Jesus, whose death is in the past. Some are therefore tempted to translate "crucify again." But the prefix *ana* in the verb *anastauroun* does not mean "again" but refers rather to "lifting up" in crucifixion. Hebrews makes clear the metaphorical sense through the phrase "in their own regard" (*heautois*). Their rejection of the gift won by his death is equivalent to participating in his state execution. They thereby also "mock" (*paradeigmatizein*) him. The verb is used outside the New Testament precisely for a shameful exposure through public hanging (see Num 25:4; Ezek 28:17; 3 Macc 7:14; Plutarch, *On Curiosity* 10 [*Mor.* 520B]). Hebrews will later say that Jesus "despised its shame" when he endured the cross (12:2) because of the joy that was set before him. But when the joy of the gift that he gives is itself spurned by one who has publicly partaken in it (6:4–5), then the Son of God is held up for ridicule. Such a one exposes Jesus to the same shame he experienced in his crucifixion. The effect of apostasy is so devastating because of the extraordinary character of the gift received and the cost to Christ of its giving.[5]

In a manner similar to Hebrews, Paul lays out in 1 Cor 10:1–4 the initial privileges of those in the wilderness generation who displeased God. Paul says that

4. For a study of the wilderness generation as backdrop to the present passage, see D. Mathewson, "Reading Heb 6:4–6 in Light of the Old Testament," *WTJ* 61 (1999): 209–25.

5. L. Sabourin, "'Crucifying Afresh for One's Repentance' (Heb 6:4–6)," *BTB* 6 (1976): 264–71, argues that the phrase "crucifying again" should go with "it is impossible," thus heightening the once-for-all character of Christ's sacrificial death.

"our fathers": (a) all were under the cloud; (b) all passed through the sea; (c) all were baptized into Moses; (d) all ate the same spiritual food; and (e) all drank the same spiritual drink—they drank from the rock following them, which was Christ. Then Paul adds, "But God was not pleased with most of them and they were scattered in the wilderness" (1 Cor 10:5). So also here, Hebrews enumerates the gifts that the apostates once enjoyed. The adverb *hapax* can be used simply in the sense of "once," but the term occurs so frequently in this composition for the singularity of Christ's work (9:7, 26, 27, 28; 10:2) that it may well bear some of the weight of *ephapax* ("once for all"), used by Hebrews in the same connection (7:27; 9:12; 10:10). If so, then the first repentance and the experiences attached to it have the same "once-for-all" definitiveness to them as does Christ's sacrifice, thus enabling the author to regard those who reject them as "crucifying and mocking" of the one who "once for all" (*ephapax*) died for their sake.

There is a rough sort of equivalence between this set of experiences and the "basic instruction about the Messiah" that is enumerated in 6:1–2, but no more than that. It is, indeed, by no means clear that this list actually refers to separate realities. It may provide alternative ways of speaking of the same reality. Although his language is indirect, the author seems to focus on the experience of Christian initiation. The word "experience" is here important. It is not merely a matter of "instruction" (*logos*) that apostates reject, but actual experience. The aorist tense of the participles therefore is significant: they *were* once for all enlightened, they *did* taste, they *had* been made partakers! The "falling away" is not from an external teaching but from the experience that the hearers have themselves had.

Light is a natural and widespread religious symbol. The term "enlightened" (*phōtisthentas*) is employed again in 10:32 with reference to the hearer's starting point. It can refer to the experience of revelation ("I have seen the light"), as in Judg 13:8; Pss 33:6; 118:130; Isa 60:1; 2 Cor 4:4–6; Eph 1:18. But in view of other New Testament passages using the metaphor, it probably refers here to the experience of baptism; see, for example, 2 Cor 4:6; Rom 13:12, and especially 1 Pet 2:9: "He called you out of darkness into his marvelous light," and Eph 5:14: "Awake, O sleeper, and arise from the dead, and Christ shall give you light."

The use of the word "taste" (*geuomai*) for "the heavenly gift" and "the noble word of God" does not suggest the Eucharist or other cultic meal; rather, as in 2:9, "taste" means simply to experience. The phrase "taste the heavenly gift (*dōreas tēs epouraniou*)," therefore, may well be another way to say, "enlightened/baptized." The same is true of "become partakers of the Holy Spirit (*metochoi pneumatos hagiou*)." It can be lined up next to "partakers in a heavenly calling" (*klēseōs epouraniou metochoi*, 3:1), and "partakers of the Messiah" (*metochoi tou Christou*, 3:14). Our author is manifestly fond of mixing and matching his characterizations, and thereby resists our efforts at an overly precise determination. We can say that participation in the life and power given by the Holy Spirit (cf. 2:4)—which is surely a "heavenly gift"—is commonly associated with baptism and the laying on of hands in early Christianity (see John 3:8; Matt 28:19; Acts 2:38; 8:18; 10:44–47; 19:6; Gal 4:6; Eph 1:13).

The tasting of "the noble word of God and the powers of the coming age" is equally obscure. I choose to translate *kalos* as "noble" rather than "good" or "beautiful" because the point throughout seems to be that the initiatory experience was one that enabled contact with the Divine. For *kalos* in connection with the word, see Deut 1:14; Prov 16:24; Zech 1:13. The closest parallel is Jas 2:7, which speaks of "the noble name (*to kalon onoma*) that is invoked upon you." Mention of the word of God and of the powers of the age to come can well be once more an invocation of the first initiation of the hearers. In Heb 2:3 the author spoke of the salvation that began with the things that were heard from the Lord, and in 2:4 of the "signs and wonders and various powerful deeds" in close conjunction to the gifts given by the Holy Spirit.

The struggle to find definite answers to the puzzles provided by these allusive lists is, to be sure, a distraction. The main point is perfectly straightforward: the enormity of apostasy is measured by the greatness of the experience of God it abandons. That is why it is impossible to "renew to repentance" people who have proven capable of turning away from their own most powerful and transforming experience.

This passage, together with 10:26–29, has challenged readers from the start because of the author's implacable position with regard to repentance. In the early church, as noted in the Introduction (p. 4), the Shepherd of Hermas appeared to reject a position close to that enunciated by Hebrews (see *Mand.* 4.3.1–7; *Vis.* 2.2.4–5; *Sim.* 9.26.5–6), leading Tertullian in turn to reject Hermas (Tertullian, *On Modesty* 20). In third-century North Africa, the Novatians cited Hebrews as a basis for the refusal to readmit those who had caved in under persecution (see Epiphanius, *Panarion* 59.1.1–3.5), whereas Cyprian argued for the readmission of the *Lapsi* (Cyprian of Carthage, *Letter* 51). Ambrose of Milan argued for readmission but no rebaptism (*On Penance* 2.2).

Here is one more way in which the author's perspective—and that of a considerable part of the ancient church—seems far away from that of present-day readers, for whom the very concept of "apostasy" appears strange, and who consider themselves to live in a world in which everything can be forgiven. When the very reality of sin has been reduced to a form of sickness or inadequacy, then meaningful discussion of conversion is not possible. Hebrews, in contrast, has a strong sense of sin as refusal and rejection of both the gift and the one who gives it, and therefore has a correspondingly strong sense both of the need for conversion and of the impossibility of converting when the ground of conversion has itself been rejected.

The warning about the impossibility of renewing to repentance has something to do with Hebrews' strong sense of eschatological urgency, for the author reminds the readers in 12:17 that Esau "found no opportunity to repent," and tells them to exhort one another the more as they see the day coming near (10:25). It also has something to do with the "once-for-all" quality of Christ's sacrificial death, as the language of 10:26 suggests. Most of all, however, the threat expresses the negative side of the author's positive argument concerning the greatness of the gift. To suppose that one could take or leave such a gift with impunity would be to impugn its significance. Because they have been gifted by the living God with a share in God's own life, the stakes are ultimately high.[6]

The author follows this harsh assessment with an agricultural metaphor. The contrast between a plant that matures and yields good fruit and a plant that yields only thorns and thistles has easy and natural application to the moral life (see Isa 5:1–7; Ezek 19:10–14; Mark 4:3–9; Matt 13:1–9, 24–30; Philo, *Who Is the Heir?* 204; *Special Laws* 1.246). The language of "thorns and thistles" is reminiscent of Gen 3:12–18, where God curses the earth because of human sin. The use of "blessing" and "curse," in turn, reminds us of Deuteronomy, where God sets before the people "the blessing and the curse" (30:1). The blessing comes to those who keep covenant by observing God's commandments; theirs will be prosperity in a fruitful land (Deut 30:2–16). The curse falls on those whose "heart turns away . . . and do not hear" (30:17). In the metaphor, to be sure, the fruitful plants are persons who mature in the moral life and do not fall away, while the plants producing thorns and thistles grow in destructive ways. When plants have repeatedly been cultivated and still fail to yield the expected fruit, they will be cut out and cast away (Luke 13:6–9) or burned (Philo, *Noah the Planter* 17–19). The image of such burning can therefore stand as a metaphor of judgment on worthlessness (*adokimos*); see Matt 3:10–12; 13:30; John 15:6. For *telos*, "end" in the sense of destiny, see Rom 6:21–22 and Phil 3:19; with specific reference to judgment, see 1 Tim 1:16.

[9–12] Hebrews concludes this rhetorical pause and exhortation with words of encouragement that are as positive as its warning is dire. The author acknowledges the tone of the preceding comments by the phrase "Even though we are speaking in this way," and shifts the mood by addressing his hearers for the first and only time within the composition as "beloved" (*agapētoi*). The phrase "we are confident concerning you" (*pepeismetha peri hymōn*) can indicate some concern (see, e.g., 2 Tim 1:5), but here, as in Rom 15:14, it straightforwardly expresses a genuinely optimistic viewpoint, indicating that the author's warning in the previous verses was truly a caution concerning the possibility of their falling away, rather than a response to those who had already apostasized.

6. See Koester, 311–24, for a rich exposition of this section.

As throughout this section, the author employs the rhetorical "we" (see 5:11; 6:3, 11). His confidence with respect to them concerns the "better things belonging to salvation." The term *sōtēria* ("salvation") recalls 2:3, where it was designated "so great a salvation," and 5:9, where Christ is called the cause of "eternal salvation" (see also 1:14; 2:10; 9:28). The phrase "better things" (*ta kreissona*) runs through the author's discourse (see 8:6; 9:23), indicating in particular the realities coming from God that are superior to the merely human or empirical. It is an expression of Hebrews' religious Platonism, which distinguishes less between body and soul than between what is possible to humans and what is possible only to God, and to humans by God's gift.

The reason for the author's confidence concerning his hearers is twofold. First and foremost is God's fidelity to them. Second is their demonstrated fidelity to God. They may be slow to catch on and grow to maturity, but, the author recognizes, they have not produced thorns and thistles, either. The statement that God "is not so unrighteous" (*adikos*) as "to forget" (*epilathesthai*) is an example of *litotes,* a rhetorical device to achieve emphasis by understatement or even negation. Thus Paul claims prestige for his native city of Tarsus when he declares it to be "not an insignificant city" (Acts 21:29), and he actually boasts when he says, "I am not ashamed of the good news" (Rom 1:16). Thus when Hebrews says that God is not so unjust as to forget, it actually states that God is righteous and remembers (see Gen 8:1; 9:15–16; Exod 2:24; 6:5; Pss 24:7). So also Paul asks rhetorically in Rom 3:5, "Is God unjust when he brings on the wrath?" and means, "God is surely righteous when he brings on the wrath, is he not?" To "forget" (*epilanthanesthai*) can simply mean not to be held in memory (see Matt 16:5; Phil 3:13; Jas 1:24), but it can also mean to neglect (Luke 12:6, and esp. Heb 13:6, 11). God's forgetfulness of what they had done would mean failing to acknowledge or reward their demonstration of fidelity to him, and this, says the author, God will not do.

God will remember how they have "demonstrated" (*enedeixasthe*) both labor and love "toward his name" (*eis to onoma autou*). The verb *endeiknymi* can mean show or reveal (Xenophon, *Anabasis* 6.1.19; Rom 2:15; 2 Cor 8:24; 1 Tim 1:16), but it can bear the sense of "demonstrate, give proof" in a more technical sense (see Plato, *Laws* 966B). One is almost tempted in this case to split the nuance between the two objects: they have revealed their labor and demonstrated their love. The choice of *agapē* ("love") is unexpected in this context for two reasons. First, we would have expected faith or obedience, since they have been thematic up to this point, and will be again. Second, the expression of human love toward God is relatively rare in the New Testament. More often the New Testament speaks of God's or Christ's love toward humans (see Rom 5:5, 8; 8:35, 39; 2 Cor 5:14; 13:11; Eph 2:4; 3:19; Col 1:13; 1 Thess 1:4; 2 Thess 3:5; 1 Tim 1:14; 2 Tim 1:13; 1 John 2:5; 3:1, 17; 4:9, 16; John 3:16; 15:9; 17:23) or the love that humans should show to other humans (Matt 22:37; Mark 12:30;

Luke 10:27; Rom 12:9; 13:10; 14:15; 1 Cor 13:1–13; Gal 5:6, 13, 14; Eph 4:2; 5:2; 2 Cor 9:7; Phil 1:9; 2:1; 1 Thess 3:12; 4:9; John 15:12, 17; Jas 2:8; 1 John 2:20; 3:11; 4:7). Human love toward God does also appear in passages such as Rom 8:28; 1 Cor 2:9; 8:3; 2 Tim 4:8; Jas 1:12; 1 Pet 1:8. Here that love has been demonstrated *eis to onoma autou* ("for his name"), meaning God. The use of "name" (*onoma*) for Christ or God is frequent in early Christianity (Acts 2:21, 38; 3:6, 16; 5:40; 8:12; Rom 1:5; 2:24; 10:13; 1 Cor 1:2, 10; Phil 2:9–10; 2 Tim 2:19; Jas 2:7; 5:10; 1 Pet 4:14; 3 John 7). Although Hebrews uses *onoma* for the dignity that Jesus has inherited through his exaltation to God's right hand (1:4), it otherwise applies the term to God (2:12; 13:15), as it does here. The construction "love for his name" is unique in the New Testament.

The love of God and love of neighbor are here linked, as the author states that the way in which they have demonstrated their love for the name of God has been, and continues to be, the service they show to the saints. As often in the New Testament, "the saints" (*hoi hagioi*) designates members of the community (see Acts 9:13, 32; Rom 1:7; 15:31; 16:2, 15, 16; 1 Cor 1:2; 6:1–2, 16; 2 Cor 1:1; Eph 1:1; 6:18; Phil 1:1; Col 1:2; 3:12; 1 Thess 5:27; Phlm 5; and especially Heb 13:24). The service they have shown and are still showing—the participles using *diakonein* are aorist and present—may mean only that they are helpful to each other (see Acts 19:22; 1 Tim 3:10, 13; Phlm 13; 1 Pet 1:12), but it may also have the more specific sense of providing mutual economic support (see Acts 6:2; Rom 15:25; 1 Cor 16:15; 1 Tim 5:10; Phlm 7; 2 Cor 8:19–20). Their mutual self-disposition fits the characterization of the hearers' first fervor in Heb 10:32–34, and the author's express concern that they continue to share their goods in 13:16. The author's praise of their devotion is real and indicates that the listeners, however slow they may be to grow toward full maturity, are far from being actual apostates.

In 6:11–12 the author makes a neat turn and transition to the next part of his exposition. He expresses his fervent desire (for *enthymein* see Luke 17:22; 22:15; 1 Tim 3:1; 1 Pet 1:12) that they demonstrate—using the same verb, *endeiknymi*, as in the previous verse—the same eagerness with respect to moving forward as they have in their good work in the past and present. The noun *spoudē* is sometimes used for haste (Josephus, *Ant.* 7.223; Mark 6:25), but here has its frequent sense of diligence or eagerness (Josephus, *Ant.* 13.245; Rom 12:8, 11; 2 Cor 7:11; 8:7). It is, indeed, the opposite of *nōthros* ("laziness, reluctance") that the author repeats in verse 12, picking up the same word with which his complaint began in 5:11. There the author stated that they had become reluctant listeners (*nōthroi gegonate tais akoais*). Here he desires in them such a zeal that they not become lazy.

Their eagerness is to be *pros tēn plērophorian tēs elpidos achri telous*. The basic meaning is clear. The phrase *achri telous* ("all the way to the end") points us back to the note of completion, maturity, or perfection that was sounded in 5:13–14. The construction involving the nouns *plērophoria* and *elpis* is less obvious. Like the verb form *plērophorein*, the noun can mean "full assurance" or "conviction," indicating a mental state. Such a meaning is possible in passages such as Rom 15:29 and Col 2:2. If this is what the author intends, then he would crave a zeal that would yield a mental certainty concerning their hope all the way to the end. The noun can, however, also bear the sense of "fullness, fulfillment" (see the same passages cited above, plus 2 Tim 4:5 and Heb 10:22). Read this way, the author would desire a zeal that would yield the fulfillment of what they hope for, all the way to maturity, or perfection (cf. Heb 3:6). This second rendering seems to fit better the author's overall theme of moving toward maturity.

The hearers will be able to move to that greater state of maturity if they do not follow those who showed themselves *nōthroi* in the wilderness generation of old, but rather become imitators (*mimētai*) of those who were the inheritors of the promises (*klēronomountōn tas epangelias*). Here the author anticipates two later developments in his argument. In chapter 11 he will praise all the ancestors whose faith—a way of hearing, remember—led them to seek the inheritance (11:8) and became a "cloud of witnesses" (12:1) for those who are now inheriting a heavenly salvation (1:14; 9:15), because they are the "many sons" being led by the one who has himself "inherited a better name" (1:4). The author will also later encourage his hearers to "imitate the faith" of their leaders (13:7).

We are not by this time surprised to discover that the inheritance is to be gained through faith (*pistis*), because of the way in which the faithful obedience of Jesus as pioneer has already been developed (3:1–6; 5:7–8), and we shall see faith and hope (*elpis*) inextricably linked in 11:1. But Hebrews here adds another term, *makrothymia*, which I translate as "long-suffering." In contrast to the frequently used noun "endurance" (*hypomonē*), which suggests a passive stance toward a circumstance (Plato, *Theaetetus* 177B; Ps 24:3; Job 6:11; 9:4), *makrothymia* can suggest a more active disposition of "putting up generously with another" and can therefore be used of God's attitude toward humans (Sir 18:11; 35:19, 2 Macc 6:14; Jer 15:15; Rom 2:4; 9:22; 1 Pet 3:20; 2 Pet 3:9, 15), as well as of a generous human attitude toward suffering (see 1 Cor 13:4; Gal 5:22; Col 1:11; 3:12; Eph 4:2; 2 Tim 3:10).

The mention of "those who inherit the promises" also provides a transition to the next portion of the argument, in which we find the author taking up the theme of God's oath to Abraham, whose "long-suffering" enabled him to obtain the promise (6:15).

6:13–20 God Secures the Promise with an Oath

Ancient rhetoric worked effectively when themes were introduced and developed organically, rather than according to strict outline. Hebrews is likewise effective because of the subtle manner in which the author interweaves exposition and exhortation. The present section of text clearly continues logically from 5:11–6:12, but while continuing and expanding on one theme (that of inheriting the promise, initiated in 2:16 and touched on in 6:12), also begins another, namely God's securing of the promise through an oath. This theme, however, serves to bring the author and his hearers back to the major topic broached in 5:7–10, the eternal priesthood of Jesus "according to the order of Melchizedek" (6:20), which is then expounded at length in 7:1–28.

6:13 Now when God had made a promise to Abraham, he swore by himself because he had no one greater by whom to swear. **14** He said, "I will indeed[a] bless you and I will indeed increase you." **15** And thus, because he was long-suffering, Abraham attained the promise. **16** For humans[b] swear by what is greater than them, and the oath taken as confirmation concludes all controversy among them. **17** For this reason, since God wanted to demonstrate[c] the more strongly[d] to the heirs[e] of the promise the unchangeableness of his will, he secured it with an oath, **18** so that, through two unchangeable things in which it is not possible for God[f] to lie, those of us who have fled our place in order to take hold of the hope that lies ahead might have a powerful encouragement. **19** We have it[g] as an anchor for the soul, sure, solid, and reaching into the inner place behind the veil, **20** where Jesus has entered as a forerunner in our behalf, having become a high priest forever according to the order of Melchizedek.

a. Gen 22:17 has *ē mēn* ("surely"), and this is read also by the majority of NT MSS; the reading *ei mēn*, which has the same meaning, is found in P^{46} and the great uncials.

b. The particle *men* is added by C, the second corrector of D, and the majority of MSS, possibly to sharpen the contrast between humans and God.

c. B has the adverbial form *perissoterōs* rather than the neuter comparative *perissoteron*, which also functions as an adverb.

d. A uses the present infinitive of the verb *epideiknymi*, rather than the aorist found in other MSS.

e. One MS (69) adds *klētois* ("called") immediately before "heirs."

f. Some MSS (e.g., B and D) omit the definite article before *theos*, which would make the phrase read "for a god to lie," rather than "for God to lie."

g. D and a few other witnesses have the subjunctive *echōmen* ("let us have"), which fits poorly in the context; the indicative *echomen* ("we have") is the better reading.

[6:13–15] The mention of those who inherit the promise reminds hearers of the author's earlier declaration that God "takes hold of the descendants of Abraham" (2:16), and leads directly to this clarification (note the connective *gar*) concerning the promise and the oath sworn by God.[1] Oaths are important to our

1. For this theme see esp. D. R. Worley, "God's Faithfulness to Promise: The Hortatory Use of Commissive Language in Hebrews" (Ph.D. diss., Yale University, 1981).

author above all, to be sure, because of the presence of God's oath in Ps 109:4. But we remember as well the citation of Ps 94:7–11, where God swore in anger concerning the rebellious people (Heb 3:11).

The use of the aorist tense for the circumstantial participle *epangeilamenos* is precise: God *had* made the promise to Abraham twice before the incident to which the author here alludes. The first promise was announced when Abraham was called to leave the land of his fathers in Gen 12:2–3—note again the theme of the pilgrimage, leaving a homeland in search of an unseen destination. It is declared a second time in 15:5, and because Abraham believes God's promise, he is declared righteous (15:6). So the promise stands as something that God has spoken. He has had to repeat it precisely because, in Abraham's experience, the promise does not appear to be fulfilled.

The third statement of the promise is in Gen 22:16, and is introduced by an oath, "By myself I have sworn (*kat' emautou ōmosa*)." Then God repeats the promise: "I will indeed bless you and I will indeed increase you" (22:17). The timing of the promise and oath is significant. Abraham has, in response to God's command, just shown himself willing to offer his only son Isaac as a sacrifice. If Abraham had succeeded—if God had not intervened—the promise of posterity through Isaac would surely have been voided. Since God's testing of Abraham appeared to place his own promise in jeopardy, it was appropriate that this final expression of the promise be introduced by an oath of the greatest possible authority.

The context of Gen 22:16–17 also helps us understand Heb 6:15, "and thus, because he was long-suffering, Abraham attained the promise." The willingness of Abraham to sacrifice Isaac was an expression of his faith (see later in Heb 11:17–19) that manifested itself in the "long-suffering" (*makrothymia*) involved in this terrible testing by God. Abraham is seen here as the model of the "faith and long-suffering" that the hearers have been told in 6:12 to imitate. It is striking that Abraham is the second specific figure in the Israelite tradition to be singled out for special consideration (the other is Moses in 3:2–5), and the same quality of obedient faith is stressed with regard to him (and Moses) as with regard to Jesus (see 3:2, 6; 5:8–10). The author's understanding of Jesus shapes the way he reads the story of the people. The threads he lays down in these early chapters he will weave together into the magnificent tapestry of chapter 11.

[16–18] The author now clarifies his own explanatory clause in 6:13: "He swore by himself because he had no one greater by whom to swear." We should note at once that Hebrews shares the same positive view toward oaths that is found generally in Scripture, where even God binds himself with oaths (Exod 13:5; Num 14:16; Deut 1:8). Scripture shows concern about the manner or truthfulness of oaths (see Lev 5:20–24; 19:12; Num 30:3; Deut 23:22; Ps 23:4; Wis 14:29–30; Sir 23:11; Hos 4:15), a concern carried forward also by Philo (see *Decalogue* 84–95; *Special Laws* 2.2–38). But Hebrews seems unaware of moral concerns among some about oaths (see Epictetus, *Enchiridion* 33.5; Diogenes Laertius, *Lives* 8.22; Josephus, *J.W.* 2.135; *Ant.* 15.370–72), and shows no knowledge of the prohibition of oaths associated with Jesus (see Matt 5:34–37; Jas 5:12).

In verse 16 the author states the general principles concerning oath taking as we find it in the world of Scripture. First, one swears by something or someone greater than oneself (see Matt 5:34). The oath is a form of invocation of a greater power than one's own. But since nothing is greater than God, God must swear by himself, that is, call into account his own authority. So Philo asserts that it is appropriate for God to swear by himself since he is the "best of all things" (*Allegorical Laws* 3.203). Second, an oath adds probative weight to another statement, so that disputes between humans should be settled by the interposing (*mesiteuein*) of an oath. Hebrews' language here echoes that of Exod 22:10–13: when persons are in dispute, *orkos estai tou theou ana meson amphoterōn* ("there will be an oath by God between them both"). That an oath settles a dispute is stated repeatedly by Philo (*Decalogue* 86; *On Dreams* 1.12; *Abraham* 273; *Allegorical Laws* 3.205). The use of the phrase *eis bebaiōsin* ("for confirmation") is particularly striking on several counts. The first is the way in which it appears in papyrological evidence for matters concerning property, as a guarantee (see P.Tebtunis 311.27). The second is the way in which cognate expressions in Hebrews bear the same sense of legal reassurance (see Heb 2:2, 3; 9:17). The third is the way in which the author uses such language in addressing hearers who stand in danger of dispossession and require hope for a better homeland (10:34; 11:9–11).

The author next explains the reason that God spoke the oath in Gen 22:16. The participial phrase *en hō* (lit. "in which") is equivalent, as in 2:18, to "because" or "for this reason." God's motivation is his desire to make clear to the heirs of the promise the constant character of his will to an even greater degree (*perissoteron*) than in the promise itself. This was necessary, as I have suggested, because his own command to Abraham concerning Isaac had put the promise in peril. Philo's comment on the passage makes such motivation explicit: God swore "so that his [i.e., Abraham's] mind might be established more securely and firmly than it was before" (*Abraham* 273). As when Hebrews states in 6:10 that "God is not so unrighteous as to forget" their good works, so here the "unchangeableness (*ametatheton*) of his will" points to God's fidelity and reliability. God does not need the oath, but humans do, especially in the face of circumstances that present evidence contrary to the promise.

The term *boulē theou* ("God's will") occurs less frequently in Scripture than the equivalent expression *thelēma theou* for expressing God's intentions concerning the world and especially humanity. This is its only occurrence in Hebrews (see Ps 19:4; Jer 27:45; 29:20; Luke 7:30; Acts 2:23; 4:28; 13:36; 20:27; Eph 1:11). The conviction that "the will of the Lord remains forever" is found in Ps 32:11 and Prov 19:21. Just as with language about God "speaking" (Heb 1:11) and "witnessing" (2:4) and "calling" (3:1), the language of promising and swearing and willing (6:13–17) affirms not only that *ho theos* is personal, but that God actively and powerfully engages humans as persons. The God "on account of whom and through whom all things exist" (2:10) is not removed from the world once it is created, but continually renews creation by his personal presence and power. Thus, with Abraham, he "secures" his promise with an oath. The term *mesiteuein* has the same sort of legal nuance as *bebaiōsis* (6:13) but is of particular interest because of the way Hebrews will speak later of Christ as the *mesitēs* ("mediator" or "guarantor") of a new and better covenant (8:6, 9; 9:15; 12:24).

In verse 18 the author continues to pursue the reason for God's securing his promise with an oath, but now makes the critical shift from Abraham to "the heirs of the promise," who are the followers of Jesus, by employing the first person plural: "so that we might have a powerful encouragement." The shift reminds us of Paul's declaration in 1 Cor 10:11: "these things happened to them as types (*typikōs*), but they were written for our instruction." The phrase "powerful encouragement" (*ischyran paraklēsin*) in turn reminds us of the author's characterization of his own composition as a "word of encouragement" in 13:22.

The encouragement comes to the contemporary heirs through "two unchangeable things in which it is not possible for God to lie." If we ask what the two things (*pragmata*) are, we might quickly conclude that the author alludes to the promise and oath in Gen 22:16–17, which he has been discussing. Alternatively, he might want hearers to think of the statements already quoted from Ps 109, namely that the Lord sits at God's right hand (109:1) and that God has sworn an oath concerning him that he is a priest forever (109:4).[2]

But since this comfort concerns his hearers, and since the author states at once the "fact" (*pragma*) that Christ has entered into the inner place behind the veil (6:19–20), he may also mean that both God's word and God's deed are truthful. That his present hearers have this encouragement "safe and sure" is certainly linked not only to God's speech but also to God's action in exalting Jesus to his right hand as Lord.

The author identifies himself with his hearers as those who have "fled our place." I translate *katapheugein* ("flee") thus loosely in order to capture the intended allusion to Abraham and the patriarchs, who wandered the land as aliens in search of the promised homeland (11:8–12). The use of the verb in the LXX, however, strongly supports the nuance of "fleeing to find refuge" (see Gen 19:20; Exod 21:14; Lev 26:25; Num 25:25–26) as in a city of refuge or sanctuary (Deut 4:42). The characterization in either case provides a sharp image of readers who are *not* sure of their place in the world and are in need of what is

2. See Attridge, 181–82.

stable and secure. The reason they have fled, indeed, is so that they might "seize" or "grasp" (*kratēsai*; cf. 4:14) the hope that lies before them (*tēs prokeimenēs elpidos*). The participle of *prokeimai* ("to set before") can lean either in the direction of that which is "set before us" as within our grasp (see Josephus, *Ant.* 1.14) or in the direction of that which "lies before us" as a goal yet to be reached (see Josephus, *Ant.* 8.208). The two other occurrences of the verb in Heb 12:2 can support either nuance, but I favor "lies ahead," because of the way the author has just spoken of the future "fulfillment of hope" in 5:11.

[19–20] The intrinsic ambiguity of the term *elpis* ("hope") is indicated by the declaration in verse 19 that "we have it." In one sense, hope is the human disposition regarding the present that enables it to be perceived as open positively to the future. This is the sense in which they now "have it." But hope can also refer to the reality that opens the present to a positive future. This is the sense in which the hearers have fled "in order to grasp" the hope that lies before them. The future, this statement suggests, concerns the hearers themselves. They have yet to inherit the promises in the fullest sense (see 5:11). But the present reality is Jesus Christ, who has already inherited (1:4) and who goes ahead of them as a forerunner (6:20).

Hebrews' language in these two verses is exceptionally complex, not because of the syntax, which is straightforward, but because of the use of metaphors that overlap and blend. The author makes use of three distinct conceptual domains, one nautical (hope is an anchor), one cultic (heaven is a temple), and one athletic/military (life is a race/war). They are drawn together by the verb "entering" (*eiserchesthai*), first in the form of a participle referring to the anchor (6:19), and a second time as a finite verb referring to Jesus (6:20). The effect of the blending is to create the concept, "Hope is Jesus."

The image of hope as an "anchor for the soul" is distinctive within Scripture. In Hellenistic literature, the anchor means literally the weight to which a ship is connected by a rope to prevent drifting (see Acts 27:29, 30, 40). It can serve as a metaphor for stability (Plato, *Laws* 961C; Artemidorus, *Oneirocritica* 2.23), and Philo uses the image to express the soul's security in virtue and/or in relationship to God (*Sacrifice of Abel and Cain* 90; *Cherubim* 13). The aspect of solidity and stability is reinforced by the author's use of the adjective *asphalēs*, which connotes cognitive certainty (see Luke 1:4; Acts 21:34; 22:30), and the adjective *bebaios*, which, as we have already seen, bears the sense of being solidly grounded (see Heb 2:2, 3; 3:6, 14; 9:17; 13:9). But the author then complicates the metaphor by adding the circumstantial participle *eiserchomenēn*—this is an anchor that is "entering in" or "extending" into the inner place behind the veil—thus introducing the second conceptual field, that of heaven as temple. Hebrews here initiates the symbolism that will dominate the argument in chapters 8–10, and it will be discussed in detail there. We need only note now that the *katapetasmatos* ("veil") refers to one of the two curtains in the temple that separated the holy place from the holy of holies, and the temple proper from the outer court (see Exod 26:31;

27:21; 37:5; 40:3; Lev 4:6, 17; 16:2, 12, 15).[3] The image, then, is that the anchor (we must picture a rope attached) is entering within the inner place of the temple (the holy of holies), as if it were a grappling hook to which the souls of believers were connected. Once it has secured a place, they can follow after. Once more we must remember, however, that the metaphor of temple here stands for the true "holy of holies," which is the actual presence and power of God.

They can follow after and "take hold of" the hope and inherit the promise—that is, enter themselves into God's presence—because Jesus has entered "there" before them. The term *prodromos* (lit. "forerunner") appears only here in the New Testament. Herodotus uses it for the advance units of an army (4.121; 7.203), and it can be used metaphorically of a precursor (Plato, *Charmides* 154A). The characterization of Jesus as "forerunner" matches that of "pioneer" (*archēgos*; 2:10; 12:2).

Jesus has entered into God's presence—the holy of holies of the heavenly temple—not for himself, but "for our sake" (*hyper hēmōn*). This familiar New Testament construction (see 1 Cor 11:25; 15:3; Gal 1:4; 2:20; Eph 5:2) points to the representative or vicarious character of Jesus, both in his death and in his exaltation. What he is and does, he is and does *for others.* And he does this *eis ton aiōna*, "forever." The contrast between the temporal and eternal seems, once more, thoroughly Platonic. But in the biblical Platonism of Hebrews, the temporal is the realm of human existence, and the eternal is being with God. The hearers' hope is safe and secure because Jesus has entered for them into the presence of God.

By stating that Jesus entered into God's presence "for our sake," the author of Hebrews has brilliantly returned to the definition of Jesus as a priest, for every priest is appointed "for the sake of humans in matters pertaining to God" (5:1). He is thus able to conclude by repeating that Jesus has become a priest according to the order of Melchizedek (6:20), closing his long excursus by returning to the statement originally made in 5:10. He is now ready to consider "this Melchizedek" at greater length, and then develop his long argument concerning Jesus as the eternal high priest.

7:1–10 Abraham and Melchizedek

The great theme of Jesus' priesthood begins by a return to the figure of the ancient priest and king Melchizedek. First named by citation of Ps 109:4 in Heb

3. For discussion see R. M. Davidson, "Christ's Entry 'Within the Veil' in Hebrews 6:19–20: The Old Testament Background," *AUSS* 39 (2001): 175–90; and N. H. Young, "The Day of Dedication or the Day of Atonement? The Old Testament Background to Hebrews 6:19–20 Revisited," *AUSS* 40 (2002): 61–68.

5:6, the mysterious figure according to whose order Jesus has been designated as a high priest is now examined in some detail, through analysis of the only other scriptural passage that mentions him, Gen 14:17–20.

The author starts with a brief summation of the encounter between priest and patriarch, taken from the language of the LXX (7:1–2), then draws special significance from the meaning of the king's name and place, as well as his lack of ancestry, in order to sketch a "likeness" between him and the Son of God (7:3). The heart of the Genesis passage—at least according to the excerpt provided by Hebrews—is the exchange of blessing and tithe between Melchizedek and Abraham. Hebrews draws on the peculiar character of this exchange to argue, in a manner convincing only to those already sharing his premises, for the superiority of Melchizedek's priesthood—and therefore of Christ's—over the priesthood drawn from the tribe of Levi (7:4–10).[1]

The passage begins and ends with Melchizedek as the subject (7:1, 10). After this literary tour de force, the author will enter more deeply into the implications of Jesus being a priest "according to the order of Melchizedek."

7:1 Now this Melchizedek was king of Salem, a priest of the most high
God. He[a] encountered Abraham as he had turned back from the slaughter
of the kings[b] and blessed him. **2** Abraham also gave him a tenth of every-
thing.[c] His name means, first, king of righteousness. Then he is also king
of Salem, that is, king of peace. **3** He is without father, without mother,
without genealogy. He has neither beginning of days nor an end of life. He
has been likened to the Son of God. He remains a priest forever.

4 Look at how great this man is! The patriarch Abraham gave him[d] a
tenth of the choice spoils. **5** Those among the sons of Levi who receive
the priesthood have a commandment: according to the law they are to
exact a tithe from the people, that is, their brothers, even though they
came forth from Abraham's loins. **6** But the one who is not descended
from them exacted a tithe from Abraham[e] and he blessed[f] the one who
has the promise. **7** Now it cannot be denied that the lesser is blessed by
the greater. **8** And here are mortal men receiving tithes, but there he is
attested as being alive. **9** And, in a manner of speaking, through Abraham
even Levi, the one who receives tithes, is tithed. **10** For he was still in the
loins of his father when Melchizedek encountered him.

a. Some important MSS (including א and B) have the relative pronoun (*hos*) rather than the definite article (*ho*). My translation throughout the passage turns longer Greek sentences into shorter English sentences.

1. For a helpful analysis of the *synkrisis* here, see T. W. Seid, "The Rhetorical Form of the Melchizedek/Christ Comparison in Hebrews 7" (Ph.D. diss., Brown University, 1996).

b. One MS (460) expands the text in order to better locate the passage within Genesis: "when he [Abraham] had pursued the foreigners and freed Lot and all that had been taken captive" (see Gen 14:16).

c. Two important witnesses have the singular *pantos* (B) or *pantos autō* (P^{46}) rather than the plural *pantōn*, read by the majority of MSS. The meaning would shift from Abraham giving a tenth of all possessions to demanding a tenth from each person.

d. Witnesses are fairly evenly divided over whether to include the (unnecessary) *kai* ("and"), which my translation also omits.

e. The majority of MSS have a definite article before the name Abraham, but the best witnesses omit it.

f. Many MSS have the aorist tense *eulogēsen*, rather than the perfect *eulogēken*, but there is no significant difference in meaning.

[7:1–3] The exposition of Gen 14:17–20 reveals more of the author's range of interpretive strategies, some of which we have already seen in 3:7–4:10, and shows how thoroughly at home not only in the world of Greco-Roman rhetoric but also in the world of Hellenistic textual interpretation, both Greek and Jewish, the author is. The chapter opens with a selective paraphrase of Gen 14:17–20. The actual words of the LXX are used, but not all of them. Noteworthy for their absence are the mention of Melchizedek offering bread and wine, and the actual words of blessing.

This is the only other place in Scripture apart from Ps 109:4 where the name Melchizedek appears. Having quoted the psalm verse in 5:6, the author follows the rabbinic interpretive principle called *gezerah shawah* in seeking out the Genesis passage in order to better understand the psalm. This principle is based on the premise that all of Scripture is meaningful and indeed has a single author, so that the occurrence of a word in one passage can be used to illuminate the use of the word in another passage. The two passages, indeed, can stand as mutually interpretive. The principle is all the more important when the same word (in this case, personal name) appears in only these two passages in all of Scripture!

The comparison is demanded even more by the circumstance that in both passages the name Melchizedek is connected with priesthood, and in unexpected ways. In the psalm, the Davidic "Lord" who sits at the "Lord's" right hand in enthronement is declared a priest forever "according to the order" of Melchizedek—with no explanation of who Melchizedek is or what the "order" of his priesthood might mean. What does God intend for us to understand by taking an oath in such terms? At the very least, the Davidic Messiah and the priesthood of Melchizedek seem to be aligned. Then, in the Genesis passage, the same Melchizedek encounters the patriarch Abraham, to whom the promise was given (Heb 6:13). Simply the *connections* that Scripture makes between Melchizedek, the Messiah, and the patriarch of the promise demand a careful consideration of Genesis as the interpretive key for the psalm verse.

The Genesis passage is itself exceptionally strange, both in the way its sits in the narrative flow and in the provocative things it says about the two figures. First, the story of the abduction of Lot with his family and possessions, the pursuit and conquest of the five kings by Abraham, and the encounter with the king of Salem, all seem from another world—a larger, Gentile, political world—than the tightly focused story of Abraham and his pursuit of the promised heir. The author pays tribute to this narrative anomaly by saying that Melchizedek is "without genealogy." Melchizedek literally interrupts the narrative flow, without any apparent cause or consequence. He must therefore be important in himself. Technically, Melchizedek is *agenealogētos* because he is not introduced with the tables of ancestors (Heb. *tôlēdôt*) that other prominent characters of Genesis have been to this point (Gen 5:1–32; 6:9–10; 9:8–27; 10:1–32; 11:10–32). But in contemporary terms he also lacks any narrative connections. Only God's later oath in Ps 109:4 summons him back from his narrative obscurity, and in connection with the Messiah!

Hebrews' excerpt from the LXX focuses on two elements in the story: the identity of Melchizedek, and the exchange between him and Abraham. The scriptural text provides his name and his dual office: he is king of Salem and—more fascinating—a "priest of the Most High God." Immediately we see how provocative a figure he might be: here is the first priest in all of Torah, and a priest of the "Most High God" at that, the same God who also called Abraham (for *'ēl-'elyôn* as [*theos*] *hypsistos*, see Num 24:16; Deut 32:8; Pss 56:2; 77:56). And he is simultaneously a king. Melchizedek holds both offices and is *not* descended from Abraham. He is a Gentile—as, in the strictest sense, so is Abraham at this point preceding his own circumcision (see Gen 17:22–27).

The deeper significance of Melchizedek is sought first through etymology, a common feature of biblical interpretation, both Greek (see Philo, *Preliminary Studies* 44–45; *Change of Names* 61–82) and Hebrew (see *Sifre on Deuteronomy* Berakah 343; *Targum Pseudo-Jonathan* on Gen 31:45–50). By analyzing a term through its constitutive elements one gains, it was thought, a deeper insight into the character of the one bearing that name, especially if this "translation" also gets carried into another language. Note the use of *hermēneuomai* in John 1:38, 42; 9:7, and the use of etymological interpretation in Mark 3:17 ("he gave them the name Boanerges, that is, sons of thunder") and Matt 16:17–18 ("Blessed are you, Simon Bar Jonah . . . you are Peter [*petros*] and upon this rock [*petra*] I will build my church").

Here the author's rendering of Melchizedek, which may originally have meant "Zedek is my king," as "king of righteousness" (Heb. *melek ṣĕdāqâ*; Gk. *basileus dikaiosynēs*) is attested also in Philo, *Allegorical Laws* 3.79; Josephus, *J.W.* 6.438; and *Targum Pseudo-Jonathan* on Gen 14:18. For Hebrews, that Melchizedek is "king of righteousness" matches the quality associated with the Messiah-King in Ps 44:8 quoted in Heb 1:9: "You have loved righteousness and hated lawlessness," and that required of the faithful (5:13; 11:7, 33; 12:11).

Etymology also provides the deeper significance of Melchizedek's identification as *basileus Salēm*, which might simply have been taken with reference to Jerusalem, a connection that was sometimes drawn (see Josephus, *J.W.* 6.438; *Ant.* 1.180). By understanding *salēm* as the transliteration of the Hebrew *šālôm* ("peace"), Hebrews is able to name Melchizedek as a "king of peace" (*basileus eirēnēs*). The qualities of righteousness and peace classically represent the prophetic hopes of Israel (see Isa 9:6–9; 32:17; Mic 5:5; Zech 9:10). Hebrews invokes the "God of peace" in 13:20, and combines peace and righteousness in the exhortation of 12:11.

These etymological gleanings are important to the author, for his goal is to demonstrate that Melchizedek has been "likened to the Son of God"—that is, Jesus (1:2, 5; 4:14; 6:6)—by Scripture itself. The passive participle of *aphōmoioun* can mean simply "to be like" or "resemble" (see Diodorus Siculus, *Library of History* 1.86.3; Ep Jer 63, 70), or it can have the sense of "being compared to" something (see Plato, *Republic* 517B, 564B). Here I think Hebrews wants to say that Scripture itself has drawn Melchizedek in such a fashion as to enable the reader to see a likeness between him and Jesus the Son of God. This enables a further comparison between the priesthood of Melchizedek/Jesus and that derived from Abraham through the tribe of Levi.

Hebrews therefore exploits another puzzling feature of the Genesis account in order to strengthen the comparison further. Melchizedek appears in the story without any mention of his birth or his death. Hebrews' fondness for alliteration is seen in the sequence of *a̱patōr a̱mētōr a̱genealogētos* ("*without* father, *without* mother, *without* genealogy"). Whereas a present-day reader might take the narrative silence as an indication of a discrete source inserted into the ancient text, our author follows the interpretive principle that has been called *non in tora non in mundo*. The silence of Scripture on a given point can be taken as evidence that something did not exist in the extratextual world, either (see Philo, *Allegorical Laws* 2.55; 3.79; *Abraham* 31). Thus if Scripture does not report on his ancestors, Melchizedek had none. The reader may conclude that he is without human antecedent. But Hebrews goes further. Neither does Scripture report him as having a "beginning of days or end of life" (once more, using the terms *archē* and *telos*). The reader can therefore conclude further that Melchizedek had no natural birth (beginning of days) and did not die (end of life). Melchizedek is somehow, by Scripture's own implicit testimony, eternal.[2]

Melchizedek's fullest likeness to the Son of God is found in the inference, drawn from Scripture's silence, that "he remains a priest forever." The phrase *eis to diēnekes* is a more Hellenistically elegant way of expressing *eis ton aiōna*

2. For 7:3 as read from the Reformation period to the present, see B. A. Demarest, "Hebrews 7:3: A *Crux Interpretum* Historically Considered," *EvQ* 49 (1977): 141–62; and for a reading from the side of Greco-Roman presuppositions, see J. H. Neyrey, "Without Beginning of Days or End of Life (Hebrews 7:3): Topos for a True Deity," *CBQ* 53 (1991): 439–55.

("forever"; see Josephus, *Ant.* 16.149; Appian, *Civil War* 1.4.15). The only New Testament appearance of the phrase is in Hebrews, and after this application to Melchizedek, it is used three more times with specific reference to the eternal priesthood of Christ (10:1, 12, 14). Similarly, this is the first time Hebrews uses the verb *menein* ("he remains a priest forever"). The verb will be used again for Melchizedek in 7:24; otherwise, Hebrews uses it for the "stable" character of Christian hope (10:34; 12:27; 13:14). In short, it is not only Scripture that suggests a resemblance between the ancient priest-king and Christ; it is the conscious selecting and shaping of the Scripture text that makes the resemblance impressive.

[4–10] With the words "look (*theōreite*) at how great this man is," the author of Hebrews begins to develop his third great *synkrisis*. His earlier comparisons had been between the Son and the angels (1:4–2:9) and between the Son and Moses (3:1–5). The present comparison was initiated earlier by the statement that human priests are "called by God, in the way even Aaron was. Thus even Christ" (in 5:4–5), and by the declaration in 5:10 that Christ was called by God a priest according to the order of Melchizedek (5:6). The comparison between Melchizedek and Abraham is, in effect, a *synkrisis* between the Levitical priesthood and that exercised by the priest-king who has been proclaimed as God's Son, Jesus.

The entire question of the priesthood within ancient Israel is full of difficulties. Fortunately, Hebrews itself so simplifies things that we can take its representation as the significant point of departure. The book of Exodus identifies Moses with the tribe of Levi (Exod 2:1) and calls Aaron "your brother, the Levite" (4:27). Aaron and his sons are, according to God's command to Moses, to be consecrated as priests (28:1–3, 41–43), and they are (29:1–46). Aaron and his sons are to carry out the rites in the tent, including burning incense before the ark of the testimony (30:7) and making the sacrifice of atonement once a year (30:10). The "Levitical priesthood," then, descends from Aaron because he and Moses are of the tribe of Levi. The three thousand members of the tribe of Levi who rally to Moses' side are told, "Today you have ordained yourself for the service of the LORD," but there is also a consecration of them by oil: "their anointing shall admit them to a perpetual priesthood throughout their generations" (40:15).

It is in the book of Numbers that we learn of the tribe of Levi being separated from the rest of the people, assigned to surround the tent in order to protect it from violation (Num 1:47–54; 2:33; 3:14–40; 27:57–62), while Moses and Aaron and his sons do the "rites in the sanctuary" (3:38). In Numbers as well we learn that the entire tribe of Levi belongs to the Lord as a firstborn (3:44) and therefore is to tax the people (3:44–51). The Levites have no portion of the land: "I am your portion and your inheritance among the people of Israel" (18:10), and "to the Levites I have given every tithe in Israel for inheritance in return for their service" (18:21). Of the tithe (or tenth portion of their possessions) that the people offered to the Lord, the Lord said, "I have given to the Levites" (18:24). The Levites, in turn, are to offer a tenth of what they have been given to the Lord (18:26). The book of Leviticus speaks constantly of the ritual requirements and tasks of "Aaron's sons the priests" (e.g., 1:10; 3:2, 5, 8, 12; 16:14) or "Aaron and his sons" (2:3, 10; 6:24; 21:1–22, etc.). Aaron's death is reported in Num 20:22–29. His priestly garments are taken off the body and given to his son Eleazar (also of the tribe of Levi). So although the priesthood of Aaron is "perpetual," it is also passed on through mortal men "throughout their generations" (Exod 40:15).

The author of Hebrews seems to suppose just about this much knowledge of Scripture among his hearers, for his *synkrisis* would otherwise be unintelligible to them.[3] Ostensibly, our author is simply examining the question of the relative status of Melchizedek and Abraham, based on the report in Genesis that Melchizedek blessed Abraham (Gen 14:19) and that Abraham gave Melchizedek a tenth (tithe) of his booty (Gen 14:20). But the means of explicating those gestures are not all of equal value, and the passage serves mainly to set up an opposition that will be more fully developed in the following sections.

He starts, then, with the remarkable gesture of Abraham giving Melchizedek a tenth of the spoils (*ek tōn akrothinōn*). Why remarkable? For one thing, the gesture seemed to have been a spontaneous sharing, not a demanded offering. For another, Jewish readers could not but be aware, and if they were not, our author quickly reminds them, that the Levites were commanded under the law to tax their fellow Israelites a tenth of their goods as that tribe's "inheritance" in place of land. The reference is to Num 18:21, but more significant is that the author here introduces the topic of the law and of the regulation of the cult under the law (*ho nomos*), a topic that will play an important role in his subsequent discussion of the priesthood (see Heb 7:12, 16, 19, 28; 8:4, 10; 9:19, 22; 10:1, 8, 16, 28).

The Levites were commanded to exact this tax, "even though they came forth from Abraham's loins" (7:5). The tax, or tithe, in other words, was not paid from outsiders, but from fellow Israelites. The tithe was in exchange for all the services they rendered, which could be summarized by the term "blessing." Thus, when Aaron came down from offering sacrifice for the people, he "lifted up his hands toward the people and blessed them . . . and Moses and Aaron went into the tent of meeting; and when they came out they blessed the people, and the glory of the LORD appeared to all the people" (Lev 9:22–23). In short, tithes are in exchange for blessing. But in the case of Melchizedek, one not from the people of Israel receives a tithe from Abraham, and he blesses the

3. That the small amount of data provided by Hebrews about the priesthood conforms with assumptions and debates current in Second Temple Judaism before the first revolt is argued by W. Horbury, "The Aaronic Priesthood in the Epistle to the Hebrews," *JSNT* 19 (1983): 43–71.

one who has the blessing. Is his, then, not the true priesthood, recognized by the patriarch himself?

Commenting on this exchange, Hebrews states as an incontestable principle (lit. "apart from all denial") that "the lesser is blessed by the greater." If he is thinking of the relationship of Moses and Aaron to the people Israel, then the principle holds in general, at least with respect to their social positions. But Scripture itself shows that there are contrary cases, in which the lesser blesses the greater (see 2 Sam 14:22; 1 Kgs 1:47; Job 31:20). The case here is less that Hebrews can cite a standard principle than that Hebrews sees in this specific instance that the greater blesses the lesser, which is shown, parenthetically, by the tribute paid by Abraham. The author, indeed, moves quickly to the aspect that truly distinguishes the lesser and greater, and as he does so, we can observe how he collapses the horizons between the scriptural story and the actual contrast he is interested in making.

Continuing the visual metaphor established by "look at" in 7:4, the author now says in 7:8 that there are men who are in the process of dying (the participle *apothnēskontes* is present progressive), and they are receiving tithes. He means not Abraham but the Levitical priests. And there—pointing to the tableau he has so deftly sketched—"he is attested as being alive (*hoti zē*)." Once more, the present tense suggests continuing in life: he goes on living! We shall see much more of this "being witnessed to" (*martyroumenos*) in the roll call of the faithful in chapter 11. But we should observe that Scripture does not actually say that Melchizedek goes on living. That was a deduction drawn by the author from hints in the text, or rather, not in the text, since it provided for Melchizedek "neither beginning of days nor an end of life," so "he remains a priest forever" (7:3). But the one who truly "lives forever" is Jesus, and he is the one whom Hebrews really has in mind when it says that "he is attested as being alive." The real difference between the Levitical priesthood and that of Jesus, then, is that they are mortal and he is the living one. This is precisely the difference that establishes the priesthood of Jesus as "the greater" as the *synkrisis* continues in subsequent sections of the text.

The final observation is something of a throwaway line, as indicated by the author's introductory phrase, "in a manner of speaking" (for *hōs epos eipein*, see Josephus, *Ant.* 11.387; Philo, *Creation of the World* 13; *On Drunkenness* 51). That Levi himself was being tithed because he was still in the loins of Abraham (who was paying a tithe to Melchizedek) is a conceit that relies on the notion that the deeds of the ancestors are determinative of the destiny of their offspring. It is not, to be sure, a notion foreign to the New Testament (see Rom 5:12–21). The obvious logical difficulty, however, does not seem to have occurred to the author, namely that the Messiah Jesus also was in the loins of Abraham, and would therefore also be paying tithes to Melchizedek. But the seriousness of the point has already been reduced by the introductory phrase—

the author knows he is stretching—and Hebrews is prepared to move on to the more critical part of its exposition, which relies on the premise that Jesus lives forever, whereas the Levitical priests are merely mortal.

Excursus 4: The Mysterious Melchizedek

Hebrews is the only New Testament composition to pay any attention to Melchizedek, but it is scarcely the only Jewish writing to find the sudden appearance of the priest-king a fascinating subject to explore.[4] It cannot be demonstrated that the author of Hebrews depended on any other source for his interpretation, even though some of his interpretive moves are found in other writings. One reason is that Hebrews itself is among our earliest extant sources for Melchizedek speculation; another is that the manner of reading in antiquity allowed different readers of the same text to reach similar conclusions. One can say that Hebrews read Genesis in a manner similar to his Jewish predecessors and peers, namely, with close attention to the minutest nuances of the text, and with an eagerness to draw contemporary implications from the hints that God had embedded in the ancient text. A rapid survey of the ways in which Melchizedek was construed across a wide range of compositions shows that Hebrews stood within a broad interpretive tradition, even as it made claims that those outside the Christian confession would not have accepted.

Compositions that, in one way or another, retell the biblical story are relatively modest and circumspect in their interpretive creativity. The *Genesis Apocryphon* from Qumran, for example, remains close to the narrative of Genesis, only adding minor details: that Salem is to be identified with Jerusalem, and that Abraham's tithe was drawn from "all the flocks of the king of Elam and his allies" (1QApGen 22:12–17). The periphrastic book of *Jubilees* tells of the capture of Lot and of Abraham's resolve to capture him (13.22–25), but breaks off before recounting the meeting with Melchizedek. The original must have had that scene, however, because the present narrative picks up with the giving of tithes. But in contrast to Hebrews, *Jubilees* understands the story to say that Melchizedek gave tithes to Abraham—and the Hebrew can be read that way. The conclusion? "The Lord ordained it as an ordinance forever that they should give it to the priests, to those who minister before him so that they may possess it forever" (13.26–27). The story, in short, does not undermine but supports the place of the Levitical priesthood.

Targum Onqelos on Genesis identifies Melchizedek as "king of Jerusalem" and reads the statement about giving tithes as though it were part of the blessing pronounced by the priest-king: "Blessed be God Most High . . . who has given him [Abraham] a tenth of everything" (14:18–20). More expansive is *Targum Neofiti* on Gen 14:18–19: Melchizedek is king of Jerusalem, but is also identified as "Shem the Great," who "ministered

4. The Melchizedek material is well researched; see F. L. Horton, *Melchizedek Tradition through the First Five Centuries of the Christian Era and in the Epistle to the Hebrews* (SNTSMS; Cambridge: Cambridge University Press, 1976); M. Delcor, "Melchizedek from Genesis to the Qumran Texts and the Epistle to the Hebrews," *JSJ* 2 (1971): 115–35; M. McNamara, "Melchizedek: Gen 14:17–20 in the Targums, in Rabbinic and Early Christian Literature," *Bib* 81 (2000): 1–31; J. A. Fitzmyer, "Melchizedek in the MT, LXX, and the NT," *Bib* 81 (2000): 63–69.

in the high priesthood." The identification with Shem is possible because of the peculiar chronology of Gen 11:10–26, which would make Noah's son still available for an encounter with Abraham. *Targum Pseudo-Jonathan* is still more expansive: "The righteous king—that is, Shem, the son of Noah—king of Jerusalem, went out to meet Abraham." This targum makes clear that it was Abraham who gave tithes to Melchizedek "of all that he had brought back" (on Gen 14:18–20).

Narrative renderings in Greek include Josephus's *Ant.* 1.179–81, which speaks of "the king of Solyma, Melchizedek; this name means 'righteous king,' and such was he by common consent, insomuch that for this reason he was made priest of God; Solyma was in fact the place afterwards called Hierosolyma." After mentioning the priest's blessing of the patriarch, Josephus adds, "Abraham then offered him the tithe of the spoil, and he accepted the gift" (see also *J.W.* 6.438). Perhaps the strangest reading is that in the fragment of Pseudo-Eupolemus preserved in Eusebius's *Preparation for the Gospel* 9.17.5–6: "Abraham was treated as a guest by the city in the temple Argarizim, which means, 'Mountain of the Most High.' He received gifts from Melchizedek, its ruler and priest."

In Philo's paraphrase of Gen 14, he states, "when the high priest of the most high God saw him approaching with his trophies . . . and thinking, as indeed was natural, that such success was not won without God's directing care and help to their arms, he stretched his hands to heaven and honoured him with prayers on his behalf and offered sacrifices of thanksgiving for the victory . . . sharing their gladness as though the success were his own; and so indeed it was, for 'the belongings of friends are held in common,' as the proverb says, and this is far more true of the belongings of the good whose one end is to be well-pleasing to God" (*Abraham* 235). Philo has carefully shaped the story as a moral lesson concerning the ancient ideal of friendship. Because both the patriarch and the priest-king are devoted to the supreme good, which is service of God, they are bound together as true friends. Therefore, in accord with the proverb, it is appropriate that they share their possessions.

In his *Preliminary Studies* 99, Philo moves slightly beyond the literal sense when he interprets the tithe given by Abraham to Melchizedek as a sharing in sense, speaking, and reason. And in *Allegorical Laws* 3.79–82, Philo provides a still fuller reading. He identifies Melchizedek as "king of peace, for that is the meaning of Salem, and his own priest." Philo also here calls Melchizedek "the righteous king." After developing the moral implications of the sobriquet, Philo avers that Melchizedek's offer of bread and wine is "to give to souls strong drink, that they may be seized by a divine intoxication, more sober than sobriety itself. For he is a priest, even Reason [*logos*], having as his portion Him that is, and all his thoughts of God are high and vast and sublime, for he is a priest of the Most High." (For other passages in which the high priest is identified with the rational soul or the divine word, see *Dreams* 1.215; *Giants* 52; *Flight and Finding* 108.)

Up to this point, sources have stuck close to the biblical narrative and have speculated about the Melchizedek of the past. Quite another stream of speculation is revealed by the fragmentary Qumran composition designated *11QMelchizedek*, in which the priest-king appears as a figure of future expectation: "He will proclaim liberty for them . . . [he] will carry out the vengeance of God's judgments . . . Melchizedek will free them from the hand of Belial" (2:6–25). And in the Qumran *Songs of the Sabbath Sacrifice*, Melchizedek appears to play a role in the present heavenly liturgy (11:1–3; 22:1–3).

Melchizedek similarly appears in the Nag Hammadi library. In the tractate called *Melchizedek*, the ancient priest-king once more seems to have a salvific role to play in the future, although the text is so fragmentary that his exact activity is difficult to discern. Likewise, in the composition known as *2 Enoch* (Slavonic), whose provenance and date are both uncertain, Melchizedek is given specific attention as a figure who has a miraculous birth and a future cosmic role (*2 En.* 71–72).

Just the opposite tack is taken by some rabbinic texts that seek to diminish the significance of Melchizedek, especially his priesthood. Some texts emphasize that Melchizedek was circumcised, apparently to remove the implication that he was a Gentile priest of the Most High God (*Gen. Rab.* 26.3; *Abot de Rabbi Nathan* [A] 2). The passage in the Babylonian Talmud, tractate *Nedarim* 32b, reads the Hebrew text of Genesis in a manner quite distinct from the way Hebrews read the LXX, understanding Melchizedek to have committed a profound error by blessing Abraham before blessing God. "R. Zechariah said in the name of R. Ishmael: God at first wished the priesthood to come from Shem, as it is written, 'And he was a priest to God most high.' But when he put Abraham's blessing before God's own, God resolved to have the priesthood descend from Abraham instead . . . and thus it says, 'The Lord has sworn and will not change his mind, 'you are a priest forever after the order of Melchizedek.' *After the order* should be interpreted as 'because of the word of Melchizedek.' Likewise it says, 'And he was a priest to God most high'—*he* was a priest, but not his descendants" (see also *Gen. Rab.* 43.6–8; *Lev. Rab.* 25.6). It is not possible to prove that the polemical tone here is directed against the claims made for Melchizedek by Christians following Hebrews (see Clement of Alexandria, *Stromateis* 4.161.3; Tertullian, *Against the Jews* 2), but it is definitely plausible. What can be said with certainty is that the same two texts (Gen 14 and MT Ps 110 [LXX 109]) are being brought together according to the same principle of *gezerah shawah* but are being read in Hebrew rather than Greek, and in light of sharply different premises.

7:11–19 The Change of Priesthood

The argument of Hebrews now shifts from a comparison between the two ancient figures in the Genesis account to the author's explicit concern, the superiority of the priesthood of Jesus to the cult of Israel, established by the law of Moses and exercised by the Levitical priests. In a manner similar to the reflection on Ps 94:7 in Heb 4:7–8, the author muses not only on what Ps 109:4 says, but also on the significance of its being said at all, so many years after the establishment of the law (Heb 7:17). There must be a reason why the one declared to be "Lord" because of his elevation to God's right hand is also designated as "priest according to the order of Melchizedek." God does not speak in vain.

The argument therefore picks up from the phrase "according to the law" in the previous section (7:5), and develops an opposition between the eternal priesthood of Christ, founded in the "power of indestructible life," and that of Aaron, which is weak and ineffectual because it is based only in a human commandment. The section is bracketed by the language of perfection, beginning in 7:11 with a condition contrary to fact, and ending in 7:19 with a flat assertion that the law perfected nothing. Language of "establishment" (*tithēmi*) also runs through the section: the law is established (*nenomothetētai*, 7:11), but then is changed (*metatithemenēs*, 7:12), and then is set aside (*athetēsis*, 7:18). There is also a subtle use of language concerning "arising" in 7:11, 14, and 15.

Two sets of assumptions must be granted for the argument to be convincing. One concerns the relationship of priesthood to law and the purpose of the law: Hebrews virtually equates the law with its legislation concerning the cult, and regards the law's function as that of perfecting humans. If it fails to do this, then both law and priesthood are useless and need changing. The second set of assumptions—which the author regards as "obvious"—concerns Jesus' relationship to the law: he arose from a tribe not mentioned by the law, and his "arising" was not merely an election, but an entry into God's own eternal life.

7:11 If therefore perfection came through the Levitical priesthood[a]—for the people received the law[b] on its basis[c]—what further need would there be for another priest to arise and not one said to be "according to the order of Aaron"? **12** For once the priesthood has been changed, there is also of necessity a change of law. **13** For the one about whom these things are being said belongs to a different tribe.[d] From it no one served at the altar. **14** For it is obvious that our Lord[e] arose from Judah. Moses said nothing about priests[f] in that tribe. **15** And it is even more abundantly obvious if another priest is raised up according to the order of Melchizedek, **16** one who became priest not according to a law of fleshly commandment[g] but according to the power of indestructible life. **17** For it is testified that,[h] "You are a priest according to the order of Melchizedek." **18** So on one side[i] there is a setting aside of a previous commandment because of lack of power and effectiveness—**19** for the law brought nothing to perfection—and on the other side, there is the introduction of a better hope through which we are approaching God.

a. B and a few other witnesses omit the imperfect of the verb "to be" (*ēn*), but its presence is secured by the weight of evidence of other MSS.

b. Witnesses differ on the proper case of the pronoun following the preposition *epi*: some have the dative, others the accusative, and the best MSS have the genitive, which is the basis of the translation.

c. The second hand of D and many other MSS have the imperfect passive ending-*thetēto* for the verb *nomotheteō*, "was established."

d. A variety of witnesses read the aorist tense here (*meteschen*), which would suggest a single act in the past, rather than the perfect tense (*meteschēken*) read by the majority of MSS, and which suggests a participation begun in the past that continues into the present.

e. A handful of MSS add *Iēsous* ("Jesus") to the phrase "our Lord," a natural reflex, especially since Hebrews uses the full phrase in 13:20.

f. Many MSS have "about the priesthood" rather than "about priests," an understandable correction, since that noun occurred just previously, and is the overall topic.

g. Some MSS have the adjective *sarkikēs* rather than *sarkinēs*. In the New Testament, the terms are used more or less interchangeably, although *sarkikēs* has more the nuance "belonging to the flesh" and *sarkinēs* that of "composed of flesh," i.e., human.

h. Some witnesses have the active voice, "he witnesses," instead of the passive, "it is witnessed that."

i. My translation makes the contrast established by the particles *men* . . . *de* explicit and emphatic.

[7:11–14] Remarkably, although the term "priest" (*hiereus*) occurs in the LXX over 750 times, "priesthood" (*hierosynē*) appears only 9 times (1 Chr 29:22; 1 Esd 5:38; Sir 45:24; 1 Macc 2:54; 3:49; 7:9, 21; 4 Macc 5:35; 7:6). And the only time "priesthood" appears in the New Testament is in this chapter of Hebrews (7:11, 12, 24). We see, then, that our author has shifted from a comparison of biblical figures to the real subject with which he is concerned, namely the adequacy of the priesthood as such—meaning thereby the entire organized system of mediation between God and humans within Israel. Since so much of the law (*nomos*) is dedicated specifically to cultic regulation (the arrangement of the sanctuary, the consecration of priests, the carrying out of sacrifices, the maintenance of holiness), the inadequacy of the cult calls into question the adequacy of the law itself as the expression of the covenant between God and the people.

The close linkage of law and cult is asserted at once: the people "received the law on its [i.e., priesthood's] basis." The passive of *nomothetein* ("to legislate") appears this way in Philo (*Life of Moses* 2.9) and Josephus (*Ag. Ap.* 1.284). For the construction, compare especially Philo, *Migration of Abraham* 91. If the connection is granted, then the corollary stated in verse 12 is obvious: "once the priesthood has been changed, there is also of necessity a change of law." Note the phrase "of necessity" (*ex anankēs*): the necessity is a logical one, based on the assumption that the entire purpose of the law has to do with the relations between God and people expressed through the priestly cult.

The author of Hebrews assumes that the purpose of the cult, in turn, is the "perfection" (*teleiōsis*) of the people. If this is lacking, then the cult itself is ineffectual and needs reform or replacement. The noun *teleiōsis* appears only here in Hebrews, though, as noted before, the cognates occur in 2:10; 5:9, 14; 7:19, 28; 9:9, 11; 10:1, 14; 11:40; 12:2, 23. What does Hebrews understand by perfection? Readers of the LXX might catch an allusion to the "sacrifice of ordination" of the Levitical priests (see Exod 29:22–34 and Lev 7:27; 8:21–33), but although the sacrificial nuance is intriguing, that does not get us to the heart of Hebrews' understanding. For Hebrews, perfection is a matter of human transformation rather than cultic transaction. It combines elements of maturity and moral growth (see 5:14). Negatively, perfection means abandoning or overcoming sin (9:27; 10:4) and cleansing the conscience (9:9). Positively, it means a process of sanctification (9:13; 10:10, 14)—entering into a state of holiness—through an opening to God's power and presence through faithful obedience (5:7–10; 12:1–2).

Such holiness demands more than the "setting aside" of a material thing (calf, goat, or ox) as a sign of dedication to the Lord. It demands the total dedication of the human spirit to God and the progressive openness of human freedom to the will of God. Such transformation is possible for other humans because it has been accomplished first through Christ the priest. Only the one who has become perfect in this way can make others perfect in this way. By thus becoming "perfect," Jesus has in turn become "the cause of eternal salvation" to those who obey him (5:9).

The inadequacy of the Israelite cult becomes fully apparent, to be sure, only when the definition of the purpose of the cult changes, and the terms of understanding can change only in light of a new reality, indeed a new experience of personal transformation brought about by God through Jesus: "we have been sanctified through the offering once for all of the body of Jesus Christ" (10:10). This is not merely, as in Platonism, an issue of the superiority of the interior (moral) to the physical (ritual). It is an issue of whether perfection means entering into actual contact with God. In the case of Christ, Hebrews avers, God has made contact with humans at the most intimate level possible and thus enables humans to enter into contact with God at the most intimate level.

The experience of Christ is necessary for the new perception. But once that experience is grasped, it is possible to see that God had already spoken of the new reality in Scripture. In Ps 109:4 God declares of "the Lord" that he is a priest forever according to the order of Melchizedek (Heb 7:11). Here we see the same sort of argument that we observed earlier in the case of Ps 94:7–11: If the rest had already been achieved, God (in the psalm) would not have spoken of a "today" in which people could still enter it (Heb 4:3–11). Similarly, we shall see in Heb 8:9–13 that the author will derive from Jeremiah's speech about a new covenant "not like the covenant that I made with their fathers" an indication at once of a new covenant and an indication about the inadequacy of the previous one. So here as well, the psalmist speaks of a priest "according to the order of Melchizedek" and *not* "according to the order of Aaron" long after the establishment of the Levitical priesthood by the law—and speaks in this manner of the Messiah-King. The author takes this as a clear indication that even Scripture knew that perfection did not come through the Levitical priesthood. Otherwise, why did it speak this way?

In speaking of a priest "according to the order of Melchizedek" here and immediately after in 7:15, the author twice uses the verb *anistēmi*—the only two times in the entire composition. Does he mean readers to understand this simply in the sense of "arising," that is, "appearing in history" (see 1 Macc 2:1; 14:41; Acts 7:18)? Or does he intend it to be understood with reference to Jesus' "arising" from the dead? The verb is, after all, used with reference to the resurrection of Jesus with some frequency in the New Testament (Matt 17:9; 20:19; Luke 18:33; Acts 17:3; 1 Thess 4:14; Rom 6:1). Since the second occurrence in Heb 7:15 comes in close connection with "the power of indestructible life," we may entertain the possibility that Hebrews is playing on the polyvalent potential of the verb: Jesus is priest above all because of his resurrection and exaltation to God's right hand.

The author not only wants to align Jesus' priesthood with Melchizedek; he also distances it from the law by a straightforward assertion in 7:13–14: Scripture says nothing about anyone from the tribe of Judah being a priest (i.e., "doing service at the altar"). The priesthood is explicitly and exclusively reserved for the tribe of Levi. Yet it is obvious (*prodēlon*) that "our Lord arose from [the tribe of] Judah." The sentence structure is neatly chiastic: *a.* the one about whom these things are said belongs to a different tribe; *b.* no one from it served at the altar; *b′*. our Lord came from Judah; *a′*. Moses said nothing about priests in that tribe.

Two aspects of this declaration deserve attention. The first is the author's diction: the perfect active verb *anatetalken* alludes to a complex scriptural tradition. The verb *anatellein* is used literally for the "rising" of the stars (Philo, *Special Laws* 3.187) or the sun "in the east" (Josephus, *Ag. Ap.* 1.65; Matt 2:1); but influenced by the prophecy of Num 24:17, "a star shall arise from Jacob" (*anatelei astron ex Iakōb*), it can also suggest the coming of the Messiah (see Jer 23:5; Zech 3:8; 6:12; Matt 4:16; Luke 1:78; see also Isa 11:1). As with the verb *anistēmi* (see above), the author may deliberately intend this allusion, which gains even further depth if "arising" also includes the resurrection and exaltation of the Messiah.

The second thing to note is the author's assumption that such knowledge about Jesus is "obvious" (*prodēlon*) to his readers. This suggests a pervasive awareness among early Christians that Jesus was "according to the flesh" from David (Rom 1:3; 2 Tim 2:8; Rev 5:5; 22:16; Matt 1:1, 6; 9:27; 15:22; Mark 10:47; Luke 1:27, 32; 2:4; 3:23–33; 18:38; Acts 2:30–31; 13:22–23), who was, in turn, from the tribe of Judah (1 Sam 17:12; see Matt 1:1–3; Luke 3:23; Rev 5:5). The tribe of Judah was particularly associated with kingship (Gen 49:10) rather than priesthood, although the *Testament of Levi* speaks of a descendant of Judah as establishing a new priesthood: "a king shall arise in Judah, and shall establish a new priesthood after the fashion of the gentiles" (*T. Levi* 8.14). Hebrews is certainly correct, however, in asserting: "Moses said nothing about priests in that tribe." For Hebrews, as we have seen, Jesus combines the roles of king and priest. For the present argument, however, the point is simply that if Jesus arises as a priest from a tribe that the law does not associate with priesthood, that stands as evidence of God's desire to establish a priesthood apart from the law—and once there is a change of priesthood, "of necessity" there is a change of law as well (7:12).

[15–19] The most fundamental difference in the priesthood of Jesus is not his earthly origin but his heavenly destination. Jesus' priestly identity is based on his exaltation to God's right hand (1:3), a connection perhaps suggested already by the designation of Jesus as "our Lord" (*ho kyrios hēmōn*) in 7:14. The phrase *kai perissoteron eti katadēlon estin* ("and it is even more abundantly obvious") also picks up from *prodēlon* ("it is obvious") in verse 14.

What is even more obvious is that a change of priesthood demands a change in the structure of the relationship between God and humans. Why is it more obvious? Here we come to the point toward which our author has been moving since his introduction of Melchizedek. We saw earlier that the phrase *kata tēn taxin* ("according to the order") could mean either "on the same basis" or "in the sequence." The ambiguity is exploited in the use of the preposition *kata* in verses 15–16. This "other priest" is raised up both "according to (*kata*) the order of Melchizedek" and "according to (*kata*) the power of indestructible life" (*kata dynamin zōēs akatalytou*). The last phrase refers to the *basis* of Jesus' priesthood, his exaltation to God's own life, which never ends. Because he shares God's life, Jesus can also share it with others. In contrast, the Levitical priesthood is based on (*kata*) "a law of fleshly commandment" (7:16).

The two phrases balance each other perfectly. Corresponding to law (*nomos*) is power (*dynamis*), and corresponding to commandment (*entolē*) is life (*zōē*). To put the same contrast in different terms: life is a matter of internal participation and transformation, whereas commandment is a matter of external norm and observance. Finally, corresponding to "fleshly" (*sarkinēs*) is "indestructible" (*akatalytou*). If this were mere Platonism, then the contrast would be between the material and the spiritual, or between the external and the internal. The perspective is not, as we have noted, foreign to Hebrews. But the essential contrast between "fleshly" and "indestructible" is that between the merely human and God.

The adjective *sarkinēs* (the textual variant is *sarkikēs*, virtually a synonym) is associated with the law also in 2 Cor 3:3. Otherwise the New Testament uses the term for material things (Rom 15:17; 1 Cor 9:11) or for a human condition that is weakened and/or wicked (Rom 7:14; 1 Cor 3:1, 3; 2 Cor 1:12; 10:4; 1 Pet 2:11). That the commandment is "merely human" means that it lacks the power to communicate God's own life. Only life can generate life. And, in virtue of the resurrection, Jesus' life is now "indestructible," for it is a share in God's own existence. The author seals this statement with another reference to Ps 109:4. This is the second time he has used the introduction, "it is testified" (by God, through the psalmist). The first was in 7:8, "there he is attested as being alive," with reference to Melchizedek. Here the testimony of God bears on the phrase *eis ton aiōna* ("forever"). Jesus' priesthood is like that prefigured by the ancient priest-king, because Jesus truly lives forever.

The author concludes this portion of his argument with a formal and well-balanced statement. My translation deliberately expands ("on one side . . . on the other side") in order to exploit the *men . . . de* construction that holds the clauses in tension. The author contrasts the powerlessness of the commandment with regard to the most fundamental goal of all religion, which is access to the life and power of God, to the "better hope" through which, he claims, "we are approaching God." The use of the present progressive in this last phrase is telling: the author speaks out of the experience that is available through the resurrected and exalted Lord Jesus. It is in light of Jesus' own access to God, and the hope of such access that Jesus provides others, that the commandment is now perceived as "merely human," or, as this verse states it, "lack of power and effectiveness." Thus the short interjection at the start of verse 19, "for the law brought nothing to perfection."

From the perspective of ancient Israelite religion, this would be considered a false charge, for the Levitical priesthood accomplished its purpose of maintaining the covenant between God and the people. But from the perspective of what Hebrews regards as "perfection," namely a participation in God's own life, the law—that is, the cult of sacrifice—falls far short. This is the only time Hebrews uses the adjective "weak" (*asthenes*), a term familiar from Paul's writings in connection with forms of incapacity (see Rom 5:6; 8:3; 1 Cor 1:27; 2 Cor 10:10). Similarly, *anōpheles* (see Titus 3:9) has the sense of "useless" (see Lucian, *Dialogues of the Dead* 15; Wis 1:11)—in Isa 44:10 and Jer 2:8, the adjective is applied to idols! There is, therefore, a "setting aside" (*athetēsis*; see v. 12) of the previous (lit. "going before") commandment. The idiom is legal. The term *athetēsis* has the sense of "cancel" or "abrogate" with respect to a standing arrangement (Polybius, *History* 8.36.5; Cicero, *To Atticus* 6.9.3; 1 Sam 2:17; Luke 7:30; 10:16; Gal 2:21). In contrast to this "canceling" (cf. Gal 3:15), is a "leading in" (*epeisagōgē*; see Xenophon, *Anabasis* 18.16; Josephus, *Ant.* 1.38) of something new (Plato, *Republic* 575D), perhaps in place of something else (Josephus, *Ant.* 11.196). The careful reader of Hebrews will catch the echo of the "leading in" of the firstborn into the world in 1:6.

The introduction here is of a "better hope" (*kreittonos elpidos*). For the comparative adjective "better" in Hebrews, see 1:4; 6:9; 7:7, 22; 8:6; 9:23; 10:34; 11:16, 35, 40; 12:24. The hope is not simply a subjective expectation on the part of the author and his readers, although it includes that (see 6:11). Here, as in 6:15–19, the term "hope" (*elpis*) is a way of designating Jesus himself. Because he has entered into God's presence (6:20), the author and his readers can declare with confidence that "through it" (the hope that is Jesus) they are "approaching God." Although the language of "approach," as in 4:16, certainly suggests the entrance into the holy place in the ritual of sacrifice—the symbolic place of God's power and presence among the people—Hebrews clearly understands their approach not as a matter of ritual alone but as a reality that is accomplished in Jesus, who now sits at the right hand of the majesty on high (1:3), and can also be accomplished in them.

7:20–28 The Son Is an Eternal High Priest

The demonstration of Jesus' superiority as high priest—centered on an interpretation of Gen 14 and Ps 109—continues in this section. In 7:20–22 still another clue concerning Jesus' priesthood is lifted from Ps 109:4, namely, that it is secured by an oath, just as was God's promise to Abraham (Heb 6:13–18). This point leads to still another variation on the mortal/immortal contrast (see 7:8): because the exalted Christ lives forever, his priesthood is permanent (7:23–25). The author then asserts for himself and his readers the "fittingness" of having such a high priest (7:26–27), just as in 2:10 he had affirmed for God the "fittingness" of the Son being perfected through suffering. This section concludes by reconnecting with 7:11–19. The contrast between the law and the oath spoken by God in the psalm is in effect a contrast between the weakness of the Levitical priesthood and that of the Son, who has been eternally perfected.[1]

> **7:20** Moreover, insofar as an oath is involved—for they became priests without an oath, **21** whereas he became one with an oath, through the one who says to him, "The Lord has sworn and will not change his mind. You are[a] a priest forever"[b]—**22** in this respect[c] also[d] Jesus has become the pledge of a better covenant. **23** Also there were many becoming priests because they were prevented from continuing on by death. **24** In contrast, because he remains forever, he holds the priesthood permanently. **25** For this reason, he is able also to save completely those approaching God through him, since he is alive always to intercede for them. **26** It was indeed[e] fitting that we should have such a high priest. He is holy, blameless, undefiled. He has been separated from sinners. He has been exalted above the heavens. **27** He has no need, like the high priests,[f] to first offer sacrifices[g] every day for his own sins and then those of the people. For he has done this once for all when he offered himself.[h] **28** Now the law establishes as high priests[i] those who have a weakness. But the word of the oath that came after the law establishes a Son who has been perfected forever.

a. P^{46} and the second corrector of D, together with some other witnesses, add "are." The addition is attributable to the influence of the LXX, even though Hebrews lacks the verb in its citations at 5:6 and 7:17.

1. For more on priethood in Hebrews, see A. Vanhoye, *Old Testament Priests and the New Priest According to the New Testament*, trans. J. B. Orchard (Petersham, MA: St. Bede's Publications, 1986); and J. M. Scholer, *Proleptic Priests: Priesthood in the Epistle to the Hebrews* (JSNTSup 49; Sheffield: JSOT Press, 1991).

b. The same sort of textual issue here: the second corrector of א, as well as the original hands of A and D, all add "according to the order of Melchizedek," under the influence of the LXX. In this case P[46], the original hand of א, and B all have the shorter reading.

c. The best evidence supports the neuter *kata tosouto*, which corresponds to the phrase *kath' hoson* in v. 20, rather than the masculine *kata tosouton*, found in some witnesses.

d. Some MSS lack the *kai*, which can be understood as emphatic, yielding "an even greater covenant" (Attridge, 206). But I take the *kai* as a simple copulative ("also") similar to the *kai* in v. 20.

e. The *kai*, which in this case does serve adverbially to provide emphasis, is lacking in a large number of MSS, but is read by P[46] and important uncials (B, A, D).

f. The original hand of D has the singular, "the high priest," and a few other MSS have simply "the priests."

g. D and some other witnesses have the singular *thysian* ("sacrifice") rather than plural *thysias* ("sacrifices").

h. Some MSS have *prosenenkas* ("offered"), as in 5:7, rather than the *anenkas* ("offered up"), which is found in the best witnesses.

i. Again, some witnesses have "priests" rather than "high priests."

[7:20–22] Hebrews has been closely examining Ps 109:1–4 and Gen 14 in each other's light, seeking to find in Scripture a legitimation for regarding the death and resurrection of Jesus as the establishment of a new priesthood, and with it, as we shall see, a new covenant (*diathēkē*) other than that based on the law (*nomos*). The point concerning the covenant as such will occupy the next stage of the argument. In these final verses of chapter 7, the author comes at the topic of the priesthood once more. He begins by picking up the phrase of Ps 109:4, "the Lord has sworn and will not change his mind," and uses it to make one more point in favor of the superiority of Christ's priesthood.

The structure of verses 20–22 is provided by the correlative *kata* phrases beginning verses 20 and 22. Literally, *kath' hoson* and *kata tosouto* can be translated as "to the degree that . . . so to the same degree." The neat balance, however, is upset by the lengthy interjection that takes up most of verses 20–21, which states parenthetically—perhaps for a rhetorical effect that now escapes us—what would have been expected as evidence supporting the assertion in verse 22. My translation aims for clarity: If you are looking for an oath as a sign of certitude, Jesus has it, and they don't!

The Levitical priesthood received no special affirmation from God apart from the legislation provided by the law. This is in sharp contrast to the oath spoken to Abraham as confirmation of the divine promise (Gen 22:16–17). In Heb 6:13–18 the author stressed the importance of God's providing such extra support to his promise. What are we to conclude, then, if in the classic resurrection psalm, the same divine voice speaks to the Messiah-King in the same mode: "The Lord has sworn and will not change his mind: 'You are a priest forever'" (Ps 109:4)? Not only is the new priest's position secured by an oath, but in addition, because God "will not change his mind" (*ou metamelēthēsetai*; cf. Matt 21:30, 32; 27:3; 2 Cor 7:8), this priesthood will last forever with God's approval. Just as in Gal 3:14–18 Paul displaces the law by appeal to the covenant established by the promise to Abraham, so Hebrews relativizes the priesthood of Aaron (and thereby the covenant of law) by appeal to the living voice of God that spoke to the Messiah-King just as he had to confirm that promise to Abraham.

Because of this oath, the author concludes that Jesus—the assumed "Lord" addressed by "the Lord" in the psalm—has become the pledge of a better covenant (v. 22). This is the first mention in the composition of "covenant" (*diathēkē*), a term more inclusive and fundamental than "law" (*nomos*). The author draws on the biblical tradition concerning the covenants (Heb. *bĕrît*) that God made with Noah (Gen 6:18; 9:9–17) and with Abraham (15:18; 17:2–21), the covenant remembered by God at the time of the exodus (Exod 2:24), established again at Mount Sinai through Moses (Exod 19:15; 23:22; 34:10; Lev 2:13; 24:8; 26:9; Num 25:12; Deut 4:13, 23, 31; 5:2; 29:1), and renewed through Joshua (Josh 24:25). The theme of a new covenant that is mediated by Christ will become explicit in Heb 8:6–13.

A covenant is a binding treaty between two parties. The Hebrew *bĕrît* escapes reduction to the contractual by being defined in terms of open-ended attitudes or dispositions. From one side, God pledges faithfulness and love (Exod 34:6–7), and from the side of the people God asks for corresponding loyalty and obedience (Deut 6:4–5). Such fidelity, in turn, was spelled out by the commandments of the law (Deut 6:6–9). When the LXX translated *bĕrît* by *diathēkē*, it maintained the broader idea of covenant, but also inevitably imported some sense of the prior usage of the term in secular Greek, which was primarily legal. The word was used especially—as seen in Greek inscriptions and papyri—for a last will or testament (see P.Oxy. 489.13; 490.4; *OGIS* 753.8; *BGU* 1113.5). In the New Testament, therefore, we find *diathēkē* used both in the broad sense of covenant (Luke 1:72; Acts 3:25; 7:8; Rom 9:4; Eph 2:12) and also in the narrower sense of testament (Matt 26:28; Mark 14:24; Luke 22:20; and esp. Gal 3:15). In Hebrews we find the entire spectrum of nuances attaching to *diathēkē* (see 8:6, 8–10; 9:4, 15, 16, 17, 20; 10:16, 29; 12:24; 13:20).

Later in the composition, the author will call Jesus the "mediator of a better covenant" (8:6) and "mediator of a new covenant" (12:24). The term *mesitēs* suggests an agent who negotiates or manages a covenant/contract between two parties. Here, however, Jesus is called the *engyos* of a better covenant. This term has the sense of a pledge, surety, or guarantee, for a contract. One party puts up such a pledge to ensure the other party that the contractual obligations will be met, at loss to himself if he fails to meet the obligations. Property could be placed in pledge, or a person could stand as surety for another (see Plutarch, *Alcibiades* 5.4). In the present context, it is God who has sworn an oath concerning the eternal priesthood of Jesus, and Jesus is God's "pledge" or "guarantee" of a better covenant based on that priesthood.

The two passages in the LXX where *engyos* appears throw some light on the present use. In 2 Macc 16:28 Jewish soldiers fight the Greeks, "having as pledge (*engyos*) of success and victory not only their valor but their reliance on the Lord." In Sir 29:15, after stating that a good man will be surety (*engyos*) for a neighbor, the sage admonishes, "do not forget all the kindness of your surety (*engyos*), for he has given his life for you." In the view of Hebrews, that is precisely how Jesus is God's pledge of a better covenant, by giving his life for us.

[23–25] Having shown that Christ's priesthood is secured by God's oath, our author returns to the contrast between mortal and immortal (7:15), which is, in effect, a contrast between inefficacy and efficacy. Once more, the contrast is set up in Greek by a *men . . . de* construction. On one side are many who became priests. The reason there were many is that no one of them could remain, and the reason for such inability is that they died. Mortal priests are therefore necessarily multiple. We remember how in Platonism the many are always regarded as inferior to the one (see the comment on 1:1–3).

On the other side, then, there is the one who himself remains forever (in virtue of his exaltation to God's right hand, 1:3). The result? His priesthood is *aparabaton*, a term that appears only here in Scripture. It derives from *parabainō*, "to go beyond or transgress": the alpha-privative construction of the term indicates that this priesthood cannot be gone beyond or transgressed (see Epictetus, *Discourses* 2.15.1; Philo, *On the Eternity of the World* 112). Thus, in legal contexts, a decree that is *aparabatos* is absolute (see *BGU* 4:1020.9; see also Epictetus, *Enchiridion* 51.2). In the present context, it signifies that Jesus' priesthood will not be replaced. It is not relative but absolute in character. Unlike earthly priests who are conquered by death, Jesus has instead passed through death and conquered the one who had the power of death, the devil (2:14).

The adverb *hothen* ("whence/for this reason") connects the power of this priesthood precisely to the fact that he "remains forever" (7:25). The author has already identified Jesus as the "cause of eternal salvation to those who obey him" (5:9) because he had "been made perfect." Now that perfection is explicitly connected to the eternal life that Jesus shares with God. He is able to save *eis to panteles* those who approach God through him. The phrase *di' autou* ("through him") points to Jesus' mediational role: God's gift to humans comes through Jesus, and likewise their access to God passes through him. The author here uses the third person plural, "those approaching," shifting from the personal and confessional version in 7:19: "through which [hope] we are approaching God." The identity in construction, though, supports my earlier suggestion that by "hope" in 7:19 Hebrews means simply, Jesus.

But what is the significance of the prepositional phrase *eis to panteles*, found only here in the New Testament apart from Luke 13:11? It is equivalent to an adverb, and it is most natural to take it as complementary to *aparabatos*, understanding it to mean "completely" (cf. Philo, *Legation* 144; Josephus, *Ant.* 1.267). Thus, negatively, the bent woman in Luke 13:11 could not straighten "at all." The term can, however, also be used temporally (see Julian, *Oration* 2.61C), and in this context could be taken as "forever." Both understandings fit within our author's overall conception of things: the absolute power of Christ's priesthood, after all, derives from his sharing in God's eternal life. The temporal sense might at first appear to be strengthened by the next clause, "since he is alive always (*pantote zōn*) to intercede for them (*eis to entynchanein hyper autōn*)." But since the ability to save is in any case also connected to the "power of indestructible life" (7:16), the participial clause might equally support the reading of *eis to panteles* as "completely."

More significant in verse 25 is the glimpse we get of Jesus' enduring priestly activity. The verb *entynchanein* fits a legal as well as a religious context. The verb has the basic sense of engaging someone or something, and in situations of encounter between inferior and superior, takes on the sense of "making an appeal" (Polybius, *History* 4.766.9). One can therefore make an appeal "in behalf of" someone (1 Macc 8:32; 2 Macc 4:36; 3 Macc 6:77; Acts 25:24), or appeal to a higher authority "against" someone (Dan 6:13; 1 Macc 10:61, 63, 64; 11:25; Rom 11:2). When the one appealed to is not simply another human king but God, then the appeal can be understood as a prayer of intercession (Wis 8:20; 16:28). The passage closest to this one in the New Testament is Rom 8:27, where Paul states that "the Spirit interceded for the saints (*entynchanei hyper hagiōn*) according to the mind of God." Hebrews does not picture the exalted Christ as otiose, but as "living always" and active in the effort to save his fellow humans through his advocacy before God.

[26–28] In 2:10 the author said that it "was fitting" (*eprepen*) that God should perfect the pioneer of salvation through suffering. Now he uses the impersonal construction again with reference "to us" and to the kind of priest Jesus is. The point of being "fitting" is not "what we have deserved," but rather "what we truly needed," a priest who, as one of us, offered himself to God once for all (v. 27), and as exalted Lord, provides humanity with full access to God (v. 26).

This characterization of Jesus as "high priest" (*archiereus*) is purely encomiastic, with five distinct attributes ascribed to him asyndetically (i.e., without copulatives). To provide the equivalent rhetoric in English, I have joined the first three statements asyndetically, and then constructed two independent clauses that correspond to the longer participial clauses with which the author ends the sentence. The use of alliteration is again evident in the author's repeated use of words beginning with alpha (*akakos, amiantos, apo tōn hamartōlōn*). The author's affection for assonance is found in words like *hosios, akakos*, and *hypsēloteros*.

The list of qualities moves from moral disposition to status. Jesus is first of all *hosios*. Although the adjective is sometimes applied to a god (see *Orphic Hymn*

77.2; Deut 32:4; Ps 145:17; Rev 15:4; 16:5), it is more often applied to a person who is "holy" or "just" in relation to God (Plato, *Laws* 663B; Pss 4:3; 11:1; 29:4; 1 Tim 2:8; Titus 1:8). From the negative side, the same quality is suggested by the adjective *akakos* ("blameless, removed from evil, innocent"). It is used to describe Job (2:3; 36:5), and has the nuance of guilelessness (see Prov 1:4; 8:5; Rom 16:18). Jeremiah uses it for the innocent lamb who is led to the slaughter (Jer 11:19). Similarly, *amiantos* means "without defilement," whether applied, as frequently, to things (2 Macc 14:36; 15:34; Josephus, *J.W.* 6.99; *T. Jos.* 4:6; 1 Pet 1:4), or the body (Wis 8:20), activities (Jas 1:27), or, as here, a person.

These first three characteristics combine to depict Christ's complete separation from any aspect of moral evil. The next phrase makes that separation explicit: "he has been separated from sinners." In contrast to the three adjectives used of Jesus, this participial phrase in the perfect describes what has happened to him. It is undoubtedly to be taken with the final phrase, "he has been exalted above the heavens," as descriptive of Jesus' elevation to God's presence after his death (cf. 4:14, and, immediately following this passage, 8:1). Therefore, it is descriptive of his present location and status—with God—rather than his personal qualities or dispositions.

Verse 27 presents difficulties of two kinds. The first is factual, the second is logical. The author declares that in contrast to the high priests, Jesus had no need to offer sacrifices every day first for himself and then for the people. The factual problem is not the offering for the self and for the people (see 5:3), but the use of the term "every day" (*kath' hēmeran*). The requirement for the high priest to offer such a double sacrifice was only yearly, on the Day of Atonement (see 9:7). The author may simply have erred here, perhaps by mistaking the *tāmîd* offering—the twice-daily animal sacrifice described in Exod 29:28–42 and Num 23:3–8—as the duty of the high priest, which it was only in the week preceding the Day of Atonement. The logical difficulty is the author's stating that Christ "has done this once for all when he offered himself." If "this" is taken as referring to the sacrifices for the priest's own sins as well as those of the people, then the implication would be that Christ needed to offer sacrifices for his own sins, a premise that the author's own insistence on Jesus' sinlessness would seem to preclude (Heb 4:15; 7:26).

Perhaps the best way to deal with both difficulties is by beginning with the author's positive affirmation and then asking what he intends to be the point of contrast. First, he wants his hearers to appreciate the complete adequacy and singularity of Christ's self-offering, expressed by the adverb *ephapax* ("once for all"), which he will repeat in 9:12 and 10:10. Second, he wants them to acknowledge in contrast the *multiplicity* inherent in the Levitical priesthood—the plurality of priests, the plurality of sacrifices (for priests and for people), and the plurality of their temporal repetition. He may get some of the details wrong, but his central point is correct: Christ's *self*-sacrifice was absolute in a way that the earlier cult's sacrifices could not be, because they were performed by mortals alone, whereas Christ's was both human and divine.

The author concludes chapter 7 with a balanced statement that summarizes the argument he has been making. We observe again the contrast between the law (*nomos*), by which he means all the legislation concerning the cult, and the "word of oath," by which he means the declaration by God to the King-Messiah in Ps 109:4. Note the significance of the short phrase concerning the oath, that it happened "after the law": the living God continues to reveal his will. The word of God is living and God is capable of new things. We also observe the contrast between the priesthood that inherently involves weakness (*astheneia*) established by the law, and the priesthood established by God's oath in the psalm: the priesthood of Christ is that of a Son who has been perfected forever. With this final phrase, the author reasserts the identity of Jesus as Son that was delineated so thoroughly in chapters 1–5: he is the Son, who through his faithful obedience became the cause of eternal salvation to all who obey him, a priest according to the order of Melchizedek (5:7–10).

8:1–6 The Son Is Mediator of a New Covenant

Although the opening of this section sounds like a major summary of the foregoing argument, the section as a whole (extending from 6:1–13) serves as a major transition within the composition. Having established that Christ is indeed the "high priest according to the order of Melchizedek," the author will shortly begin to elaborate much more fully the distinctive character of his priesthood, which has to do not only with who he is but also with what he offers, namely himself. This theme is initiated, almost parenthetically, in 8:3–4, which states that every priest must have something to offer. Christ does not offer gifts and sacrifices on earth like the Levitical priests. So what does he offer? The contrast drawn immediately between the "shadow" worship of the Israelite cult and Jesus' worship in the "genuine" sanctuary shifts quickly to another link between Jesus' priesthood and the covenant. In 8:7–13 the scriptural basis for a new covenant will be examined, and then all of 9:1–10:18 will elaborate the great theme of Christ's self-sacrifice. In effect, this section wraps up what preceded and prepares for what follows.

> **8:1** Now the point[a] of what is being said is that we have such a high priest. He has taken a seat at the right hand of the throne of majesty in the heavens.[b] **2** He is minister of the sanctuary and of the genuine tent, which the Lord,[c] not a human, has built. **3** Since every priest is appointed in order

to offer gifts and sacrifices, it follows that this one also must have something that he offers. 4 If therefore[d] he were on earth, he would not even be a priest, because there are those[e] who offer the gifts according to law.[f] 5 They are serving in a copy and shadow of the heavenly things, just as it was revealed to Moses when he was about to construct the tent, saying, "See that you make everything according to the pattern that was shown to you on the mountain." 6 But now he has obtained[g] a ministry as much greater as he is also[h] mediator of a better covenant, which is established upon better promises.

a. A and a few other witnesses have the preposition *en* ("in") rather than *epi* ("concerning"). There is no significant difference in meaning.

b. The reading "high places" (*hypsēlois*) is found in a few minor witnesses, undoubtedly under the influence of 1:3; "heavenly places" is read by some other MSS.

c. Some important MSS (the second hand of א, A, and the second hand of D) add *kai* ("and") to relieve the asyndeton between "Lord" and "human," but the harder reading is supported by P^{46}, the original hand of א and D, as well as B.

d. The reading of *oun* ("therefore") is supported by the best witnesses over *gar* ("for").

e. The shorter reading—lacking the word "priests" or the phrase "other priests"—is attested by P^{46}, the original hand of א, A, and B.

f. MSS are fairly divided whether to include the definite article with *nomos* to form "the law." The shorter and more difficult reading is to be preferred.

g. There are a couple of variations in the form of this perfect tense of *tynchanein* ("to reach/ attain"), none of which is significant.

h. The original hand of D and a few other witnesses omit the *kai* ("also"), but it should be read.

[8:1–2] The first verses of this section remind hearers of the main point (*kephalaion*) of the discussion that has extended from 5:1 forward. The noun *kephalaion* is used widely to identify a central point (see Plato, *Phaedo* 95B; Philo, *Allegorical Laws* 2.102), and can also mean a summary (Xenophon, *Cyropaedia* 6.3.18). In this case, the author simply wants to identify and punctuate the fact that all this discussion about a priest like Melchizedek has a real pertinence to his hearers. In 7:26 he had declared that "such a high priest" (*toioutos archiereus*) "was fitting for us," and now he asserts, "we have such a high priest" (*toiouton echomen archierea*). Jesus has all the qualities identified in 7:26–27, and "we have" Jesus!

The author's discourse about Jesus as Son and Jesus as priest is brought together nicely by the following clause, which recalls the language of the prologue (1:3) as well as the start of Ps 109, which has governed the entire discussion. The psalm invited the Lord to "sit at my right hand" (109:1). The author now declares, "he has taken a seat at the right hand." And for the "my" of the psalm, the author supplies, "of the throne of majesty in the heavens."

The next statement serves to summarize a number of affirmations concerning Jesus as high priest that have been dropped in passing, and to prepare for the next stage of the argument. In 4:14 the readers are said to have a great high priest who had passed through the heavens. In 6:19 Jesus is identified as the forerunner who had reached "the inner place behind the veil" as the "high priest according to the order of Melchizedek" (6:20). In 7:3 Melchizedek is likened to the Son of God as one who is a priest forever. In 7:24 Jesus is said to remain forever, in 7:25 he is said to live always to make intercession, and in 7:27 he is declared as exalted higher than the heavens. In sum, the place where Jesus is now the eternal priest is in God's presence.

The language of "passing through" and "behind the veil," however, has anticipated the great imaginative leap of this composition: picturing heaven as the true sanctuary. The logic is impeccable. If what defines a sanctuary is the presence of God, where God essentially and eternally exists must be the real "holy place." All of the subsequent argument flows from this simple imaginative premise. Jesus is therefore said in 8:2 to be "minister of the sanctuary and of the genuine tent, which the Lord, not a human, has built."

Several aspects of this dense statement deserve attention. First, we can note the use of *leitourgos*, here translated as "minister." In the ancient Greek world, the verb *leitourgein* (from which we derive the term "liturgy") refers generally to the performance of public service, most often at one's own expense (Xenophon, *Memorabilia* 2.7.6; Aristotle, *Politics* 1291A). The *leitourgia*, in turn, is the public work, and the *leitourgos* is the one who puts it on (P.Oxy. 82.3). Given the public and pervasive character of ancient polytheistic religion, such public service—the providing of festivals and the like—naturally took on a religious coloration. It was appropriate, therefore, that the LXX used this language for the "public work" of worship in Israel (*leitourgein*, Exod 28:35; 29:30; *leitourgia*, Exod 37:19; Num 8:22). In light of such usage, it is striking that the LXX does not employ the term *leitourgos* for the priests engaged in the cult. Only in Isa 61:6 are priests referred to as *leitourgoi theou*. Instead, it used *leitourgos* for servants in the broader sense (see Josh 1:1; 2 Sam 13:18; Sir 7:30; 10:2; 3 Macc 5:5). In the New Testament, so also does Paul (see Rom 13:6; 15:16; Phil 2:25). Indeed, Hebrews itself employs the term in this broader sense in 1:7 with reference to the angels (citing Ps 103:4). This broader sense of "public work" should perhaps be kept in mind when Hebrews uses the substantive *leitourgia* in 8:6 and again in 9:21.

Second, there is the question of how to translate the phrase *tōn hagiōn . . . kai tēs skēnēs tēs alēthinēs*. It is clear enough that the author is pointing to the heavenly realm, and identifying it as the "genuine tent." The adjective *alēthinos* is used here (see also 9:24 and 10:22) as it is in the Gospel of John to distinguish the "real thing" from that which may distantly approximate it. So in John's Gospel, Jesus is the "genuine light" (*to phōs to alēthinon*, 1:9), the "genuine bread" (*arton . . . ton alēthinon*, 6:32), and the "genuine vine" (*ampelos hē alēthinē*, 15:1). Likewise for Hebrews, there is a tent on earth, but Jesus ministers in the "genuine tent" in heaven.

The noun *skēnē*, in turn, equally clearly alludes to the sanctuary that Moses had constructed for the dwelling place of God (Exod 25:8) in the wilderness, the place of worship carried out by the sons of Aaron, the Levitical priests (Exod 26:1–36; 27:9, 21; 35:11; 40:2–38; Lev 16:7–33). The arrangements of this earthly *skēnē* will be described in Heb 9:1–5. For now it need only be observed that when Hebrews uses the term *alēthinos* of the heavenly tent, its earthly counterpart is necessarily deprecated.

The translation of *ta hagia* and its relation to the "genuine tent" is a bit more difficult. The noun means simply "holy things," and it would theoretically be possible to translate the entire phrase as "minister of the holy things and of the genuine tent." In some passages of the LXX, however (see Jdt 4:12; 16:20; 1 Macc 3:43, 59) and in some Hellenistic Jewish writers (Philo, *Flight and Finding* 93; Josephus, *J.W.* 2.341), the phrase *ta hagia* is used specifically to indicate "the sanctuary." Other uses in Hebrews clearly bear that meaning as well (see 9:3, 12, 24, 25; 10:19; 13:11). But if *ta hagia* can mean sanctuary, why is it linked to "the genuine tent" by the copulative "and" (*kai*)?

Two possibilities present themselves. One is to take "sanctuary and genuine tent" as a hendiadys (saying one thing through two phrases). So Koester (341) translates, "Of the sanctuary, that is, of the true tent." The other possibility is to consider Hebrews to be making a distinction (as some other authors did) between the inner sanctuary (*ta hagia*) and the tabernacle as a whole (*hē skēnē*), as in Lev 16:16, 20, 33. So Attridge (216) translates, "of the sanctuary and of the true tabernacle." But the decision is not a critical one, for the author's real interest is in the distinction between the heavenly worship carried out by Jesus and that conducted on earth. Both *ta hagia* and *tēs skēnēs tēs alēthinēs* fall on the heavenly side of the contrast, as the next phrase makes clear.

The third aspect of the statement in 8:2 is that the tent/sanctuary where Jesus serves is one "built by the Lord, not a human." The verb *pegnynai* (found only here in the NT) means literally to "pitch" a tent (see Gen 26:25; 31:25), and is used by the LXX for the "pitching" of the tent of testimony (Exod 38:6; Josh 18:1). The construction "tents that the Lord had pitched" occurs in Num 24:6 with reference to "the houses of Jacob" rather than the sanctuary. Here the contrast between divine and human construction gives further nuance to the "genuine tent," and echoes the deprecation of "things made by hands" throughout Scripture, whether temples or gods or rituals (see Lev 26:1, 30; Judg 8:18; Wis 14:8; Isa 2:18; 10:11; 16:12; 21:9; Dan 5:4, 23; 6:27; Acts 7:48; 17:24; Mark 14:58; 2 Cor 5:1; Col 2:11; Eph 2:11).

[3–6] The next four verses serve to prepare readers for the following stages of the argument. Having stated that Christ's priestly service is in the heavens, and that this is the "true tent" of God's presence, the author quickly raises the question of Christ's offering (v. 3), as a way of again asserting that his priesthood is not on earth (v. 4). He then explicitly identifies the Israelite cult as a shadow of the reality (v. 5) before concluding with a statement concerning the superiority of Christ's priesthood in direct connection with the superiority of the covenant that he mediates (v. 6). Each of these statements will be unfolded further in the succeeding chapters, but in reverse order: the new covenant will be examined in 8:7–13, the "shadow" character of worship under the old covenant is described in 9:1–10, and the nature of Christ's self-sacrifice is defined in 9:11–10:18.

In 8:3 the author makes a general statement about high priesthood almost identical to the one he made in 5:1. There he declared that every high priest is appointed (*kathistatai*) to represent humans in matters concerning God (*ta pros ton theon*), and spells that out in terms of "offering gifts and sacrifices in behalf of sins." Here the same point about being appointed (*kathistatai*) to offer gifts and sacrifices leads to the inference that if this is the case for "all high priests," then it is necessarily also the case for "this one" (*touton*), namely Jesus. He also must have something to offer. But what can he possibly offer God in the heavenly places?

Hebrews begins by eliminating the possibility that Jesus offers "the gifts according to law." There are already priests who do that, and they are on earth. But Jesus is in heaven! The contrary-to-fact conditional sentence says everything about Hebrews' perception of Jesus' present and ongoing existence: "if he were on earth, he would not even be a priest." As the author showed already in 7:13–19, Jesus does not fit the ordinance of the law concerning Israelite priests. The form of his priesthood, rather, is his eternal existence with God (7:23–25).

The contrast between the location of his ministry and that of the Levitical priests is made even more explicit in verse 5, where the author takes as evidence that the merely human priests serve "in a copy and shadow of the heavenly things," the divine instruction given to Moses when he was about to build the tent in the wilderness: "see that you make everything according to the pattern that was shown to you on the mountain" (Exod 25:40). The citation corresponds closely to the LXX, although Hebrews adds the word *panta* ("everything") and replaces the LXX's perfect passive participle (*ton dedeigmenon*) with an aorist passive participle (*ton deichthenta*). This is a statement of great importance within Hebrews, because it supports not only this portion of the argument, but also the entire worldview of the composition.[1]

1. For background see L. Goppelt, *Typos: The Typological Interpretation of the Old Testament in the New*, trans. D. H. Madvig (Grand Rapids: Eerdmans, 1982), esp. pp. 1–60; and M. Wilcox, "'According to the Pattern (*tbnyt*) . . .': Exodus 25,40 in the New Testament and Early Jewish Thought," *RevQ* 13 (1988): 647–56.

We should notice that the author does not only quote the scriptural text but typically characterizes it in terms of an oral proclamation from God. The verb *chrēmatizein* is used for the delivery of an oracle (Philo, *Moses* 2.238; Josephus, *Ant.* 5.42) or of a revelation (see Matt 2:12, 22; Luke 2:26; Acts 10:22; 11:26). In the present case, there is a slight nuance of "warning" as well, a sense supported also by the two other instances of the verb within the composition (Heb 11:7; 12:25), as well as by the imperative *hora* ("see to it")! The reception of this oracle while "on the mountain," furthermore, is another way of saying in God's presence, for in the exodus narrative, the mountain is where Moses converses with God and receives his instructions (Exod 19:3–23; 24:4–18; 26:30; 34:1–4).

What was Moses shown in God's presence? He was shown the *typos* "according to which" (*kata*) he was to make all things in the sanctuary. Here is the key word in the citation for Hebrews. The Greek *typos* translates Heb. *tabnît*, which itself simply means "building" or "construction." In the original Hebrew, then, Moses is simply told to build a tent like the one he saw on the mountain. The LXX, however, does not translate with the noun *oikodomē*, but instead uses *typos*. In the next verse, the LXX continues, "and you will make for me according to everything that I have shown to you on the mountain, the model (*paradeigma*) for the tent and the model (*paradeigma*) for all its vessels. Thus shall you make."

The Greek translation allows an inference not suggested by the Hebrew. The Hebrew can be understood as supporting the sanctuary constructed by Moses as conforming in every respect to the building God showed him. But readers of the LXX (like Philo and the author of Hebrews) could scarcely avoid another sort of inference, suggested by the use of *typos* and *paradeigma*. They could conclude that the earthly, material edifice was but a pale imitation of an ideal prototype, and as a consequence that the earthly sacrifices carried out every day were but an imitation of something more real taking place in heaven. So Philo contrasts the realities that Moses was shown with the shadows of those realities that Moses' builder Bezalel (Exod 31:2) constructed (see *Allegorical Laws* 3.96; *Dreams* 1.206).

The contrast between the *typos* in heaven and the *skia kai hypodeigma* that are on earth perfectly illustrates what I have called in the introduction to this commentary the Platonic worldview of Hebrews, which marries the philosophical dualism of the Greek philosopher to biblical cosmology. Although the noun *typos* has wide applicability as an impression or shape, it is most associated philosophically with the work of Plato, where, in a variety of contexts, it can be used of an archetype, pattern, or model (Plato, *Republic* 379A, 380C, 396E), or of a general character (*Theaetetus* 171E; *Republic* 402D), or of an outline or sketch (*Republic* 403E; *Laws* 876E). Within a Platonic framework, the ideal or spiritual realm holds the *typoi* of which the material representations are mere copies or imitations. The imitation depends on the ideal type, so there is a real connection, but it is always derivative and secondary. There is both ontology and axiology involved in Platonic dualism: the ideal is more real than the material representation, and the ideal is also better, more worthy, than the physical imitation.

For Hebrews, to be sure, something more than Platonism is at work here. The ideal realm is not merely a matter of the mental but of the divine. The fundamental contrast is between the sphere of God's existence and the entire realm of creation. But the language for expressing the contrast is undoubtedly that associated with Plato. The *typos* shown Moses on the mountain is the "genuine tent" and the "sanctuary" of God's presence. No material sanctuary can adequately capture that reality. Thus the author contrasts to this *typos* the *skia* and *hypodeigma* where the Levitical priests carry out their ministry. These last terms are generally clear, although the fact that *hypodeigma* can also be used in the sense of "example to be followed" adds some ambiguity (see Philo, *Who Is the Heir?* 256; Josephus, *J.W.* 6.103; Sir 44:16; John 13:15; Jas 5:10; 2 Pet 2:6). Indeed, Hebrews itself uses *hypodeigma* this way earlier with reference to the wilderness generation (4:11). In context, however, there is no doubt that here *hypodeigma* stands with *skia* on the secondary and derivative side of the contrast with the ideal type (see also Heb 9:23). In our literature, *skia* ("shadow") consistently is opposed to reality (see Philo, *Dreams* 1.206; *Allegorical Laws* 3.102; Col 2:17). In Plato's *Republic* 715A-B, the allegory of the cave contrasts "shadows" to realities. One might even translate the two terms here as a hendiadys: "shadowy outline."

In short, the author of Hebrews, like Philo, is comfortable reading the LXX from the perspective of a Platonic metaphysics and epistemology, and finds nothing "unbiblical" about such reading (cf. Philo, *Dreams* 1.188; *Allegorical Laws* 3.97–99). This text of Scripture, furthermore, serves precisely to ground such a view of reality, in which a sharp distinction is made between realms of being, between the real and the imitation. It is, to be sure, of the first importance to remember that for Hebrews the Platonic distinction itself must ultimately be transcended, precisely because the Son of God entered fully into God's creation and into the flesh of humans. Nevertheless, the language of Platonism serves our author well as a means to emphasize the qualitatively different character of Christ's ministry from that of the Levitical priesthood.

In the discussion of 7:11–19, we saw that a critical premise for Hebrews is that priesthood and covenant are inextricably linked, so that a change in one demands a change in the other. That principle reappears in 8:6. But now, instead of asserting *what* Jesus has to offer in place of the sacrifices and gifts brought by the sons of Aaron—that will be developed in the chapters to follow—the author simply affirms again in slightly different language the point of verse 2: he has obtained a ministry (here *leitourgia*, the public act itself) commensurate to the covenant of which he is the mediator.

We saw that Jesus was identified as an *engyos* of a better covenant in 7:22. Here he is called a *mesitēs*, another legal technical term in the Hellenistic world (used by the LXX only in Job 9:33). A *mesitēs* is one who helps two parties resolve a dispute or reach a common goal (see P.Oxy. 1298.19; P.Lon. 1.113.1.26). Thus Paul designates Moses as a *mesitēs* of the law in Gal 3:19–20. Mithras is identified as a *mesitēs* between two gods by Plutarch (*Isis and Osiris* 46 [*Mor*. 369E]). Paul speaks of Jesus as a *mesitēs* between God and humans (1 Tim 2:5). Although the term can occur as roughly equivalent to *engyos* ("pledge," as in 7:22; see Diodorus Siculus, *Library of History* 4.46.4; 4.54.7), Hebrews clearly sees Jesus as the effective agent of a covenant (*diathēkē*) between God and humans that is characterized as "better" (8:6), and "new" (*kainē*, 9:15; *nea*, 12:24). How it is better and new, the composition has yet to reveal.

This conclusion, nevertheless, sets up the long citation from Jeremiah concerning the new covenant that God promised through the prophet. This "better covenant" is established, he says, (note the use of *nomoethetein*, as in 7:11) upon "better promises." He means, better than those of the law. But what are they? Certainly, the author must want to include the oath made in the psalm to the messiah king like Melchizedek that his priesthood would last forever. But he probably also means the prophetic promise spoken by Jeremiah of a covenant that would be grounded in the hearts and minds of humans. As throughout his long argument, the author finds in the words of Scripture clear intimations of the claims that he (and his community) make for Jesus. The best promise of all, of course, is the experience of the power of this exalted Lord, shared by the author and his hearers: "we have such a high priest!"

8:7–13 The Promise of a New Covenant

The theme of a new covenant is as prominent in this composition as the theme of a new priesthood. Indeed, as we have seen, for Hebrews the two are intertwined. Jesus was called the pledge of a better covenant in 7:22, and the section immediately preceding this one ended by designating him the mediator of a better covenant (8:6). The term "covenant" (*diathēkē*) will appear repeatedly in the succeeding chapters (see 9:4, 15, 16, 17, 20; 10:16, 29; 12:24; 13:20). The theme is formally initiated, however, by this passage, whose structure is simple. An introductory sentence leads to a long, explicit quotation from the prophet Jer 31:31–34 (LXX 38:31–34), and the section concludes with a flat statement concerning the implication of the prophetic language. The wording of the citation is critical to the author's understanding of the supremacy of the covenant mediated by Jesus, for it points to a relationship with God that is direct and internal. After the commentary on this section, a short excursus will examine Hebrews' understanding of the new covenant and its implications for Christians today.

8:7 Now if the first covenant had been without fault, a place would not
have been sought for a second.[a] **8** For, when he finds fault with them, he
says, "Behold, days are coming, says the Lord, and I will complete with
the house of Israel and with the house of Judah a new covenant. **9** It will
not be like the covenant that I made with their fathers in the day[b] when I
grasped their hand to lead them out of the land of Egypt, because they did
not remain in my covenant and I grew unconcerned about them. **10** Because
this is the covenant[c] that I will make in the house of Israel after those days,
says the Lord: I will give my laws into their minds and I will engrave[d]
them on their hearts.[e] And I will be their God and they will be my peo-
ple. **11** And each one will not teach his countryman[f] or each one say to
his[g] brother, 'Know the Lord.' Because all of them will know me, from
the little[h] to the great among them. **12** For I will be merciful with regard
to their injustices, and their sins[i] I will not remember any longer." **13** By
saying "new," he has made the first old. And that which has been made
old is also aging to the point of destruction.

a. B has *heteras* ("another") rather that *deuteras* ("second").

b. B and a Sahidic MS has the plural "days" (*hēmerais*) rather than the singular "day" (*hēmera*).

c. A and D add the possessive pronoun *mou* ("my"), under the influence of the LXX, which also has it. The difference would be: "this is my covenant."

d. P[46], B, and other witnesses follow the LXX in reading *grapsō* ("I will write") rather than *epigrapsō* ("I will engrave").

e. MSS reveal considerable uncertainty with respect to the number and case of the Greek "heart" (*kardia*). Some have the singular accusative, some the singular or plural dative. The reading *kardias*, found in the majority of witnesses, can be either genitive singular or accusative plural.

f. The Greek noun *politēs* ("countryman") follows the LXX, and is found in P[46] and the major uncials. MSS that change it to *plēsion* ("neighbor") were probably impressed by the relative rarity of *politēs* in the LXX.

g. Although the personal pronoun "his" (*autou*) would in any case be assumed with a relational term like "brother," its absence from P[46] and the original hand of D is difficult to understand, given its presence in the LXX.

h. Following the LXX, the second hand of D and a large number of other witnesses add "their" (*autōn*).

i. Under the influence of Heb 10:17, a substantial number of important witnesses add *kai tōn anomiōn autōn* ("and their lawless deeds") to this citation. The shorter version found in P[46] and the original hand of B is probably correct. The LXX has "their injustices and their sins" (*adikias autōn kai tōn hamartiōn autōn*) (Jer 38:34).

[8:7–9] For Hebrews, the introduction of a new covenant by God is not arbitrary. It is prepared for by a promise made by God through the prophet Jeremiah, and that promise reveals a problem in the earlier covenant made on Mount Sinai. We note that the author does not challenge the covenant made with Abraham (see 2:16–18; 6:13–20), but only that mediated by Moses. He begins in 8:7 with a contrary-to-fact conditional sentence: there would have been no search for a second covenant if the first had been without blame. The very structure of the syntax implies that there was such fault to be found.

The adjective *amemptos* corresponds to the verb *memphomai* ("to blame, find fault with") in 8:8. It therefore means "blameless" not quite in the sense of "innocent," but in the sense that no one has found fault with it. But the attachment of blame to the covenant as such is somewhat puzzling, since in the next verse (8:8) blame is directed to those who failed to remain in the covenant. To be fair, the failure of people to keep a covenant does not by itself condemn the terms of the covenant or require a new framework for the relationship. But however illogical, that is the line our author follows. It is important to remember that for the author, it is precisely the failure of the people to keep it that reveals the inadequacy of the first covenant. Why? Here we again see the author's conviction that the worth of a covenant is measured by its efficacy in perfecting persons. Their failure to be perfected is a failure of the covenant as such.

Consonant with the rest of the composition, this citation from Jeremiah is not ascribed to him as such, nor is it cited as Scripture. Rather, it is regarded as God's own speech (*legein*) as he expresses his complaint against the people within the first covenant (see Heb 1:1). Before considering the content of this unusually long passage, it may be helpful to examine its original context within the book of Jeremiah, the ways in which the LXX differs from the Hebrew (MT), and how Hebrews itself differs from the LXX.[1] Because the English translations based on the MT are more easily accessible, I follow their chapter and verse numbers throughout this discussion.

The solemn declaration that "days are coming" in Jer 31:31 (LXX 38:31) is one of a series of oracles that begin in 30:1 (LXX 37:1). The phrase "days are coming" is repeated throughout (30:3; 31:27, 31, 38), and throughout as well the miseries to befall the people are interspersed with assurances concerning God's faithful love (see 31:1–6, 19–20, 23–29), culminating—immediately after the promise of a new covenant—with the pledge that never shall "the descendants of Israel cease from being a nation before me forever." In the original context of the Hebrew Bible, therefore, this promise of a new covenant is

1. For discussion see M. Weinfeld, "Jeremiah and the Spiritual Metamorphosis of Israel," *ZAW* 88 (1976): 17–56; and F. A. Malone, "A Critical Evaluation of the Use of Jeremiah 31:31–34 in the Letter to the Hebrews" (Ph.D. diss., Southwestern Baptist Theological Seminary, 1969).

to be seen as an intensification and internalization—a new "realization"—of the Sinai covenant itself, rather than its replacement.

The LXX translation differs from the original Hebrew in three places. First, in the framing of the complaint, the MT has "my covenant that they broke, though I was their husband," whereas the LXX has "they did not remain in my covenant and I grew unconcerned about them." The *egō ēmelēsa* (v. 32) asserts a corresponding response of the Lord to the people's infidelity that is absent from the Hebrew. Second, the MT has "I will put my law within them," and the LXX has "I will give my laws into their minds" (v. 33). Finally, the MT has each one teaching "his neighbor," whereas the LXX has each one teaching his "countryman" (v. 33).

The version of the Jeremiah passage in Hebrews also differs in some respects from the LXX. Hebrews has *syntelesō* ("I will complete") rather than the LXX *diathēsomai* ("I will make covenant"). Throughout the citation, Hebrews replaces the LXX's verb for speaking (*phēsin*) with *legei* (there is no difference in meaning). Hebrews 8:9 uses the verb form *epoiēsa* ("I made") rather than the LXX *diethemēn* ("I established"). According to the best manuscripts, Hebrews drops the personal pronoun *mou* ("my") in 8:10, as well as the verb *dōsō* (" I will give"). Hebrews uses the verb *epigrapsō* ("I will engrave") rather than the LXX *grapsō* ("I will write"). Finally, in 8:11 Hebrews omits LXX *autōn kai* in the phrase "from the little to the great among them." The introduction to the citation is also noteworthy, since the author has chosen to pick up the term *amemptos* ("blameless") in 8:7 by using the participle *memphomenos* ("when he finds fault with them"). The author thus places at least as much emphasis on the negative as on the positive by the way in which he frames the scriptural passage.

The first line of Jeremiah's prophecy has three noteworthy aspects. First is the phrase "days are coming." The author of Hebrews naturally understands this to refer to "these final days" in which he and his hearers live (see 1:1). Second is the address to the house of Israel and the house of Judah: historically, this split designation reflects the divided kingdom; eschatologically, it points to the restored and united Israel (see "house of Israel" below). Third is the phrase "new covenant," which occurs here for the only time in the Old Testament.

This language fits, however, within the more frequent language of Jeremiah, Isaiah, and Ezekiel, about the "new things" God will accomplish in the future. A few verses before this promise of a new covenant, Jeremiah says (LXX 38:22) that the Lord has created a salvation for a new planting. Isaiah 43:19 has the Lord declare, "I am making new things" (see also 48:6); Israel, says the prophet, will be called by "a new name" (62:2; 65:15); and God will create a "new heaven and a new earth" (65:17; 66:22). Ezekiel has the Lord promise to give the people a "new spirit" (11:19), and twice that he will give them a "new heart and new spirit" (18:31; 36:26). Jeremiah's promise of a "new covenant" in which people will know the Lord from the heart, then, fits within a fairly widespread prophetic longing for a deeper and more personal level of commitment to God, and the expectation that God will act to create such a new reality.

The announcement of God's intention to form a new covenant leads immediately to a contrast: it will "not be like" (or "not according to," *ou kata*) the Sinai covenant (8:9). The reference to Sinai is unmistakable: "on the day when I grasped their hand to lead them out of the land of Egypt." The phrase "grasping their hand" (*epilabomenou tēs cheiros autōn*) reminds us of the statement in Heb 2:16, that the Son did not "take hold" of the angels but rather "took hold" of the seed of Abraham. The reference to coming out of Egypt also echoes the negative portrayal of the wilderness generation in 3:7–19, which also opened to the possibility of a later generation entering into the "true rest" (4:1–11).

Jeremiah does not, we note, identify a problem with the terms of the first covenant as such. But his (i.e., God's) complaint concerns the failure of the people to be obedient to those terms: they "did not remain in my covenant." They did not, to put it another way, remain faithfully within the relationship with God spelled out by the first covenant. As I observed above, the MT and LXX diverge dramatically at this point. In the Hebrew, Jeremiah accentuates the infidelity of the people by asserting that the Lord was their husband. We remember that in the prophets, covenant is constantly symbolized by marriage, as in Jer 31:3–5. The LXX and Hebrews, in contrast, have the Lord respond in kind to the people's neglect: "and I grew unconcerned about them" (*kagō ēmelēsa autōn*). The verb *amelein* can scarcely be understood in any other way. The LXX of Jer 4:17 uses it for the people's rebellion against God; in Wis 3:10 it is used for the wicked people's neglect of the righteous one; and in 2 Macc 4:14 it refers to the priests' neglect of the sacrifices of the temple. A fundamental flaw of the first covenant would appear to be, then, its fragility and uncertainty, on both sides. The new covenant, says the prophet, will not be "like that one."

[10–13] God's new covenant will be "unlike" the earlier one with respect to both parties, the people and the Lord himself. The new covenant will have the people respond from the mind and the heart with direct knowledge of the Lord. Here is the contrast between external and internal dear to Platonism and to the author of Hebrews: not the external practices of ritual but the internal dispositions of the human person lie at the center of the new covenant. But did they not of the first covenant as well? Yes, but in the eyes of our author, ineffectively.

What is needed is the participation of God's Son on the side of humans as their anchor of hope and pledge of the covenant. So, says Jeremiah, God will "give my laws into their minds and I will engrave them on their hearts." The phrase "mind and heart" echoes the Shema in Deut 6:6: God's commandments are to be "in your heart (*kardia*) and in your soul (*psychē*)." What is different is not the desired end, but the divine agency to accomplish that end. This is a covenant that God will not only "make" (*poiein*), but will "complete/fulfill" (*syntelein*). For Hebrews, God has accomplished this by the human response of Jesus, who was perfected through his faithful obedience.

As a result of this internal knowledge and obedience, promises the Lord, "I will be their God and they will be my people" (in the Greek, lit., "I will be God with respect to them and they will be a people with respect to me"). Once more, this is a statement that echoes the covenantal pledge sounded throughout the Hebrew Bible. In Exod 6:7 God declares, "I will take you for my people. And I will be your God." Leviticus 26:12 has God promise that if the people keep all his statutes, "I will walk among you and will be your God and you shall be my people" (see also Deut 26:17–19). Likewise in Jer 7:23, "Obey my voice and I will be your God and you shall be my people" (see also Jer 11:4). And Ezekiel promises that when the new spirit breathes on the people and they observe all God's statutes, "I will make a covenant of peace with them, and I will bless them and multiply them, and will set my sanctuary in the midst of them forever. My dwelling place shall be with them; and I will be their God and they shall be my people" (Ezek 37:26–27). The terms are not changed, only the agency by which they will be accomplished and the fullness of their realization.

The effectiveness of the new covenant will be shown by the immediacy and the intimacy of relationship to God that it enables. Immediacy: no one will need to teach fellow countrymen, as Moses taught God's commandments to Israel (Deut 4:5; 11:19–20) and enjoined them in turn to teach their children (4:9–10; 6:7–9; 11:19–20). The instruction, "Know the Lord" (*gnōthi ton kyrion*), is unattested in this form otherwise in Scripture, but it contains the essence of a variety of statements that, on one side, call for an acknowledgment ("knowing") *that* the Lord is their God ("you will know that I am the Lord your God," Exod 6:7; see also 7:17; 10:2; 29:46; 31:13; Deut 29:6; Pss 45:10; 99:3; Isa 45:3; 49:23; Jer 9:24; Ezek 6:13; 7:27; 13:23), and, on another side, a response to the Lord of obedience in life (see Judg 2:10; 1 Sam 2:10 [only in LXX]; Ps 9:10; Isa 1:3; 60:16; Jer 4:22; 5:1; 8:7; 9:3).

Such knowledge will not need to be taught to them, for it will be universally shared, "from the little to the great among them." They will all, the prophet promises, "know me." What the first covenant hoped to accomplish, through a process of external observance and mediated instruction, God will directly accomplish for all. According to the LXX text used by Hebrews, a defect in the first covenant was not simply the people's failure to remain within it, but also the consequent "neglect" of them by the Lord. In the new covenant, however, the direct and internal knowledge of the Lord from the side of the people will have corresponding to it—or better, causing it (*hoti*)—the positive disposition toward them of the Lord. He will show mercy toward their unjust deeds. Mercy (*eleos*) is one of the Lord's essential covenantal qualities (Exod 20:6; 34:7; Deut 5:10; 7:9) and is constantly sought by sinners in prayer (Pss 5:7; 6:4; 12:5; 16:7; 22:6; 24:10; 30:16; 39:10–11; 50:1, etc.). God will also no longer remember their sins. "Not remembering" here is startling, for the language of Scripture constantly calls on God to "remember" his covenant with the people (Gen 9:15; Exod 2:24; 6:5; Pss 24:6; 73:2, 18; 88:50; 105:4; 113:20; 131:1; Luke 1:54, 72), and, indeed, to remember his mercy toward them (Ps 24:6–7). But the construction makes sense here, as corresponding to the "not being concerned" of Heb 8:9, which expressed God's response to the people's infidelity in the first covenant. Here, "not remembering" their sins (see Ps 78:8) is precisely a way of "remembering" *them* and showing them mercy. It is precisely to remain "concerned about" them forever.

As he does with other citations from Scripture, the author concludes this passage from Jeremiah with a closing comment (see 1:14; 10:18, 39; 11:7). The precise weight of this one is difficult to assess, making for real differences in translation. At one level, the author begins by making an obvious linguistic point: by using the term "new," Jeremiah has automatically made the first covenant "old." But how strongly should the verb *pepalaiōken* ("to make old") be translated? Some interpreters opt for the very strong "made obsolete" (see RSV, Koester), and regard Hebrews as formally stating a nullification of the first covenant, just as the earlier declaration in 7:18 about a "setting aside" of the previous commandment was taken to mean a legal abrogation (Koester, 355). One can see the legal dimension of such language when *diathēkē* is taken to mean the same thing in every place as "will/testament," for it is patent that a new will cancels the old one.

In the present passage, however, it is not at all clear how much the sense of "will" is present. The term *diathēkē* appears here to have the classical sense of an agreement or treaty between persons. Furthermore, as we have seen, the terms or goals of the first covenant are not here changed. The promise is, rather, that they will be realized. The translation of "obsolete" in the first clause seems, therefore, to be overly definite, and I have chosen instead to render the verb simply as "made the first old."

Equally difficult is translating the next phrase, *gēraskon engys aphanismou*. Once more, we can move from the clear to the unclear. First, the author is describing a process that is underway rather than a finished reality; but does he mean it was underway already in the time of Jeremiah, or in "these last days"? Second, the verb *gēraskon* (here in the present participle) is used frequently by the LXX for the normal process of human aging (Gen 18:13; 24:36; 27:1; Josh 23:2; 1 Sam 8:1, 5; 12:2; Tob 14:3; Ps 36:25; 1 Macc 16:3). In some of these passages, however, there is the implication that aging also brings with it a loss of vitality and strength (see especially Gen 1:18; 1 Sam 8:1; Ruth 1:12). In this light, to characterize the first covenant as "aging" suggests in another way its "weakness and ineffectiveness" (see Heb 7:18, 28).

Third, and most difficult, is the noun *aphanismou*, which the aging covenant is said to be "approaching" (*engys*). In broader usage, the verb *aphanizein* can mean simply to hide, make unseen, or "disappear" something. But the noun constructed from the passive verb is also used for "destruction" (Polybius, *History* 5.11.5), whether of cities (Diodorus Siculus, *Library of History* 15.48) or of body and soul (Plutarch, *Letter to Apollonius* 12 [*Mor.* 107D]). This does not suggest a mere "vanishing" but a more deliberate "destroying." The usage in the LXX makes this nuance the more likely in the present passage. In the LXX the verb *aphanizein* is used often for the destruction of foes (Deut 7:2; 19:1; 2 Sam 21:5; Pss 12:7; 14:11; Wis 3:6; Mic 5:14). More tellingly, the noun *aphanismos* is used for destruction rather than simply disappearance (Deut 7:2; 1 Kgs 9:7; Jdt 4:1; Esth 8:13; Mic 1:7; 7:13; Zech 1:13; Mal 1:3; Jer 9:11; Ezek 6:14). Given Hebrews' superb grasp of the diction of the LXX, it is difficult to see how the author could not have been aware of this nuance, and it is therefore the more likely that *aphanismos* has a similar sense here: the first covenant is not only old and weak, it is destined for an imminent destruction.

Excursus 5: Old and New Covenants

Hebrews' language about the first (old) covenant and the new covenant would not have appeared problematic to many generations of Christian interpreters. But it has become problematic for those of us who take seriously the experience of the Holocaust in the twentieth century and the way it opened our eyes to the consequences of a centuries-long history of Christian supersessionist readings of Scripture. In supersessionist readings, the failure of Jews to acknowledge Jesus as Messiah was regarded as a rejection of God's plan for them, and therefore the nullification of their status as God's elect people. Jews were therefore no longer God's people and Christians were. God's making of a new covenant was not simply a rejection of the old covenant but as well the rejection of the people that continued to live within that earlier covenant. Christians consequently were not only the "new people of God" living within the "new covenant," but they had the right to define the identity of Jews (they are those who still await a messiah) and declare on their fate (they live under God's curse).

History is notoriously written by winners, and the right to define Judaism's place in history seemed to belong to Christians because history for so long seemed to be on the Christian side. Jews lost their temple and their land, and their very ability to exist was owed to the pleasure and patience of a Christian state. In such triumphalistic readings, Hebrews—together with a handful of passages in Paul—seemed to provide a perfect set of proof texts to support the obvious evidence offered by historical events. Thus it was not with reluctance but with relish that Christian translators would render Heb 8:13 in as harsh a manner as possible. The first covenant is not only old but obsolete. It is near to obliteration.

It is not only the sense of moral revulsion created by Christians' awareness of their role in the suppression and murder of Jews, and the sense of theological revulsion generated by Christian awareness of how distorting such supersessionist views are of Christianity itself, but equally the way in which historical events have forced Christians to reexamine the premise that they are history's darlings, that lead contemporary interpreters to a chastened attitude when dealing with language about old and new covenants. Recent history has not been particularly kind to Christian pretensions: Christianity has been politically disestablished and intellectually marginalized within modernity. Christian theologians are called to recover grounds for Christianity's truth more significant than its simply not being Judaism. Christian exegetes are therefore correctly cautious when they tread warily among language that their predecessors took for granted.

A short excursus in a commentary on Hebrews is not the place to sort out all the theological issues raised by the New Testament's rhetoric concerning Jews, but it is an appropriate place to sort out the specific language used in this passage and throughout Hebrews concerning old and new covenants.[2] I will therefore touch first on some theological issues, and then focus on Hebrews' language in the context of other contemporary Jewish literature.

From the perspective of early Christian experience and conviction, Hebrews' declarations are perfectly legitimate. They have their basis in the experience of Jesus as exalted Lord and a tradition that may well go back to Jesus himself (see below), namely, that his death is the basis for a new covenant between God and humans. The author of Hebrews is not a neutral student of religion, but speaks passionately as an advocate of this "new thing" that God has brought about through his Son in "these last days." From that standpoint it is also legitimate, perhaps even inevitable, that Hebrews criticizes the earlier covenant on the grounds that it was weak and ineffective.

But we must also recognize that Hebrews is, in effect, reinterpreting the purpose of the covenant from the perspective of present experience and conviction. To put it another way, it is in light of what Jesus accomplishes that the author finds the earlier covenant insufficient. What has Jesus accomplished? The perfecting of persons, their transformation. Jesus is the pioneer and perfecter of this transformation. What he has reached, others can now attain. The first covenant did not accomplish this.

Such redefinition is fair enough, so long as it is recognized as a changing of the terms. A Jew standing outside the experience of Jesus as exalted Lord, and unconvinced—for whatever reasons—by the claims made for Jesus as the mediator of a new covenant, might with equal legitimacy reject that redefinition. A Jew might insist that the covenant was never intended to secure the perfection of individual persons but rather the safety, stability, and sanctity of the people as a community dedicated to the one God of Israel. By such a definition of the covenant's goals, the first covenant was not weak and ineffective but perfectly adequate, especially since it was in the name of that covenant that God constantly drew the people back to himself when they strayed.

We must pay careful attention to what Hebrews is actually saying and what it is not saying. First, the author of Hebrews does not stand outside the original covenant that God established with the "seed of Abraham" and the promise that God secured by his unfailing oath (2:16; 6:13–18); rather, the author stands within the commitments and story of this covenanted people. Nowhere does the author suggest that God's word through the Son is a disavowal of the words spoken to "our fathers" of old (1:1). Rather, the author makes a claim for a new covenant precisely for this people.

2. See further S. Lehne, "The Concept of the New Covenant in Hebrews" (Ph.D. diss., Columbia University, 1989).

It follows from this, second, that Hebrews contains no trace of the rejection of the people of Israel or their replacement by another people. There is here no contrast between Gentiles and Jews. There is certainly as yet no "Christianity" facing off against an equally defined "Judaism." Hebrews does not therefore speak as representative of a Gentile Christianity that claims to have superseded Judaism. Hebrews' voice, rather, is like that of the covenanters at Qumran (see below) who claimed a better covenant mediated by their teacher without in the least rejecting the earlier covenant, much less their claim to authentic Jewish identity.

Third, the author of Hebrews does not suggest that the first covenant was wrong or a mistake, any more than he regards the bringing of the people into the land under Joshua to have been a mistake—even though they did not reach God's rest (3:7–4:13). The covenant simply was unable to accomplish what, by Hebrews' definition (in light of the experience of the exalted Lord Jesus), a "better covenant" should be able to accomplish. The first is seen as old and weak and disappearing only because of the new and powerful work of God in Christ, who has provided access to the presence of God.

Finally, Hebrews does not even take up—indeed, was not in a position to take up—the status of Judaism (as a religion among other religions!) in light of the experience of Jesus as exalted Lord. What Hebrews does take up—and is competent to take up and speak truthfully about—is the call of God to a deeper obedience of faith revealed and demonstrated by the crucified and raised Messiah Jesus. It follows, I submit, that present-day theologians who are tempted to discourse about Jewish and Christian relations should not make Hebrews speak absolutely or anachronistically, but should recognize the gap between the situation faced by Hebrews and the questions posed by circumstances today, and should therefore hear Hebrews (and all other scriptural witnesses) with a certain degree of subtlety. Theologians today might do well to focus less on what Hebrews says about the first covenant than on what Hebrews insists is the rigorous demand of obedience imposed by the new covenant, and rather than seek to discourse about the fate of the Jews in God's plan, might seek to discover the dimensions of following the fidelity of Jesus to God's plan.

Once appropriate theological caution is exercised, it is nevertheless also good to recognize the startling claims being made by Hebrews concerning the old and new covenants. As I noted in the commentary, the prophet Jeremiah is not alone in promising that God will do "new things," even of a fundamental character (like creating a new heaven and a new earth!), but Jeremiah is alone in applying the language of newness to the covenant. When Scripture speaks of the covenant God made with Abraham, its eternal character is frequently asserted (Gen 17:7; 1 Chr 16:15–18; Ps 104:10; Sir 44:18; 2 Esd 3:15; see also Pseudo-Philo, *L.A.B.* 8.4). Nor does Hebrews, as we have seen, challenge the Abrahamic covenant. With somewhat less frequency, Jewish literature also affirms the eternal character of the Sinai covenant (the one to which Jeremiah contrasts the new covenant; see Sir 17:12; 45:7, 15; *4 Ezra* 9.36–37; *2 Bar*. 77.15; Philo, *Moses* 2.14–15; Pseudo-Philo, *L.A.B.* 11.2). Until the discovery of the Dead Sea Scrolls, indeed, the appropriation of the idea of a new covenant among early Christian writings appeared to be unique.

Now we see that the language of Hebrews and other New Testament compositions concerning covenant finds its closest analogy in the sectarian writings from Qumran. Here are Jews—in all likelihood contemporary to the composition of Hebrews—withdrawing into the wilderness "to prepare for the coming of the Lord" by the closest observance of Torah (1QS 8:13–16), the complete removal of the impure from their midst (5:1–3; 7:24–25; 8:22–24), and a total sharing of possessions as a community of the pure (1:11–12; 6:17–22; 6:24–7:27). Five aspects of this intriguing sect are of special interest.

First, they observed the law of Moses accurately, but according to the specific interpretation of the law provided by their "Teacher of Righteousness," who had special insight into its meaning (CD 20:1; 1QpHab 2:2; 9:9–10). Second, they regarded their community as a "house of holiness" for the Lord that offered spiritual sacrifices of praise and study (4QFlor 1:6; 1QS 8:6–8; 9:3–11), guided by a leadership of priests and Levites of the order of Zadok (1QS 2:19–20; 5:1–3). Third, this self-appropriation of temple imagery and ideology accompanied an intense hostility toward the "wicked priests" of the temple priesthood in Jerusalem, whom they regarded as having profaned the temple and polluted the land (1QpHab 8:9; 9:9). Fourth, they saw themselves in some sense as living in the last days, anticipating the inbreak of God's kingdom and the rule of the Messiah (1QSa 1:19–26; 2:16). Fifth, all these claims were made, not by a group that sought to replace Israel, but by a group that saw itself as the authentic and purified remnant of Israel, the realization of what God wanted Israel to be.

Most pertinent for our present topic is the way the sectarian writings speak of their community (*hayyaḥad*) in terms of covenant (*bĕrît*). Certainly we find no sort of fundamental break with the covenant made with Abraham (CD 12:11) or that made at Sinai (1:4). Indeed, it is the law of Moses, the "covenant from the first" (4:9; 6:2) that the sectarians pledge to observe (1:17–20). At the same time, however, the law of Moses is observed precisely according to the interpretation revealed by the Teacher of Righteousness—and *not* according to the deceitful teachings of lesser interpreters (1QS 5:9). Their "covenant of conversion" (CD 19:3), was therefore in effect, a covenant they made with each other and God to follow the law of Moses according to a certain interpretation (1QSA 1:5, 7) as a "covenant of grace" (1:8) and "covenant of justice" (8:19).

To "enter the rule of the community" (1QS 1:16) was therefore also to enter "this covenant" (2:12, 18, 25–26; 5:10). They themselves together "establish a covenant" (5:18; 8:10) and "enter into covenant" (1:18, 20; 2:10, 18; 5:8, 20; 6:15; 10:10; CD 2:2; 6:11; 15:5–6; 19:24; 20:25), a covenant that they consider to be everlasting (CD 3:4; 1QS 3:11; 4:22; 5:5). By so doing, they separate themselves from those who "do not know the covenant" (1QS 5:19), and themselves become "men of the covenant" (1QSA 1:2–3; 1QS 6:19; 8:16) who protect and persevere in this covenant (1QS 5:2–3). To enter the community at Qumran *is* to enter "the covenant of God" (CD 13:14; 14:2).

The *Damascus Document* in particular distinguishes the "covenant from the first" (CD 4:9; 6:2) that was made on Sinai—and that the people failed to keep (3:12)—from God's establishment of a covenant in Israel forever (according to the secret instructions of the Teacher of Righteousness, 3:12). Although we have as yet no evidence that the sectarians at Qumran read or were influenced by the prophecy of Jeremiah, the *Damascus Document* speaks forthrightly three (and possibly four) times of the sectarians as the "new covenant" (*habbĕrît haḥădāšâ*) that God established in Damascus (6:19; 8:21; 19:13; and possibly 20:12).

At the very least, the Qumran writings show us the possibility of using "new covenant" language at a time contemporary to Hebrews, and in a situation of competition and rejection of the Hasmonean priesthood in the Jerusalem temple, as a way not of forsaking

Jewish identity but rather of asserting it in a powerful fashion. While these writings do not characterize the Sinai covenant as inadequate or weak, the necessity of establishing a covenant of conversion on the basis of a distinctive interpretation of that covenant at the very least shows us that a Jewish community could claim absolute loyalty to the God of the Abrahamic covenant while negotiating changes in the Sinai covenant.

At the same time, the Qumran writings remind us of the difference between the claims made for the Teacher of Righteousness (he revealed the true way to observe the law to enable a community to be ritually pure), and the claims made for Jesus (he has entered into the presence of God as the forerunner of many children who will follow him to God's rest). It is because of the difference in the experiences and claims of the respective communities associated with the Teacher and with Jesus that the Sinai covenant is differently assessed.

Although among New Testament compositions Hebrews is most extravagant in its use of "new covenant" language, it is by no means unique. Hebrews should be seen less as asserting a theological position than as expressing a community conviction. In the Acts of the Apostles, the term *diathēkē* appears twice, both times with reference to the covenant God made with Abraham (Acts 3:25; see "covenant of circumcision" in 7:8). But whereas Mark 14:24 reports Jesus' words at his last supper as "this is my blood of the covenant which is poured out for many," and Matt 26:28 adds "for the forgiveness of sins," Luke 22:2 has "this cup which is poured out for you is the new covenant in my blood." Whether the term "new" is present or not, all three versions report the remarkable language ascribed to Jesus himself: that his bloody death is the sacrificial seal of a covenant like that of Sinai (see Exod 24:7–8).

The possibility that Jesus actually interpreted his own death in such covenantal and sacrificial terms is heightened by the way in which Paul reports the words of Jesus some twenty years after his death (and therefore well before the Gospels' composition) in his first letter to the Corinthians: "In the same way also the cup, after the supper, saying, 'This cup is the new covenant in my blood. Do this, as often as you do it, in remembrance of me'" (1 Cor 11:25).

For Luke and for Paul (explicitly) and for Matthew and Mark (implicitly), Jesus himself interpreted the significance of his death as a sacrifice to secure a new covenant between God and humans. Paul does not regard this initiative as inconsistent with God's precedents, for God had already established multiple covenants with the people. In Rom 9:4 Paul speaks of "the covenants" (*hai diathēkai*) in the plural as among the blessings that God bestowed on "my brethren, my kinsmen by race." In Eph 2:12 he speaks of Gentiles as having been strangers to "the covenants of the promise" (*xenoi tōn diathēkōn tēs epangelias*). Then, in Rom 11:27, Paul quotes Isa 59:20–21 and 27 with reference to the future salvation of "all Israel" when Gentiles shall also be included in God's people: "The deliverer will come from Zion, he will banish ungodliness from Jacob; and this will be my covenant with them when I take away their sins." Please note that Paul finds in the Isaiah passage the same connection between "my covenant" and the "taking away of sins" that the author of Hebrews found in Jeremiah. But in "the deliverer" Paul is also able to connect this covenant more explicitly to the figure of the Messiah. It is noteworthy also that Paul earlier in Romans clearly uses language with respect to Jesus' death that recalls the sacrifice and sprinkling of blood on the mercy seat on the Day of Atonement (Rom 3:21–26)—the imagery that Hebrews exploits at considerable length.

Paul's language about the law of Moses is most vigorous and polemical in his Letter to the Galatians, where we find two important statements about covenant. In Gal 3:15–17 Paul opposes the covenant that God made with Abraham—which carried with it the blessings to be received by faith—to the law of Moses that was revealed 430 years later, and insists (using the analogy of a human will/covenant) that the law does not nullify that earlier covenant. It is significant that Paul does not use the term "covenant" here with respect to the law of Moses, but only of the promise to Abraham. Paul does use *diathēkē* for the giving of the law on Sinai in Gal 4:21–31. Indeed, Paul's allegory of Sarah and Hagar is intended precisely to contrast "two covenants" (*dyo diathēkai*), one from Mount Sinai that "bears children for slavery" that corresponds to the present Jerusalem, and the other from "the Jerusalem above, our mother, who is free" (4:26). Paul's readers are the children of the promise, like Isaac (4:28), born according to the Spirit (4:29), in contrast to those now belonging to the covenant of Sinai, who are "born according to the flesh" (4:29).

Finally, in 2 Corinthians Paul explicitly opposes the "new covenant" (*kainē diathēkē*), which is "not of the letter but of the spirit" (3:6), to an "old covenant" (*palaia diathēkē*), which continues to be read without insight by those who do not recognize that it points to the Lord Jesus (3:14). Here Paul states with unparalleled simplicity, "the letter kills, but the spirit gives life" (*to gar gramma apoktennei, to de pneuma zōopoiei*, 3:6). For Paul, as for Hebrews, it is retrospectively, in light of what God has accomplished through the "last Adam," who has become "life-giving spirit" (*pneuma zōopoioun*, 1 Cor 15:45), that the earlier covenant must be considered as inadequate (see Rom 7:1–8:11) and "old." Is this fair to Jews who stood then and stand now outside the experience of life given by the Lord Jesus? No. But is it true to the experience and convictions of those who experience Jesus as the one who goes before them as pioneer and perfecter of faith? Yes.

9:1–10 The Worship of the Old Covenant

The rhetorical progression of Hebrews' argument concerning the priesthood of Jesus is both steady and subtle. The section considered here was anticipated by 8:4–6, which drew a contrast between the service of Jesus in the "true tent" that is God's presence, and that carried out in the "copy and shadow" that was the earthly tabernacle. The author then appeared to detour into another topic in 8:7–13, with a discussion of the old and new covenants. But as we have seen, it was no digression: for our author, cult and covenant go hand in hand (see 7:12). The discussion of the old and new covenant was in fact another stage of preparation for the present exposition, which returns explicitly to the theme set by 8:4–6.

Here, then, Hebrews lays out the *dikaiōmata latreias* ("regulations for worship") that obtained under the Sinai covenant, before developing the worship of the true tent accomplished by the death and resurrection of Jesus. The author begins with a quick description of the arrangement and furnishings of the sanctuary constructed by Moses in the wilderness (9:1–5), then summarizes the practices of the cult within it (9:6–7), before closing with another deprecating characterization of the earlier cult's failure to perfect the conscience of the worshiper (9:9–10) because it dealt only with *dikaiōmata sarkos* ("regulations for the flesh"). The present passage, in turn, prepares for the long exposition of Christ's offering of himself in 9:11–10:18, which builds on the statement in 8:3 that every priest must have something to offer.

9:1 Now the first[a] also[b] had regulations for worship and the earthly sanc-
tuary. **2** For the first tent was erected, in which was the lampstand and the
table and the presentation of the breads.[c] It is called the sanctuary.[d] **3** And
behind the second veil was a tent called holiest sanctuary.[e] **4** It had a
golden incense altar[f] and the ark of the covenant—covered all over with
gold—in which was the golden jar containing the manna, and the[g] flow-
ering staff of Aaron and the tablets of the covenant. **5** And above it the
cherubim of glory were overshadowing the mercy seat. Now is not the
time to speak of these things in detail.

6 But with these things thus arranged, the priests regularly enter the
first tent to carry out acts of worship. **7** The high priest alone, however,
goes into the second once a year, not without blood, which he offers in
behalf of himself and in behalf of the unintentional sins of the people. **8** The
Holy Spirit is making this clear: while the first tent still has standing,
the way into the sanctuary does not yet appear. **9** This[h] is a symbol for the
present time, namely[i] that gifts and sacrifices are being offered that are
not able to perfect the worshiper with respect to conscience. **10** They are
regulations[j] of the flesh laid down until a time of correction, dealing only
with foods and drinks and various washings.

a. In the best Greek MSS the adjective *prōtē* lacks a substantive. The natural referent is the first covenant (8:1–13). But a number of MSS supply *skēnē* ("tent"), which is clearly a misunderstanding.

b. Textual evidence is split concerning the presence of the adverb *kai*. P[46] and B lack it, while ℵ, A, and D have it. I do not agree with Attridge (230) that the presence of the word makes the argument self-contradictory.

c. B and some Sahidic MSS place "and the golden incense altar" (*kai to chrysoun thymiatērion*) here rather than in v. 4 with all other witnesses. See discussion in the commentary.

d. We can appreciate the scribal uncertainty here and in the next verse concerning the author's intended meaning, not least because the usage of the LXX itself is so inconsistent (see the commentary). The witnesses range from *hagia* ("holy" accented as a feminine adjective), through *ta hagia* ("holy things" = "sanctuary"), to *hagia tōn hagiōn* ("holy of holies" = "holiest sanctuary"). I follow Nestle-Aland[27] in reading the anarthrous accusative neuter plural *hagia* as equivalent to "sanctuary" (with Koester, 394, against Attridge, 230), consistent with the earlier usage *ta hagia* in 8:2.

e. As might be expected, MSS also differ on this designation. Again, I follow Nestle-Aland[27], which reads the anarthrous neuter plural *Hagia Hagiōn* (lit. "holies of holies") as equaling "holiest sanctuary" (with Koester). This is read by the original hand of א, A, and D. The next best attested reading adds a definite article to both words: *ta hagia tōn hagiōn*.

f. See note c above for the transposition of this phrase found in B and a few Sahidic MSS.

g. B (with a few others witnesses) again follows its own course in this section by omitting the definite article before "flowering."

h. The original version of D adds the word "first" (*prōtē*), probably as an attempt to clarify the referent of the relative adjective *hētis*, which I translate as "this."

i. The second hand of D and a number of later witnesses have *kath' hon* here rather than *kath' hēn*. The effect is to make "the present time" the antecedent rather than "parable" or "standing" or "way"—all nouns in the feminine gender.

j. There are a number of variations among the witnesses for *dikaiōmata* ("regulations"), all of which miss the fact that the noun is in apposition to "gifts and sacrifices" in the previous clause, and creates an *inclusio* with *dikaiōmata* in 9:1.

[9:1–5] For most readers, this section of Hebrews is at once most fascinating and most difficult. It is fascinating because Hebrews elaborates a complex and vivid comparison (*synkrisis*) between the ancient cult and the priestly act of Christ. The comparison involves an evocation of the ritual of the Day of Atonement according to Scripture, and this has a certain intrinsic antiquarian charm. The closer we read, however, the more difficult the section becomes. The difficulty has two sources. The first is created by the readers' (and before that, the author's) desire to stabilize a picture of ancient worship so as to have a firm and coherent basis for comparison to Christ. But there is instability everywhere. The accounts given of worship in the Hebrew versions of Exodus, Leviticus, and Numbers are not always consistent—or at least are not obviously consistent. The LXX, furthermore, sometimes differs from the Hebrew version in each of these books. Then Hebrews tries to select and shape a "standard" account from these sources.

Finally, Christian scribes tried to "correct" Hebrews in accord with their own understanding of the LXX. A good example is the distinction Hebrews makes between "sanctuary" and "holiest sanctuary" (or "holy place" and "holy of holies"). Not only is the present-day interpreter confronted with a plethora of textual variants, forcing a decision on what Hebrews itself might have intended, but the LXX—although it can make the distinction Hebrews does (see Exod 26:33–34)—is by no means consistent in its terminology for the spaces in the wilderness tent. Nor can we line up the ritual described by Hebrews precisely with the instructions for the Day of Atonement provided by Lev 16; Hebrews selects and simplifies. Hebrews makes it appear that the high priest enters the inner tent only once, for example, and it leaves out altogether the ritual involving the "scapegoat" that bears the sins of the people (see Lev 16:20–28). The best we can do with this particular difficulty is to focus on what Hebrews presents as the case and not get distracted by his simplification of the sources. The point, after all, is that the *author's* understanding is what forms the basis of the comparison to Christ.

The second source of difficulty is the complexity of the analogical or metaphorical framework that Hebrews employs. The author works with two basic axes. One is spatial, the other is temporal. Each axis, however, is itself polyvalent; and, to make matters even more confusing, Hebrews is capable of merging the two. At its most straightforward, the spatial axis can be regarded as "horizontal": it presents an architectural floor plan of the sanctuary in the wilderness—again, we must not confuse the issue by invoking physical descriptions of the temple. Hebrews distinguishes an outer ("first") and inner tent, and there is a veil before each tent (9:2–3). The author asks us to picture priests entering the outer tent to perform their duties (9:6), and the high priest alone entering the second (inner) tent once a year (9:7). Already we see that the spatial and temporal mix: outer and inner, the many and the one, the constant and the once! But the spatial axis is also turned "vertically," so that the outer and inner tents correspond to the cosmological distinction between earth and heaven. Now passage from first tent to second is a passage from earth to heaven. But this vertical turn of the spatial axis also has an ontological dimension: the outer and inner correspond to what is less real and more real, less true and more true, what is material and what is ideal, what is human and what is divine.[1]

The temporal axis is only slightly less complex. There is the contrast between the past and the present (or the "old" covenant and the "new" covenant), but there is also the contrast—in Platonic terms—between the temporal as such (the realm of materiality and change) and the eternal (where there is no change). The "outer tent" therefore can stand *both* for earthly, temporal worship *and* for the worship of the first covenant. Likewise, the "inner tent" corresponds *both* to the new covenant *and* to heaven/the eternal/God's presence. It is small wonder, given these two kinds of difficulties, that Hebrews sometimes grows obscure, and readers sometimes get confused.

The main point in 9:1–10 is to set the stage for the *synkrisis* with Christ that begins in 9:11. The first verse (9:1) indicates the agenda. It uses the particle *men* ("on the one hand") that anticipates the corresponding *de* ("on the other hand") in 9:11. The sentence announces the two dimensions of the "first covenant" (*prōtē*) that are to be discussed, although in reverse order: its regulations for worship (*latreia*; see also 9:6, and the use of the verb form *latreuein* in 8:5; 9:9, 14; 10:2; 12:28; 13:10), and the arrangements of the "earthly sanctuary" (*to hagion kosmikon*). Although the adjective *kosmikos* can be used of "worldly"

1. For discussion see A. Cody, *Heavenly Sanctuary and Liturgy in the Epistle to the Hebrews* (Saint Meinrad, IN: Grail, 1960).

in the sense of "opposed to God" (see Titus 2:12), its meaning here is clearly cosmological.

This is the worship carried out on earth—and merely human—in contrast to that taking place in heaven—in the presence of God (see 7:26; 8:1–2). The use of *to hagion* (lit. "the holy thing") for the sanctuary as a whole has precedent in the LXX (Exod 36:3; Num 3:38; Ezek 45:4), but it is used with this meaning only here in Hebrews. It bypasses the terminological confusion of the next two verses, while at the same time illustrating the fluidity of the vocabulary available for the subject. The next verses will take up the stated theme: verses 2–5 describe the sanctuary, and verses 6–7 describe (some of) the rules for worship.

The author shows more of his rhetorical ability in verses 2–5 with a brief but vivid *ekphrasis* of the arrangement and furnishing of wilderness sanctuary, evoking through words a visual impression that his readers can imagine. The effect is enhanced by his use of a single long sentence that is cut short by the use of a conventional rhetorical turn, "now is not the time to speak of these things in detail" (cf. 2 Macc 2:28–32; Philo, *Questions on Exodus* 25.22; *Who Is the Heir?* 221). The author's interest is not in the furnishings themselves, or in how they might be given individual symbolic meanings (see Philo, *Life of Moses* 2.97–104; *Who Is the Heir?* 226; Josephus, *J.W.* 1.152; 5.216; *Ant.* 3.139–50), but simply in setting up the *synkrisis* with Christ.

The first (or outer) tent is described quickly in verse 2. The author provides the name *hagia* ("sanctuary") here (for the complexity, see the textual notes) and the briefest possible tour of its furnishings: the lampstand and the table, and the presentation of the breads. The lampstand (*lychnia*) is the one described as seven-branched and made of pure gold in Exod 35:31–40; 37:17–24; 40:4, 24. The table (*trapeza*) and the presentation of breads (*prothesis tōn artōn*) are distinguished by Hebrews, but the table—described in Exod 25:23–30 as made of acacia wood and covered with gold—served as the place where the loaves of bread were placed before the Lord (Exod 25:30; 39:36; 40:23) as a sign of the covenant. Twelve loaves were placed on the table each week, prepared by a special group of priests (1 Chr 9:32), and were to be consumed by Aaron and his sons as their perpetual due (Lev 24:5–9). These are the loaves consumed by David and his men when they were hungry and had no other food (1 Sam 21:4–6), to which Jesus refers in his controversy with the Pharisees over eating grain on the Sabbath (Matt 12:1–8; Mark 2:23–28; Luke 6:1–5). For the piety associated with the twice-daily offerings in this space, see 2 Chr 13:10–12.

As Hebrews turns to the arrangements of the "tent called holiest sanctuary" (or holy of holies) that lies behind the second curtain (cf. Heb 6:19), we are struck by the placement of the golden incense altar within this second tent (9:4). At least one major manuscript (B) considered the placement wrong and placed it in the first tent! The oddity here is that the *thymiatērion* does not actually appear in the accounts of the construction of the sanctuary at all (Exod 25:1–31:11; 36:2–39; 40:1–38). But among instructions concerning the consecration of the priests, there is one to "make an altar to burn incense on" (30:1), and it was to be placed "before the veil that is by the ark of the testimony before the mercy seat" (30:6; 40:26–27). The indication of location is obscure. Later Jewish authors speak of the incense altar as being in the outer tent (Philo, *Who Is the Heir?* 226; *Life of Moses* 2.94, 101; Josephus, *J.W.* 5.218; *Ant.* 3.147, 198; *m. Tamid* 1.4; 3.1, 6, 9; 6.1). But the language of the LXX is sufficiently vague to allow a reader—such as the author of Hebrews—to suppose that it was placed near the ark of the covenant within the second tent.

Hebrews next mentions the "ark of the covenant." The ark is a box or chest (*kibōton*) that is also called by the LXX the *kibōtos martyriou* ("ark of the testimony") (Exod 25:10). Exodus 25:16 says simply that Moses is to put into the ark "the testimonies (*ta martyria*) that I will give you." The term means "evidences," and the author elaborates three such concrete pieces of evidence for God's presence among the people—only one of which Exodus itself specifies, namely "the tablets of the covenant" (see Deut 10:1–5; 1 Kgs 8:9; 2 Chr 5:10) given to Moses from the hand of God (Deut 9:9–10). The other two items were also signs of God's presence and protection. The miraculous manna (Exod 16:31) fed the people in the wilderness, and some of it was preserved in a jar (Exod 16:32–34) that the LXX characterizes as "golden" (Exod 16:33; see also Philo, *Preliminary Studies* 100). Moses was told to place the jar "before God," but not specifically in the ark. The flowering rod of Aaron was equally a sign or "evidence" of God's protection, through the selection of Aaron as the one whom God wanted to approach the tent of testimony, and put an end to the murmuring of the people (Num 17:16–26). Once more, Moses is instructed to place the rod before the testimony "as a sign for the sons of rebellion" (Num 17:25), though not in the ark, as Hebrews has it.

Finally, and climactically, Hebrews draws its listeners to imagine the "mercy seat" with its overshadowing cherubim (9:5). The instructions of Exod 25:17–22 are explicit and correspond to Hebrews' brief description. The "mercy seat" (Heb. *kappōret*; Gk. *hilastērion*) is basically the lid or cover of the ark of the covenant. The cherubim are figures of hammered gold at either end of the mercy seat; they face each other, and their wings are to overshadow (LXX *syskiazontes*) the mercy seat (see also Exod 38:7–9). According to Hebrews, then, the inner tent contained a golden incense altar and the ark of the covenant. The ark contained three objects: the jar of manna, the rod of Aaron, and the tablets of the covenant. The ark was covered by a mercy seat over which loomed the figures called cherubim.

Three nuances or implications of Hebrews' description—especially of the inner tent—would be obvious to the careful reader of Scripture, and undoubtedly were important to the author of Hebrews himself, since each plays a role in his overall argument. The first is that precisely this is the place where God promised to take up his presence among the people. As Exod 25:22 says, "There I will meet with you, from above the mercy seat, from between the two cherubim that are upon the ark of the testimony, I will speak with you of all that I will give you in commandment for the people of Israel." To be sure, the tent as a whole is filled with God's glory (Heb. *kābôd*; Gk. *doxa*)—that is, his effective presence. As Exod 40:34 has it, "The cloud covered the tent of meeting and the glory of the Lord filled the tabernacle."

But it was precisely at the mercy seat from which God spoke: "When Moses went into the tent of meeting to speak with the Lord, he heard the voice speaking to him from above the mercy seat that was upon the ark of the testimony, from between the two cherubim; and it spoke to him" (Exod 25:21; see also Lev 16:2: "I will appear in the cloud upon the mercy seat"). Because the ark covered by the mercy seat was the preeminent place of God's presence, and because the term *doxa* refers explicitly to God's presence, the phrase *autēs cheroubin doxēs* should be translated not as "glorious cherubim" but as "cherubim of glory." Thus, when Ezekiel describes God's presence leaving Israel, he says, "The glory of Israel went up from upon the cherubim" (Ezek 9:30; see also all of Ezek 10:1–22). The implication, then, is that someone who has entered the true inner tent has entered into the place of God's presence.

The second nuance is that this arrangement of ark, mercy seat, and cherubim is also understood to be God's *throne* from which he rules. Thus both Pss 79:2 and 98:1 speak of the Lord "sitting upon the cherubim," with 98:1 making the royal imagery explicit: "The Lord has ruled (*ebasileusen*), let the peoples tremble; he sits upon the cherubim, let the earth quake." The Song of the Three Young Men 32–33 (LXX Dan 3:54–55) says, "Blessed are you seated upon the cherubim . . . upon the throne of your kingdom." Similarly, 1 Sam 4:4 speaks of "the ark of the Lord sitting on the cherubim," and 2 Sam 6:2 has "the ark of God, which is called by the name of the Lord of hosts who sits enthroned upon the cherubim" (see also Lev 16:2, and especially Ezek 1:26–28). Such an association helps us understand Hebrews' language about Jesus' exaltation to God's right hand. If the mercy seat is, in effect, the place of God's presence and the throne of God's rule, then the Son who has taken his seat at "the right hand of the majesty on high" (Heb 1:3; 8:1) has taken a seat "at the right hand of the throne of God" (12:2). This Son therefore shares God's rule and can be addressed in the words of the psalm, "Your throne, O God, is forever and ever" (1:8). And those approaching him approach "the throne of grace" from which they can expect to receive "mercy and grace" (4:16).

The third nuance concerns the high priesthood. It is on the mercy seat covering the ark of the covenant (in the very presence of God's throne) that the high priest once a year sprinkles the blood of sacrifice (of a bull and a goat). According to Lev 16:14, "And he shall take some of the blood of the bull and sprinkle it with his finger on the front of the mercy seat, and before the mercy seat he shall sprinkle the blood with his finger seven times." Then likewise with the blood of the goat: "he shall do with its blood as he did with the blood of the bull, sprinkling it upon the mercy seat and before the mercy seat" (Lev 16:15). The combination of these three elements helps us understand how, for the author of Hebrews, the resurrection/exaltation of Jesus was simultaneously an entry into God's glory/presence, a royal enthronement, and an act of high priestly sacrifice.

[6–10] Having described the arrangement of the first sanctuary ("with these things thus arranged"), Hebrews turns even briefer attention to the "regulations for worship." By no means is the discussion of the cult complete. Indeed, its focus is entirely determined by the comparison the author seeks to make. The major comparison is that between the worship of the first covenant (= first tent) and that of the second covenant mediated by Christ (= the true tent). To make that comparison, however, the author makes another: between the bustling activity of ordinary priests in the daily round of worship and the activity of the high priest once a year on the Day of Atonement.

The author proceeds by setting up in verses 6–7 another *men . . . de* ("on one hand . . . on the other hand") construction. Ordinary priests regularly enter the first tent in order to carry out their acts of worship (or "service," *latreia*). The participle *epitelountes* here expresses purpose: they enter for this purpose. The verb *epiteloun* appears elsewhere for the performance of ritual acts and sacrifices (Herodotus 2.63; 4.26; Philo, *Dreams* 1.214–15; Josephus, *Ant.* 4.123; 9.273). The adverbial phrase *dia pantos*—which I translate as "regularly"—suggests ongoing, constant activity (see Heb 13:15; also Luke 24:53; Acts 2:25). The phrase is used a number of times in the LXX for the lighting of the lamps (Exod 27:20), the offering of the loaves of bread (25:29), and for the daily incense offering (30:8). The author uses the present tense of *eiseimi* ("go in"). This could suggest that such worship continues in the present (the section on "Date" in the Introduction takes up the possible implications for the dating of the composition). It is also possible that the author uses the present tense in order to state a general truth on the basis of Scripture (see 5:1–4). Whichever is the case—and I will return to the issue below—the emphasis is clearly on the regular or constant activity of the first tent.

The contrast (*de*) is to the activity of the high priest, which Hebrews elaborates more fully. We note first that the singularity (*monos*) of the high priest stands in contrast to the many ordinary priests, and remember that in the Platonic worldview, the many is always inferior to the one. Then, in contrast to the constant bustle of the priests (*dia pantos*), there is the singularity of the high priest's act; he goes in once (*hapax*) in the year (*eniautou*; Lev 16:2, 3). As observed above, Hebrews simplifies the ritual of the Day of Atonement (Yom Kippur). According to the scriptural instructions, there is a more complex sequence of events that the high priest accomplishes: (1) He enters the holy place with a young bull for a sin offering and a ram for a burnt offering, and takes from the people two goats and a ram (16:3–5). (2) He offers the bull as a sin offering for himself, then casts lots over the two goats, and sacrifices as a sin offering the one selected for the Lord (16:6–10). (3) The high priest then presents the bull as a sin offering for himself and his house, sprinkling the blood of the bull on the mercy seat (16:11–14). (4) He does the same with the blood of the goat (16:15–17). (5) He next takes some of the blood of the bull and the goat and smears it on the horns of the altar—outside the holy of holies—sprinkling more blood on it (16:18–19). (6) Then the other goat has the sins of Israel pronounced over it and is sent bearing those sins into the wilderness (16:20–22). (7) Finally, the high priest washes his clothes and offers his burnt offering and the burnt offering of the people (16:23–28).

Hebrews focuses only on the singularity of the event, that it is "not without blood," and that the offering is for the high priest himself and for the "unintended" sins of the people. This last term, *tou laou agnoēmatōn* (lit. "the ignorances of the people") is strange and not well attested in the LXX (see Jdt 5:20; Tob 3:3; Sir 23:2; 1 Macc 13:39), but it apparently reflects a distinction made by Num 15:22–30 and Lev 4:2–17 between "unwitting" (*akousiōs*) sins and others. The distinction does not, however, occur among the regulations for the Day of Atonement. Leviticus 16:16 and 30 declare that "all sins" are expiated by the ritual (see also Philo, *Posterity of Cain* 48; *Special Laws* 2.196).

Later Jewish tradition, however, appears to agree with Hebrews that Yom Kippur atones only for unintended sins (*m. Yoma* 8.9). Hebrews itself warns against sinning intentionally after once being forgiven: "if we sin deliberately after reaching knowledge of the truth, there no longer remains a sacrifice for sins" (Heb 10:26; see also 6:4–6). The emphasis here on the people's "inadvertent sins" expiated on the Day of Atonement also provides the author with a contrast to the priestly act of Christ that cleanses the conscience of sin (9:28; 10:2, 12, 17).

All of this is clear enough. The passage becomes considerably more confusing, however, when the author turns to the lesson that he wants his hearers to derive from the description he has provided (9:8–10). We have learned that the author thinks of Scripture as "spoken" by the Holy Spirit (see 3:7 and 10:15), and has just described Scripture's account of the worship of the first tent. Now the author seeks to characterize what the Holy Spirit is "making clear" through this description. The verb *dēloun* can mean simply to report (Exod 33:12; 1 Cor 1:11; Col 1:18) or to reveal (Exod 6:3; Deut 33:10; Josh 4:7; Ps 147:9; 1 Sam 3:21; 1 Pet 1:11; 2 Pet 1:14). But it can also have the specific sense of making clear what is otherwise obscure or hidden (Ps 50:6; Dan 2:5–47; 1 Cor 3:13), and that is its sense here (cf. Heb 12:27). It fits the basic Platonic framework within which Hebrews operates: if the worship of the first tent is a "copy and shadow" (8:5), it is necessarily obscure and requires interpretation. The interpretation, to be sure, is available only "in light of" greater truth.

Unfortunately, the clarification offered immediately by the author is not itself entirely perspicuous. His statement involves a temporal contrast ("while . . . not yet") and a form of condition (if this does not change, that cannot happen). Here a "way into the sanctuary" (*tēn tōn hagiōn hodon*) is not yet revealed so long as "the first tent has standing." The difficulty here is knowing the degree to which the author has merged his image and its interpretation. I think that the author considers that "the Holy Spirit wants us to see" something in the image that he has constructed.

The key may lie in the translation of *phaneroun*, which is here in the perfect passive, and the phrase *echein stasin*. In the LXX, *stasis* is used primarily for a "place" in the spatial sense (see Deut 28:65; Josh 10:13; 1 Chr 28:2; 1 Kgs 10:5; 2 Chr 9:4; 24:13; 30:16; 35:10, 15; Neh 8:7; 9:3, 7; 13:11; Isa 22:19), so that the phrase *echein stasin* would mean "hold position" (see Dan 8:17). If this phrase has a straightforward spatial meaning, the same may be true of the *phaneroun* in the perfect passive infinitive: a way to the inner sanctuary does not yet appear so long as the business of the outer tent is being carried on. To rephrase: so long as ordinary priests are coming and going in the outer tent, the way to the inner tent taken once a year by the high priest is obscured. Or, alternatively, the way that is open to the high priest is not open to others, so that it is not "revealed/obvious" in terms of its physical arrangement and its status.

This reading may seem terribly pedestrian, but it is important to remember that this first observation by the author serves as a *parabolē* for something else.[2] It is not itself the interpretation, but what needs to be interpreted. I have translated "while the first tent still has standing" (in agreement with Koester, 397) to catch the double meaning that the author quite likely intends. I regard as overly definite translations such as the RSV: "the way into the sanctuary is not yet opened [!] as long as the outer tent is still standing."

The author proposes the situation just described as a *parabolē* for "the present time" (*ton kairon ton enestēkota*). The term *parabolē* here means "symbol" or even a "type"; see 11:19, where the author calls the rescue of Isaac a *parabolē* of the resurrection of Jesus. We remember that we remain within the framework of a complex sort of Platonic worldview, in which the arrangements of the "earthly sanctuary" serve as "shadow and copy" of the "true tent" in heaven.

Here we see the author employing both the spatial and temporal axes of his analogical imagination. Not only does the first tent (horizontally considered) operate as though it were all that was necessary—except for that one day a year—but the entire first sanctuary (in the horizontal temporal sense) served as a "veil" that could hide the reality of the "true sanctuary" (in the vertical sense).

That "first tent" (in the temporal sense) considered as the worship of the earlier covenant could similarly claim a reality for itself that obscured or denied

2. See S. Stanley, "Hebrews 9:6–10: The 'Parable' of the Tabernacle," *NovT* 37 (1995): 385–99.

the need for access to a "truer tent." When the shadow is taken to be the reality, human hopes are misplaced. The present, then, is a "season of correction" (*kairou diorthōseōs*) insofar as the true reality has made clear—for those who can see—the inadequacy of the former cult. This is precisely because, as we shall see, Christ has "opened the way" to that true presence of God.

This seems, in general, what the passage means. The devil, however, is in the details. I take the Greek relative adjective *hētis* at the beginning of verse 9 as the equivalent of "this," but the possible feminine singular antecedents are multiple. It could refer back to "way" (*hodos*) or "tent" (*skēnē*) or "standing" (*stasis*). Or it could simply refer to "all that I have just said!" The decision on this also affects the translation of the phrase *kath' hēn* (once more a feminine singular). I have taken it broadly as referring to the entire situation before the "time of correction," and have translated as "namely": this is the shape of the symbol, or this is the situation in the continued standing of the first tent. Literally, the phrase means "according to which," and the author uses it to characterize the worship of the first tent in a strongly polemical fashion.

The phrase "offering gifts and sacrifices" echoes 5:1 and 8:3–4. This is how Hebrews understands the duty of the priesthood. But the gifts and sacrifices offered in the "earthly sanctuary" (9:1) deal only with externals. They are "regulations of the flesh," or, alternatively, "fleshly regulations": they have to do only with human realities, and that at the most physical level. We are reminded of 7:16, where Hebrews spoke of a "law of fleshly commandment" in contrast to the "power of indestructible life."

Hebrews spells out these fleshly regulations in terms of "foods and drinks and various washings." The author could be referring specifically to the regulations governing worship. Parts of some sacrifices were consumed by those who offered them (Lev 2:3, 10; 5:13; 6:18, 24–30); drink offerings were made (Num 15:5, 7, 10; 28:7–10, 15); and animal sacrifices required washings before and after (Exod 29:4; Lev 8:6; 16:4, 28; Num 19:7). Alternatively, the author could be referring to the "fleshly commandments" (7:16) regulating life under the first covenant generally, which kept people in a state of ritual purity and therefore in a position to participate fully in the life of worship.[3] Here rules regarding washings are particularly important (Lev 12:1–15:33; Num 19:11–22), as are those for the appropriate foods to be eaten (Lev 11:1–42; Deut 14:3–21). Drinks receive relatively little attention in Torah, although the purity of the vessels from which people drink is important (Lev 11:32–38) and the *Let. Aris.* 128 refers to "meats and drink and beasts to be considered unclean" as a concern for all humankind as well as Jews. The same composition says, "he hedged us in on all sides with strict observances connected with meat and drink

3. For discussion see J. Neusner, *The Idea of Purity in Ancient Judaism* (SJLA 1; Leiden: Brill, 1973).

and touch and hearing and sight" (*Let. Aris.* 142; see also 158, 162). Hebrews' polemical edge here is not accidental or casual. In 13:9 the author warns his readers away from various and strange teachings having to do with "dietary laws that offer nothing useful to those who practice them."

This brings us to the real critique of the worship of the first tent, namely that such external things could not "perfect the worshiper (*teleiōsai ton latreuonta*) with respect to conscience (*kata syneidēsin*)." We see again how the author of Hebrews redefines the goal of worship even as he criticizes the failure of the earlier cult. He makes the "perfecting" of the worshiper (singular, not plural) the implied goal of the cult (= religion). This is in tension with the implied goal of the cult according to Scripture, which was a state of "at-one-ness" between God and the people of Israel considered as a whole. The aspect of "perfection/maturity" (*teleioun*) is, we recognize, precisely what Hebrews has previously denied to the Levitical priesthood (7:11), and already claimed for the priestly work of Christ (2:10; 5:9; 6:1; 7:28), a contrast that will be continued as the argument moves forward (9:11; 10:1, 14; 11:40; 12:23). We saw earlier as well that Hebrews connected "perfection" to a moral maturity (5:14). Now the author makes clear that regulations pertaining only to the body or flesh cannot by themselves affect the conscience. Here is the classic Platonic distinction between the outer and the inner, between the material and the spiritual—another turn in this complex passage, corresponding roughly to the contrasts made earlier.

The noun *syneidēsis* basically means "consciousness" (Diogenes Laertius, *Lives* 7.85; Josephus, *Ant.* 16.212), and Hebrews uses it in this sense in 10:2: "consciousness of sin" (cf. also Qoh 10:11; Sir 42:18; 1 Pet 2:12). But it comes to mean also the capacity for "moral consciousness," or what we call "conscience" (see Wis 17:20; Josephus, *Ant.* 16.103; *T. Reu.* 4.3). This is the predominant sense of the term in Paul's letters (Rom 2:15; 9:1; 13:5; 1 Cor 8:7, 10, 12; 10:25–29; 2 Cor 1:12; 4:2; 5:11; 1 Tim 1:5, 19; 3:9; 4:2; 2 Tim 1:3; Titus 1:15) and other New Testament writings (Acts 23:1; 24:16; 1 Pet 3:16, 21).

Hebrews uses the term in this narrower meaning also in 9:14 ("will cleanse our conscience from dead works"), 10:22 ("our hearts cleansed from an evil conscience"), and 13:18 ("persuaded that we have a good conscience"). It is evident, therefore, that Hebrews understands perfection in personal terms (it concerns every individual) and in spiritual/moral terms (it is to affect their inner moral awareness). This sort of perfection the law and its cult could not accomplish, and therefore required "correction."

It remains to ask whether the polemical stance reflected in this section of the argument is simply literary or has in mind actual cultic practices within contemporary Judaism. The basis of the argument, as I have noted repeatedly, is definitely literary. Hebrews does not describe the practice of the Jerusalem temple, but the portrayal of the cult in the Torah. But does this mean that the author is necessarily writing with no reference to the temple cult? That position cannot be demonstrated. As I have shown in the section on "Date" in the Introduction, there is no reason for dating this composition after the fall of the Jerusalem temple in 70. Indeed, the absence of any supersessionist argument based on the destruction of the temple (God showed that it was ineffectual by destroying it) is striking. It is harder to imagine the author refraining from any mention of an event so cataclysmic (for Jews) and so confirming (for messianists) if it had already happened. In this light, that the author here speaks of the cult as though it were still going on (the present tense), and the polemical tone concerning foods, drinks and washings (here and in 13:9–10) tilt the probability in the direction of the argument being made while the sacrificial cult of the temple was still in operation.

Excursus 6: Sanctuaries Material and Ideal

As with its language about a new covenant, so does Hebrews' contrast between an earthly and a heavenly sanctuary fit within contemporary Jewish religious literature. It is not possible to say that Hebrews is directly attacking the sacrificial cult that continued within the Jerusalem temple until its destruction in 70 C.E. The composition's point of reference is the worship prescribed for the tent of the wilderness in the Torah. It is difficult to imagine, however, that either the author or his readers would not automatically have the Jerusalem temple in mind. Other Jews also found fault with actual sanctuaries throughout the history of Israel, and expressed their disenchantment or disapproval by appeal to an imagined ideal sanctuary either in heaven or to come, or both. When reading Jewish literature roughly contemporary to Hebrews, indeed, it is remarkable how powerful and pervasive is the symbol of the temple as the place of God's power, presence, and protection of the people.[4]

David's desire to provide a permanent sanctuary—a house—for the ark of the covenant was rejected by the Lord (2 Sam 7:1–8), who promised instead to build a house (dynasty) for David (2 Sam 7:12–16). Solomon constructed the first great temple in Jerusalem (1 Kgs 6:1–7:51), and when the ark was placed in the "inner sanctuary of the house in the most holy place" (1 Kgs 8:6), "a cloud filled the house of the LORD, so that the priests could not stand to minister because of the cloud; for the glory of the LORD filled the house of the LORD" (8:11). But this presence was conditional on the people keeping the covenant faithfully. Only if they do this will God "dwell among the children of Israel, and will not forsake my people Israel" (6:12–13).

It is against this backdrop that we understand Jeremiah's threat: those who rely on the temple as the guarantee of God's protection ("this is the temple of the LORD") without observing the terms of the covenant are foolhardy (Jer 7:1–4). Only observance of the commandments ensures safety on the land (7:5–6). If the people are faithless, both they and the temple will fall: "Therefore I will do to the house which is called by my name, and in which you trust, and to the place which I gave to you and to your fathers,

4. For a helpful survey of the literature, see G. Stevenson, *Power and Place: Temple and Identity in the Book of Revelation* (BZNW 107; New York: de Gruyter, 2001).

as I did to Shiloh. And I will cast you out of my sight, as I cast out your kinsmen, all the offspring of Ephraim" (7:14–15).

The prophet Ezekiel, himself a priest living in exile after the destruction of the first temple, develops the potential of the temple as a symbol. Because their abominable ways have "defiled my sanctuary," God brings punishment upon the people (Ezek 5:11). Ezekiel has a vision in which he is brought by the spirit back to Jerusalem to witness all those abominations carried out in the temple itself (8:1–9:10), and the subsequent leaving of the temple of God's glory (11:22–23) to join the exiled people as "a sanctuary to them for a while in the countries where they have gone" (11:16). Only when God fills the people with a new spirit and new heart will they again be given the land of Israel (11:17–19).

If the temple and God's protective presence are not identical, and if the term "sanctuary" can be used for God's effective presence even apart from a material tent or building, then "temple" or "tent" becomes a powerful symbol for the reality of God's presence wherever it is experienced. Thus, after Ezekiel has the vision of the renewal of the people by the spirit—"I will cause breath to enter you and you shall live . . . you shall live and you shall know that I am the LORD" (36:5–6)—he is shown in another vision (40:2) the restoration of the people itself in terms of a future temple (40:3–47:12), one in which the glory of the Lord again dwells: "The spirit of the LORD lifted me up, and brought me into the inner court; and behold the glory of the LORD filled the temple" (43:1–5). As a result, the very name of the city is to become, "The LORD is there" (48:35).

The postexilic temple could not pretend to match the splendor of Solomon's temple (see Ezra 3:12–13) or the sanctity of Ezekiel's ideal vision (see Neh 13:4–29). The corrupt struggles for the priesthood during the time of Hellenistic hegemony (see 2 Macc 4:7–10), and the widespread hellenization of Palestine during the same period, led to a further loss of prestige in the national sanctuary of Jerusalem (1 Macc 1:21–28, 54–61; 2 Macc 6:1–6). The Maccabees purified the sanctuary (1 Macc 4:36–58; 2 Macc 10:3–8), but it remained under threat (2 Macc 14:31–36). The high priesthood granted to the Hasmoneans Jonathan and Simon (1 Macc 14:30–48) was of dubious and conditional legitimacy: "until a trustworthy prophet should arise" (1 Macc 14:41), even though the worship carried out in the temple generated admiration. The *Letter of Aristeas* comments on the vestments worn by the high priest Eleazar: "Their appearance makes one awe-struck and dumbfounded; a man would think that he had come out of this world into another one" (99).

The massive temple constructed by Herod suffered from the same ambiguity. Its size and splendor caused astonishment and pride (Josephus, *J.W.* 5.184–237; *Ag. Ap.* 2.193–198). But many pious Jews were critical of the official cult from a variety of perspectives. In Josephus's own view—writing after the destruction of the temple—the Zealots were to blame for profaning the temple by making it a place of battle. It was no longer the dwelling place of God (*J.W.* 5.419). God turned away from the temple because of their misdeeds (*J.W.* 2.539), reducing the temple to flames (6.250). God condemns the city and purges the temple by fire (4.323), taking the side of the Romans against the Jews (5.369, 412), so that the destruction of the city was to be seen as a punishment from God (6.110; 2.455).

From the time of Ezekiel, then, a variety of Jewish writers used the temple as a symbol for God's power and presence, imagining either a sanctuary to be realized in the future, or a sanctuary now existing in heaven (or both), a hope for a sanctuary "more real" and "more holy" than the dubious and often desecrated version operating in Jerusalem. As always when dealing with a religious symbol, a certain amount of ambiguity and imprecision characterizes all such imagination concerning the ideal sanctuary.

If we look at what are usually designated as apocalyptic compositions, for example, we find a range of statements concerning the temple. *Jubilees* speaks of the sanctuary that God will build in the midst of the people after their exile: "I shall dwell with them. And I shall be their God and they shall be my people truly and rightly" (1.17–18). Connected to this restoration of the temple is the restoration of the people through God's Holy Spirit (1.23) that will enable them to be called "sons of the living God" (1.25), and God will "descend and dwell with them in all the ages of eternity" (1.26). All this is not somewhere else, it is in Jerusalem, as "my sanctuary built in their midst forever and ever. And the Lord will appear in the sight of all" (1.27–28). In other places, *Jubilees* speaks of Mount Zion, "which will be sanctified in the new creation for the sanctification of the earth" (4.26). Similarly, *T. Benj.* 9.2 looks for a new temple, "and the latter temple will exceed the former in glory."

Although the language of *1 Enoch* is veiled, it appears also to envisage a future temple for a restored people. In the "Animal Apocalypse" (*1 En.* 85–90), a dream vision reveals Israel's history through the symbolism of animals. Rather than a temple or sanctuary, this apocalypse speaks of a "house." When the people enter the promised land, "that house was in their midst" and they could see (i.e., they were faithful; 89.40–41). The wilderness house then gives way to another, the temple in Jerusalem, which is abandoned—the Babylonian captivity—and the people are blinded (89.51–54). The postexilic house was also profaned, and once more "the eyes of the sheep were blind so that they saw not" (89.73–74). But when God renews the covenant with the people in the eschatological house and the sheep will dwell with the Lord, the eyes of all are to be opened (90.35), and "not a single one among them existed who could not see" (90.36). But *1 Enoch* also speaks of a heavenly temple existing now. In 14.8–25 the seer enters heaven, goes through a first and into a second house; there he sees God's throne and hears the voice of the cherubim, and "beneath the throne were issuing streams of flaming fire" (14.19). Again in 71 the seer approaches "the throne of his glory" (71.8). The vision serves as a commissioning of the seer (71.14–17), just as Isaiah's vision in the temple had commissioned him as a prophet (Isa 6).

The approach to the heavenly throne room (the holy of holies of the temple) is the central theme, indeed, of Jewish Merkabah mysticism. A classic expression is found in another Enoch book. In *3 Enoch* 1, Rabbi Ishmael recounts an ascent into heaven that reaches the "throne of glory," where the angels "below the throne of glory and above the throne" cry out "Holy, Holy, Holy" (see Isa 6:3), and "blessed be the glory of the Lord in his dwelling place" (see Ezek 3:12). The word "temple" is not used, but there is no need for it; no one would miss the symbolism by which the power and presence of God is signified.

The image of a heavenly temple is found in three other apocalyptic writings. In the *Testament of Levi*, the patriarch, from whose line the priesthood came, ascends into heaven to be shown mysteries that he will reveal to others (*T. Levi* 3.4–6). In *T. Levi* 5.1, the reader is given another: "at this moment the angel opened for me the gates of heaven and I saw the most high sitting on the throne. And he said to me, 'Levi, to you I have given the blessing of the priesthood until I shall come and dwell in the midst of Israel'" (5.1–3). Here the earthly priesthood is received from heaven, but awaits a more perfect realization of God's presence. In *2 Baruch* as well, a distinction is made between the earthly city of Jerusalem with its temple and a heavenly one, which was shown to Moses on Mount Sinai and which had been shown to Adam before he sinned: "It is not this building that is in your midst now; it is that which will be revealed, with me, that was already prepared from the moment I decided to create paradise" (*2 Bar.* 4.3–7).

The apocalyptic composition *4 Ezra* was written after the destruction of the material temple in Jerusalem (70 C.E.). In 10.19–24, the seer speaks of "the sanctuary being laid waste, our altar thrown down, our temple destroyed," but is also given a vision of an "established city" that is Zion: "For now the Most High, seeing that you are seriously grieved and profoundly distressed for her, has shown you the brightness of her glory, and the loveliness of her beauty" (10.38–54).

Another appropriation of the temple as symbol is found among Jewish writers who connect God's presence to human moral endeavor. In Philo, for example, the human soul that acts virtuously is portrayed as the dwelling place of God. In *Dreams* 1.149 Philo apostrophizes the soul: "Be zealous, therefore, O soul, to become a house of God (*theou oikos*), a holy temple (*hieron hagion*), a most beauteous abiding-place; for perchance, perchance the Master of the whole world's houshold shall be thine too and keep thee under His care as His special house, to preserve thee evermore strongly guarded and unharmed." In *Cherubim* 98 Philo says, "seeing then that our souls are a region open to his invisible entrance, let us make that place (*topon ekeinon*) as beautiful as we may, to be a lodging fit for God." Likewise, in *Sobriety* 62 he declares, "for what more worthy house could be found for God throughout the whole world of creation, than a soul that is perfectly purified?" Finally, "Let him then dwell in the houses of the soul of him who holds that moral beauty is the only good, and merely sojourn in the houses of the others, who value also bodily and external things" (*Sobriety* 68).

A similar appropriation of temple imagery to human moral activity occurs in rabbinic materials. Dating rabbinic traditions is notoriously difficult: compositions tend to be written considerably later than the time of the New Testament (after 200 C.E.), but also contain earlier sayings that were preserved in oral transmission. The point here, however, is not to show dependence or even influence, but merely patterns of symbolic usage, so the issue of dating—for these or any of the materials surveyed to this point—is not absolutely critical. Indeed, there is clear evidence that the destruction of the temple in 70 had a genuine impact on the Pharisaic tradition. The distinctive angle in these sayings is provided by the rabbinic understanding of the *shekinah* as God's presence. The tent in the wilderness, it is said, was filled with the radiance of the Shekinah (*Num. Rab.* Naso 12.4; see also Naso 13.6, and *Sifre on Numbers* 12.6). But the Shekinah left the first temple because of the sins of the people (*Lam. Rab.* Int 246), and never dwelt in the postexilic temple: "When the temple was rebuilt, the Shekinah did not rest upon it. For God had said, 'if all the Israelites return, the Shekinah will rest upon it, but if not they shall be served only by the heavenly voice'" (*Pesikta Rabbati* 160a). The absence of the Shekinah is one of five ways in which the second temple differed from the first (*b. Yoma* 21b).

There is some speculation among the rabbis concerning the heavenly temple where the Shekinah now dwells (see *Mekilta on Exodus* 15.17), and Merkabah mysticism flourished in the heart of the rabbinic tradition (see *3 Enoch* above). We also find statements about the messianic temple: "Five things will God restore when he will erect his house and temple: ark, candlestick, fire of altar, Holy Spirit of prophecy, and the cherubim" (*b. Yoma* 9b). But the rabbis tended, like Philo, to focus on the divine presence attending the work of human virtue: "In this world, because there were slanderers among you, I have drawn my *shekinah* from your midst, but in the time to come, when I root out all the evil inclination from you, I will cause my *shekinah* to return to you, you will be willing to fulfill the law and you will dwell at peace" (*Deut. Rab.* Ki Teze 6.14). The study of the law took the place of the physical temple in the lives of the devout. The Shekinah was present even to one person studying Torah, and even more so when more gathered in study (*Pirke Abot* 3.3, 7; *Sifre on Numbers* 6.25).

Among later rabbis, the synagogue replaced the temple as the primary material locus of the divine presence because there the law was studied (*Deut. Rab.* Ki Tabo 7.2; *Num. Rab.* Naso 11.2). With the fall of the Jerusalem temple, the study of the laws pertaining to sacrifice was regarded as the equivalent of performing the corresponding sacrifices in the temple: "God foresaw that the temple would be destroyed, and he said, 'While the temple exists and you bring sacrifices, the temple atones for you; and when the temple is not there, what atones for you? Busy yourself with the words of the law, for they are equivalent to sacrifices and they will atone for you'" (*Tanḥuma* B. Ahara Mot. 35a). Even the individual righteous person in some sense represented the Shekinah among the people (*Exod. Rab.* Terumah 35.4).

When reviewing language about covenant in excursus 5, we found that the sectarian community at Qumran was the most explicit in applying such language to itself. The same is true of the use of temple symbolism. We know that the ideas of a future temple and a heavenly temple were active in this group simply from the fact that they had in their library versions of *Jubilees*, *1 Enoch*, and *Testament of Levi*. But the same ideas pervade their own compositions as well. The vision of a future temple, complete with legislation for its purity, is elaborated in great detail in the *Temple Scroll* (11QTemple), and there is a real touch of Merkabah mysticism to be found in the *Songs of the Sabbath Sacrifice* (see 4QShirShabb frag. 1, 1.20). As we have seen earlier as well, the priest-king Melchizedek figures in their writings (see 11QMelchizedek).

Most of all, the community's own compositions portray the group itself as a living sanctuary, whose observance and study of the law is a sort of "spiritual sacrifice" for the atonement of the land: "In order to establish the spirit of holiness in truth eternal, in order to atone for the guilt of sin and for approval for the earth, without the flesh of burnt offerings and without the fats of sacrifices—the offering of the lips in compliance with the decree will be like the pleasant aroma of justice and the correctness of behavior will be acceptable like freewill offering—at this moment the men of the community shall set themselves apart like a holy house for Aaron, in order to enter the holy of holies, and like a house for the community of Israel for those who walk in perfection" (1QS 9:3–7; see also 5:5–7; 8:3–9). The "house that they shall establish for him in the last days" is "the temple of Israel for its sins. And he commanded to build for himself a temple of men, to offer him in it, before him, the works of thanksgiving" (4QFlor 1:1–7). The community has a leadership of priests and Levites (1QS 2:18–24; 5:7–9), in opposition to the corrupt leadership of the Jerusalem temple, represented by the one called "the Wicked Priest" (4QpHab 1:11–14; 5:10–14; 8:7–15; 9:9–10; 11:12).

The New Testament compositions fit within the framework of ancient Judaism with this critical difference: the figure of Jesus and convictions concerning the outpouring of the Holy Spirit following his resurrection serve to catalyze the use of the temple as a symbol. In the Gospels, for example, we have Jesus portrayed as "purifying" the temple (Matt 21:12–13; Mark 11:11; Luke 19:45–46) and predicting its destruction (Matt 24:1–2; Mark 13:1–2; Luke 21:5), but also see the temple imagery used to signify that Jesus is the realization of God's presence (Mark 14:58; 15:37; Matt 26:61; 27:51; Luke 23:45), a theme that is made most explicit by John: "he was speaking of the temple of his body" (John 2:13–22).

In Paul's letters the temple serves, as it does at Qumran, as a symbol for the messianic community as such, since God's Holy Spirit dwells among them (1 Cor 3:9, 16–17; 6:19–20; 2 Cor 6:16–18; Eph 2:19–22). Paul describes Jesus' death in sacrificial terms (Rom 3:24–25; 1 Cor 5:7), and Christian moral behavior is characterized as a form of "spiritual sacrifice" offered to God (Rom 12:1–2). The First Letter of Peter, which also speaks of Christ's death as a ransoming sacrifice (1 Pet 1:19), similarly uses temple imagery for the community of believers as such: "like living stones be yourselves built into a spiritual house, to be a holy priesthood, to offer spiritual sacrifices acceptable to God through Jesus Christ" (2:5). The community is "a chosen race, a royal priesthood, a holy nation, God's own people" (2:9).

The book of Revelation uses temple imagery in a particularly complex fashion. The notion of a living and eschatological temple is suggested by the letter addressed by the Spirit to the church at Philadelphia: "The victor I will make into a pillar in the temple of my God, and he will never leave it again. On him I will inscribe the name of my God, and the name of the city of my God, the new Jerusalem, which comes down out of heaven, as well as my new name" (Rev 3:12). When the seer is taken up into heaven (4:1), we are strongly aware of the way in which this vision-ascent resembles Merkabah mysticism: the seer beholds the throne of God surrounded by the living creatures who cry out, "Holy, Holy, Holy" (4:1–11). The death and resurrection of Jesus is sacrificial. He is the lamb who was slain but now dwells in the heavenly sanctuary (5:6–10). The vision of Jerusalem in the "new heaven and new earth" (21:1) that descends from heaven to dwell among humans has no temple building, "for its temple is the Lord God Almighty and the Lamb" (21:22). If the symbol "temple" stands for God's effective presence and power, then Revelation places that reality presently in heaven to be realized soon in the future in a renewed creation.

As with its language about an old and new covenant, Hebrews' distinction between an earthly and heavenly sanctuary, the first ineffective and the second effective, is far from being a rejection of contemporary Jewish sensibility. Indeed, it fits comfortably within a multifaceted spirit of longing within Judaism for a presence of God more powerful than that mediated by the cult of animal sacrifice. What distinguishes Hebrews in this, as in its language about covenant, is the author's conviction that this presence has been realized in the death and exaltation of Jesus.

9:11–28 Christ's Worship in Heaven

The lengthy argument for the superiority of Christ's priesthood—and the new covenant of which he is the mediator—continues in this section. Having described the furnishings and practice of the "earthly sanctuary" in 9:1–10, the author now turns to a point-by-point comparison that shows how, in every respect, the messianic priest (note how the title *Christos* appears by itself throughout the passage) outstrips the ancient cult, and in particular, the actions of the high priest on the Day of Atonement. Three themes are woven together. (1) The worship of Christ is superior because it takes place in the "greater and more perfect tent"—it gives access to God and is therefore both efficacious and eternal. (2) The sacrifice Christ offers is himself; this picks up the statement in 8:3 that "[Christ] also must have something to offer" as high priest. For Hebrews, Christ is both victim and priest, the one offered and the one offering. This part of the argument makes the death of Christ more explicit than in any earlier section. (3) Christ's sacrifice accomplishes the internal purification of the human conscience.

> **9:11** But Christ has arrived as a high priest of the good things that have come
> into being.[a] He has entered once for all through the greater and more per-
> fect tent, the one not made by hands—that is, not of this creation—into the
> sanctuary.[b] **12** He did not use the blood of goats and calves but his own
> blood in order to obtain an eternal redemption. **13** For if the blood of goats
> and bulls and the sprinkling of a heifer's ashes sanctify those who have
> been profaned, to accomplish the purification of the flesh, **14** how much
> more will the blood of Christ, who through the eternal spirit[c] offered him-
> self to God as blameless, cleanse our[d] conscience from dead works so that
> we might serve the living God.[e] **15** And it is on this basis that he is media-
> tor of a new covenant, so that, with the occurrence of a death for the
> redemption of the transgressions under the first covenant, those who have
> been called might receive the promise of an eternal inheritance.
>
> **16** Now wherever there is a will, it is necessary that the death of the
> will maker be established. **17** For a will is valid on the basis of people
> being dead, because when the will maker is alive, it does not yet[f] have
> effect. **18** Consequently, not even the first covenant was initiated without
> blood. **19** For when Moses had finished speaking to all the people every[g]
> commandment according to the law, he took the blood of calves[h] with
> water and scarlet wool and hyssop, and sprinkled the book itself and all
> the people. **20** He said, "This is the blood of the covenant that God has
> ordered for you." **21** And he likewise sprinkled with blood the tent and all
> the vessels for worship. **22** According to the law, nearly everything is puri-
> fied by blood, and apart from the shedding of blood forgiveness does not
> happen.
>
> **23** It is necessary therefore that the copies of the things in heaven be
> purified by these things, but the heavenly things themselves by better sac-
> rifices than these. **24** For Christ did not enter into a sanctuary made by
> hands, a copy of the real things, but into heaven itself, now to appear

before the face of God in our behalf. **25** Nor was it to offer himself many times in the manner that the high priest enters the sanctuary[i] year by year with blood not his own, **26** because then it would be required of him that he suffer[j] from the creation of the world. Rather, he has now once for all, at the end of the ages, been manifested for the cancellation of sin[k] through his sacrifice. **27** Just as it is human destiny to die once, and after that is judgment, **28** so also Christ, having appeared once to bear the sins of many, will appear a second time for the salvation[l] of those awaiting him.

a. Many MSS, including א, A, and the second hand of D, have "the good things to come" (*tōn mellontōn*). The "good things that have come into being" (*tōn genomenōn agathōn*) is found in P^{46}, B, and the first hand of D. Since 10:1 has the phrase "the good things to come," some scribes may have been influenced in the copying of this phrase. But the perspective of the two statements is quite different. In 10:1 the law prefigures future events, while here the statement refers to the realities brought into being by Christ.

b. One witness (P) adds the words *tōn hagiōn* to form the phrase "holy of holies" (see 9:3).

c. A substantial number of MSS, including the original of D and the first corrector of א, have "Holy Spirit" (*pneumatos hagiou*) rather than "eternal spirit" (*pneumatos aiōniou*) found in the original hand of א, A, and B, as well as the second hand of D. The change may be due to the presence of "Holy Spirit" in the preceding 9:8.

d. Although "your (*hymōn*) conscience" is read by א, the second hand of D, and the overall majority of MSS, the more inclusive "our (*hēmōn*) conscience"—found in A and the original hand of D—makes better sense in this nonhortatory context.

e. The addition of the words "and true" to the phrase "living God" by A and some other witnesses is in all likelihood due to scribal memory of 1 Thess 1:9, "to serve (*douleuein*) the living and true God."

f. Two important witnesses (the original hand of א and D) split *mēpote* into *mē tote*, which would make the phrase an indirect question.

g. P^{46} and the original hand of D add the definite article (*tēs*) to make the phrase "all the commandment" or "the whole commandment."

h. The textual tradition here is complex, with Nestle-Aland[27] accepting the longer reading, which adds the words "and the goats" (*kai tōn tragōn*) to the phrase "of the calves" (*tōn moschōn*), on the basis of a substantial number of witnesses (including P^{46}). The shorter reading is usually to be preferred, and is supported by the original version of א, A, and C. I accept the shorter reading, since the additional phrase could have been added under the influence of the preceding 9:12. On the other hand, the shorter reading may represent an accommodation to Exod 24:5 (Attridge, 253)!

i. Once more, a handful of witnesses (including the corrector of א) add the words *tōn hagiōn*, to form "holy of holies."

j. Some minor witnesses have "to die" (*apothanein*) rather than "to suffer" (*pathein*), which is surely correct.

k. The singular "sin" (in the genitive, *hamartias*) is read by the most and best witnesses, whether with a definite article or not. The plural *hamartion* has as its main support the original hand of D.

1. A and some other witnesses add "through faith" (*dia [tēs] pisteōs*) to the phrase "for the salvation," a theological amplification probably influenced by Paul's language (see Rom 3:25).

[9:11–14] The *de* ("But") with which this section starts sets up a strong contrast, corresponding to the particle *men* at the start of 9:1. This entire pericope provides the contrast to the description of furnishings and ritual in the "first tent" that was the "earthly sanctuary" in 9:1–10. In Greek, verses 11–12 form a single long sentence. I have treated the initial participial phrase as an independent sentence, both to simplify the syntax and to sharpen the contrast between all that went before and the arrival of Christ as high priest. For the same reason, I have translated the aorist participle *paragenomenos* as "arrived" (see Herodotus 6.95; Matt 2:1; Luke 12:51; 14:21), rather than as "appear" (see RSV). Precisely because of this passage's stress on full redemption through Christ, the version of the Greek text that has "the good things that have come into being" is also preferable to the variant reflected in some translations, "the good things to come" (see 10:1). This is now the "present time" and "the time of correction" (9:9–10) of which the earthly cult was a *parabolē*. The content of "the good things" is not spelled out—it refers to everything now celebrated by those who have embraced this new age in Christ (see 2:4; 6:1–5).

The Platonism of Hebrews expresses itself in this passage first in the contrast between the temporal and the eternal (the earthly and the heavenly), and second in the contrast between the external and the internal. On the first, we note that the author characterizes Christ's priesthood in terms of entering the sanctuary "through the greater and more perfect tent, the one not made by hands—that is, not of this creation," that he entered "once for all" (*ephapax*, 9:11), that he obtained an "eternal redemption" (9:12), and that he offered himself "through the eternal spirit" (9:14).

The opening characterization sets the frame for the others: Jesus enters into God's own existence rather than into anything "made by hands"; the distinction between Creator and creation is absolute, and the Son stands on the side of the Creator, since it was "through him that he created the universe" (1:2). The phrase "not made by hands" (*ou cheiropoiētou*) will be used again in 9:24 to describe the sanctuary, and echoes 8:2 ("which the Lord, not a human, has built"; see also 2 Cor 5:1). God's presence—or heaven—is "the greater and more perfect tent." Earlier, the author called it the "genuine tent" (8:2), in contrast to the earthly copy. The comparative adjective "greater" does not refer to dimensions but to dignity (see Philo, *Cherubim* 29; Josephus, *Ant.* 8.319); the author of Hebrews uses it to refer implicitly to God when he speaks of "swearing by one greater" (6:13, 16), and to God's reward as "greater than the wealth of the Egyptians" (11:26). The choice of the comparative adjective "more perfect" (*teleioteras*) is particularly apposite, since, for Hebrews, the process of human perfection is one that passes through suffering and enters into God's glory (2:10; 5:9; 7:28; 10:14; 11:40; 12:2, 23), that is, God's own life. This is something, the author repeatedly asserts, that the cult under the law cannot do (7:19; 9:9; 10:1).[1]

A contrast to the temporal is found as well in the "eternal" used in connection with the spirit (*pneuma*) through whom Christ offers himself. What the author means by this expression is not at all clear. Some scribes alter it to read "Holy Spirit," and it is possible that Hebrews meant this (see 2:4; 3:7; 6:4; 9:8; 10:15). But it is perhaps more likely that the author intends to describe the mode of Christ's offering. He has stated that God's messengers are spirits (1:7, 14), and will declare in 12:9 that God is the "father of spirits." Most strikingly, he speaks in 12:23 of the "spirits of those who have been perfected." If spirit is the realm of God's existence, then Christ's entry into that presence is appropriately described as "through the eternal spirit."

Also eternal is the redemption that Christ secures (*aiōnian lytrōsin heuramenos*). The noun *lytron* is literally the price paid for the release of something held by another, thus a "ransom" or "redemption" (Herodotus 5.77; Plato, *Republic* 393D); *lytrōsis*, in turn, is the act of paying such a ransom, thereby accomplishing the liberation of that which had been held (see Lev 25:29, 48; Pss 48:8; 110:9; 129:7). In the LXX, the verb form *lytroun* is used frequently for the action of the Lord in liberating the people Israel from bondage (Exod 6:6; 13:15; 15:13; Deut 7:8; 9:26; 13:5). Hebrews will use the noun *apolytrōsis* in 9:15 and 11:35, but this is the only time *lytrōsis* occurs (for the noun, cf. Luke 1:68; 2:38; and for the verb, see Luke 24:21; Titus 2:14; 1 Pet 1:18). An "eternal" redemption is such because it is through an eternal spirit. Acts of liberation on earth (of a people from bondage) can only be temporary. But this is not simply a Platonic contrast between matter and spirit (therefore time and eternity); it is also a contrast between what humans can accomplish on their own and what can be accomplished only by God. In this sense "eternal redemption" is equivalent to "a liberation that God has brought about" (cf. Heb 5:9; 6:2).

More difficult in this phrase is the construal of the participle *heuramenos* (from *heuriskein*, "to find"). In the middle voice, it can mean to "find for oneself/obtain" or even "earn" (Herodotus 1.196; Thephrastus, *Characters* 15.4; Xenophon, *Memorabilia* 2.5.5). The aorist tense of the participle does not designate time but the kind of action, here punctiliar rather than continuous ("once for all"). The real difficulty is deciding on the syntax. Does the circumstantial participle indicate something antecedent, coincident, or even subsequent to the main verb? Exegesis must decide (see Ellingworth, 453). The RSV translates as

1. See J. Swetnam, "'The Greater and More Perfect Tent': A Contribution to the Discussion of Hebrews 9,11," *Bib* 47 (1966): 91–106; and Ch. T. Fritsch, "*To Antitypon*," in *Studia Biblica et Semitica* (FS T. C. Vriezen), ed. W. C. van Unnik and A. S. van der Woude (Wageningen: Veenman, 1966), 100–107.

coincident/subsequent: "thus securing an eternal redemption" (see also Koester, 406; Attridge, 244). The circumstantial participle can, however, express purpose,[2] and translating it as purpose here brings it into accord with the phrase *eis apolytrōsin* ("for the redemption") in 9:15.

The second form of Platonic distinction in these verses is between the outer and the inner, which is typically worked out in a fairly subtle manner. The author begins by contrasting the blood of animals (brought by the high priest to the inner sanctuary on the Day of Atonement, Lev 16:14–27) and Christ's own blood (9:12). Here Hebrews begins to develop more fully the role of Christ's death in his priestly ministry. In 2:14 the author stated that "through death he might destroy the one holding the power of death," and in 5:7, when speaking of Christ's learning obedience through suffering, he says that Christ "offered prayers and supplications to the one able to save him from death." Apart from these intimations, however, everything said about Christ's priesthood to this point has focused on his exaltation. Now, through the offering of his blood, the importance of Christ's death is developed (for *haima* in Hebrews see 9:13, 14, 18, 19, 20, 21, 22, 25; 10:4, 19, 29; 11:28; 12:4, 24; 13:11, 12, 20).

Implicit through this entire discussion is the axiom stated by Lev 17:11, "for the life of the flesh is in the blood," and Lev 17:14, "for the life of every creature is in the blood of it." The shedding or effusion of blood is ritual synecdoche for the offering of one's life. As stated in the Introduction (pp. 25–27), the symbolism works best when one is dependent for one's own biological life on the creature that is slain in offering to God. But when any animal is sacrificed, the giving of human life is still only symbolized, at best indirectly offered. When Hebrews speaks of Christ entering the sanctuary with his own blood, it means that Christ's entry into God's presence was through the violent and bloody death on the cross. For blood in association with Christ's death elsewhere in the New Testament, see John 19:34; Matt 27:24–25; Acts 20:28; Rom 3:25; 5:9; Col 1:14, 20; Eph 1:7; 2:13; 1 Pet 1:2, 9; 1 John 1:7; Rev 1:5; 5:9; 7:14; 12:11; 19:13), and especially in connection with the meal in remembrance of his death (Matt 26:28; Mark 14:24; Luke 22:20; 1 Cor 10:16; 11:25, 27).

In verses 13–14 the contrast shifts to the issue of efficacy by means of a conditional sentence whose protasis is verse 13 and apodosis is verse 14. The external offering of the blood of goats and bulls and the sprinkling of a heifer's ashes serve to cleanse outwardly (Num 19:9–17). Those who have been "profaned" or "made common" (*kekoinōmenous*; cf. Mark 7:15–23; Acts 10:15; 11:9; 21:28) are ritually "sanctified" (*hagiazei*) by such means: they are qualified to participate in the public cult through the "purification of the flesh." There is a

2. See H. W. Smyth, *Greek Grammar*, rev. G. M. Messing (Cambridge: Harvard University Press, 1956), 458, par. 2065. Smyth, however, lists examples using only the future or present participle.

double edge to this statement, for it denotes the cleansing of bodily conditions—much of ritual "impurity" resulted from touching things that polluted—and at the same time connotes the "merely human" ("fleshly") character of such rituals. Nevertheless the protasis recognizes that there was a real effectiveness to such use of blood: it accomplished an external and physical effect.

The apodosis of the conditional is introduced by the phrase *posō mallon* ("how much more"), familiar from Paul's letters (see Rom 11:12, 24; Phlm 16; and also *pollō mallon*, Rom 5:9, 10, 15, 17; 1 Cor 12:22; 2 Cor 3:9; Phil 1:23). The phrase sets up the argument from the lesser to the greater: if the effect of external ritual enabled Israelites to approach the earthly sanctuary in public worship, the effect of the offering of Christ's own blood should be correspondingly greater. Hebrews emphasizes the distinction in cause by elaborating the offering itself. It was "through an eternal spirit" and "blameless" (*amōmos*; cf. esp. 1 Pet 1:9). These phrases point to the importance of Christ's internal disposition, a theme that will be taken up specifically in Heb 10:5–10. It is not merely that Jesus offered his own lifeblood, but that he did so as the eternal Son and as a blameless human being. The choice of the adjective "blameless" is particularly intriguing, since in the LXX it is used specifically for a sacrificial animal without *physical* blemish—thus the external (Exod 29:1; Lev 1:3; Num 6:14; 19:2; Philo, *Dreams* 1.62)—but when used of persons, it points to a *moral* quality of innocence and integrity (see Pss 14:2; 17:23, 30; 36:18; Prov 11:5). It is not, in short, Christ's physical lack of blemish, but rather his moral/spiritual disposition that distinguishes his offering of himself.

The greater effect accomplished by Christ's offering is likewise internal rather than external, moral rather than ritual: the blood of the Messiah "will cleanse our conscience." In language that deliberately echoes that of the "cleansing of the flesh" in ancient purification rituals, the author declares that Christ's death does what external observances cannot, that is, perfect the conscience of the worshiper (9:9). Since the Christ who offers himself—through the spilling of his blood—is in fact "blameless," he is "perfected" (see 5:7–10), but does not need his conscience cleansed. He therefore obtains "eternal redemption," not for himself, but for us, his fellow humans. Our conscience is cleansed.

The cleansing of the conscience leads to a final contrast in verse 14. The author states a negative: we are purified "from dead works" (*apo nekrōn ergōn*) and a positive: "to serve the living God." The phrase "from dead works" echoes 6:2, and the options for the point of reference are discussed there. In the present context, it means that serving the living God demands precisely a clean conscience, that is, moral transformation of the worshiper (9:9). This is now the second time that Hebrews has used the expression "the living God." In 3:12 readers were warned not to fall "away from the living God" (*apo theou zōntos*), which neatly matches *apo nekrōn ergōn* in the present passage. God will be called "living" again in 10:31 and 12:22. The point of the entire section is nicely summarized in this final contrast. The earthly cult met its own goals—it assured the ritual purity of the people—but those very goals fell short of the moral transformation demanded of those who seek to approach the living God, and in that light, must be regarded as "dead works."

[15–17] The phrase "and it is on this basis" (*kai dia touto*) explicitly links the statement concerning Christ's mediation of a new covenant to the character of his priestly work. Once more, we see how Hebrews closely connects the realities of covenant and cult (see 7:12). In 8:6 the author designated Jesus as *mesitēs* of a "better covenant." The use of "new covenant" here draws from the exposition of Jeremiah in 8:7–13.

In light of the previous passage, we can appreciate how appropriate yet how striking is the term *mesitēs* for Jesus. This mediator does not serve simply as one who negotiates externally between two parties. He bears both parties within himself. His offering of his own blood makes him at once priest and sacrifice. Because he is at once the one bearing the express image of God (1:3) even as he is like his brothers in every way apart from sin (4:15), Christ mediates and reconciles within himself. Christ's "blameless" offering of himself shows, as Jeremiah prophesied, that this covenant is not only "new" chronologically but ontologically, for it essentially engages the internal dispositions of humans, enabling them to "know God" (8:11).

The purpose clause introduced by *hopōs* connects the mediation of covenant to Jesus' death—stated periphrastically as "with the occurrence of a death"—and the two goals his death was to accomplish. The first was "redemption of the transgressions under the first covenant." The term "redemption" (*apolytrōsis*) picks up from "eternal redemption" in 9:12. The choice of "transgressions" (*parabaseis*) for offenses rather than "sins" once more emphasizes the external, legal character of the first covenant; compare 2:2, which speaks of "every transgression and disobedience" against the message declared by angels (viz. the law). The prepositional phrase *epi . . . diathēkē* means literally "on the basis of . . . covenant" (as in 8:6); here the sense is close to the *ep' autēs* used of the Levitical priesthood in 7:11 (see also 9:10, 17). The redemption is from the transgressions committed against or with respect to the commandments spelled out in the Sinai covenant.

The second goal of Christ's mediation is that "those who have been called might receive the promise of an eternal inheritance." The language resembles that in Rom 3:24–26: Paul speaks of "the redemption which is in Christ Jesus, whom God put forward as an expiation (*hilastērion*) by his blood through faith. This was to show God's righteousness because in his divine forbearance he had passed over former sins; it was to prove at the present that he himself is righteous and that he makes righteous the one who shares the faith of Jesus." The elements of redemption, blood, and expiation are shared with Hebrews. The role of Jesus' faith has been stated already by Hebrews (3:1–5) and will be developed further (10:5–10; 12:1–2). Paul's statement about the former time and the present time also bears some resemblance to the two goals stated by the present passage. Such resemblances suggest a tradition shared by each author. They also diverge: in Romans the emphasis is on righteousness, and in Hebrews the emphasis is on inheritance.

The expression "those who have been called" (*keklēmenoi*) reminds hearers of the author's designation of them as "sharers of a heavenly calling" in 3:1, and anticipates his reference to Abraham as "called" in 11:8. The two references are pertinent to the present passage. For Hebrews, there is real continuity of call between Abraham and his hearers. The covenant with Abraham, I repeat, is never abolished or repealed; see 6:14–18 for God's unchangeable purpose regarding the promise (*epangelia*) to Abraham. And "those who have been called" are not distinguished as a separate population from those who may have transgressed under the Sinai covenant.

Indeed, the author will claim that Abraham himself looked for the same heavenly inheritance that is now being offered the hearers (11:8–16). The difference now is that Christ's death enables those who are called to receive (or perhaps "take hold of") the promise that is an eternal inheritance. Why? Because Jesus is the first of many sons, and is himself the "heir" of all things (1:2, 4)—he opens the way for others to receive their promised inheritance (1:14; 6:12, 17; 11:7).

It is this mention of "inheritance" (*klēronomia*) that provides the logical basis for a semantic shift that otherwise seems arbitrary. In verse 15 *diathēkē* means, as it had in every previous instance, "covenant"—as in the binding treaty between God and humans. But in verse 16 *diathēkē* clearly has the sense of "will" or "testament." The shift is not arbitrary, because the new covenant is precisely about the inheritance. Note that in Gal 3:15, Paul makes a roughly similar point concerning *diathēkē*.[3] If Christ as Son is, as we have seen, "heir of all things," and through his exaltation to the right hand of God "inherited a name greater than that of the angels" (1:2, 4), then his death becomes an opportunity for the "many sons" (2:10) who are his brothers (2:11) to participate in the inheritance he has won. So the author states as a general principle that wherever there is a will, there must be the death of the will maker (v. 16), because while the will maker still lives, the disposition of the inheritance he has placed in the will is not yet "valid" or "secure" (*bebaios*; see 2:2–3; 3:6, 16; 6:16, 19; 13:9)—it does not yet have effect (*ischyei* = have force, power; v. 17). The idea here, then, is that the death

3. For discussion see J. S. Wiid, "The Testamental Significance of *diathēkē* in Hebrews 9:15–22," *Neot* 26 (1992): 149–56; and J. J. Hughes, "Hebrews ix 15ff. and Galatians iii 15ff.: A Study in Covenant Practice and Procedure," *NovT* 21 (1979): 27–96.

of Christ makes the inheritance intended for his brothers—and all those whose longing for a heavenly inheritance will be praised in chapter 11—effective.

[18–22] The author has consistently followed a pattern of alternation as he develops his extended *synkrisis*. Having established the link between the death of Jesus and his mediation of a new covenant, Hebrews now returns to the role that blood played in the establishment of the first covenant. The author chooses a verb (*enkainizein*) that, together with its cognate (*enkainismos*), is used by the LXX for any dedication (see Deut 20:5; 1 Sam 11:14), but above all for the dedication of the altar or sanctuary (2 Chr 2:7; 7:5; 15:8; Num 7:10–11, 84; 1 Macc 4:36, 54–56, 57–59; 5:1; 2 Macc 2:9, 19). Once more, we observe the implicit bond between covenant and worship, although the author also finds explicit warrant for the connection in the LXX's description of the initiation of the Sinai covenant.

The paraphrase of the scene described by Exod 24:3–8 is extremely loose. Even the explicit citation of Exod 24:8 in 9:20 differs from the LXX in five ways: (a) Hebrews has "this is" (*touto*) rather than the LXX "behold" (*idou*); (b) Hebrews has "ordered" (*eneteilato*) in place of the LXX "made" (*dietheto*); (c) Hebrews has "God" (*ho theos*) as the subject rather than the LXX "Lord" (*kyrios*); (d) Hebrews reverses the word order from *kyrios pros hymas* to *pros hymas ho theos*; (e) Hebrews omits the LXX "concerning all these words" (*peri pantōn tōn logōn toutōn*). Among these changes, the use of *touto* is the most intriguing, because it makes the words of Moses more closely resemble those ascribed to Jesus at the Last Supper: "for this (*touto*) is my blood of the covenant" (Matt 26:28; Mark 14:24; Luke 22:20; 1 Cor 11:25). It is possible that, consciously or unconsciously, Hebrews' wording accommodates Moses' words to those of Jesus.

The author takes even more liberties in describing Moses' activity by adding to, subtracting from, and altering the LXX. Hebrews retains the sprinkling of the people with blood (Exod 24:8). It drops from the Exodus account the fact that Moses built an altar (24:4), and the twofold response of the people that they would "do and hear" all that God commanded (24:3, 7). Hebrews alters the wording concerning Moses' delivery of the commands to the people (24:3) and rather than the "holocausts and young bulls" sacrificed by Moses (24:5), Hebrews has the "blood of calves and goats." Oddly, Hebrews adds the elements of water, scarlet wool, and hyssop, which probably derive from other purification rituals described in Lev 14:4 and Num 19:6. Most striking, Hebrews has Moses sprinkle blood on "the book" (*to biblion*), presumably because, when reading the LXX, the author assumed that when Moses "wrote all the words of the Lord" and then built an altar (Exod 24:4), he also sprinkled the commandments when he sprinkled the altar (Exod 24:6), and therefore he sprinkled "the book." In Exodus, however, Moses picks up the book and reads all the commandments to the people (24:7–8). It is also perhaps not incidental that the author of Hebrews singles out the book (*to biblion*) as he speaks of the covenant, since in 10:7 he has the Messiah declaring, of his own response to God, "In the head of the book it stands written concerning me, to do your will, O God" (Ps 39:8).

When the author asserts that Moses "likewise" (*homoiōs*) sprinkled the tent and its vessels (*skeuē*) with blood, he is again inaccurate. The account of the inauguration of the covenant precedes the building of the sanctuary, and it is dedicated by oil rather than by blood (Exod 40:9–10). The altar was sprinkled with blood for the ordination of Aaron (Lev 8:15, 19), and on the Day of Atonement the high priest purified the sanctuary by means of the sprinkling of blood (Lev 16:15–19). But these examples fall far short of what Hebrews claims Moses did. When the author declares further that according to law "nearly everything" (*schedon panta*) is cleansed by blood, he again narrowly escapes exaggeration. In addition to its use on the Day of Atonement and in the ordination of priests (Exod 21:20–21), blood was used for cleansing people from leprosy (Lev 14:6–7, 14). But the law prescribes other means of cleansing as well (Lev 5:11; 15:1–33; 16:26; 22:6; Num 16:46; 31:21–24, 50).

Nevertheless, Hebrews' final clause in this section (9:22) cuts close to the reality "under the law." The noun used for the "shedding of blood" or "effusion of blood" (*haimatekchysia*) is not attested before this composition.[4] But the use of the verb "pour out" (*ekchein*) appears several times with reference to sacrifices (Exod 29:12; Lev 4:7, 18, 25, 30; 17:4, 13; see esp. Num 35:33, and the use of *ekchysis* in Lev 4:12). There is also a close connection in some Scripture passages between such shedding of blood through sacrifices and forgiveness of sins (see Lev 4:20; 19:22; Num 15:25–26, 28). Although the author does not in this case use the full phrase "forgiveness of sins" (*aphesis hamartiōn*), because of the frequent use of the expression elsewhere in the New Testament (Mark 1:4; Matt 26:28; Luke 1:77; 3:3; 24:27; Acts 2:38; 5:31; 10:43; 13:38; 26:18; Eph 1:7; Col 1:14) and the later development in Heb 10:17–18, it may be assumed here as well. The same connection is made by Lev 17:11: "Since the life of a living being is in its blood, I have made you put it upon the altar, so that atonement might thereby be made for your lives, because it is the blood, as the seat of life, that makes atonement" (see also Philo, *Special Laws* 1.205; *b. Men*. 93b and *b. Zeb*. 6a).

[23–26] The author has shown the role of blood in the sacrifices carried out in the first covenant, and now turns to the comparison between earthly and heavenly realities (see 9:11). For the fourth time, he uses the noun *anankē* in verse 23 to express a kind of logical necessity (see 7:12, 27; 9:16), but in this case the noun sets up an infinitive clause, having the effect of a conditional clause: "if

4. For discussion see T. C. G. Thornton, "The Meaning of *haimatenchysia* in Heb IX. 22," *JTS* 15 (1964): 63–65; and N. H. Young, "*Haimatenchysia*: A Comment," *ExpT* 90 (1979): 180.

these things apply here, better ones apply there." The sprinkling of the blood of animals ("these things") serves to purify the "copies" (*hypodeigmata*; see 8:5) of the "things that are in heaven." The use of the plural here may be intended to indicate specifically the heavenly sanctuary (see *ta hagia* in 8:2; 9:8, 12, 24, 25). These copies are contrasted to "the heavenly things themselves" (*auta ta epourania*). Within the biblical Platonism of Hebrews, as I have stated several times, the poles earth/heaven correspond to less real/more real. Therefore, the heavenly sanctuary must logically have "better sacrifices than these," namely those carried out on earth (for "better" [*kreitton*], see 1:4; 6:9; 7:7, 19, 22; 8:6). The only surprise in this statement is the plural "sacrifices" (*thysiai*), since the argument emphasizes the singularity and once-for-all-ness of Christ's offering. This may be a case where grammatical choice is governed by the logic of the image rather than by the logic of the argument.

The author hammers the contrast by means of a fourfold statement arranged chiastically: *a*. Christ did not enter a sanctuary made by hands; *b*. a copy of real things; *b′*. into heaven itself; *a′*. to appear before God. The two inner terms are more Platonic in tone. The contrast between the *antitypa* of the "true things" and "heaven itself" (*auton ton ouranon*) is a perfect expression of biblical Platonism, in which heaven is the realm of the true and real, and earth the place of the imitation and shadow. The verb *antitypein* means literally to strike against something hard and thus form an image (Plato, *Cratylus* 420D), and is used for making a copy or representation (LXX Esth 3:13; P. Oxy. 1470.6). Hebrews here uses the plural neuter adjective as equivalent to a substantive, with a meaning virtually identical to *hypodeigma*. The only other use of the term in the New Testament is in 1 Pet 3:21, where the story of Noah in the past serves as a model (*antitypos*) for the reality that is baptism in the readers' present experience.

The outer members of the chiasm are more recognizably biblical in expression. Jesus enters a sanctuary "not made by hand" (*ou cheiropoiēta*). This repeats 9:11, which also added, "that is, not of this creation." References can be found in the discussion of that passage. Most important, and theologically most explicit, Jesus "now appears before the face of God in our behalf." The passive infinitive of the verb *emphanizein* means simply "to appear" (see Wis 1:2; 17:4; Philo, *Allegorical Laws* 3.101). The phrase "before the face of God" (*tō prosōpō tou theou*) is a biblical anthropomorphism for God's presence (see Gen 3:8; 4:16; Lev 26:17; Pss 4:6; 9:3; 15:11; 23:6; 26:8; 41:2; 45:5; 49:21). This makes explicit what Hebrews has meant by "heaven" all along: it is the "place" of God's presence and power. Two further small details deserve attention. The first is that Christ's appearance before God is not for himself but "in our behalf" (*hyper hēmōn*). The phrase reminds us of Heb 7:25, which says that Christ is able to save those who approach God through him, since he is always alive "to make intercession in their behalf." Jesus' entire existence is dedicated to his brothers and sisters (see 2:9; 5:1; 6:20). The second is that Jesus appears "now" (*nyn*). As in 8:6, the author insists on the present reality of Christ's presence before God and his intercession for humans.

There follows in 9:25–26 a double comparison. The first is between the single offering made by Christ and the frequent offerings made by the high priests on the Day of Atonement "year by year" (*kat' eniauton*). The second is between the high priest's offering "with blood not his own" (*en haimati allotriō*) and Jesus' offering of "himself" (*heauton*). The implication of offering "himself" and not just "his own blood" will be developed more fully by 10:1–10. In the present section, the author concentrates on the temporal contrast. He twice uses the adverb *pollakis* ("many times") to draw attention to the contrast between repetition and singularity. Anyone sharing a Platonic worldview would immediately grasp that the one is superior to the many (see also Heb 10:11). The stress on repetition is accentuated by the clause begun by the conjunction *epei* ("because"), which here introduces a contrary-to-fact statement (cf. Rom 3:6; 11:6; 1 Cor 5:10). The author proposes that offering himself "many times" would mean that of necessity (for *dei* see also 2:1 and 11:6) Christ would have suffered from the creation of the world (for *katabolēs kosmou*, cf. 4:3). The author clearly regards this as a reductio ad absurdum, but it is only such if we take "suffering" (*pathein*) as equivalent to "dying" (*apothnēskein*), an equation some manuscripts actually apply.

Once this is granted, then the proposition does appear as absurd, and the logic of verses 27–28 becomes more apparent. Humans do not die "many times." If Jesus had made an offering with the blood of animals, then he could have made such sacrifices through the ages from the start of the world. But because he mediates the new covenant through his death as a human, he can do it only once. The eternal and internal dimensions of Platonism here meet in the figure of Jesus.

In contrast to that hypothetical repetition from start of the world (and temporality), Christ has "been manifested" now (*nyn*) once (*hapax*) and at the end of the ages (*synteleia tōn aiōniōn*). For *phaneroun* ("manifested") see 9:8, and compare Rom 3:21; 16:26. The repetition of "now" echoes verse 24, and "once" echoes the use of the term *ephapax* ("once for all") in 7:12 and 9:12. The phrase *synteleia tōn aiōniōn* (cf. Dan 9:26–27; 11:35; 12:13), in turn, stresses the eschatological character of Christ's appearance. An equivalent phrase (*synteleia tou aiōnos*) is used for the end time in Matt 13:39, 40, 49; 24:3; 28:20. Three aspects of this phrase are intriguing. The first is that it corresponds to "the last of these days" with which the composition opens: for Hebrews, eschatology is access to the living God. The second is that the noun *synteleia* bears with it some of the nuance of *syntelein* ("to fulfill, accomplish")—it is the "perfection" of time. The third is that this allusion to eschatology sets up the analogy to human death/judgment in verses 27–28.

Finally, the phrase "for the cancellation of sin" (*eis athetēsin tēs hamartias*) echoes 7:18, which spoke of "the setting aside" (*athetēsis*) of the preceding commandment because of its weakness and ineffectiveness. The law could not "put aside sin," so had itself to be "put aside." Only Christ's priestly sacrifice accomplishes the cancellation of sin.

[27–28] The phrase "end of the ages" triggers the most explicitly eschatological statement in the composition. The structure of the statement derives from the singularity of human death, a point that was just raised with respect to Christ's sacrifice. The analogy is set up by the phrase *kath' hoson* ("just as") in verse 27 and *houtōs kai* ("so also") in verse 28, and is based on ordinary individual human experience of the end, which, our author proposes, falls into two stages: death and then judgment.

I have translated *apokeitai tois anthrōpois* loosely as "it is human destiny." The verb *apokeimai* has the basic sense of "being laid up" for something or someone (see Xenophon, *Anabasis* 2.3.15; *Cyropaedia* 3.1.19; cf. Luke 19:20; Col 1:15; 2 Tim 4:8). It is one in a series of expressions in this section signifying necessity (see *anankē* in 9:23, *edei* in 9:26). The idea that all humans are mortal is scarcely novel (see 4 Macc 8:11). Nor is the conviction that after death humans face a judgment on their deeds. It is found equally among Greeks (see Plato, *Republic* 614B–621D; Plutarch, *Divine Vengeance* 23–26 [*Mor.* 563F–565D]; Lucian, *Dialogues of the Dead* 3), Jews (see Dan 7:26; 2 Macc 6:26; 7:17, 19; *1 En.* 1.7; 5.6; 50.1–5, 53–56), and other early Christian writings (Matt 25:31–46; 2 Thess 2:12; John 5:25–29; Rom 2:16; 14:10–12; Rev 20:12).

How, then, does the analogy apply to Jesus? In a fascinating and partially surprising fashion: corresponding to the death of humans is Christ's offering of himself. Hebrews here uses the passive voice: Christ was offered (*prosenechtheis*) once (*hapax*) to bear the sins of many (*pollōn anenenkein hamartias*). The Greek of this last phrase echoes that used by the LXX for the Suffering Servant in Isa 53:12, and in other New Testament passages concerning the vicarious death of Jesus (1 Pet 2:24; Mark 10:45; 14:24; Matt 26:28). It also echoes Heb 7:27. Corresponding to the "judgment" faced by a human after death is Hebrews' most explicit statement concerning Christ's second coming: he will "appear a second time" (*ek deuterou ophthēsetai*).

But Hebrews says nothing about judgment! Christ will appear *chōris hamartias* ("apart from sin")—for the sake of salvation (*eis sōtērian*) for those awaiting him (*auton apekdechomenois*). For the verb "awaiting," see Rom 8:19, 23, 25; 1 Cor 1:7; Gal 5:5; and for "expecting a savior," see Phil 3:20. Salvation runs as a theme throughout Hebrews (see 1:14; 2:3, 10; 5:9; 6:9), and this eschatological statement reminds readers of similar statements in Paul: "to await his Son from heaven, whom he raised from the dead, Jesus who will rescue us from the wrath to come" (1 Thess 1:10), and "our citizenship is in heaven, from whence we await our Savior, Lord Jesus Christ" (Phil 3:20).

10:1–18 The Efficacy of Christ's Priestly Act

We now reach the conclusion of the long exposition that began in 7:1 and, from multiple perspectives, compared the Levitical priesthood unfavorably to that of Jesus. The passage provides the climax to this exposition, and leads to the exhortation that runs from 10:19 to 10:31. The focus in this section is on the effectiveness of Christ's priestly act. Once more the contrast between the shadow and the real, between the earthly and heavenly, is invoked, to show the failure of the law's ritual practices to achieve what Hebrews considers to be the real aim of worship, namely gaining access to God's presence, which requires the cleansing of the conscience, not simply the washing of the hands (10:1–2). The simple fact that sacrifices continue to be made indicates their lack of efficacy.

At the heart of this passage is another exposition of Scripture (10:5–10). This time, Ps 39:6–8 is applied to the Messiah Jesus. He does not offer animal sacrifices, but comes into the world precisely to perform God's will. By this means Hebrews reconnects with the theme of Christ's obedient faith (see 3:1–5; 5:7–10) as essential to his own perfection as Son, and to his becoming the source of eternal salvation for others. Jesus offered his own blood, yes, but the essence of his sacrifice is his commitment, from the beginning of his life, to "learn obedience through the things he suffered" (5:8), so that he could become the "pioneer and perfecter of faith" (12:2) for his brothers and sisters. The total offering of the Son "once for all" accomplishes that "sanctification," which is internal as well as external (10:10–14).

The passage concludes in 10:15–18 with a return to a portion of the Jeremiah 31 passage that the author had quoted more fully in 8:8–12. This citation focuses not on the failure of the first covenant but on the efficacy of the second. God's laws are written in people's minds and hearts, and the sins and lawlessness of the people will not be remembered. It is just this that Jesus has accomplished. And because he has brought about so complete a forgiveness/remission/cancellation of sin, there can be no further need of offerings (10:18).

> **10:1** Because the law holds but a shadow of the good things to come and
> not the very image[a] of the things, it is never able[b] to perfect those who
> approach with the same sacrifices[c] that[d] they continually offer year by
> year. **2** Otherwise, would they not have ceased being offered, since the
> worshipers, once cleansed, would no longer have an awareness of sins?
> **3** Instead, every year they are a reminder of sins. **4** For it is not possible
> that the blood of bulls and goats takes away sins.

5 Therefore, as he comes into the world, he says, "You have not desired
a sacrifice and offering. Rather, you have made for me a body. **6** You did
not take delight in holocausts and offerings for sins. **7** Then I said, in the
scroll of the book it stands written[e] of me, 'Behold, I am here to do your
will, O God.'" **8** He states above that "sacrifices and offerings and holo-
causts and offerings for sins you neither desired nor took delight in"—
such things are offered according to law.[f] **9** Then he says, "Behold, I am
here to do your will."[g] He removes the first in order to establish the sec-
ond. **10** By this will we have been sanctified[h] through the offering once
for all of the body[i] of Jesus Christ. **11** Now every priest[j] stands each day
in service and offers many times the same sacrifices that are never able
to remove sins.[k] **12** But this one,[l] having offered one sacrifice for sins, has
taken a seat at the right hand[m] of God forever. **13** He now waits until his[n]
enemies are put as a footstool beneath his feet. **14** By one offering[o] he has
made perfect those who are being made holy.[p] **15** And the Holy Spirit also
testifies to us. For after saying, **16** "This[q] is the covenant that I will make
with them after those days," the Lord says, "I will put my laws in their
hearts and I will inscribe them on their mind,[r] **17** and[s] I will no longer
remember[t] their[u] sins and their lawless deeds." **18** And where there is for-
giveness of these,[v] an offering for sin is no more.

a. Although there are several lesser variants here, the reading of P^{46}, which has *kai tēn eikona* ("and the image"), is the most significant, since it serves to coordinate "shadow" and "image." The majority of witnesses have the much harder reading *ouk autēn tēn eikona* ("not the very image"), which underlies the present translation.

b. The MS evidence is fairly evenly split between the singular *dynatai* and the plural *dynantai*. My translation follows Nestle-Aland^{27} in reading the singular, which makes "the law" (*nomos*) the distant subject.

c. Some witnesses (including א) have "their" same sacrifices; it seems to be a scribal addition meant for clarification.

d. The disagreement among MSS concerning the case of the relative pronoun (accusative or dative) does not affect the meaning.

e. P^{46} and the original hand of D add *gar* ("for"), absent from the LXX, so that the odd phrase "in the scroll of the book it stands written of me" appears as explanatory.

f. There is the recurrent scribal confusion here on the presence or absence of the definite article: should it be "the law" or, as I have it, simply "law"?

g. MSS are evenly split between including the vocative "O God" (*theos*) (in agreement with the psalm citation above) or omitting it. The shorter reading is ordinarily to be preferred, and it is here.

h. We can detect doctrinal interests at work in shaping versions of the text in this verse. The majority of MSS add the definite article *hoi* after "we have been sanctified," which has the effect of making the group definite. Another handful of MSS (323 and a few others) adds "we" (*hēmeis*), which makes the group exclusive.

i. Also in this same verse, the original hand of D has "blood" instead of "body," which would put this bold statement more in line with standard teaching.

j. A considerable body of witnesses has "high priest" (*archiereus*) rather than the simple "priest" (*hiereus*), perhaps influenced by the earlier statements of high priestly duties in 5:1 and 8:3.

k. P[13] and some Coptic versions have the singular "sin" (*hamartian*) rather than the plural "sins" (*hamartias*). As Attridge (278) notes, this may be another instance of a concern to bring a statement into harmony, this time with Paul's statements in Rom 5:12–21.

l. The corrector of D and the majority of witnesses have the intensive personal pronoun *autos* ("he himself") rather than the demonstrative pronoun *houtos* ("this one"). The earliest papyri (including P[46]) and the best uncials all have the demonstrative, which I follow in my translation.

m. Some MSS have variants of the phrase "at the right hand," but they do not affect the meaning.

n. P[13] alone omits *autou* ("his") from the phrase "his enemies."

o. A few MSS have the nominative rather than the dative of *mia gar prosphora*, which would yield "for one offering has made perfect," instead of "by one offering he has made perfect."

p. P[46] alone has the strange reading *tous anasōzomenous* ("those who are being saved") rather than *tous hagiazomenous* ("those who are being made holy").

q. The original hand of D and P[13] add the particle *de*, so that the clause reads, "But this is the covenant. . . ."

r. The plural "minds" rather than "mind" is read by a substantial number of textual witnesses, but the singular is well attested and corresponds to the LXX.

s. Imitating the author's interjections in vv. 8 and 9, some MSS here insert "after saying" and "then he said," which are lacking in the best witnesses.

t. This translation follows the choice of Nestle-Aland[27] to follow P[13], the original hand of א, and other important witnesses in reading *mnēsthēsomai* rather than the *mnēsthō* of the LXX. If this is the original reading, then the other witnesses are seen to be correcting in the direction of the LXX.

u. P[46], the original hand of D, and apparently also P[13] omit "their" (*autōn*) from the phrase "their sins," but it is found in the other best textual witnesses.

v. The original hand of א and a few other MSS omit the pronoun *toutōn* ("these").

[10:1–4] In the previous section, the contrast between "the copies of the things in heaven" (the earthly sanctuary) and "the heavenly things themselves" (9:23) served to establish a correlation: what was required in the lesser cult could also be assumed in the greater. Now we find a similarly constructed contrast, but the purpose of this one is to make the opposite point: what the earthly cult could not accomplish, the priestly act of Jesus has achieved. The functional equivalence of 9:23 and 10:1 is significant, however, because it helps us sort through what otherwise might be interpretive tangles. We can take "the shadow of the good things to come," for example, as equivalent to "the copies of the things in heaven." Virtually the same phrase, *skia tōn mellontōn* ("shadow of things to come"), occurs also in Col 2:17 precisely for ritual observances under law. The "good things to come" need not here have future reference with respect to the author's hearers, for in 9:11 Hebrews said that Christ has become high priest of "the good things that have come to be." If there is a temporal dimension, it is from past to present: the law was a shadow of the present reality in Christ.

Likewise, the phrase in 10:1, "the very image of the things" (*autēn tēn eikona tōn pragmatōn*), is roughly equivalent to 9:23, "the heavenly things themselves" (*auta ta epourania*). The "things" here are the realities as opposed to the shadows —Plato uses the term in contrast to shadows and names (*Cratylus* 391B, 439A). In 6:18 Hebrews had spoken of "two unshakeable things/realities" (*dyo pragmatōn*), and in 11:1 will define faith as a "proof of things not seen" (*pragmatōn elenchos ou blepomenōn*). In this context, the use of "image" (*eikon*) cannot mean a diminished form of being—as though equivalent to "shadow" (*skia*)—but must mean a full participation in the heavenly realities. The meaning of "image" here is close to "form" (*morphē*), as it is also in Paul (see especially Rom 8:29; 1 Cor 11:7; 15:49; 2 Cor 3:18; 4:4; Col 1:15; 3:10), a point made emphatically by the use of the intensive pronoun *autēn*, "the very image," or "the image itself."

The purpose of this language, to be sure, is to assert that the cult based on the law was only the shadow and not the reality, and therefore was not efficacious—by the measure, I must again insist, of the author's own understanding of the cult's goal, which is not one shared by Torah. The author's characterization of the Levitical cult therefore stresses its futile repetitiveness. The repetitiveness, indeed, proves its futility: "the same sacrifices" (*tas autas thysias*) are offered "year by year" (*kat' eniauton*) and "continually" (*eis to diēnekes*). Yet, for all this effort, they can "never" (*oudepote*) accomplish the one thing that, according to Hebrews, they must do, namely "perfect those who approach" (*tous proserchomenous teleiōsai*). The sentence echoes 7:19 ("the law brought nothing to perfection") and 9:9 ("gifts and sacrifices are offered that are not able to perfect the conscience of the one who ministers").

The rhetorical question in 10:2 makes clear the author's same understanding of perfection: if such sacrifices had only "once cleansed" worshipers, they would no longer have "an awareness of sins" (*syneidesis hamartiōn*; cf. 9:9 and 9:14). The proper effect of priestly activity is therefore moral rather than simply ritual. Ritual cleansing worked to prepare a people for participation in the public cult of Israel and to "approach God" in the earthly sanctuary. But only if the conscience is cleansed from the "awareness of sins" are people morally capable of approaching the living God.

The author proposes a condition that has not been met: if these sacrifices had finally perfected the conscience of worshipers, they would have ceased—there would no longer be need for them. But the opposite is the case: their continued performance serves as a "reminder" (*anamnēsis*) of sins, year by year (10:3). The sheer fact of repetition argues against efficacy. The mention of memory anticipates the second citation from the prophecy of Jer 31:31–34 in 10:17, which concludes with the declaration that in the new covenant, God will no longer remember the sins of the people. The point made by 10:2–3 would fit the situation when temple sacrifices were still being carried out in Jerusalem, and provides real, though not conclusive, support for a dating of the letter before the cessation of the temple cult.

This section concludes with the flat denial: it is impossible (*adynaton*) for the blood of bulls and goats to take away sins. The impersonal *adynaton* picks up from the "never able" (*oudepote dynatai*) in 10:1. Why can't they accomplish this? Because sin is, for Hebrews, a moral issue rather than simply a cultic issue. It is a question of the human will in relation to God. Something has to happen within human freedom for sin to be released.

[5–10] Hebrews leads into the positive exposition of Christ's priestly act—the essence of his offering—with the strong conjunction *dio* ("Therefore, on this account"), as in 3:7, 10, and 6:1. What is now said about Christ is in reply to the inability of the Levitical cult to perfect the conscience. The speaker of the words is Christ, even though he has not explicitly been mentioned since 9:28. We should note particularly that these words are ascribed to Christ "as he comes into the world" (cf. 1:6): the faithful obedience that is the essence of Christ's priesthood is also the essence of his character, not only at his death, although that is its final and perfect expression, but also from the first moment of his human existence. He is the Son who "learned obedience from the things he suffered" (5:8), and did so from the beginning, as he progressively opened, in his human freedom, to the immensity of the divine will.

This is only the second time that Hebrews has Jesus himself speak. In both cases, Jesus speaks with the words of Scripture. In 1:12–13 the Son spoke of himself, using the words of Ps 21:23 and Isa 8:17–18. Here the Son enters the world reciting the words of Ps 39:6–8. The two statements placed in Jesus' mouth together express Jesus' mediational role as priest. In 1:12–13 he states his complete solidarity with his brothers; in 10:5 he declares his utter commitment to God's will.

The choice of these particular psalm verses is inspired. Psalm 39:6–8 states the contrast between the external sacrifices of the first covenant's cult—in which God takes no pleasure—and the internal response of faithful obedience to God's will, which Hebrews regards as the essence of the "perfection of conscience" brought about by Jesus. Before turning to the cited verses, however, we can ask whether the author found other aspects of the psalm congenial to his argument, and perhaps, assuming a certain scriptural competence among his listeners, expected such aspects to be appreciated by his hearers as well.

Psalm 39 is a psalm of David, and therefore appropriately sung by the Messiah as he comes into the world (see the earlier discussion of 1:5–13). The psalm expresses confidence and hope in God even in circumstances of opposition and persecution (39:11–17). In addition to the verses quoted by Hebrews, four other aspects of the psalm are echoed by Hebrews' portrayal of Jesus. First, the psalmist has "proclaimed the good news of God's righteousness in the great assembly (*ekklēsia*) and has not hidden God's mercy and truth from the great congregation (*synagōgēs*)" (Ps 39:10–11), which resembles our composition's characterization of Jesus as first speaking salvation (Heb 2:3) and—again using the words of a psalm—proclaiming God's name to his brothers in the midst of the assembly (*ekklēsia*, Heb 2:12). Second, the psalmist has had a new song put in his mouth, a hymn of God (Ps 39:3), and Hebrews has the Son singing a hymn to God in the assembly (2:12). Third, the psalmist declares that God "has brought me up out of a pit of misery and from miry clay; and he set my feet on a rock, and set my goings aright," Ps 39:2), which resembles the final verses of Ps 109, so well loved by the author, and which can be read as an oblique reference to the resurrection. Fourth, and most striking, the psalmist begins by saying, "I waited patiently for the Lord, and he attended to me, and hearkened to my exhortation" (Ps 39:1), which cannot but remind readers of Hebrew's characterization of Jesus as one who was "heard because of his piety" (Heb 5:7).

The actual citation stays close to the LXX, with two minor and two more significant alterations. Minor: the best manuscripts of Hebrews have the plural of *holokautōmata* ("holocausts") rather than the LXX's singular, and Hebrews reverses the word order of "your will" and "God" while also dropping the personal pronoun, "my," in favor of the straight vocative, "O God." More significant is Hebrews' having "you did not take pleasure in" (*ouk eudokēsas*) instead of the LXX "you did not seek" (*ētēsas*). Hebrews also omits the LXX's ending of verse 9. Hebrews has "to do your will, O God," whereas the original has "I chose (*eboulēthēn*) to do your will, O my God," and continues, "and your law in the midst of my heart" (*kai ton nomon en mesō tēs koilias mou*). This omission is all the more striking since the author was surely aware that "having the law in the heart" was precisely what was promised by the Jeremiah prophecy that he himself will quote for a second time in 10:16. Then why omit it from this citation? Perhaps only to focus attention more directly on the fundamental character of obedience to God's will in all circumstances, and to avoid the possible misunderstanding that the "law in the heart" should be identified with the Sinai covenant. But we cannot know for sure.[1]

Hebrews follows the LXX also in reading "you have made a body (*sōma*) for me," whereas the MT has "you have dug ears for me." The MT would have worked well with the theme of faithful obedience in Hebrews. But the author's glad acceptance of the LXX version is indicated by his repetition of *sōma* in 10:10. Jesus' obedience is not only a matter of hearing; it is enacted by his entire bodily existence.

1. See K. H. Jobes, "Rhetorical Achievement in the Hebrews 10 'Misquote' of Psalm 40," *Bib* 72 (1991): 387–96.

The citation's main interpretive difficulty is presented by 10:7 (Ps 39:7). First, the phrase "in the scroll of the book it stands written of me" stands as something of an interjection in the LXX, between "Behold, I am here" (*idou hēkō*) and "to do your will, O God." In my translation, I decided to remove the awkwardness by making the clause an introduction rather than an interjection. The meaning is not fundamentally changed.

Second, the precise meaning of "in the scroll of the book" is not entirely clear. The *kephalis* is the knob at the end of the rod on which a scroll of Torah was wrapped. We find the term used in other LXX passages for the scroll itself (Ezek 2:9; 3:1–3). In Deut 17:18 there is reference to a "copy of this law made from the scroll that is in the custody of the Levitical priests." The commandments mentioned in the context of this statement spell out some of the requirements of the Israelite king. In this psalm ascribed to David, the reference may simply be to the way in which the will of God that is written in such scrolls is also written in this archetypal king's heart: he is entirely devoted to doing what God desires.

The citation's point is made even clearer by the author's parsing of it, which makes the Scripture passage fit even more neatly into the argument he has been developing. He isolates and divides two key statements. The first is that God was not pleased with the sacrifices brought by the people, and the author adds this comment, "Such things were offered according to law." The second is Christ's declaration "I am come to do your will." The author interprets the sequence in this fashion: "he removes (*anairei*) the first in order to establish (*stēsē*) the second." This comment reminds us of the author's interpretation of the Jer 31:31–34 passage in Heb 8:13. As in that earlier statement, he here uses legal language. For the "dissolving" of laws, see Aristotle, *Athenian Constitution* 29.4; Dio Chrysostom, *Oration* 76.2; Josephus, *J.W.* 2.4. For the dissolving of a will, see Demosthenes, *Oration* 28.5. In contrast, we see "making stand" (*histēmi*) used with reference to the covenant in Gen 6:18; 17:7; Exod 6:4; Deut 28:29.

Because of the formal nature of the language, and because of the long tradition of Christian supersessionism that builds on such language, it is appropriate to note exactly what the author's language signifies. It does not declare that God's covenant with Israel is nullified and replaced by another with Christians. As we have seen, Hebrews nowhere suggests a shift of God's attention and care from the Jewish people. The covenant with Abraham and its promise remains. Nor does the statement represent a rejection of law as such, for the point is precisely that God's will can be expressed by the scroll of the book as well as in the heart. What the author is saying is that the claim of the Levitical cult (established by the law of Moses) to provide access to God is shown—on the evidence of Scripture itself—to be false. What God desires is faithful obedience. Hebrews therefore here stands within the tradition of the prophets who deny the efficacy of ritual when the deeper covenantal obligations are being neglected (see Isa 1:11–31).

The goal of the Levitical cult was the sanctification of the people, that is, setting Israel apart as the distinctive possession of the Holy God: "Be holy as I am holy" (Lev 20:7). Such ritual holiness (separation) could be accomplished through external actions, even without reference to internal dispositions: "sanctify yourselves" (Lev 20:7). The deeper sort of obedience that Hebrews understands as sanctification—approaching the presence of the living God—is not possible through such observances. Indeed, the possibility of such transformation is only given to humans through the intervention of a mediator who bears within him both divine life and human mortality. The author therefore declares not that we have sanctified ourselves, but rather that "we have been sanctified" by means of that "will of God" (*thelēma theou*) of which the psalmist spoke.

But our sanctification through God's will has been wrought "once for all" (*ephapax*) through the faithful obedience—leading to his death—of Jesus our brother. It is "through the offering of the body (*sōma*) of Jesus Christ" that we have been made holy with God's own holiness. The author picks up "body" from Ps 39:6. Jesus' faithful obedience—or obedient faith—was enacted through the body that he offered to God. We are close to Paul's statement in Rom 3:25, where he speaks of God putting forward Jesus "as an expiation (*hilastērion*) through faith (*dia pisteōs*) in his blood (*en tō autou haimati*)." The offering of Jesus was complete, involving his entire somatic existence. Therefore, the "cleansing" accomplished by Jesus was complete.

[11–14] Having used the authority of Scripture to support the presentation of Christ as one totally committed to God and therefore obedient from the heart, the author turns for a final contrast between him and the Levitical priesthood, in terms of efficacy. The author approaches once more from the side of temporality: those who serve under the law do so "every day" and offer "the same sacrifices" and "many times." They are never able to remove sins. This is virtually a restatement of 10:1.

The one distinctive note here is the author's description of the Levitical priests as "standing." We see the significance in the next statement concerning Christ. Having offered "one sacrifice for sins," he now "sits forever at the right hand of God." The central thematic role of Ps 109 reasserts itself. Compare the prologue: "having accomplished purification for sins, he has taken a seat at the right hand of the majesty on high" (Heb 1:3). Christ's one sacrifice was fully effective. Although Hebrews spoke of him earlier as "living forever to intercede on their behalf" (7:18), he does not need to offer himself bodily time and again.

Instead—to continue with Ps 109—he waits until his enemies are put as a footstool beneath his feet. Christ has entered as our pioneer into God's own sabbath rest (4:1–11). Why is he able to sit rather than stand? Because, the author declares, "by one offering" he has perfected those who are sanctified "forever" (*eis to diēnekes*). There is a deliberate contrast here with the Levitical priests in 10:1 who offer many sacrifices "forever" (*eis to diēnekes*), precisely because such sacrifices are ineffective in perfecting those who approach God.

[15–18] The prophecy of Jer 31:31–34 now reappears (see Heb 8:8–12) as another "witness" to the efficacy of Christ's sacrifice. This is the third time that Scripture is said to "bear witness" (*martyrein*; see also 7:8, 17), and also the third time that the Holy Spirit is said to speak or reveal through Scripture (see 3:7, and, by implication, 9:8). Characteristically, the Scripture is understood as spoken, and as addressed "to us" (*hēmin*) rather than simply to the past.

Only a small portion of the Jeremiah passage is excerpted here. The first two verses, which spoke of the Sinai covenant that the people broke, are not mentioned. The author begins with the covenant that God will make "after those days," touching on the inscription of the law in human hearts (Jer 31:33) and then skipping to the statement that God will no longer remember their sins (Jer 31:34), leaving out the intermediate material dealing with the knowledge of the Lord. Out of 131 words in the Jeremiah passage as it appears in Heb 8:8–12, only 32 reappear in this excerpt. It is all the more striking, then, that this version of the citation also has notable alterations/additions. In 10:16 the phrase *pros autous* ("with them") replaces the lengthy characterization of "their fathers" in the original. In 10:17 the author adds, "and their lawless deeds" (*kai tōn anomiōn autōn*) to "their sins" (*tōn hamartiōn autōn*) as no longer remembered by God.

The introduction, "after saying," in 10:15, seems to demand another introductory phrase, such as the "he says afterward," found in a number of MSS, following the pattern of introductory phrases in 10:8 and 10:9. But it is more likely that the phrase internal to the citation, "the Lord says" (*legei kyrios*) in 10:16, provides the link between the two parts of the citation (Attridge, 281). The point of the citation is revealed by the author's selection of verses and by his final statement: "where there is forgiveness of these, an offering for sin is no more." Because Christ's sacrifice has perfected the conscience through the cleansing that comes from the perfect obedience to God's will, the forms of ritual observance are no longer required.

10:19–31 Exhortation to Enter and Not Fall Away

We have followed the longest stretch of exposition in the composition, extending from 6:13 to 10:18. In his characteristic manner, the author now renews his exhortation to his listeners. In 10:19–31 the exhortation falls into two distinct phases, the first fundamentally positive (10:19–25), the second taking the form of a warning (10:26–31). After this exhortation, the author will turn again for his final long exposition on the nature of faith as revealed in the heroes of old (11:1–40).

The positive encouragement builds directly on the long argument concerning Jesus as the great high priest: since he has given them access to God's presence, they should enter with the same dispositions that he demonstrated. Such moral dispositions, in turn, are to find nourishment through the way the listeners mutually exhort each other, and remain loyal to their community commitments.

The negative warning has all the severity that we have come to expect from the author (cf. 2:3; 4:11; 6:4–8). Using still another "lesser to the greater" argument, he declares that the punishment of death decreed by Torah for those who reject it is less severe than the punishment awaiting those who spurn the gifts that have been given them through Christ. The living God is the source of all blessing, but the living God never ceases being fearsome.

> **10:19** Therefore, brothers, since by the blood of Jesus we have boldness to enter the sanctuary through the new and living way **20** that he has dedicated for us, through the veil, that is, his flesh, **21** and since we have a great priest over the house of God, **22** let us approach[a] with true hearts in a fullness of faith, having been sprinkled in our hearts from an evil conscience and having our bodies washed with pure water. **23** Let us hold on to the secure confession of hope,[b] for the one who has made the promise is faithful. **24** Let us consider how to arouse[c] one another to love and good deeds, **25** not abandoning[d] our assemblies, as some are accustomed to do, but exhorting[e] one another, and this all the more as you see the day approaching.
>
> **26** For[f] when we sin deliberately after we have received recognition of the truth, there no longer remains[g] a sacrifice for sins.[h] **27** Instead, there is a certain dread expectation of judgment and a fiery zeal ready to consume opponents. **28** Anyone who rejects Moses' law "will die" without compassion[i] on the "witness of two or three." **29** Of how much worse a punishment do you suppose the one worthy,[j] who has shown contempt for the Son of God, and who has reckoned as profane the blood of the covenant by which he was sanctified, and who has insulted the spirit of grace? **30** For we know the one who said, "To me belongs vengeance, I will repay,"[k] and again, "The Lord will judge his people." **31** Falling into the hands of the living God is a fearful thing.

a. Although the indicative of *proserchometha* ("we are entering") is read by P^{46} (together with *gar*) and D, as well as a number of lesser witnesses, the subjunctive, "let us enter" (*proserchōmetha*) is surely the best reading.

b. The original hand of א, together with some Latin and Syriac witnesses, add "our" (*hēmōn*) to the word "hope," which is, in any case, to be understood.

c. P^{46} has "out of arousal" (*ek paraxysmou*), rather than "to arousal," which would make "an arousal of love" to be the stimulus for mutual exhortation.

d. P46 and the original hand of D have a shorter, less intense version of the participle read by other MSS (*kataleipontes* rather than *enkataleipontes).*

e. Some MSS add "each other" (*heautous*), but it is in any case to be understood, as in my translation.

f. P46 and some Vulgate MSS lack the inferential conjunction *gar* ("for"), reducing the logical link between the positive and negative exhortations.

g. As in v. 25, P46 and D go their own way with a different version of the participle (here *kataleipein* and *perileipein*, respectively, rather than *apoleipein*).

h. Perhaps under the influence of 10:8, some MSS (P46 and the original hand of D among them) have the singular *hamartias* rather than the plural *hamartiōn.*

i. The original hand of D and the Harclean Syriac add the phrase *kai diakryōn* ("and tears"), perhaps echoing a commonplace (*oikton kai dakrya*) such as is found in 3 Macc 1:4; 6:22.

j. Once more P46 has a different version of the verb, having *katiaxioō* rather than *axioō.*

k. A great many witnesses add "says the Lord," as in the citation of the same verse from Deut 32:35 in Rom 12:19.

[10:19–22] The exhortation builds on the entire argument so far developed, and artfully uses terms that echo parts of that earlier development. In verses 19–21 the author states what he and his hearers "have" (*echontes*) as a result of Christ's work, and in verse 22 he summons them to "approach" (*proserchōmetha*). The language merges the image of ritual entrance to worship (argued in chaps. 7–10), and of reaching the goal of pilgrimage (argued in chaps. 3–4).

Through "the blood of Jesus"—that is, through Jesus' obedient offering of himself in death—they have been given "boldness" (*parrēsia*). In 3:6 this quality was associated with the hearers' belonging to God's house, and in 4:16 with their approach to the throne of grace. Here confidence and boldness enable them to enter the true sanctuary of God's presence. The term *eisodos* can be used for any sort of opening, as to a temple (see Euripides, *Ion* 104), but can be used also for a right of access (Herodotus 3.118), or for the act of entering itself (Ps 120:8; 1 Sam 29:6). Here it is appropriate both for the sense of entry into the sanctuary, and for the "making a path" in pilgrimage (cf. 1 Thess 1:9; 2:1). The notion of access to God gained by the sacrifice of Jesus is strikingly similar to Paul's argument in Rom 3:21–26 and 5:1. The verb *enkainizein*, as we saw in Heb 9:18, can mean "to initiate," but here must surely be read in the ritual sense of "dedicate" or "consecrate" (see Deut 20:5; 2 Chr 7:5; 1 Kgs 8:63).[1]

In 9:8 the author stated that, while the first tent still had standing, the way (*hodos*) into the sanctuary does not yet appear. Now he declares that Christ has dedicated the "new and living way (*hodos*)." Each of the two descriptors is

1. See N. A. Dahl, "A New and Living Way: The Approach to God according to Hebrews 10:19–25," *Int* 5 (1951): 401–12.

striking. The adjective *prosphatos* is a New Testament *hapax legomenon*, although the adverb appears in Acts 18:2 with reference to the "recent" arrival of Aquila and Priscilla in Corinth. And that is the basic sense of the term; when used of corpses, it means fresh rather than decomposed (Homer, *Il.* 24.757); when used of water, it means fresh rather than stale (Plutarch, Table-Talk 6.14, *Mor.* 690C); and when used of time, it means recent rather than ancient (Aristotle, *Rhetoric* 1375B). It means simply "new" in Qoh 1:9 ("nothing new under the sun"), and in Ps 80:10 ("nothing new with God"; see also Hermas, *Sim.* 9.2.2).

The term "living" (*zōsan*), in turn, reminds us of Hebrews' characterization of the priesthood of Melchizedek and the Son of God in 7:8 and 7:25, of the word of God in 4:12, and of God ("the living God") in 3:12; 9:14; and 10:31. The "new and living way" that Christ opens leads from his death ("in his blood") to the presence of the living God. Hebrews uses one more bit of sanctuary imagery, when it speaks of this way passing "through the veil," that is, Jesus' flesh. As we saw earlier, the *katapetasma* separated the holy place from the holy of holies (see Exod 26:37; 36:18; Num 3:26; and Heb 6:19; 9:3).[2] In Hebrews, *sarx* ("flesh") consistently refers to the realm of human existence characterized by mortality (2:14; 5:7; 9:10, 13; 12:9). The image of passing through the veil of the flesh, then, suggests that Jesus himself is the "way" that gives access to God. His mortal body is the "veil" that must be passed through in order to find full access to the living God.[3]

It would be difficult to imagine a more complete anthropological realization of the cult, for even as Jesus' flesh and blood are the means of sacrifice, so is this same dying and rising Jesus "a great priest (*mega hiera*) over the house of God" (cf. Heb 4:14). But as Hebrews has clearly shown, the "house of God" is to be conceived not as a physical building but as a living people: "Christ is son over all the house, whose house we are" (3:6).

The "approach" of the author and hearers (see 4:16) that is encouraged in 10:22 is, therefore, a moral and religious response to God similar to that of Jesus, rather than a performance of external rituals (see 11:6; 12:18, 22). This will become explicit in 13:8–16. To speak of a moral and religious response does not imply that it is simply mental, for the author immediately shows how this response involves the common practices of the nascent Christian movement. But they are practices that are enlivened by a renewed spirit within those who enact them. They can approach God with a "true heart." It is not by accident that the term "heart" is repeated in these verses. We remember how the failure to respond to God through obedience by the wilderness generation was

2. For the history of religions context, see O. Hofius, *Der Vorhang vor dem Thron Gottes* (WUNT 14; Tübingen: Mohr [Siebeck], 1972).

3. For discussion of the function of "of his flesh," see N. H. Young, "*Tout' estin tēs sarkos autou* (Heb. x.20): Apposition, Dependent or Explicative?" *NTS* 20 (1973–74): 100–114.

due to a wicked, hard, wandering, and faithless heart (3:8, 10, 12; 4:7), and how the word of God was described as discerning the thoughts and intentions of the heart (4:12), and how the new covenant was to be one inscribed on the hearts of humans (8:10; 10:16). The effect of Christ's gift to them is that his followers can now approach God with a heart (i.e., disposition) that is true, even as they enter into the "true things" of the heavenly sanctuary (8:2; 9:24), and have come to "the recognition of the truth" (10:26).

The truthfulness of the heart is expressed by a fullness (or, full conviction) of faith (*plērophoria pisteōs*). The ambiguity of *plērophoria* was discussed when we looked at its use in 6:11. There it was connected with hope (*elpis*), and in just a few verses, the author will bring faith and hope into a mutually defining relationship (11:1). Given the thematic importance of faith throughout this composition, and above all the role that the faithful obedience of Christ played in his priestly act, the choice of *pistis* here cannot be considered arbitrary. Their "perfecting" is to have a maturity—fullness—of faith. They are to respond to God in a way that the wilderness generation did not because of its faithlessness (*apistia*; see 4:2), and they will shortly be shown, in the roll call of the heroes of faith in chapter 11, how they can "become imitators of those who through faith and long-suffering inherit the promises" (6:12).

The fullness of faith should be read in conjunction with the two following phrases. First, the "sprinkling" (*rhantizein*) alludes to the ancient cultic practice (see 9:13, 19, 21), whether with blood or water. But now it is not a ritual location or the outside of bodies that is thus purified/dedicated. It is once again the "heart" or the seat of human freedom, which is purified from an evil conscience. Christ has brought about the purification of moral consciousness that the law could never accomplish (9:9, 14; 10:2, 11–14). Hebrews then adds a second term for cleansing, namely "washing." The verb *louein* occurs only here in the New Testament, but the noun *loutron* appears twice in connection with baptism (Eph 5:26; Titus 3:5). Perhaps baptism is also meant here, but it is also possible that "washing" simply carries forward the image of purification, extending it to the body (*sōma*) as the outward symbol and instrument of faithful obedience (see 10:5, 10), so that as Christ's faith was enacted by the disposition of his body, so is the faith of his followers expressed fully when the purified internal attitude is expressed in the pure disposition of their bodies.[4]

[23–25] The author shifts from the imagery of the cult to the straightforward language of communal life. He exhorts his hearers to "hold fast" (*katechein*) to the "confession." The notion of grasping or holding on echoes the earlier exhortation of 3:6 and 3:14, while the specific command to hold to the confession (*homologia*) repeats 4:14 (see also 3:1, "consider [*katanoein*] our confession").

4. For the argument that baptism is intended, see P. J. Leithart, "Womb of the World: Baptism and the Priesthood of the New Covenant in Hebrews 10:19–22," *JSNT* 78 (2000): 49–65.

Describing this confession (or commitment) in terms of hope (*elpis*), the author brings the terms "faith" and "hope" into position for their mutually defining role. In 3:6 he told his hearers to "look to the boast that is our hope" (*kauchēma tēs elpidos*); and as he speaks of a "fullness of faith" here, in 6:11 he spoke of *plērophorian tēs elpidos* ("a fullness of hope"). In 6:18, in turn, he also spoke of believers as "taking hold (*kratēsai*) of the hope that lies ahead." And in 7:19 he declared a "better hope through which we are approaching God." As I mentioned above, this identification will become complete in 11:1, when faith is defined as "the substance of things hoped for."

In this exhortation, the "confession" is modified by the adjective *aklinē*, another New Testament *hapax legomenon*. In Plato's *Phaedrus* 109A it has the sense of "unswerving" (as from side to side; see also Philo, *Moses* 1.30; *On Virtue* 158). In 4 Maccabees the adjective is used to describe a determination that does not flinch (4 Macc 6:7; 17:3). Here it attaches grammatically to "confession"—thus the translation as "secure"—but it is a natural temptation to make it translate the unswerving conviction of the believers, as though it were an adverb. Nevertheless, the emphasis here is on the confession itself as steady, as the next clause makes clear: they can hold on, because the one who has made the promise is "faithful" (*pistos*). In earlier passages, the author spoke of Christ as *pistos*, but here it is God whose faithfulness to his promise is affirmed; we remember the lengthy defense of the security of God's promise in 6:13–18. And in 11:11 the author will say of Abraham that he reckoned the one who had made the promise to him as "faithful" (*piston hēgēsato ton epangeilamenon*).

Holding to the confession is not a matter of grim determination, but of active and mutual commitment and upbuilding. The translation, "Let us consider how to arouse one another," is something of a compromise. The phrase *katanoōmen allēlous* is literally, "Let us consider one another." The verb *katanoein* has the ordinary sense of "contemplate" or "consider" in a noetic manner (see Herodotus 2.23; Jas 1:23–24; Matt 7:3), and has that same meaning when the author uses it earlier: "consider the apostle and high priest of our confession" (3:1). Here, however, the sense is closer to "pay attention to one another," or "put your minds to one another" by way of helping one another concentrate—compare the use of *blepein* ("see to it") in 3:12 and 12:25. The phrase *eis paraxysmon* defines the goal of that mutual attention, that they all be stimulated to love and good deeds. The noun *paraxysmos* is often used negatively as "irritate" or "exasperate" (see Jer 39:37; Deut 29:27; Acts 15:39), and the verb also can have that meaning (see 1 Cor 13:5; Acts 17:10). But it can also be used more neutrally as "urging" or "stimulating" someone (see Xenophon, *Cyropaedia* 6.2.5), and even in the positive sense of stimulating someone to good deeds (Xenophon, *Memorabilia* 3.3.13).

The phrase "love and good deeds" occurs here for the first time in the composition, and may be considered as something of a hendiadys: love is not a vague principle or emotion, but is shown by the doing of good deeds. We remember that the author had earlier assured the hearers that God would not forget their "work and the love" that they had demonstrated toward his name, which was spelled out in terms of "having served and still serving the saints" (6:10). Here they are exhorted to continue in the manner in which they had begun (for *kala erga* elsewhere, see 1 Tim 5:10, 25; 6:18; Titus 2:7, 14; 3:8, 14; 1 Pet 2:12). The author speaks of "love" as a moral disposition only here and in 6:10—the verb *agapan* ("to love") is ascribed to Christ and to God (1:9; 12:6)—and in both cases it forms the triad of "faith, hope, love" (cf. 1 Cor 13:13; 1 Thess 1:3).

The means of stimulating one another is mutual exhortation. The verb *parakalein* surely has the sense here of exhorting rather than comforting (as it does in 6:18). They are to do with one another and for one another what the author does for them (13:19), and writes this composition to accomplish (13:22).

Such exhortation is to be even more urgent "as you see the day approaching," a phrase that echoes the earlier encouragement of the hearers to "admonish yourselves every day, as long as it is called 'today'" (3:13). That earlier exhortation was based on the appreciation that every day is one in which God calls people to fidelity and obedience. In this passage, however, "the day" has specific eschatological overtones derived from the prophetic tradition that spoke simply of a "day" in which God would act for judgment (Isa 2:12–22; Joel 1:15; 3:14; Zech 14:1; Amos 5:18–20; 8:9–14; Zeph 1:14–18), a tradition carried forward by the New Testament compositions, whether simply as "the day" (1 Thess 5:4; 1 Cor 3:13), or as "the day of the Lord" (1 Cor 1:8; 5:5; 1 Thess 5:2; 2 Thess 2:2; 2 Cor 1:14; 2 Pet 3:10).

The use of the verb *engizein* ("approach"), in addition, echoes the language of the Gospels concerning the "arrival of the kingdom of God" (Matt 3:2; 4:17; Mark 1:15), and of Paul and James concerning the end time. In Rom 13:12 Paul declares that "the day has approached" (*hē de hēmera ēngiken*), and James says that "the appearance of the Lord has approached" (*parousia tou kyriou ēngiken*, Jas 5:8). This element of eschatological urgency is not isolated within Hebrews, and marks one of the ways in which the composition's strong Platonic worldview is modified by the symbolic world of Scripture and the experience of Jesus as Lord. The composition maintains with full vigor the early Christian expectation of a future climax to history (see 3:3; 4:1; 6:2, 5, 8; 9:28; 10:13; 12:26–28). It will, in fact, recur again immediately in the next verses (10:26–27) and in the next section (10:37).

The call to mutual stimulation to faith, love, and hope, as well as to mutual exhortation, indicates the communal character of the composition's commitment, and its awareness that a distinctive manner of life within this "house of God" will depend on the sort of shared construction of identity upon which all intentional communities—since they are inherently fragile—depend. Opposed to such communal activity, then, is the sort of individualistic attitude that finds the abandonment of the group's assemblies—as some are in the habit (*ethos*) of doing—to be a matter of no moment. In the Introduction (pp. 33–38), I suggested that this verse is one of the keys to a possible reconstruction of the rhetorical situation faced by the author. A sense of discouragement and lack of hope has a concrete expression in a distancing of the self from the community, resulting in a still more perilous condition for the remaining members, all of whom rely on a shared and enthusiastic commitment if they are to persevere in a paradoxical and painful manner of life.

The seriousness of abandoning such assemblies (for *episynagōgē* see 2 Thess 2:1; 2 Macc 2:7) is suggested by the author's use of the verb *enkataleipein*, which has the nuance of "leaving in the lurch" (see Plato, *Symposium* 179A; Xenophon, *Cyropaedia* 8.8.4; Josephus, *Life* 205; Mark 15:34; Matt 27:46). It is striking that, just as the obedient response to God is expressed through mutual support within the community, so does the abandonment of community gatherings express infidelity and apostasy.

[26–27] The threat reminds us most of the earlier warning in 6:4–8. There the author declared that it was impossible, once one had been enlightened, to fall by the side, and still be renewed to repentance. Here he speaks of sinning (*hamartanontōn*) after "receiving the recognition of the truth" (*epignōsin tēs alētheias*). Despite all the language about "sins" in this composition, this is only the second time that the author speaks of "sinning" (using the verb). In 3:17, as here, it is a matter of those who had fallen away after being gifted by God. In that earlier passage, the gift was their liberation from Egypt. In this case, it is receiving recognition of the "truth." Once more, we are given pause by the term. Although Hebrews has used the adjective *alēthinos* (8:2; 9:24; 10:22) with reference to the heavenly cult in contrast to the earthly, this is the only time it uses the noun *alētheia*. The phrase "recognition of the truth" occurs in a roughly equivalent way in 1 Tim 2:4; 2 Tim 2:25; 3:7; Titus 1:1 to mean entry into God's people. Coming to the recognition of the truth means entering into the community that is defined by the true God. The phrase is therefore equivalent to "being enlightened" in Heb 6:4.

Consistent with the entire argument to this point, the statement that "there no longer remains a sacrifice for sins" (see 10:2, 18) brings home both the promise and the peril of the priestly work of Jesus. On the positive side, there is the possibility that those joined to him can be perfected through the "cleansing of conscience" that he accomplished once for all. On the negative side, a deliberate turning away from this gift means being cut off not only from its benefits, but also from any chance of resuming (with any sense of satisfaction) the old cult that could purify only externals.

The key term here is certainly *hekousiōs*, which I have translated as "deliberately." When the adjective is used with reference to actions, it signifies their voluntary as opposed to their involuntary character (Plato, *Republic* 556B;

Xenophon, *Memorabilia* 2.1.18; Aristotle, *Nicomachean Ethics* 1109B). It is used for "freewill offerings" in the law (Lev 23:38; Num 15:3; 29:39; Deut 12:6–8), and the adverb—used here—has the same force (see Phlm 14; 1 Pet 5:2). Without using these terms, the law distinguishes between sins that are committed "inadvertently," and for which sacrifices are efficacious, and sins that are "defiant" or "high-handed" or "insolent." Those who sin this way must be cut off from the people (see Num 15:22–31; Deut 17:12–13; also Heb 9:7): "But anyone who sins defiantly, whether he be a native or an alien, insults the LORD, and shall be cut off from among his people" (Num 15:20). Just as in the present passage, the reason for the severity is that such defiance is a direct challenge not only to the gift, but to the one who has given the gift: "Since he has despised the word of the LORD and has broken his commandment, he must be cut off. He has only himself to blame" (NAB).

The sin that is freely chosen, then, is not a minor transgression, but apostasy, a turning away (cf. Heb 3:12–19). As in 6:4–8, the sinner cannot turn back again, for the sinner is denying the basis for such return. Not only do apostates now lack a way of being reconciled with God, they face the same destiny as God's enemies. The author's use of "expectation" (*ekdochē*) here is intriguing. The exalted Jesus has the expectation that his enemies will be placed as a footstool beneath his feet (10:13; Ps 109:1). And those on the pilgrimage of faith with Abraham have an expectation: they await a heavenly city (Heb 11:10). The apostates, however, have only an expectation of a certain dread judgment (*phobera de tis ekdochē kriseōs*). The author stated in 9:27 that after death there is judgment. The apostate's judgment is fearsome for two reasons. The first is that it will consist in condemnation, of being "cut off from the people." The second is that the judgment is carried out by the all-seeing and fearful God.

The adjective *phoberos* ("dreadful/fearful") occurs here, again in 10:31 as an attribute of God, and once more in 12:21 in a description of the appearance of God at Sinai. In the LXX, the term is consistently associated with God's appearance (Gen 28:17; Deut 1:19; 2:7; 8:17; Judg 13:6; 1 Chr 16:25; Neh 1:5; 4:14; Pss 46:2; 75:7; 95:4; 98:3; 110:9). In Heb 4:1 the author tells his readers that they should fear lest they be thought to fall away from this God. When God is feared—through faithful obedience—there is no need to fear anything else, not death (2:15), nor human rulers (11:23, 27). Quoting Ps 117:6, the author will declare, "The Lord is my help, I will not fear; what can a human do to me?" (13:6). But those who do not "fear God" in their lives must face God as a fearsome, even dread, judge, because they have become, through their own choice, God's "enemies." The term *hypenantos* is used for opponents in battle (Thucydides, *Peloponnesian War* 2.2.2; Xenophon, *Cyropaedia* 1.6.38). Apostates are now among those "enemies" who are to be placed beneath the feet (Ps 109:1).

To express the mode of this judgment—"a fiery zeal ready to consume"—the author uses imagery associated especially with the prophets. The phrase "fiery zeal" appears in Ps 78:5 and Zeph 3:8. Zephaniah 1:18 speaks of "the fire of God's wrath," and Isa 66:15 declares that the Lord will come in fire against his enemies. (For other passages of God's "jealous/zealous wrath," see Deut 29:20; 2 Kgs 19:31; Judg 9:4; Ps 68:9.) Fire continues to be associated with God's judgment throughout the New Testament (Matt 3:10–12; 5:22; 7:19; 13:42; 25:41; John 15:6; 1 Cor 3:13; 2 Thess 1:8; 1 Pet 1:7; 2 Pet 3:7; Rev 17:16; 18:8; 20:14). For "eating/devouring" as part of the eschatological threat, see Jer 21:14 and Jas 5:3. The prophetic passage that Hebrews most obviously echoes, however, is Isa 26:11: "A wrath will take an undisciplined people, and now a fire will consume enemies."

[28–31] The author of Hebrews has consistently used the "lesser to greater" form of argument throughout the composition, both for exposition and for exhortation. In 2:1–4, for example, he asked how those who heard this greater word of salvation could flee, if those who earlier heard the word spoken by angels and yet disobedient were appropriately punished.

The same argument returns here. Those who "reject" Moses' law, he says, were to be killed without compassion. The weight of the verb *athetein* must be taken seriously. It is used for putting aside a wife in Deut 21:14, for alienation in Judg 9:23, and for rejecting God's sacrifices in 1 Sam 2:17. So it means more than "setting aside," suggesting as well "dealing treacherously," or "breaking faith" (see Polybius, *Histories* 9.36.10; Isa 1:2; Mark 6:26; 1 Tim 5:12). For such rejection in the New Testament, see Mark 7:9; Luke 7:30; 10:16; John 12:48; Gal 2:21; 3:15; 1 Thess 4:8. Hebrews uses the noun form *athetēsis* twice, once with respect to the "nullification/putting aside" of the first commandment (law of Moses) by Ps 109:4 (Heb 7:18), and once with respect to the "nullification/setting aside" of sin by Christ's sacrifice (9:26). The author is therefore not speaking here of transgressions or "unintentional sins," but precisely of the sort of apostasy that is the equivalent of "sinning deliberately" (10:26).

The language of verse 28 combines, in our author's typical manner, a strict adherence to biblical diction, together with considerable liberty in adaptation. The tradition of requiring two or three witnesses is itself complex. In Num 35:30 we find only that more than one witness is required in capital cases. In Deut 17:6 the principle is refined and again connected to putting someone to death, but without specifying the cause. It is the language of this passage that Hebrews most echoes. Finally, in Deut 19:15 the principle of two or three witnesses is extended to every serious case: "a judicial fact shall be established only on the testimony of two or three witnesses." It is this Deuteronomic version that is echoed in other New Testament passages (see Matt 18:16; 2 Cor 13:1; 1 Tim 5:19).[5]

5. See H. van Vliet, *No Single Testimony: A Study of the Adoption of the Law of Deut. 19:15 Par. into the New Testament* (Utrecht: Kemink en Zoon, 1958).

The author seems deliberately to allude to the entire passage in Deut 17:2–6, which envisages the killing of an Israelite who has transgressed the covenant by worshiping other gods. Idolatry is as fundamental a rejection of covenant as can be imagined. But that passage lacks any reference to "without compassion" (*chōris oiktirmōn*). The language of compassion in Scripture is almost entirely associated with the Lord (Exod 34:6; Deut 4:31; Ps 77:38). In Ps 108:12 the Lord is asked not to show compassion to the orphans of the psalmist's enemies. But we do find "without compassion" in a passage parallel to Deut 17:2–6, namely 13:6–10, where the punishment of death is demanded for those who tempt others to idolatry. The injunction "show no pity" appears also in 19:21, with reference to the killing of false witnesses. The author has combined elements from several scriptural passages to make his point with great efficiency.

As in Heb 2:1–4, the "how much greater" part of the argument is couched in terms of a rhetorical question. The author asks his hearers to "suppose" (*dokeite*), thereby appealing to their imaginations (for other examples of *dokein*, see Matt 17:25; 18:12; 21:28; Luke 22:24): what sort of "worse punishment" would someone deserve who rejects the gift of God in Christ? The verb *axioun* ("deserve") appears also in Heb 3:3, where it refers to the greater honor than Moses that Christ deserves. The noun *timōria* ("punishment") has the specific sense of a punishment that is not corrective, but is rather a form of vengeance (for the distinction see Aristotle, *Rhetoric* 1369B, and the uses in Euripides, *Orestes* 400, 425; Wis 19:13; 2 Macc 6:12, 26; 4 Macc 4:24). This is not to be confused with "discipline" (*paideia*) that God brings upon his sons (Heb 12:7–11); it is, rather, the fearful judgment of the end time. Like any good rhetorician, the author does not go into specifics beyond the prophetic imagery in 10:27. He leaves the form of punishment to their imagination and turns his attention instead to developing the enormity of the crime involved in such apostasy.

The grievousness of "sinning deliberately" is elaborated by three parallel phrases that echo themes established earlier in the composition. First, such sin shows contempt toward the Son of God. If the verb *patapatein* were read literally, the phrase would be even more powerful. It was the verb used for the "trampling underfoot" of seeds by swine (Herodotus 2.14). In Ps 7:5 it retains some of that meaning: the psalmist complains that his enemies have "trampled his life into the ground." In 1 Sam 14:48 and 17:53, however, the term has the extended meaning of defeating another. The use here has the still more extended sense of "showing contempt toward." Homer uses it for scorning oaths that had been taken (*Il.* 4.157), and Plato uses the verb for the scorning of laws (*Laws* 714A; *Gorgias* 484A). Its use here is particularly striking in that this is only the fourth time (see Heb 4:14; 6:6; 7:3) that the author uses the full solemn title for Jesus, "Son of God" (*huios tou theou*). As in 6:6, the full title emphasizes the shocking character of the apostasy: it not only falls from grace, it mocks the giver of the grace.

The sin of apostasy can be expressed also through the language of the cult as "reckoning as profane the blood of the covenant by which he was sanctified." The verb *hēgeomai* has the sense of mental calculation or evaluation (see esp. Phil 2:3, 6, 25; 3:7; Jas 1:2). The apostasy, in effect, reverses the effect of Christ's priestly work. The "blood of the covenant" is not that sprinkled by Moses on altar and laws (Heb 9:20), but the "blood of Jesus" that has enabled access to God through the rending of the veil of his flesh (10:19), a blood "so much greater" than that of bulls and goats (9:13–14). It is precisely through the death and exaltation of Jesus that they have been "sanctified" in the most proper sense, that is, given access to the most holy God (see 2:11; 9:13; 10:10, 14; 13:12). The one who voluntarily turns away from such a gift renders that which is holy "profane" or "common" or "unclean." The term *koinos* ordinarily signifies that which is "common" in the sense that it is shared, but it can take on the connotation of "ordinary" (Aristotle, *Rhetoric* 1355A), and is occasionally used in Judaism and in the New Testament for that which is not sanctified (*Let. Aris.* 315; Josephus, *Ant.* 12.112; Mark 7:2; Acts 10:14, 28; Rom 14:14; Rev 21:17).

The third characterization of the one who "sins deliberately" is that he has "insulted the spirit of grace." The verb *enybrizein* is a New Testament *hapax legomenon,* but it plainly intensifies *hybrizein*, which, in an honor-shame culture, means to reduce the honor that is due to another, that is, to "insult" the other (cf. Luke 11:45). The verb *enybrizein* is used in this sense in Polybius, *Histories* 10.26.3; and Sophocles, *Philoctetes* 342. The phrase "spirit of grace" draws together for the first time two terms, each of which points to the presence and power of God among humans. We have seen earlier that the *pneuma* ("spirit") speaks through Scripture (Heb 3:7; 9:8; 10:15), and is the source of the many gifts distributed to believers (2:4), who have, indeed, become "partakers of the spirit" (6:4), because Christ entered God's presence "through the eternal spirit" (9:14).

The author here connects "spirit" to "grace" (*charis*), another term that has run through the composition. In 2:9 the author states that it was by the grace of God that Christ tasted death in behalf of all, and in 4:16 that those who belong to Christ can "approach the throne of grace" and "find grace." In 12:15 the author will warn against "falling short of the grace of God," which is the grace of an "unshakeable kingdom" (12:28). In 13:9 he states that his hearers' hearts are secured by grace, and in 13:25 he wishes grace upon them all. In brief, the apostate insults everything that has come from God, and therefore also insults God.

Such arrogance demands a dreadful and certain penalty, delivered by the one who is thus insulted. In verse 30 the *gar* ("for") serves to connect this statement about God as judge to the statement in verse 27 about the expectation of a dread judgment. The apostate can expect it, because "we know the one who said (*ton eiponta*)." The "knowing" in this case is based on the human experience of God in the past, particularly as it has been disclosed in Scripture, a passage of which the author now quotes as evidence of God's ability and willingness to punish those who despise his claim on them. The biblical citation comes from Deut 32:35–36, and its two parts are separated by the phrase "and again" (*kai palin*), a method of stringing together texts used earlier by the author (Heb 1:5; 2:13). The first statement, "to me belongs vengeance (*ekdikēsis*), I will repay (*antapodōsō*)," does not correspond exactly either to the Hebrew ("vengeance is mine and recompense," NRSV) or to the LXX, "In a day of vengeance, I will repay." The version in Hebrews agrees with the form of the citation found in Rom 12:19, except that Paul adds, "says the Lord" (also added by some MSS of Hebrews).

The second statement, "The Lord will judge his people," agrees with Deut 32:36 as well as a parallel text in Ps 134:14. In both passages, however, the statement about God's judgment is followed by an affirmation that comfort will come to his servants. In Paul and Hebrews, the statements serve to assert the absolute sovereignty of God as judge of the world, who can and will deliver *ekdikēsis* and *antapodosis*. The first of these terms means to exact vengeance for a wrong and is frequently associated with God's actions (see Exod 7:4; 12:12; Num 31:2; 33:4; Judg 11:36; 2 Sam 4:8; Pss 17:47; 93:1; see also Luke 18:7–8; Acts 7:24). The second term means simply to "pay back" (as a loan; see Aristotle, *Nicomachean Ethics* 1133A). It is used in the LXX for God's "paying back" evildoers with punishment (Lev 18:25; Deut 32:6, 41, 43; Judg 1:7; Pss 7:4; 30:23; 40:10).

The final sentence of the admonition is chilling in its simplicity. The statement plays upon a scriptural topos. "Falling into the hands" of someone means coming under their power (see Judg 15:18; Sir 8:1; Sus 23). Three passages in Scripture declare how much better it is to fall into the "hands of the Lord" than into the "hands of a man" (2 Sam 24:14; 1 Chr 21:13), for, as Sir 2:18 states, "equal is his majesty to the mercy that he shows." In such passages, "falling into God's hands" is a reassurance. But that is not what Hebrews offers. Rather, falling into God's hands is "fearsome"—the author uses the same adjective (*phoberos*) used to describe the "dread" judgment in 10:27.[6]

The judgment will be fearsome, because it will be carried out by "the living God." We have seen this phrase used earlier. In 3:12 the people in the wilderness turned away from "the living God." In 9:14 Christ's sacrifice has brought the hearers to worship "the living God." And in 12:22 they will be reminded that they are not approaching Mount Sinai (itself a "fearsome" place), but the city of "the living God." Set among these passages, the statement in 10:31 reminds the first hearers—and today's readers—that the worship of the living God is quite unlike the worship of an idol, whose existence depends on human service. The living God is fearsome precisely because, like his own word, he

6. For the argument that there is a positive element here, see J. Swetnam, "Hebrews 10, 30–31: A Suggestion," *Bib* 75 (1994): 388–95.

sees deeply and truly into the heart of his own creatures, and demands of them a truth commensurate with his own. It is not a game. It is the most ultimate reality, and therefore, quite properly, "fearful."

10:32–39 Memory of the Past as Encouragement for the Future

The author has several times touched on the earlier experience of his hearers: the mighty deeds and outpouring of the Spirit that accompanied the proclamation of the word (2:3–4), their experience of initiation into the community (6:4–5), and the labor of love they had demonstrated in serving the saints (6:10). Now, having shown the greatness of the gift given through Christ's sacrifice (10:1–22), having exhorted his hearers to mutual encouragement and support of their assemblies (10:23–25), and having warned them of the punishment awaiting those who fall away (10:26–31), he again summons them to remember their earlier devotion (10:32–34), in order to exhort them again to fidelity (10:35–39), before turning to his great encomium on faith (11:1–40).

> **10:32** But remember the earlier days,[a] when after you were enlightened,
> you endured a great contest of sufferings. You were both publicly shamed[b]
> by revilings and afflictions, and you became partners of those who lived
> that way. **34** For you even shared the suffering of prisoners[c] and you ac-
> cepted the seizure of your property with joy, since you knew that you
> yourselves[d] had a better and permanent possession.[e] **35** So don't lose your
> confidence. It has a great reward. **36** For you need to have endurance, so
> that, by having done God's will, you might receive the promise. **37** Now,[f]
> "Yet a little while—he who comes will arrive and he will not delay, **38**
> and my righteous one will live from faith," and, "if he draws back, my
> soul will not be pleased with him." **39** But we do not draw back—to our
> destruction. Rather, we have faith—to the securing of our life.

a. The first corrector of א adds "your" (*hymōn*) to "days," which is in any case understood. The corrector was certainly closer than the original hand of that MS, which had "your earlier sins."

b. The original hand of D, perhaps not grasping the negative sense of *theatrizomenoi*, has instead *oneidizomenoi* ("being reviled").

c. Some MSS, e.g., P^{46}, have *desmois* ("chains") rather than *desmiois* ("prisoners"), and then add various identifiers: "my chains" (e.g., א), or "their chains" (some Latin MSS).

d. D and the majority of MSS, missing the accusative + infinitive construction, have *heautois* ("for themselves"), while 1881 and a few other witnesses have *en heautois* ("in themselves").

e. A large number of MSS (including the second hand of both א and D) add the words *en ouranois* (“in heaven”), but this is undoubtedly a scribal clarification.

f. P[13] and a few other witnesses lack the *gar* (“for”), which is absent from the LXX of Hab 2:3 as well.

[10:32–34] The hearers of this discourse find themselves between “the days” after their first enlightenment and “the day” of the Lord’s coming. In 10:25 they were urged to exhort one another “all the more” as they saw that final day approaching. In the present passage, the note of eschatological urgency is struck again: “He who comes will arrive and will not delay” (10:38). In this in-between time, the author summons his audience to an act of anamnesis (for *anamimneskesthai* see 1 Cor 4:17; 2 Cor 7:15; 2 Tim 1:6) as a means of encouraging them to endurance as they await that climax to history. The act of memory is not a simple recall of facts from the past. It is rather making present to mind and heart the experiences that shaped and continue to shape their identity. Their “earlier days” serve as a counterpoint to the present temptation to neglect the assemblies and turn away from their commitment.

The days they are to remember are those following their “enlightenment” (*phōtisthentes*). As in 6:4, the participle could refer to the rite of baptism (see Eph 5:12–14), but in any case signifies their “recognition of truth” (10:26) at their entrance into the community. It is the community’s behavior after that enlightenment on which the author focuses.

He reminds them that they then “endured a great contest of sufferings.” The precise translation of the phrase *pollēn athlēsin . . . pathēmatōn* is difficult for two reasons. The first difficulty is that no English term adequately captures the meaning of the Greek *athlēsis*. Today’s English term “contest” suggests any form of competition, but Hebrews uses the term as the starting point of development for one of the composition’s key metaphors, that of the athletic games of ancient Greece. Such use of the games, especially those at Olympus, as a metaphor for the moral life is common among Greco-Roman philosophers (see Epictetus, *Discourses* 2.18.28; 3.22.59; 3.25.1–4). The author of Hebrews will extend and elaborate the metaphor in 12:1–11. The second difficulty is aligning the genitive “of sufferings” (*pathēmatōn*) to the noun “contest.” It is clear enough that the author means the genitive to function adjectivally, to characterize the “great contest/struggle”: it was not only accompanied by suffering—the corollary of any strenuous effort—but actually *consisted* in their sufferings. The contest, in a word, was how they could deal with the sufferings that came upon them because of their holding to the confession of Christ. Their “enduring” (*hypemeinate*) marks their success in the contest. They did not fall away or leave the game. They stayed the course.

The nature of the sufferings is now spelled out more fully, first in general terms (v. 33) and then in more specific terms (v. 34). The hearers have “both” (*touto men*) undergone sufferings "and" (*touto de*) joined themselves to those who also suffered. Although the overall sense of the sentence is clear enough, it does offer some difficulties. For example, the participle *theatrizomenoi* is unusual—in fact, a New Testament *hapax legomenon*. A *theatron* of an ancient city was the place where dramas were performed (Herodotus 6.67), and often where the populace of the city gathered as an *ekklēsia* (see Acts 19:29, 31). It is a public place. The (also rare) verb *theatrizein* means, logically enough, to perform a play or put something on display in a public manner. The verb here is in the passive voice, and would seem to mean "to be made a spectacle" or "to be put on public display." Given the low repute of actors in the honor-shame calculus of antiquity, and given the involuntary nature of "being put on display" suggested by the passive form of the verb, we are justified in reading the display as a sort of shaming. The closest analogy in the New Testament is Paul's statement that he and his associates "have become a spectacle (*theatron*) to the world" (1 Cor 4:9). In Heb 12:1–3 the athletic imagery also evokes a theater, when the author speaks of "a great cloud of witnesses" (12:1), who support the faith of those who follow the pioneer and perfecter of faith, Jesus. Here, however, the great contest of suffering is carried out before a public gaze that is hostile.

The two terms describing the means of such public shaming are found throughout the New Testament in similar settings. The verb *oneidizein* ("to revile or reproach") is used frequently for the rejection of Jesus (Matt 27:44; Mark 15:32; Rom 15:3), or for the response to be expected from others by those associated with Jesus (Matt 5:11; Luke 6:22; 1 Pet 4:14). The choice of the noun *oneidismos*—a reproach or censure, usually verbal in form, and with the nuance of bringing shame on the reproached (see Herodotus 2.36; 9.71; Plato, *Republic* 590C)—is especially significant here, because the author will shortly speak of how Moses preferred the reviling for Christ he received rather than the wealth of Egypt (11:26), and in 13:13 will summon his hearers to go out of the city, bearing his (Christ's) reproach. The shame to which they have been exposed is that borne already by Jesus.

The noun *thlipsis*, in turn, has a definite physical dimension. The verb means bringing pressure on another or oppressing another (Aristotle, *Politics* 1307A). In the LXX the noun is used for the hard things that come upon the people (Gen 35:3; 42:21; Exod 4:31; Deut 4:29; 28:53; Judg 10:14; 2 Sam 4:9; Pss 9:9; 21:11; 24:22). In the New Testament, as well, *thlipsis* tends to be associated with the troubles or afflictions experienced because of being associated with the Christ (Matt 13:2; 24:9, 29; John 16:33; Acts 11:19; 14:22; 20:23; Rom 5:3; 2 Cor 1:4; Eph 3:13; Phil 4:14; Col 1:24). The two terms in combination suggest that the hearers have undergone both verbal and physical abuse in public at the hands of others. And, the author declares, they have endured.

In addition to the ridicule and pain they themselves have suffered, they have made themselves partners (*koinōnoi*) of those likewise situated. The translation "those who lived that way" seems best to respect the ordinary middle-passive sense of *anastrephein*, namely "manner of life." The translation "those so treated" (NRSV, Attridge) makes the verb transitive and simply passive, placing the stress on the indignities suffered. The *houtōs* ("likewise"), however, can equally refer to the endurance that the hearers have shared. They have therefore made themselves partners to those who likewise *endure* various hard things. Also significant here is the word choice of *koinōnos* ("partner/sharer"). They have shown the same disposition to share in the sufferings of others as has the Messiah Jesus, who joined the destiny of those who "share in flesh and blood" (2:14), and therefore also in suffering and mortality.

The author next spells out their suffering in reverse sequence, touching first on the specific way they partnered the suffering of others, then turning to their own experience of deprivation. The verb *sympathein* means to "have sympathy toward," as a moral disposition (see 4 Macc 13:23; Josephus, *Ant.* 16.404; *T. Sim.* 3.6). But the contemporary usage is so weak that I have (with Attridge) translated the verb as "shared the suffering" of prisoners. This strong rendering also better suits the conception of them as "partners" (*koinōnoi*). Once more, the word choice is deliberately evocative.

The same disposition is ascribed to Christ: in 4:15 the author declares that their high priest is himself tested in every way, and therefore able to sympathize with their weaknesses. In this case, the hearers have identified themselves with prisoners (*desmioi*). It is not stated explicitly that the prisoners are members of the community, or that they are in prison because of their commitment to Christ. But the experience of Peter and Paul supports the view that Christianity at its inception was a dangerous profession that could lead to incarceration. Acts speaks of Peter's imprisonment by Herod (12:3–5), and of Paul's captivity at Philippi (16:24–34), Jerusalem (22:24–29), Caesarea (24:24–27), and Rome (28:20–31). Paul himself mentions his frequent imprisonments as a servant of Christ (2 Cor 11:22), and wrote five of his letters from conditions of captivity (Philemon, Philippians, Colossians, Ephesians, 2 Timothy). As for ordinary believers, Acts describes Saul as having imprisoned followers of Jesus while he was a persecutor (Acts 8:3; 9:2). According to Matthew's vision of the final judgment, visiting those in prison is a mark by which disciples are to be judged (Matt 25:36, 39, 43, 44). That the author of Hebrews takes the responsibility of visiting prisoners as a fundamental duty is shown as well by his command in 13:3: "be mindful of prisoners, as though you also were imprisoned."

The most immediate and concrete form of *thlipsis* to come upon the hearers in the early days is the forcible seizure of their property. The sort of property is not specified: *hyparchonta* can refer to any possession (Luke 8:3; 11:21; 12:15, 33, 44; 16:1; Acts 4:32; 1 Cor 13:3). The loss of property that is most painful is that of one's home, and the image developed in chapter 11 of the patriarchs wandering in tents and of those persecuted wandering over deserts and mountains and dens and caves of the earth (11:8–10, 38) supports the suggestion that the loss suffered was one of "place." Nor does the author specify the manner of its being lost, although the noun *harpagē* makes us think in terms of a violent seizure. (For the verb *harpazein*, see Xenophon, *Memorabilia* 2.3.14; Josephus, *Ant.* 20.214; Matt 11:12; 13:9; John 6:15; 10:12; for the noun *harpagmos*, see Plutarch, *Education of Children* 15 [*Mor.* 12A]; Phil 2:6; and for the noun *harpagē*, see Thucydides, *Peloponnesian War* 4.104.2; *T. Jud.* 23.3; Matt 23:25; Luke 11:39.) That the property of a rival sect could be confiscated is shown by the experience of the community at Qumran, for whom the seizure of the property by the "Wicked Priest" became something of a primal trauma (see 1QpHab 12:1–10). The language used by the author in Heb 10:33 suggests that such loss of property was an experience of public exposure and shame. The natural response would be a combination of grief and anger.

The author's focus is not on what they lost or how they lost it, but on the moral manner in which they experienced this *thlipsis*. The verb *prosdechomai* here has the nuance of not only "accepting" (see Heb 11:35), but even of "welcoming" (see *Let. Aris.* 257; Luke 15:2; Rom 16:2; Phil 2:29), and that nuance is made explicit by the phrase "with joy" (*meta charas*). The term "joy" is a distinctive part of the early Christian lexicon of virtues (Matt 25:21, 23; 28:8; Luke 1:14; 2:10; 15:7, 10; 24:52; John 15:11; 16:20; Acts 13:52; 15:3; Rom 15:13; 2 Cor 8:2; Gal 5:22; Phil 2:2, 29; Col 1:11; 1 Thess 2:19). I use the term "virtues" advisedly, because joy is more than an emotion. It is a moral disposition. Unlike happiness, for example, which is dependent on positive circumstances, joy is a moral disposition of contentment/receptivity even in the midst of suffering (see 2 Cor 7:4; 1 Thess 1:6; Jas 1:2). As with other terms in this passage, the diction serves the author's rhetorical purpose. He will say in 12:11 that those experiencing discipline at the hands of their father do not "consider it joy" while it is happening, but afterward it brings about the peaceful fruit of righteousness. More directly, he will speak of Jesus as enduring the cross and "despising its shame" because of "the joy that was set before him" (12:2).

The joy with which the hearers welcomed their affliction was grounded in a certain perception of reality. They were able to have "joy" when their human property was taken away "because they knew" (*ginōskontes*): their understanding of the nature and certainty of the promise made by God was then sufficient not only to endure but to endure joyfully, rather than "abandon their assemblies" as some of them are now doing (10:25). What they "know" is what the author has been trying to demonstrate throughout the composition, and what he will shortly develop far more extensively: they themselves have a better (*kreittona*) and permanent (*menousan*) possession (*hyparxin*). The noun *hyparxis* is equivalent to *hyparchonta* (see Acts 2:45). This "possession," however, is not to be something merely material and transitory. It is the realization of God's presence through the exaltation of Christ. Once more, the author's language deliberately anticipates the encomium on faith in chapter 11, where he portrays the patriarchs as "desiring a better (*kreittonos*) country, that is, a heavenly one" (11:16).

[35–39] Those listening to the author's discourse were given *parrēsia* ("boldness/confidence"; see 3:6; 4:6; 10:19) in their confession of Christ. Now the author tells them not to throw it away. The negative command, using the aorist tense, does not suggest that they have already done so (like the "some" in 10:25), but they are clearly being tempted. The same phrase, *apobalein parrēsian,* is found in Dio Chrysostom, *Oration* 17.39. The verb can mean simply "lose" something (see Epictetus, *Discourses* 2.10.15; Deut 26:5; Philo, *Abraham* 235), but in the present exhortation, the deliberate action of "tossing it aside" (see Mark 10:50) seems preferable—we are in the realm of choice (see *hekousiōs* in 10:26, and cf. Lucian, *Dialogues of the Dead* 10).

The reason they are not to throw it away is that this is the sort (*hētis*) of boldness that "possesses a great reward." The noun *misthapodosia* ("reward/recompense") was used with its negative sense in 2:2, but will be found again positively in 11:26: Moses endured suffering for the Christ because he "looked to the reward." In 11:6 the author will state that those who approach God must believe that he exists and that he "is the rewarder of those who seek him." The "great" (*megalē*) reward corresponds to the "great" (*pollē*) contest that they endured in former days.

The next verse seems at first simply to repeat the point, but there is a subtle difference. The boldness has a great reward, but only if they hold on to it the way they did in the past. They "endured a great contest of sufferings" after their enlightenment, and now they need to endure (*hypomenein*). This will be the powerful lesson driven home in the next chapter: all of the heroes of old held on to faith. Their faith was not simply belief, or even trust or obedience; it was all of these extended through trial by endurance. Jesus, the pioneer and perfecter of faith, "endured the cross" (12:2–3), and they are to endure for the sake of the same "education" in perfection (see the discussion of 12:7).

This verse also spells out more fully the character of the endurance that wins a reward: it is one that imitates the faith of Jesus. He entered the world proclaiming, "I have come to do your will, O God" (10:7, 9), and "by that will" they have been sanctified (10:10). Now they also are to "do God's will" in order to receive the promise that is a share in God's own life made available to them by Jesus (for the promise [*epangelia*], see 4:1; 6:12, 15, 17; 7:6; 8:6; 9:15). This exhortation also prepares the way for the encomium on the heroes of faith in 11:1–40, for all of them endured for the sake of the promises (11:9, 13, 17, 33, 39).

Just as he did in 10:30–31, the author closes this exhortation with a (mixed) citation from Scripture and a final gnomic declaration. Strikingly, though, this time the citation has no introduction at all. With the addition of "for" and "and," the author has seamlessly made the words of Scripture his own words.

No better evidence could be found for his conviction that the prophets speak directly to his own time.[1]

The citation is introduced by an allusion to Isa 26:20, "yet a little while." I have placed a dash between these words and the rest of the citation to preserve the anacoluthic character of the mixed citation. The words from Isaiah heighten the eschatological urgency that we have already noticed as a feature of this part of the composition (see Heb 10:25, 30). The main part of the citation is from Hab 2:4, a passage favored by other Jewish writers of the first century. The sectarians at Qumran devoted a *pesher* interpretation to this prophet, and the text of Hab 2:4 was interpreted by them in terms of their own community experience and their faith in the Teacher of Righteousness. Paul twice quotes the same passage in a more abbreviated form in his arguments concerning the righteousness that comes to humans through the faith of Jesus (Rom 1:17; Gal 3:11).

The Habakkuk citation depends entirely on the LXX rather than the Hebrew. The original Hebrew version contained a vision concerning God's judgment, delivered to the prophet, who had taken his stand on the watchtower: "it will surely come; it will not delay" (RSV). Hebrews makes the present participle *erchomenos* (already in the LXX) both personal and specific by adding the definite article, thus forming, "the one who is coming." As a result, the passage seems clearly to speak of the judgment to be carried out by the Messiah (for "the coming one" with reference to Jesus, see Matt 3:21; Luke 7:19; John 1:9; 3:31; 6:14), as Hebrews already stated Jesus would come to carry out (see 9:28).

The remainder of the passage from Habakkuk reads in the Hebrew, "Behold, he whose soul is not upright in him shall fail, but the righteous shall live by his faith" (RSV). The LXX, followed by Hebrews, translates the first clause as "if he draws back, my soul will not be pleased with him." Our composition also reverses the sequence of the clauses, so that the statement concerning the righteous one precedes that concerning the one who draws back (*hyposteilētai*). In Hebrews, then, the verses stand not for two classes of people on whom judgment will fall, but for two ways of responding to God's visitation, the way of the apostate and the way of the faithful.

Finally, both the LXX and Hebrews use the personal pronoun "my" rather than the MT "his." In some LXX manuscripts, the "my" modifies the noun "faith," to make "the righteous one will live out of my [God's] faithfulness." Hebrews, however, agrees with those LXX manuscripts in which "my" modifies the righteous one, making, "my righteous one (*dikaios*) will live out of faith (*ek pisteōs*)." This is the first of three occurrences of "righteous" in the composition. In 11:4 we learn that it was because of his faith that Abel was testified to as righteous (*dikaios*). In 12:23 the hearers are told that they are approaching the

1. For a particularly full examination of the passage, see R. Gheorghita, *The Role of the Septuagint in Hebrews* (WUNT 2/160; Tübingen: Mohr [Siebeck], 2003).

city of the living God—and the spirits of righteous ones (*dikaioi*) who have been made perfect. As for faith (*pistis*), it will immediately become the metronomic introduction to every hero of Israel's past whose praises the author will shortly tell—all of them lived "in faith."

Like all gnomic utterances, the final sentence challenges the translator because of its compressed manner of expression. The sentence begins "but we are not" (*ouk esmen*), followed by two genitives: "of drawing back" (*hypostolēs*) and "of faith" (*pisteōs*), and each of these is followed by prepositional phrases forming final clauses (*eis apōleian, eis peripoiēsin psychēs*). The final phrase is especially ambiguous. Does *psychē* here mean "soul" or "life" (see Heb 4:12; 6:19; 12:3; 13:17)? And should the noun *peripoiēsis* have its possible sense of "acquire as a possession" (see Eph 1:14; 1 Pet 2:9; 1 Tim 3:13; Acts 20:28)? The most striking parallel is Luke 17:33, "Whoever seeks to possess/secure his life/soul (*psychē*) will lose it." The nuance "gain as a possession" is certainly appropriate in the context of their being tested by the expropriation of their material property. In my translation, I change the phrases to verbs ("we do not draw back" and "we have faith"), and use dashes to help signify the result clauses. That destruction is the consequence of drawing back or apostasy has been the burden of the author's exhortation in the preceding passages.[2] That the saving of life (or securing of the soul) is the consequence of faith is what will be demonstrated by the roll call of the heroes that immediately follows.

11:1–7 The Faith of the Ancients

In chapter 11 we have one of the deservedly famous set pieces of New Testament rhetoric: the roll call of the heroes of faith. Since the rhetoric of Hebrews is so seamless, however, any division of material is artificial. The long encomium on faith—and its exemplars—that seems to begin in 11:1 actually builds on the theme of endurance and faith stated in 10:35–39, developing in particular the proposition of Hab 2:4, that "my righteous one will live from faith" (Heb 10:38).

This section also reaches back to the theme of pilgrimage toward God's rest that preceded the lengthy exposition (in chaps. 5–10) on Christ's priesthood. In 3:7–19 the author reminded his hearers of the wilderness generation that failed to enter into the land with Joshua because of its faithlessness, and in 4:1–10 summoned them to take up the opportunity of entering into God's true rest provided

2. For the argument that something less than apostasy is meant here, rather a withdrawal from the possibility of public reproach, see T. W. Lewis, ". . . 'And If He Shrinks Back' (Heb X. 38b)," *NTS* 22 (1975–76): 88–94.

by "every day while it is still today." The present discourse on those in Israel's past who demonstrated faith therefore provides positive incentive for the hearers to endure their own difficulties. They are not to be "sluggards" (6:12) or "draw back" (10:39) but are to "become imitators of those who through faith and patience inherit the promises" (6:12). The heroes of faith here presented are precisely the models they are to imitate, culminating in the "pioneer and perfecter of faith," Jesus himself (12:1–3).

Not surprisingly, then, this recitation strikes certain notes repeatedly, echoing exhortations from earlier in the composition (especially 10:19–39) and building to the climactic exhortation in chapter 12.[1] Most obvious is the term "faith": the phrase "by faith" (*pistei*) recurs eighteen times, but the word "faith" (*pistis*) occurs six other times as well. Similarly, we find repeated mention of God's testimony or approval (11:2, 4, 31), of his being one who rewards (11:6, 26), and of being an heir (11:7, 9) of his promises (11:9, 11, 13, 17, 33, 39). The note of dying is struck seven times (11:4, 12, 19, 21, 22, 35 [bis]), five times in combination with resurrection from the dead (11:4, 12, 19, 35 [bis]).

The roll call mentions eighteen biblical characters by name, including two women (Sarah in 11:11 and Rahab in 11:31). The "sons of Israel" are named as a group in 11:22, as are "the prophets" in 11:32. As might be anticipated in an exhortation stressing the need to endure, most of those mentioned experience specific tribulations. Part of the section's dramatic impact comes from the way it begins in such leisurely fashion, lingering over named figures, with an emphasis on God's promises and rewards, and then builds toward an ever more rapid recitation of hardships suffered by unnamed forebears in the faith, who, though anonymous, are remembered by the author as those "of whom the world was not worthy" (11:38).[2]

In a commentary such as this one, it is necessary to divide the text into manageable portions, but readers are advised to experience chapter 11 at least once in one go, read aloud and at full voice. Only in that fashion can its real power be fully experienced. This first section begins slowly, mixing propositions about the nature of faith itself (11:1, 3, 6) with pointed portrayals of Abel (11:4), Enoch (11:5), and Noah (11:7). In 11:2 and 4 the note of God's bearing testimony (*martyrein*) is struck twice, and will not be repeated until 11:39. We are to understand that for all these figures, named and unnamed, God stands as the witness.

1. For the formal analysis of the chapter in comparison with other such rhetorical lists, see M. R. Cosby, *The Rhetorical Composition and Function of Hebrews 11* (Macon, GA: Mercer University Press, 1988).

2. For studies of the chapter as a whole, see P. M. Eisenbaum, *The Jewish Heroes of Christian History: Hebrews 11 in Literary Context* (SBLDS 156; Atlanta: Scholars Press, 1997); and C. Rose, *Die Wolke der Zeugen: Eine exegetische-traditionsgeschichtliche Untersuchung zu Hebräer 10,32–12,3* (WUNT 2/60; Tübingen: Mohr [Siebeck], 1994).

11:1 Now faith is the substance[a] of things hoped for, a proof of things not seen. **2** For by this,[b] the ancients were attested. **3** By faith, we understand that the ages were fashioned by God's word, so that what we see[c] comes from what we do not see. **4** By faith, Abel offered to God a greater sacrifice than did Cain. Through it, he was attested as righteous, since God himself[d] testified over his gifts. And through it, although he died, he continues to speak.[e]

5 By faith, Enoch was taken away so that he would not see death, and he was not found, because God had taken him away. For he was attested before being taken away[f] that he had pleased God. **6** And apart from faith it is impossible to please, for the one approaching God must believe that he exists and that he is the rewarder of those who seek him. **7** By faith, Noah built an ark to save his household, out of reverence, when he was warned about things not yet seen. Through this, he condemned the world, and became an heir of the righteousness that is according to faith.

a. P^{13} has an odd reading, *pragmatōn apostasis*, a "turning away from things." The reading is difficult to account for and is found in no other witnesses.

b. P^{13}, this time with a few other MSS, has the personal pronoun *autē* ("it") rather than the demonstrative pronoun *tautē* ("this"), an understandable correction.

c. The plural *ta blepomena* ("things that are seen") is found in the second hand of D and a majority of later MSS. The singular *to blepomenon* ("that which is seen") is found in P^{13}, the original hand of D, as well as A and א.

d. The sequence of words *autou tou theou* ("God himself") is found in the original hand of P^{13} and P^{46}, as well as the second corrector of א and D. P^{13} has been corrected to *autō tou theou*, yielding the sense, "God testified to him" (i.e., Abel), while the original versions of א and D have *autou tō theō*, yielding "he [Abel] testified to God."

e. D and the majority of later MSS have *laleitai* ("he is still spoken of"), rather than *lalei* ("he speaks"), read by the best witnesses.

f. The first corrector of D and the second corrector of B add *autou* ("his") to the phrase "being taken away."

[11:1–4] The passage begins with a justly renowned declaration on the character of faith. Unfortunately, the author's word choices leave translators in a considerable quandary.[3] Two phrases are absolutely clear: "things hoped for" (*elpizomenōn*) picks up a familiar and important theme of Hebrews, although this is the first time the participle form has been used. In 3:6 we saw that the hearers were to "keep hold of the boldness and the boast that is our hope" to the end. In that statement, boldness and boasting are connected by hope to a future realization. In 6:11, again, the author desires that each of them "demonstrate

3. See O. Betz, "Firmness in Faith: Hebrews 11:11 and Isaiah 28:16," in *Scripture: Meaning and Method*, ed. B. P. Thompson (Hull: Hull University Press, 1987), 92–113.

the same enthusiasm all the way to the end for the completion of your hope," and in 6:18 speaks of "having fled our place in order to lay hold of the hope that lies ahead." In 7:19 the author mentions "a better hope through which we are approaching God," and just before the present passage, he speaks once more of the need to "hold on to the secure confession of hope" (10:23).

Hope, then, has to do with the future, but it enables people to have boldness and confidence in the present as they move toward that future. What is in the future for the hearers, as for the ancients, is the complete realization of the promises. Immediately after speaking of hope in 6:12, the author tells them to "become imitators of those who through faith and patience inherit the promises," and immediately before speaking of hope in 10:23, the author speaks of approaching God "in a fullness of faith." It is clear that for the author of Hebrews, faith and hope are closely linked. But what does he mean by calling faith a *hypostasis* of the things hoped for? Here the possible meanings of *hypostasis* make precise interpretation difficult.

Similarly, the phrase *pragmatōn ou blepomenōn* ("things not seen") is not itself difficult. The author's use of *pragma* ("thing/reality") in 6:18 and 10:1 is straightforward. The latter case points us toward the distinction within the Platonic outlook between inner and outer, material and spiritual, visible and invisible. The phrase as a whole, indeed, seems to be a way of restating "things hoped for," since, not having been realized, they are certainly "unseen." Moving from the known, therefore, we can confidently state that Hebrews seeks to make a positive link between a present human moral disposition called faith and future realities. Once more, however, the term *elenchos* that precedes "not seen" is problematic, forcing us to consider together the two troublesome nouns that the author has placed in apposition.

The basic meaning of *hypostasis* is something that stands under or supports something. Of the multiple specific applications of the term in antiquity, six are possible for Hebrews; let us consider three that are less likely: (1) a foundation or a substructure, as of a temple (Nah 2:7; Ezek 43:11); (2) "substance" in the philosophical sense, that is, reality as opposed to appearance (see Artemidorus, *Oneirocritica* 3.14; Aristotle, *De mundo* 395A); (3) real nature or essence (see Heb 1:3). Now it is possible that the author means "faith is the reality of things hoped for" (cf. Heb 3:14), but this would seem to negate the point he is trying to make. He surely does not want to say that faith is the reality and "things hoped for/unseen" are unreal. Nor, I think, is he proposing that faith is the same thing as "things hoped for/unseen."

Three other applications of the term offer a stronger case: (1) in some papyri, the noun seems to have the sense of a promise or pledge (P.Elephantine 15.3; P.Tebtunis 61 [b].184). (2) Closely related to this sense is the way *hypostasis* can be used for wealth or property (Deut 1:12; 11:6; Judg 6:4), and indeed, for property title deeds (P.Oxy. 237.viii.26). If we understand the term this way, then faith can be seen as a kind of "down payment" or "pledge" on future realities. Faith participates in them in a partial and preliminary way. This nuance would nicely fit the situation of those whose property had been expropriated (Heb 10:34), and who are to imitate those who wandered without property in search of a lasting city (11:14–16). (3) Finally, there is a usage that finds favor with some translations (e.g., RSV, NRSV, NAB): "conviction" or "assurance." The translation is based on a number of passages (e.g., Polybius, *History* 4.50.10; Ruth 1:12; Ezek 19:5; Ps 39:7; Josephus, *Ant.* 18.24). Each of these passages, however, has more the sense of "basis for assurance" or "basis for boasting," rather than the simple "confidence" or "conviction" would suggest (see, e.g., 2 Cor 9:4; 11:17). Choosing among these possibilities is not easy.

Does the second term, *elenchos*, provide any help? Not as much as we might desire. This is the only occurrence of the noun in the New Testament. In the wider Greek world, the noun has two meanings. The first is the same as the verb form *elenchein* that is used in the New Testament (1 Cor 14:24; 1 Tim 5:20; 2 Tim 4:2) in its sense of reproof or reproach (see also Homer, *Od.* 21.329; Prov 12:1; 13:8; 15:10; Wis 2:14; 11:6). This clearly cannot be the meaning here. The second meaning of the Greek noun is an argument of disputation or refutation through cross-examination (Plato, *Phaedrus* 276A; Aristotle, *Rhetoric* 1410A; Philo, *On Punishments* 4). But it can also be used in the sense of a proof or demonstration (Plato, *Apology* 39C), or even for evidence used in a proof (Thucydides 1.135). Some translations take it, as they do *hypostasis*, in a subjective sense, "the conviction of things not seen" (RSV, NRSV). But this seems to stretch the term too far, especially since compelling parallels with that meaning have not been located.

To be sure, our author, like other creative writers in any language, is capable of extending the sense of words. It has even been suggested that *hypostasis* represents a play on *hypostolēs* in 10:39 (Attridge, 309). The "subjective" reading of *hypostasis* and *elenchos* also owes something to an understanding of the context. The author, remember, has just exhorted his audience not to "throw away their boldness," for it has a great reward (10:35). If 11:1 is taken in light of that exhortation, then the subjective renderings are acceptable: faith is the assurance of things hoped for and a conviction concerning things not seen.

In favor of the more "objective" (less psychological) reading—as in my translation—is that the author clearly wants to say something about faith that is in addition to the exhortation concerning boldness, and the fact that objective senses are better supported by ancient evidence. What does the author appear to be saying, then, when he speaks of faith as a "substance" of things hoped for? I would argue that he thinks in terms of a pledge, down payment, and even a participation in those realities. Faith, in this understanding, makes actual, or makes "real," for the believers the things that are hoped for, as though they were present. Similarly, faith is an "argument" or "proof" for things unseen, for it is the case that faith acts on unseen things as though they were capable of being seen, because they are understood to be as real, or even more real, than things that can be "seen," that is, verified by the senses.

This is perhaps why the author uses a *gar* ("for") to link verses 1 and 2. The second statement is to explain how faith is "substance" and "proof"—because the ancients (lit. "the elders," *hoi presbyteroi*) were "by this" (namely, faith) attested. Hebrews here uses the verb *martyrein* in the passive voice, indicating, by biblical convention, that it is God who did the attesting. That point is made even more obvious when two other things are considered. First, everywhere else in the composition to this point, it is God—through Scripture or the Holy Spirit—who has "borne witness": in the many wonders accompanying the early Christian proclamation (2:4); to the eternal priesthood of the Son (7:8, 17); to the wiping away of sins by Christ's sacrifice (10:15). Second, in his first two examples, the author speaks of God's witness concerning Abel's gifts (11:4), and of Scripture testifying to Enoch's having pleased God (11:5).

The language of "bearing witness" or "attesting," with its forensic overtones, fits within the characterization of faith as a "proof of things not seen." What we will seek in the author's examples, then, are indications of the ways in which "my righteous one will live from faith," as the Hab 2:4 citation stated. We will look for the heroes being "testified to" as righteous or as faithful, or as living despite their death.

Before beginning his roll call of heroes, however, the author explicates the second element of his characterization of faith: that it is a proof or demonstration of things not seen. He speaks not only of the ancients, but also of "we" in the present—as so often in this composition, claiming a close tie between himself and his hearers. And it is faith that links them. This faith, he declares, involves a kind of knowledge (*nooymen*, "we understand"). The verb *noein* has a slight nuance beyond simple knowing, suggesting also a certain grasp or insight into something (Xenophon, *Anabasis* 3.4.44; Josephus, *Life* 298; 2 Macc 14:30; Matt 15:7; 16:9, 11; 24:15; Eph 3:4; 2 Tim 2:7). Now we cannot really "know" or "understand" something that does not exist in some fashion. Faith, then, connects to something real.

In the present case, it is to this truth: "the ages were fashioned by God's word." The same difficult translation decision arises here as in 1:2 concerning *aiōn*. There I translated as "created the universe," and some translations have "the world" here as well (see RSV). This is certainly at least part of what the author means. Yet when he wants to say simply "world" (*kosmos*), he does so (4:3; 9:26; 10:5; 11:7, 38). His use of "age," in contrast, is more complex, having a temporal dimension (1:8; 5:6; 6:5; 7:17, 21, 24, 28; 9:26; 13:8, 21), yet also a spatial one (6:5, 20). I have translated as "ages" here because it encompasses both this present reality and the one to come. The verb *katartizein* is also subtler in its connotations than "make" or "create." It means basically to arrange or put in order (Plutarch, *Marcellus* 10; Epictetus, *Discourses* 3.20.10; Pss 73:16; 88:37; Matt 4:21; cf. Heb 10:5), so that "arranging the ages" could refer both to the creation of the universe and the arrangement of the sequence of its "ages." Quite apart from these nuances of language, the understanding given by faith is not one reached by empirical observation alone. It is an "understanding" that itself construes reality.

Faith's understanding that the universe is fashioned by the word of God (cf. 1:3) changes the human perception of all things: "so that what we see comes from what we do not see." This is the most fundamental of insights, the one that distinguishes believers and atheists: this sensory world is not self-contained, self-derived, or self-sufficient, but derives from a power greater than itself, which remains inaccessible to the senses, even as it brings forth everything that the senses encounter. This conviction is not simply a matter of a Platonic worldview, although it helps explain why Platonism was the favorite philosophy of early Christians.

The conviction is thoroughly biblical in character. The author clearly alludes to the creation account in Genesis 1, where God creates by a word alone (see also Ps 32:6; Wis 9:1; Sir 42:15; 2 Pet 3:5; Philo, *God's Immutability* 57). It is by the authority of "the word of God" that faith gains the understanding that the world comes to be "by the word of God." And if the things that are seen always arise out of what is not seen, then the world perceptible to the senses is always not only dependent on, but also inferior to, the power that brings it into being, even while it is through the sensible that the insensible finds expression. Since faith defines a life based on what is not seen rather than what is seen, it thereby also becomes a "proof"—in the very lives of the humans who live by it—of the reality of the unseen.

How does Abel exemplify the insight that the author claims faith provides?[4] He offers a "greater sacrifice" than that offered by his brother, Cain. The biblical account in Gen 4:2–7 does not explicitly state that it was a greater sacrifice, but its details allow such an inference. Cain simply offers "from the fruits of the earth," but Abel offers "from the firstborn (*prōtotokōn*) of his sheep and from their fat portions." In the ancient system of values, animals are worth more than vegetables or grain, as the entire subsequent legislation on sacrifices will demonstrate. Josephus states that God is more honored by things that grow spontaneously than by products forced from nature (*Ant.* 1.54). The offering of "the firstborn" of the animals also represents a greater sacrifice than simply choosing any animal from a herd (see Philo, *Questions and Answers on Genesis* 1.60). This may be an instance where Hebrews does not exploit something in the biblical text even though it is significant; see Christ as "firstborn" in Heb 1:6 and "the firstborn" of Egypt in 11:28. Although the biblical text does not

4. See S. Bénétrau, "La foi d'Abel: Hébreux 11/4," *ETR* 54 (1979): 623–30.

deprecate Cain's offering, the description of Abel's sacrifice enables us to see him as one exemplifying faith's perception of a power greater than that of the world, to whom the best of what is created should be offered.

The Genesis account goes on to say that "God looked upon Abel and upon his gifts but upon Cain and his gifts he had no regard" (Gen 4:5). The distinction between the person and the offering in each case legitimates an ancient author's concluding that there may well have been not only a disparity in what was offered but also in the disposition of those making the offering, a point made succinctly by Philo (*Questions and Answers on Genesis* 1.61). Hebrews interprets this as God's testifying over his gifts, and this is taken, in turn, as a "witness" to the fact that Abel was a "righteous one" (*dikaios*), even though this is also not stated explicitly in the LXX. But as the citation from Hab 2:4 has shown (Heb 10:38), faith and righteousness are correlative. For Abel as "righteous" elsewhere in the tradition, see Josephus, *Ant.* 1.53; *Ascen. Isa.* 6.8; *T. Iss.* 5.4. What is said about Abel being righteous can be taken as well for all the subsequent figures enumerated, for the roll call will conclude with the affirmation that they were all "attested" (11:39), and the author will tell his hearers in 12:23 that they will approach the "assembly of firstborn . . . and spirits of righteous people (*dikaioi*) who have been brought to perfection."

But Abel also shows the truth of the Habakkuk citation in another way. Through his faith (the phrase *di' autēs*, like *di' hēs* in the previous clause, refers back to *pistis*), although he died (*apothanōn),* he continues to speak (*eti lalei*). The statement relies on the account in Gen 4:10: after Cain killed Abel, God told him, "the voice of your brother's blood is crying to me from the ground." Abel's "crying out" is taken by our author as a sign that Abel must still, in some fashion, be alive. Note the force of the present tense: it is not a matter simply of the past, his voice continues in the present. In 12:24 the author will speak—with respect to Jesus as the mediator of a new covenant—of a blood that speaks better or more greatly (*kreitton*) than does Abel. In an obscure fashion, then, Abel anticipates resurrection and demonstrates that "the righteous one will live from faith."

Although some Jewish interpretations of the Genesis account give only passing notice to Abel, noting his death at the hands of Cain (*Apoc. Ab.* 24.5; *Jub.* 4.7–8; *L.A.E.* 24.2; *L.A.B.* 2.1; 2 Macc. 18:11), others elaborate aspects of the story. Some texts focus on the death of Cain in punishment for the murder of his brother (*T. Benj.* 7.4; *Jub.* 4.31–34). Others focus on Abel himself. Philo argues that God hears the voice of Abel because the righteous, even when they are dead, "live an incorporeal life" (*Questions and Answers on Genesis* 1.70). In Hellenistic synagogue prayers, Abel is explicitly designated as a priest (*Apos. Cons.* 8.5.11), whose sacrifice was pleasing to God (7.37.3): "as from a devout man you favorably accepted a sacrifice; from the brother-murderer Cain, you turned aside the offering as from an accursed person" (8.12.53–54).

The voice crying out to God is extensively developed in *1 Enoch.* The spirits of the dead are gathered until the day of judgment: "I saw the spirits of the children of the people who were dead, and their voices were reaching into heaven until this very moment." The seer asks whose voice it is and is told, "This is the spirit which had left Abel, whom Cain, his brother, had killed. It (continues to) sue him until all of (Cain's) seed is exterminated from the face of the earth" (*1 En.* 22.5–7). More than a plaintiff, Abel is figured as a glorious judge of the entire creation in *T. Abr.* 13.2.

[5–7] Enoch's story is a short one in Gen 5:21–24. After speaking of the length of his life and of his children, the Hebrew text concludes, "Enoch walked with God; and he was not, for God took him." The LXX expands on this brief recital, and it is the LXX that Hebrews uses when it presents Enoch as the second example of faith. In Gen 5:22 the LXX adds, "And Enoch pleased God (*euērestēse de Enōch tō theō*) after the birth of Methuselah." And in 5:24 the LXX reads, "and Enoch pleased God (*kai euērestēsen Enōch tō theō*) and he was not found (*ouk hēurisketo*), because God took him away (*hoti metethēken auton ho theos*)."

In 11:4 Hebrews quotes directly from the LXX of Gen 5:24, but expands the LXX even further. The author adds that it was "by faith" that Enoch was taken away, and supplies either the result or the purpose (the articular infinitive can express either, and I have taken it as expressing purpose, as in 10:7): he was taken up by God so that he would not see death. The purpose clause makes better contextual sense because the author will immediately state that God is a "rewarder." If Enoch's being taken away meant only that, as a result, he did not experience death, the author's point is not made. If the taking away has the purpose of his not experiencing death, then God's action is a reward for Enoch's having pleased him.

Finally, Hebrews provides an exegesis of the LXX version, by informing the hearers that it was "before being taken away" that Scripture declared Enoch to have pleased God (see Gen 5:22). It was, then, his disposition of faith during his life that leads to God's gift of continuing life. Just as our author drew an inference about Abel being righteous (and therefore faithful) from his "greater sacrifice," so does he in the case of Enoch infer faith from the LXX statement about "pleasing God," as his subsequent statement in 11:6 will make plain.

Hebrews' expansion of the LXX in the case of Enoch is more modest than its full-bore exploitation of the figure of Melchizedek. In that case, we saw that Hebrews stood within a broad stream of Jewish speculation on the Old Testament (read by the author, of course, in Greek). The same is true of his interpretation of Enoch, who finds even greater posthumous glory in Jewish literature than did the Gentile priest-king. Enoch's being "taken away" by God, when understood as "walking with God" (in the MT), makes Enoch the first human figure to ascend into heaven. For one stream of interpretation, therefore, Enoch was in the presence of God (*2 En.* 22.5), and the source of human knowledge of all things (Pseudo-Eupolemus, in Eusebius, *Preparation for the Gospel* 9.17.9).

Thus there is a substantial body of Merkabah (or apocalyptic) literature connected to Enoch (*1 Enoch, 2 Enoch, 3 Enoch*), based on his ascent into heaven and his vision of the heavenly courts and throne room (see *1 En.* 70.1–3 and throughout). According to *Jub.* 4.22–24, Enoch ascended to the garden of Eden, where he stood as witness against the wickedness of humans, and in *Jub.* 10.17, Enoch is declared as even more righteous than Noah. Other texts associate Enoch with Elijah—another "prophet" taken up by God (2 Kgs 2:11–12)—and therefore able to reveal divine secrets and be available to return (see *Apoc. El.* 4.7–19; 5.32).

Just as some interpretations of Melchizedek countered the tendency to glorify him with a more sober assessment, a second stream of interpretation of Enoch is less extravagant and cosmic in the claims made for him. Wisdom 4:10 draws from the LXX that Enoch "pleased God and was loved by him," but interprets his being taken up by God as a rescue from sinners, "lest evil change his understanding or guile deceive his soul." Sirach 44:16 agrees that Enoch "pleased God and was taken up," but sees him as "an example of repentance to all generations." A similar understanding probably lies behind Philo's statement that God took Enoch away from a wicked way of life (*Abraham* 17; *Questions and Answers on Genesis* 1.83; see also *Gen. Rab.* 25.1).

Hebrews' own interpretation is entirely moral and religious: because Enoch pleased God, he was rewarded. In 11:6 the author draws out the implication of Enoch's example with his third general proposition concerning faith itself (see 11:1 and 3), this one moving directly to faith as a way of responding to God. He begins with the flat denial that anyone can please God "apart from faith" (*chōris pisteōs*). That negative is followed by an apodictic positive: the one approaching God must (*dei*) believe (*pisteusai*) two things: that God actually exists (*estin*), and that he is one who rewards (*misthapodotēs*) those who seek him.

We observe that "pleasing God" has subtly shifted to "approaching God," which continues a theme that runs throughout the composition (4:16; 7:25; 10:1, 22; 12:18, 22). The equation provides a useful reminder that the "approaching" of which Hebrews speaks is not physical or ritual (although cultic overtones remain), but moral: it is a matter of disposition toward and relationship with God. As throughout, spiritual/moral transformation is given expression by physical and ritual language.

The first requirement of faith is to believe that God exists. This makes explicit the conviction that "the ages were fashioned by the word of God" and that "what is seen arises from what is not seen." The power that brings everything into existence is itself most real. Faith is consequently not a delusion or mere projection of desire. Faith understands that the object of faith is the source of all that is real, and "exists" in a manner beyond the manipulation of any creature.

The second requirement follows from the first. Only if God is all-powerful creator can God reward those who seek him. This is the only time that Hebrews uses the noun *misthapodotēs* ("rewarder"), although it speaks earlier of *misthapodosia* as punishment (2:2) and reward (10:35), and later as a reward in 11:26. The term may be the author's own coinage, since Hebrews is the only place it appears before it is taken up by Christian literature. To be sure, the phrase *misthos apodidonai* ("to give back, or recompense") is common (Euripides, *Andromache* 609; Thucydides, *Peloponnesian War* 6.8; Wis 10:17; Matt 20:8), and the idea of receiving a reward for pleasing God is standard in Judaism (in the NT alone, see Matt 5:12; 6:1–16; 10:41–42; Luke 6:23, 35; Rom 4:4; 1 Cor 3:8, 14; 2 John 8; Rev 22:12). The language of "seeking God" is also familiar, especially from the Psalms (see Deut 4:29; 1 Sam 13:14; Pss 23:6; 26:8; 69:4; 82:16; 104:3, 4; Sir 2:15; Wis 13:6; Prov 16:5; 28:5; Isa 31:1; 55:6; Jer 27:4). Like "those who approach" God, the spatial language retains connotations of "seeking the Lord" in the cult, although here it is a matter of moral disposition and relationship.

In his treatment of Noah—the third of his exemplary figures and, like Abel, one who offered sacrifice to the Lord (Gen 8:20–21)—the author concentrates on events before the flood, once more relying on the LXX of Gen 6:9–7:5.[5] In particular, Hebrews picks up on the divine warning in 6:13, using the verb *chrēmatizein* (which appears frequently in scenes of divine communication: Plutarch, *Obsolescence of Oracles* 45, *Mor.* 435C; Philo, *Moses* 2.238; Josephus, *Ant.* 5.42; Matt 2:12, 22; Luke 2:26; Acts 10:22; in Hebrews, see 8:5), Noah's obedience in carrying out God's command ("he built an ark," Gen 6:14), and the fact that it was to save his household (*oikos autou*; see Gen 7:1). The rest is interpretation built on the Genesis account, and shows similarities to some other strands in Jewish and Christian interpretation of this ancient figure. Some aspects of the Genesis account are not exploited by the author. Hebrews does not, for example, make use of the plain statement in Genesis that Noah was a righteous man (*anthrōpos dikaios*), even though that is clearly implied in everything the author ascribes to Noah's faith, as well as his final statement in verse 7. More fascinating is the author's omission of another phrase in Gen 6:9, namely that Noah was "perfect (*teleios*) in his generation," especially when compared to the focus on these terms in Philo's *Questions and Answers on Genesis* 1.97; *Abraham* 27–34. The omission may be accounted for by the author's conviction that full perfection is only possible, even for the ancients, in the present because of Christ (see Heb 11:40).

The interpretation in Hebrews focuses primarily on Noah's response to God. Most obviously, he makes Noah's response one of "faith," which is not found in Genesis, although the basis for the characterization is found in the repeated

5. For traditions on Noah, see J. P. Lewis, *A Study of the Interpretation of Noah and the Flood in Jewish and Christian Literature* (Leiden: Brill, 1968).

declaration, "Noah did everything that the Lord commanded him, thus he did" (Gen 6:22; 7:5). Noah fits within Hebrews' own understanding of faith as obedience (see 5:8). This is made clearer when we note that Noah is said to respond "out of reverence" (*eulabētheis*). As we saw in the author's use of the cognate noun in 5:7, the verb *eulabein* can be translated as "fear," and this interpretation is given to Genesis (even though the term is lacking there) by *Sib. Or.* 1.147: "An irremovable fear seized the man." But the translation of "reverence" better conforms to the portrait of Noah in Genesis, and respects the author's intended link between the faith of Noah and the faith of Jesus. Similarly, Hebrews calls Noah an "heir of the righteousness that is according to faith." The statement connects Noah to the programmatic statement of Habakkuk in 10:38, to the entire theme of inheriting the promises (Heb 1:2; 6:17; 9:15), and to the presentation of the patriarchs as heirs of the promises in the section to follow (11:7–8).

Another element of interpretation is the author's clarification that Noah had faith "concerning things not yet seen," which makes him exemplify the programmatic statement of 11:1, that faith is "a proof of things not seen." In this respect as well, Noah anticipates the presentation of the patriarchs to follow. Finally, Hebrews adds a further element not explicitly stated in the Genesis account: Noah "condemned the world." Does the author mean simply that Noah's fidelity was an implicit rebuke to the faithlessness and corruption of his contemporaries? Or do we catch a glimpse of a tradition that saw Noah as a preacher between the time of the warning and the coming of the flood?

Jewish interpretations of the Genesis story turn the figure of Noah in different ways. In *2 En* 70–72, for example, he is linked to the figure of Melchizedek; and in the prayers of the Hellenistic synagogue now preserved in the *Apostolic Constitutions*, Noah is singled out as a saint (7.39.2–4) and a priest (8.5.1–4), whose sacrifice after he came out of the ark was accepted by God (7.37.1–5). In *4 Ezra* 3.11 Noah is the start of a remnant of the righteous: "You left one of them, Noah with his household, and all the righteous who have descended from him." The link between Noah's righteousness and his deliverance is made clear by *Jubilees*: "Noah alone found favor in the sight of God" (5.3), it says, and adds, "[God] showed partiality to Noah . . . because he was righteous in all his ways just as it was commanded concerning him. And he did not transgress anything which was ordained for him" (*Jub.* 5.19). Likewise, Pseudo-Philo notes, "Noah found favor and mercy before the Lord . . . Noah, a righteous man and blameless in his generation, pleased the Lord" (*L.A.B.* 3.4).

The importance of Noah is developed particularly in the *Sibylline Oracles*. The composition praises his righteousness: Noah was "upright and true," with "trustworthy, noble deeds" (1.125–35, 269), the "most righteous of men" (1.280). But it also says that God ordered Noah to preach repentance to all the people so that they might be saved from the cataclysm (1.128–29); and even though overcome with fear (1.147), Noah did preach repentance to the people (1.150–98). The same picture of Noah as preacher of repentance is found also in the rabbinic tradition (*Sifre* 43; *Mekilta,* Shirata 5 [38b]), and in some Christian texts (*1 Clem.* 7.6; Clement of Alexandria, *Stromateis* 1.2.1).

The distinctiveness of Hebrews' portrayal of Noah emerges from comparison to the other three places in the New Testament where he appears. In Matt 24:37–38 (par. Luke 17:26–27), the behavior of Noah's contemporaries before the flood is compared to the behavior of people before the coming of the Son of Man. In this passage, the emphasis is not at all on Noah, but on the activities that brought on God's punishment. In 1 Pet 3:20–22, similarly, the lesson drawn from Noah and the building of the ark is not his faith, but rather God's patience before the flood and the saving of eight persons "through water," which is taken as a type of the baptism experienced by Peter's readers. In 2 Pet 2:5 Noah is described as the "preacher of righteousness," but the point of the allusion in this case is the punishment of the wicked, whom God "did not spare" —this is an example that goes to prove that God "knows how to rescue the godly from trial and keep the unrighteous under punishment until the day of judgment" (2 Pet 2:9). In contrast to these accounts, Hebrews places a strong emphasis on Noah himself: his faith, his reverence, his building of the ark, his judging the world, and in all this, his being "an heir of the righteousness that is according to faith."

11:8–22 The Faith of the Patriarchs

The next stage of the encomium continues to concentrate on the heroes of faith described in Genesis. The author begins with the specific responses of faith by Abraham (11:8) and Sarah (11:11), including a general reflection on the experience of the patriarchs as wanderers seeking a heavenly city (11:9–10, 13–16), then moves to the testing of Abraham (11:17–19), and finally the statements concerning the future made by Isaac, Jacob, and Joseph (11:20–22). These descriptions are drawn from the LXX, but owe much to the author's own interpretation.

The troubles of the patriarchs are noted: they were without real homes (11:9), experienced infertility (11:11), were tested (11:17), and died (11:13, 21, 22). But this is not the side of things the author stresses. His emphasis, rather, is on one aspect of their faith and several truths about God. The faith of the patriarchs was in "things not seen." They were able to follow God, not knowing where they were going (11:8), and through various tribulations and trials, because of their faith (11:8, 10, 11). They greeted from afar what they hoped for in the future (11:13), trusted that God could give back what he took away (11:19), and blessed their children for the future (11:20–21), and, even as they themselves came to an end, saw a future for the people (11:22). And the truths about God? That he is, in fact, their God (11:16), and is able to bring the dead to life (11:12, 19), and is all powerful to shape the future for which humans long (11:16, 19).

> **11:8** By faith,[a] Abraham, when he was called, obeyed by departing to a[b] place that he would receive as an inheritance, and he departed without knowing where he was going. **9** By faith he sojourned in the land of promise as if it were foreign. He dwelt in tents with the fellow heirs to the same promise, Isaac and Jacob. **10** For he was expecting the city that has foundations, whose designer and maker is God. **11** By faith, even Sarah herself, being sterile,[c] received a capacity for the planting of a seed,[d] even though she was past the age,[e] because she considered the one who had made the promise to be faithful. **12** Therefore also there were born[f] from one man, and him indeed nearly dead, descendants as many as the stars in the sky and as countless as the sand on the seashore.
>
> **13** These all died according to faith. They did not receive[g] the promises. But seeing from a distance, they both greeted them and confessed that they were strangers and aliens on the land. **14** Those who say such things make clear that they are seeking a homeland. **15** And if they were remembering[h] the one from which they had set forth,[i] they would have the opportunity to go back. **16** But now they desire a better, that is, a heavenly, one. Therefore, God is not ashamed to be called their God, for he has prepared a city for them.
>
> **17** By faith, when Abraham was tested, he sacrificed Isaac, and the one who had received the promises began to offer up his only son, **18** concerning whom it was said, "Out of Isaac your seed shall be named." **19** He considered that God was powerful enough even to raise the dead.[j] So also, in symbolic fashion, he received him back. **20** By faith also, Isaac blessed Jacob and Esau concerning the things to come. **21** By faith, Jacob blessed each of the sons of Joseph as he was dying, and bowed over the head of his staff. **22** By faith, as he was coming to an end, Joseph remembered the exodus of the children of Israel and gave commands concerning his bones.

a. P[46], A, and the original hand of D add the definite article (*ho*) to form an attributive rather than predicative participle, "He who is called Abraham." The weight of MS evidence and syntax argue for the circumstantial participle.

b. A large number of witnesses, including the second correctors of א and D, add the definite article *ton* to form "the place." P[46] and the original hands of other major uncials lack the definite article.

c. Some MSS (e.g., P[13] [apparently], א, and A) lack the adjective *steira* ("sterile"), having only "Sarah herself." A few add a participle (*ousa*) to form, "Sarah herself being strerile"; and some add a definite article, "Sarah herself, the sterile." In all these versions, however, only the nominative case appears, making Sarah the subject of the sentence.

d. The original hand of D and a few other witnesses add *eis to teknōsai* ("to bear a child"), which clearly ascribes the faith to Sarah,

e. This shorter version is contained in both the earliest papyri (P^{13}, P^{46}), and in the original hands of D and A. In corrected versions of א and D, and in the majority of later MSS, there is an addition, "she gave birth" (*eteken*).

f. Manuscript evidence is fairly well divided between "came to be" (*egenēthēsan*) and "were born" (*eggenēthēsan*). I consider "were born" the harder and correct reading because it could be taken as attributing childbearing to Abraham.

g. The participle *labontes* ("having received") is found in P^{46} and the majority of witnesses. The alternate readings, *komisamenoi* (same meaning) in א (with a number of other witnesses) and *prosdexamenoi* ("expecting") in A, seem to be secondary.

h. Some MSS, including P^{46}, have the present tense of *mnemoneuein* ("to remember") and a few others have the aorist tense of the same verb, but the imperfect tense found in the majority of MSS better fits the usual syntax of the contrary-to-fact conditional.

i. The second corrector of א and of D, as well as the majority of witnesses, have the more common *exēlthon* ("they left") rather than *exebēsan* ("they went forth"), found in the best witnesses.

j. There are two slight variations in this verse. Some witnesses have the aorist rather than the present infinitive *egeirein*, and rather than the cryptic *dynatos ho theos* ("God is powerful"), some MSS add the verb "to be" (*estin*), or change to the verb form *dynatai* ("he is able").

[11:8–12] This is now the fourth time that Abraham has appeared in Hebrews. In 2:16 the author affirmed that the Son had involved himself not with angels but with "the seed of Abraham." In 6:13 Abraham is identified as the one to whom God made the promises and confirmed the promises with an oath. In chapter 7, now explicitly called "the patriarch" (*ho patriarchēs*, 7:4), Abraham pays tithes to the priest-king Melchizedek, who in turn "blessed the one who had the promises" (7:6). Now the author celebrates the character of Abraham's response to God and how he serves as a model for those who are told to "imitate those who through faith and patience inherited the promises" (6:12).

The importance of Abraham to our author, as to Paul, can be measured by the amount of attention paid to him (for Paul cf. Gal 3:6–18; 4:21–32; Rom 4:1–25; 9:6–13; 11:1).[1] Abraham takes up the largest portion of this encomium. The author's exposition focuses on three specific aspects of the patriarch's story: the call and wandering in the land, the astonishing birth of Isaac to aged parents, and the offering of Isaac as a sacrifice. But Abraham's story is not his alone. Sarah plays a critical role through her faith (11:11). Abraham's "fellow heirs"

1. For a survey of the treatment in NT authors, see R. Longenecker, "The 'Faith of Abraham' Theme in Paul, James, and Hebrews: A Study in the Circumstantial Nature of New Testament Teaching," *JETS* 20 (1977): 203–12; and B. E. Schein, "Our Father Abraham" (Ph.D. diss., Yale University, 1972).

Isaac and Jacob are also taken up, proleptically, in Abraham's story (11:9) before receiving attention on their own (11:20–21).

Although Hebrews follows the account in Gen 12–22, it does not, apart from the explicit citations from Gen 21:12 in 11:18 and Gen 47:31 in 11:21, make heavy use of the LXX language as such, apart from such obvious touches as "tents" (*skēnai*, Gen 12:8; 18:1), "dwell" (*katoikein*, 13:12), "inherit" (*klēronomein*, 15:8), and "test" (*peirazein*, 22:1). Apart from the direct citations, the statement that Abraham's descendants would be numberless in Heb 11:12 clearly echoes both Gen 13:16 and 22:17, and the statement that the patriarchs were "strangers and aliens" echoes Gen 23:4. Strikingly, Hebrews does not make use of the one passage in Genesis that explicitly ascribes faith to Abraham (Gen 15:16), instead placing everything Abraham did under the rubric "by faith" (Heb 11:8, 9, 11, 17).

As with Abel, Enoch, and Noah, therefore, this portrayal of Abraham uses the framework of the Genesis account and details of its language to construct Hebrews' own interpretation of the patriarch's significance. The level of interpretation can be indicated by a single detail. Although Abraham is associated with "the promises" (*epangeliai*) in 6:12 and 7:6, and the promises are mentioned again here in 11:9 (bis), 11, and 17, that term never occurs in Genesis, or indeed in any of the major narrative books of Scripture. The key term for interpreting Abraham in the New Testament (see also Acts 2:39; 7:17; 13:23; 26:6; Rom 4:13–20; 9:8–9; Gal 3:14–29; 4:23, 28; Eph 2:12) is never connected to him in the LXX. This is, please note, a matter of diction, for the actual making of statements about the future or predictions by God runs through the entire Abraham account (Gen 12:2–4, 7; 13:15–16; 15:5, 13–14, 18–21; 17:2–8, 16; 18:10; 22:16–17).

Similarly, in 11:8 Hebrews says that Abraham was "called" (by God). The verb *kalein* ("to call") occurs frequently in the biblical accounts of election and command (see, e.g., Exod 3:4; 19:3; 24:6; Isa 42:6; 43:1; 45:3; 51:2; Jer 7:13), but it appears in the Abraham story only in the literal sense of speaking in Gen 22:11, 15. The author's use of "call" to introduce Abraham enables him to connect Abraham to the "calling" of the high priest Jesus (Heb 5:4), and the "calling" of the hearers themselves—those who are to receive the promised inheritance (9:15). Likewise, the LXX does not characterize Abraham's response to the call as "obeying" (*hypēkousen*), although Gen 12:4 says that Abraham went out "just as the Lord had spoken to him." The author's use of obedience language, however, once more enables him to link the faith of Abraham to that of Jesus (see Heb 5:8) and of believers (5:9). Finally, this obedience is summarized by a virtual restatement of the thesis in 11:1: Abraham "did not know where he was going." His faith, therefore, serves as a "proof of things not seen," since he acted on the promise as though it were actually present.

Hebrews' boldest interpretation is to read the experience of the patriarchs' wandering in the land in terms of a pilgrimage to God's presence (11:9–10).

The author first identifies Canaan as the "land of the promises" and the patriarch's children as "fellow heirs of the same promise." The land, then, belongs to them by a promise from God. Yet they "sojourn" (*paroikein*) in that land "as though it were foreign" (*allotrian*, "belonging to another"). The verb *paroikein* (lit. "to dwell beside") is used with some frequency in the LXX for inhabiting a place without possessing actual ownership or citizenship (see Gen 12:10; 17:8; 19:9; 20:1; 21:23; 35:27; 37:1; Exod 6:4; 20:10; Deut 5:14; 18:6; 26:5) and that sense continues in the New Testament (Luke 24:18; Acts 7:6; Eph 2:19; 1 Pet 2:11). The first contrast, then, is between alien status and citizenship. Philo also develops this dimension in terms of the physical life on earth in contrast to the heavenly homeland of the soul (see *Cherubim* 120; *Who Is the Heir?* 267). Hebrews' second contrast, however, is between the inherently unstable condition of living in tents, as opposed to dwelling in "a city having foundations." The situation of the patriarchs in their wandering was one of "expectation" for such a city. Their sojourning was not restless or random, but rather a form of patience in view of a future realization.

And the solid city they expect? It is one whose "designer" (*technitēs*) and "maker" (*dēmiourgos*) is God. There is not much distinction between the two terms, and Hebrews may use them both simply for rhetorical effect. The noun *dēmiourgos* is used for skilled workmen or craftsmen, such as sculptors (Plato, *Republic* 529E) or confectioners (Herodotus 7.31). In 2 Macc 4:1 it is used for a designer of wickedness. The noun *technitēs* has much the same range: Xenophon contrasts the *technitēs* to the farmer (*Oecumenicus* 6.6; see Aristotle, *Politics* 1262B) on one side, but on the other side to the liberally educated person (*Memorabilia* 2.74). Deuteronomy 27:15 uses it for the crafters of idols, and it has the same sense in Acts 19:24, 38.

The interpretation is bold in the first place rhetorically, since it introduces an entirely new metaphor this late in the composition. This is the first time that *polis* ("city") appears, but it is not the last. In addition to its immediate reappearance in 11:16, it occurs as the heavenly Jerusalem, the "city of the living God" to which the hearers have come (12:22). And in 13:14 the author tells his hearers, "we do not have a permanent city here. We are seeking the city to come." The even bolder aspect of this interpretation, then, is that it makes the structure and goal of the patriarchs' faith the same as that of the Christian believers. They are both on pilgrimage to God. The difference is that Christ has enabled the author's generation to attain that goal. We recognize here not only the strong implicit affirmation of the Abrahamic covenant, but as well the continuity of the response of faith between Abraham and his descendants.

In light of this, two other aspects of the composition appear in a new light. It is now clear that the wilderness generation (chaps. 3–4) was culpable not only for their rebellion against God, but also for seeing the land of Canaan as "God's rest" in the first place. It is also clear why Hebrews pays no honor to Joshua, who led them into the land. He is notably lacking from the present roll call of the faithful. The implication, perhaps, is that if he had faith, he would have been seeking "the city of God" rather than the material land of Canaan.

In Genesis the dramatic story of Isaac's birth—the first installment on the fulfillment of God's promise to make Abraham into a great nation—is the obvious next high point. Yet it comes as something of an intrusion in this encomium. Readers (or the first hearers) could easily move directly from 11:10 to 11:13 without a great sense of deprivation, since verse 13 picks up the same theme of wandering in the land as strangers. The real difficulty presented by the story, however, is deciding whether the author wants us in this instance to regard Abraham or Sarah as the one with faith. I follow the overwhelming textual evidence and make Sarah the subject. She is the one who believed, and she received the power to conceive.

The decision to read 11:11 this way, a decision reflected also in most translations, should candidly acknowledge the real difficulties it must overcome. There are four problems. First, the wording with regard to Sarah is uncertain (see textual notes). Second, the phrase I have translated "for the planting of a seed" is *eis katabolēn spermatos*, which is ordinarily used for the male role in conception (Philo, *Creation of the World* 132; *Cherubim* 49; Epictetus, *Discourses* 1.13.3), on analogy with a farmer's planting: "as a farmer casts down (*kataballei*) the seed (*sperma*) of corn into the earth, so a man casts down (*kataballei*) his seed (*sperma*) into a woman's place" (Gk. *Apoc. Ezra* 5.12). It was widely assumed in antiquity that the male was active and the female passive in procreation (Philo, *Questions and Answers on Genesis* 3.13). Third, verse 12 begins with the phrase *aph' henos*, which can only be translated as masculine, "from one man," with the presumed antecedent being Abraham. Fourth, the picture of Sarah as regarding the one who made the promise as faithful does not seem to comport with the portrayal of her in Gen 16:1–6 and 18:9–12.[2]

These problems are not, however, insurmountable. Once we take Sarah as the subject, then the textual difficulties become a matter of minor variations: they all consider her as the subject. As for her attitude in Genesis, it is no more skeptical than Abraham's (see Gen 17:16–21); indeed, when it came to the conflict over Hagar and her son Ishmael, Sarah appeared to have a clearer grasp of the implication of the promise than the emotionally divided patriarch (see Gen 21:8–13). The phrase "casting a seed" can also be resolved in Sarah's favor if

2. For discussion see J. H. Greenlee, "Hebrews 11:11—Sarah's Faith or Abraham's?" *Notes on Translation* 4 (1990): 37–42; J. Irwin, "The Use of Hebrews 11:11 as Embryological Proof-Text," *HTR* 71 (1978): 312–16; and especially the research into medical language that suggests it is possible to regard Sarah as an active agent in conception, found in P. W. van der Horst, "Sarah's Seminal Emission: Hebrews 11:11 in Light of Ancient Embryology," in *Greeks, Romans, and Christians: Essays in Honor of Abraham J. Malherbe*, ed. D. L. Balch, E. Ferguson, and W. A. Meeks (Minneapolis: Fortress Press, 1990), 287–302.

we align two other phrases, namely her being "sterile" and receiving "a power," and then take *eis katabolēn spermatos* as a final clause. Indeed, this construction makes more sense when read as the capacity to receive such a casting of sperm than if Abraham were the subject, for in that case the infinitive *kataballein sperma* would have been a more natural complement to "receiving a power" (*dynamin labein*). Here Abraham casts the seed, but Sarah receives the power for it to happen. Finally, if we read this way, then the phrase "from one man" does not exclude the role of Sarah's faith. In fact, it is her faith that enables the one man to have so many descendants.

Sarah's faith takes the form of "considering" or "reckoning" (*hēgoumai*; cf. 10:29 and 11:26) God the promiser as "faithful" (*pistos*). Here Sarah exemplifies precisely the disposition that the author desires in his hearers. He told them in 10:23 to hold to the unswerving confession, "for the one who made the promises is faithful (*pistos*)." Sarah's faith also shows how God can bring life from death, and therefore anticipates the resurrection of Jesus. Sarah is "sterile" (*steira*) and is therefore not able to be the source of life. She is, moreover, past the age for bearing children. Abraham and Sarah are both, according to Gen 18:11, "old, advanced in age," and "it had ceased to be with Sarah after the manner of women" (RSV). But her faith in God enabled her to receive the seed of new life, and thus from a man himself "nearly dead" (*tauta nenekrōmenou*) there were born countless offspring (11:12; see Gen 22:17). Paul also saw the birth of Isaac as analogous to resurrection, emphasizing Abraham's faith despite his advanced age, the "deadness" of his body (*sōma nenekrōmenon*), and the "deadness" (*nekrōsis*) of Sarah's womb (Rom 4:19–24).

[13–16] The author picks up again from the thought in 11:8–10. All these died "according to faith." The phrase *kata pistin* breaks the rhythmic repetition of "by faith," and has, I think, a slightly different nuance. It is not that they died because of their faith or by means of their faith, but that they died as people who had lived faithfully, despite the fact that they had not received the fulfillment of the promises. They have only "seen" the promises from afar and "greeted" them. Their faith acted as a "demonstration of things not seen" and the "substance of things hoped for" (11:1). And they confessed that they were "strangers and aliens on the land." This declaration continues the theme established by 11:9. The statement is based on Abraham's declaration when negotiating with the Hittites over the field of Machpelah, "I am a sojourner (*paroikos*) and alien (*parepidēmos*) among you" (Gen 23:4). Hebrews here replaces *paroikos* with "stranger" (*xenos*; though see 11:9 for *paroikein*). The two terms are functionally equivalent; for *xenos* see Ruth 2:10; Philo, *Posterity of Cain* 109; Josephus, *Ant.* 11.159; for *parepidēmos* see Polybius, *History* 27.6.3; 32.6.4; Ps 38:12. Both indicate that someone is not a full participant in civic rights in this place, and suggest that they do have such rights elsewhere.

It is precisely this last nuance that the author exploits. If they were aliens in the land of Canaan, even though it was theirs by promise, where was their real homeland (*patris*)? Their speech is a "confession" (*homologein*), just as the author's listeners have a "confession" to which they must hold. The patriarchs' statement that they are not at home in this place "makes clear" (*emphanizein*; see Acts 24:1) that they are "seeking a homeland." Like the author's use of "city" in 11:10, the term "homeland" has a definite political rather than cultic connotation (see 2 Macc 8:21; 13:14; Josephus, *J.W.* 1.246). But if the patriarchs are not referring to Canaan as their real homeland, then what can they mean? The author immediately excludes the obvious option: if they meant the land from which they had come, they could simply go back (11:15). The premise here is that everyone wants to be at home rather than a stranger. So there is another inference to be drawn from the patriarchs' behavior and confession. Why do they persist in their alien status? It is because they do not want to go back (as did the rebellious wilderness generation), but instead to go forward.

They desire a better homeland, a heavenly one. The verb *oregomai* means literally "to stretch out for something" (Homer, *Il.* 15.371; *Od.* 17.366), and figuratively "to strive for something" (Plato, *Republic* 439B; 1 Tim 3:1; 6:10). The comparative adjective *kreitton* ("better") runs throughout this composition (Heb 1:4; 6:9; 7:7, 19, 22; 8:6; 9:23; 10:34), as does "heavenly" (*epouranios*) with respect to the goal of faith (3:1; 6:4; 8:5; 9:23; 12:22). The same *synkrisis* that was worked out in cultic terms is here expressed in political terms. As I pointed out already in the comment on 11:10, the difference is that the author here effectively makes the structure and goal of the patriarchs' faith the same as the Christians'.

Another link to the Christian experience is made by the author's next statement: because of their confession, God "is not ashamed to be called their God." The allusion is to the way in which God is self-designated by the names of "Abraham, Isaac, and Jacob" (see Gen 28:13; Exod 3:6). Within the honor-shame glossary of Hebrews, the litotes "not ashamed" is equivalent to "is honored" (cf. Rom 1:16). Since they honored God by claiming him as their God, God is honored to be associated with them. The language of "not ashamed," moreover, creates a deliberate connection to the author's earlier statement with respect to the "seed of Abraham," namely, that the Son "is not ashamed to call them brothers" (2:11).

Finally, this passage serves the author as another example of how God is the rewarder of those who seek him (11:6). God has, in fact, "prepared a city" for the patriarchs. The use of the verb "prepare" (*hētoimazein*) echoes scriptural language for God's care of the people (Pss 22:5; 64:9; 77:20; 88:4; 118:73; 131:17) that is continued in New Testament passages speaking of eschatological realities (Matt 25:34, 41; 1 Cor 2:9; Rev 12:6; 19:7; 21:2). The city that God has prepared for the patriarchs is not an earthly one, but is located in the very homeland they seek; it is God's own city, toward which the author's hearers are themselves streaming in their faithful pilgrimage (Heb 12:22). Again, the pilgrimage of the people of faith is continuous, having from beginning to end the same structure of obedience and loyalty, the same goal of the presence of the living God.

[17–19] Hebrews takes up next the remarkable story of Abraham's offering of Isaac, recounted in Gen 22:1–19, and renowned in Jewish lore as the "binding of Isaac" (*Aqedah*). Jewish reflection on this passage is ancient (see Sir 44:20; Wis 10:5; 2 Macc 2:52; 4 Macc 16:20; *Jub.* 18.1–19; Josephus, *Ant.* 1.222–36; Philo, *Abraham* 167–207; *m. Abot* 5.3) and continuous. Paul probably alludes to the "handing over" of Isaac in Rom 8:22, and Jas cites it as the specific demonstration that faith is perfected through deeds (Jas 2:21–24).[3] Hebrews 11:17–19 stands within this interpretive tradition. As always, however, the author contributes distinctive touches of his own.

By referring to Abraham as "being tested" (*peirazomenos*), the author is faithful to the text of Gen 22:1, which states that "God tested Abraham (*epeirasen ton Abraam*)." The *Aqedah* is always included among the "ten trials of Abraham" (*m. Abot* 5.3; *Abot de Rabbi Nathan* 33). At the same time, the author establishes another link between the faith of the patriarchs, Jesus, and those associated with him. In 2:18 he stated that since Jesus himself had been tested, he is able to help those who are being tested; and in 5:15 he declared that Jesus as a high priest had been tested in every way apart from sin.

Abraham also did not sin in this matter, but responds *en pistei* ("by faith") to the command of God, offering his "only son" (*monogenē*). Hebrews uses a different term than the LXX of Gen 22:2, which reads, "Take your son, the beloved (*ton agapēton*), whom you love (*hon ēgapēsas*)." The LXX *agapētos* translates (as it does also in Amos 8:10; Zech 12:10; Jer 6:26) Hebrew *yāḥîd*, which means "only." In the strict sense, to be sure, Isaac was not Abraham's only son, since Hagar had given birth to his son Ishmael. It is possible that the LXX's diction resolves that technicality.

The use of *monogenēs* by our author also goes back to an alternative translation of *yāḥîd* in the LXX (Judg 11:34; Pss 21:20; 24:16; 34:17). In the New Testament, *monogenēs* is used straightforwardly for only children (Luke 7:12; 8:42; 9:38), except in John, where it designates Jesus as God's "only begotten Son" (John 1:14, 18; 3:16, 18; 1 John 4:9). It is impossible to determine whether Hebrews intends any such allusion to Jesus. On one hand, it is a possibility, since the author will speak of the giving back of Isaac as a *parabolē* of resurrection. On the other hand, Hebrews may simply be following a variant in the LXX. (Aquila's translation uses *monogenēs* rather than *agapētos* in Gen 22:2.)

3. For the literature and full discussion, see J. Swetnam, *Jesus and Isaac: A Study of the Epistle to the Hebrews in the Light of the Aqedah* (AnBib 94; Rome: Biblical Institute Press, 1981).

Like Abel, Abraham makes a sacrifice to God of what is most precious to him, giving back in the most dramatic fashion what he had received dramatically from God's power alone. The cost of Abraham's obedience was great. Isaac was the one through whom God's promise was to be fulfilled: "Out of Isaac will your seed be named." The author here quotes directly from Gen 21:12. Note the placement of that promise. It occurs immediately after Abraham was told to banish Hagar and Ishmael from his household (21:1–10), a command that already seemed "very harsh" to Abraham (21:11). But he obeyed that command. Now, having staked all on the promise through Isaac, God appears to be taking that away as well. But God interrupts the sacrifice of his son. Hebrews uses the imperfect tense of the verb, signaling that it was started but not completed. Most significant here is the confirmation of the author's conviction that the most critical element in sacrifice is the obedient disposition of the offerer (see Heb 10:5–10).

Abraham's is the obedience of faith, indeed (see the exposition in Philo, *Abraham* 194–97). On what basis could Abraham do it? The author again speaks of Abraham's "considering" or "reckoning" (*hēgoumai*), using the same verb as in the case of Sarah (11:11). Abraham "reckoned" that God was powerful enough to raise even from the dead. The lesson was drawn from the birth of a child from parents "as good as dead." Abraham's faith is once more a "proof of things not seen": entering into the act of sacrificing his son was a far more radical example of "not knowing where he was going" than when he left his homeland for Canaan. Just as God responded to Sarah's faith by giving her the power to conceive, so does God reward "the one seeking him." Because (*hothen*) Abraham acted in faith, "in symbolic fashion," he received him back.

The phrase *en parabolē* points in two directions. Abraham received Isaac "back" literally, when God stopped the sacrifice and Isaac was able to accompany his father home. Philo says, "So Isaac was saved, since God returned the gift of him and used the offering which piety rendered to Him to repay the offerer" (*Abraham* 177). But this return is "figuratively" a resurrection from the dead, since, like Sarah and Abraham at the time of the child's birth, Isaac himself was "as good as dead" with the knife to his throat. As in the use of the same phrase in 9:9, however, the author may also imply another symbolic dimension, namely the resurrection from the dead that occurred in Christ and is anticipated by believers. The rescue of Isaac, at the very least, points forward to a full realization of God's power to bring life from death.[4]

[20–21] The immediate descendants of Abraham are quickly dealt with in three sentences, each introduced by the phrase *en pistei* ("by faith"). Each patriarch's faith is defined in terms of an action taken in the present time with a view

4. For the argument that Christ's resurrection runs implicitly throughout chap. 11, see G. E. Cockerill, "The Better Resurrection (Heb 11:35): A Key to the Structure and Rhetorical Purpose of Hebrews 11," *TynBul* 51 (2000): 215–34.

toward a future realization. It does not concern our author that Jacob won Isaac's blessing through conspiracy with his mother Rebekah (Gen 27:5–17). Note that in *Jub.* 24–27 Rebekah's role is greatly expanded, so that she also gives blessings. Hebrews focuses only on the fact that Jacob's blessings concern "the things to come" (*mellontōn*). To Jacob, Isaac gives the blessing of future property and of primacy over his brothers (Gen 27:27–29). Esau's belated blessing makes him a man of the wilderness who eventually wins freedom (27:39–40). Esau, we recall, had already sold his birthright for a pot of lentils (25:29–34). Hebrews will return to this event in 12:16–17, when the author tells his hearers not to be "a fornicator or profane person like Esau."

Jacob's blessing, in turn, took place "as he was dying." What he "sees" about the future, therefore, is not something that he himself will see in the future. It is "by faith" that he blesses Joseph's sons, Ephraim and Manasseh, in Gen 48:15–20. The drama of the Genesis account lay in Jacob's reversing the order of the blessing, but there is no trace of that here. Neither does our author allude to the even more dramatic blessing that Jacob pronounces over his own sons in Gen 49:1–28. Since the author notes that Jacob blessed Joseph's sons "as he was dying," the important aspect of Jacob's faith must involve his trust in God's promises for the people as a whole.

In Gen 48:21 we read, "Then Israel said to Joseph, 'Behold, I am about to die, but God will be with you and will bring you again to the land of your fathers.'" That this is the point of interest to the author is indicated by the fact that he weaves into the account of the blessing of Joseph's sons an earlier incident involving Joseph himself (47:29–31). There Joseph promised his father Jacob that he would bury the patriarch with his fathers. Hebrews cites the words of LXX Gen 47:31, "and he bowed over the head of his staff." The MT is, "and he bowed himself upon the head of his bed," indicating fatigue or illness. For our author, however, it is a sign of worship, a signal of obedient faith to the end (cf. *proskynein*, ["worship"] in Heb 1:6).

Joseph is the last of the patriarchs, and out of his tumultuous life also Hebrews draws only from his dying moments, "as he was coming to an end" (*teleutōn*). Genesis 50:25 states that Joseph took an oath before the sons of Israel, saying, "God will visit you and you shall carry up my bones from here." Hebrews interprets the first part of this sentence as Joseph "remembered the exodus of the children of Israel." The use of *mnēmoneuein* ("remember") seems strange at first, for how can one remember an event still to occur? But I think that "remember" is preferable to "make mention" (RSV) or "reflect on" (Attridge, 336), because, although the actual exodus will be in the future, Joseph's faith is demonstrated by his remembering and trusting—and acting in light of—the *promise* of God's visitation to the people that was stated already to Abraham in Gen 15:13–15. His act of memory is therefore also an act of faith (*en pistei*) that God could accomplish what he had promised.

The author summarizes the second part of Joseph's final statement in Genesis as, "he gave commands concerning his bones." He had told the children of Israel to "bring up my bones from here." Joseph will not take part in the exodus with them. Moses will carry the bones in the wilderness (Exod 13:19), and Joshua will carry them into the land and bury them at Shechem (Josh 24:32). But Joseph's disposition of his burial while he is dying in Egypt shows how utterly he believes in the future of the people in the land of the promise.

This concern for Joseph's bones draws the attention of the tradition (see Sir 49:15; Josephus, *Ant.* 2.200). But several texts pay equal attention to the transfer of the bones of the other sons of Jacob, about which Scripture says nothing at all (see Acts 7:16; Josephus, *Ant.* 2.100; *Jub.* 46.9; *T. Sim.* 8.2–7; *T. Benj.* 12.3). Philo is distinctive in his interpretation of the significance of Joseph's last moment: he notes that Joseph's bones were worthy of perpetual memory, because he "believed that God would visit" the people (*Migration of Abraham* 18).

11:23–31 The Faith of Moses and the Israelites

The main figure in this section of the encomium on faith—and the heroes of faith—is Moses. He was already the subject of a *synkrisis* with the Son in Heb 3:1–6. There we learned that Moses was *pistos* ("faithful") in all God's house (3:2, 5), and worthy of honor as a servant (*therapōn*) in that house—"to give evidence (*martyrion*) of things yet to be spoken" (3:5). The connection between Moses and Christ will be made even more explicit in this section, which indeed throws some light back on that odd phrase, "evidence of things yet to be spoken." Moses is portrayed here as one linked to the "reproach of the Messiah" (11:26).[1]

It is not Moses alone, however, whose faith is celebrated. His parents act "by faith" (11:23), and so do those Israelites who cross the Red Sea (11:29) and circle the walls of Jericho (11:30). And it is "by faith" that Rahab the harlot—the second woman (with Sarah) explicitly to be named in this honor roll—received the Israelite scouts in peace (11:31).

As in earlier sections, we find certain themes repeated: for example faith as a way of seeing what is not visible to the eyes (11:27), God as the giver of rewards (11:26), and the escape from death or near death (11:23, 28, 29, 31). Distinctive to this part of the exposition is the necessity for faith to make hard choices for God in the face of danger (although that certainly was the case for

1. See esp. M. R. D'Angelo, *Moses in the Letter to the Hebrews* (SBLDS 42; Missoula, MT: Scholars Press, 1979).

Abraham as well!), human wrath, and dishonor (11:23, 25–26, 27, 31). Faith demands fearing God rather than human rulers (11:23, 27).

11:23 By faith, when Moses was born he was hidden for three months by
his parents, because they saw that the child was beautiful and they did not
fear the king's decree.[a] 24 By faith, when Moses was grown, he rejected
being called the daughter of Pharaoh's son. 25 He chose rather to suffer
hardship with God's people than to have the temporary advantage from
sin. 26 He considered the reproach of the Messiah as greater wealth than
the treasure of Egypt, for he looked to the reward. 27 By faith, he left
Egypt, not fearing the king's wrath, for he endured as though seeing the
one who is invisible. 28 By faith, he carried out the Passover sacrifice and
the sprinkling of the blood, so that the destroyer might not touch their
firstborn. 29 By faith, they passed through the Red Sea as through dry
land,[b] while the Egyptians trying to do it were swallowed up.[c] 30 By faith,
the walls of Jericho fell after being circled for seven days. 31 By faith,
Rahab the harlot[d] did not perish with the disobedient,[e] because she had
received the scouts in peace.

a. The original hand of D, followed by a few Greek MSS and a Vulgate MS, adds another complete sentence: "By faith, when he became great Moses slew the Egyptian, perceiving the lowliness of his brothers" (see Exod 2:11; Acts 7:24). It is too lightly attested to be considered original and may have been added to solve what could have been seen as a gap in the sequence (see discussion).

b. P^{46} omits the noun *gēs* ("the land"), probably regarding it as redundant.

c. A few witnesses have, "they were cast into the sea" (*katepontisthēsan*), rather than the more vivid, "they were swallowed up" (*katepothēsan*), found in the best MSS.

d. Possibly out of a desire to soften the harshness of *hē pornē* ("the harlot"), the original hand of א, as well as the Harclean Syriac, add *epilegomenē* ("she who was called"), but see Jas 2:25.

e. P^{46} has *apistēsasin* ("those who were faithless") rather than *apeithēsasin* ("those who were disobedient"), following its tendency also in 3:18 and 4:6.

[11:23–26] It was not Moses' faith but that of his parents that enabled him to survive the deadly decree of the pharaoh "who did not know Joseph" (Exod 1:8), and who issued successive edicts intended to wipe out the burgeoning Israelite population (Exod 1:15–22). Hebrews provides two reasons why his parents defied the king. First, they saw that Moses was *asteios*. The adjective is found in Exod 2:2, and is used for physical beauty (Aristotle, *Nicomachean Ethics* 1123B; Judg 3:17; Sus 7; Jdt 11:23), and that is probably the meaning here, although Acts 7:20 gives it a religious turn, "beautiful in God's eyes." The child (*to paidion*; see Exod 2:6) was too precious for them to abandon him to certain death.

Here, then, we see an ironic reversal of the Isaac story. Abraham showed his faith by his obedience to God, even to the point of killing his son. Moses' parents show their faith by refusing to obey a human edict that would have killed their beautiful son. The difference lies in who gave the command, God or humans. The second reason for their refusal, then, is that the parents "did not fear" the king's decree (*diatagma*; see Plutarch, *Life of Pompey* 6; Epictetus, *Discourses* 1.25.4). Hebrews considers that those who appropriately fear God (4:1) will not fear any human power (11:27; 13:6), and will act with the *parrēsia* ("boldness") of faith.

Hebrews stands within a tradition of interpreting the gaps in the biblical story through extrapolation and interpretation. Here the author ascribes faith and courage to Moses' parents, something not stated—though certainly implied—by the Exodus account. Thus, although *Jub.* 47.3 and Josephus (*Ant.* 2.218) follow Exodus closely in their respective retellings, Philo elaborates that Moses was "nursed at his mother's breast" (*Life of Moses* 1.9), and Pseudo-Philo has his mother, named Jochab, keep Moses hidden in her womb for three months (*L.A.B.* 9.12)! Stephen's speech in Acts 7:20 declares that Moses was "nurtured" (*anetraphē*) for three months in his father's house.

The author of Hebrews passes over the period of Moses' upbringing that so fascinates other Jewish interpreters (see Josephus, *Ant.* 2.223–53; Philo, *Life of Moses* 1.23–31; *Jub.* 47.9; *L.A.B.* 9.19; Artapanus, *On the Jews*, Frag. 3; Acts 7:22), and moves directly to the next pivotal element in Moses' life, when he was grown (*megas genomenos*, drawn directly from Exod 2:11). This is the incident in which Moses comes to the defense of the Israelite being abused by an Egyptian. He killed the attacker, and this intervention led in turn to Pharaoh's seeking to kill Moses, requiring Moses to flee to the wilderness of Midian (Exod 2:11–15).

Once more, Jewish interpreters of this sequence differ in their readings, especially since Moses' act of killing can be regarded as an embarrassment. *Jubilees* 47.11–12 follows the biblical narrative closely, as does Acts 7:24–27 (adding only the note that Moses sought to be a peacemaker among his brethren). But Pseudo-Philo omits the incident entirely, moving directly from Moses' childhood to the plagues (*L.A.B.* 9.16–10.1). Artapanus creates a novelistic account of a rivalry between Moses and the Egyptian king: Moses killed an assassin sent to kill him, forcing him to flee (*On the Jews*, Frag. 3). Josephus also says that Moses fled because of an enemy's plot against him, but reports nothing of Moses' own act of killing (*Ant.* 2.254–56). Philo also includes the element of a royal plot against Moses (*Life of Moses* 1.43–46).

Hebrews walks carefully on the narrow path between complete omission and faithful reporting, and represents perhaps the most creative recasting of all. The author does not mention directly either the killing or the flight, but puts the event in terms of Moses' choice to align himself with God's people (his own people) and to share their suffering, rather than avail himself of the privileges that could be his as the adopted son of Pharaoh's daughter. The author represents the decision of Moses as a "rejecting" (*arneomai*) the designation of being her son and a "choosing" (*aireomai*) of God's people. The verb *arneomai* means to "deny" verbally, but also to "reject" (see Homer, *Od.* 21.345; Herodotus 3.1; 4 Macc 8:7; Matt 10:23; Luke 9:23; John 13:38; Acts 3:13–14), the sense it clearly has here. For *aireomai* ("choose") see also Phil 1:22; 2 Thess 2:13.

Moses' choice is put in two parallel ways. First, Moses chose to "suffer hardship with God's people" rather than "the temporary advantage from sin." The verb *synkakoucheomai* is a *hapax legomenon*, but its meaning is clear from its component parts and its context (as well as its resemblance to *synkakopathein* in 2 Tim 1:8 and 2:3), which indicate that, like *sympathein* in 10:33, it represents a form of identification with the hard experience of others. In this case, Moses' coming to the aid of his fellow Israelites means that he sides with them more than with the Egyptians. That other possibility is expressed in terms of a "temporary" (*proskairon*) or "fleeting" advantage that could be gained by siding with the Egyptians. In terms of the story, the advantage would be "for a time" because the Egyptians would be swallowed by the sea; in terms of Hebrews' larger vision of reality, any temporal gain is insignificant compared to the eternal God.

My translation of *hamartias apolausin* breaks with the common rendering, as "pleasure from sin" (see RSV, NRSV). That *apolausis* can mean simply "pleasure" is certain (see Aristotle, *Politics* 1314B; 3 Macc 7:16; 1 Tim 6:17), and if the phrase is read this way, it would refer to the pleasure given by the wealth available to Moses in Egypt. But the genitive construction with *apolausis* can also mean an advantage derived from something (see Xenophon, *Memorabilia* 2.1.33; Plato, *Timaeus* 83A). Sin, in this case, is not the moral vice of luxury and avarice, but precisely apostasy, a turning away from God's people (see Heb 3:13). Moses' solidarity with the suffering of his people had its cost, but he did not "neglect the assembly" as some of the hearers were doing (10:25).

The phrase *oneidismon tou Christou* ("reproach of the Messiah") is difficult, and almost impossible to translate adequately, but two points can confidently be made. First, in the honor-shame world of the author, *oneidismos* falls emphatically on the side of shame (see Josh 5:8; 1 Sam 17:26; Neh 5:9; Hos 12:18; Joel 2:19; Jer 6:10; 23:40; *T. Reu.* 4.7; *T. Jud.* 23.3). Second, just as the hearers were reminded that in earlier days they had been exposed to afflictions and *oneidismoi* and were partners of people who lived that way (Heb 10:33), so Moses here serves as a model of identifying with the shame of those who are being shamed.

The hard question concerns the identification with the Messiah (*Christos*). The author of Hebrews clearly regards the crucifixion of Jesus as something shameful in human eyes. He says that Jesus endured the cross, "despising its shame" (12:3). Christians who experience shame are, in turn, associated with the shame of the Christ. The hearers are told to go "outside the camp, bearing his reproach (*ton oneidismon autou*)" (13:13). The link between Christ and Christians is similarly made in Rom 15:3, which quotes LXX Ps 68:10, "the reproaches of those who reproach you have fallen upon me." But how are Moses and the Christ connected, so that the shame Moses embraces is the "shame of the Messiah"?

Here we can look at another psalm where the language of reproach appears. In Ps 88:51 the theme of the Davidic dynasty is prominent: God made a covenant with David his chosen one (88:3–4), whom he anointed (88:19–21), and to whom he promised an everlasting kingdom (88:27–37). He is the *christos*, the anointed one. But the king has been brought low by enemies, who "are full of wrath against your anointed" (88:39), so that "he has become the scorn (*oneidos*) of his neighbors" (88:42). The psalm concludes with David asking the Lord to remember "the reproach of your servants" (in the plural: *oneidismou tōn doulōn sou*), by which they "have taunted (*ōneidisan*) your anointed one (*tou christou sou*)" (88:51–52). According to the psalm, the reproach of the people and of the Christ are the same. Therefore, if Moses took on the reproach leveled at his people, he also took on the reproach leveled at the Messiah about whom the later psalmist would speak. It is quite likely that this is precisely what the author meant by his statement in Heb 3:5 that Moses was a servant "in order to give evidence about things yet to be spoken."

Moses' choice, like that of the earlier heroes of faith, was based on a calculation or a "knowing" of a reality that could not be seen with the eyes. He "looked forward" to the reward (*misthopodosian*), thus demonstrating the truth enunciated by the author in 11:6 that God is the rewarder of those who seek him. Moses is also a model for the hearers because, like them, his allegiance to God's people meant being associated with shame and facing the loss of material possessions ("the treasures of the Egyptians"; see 10:32–33). Above all, his faith was exemplary, for he acted not in view of a temporary advantage but in view of an eternal reward.

[27–29] Precisely what the next verses refer to is a matter of some debate. The author says that "by faith," Moses "left Egypt." Does the author want us to think of Moses' flight to Midian after the slaying of the Egyptian (see Exod 2:14–15; so Attridge, 342), or of the departure from Egypt in the exodus (Exod 13:17–15:21; so Westcott, 373)? The main objection to the first option is that Exodus explicitly says that Moses was fearful when he fled Pharaoh (Exod 2:14; see also *Jub.* 47.12), whereas he stood up to the king courageously in the period before the people's departure (see Exod 14:13). The main objection to the second option is that it disturbs the chronological sequence, making the Passover and death of the firstborn follow the departure rather than precede it, as in the biblical account (see Exod 12:21–36). Also, Moses is here singled out (the verb is singular), whereas it is all the people who leave Egypt.

The problem of Moses' fear in his flight to Midian can be resolved by recourse to a later interpretive tradition that eliminates any mention of fear in that story (Josephus, *Ant.* 2.254–56; Philo, *Life of Moses* 1.49–50; *Allegorical Laws* 3.14; Artapanus, *On the Jews,* Frag. 3.19). But the objection to the second option can also be answered: the statement provides a general category (the departure) that contains within it the several specific incidents, while the focus on Moses is natural as the one who leads the people with his unique vision; note that Hebrews says that "he" performed the Passover ritual. There is one further consideration in favor of the "exodus" position: the statement that Moses "endured as though seeing the one who was invisible." While this could refer to his experience at the burning bush in Midian (Exod 3:4), the fact that he "endured" (*karterein*) seems to work best with his consistent visionary ability as the leader of the people. Not only is it impossible finally to decide this issue, it is not really necessary to decide, for the author wants us to focus less on the event than on Moses' faith.

In this case, Moses' faith is connected to two specific qualities. The first is his lack of fear before the king. The noun *thymos* is used by Homer for spirit, strength, and courage (*Od.* 10.78, 461), but also for the seat of anger (*Il.* 2.149) or even anger itself (*Il.* 2.196). In the LXX it usually means simply anger (Exod 15:8; Ps 2:5, 12), often in combination with *orgē* (Exod 32:12, 19; Num 12:9; Deut 7:4), and this sense continues in New Testament compositions (Luke 4:28; Acts 19:28; Rom 2:8). Moses' defiance of the king's anger makes him resemble his natural parents, who saved him because they "did not fear the king's decree" (Heb 11:23). Moses was capable of acting with such disregard of fear because he persevered "as though seeing the one who is invisible." The verb *karterein* ("persevere") has the same sense as "enduring" (*hypomenein*); see Plato, *Theaetetus* 157D; Josephus, *Ant.* 1.52; Job 2:9; Sir 2:2; 12:15; Isa 42:14; 2 Macc 7:17; 4 Macc 9:9, 28; 10:1. Moses is also a model for the hearers in this respect (see Heb 10:36–39). The phrase *hōs horōn* is ambiguous. It can mean "as though he saw" or "as one who saw." The masculine case of *ton aoraton* makes clear that this is not simply a matter of "things not seen" (11:1) that pulls Moses forward, but a "seeing" of the invisible God. Besides the vision at the burning bush, Moses had continued encounters with God, some involving a visual experience, some not (see Exod 19:20; 24:9–11; 33:11; 34:27–35), a theme that is developed by Deut 34:10; Sir 45:5; and Philo (*Life of Moses* 1.158; *Allegorical Laws* 3.100; *Rewards and Punishments* 27).

Moses' faith continues in the obedience toward God he showed in carrying out the instructions concerning the Passover meal (*to pascha*; see Exod 12:21; Matt 26:19; Mark 14:16; Luke 22:13; John 19:14; Acts 12:4; 1 Cor 5:7), and the pouring—or sprinkling—of the blood. The phrase *proschysis tou haimatos* appears only here in the New Testament, but derives from the verb *proschein*, used in passages such as Exod 24:6; 29:21; Lev 9:12, for pouring or sprinkling the blood of a victim that has been sacrificed. In the case of the exodus experience, the blood is sprinkled or smeared on the doorpost and lintel of every house where the paschal lamb is to be consumed (Exod 12:7, 25), as a sign not to destroy the firstborn children of that household (12:23–27).

The blood kept the destroyer (*olothreuōn*) from touching (*thigē*) their firstborn (*prōtotokan*). The verb *olethreuōn* (the usual spelling) means "to destroy" (Num 4:18; Deut 20:20; Josh 3:10), and the noun form, "the destroyer," appears both in Exod 12:23 and Wis 18:25. In the LXX the destroyer is undoubtedly the Lord himself, who slays the firstborn of all the Egyptian children (Exod 12:29–30) but does not touch the Israelite children. The death of the Passover lamb, then, has a salvific effect: its death ensures the life of the people's children, and thereby the very future of the people; by so doing, it foreshadows the sacrificial death of Jesus that saves humans (Heb 5:9; 9:28).

In 11:28 the author shifts to the plural, declaring that it was "by faith" that they passed through the Red Sea as though dry land. Hebrews slightly paraphrases the LXX of Exod 14:21, which describes Moses lifting his staff and the people passing through the middle of the sea, with the walls of water rising on either side. It is the LXX of Exod 14:27 that underlies the statement that when the Egyptians attempted the same crossing, they were swallowed by the water. Like the retellings in Josephus, *Ant.* 2.338–44, and Philo, *Life of Moses* 1.176–80, Hebrews stays close to the biblical account.

Jubilees, in contrast, makes the event one of fit retribution: "Just as the men of Egypt cast their sons into the river he avenged one million. And one thousand strong and ardent sons perished on account of one infant whom they threw in the midst of the river from the sons of your people" (48.14). According to Pseudo-Philo, the Egyptians went into the sea because "God hardened their perception and they did not know they were entering the sea" (*L.A.B.* 10.6). Artapanus says that the Egyptians were destroyed both by the flood and by the fire that God had made to shine in front of them (*On the Jews*, Frag. 3.37). For our author, the faith of the Israelites has two dimensions: walking into the sea was an act of "not knowing where they were going," a step as dangerous and unpredictable as Abraham's leaving for a land he did not know; it was also a step that brought them to the brink of death, as did Abraham's offering of his son Isaac. But once again, God brought them to life out of a place of death.

[30–31] The author finally summarizes the combined incidents reported by Josh 6:14–26, the fall of Jericho and the rescue of Rahab, both happening "by faith." It is striking that Joshua is not even mentioned in connection with these events, in sharp contrast both to the retelling of the biblical story by Josephus, who emphasizes his role throughout (*Ant.* 5.1–120), and of Pseudo-Philo, who glorifies Joshua but omits entirely the incidents reported here (*L.A.B.* 20.1–3). The author's neglect of Joshua is consistent with his tendency to minimize the land of Canaan as the true "rest" of the people (4:8) or the people's true "homeland" (11:4).

The fall of Jericho's walls can be attributed to faith because Joshua believed it when the Lord told him, "Behold, I have handed over to your hand Jericho and its king and the powerful men of strength within it" (Josh 6:2), and because the people believed and obeyed Joshua when he told them, "The LORD has handed over to you the city." Joshua and the people acted in view of "things not seen." The city appeared impregnable, but they circled and blew their horns, and it did fall, "by faith."

As in Jas 2:25, Rahab is unabashedly designated as "the harlot" (*hē pornē*), as also in the LXX of Josh 2:1 and 6:25. Josephus bowdlerizes by identifying her as an innkeeper (*Ant.* 5.8), here agreeing with the *Targum* on Josh 2:1, where she is called an "innkeeper." In the rabbinic tradition, consequently, Rahab is best remembered as a model of hospitality as well as a proselyte (see *b. Meg.* 14b–15a; *Mekilta* on Exodus, par. Amalek Yitro 18.1; *Exod. Rab.* 27.4; *Num. Rab.* 3.2; 8.9; 16.1; *Deut. Rab.* 2.26–27; *Ruth Rab.* 2.1; *Song Rab.* I, 3, 3; I, 15, 2; IV, 1, 2; VI, 2, 3; *Qoh. Rab.* V, 6, 1).

The LXX already makes clear that Rahab's treatment of the scouts/spies (*kataskopous;* see Josh 2:1; 6:25) was motivated by faith. She tells the scouts that she had heard about all the wonders of the Lord and ends with this confession: "The LORD your God is God in heaven above and on earth below" (Josh 2:11), and expects mercy in return for her mercy when the Lord leads them into the land and to her city (2:12–13). The rescue of her and her family will be a rescue "of her soul from death" (2:14). She is, indeed, "taken alive" when the city is put to the ban (6:25).

Two small touches distinguish Hebrews' brief account of Israel's first adventures in Canaan. First, by making explicit that Rahab had received the scouts "with peace" (*met' eirēnēs*), the author enables her to be seen also as an example to the hearers, who are told by the author to "pursue peace (*eirēnēn*) with all people" (12:14). Second, by stating that Rahab "did not perish," the author distinguishes her from "the unbelievers" (*tois apeithēsasin*; see 3:18) who did perish in the fall of the city. As in the contrast between Cain and Abel, the reward and punishment are connected to the response of obedient faith.

11:32–40 The Faith of Many Witnesses

The final section of this long recital devoted to the heroes of faith picks up the pace considerably. Indeed, after confessing an inability to "tell the story" of such famous heroes whom the author rapidly names (11:32), he shifts to a summary of deeds, dispositions, and experiences that can apply to the entire lengthy story of the people as contained in Scripture—and even outside it! That the argument remains the same, however, is indicated by the way the section is framed: in 11:33 and 11:39 the phrase "through/by faith" provides a bracket around all the specific descriptions.

The rhetorical artistry of the author is difficult to miss when the section is recited aloud in Greek, but this quality is difficult to convey through translation. I try to capture some of the rhythm of the Greek through the use of short sentences that combine repetition and variation. The recital is not arbitrary. The author praises the accomplishments achieved through faith (11:33), the empowerment to overcome given by faith (11:33–34), the endurance of suffering, both physical and emotional (11:36–37), and, decisively, the experience of homelessness (11:37–38).

The most striking, and revealing, element in the exposition is the statement in 11:35 about women receiving their dead back through resurrection, and about the expectation of a "better" resurrection, which both recalls the story of Abraham and Isaac in 11:17–19, but even more clearly points forward to the resurrection of Jesus. Like the patriarchs who wandered in the land of Canaan while seeking their real homeland (11:13–14), all these heroes of whom the world was not worthy (11:38) were searching for that better realization of the promise, which God has now brought about through the Messiah Jesus, so that all God's people, defined by faith, can be brought to perfection.

> **11:32** And what more should I say? Time will fail me if I tell the story of
> Gideon, Barak,[a] Samson, Jephthah, David and Samuel, and the prophets.
> **33** Through faith they defeated kingdoms,[b] accomplished justice, obtained
> promises. They shut the mouths of lions. **34** They quenched powerful fire.
> They fled the edge of the sword. They grew powerful out of weakness,
> became strong in battle, turned back foreign armies. **35** Women received
> back their dead by resurrection. But others were tortured and did not accept
> release, so that they might attain a better resurrection.
>
> **36** Others experienced taunts and whips, even chains and prison. **37** They
> were stoned, they were sawed in half.[c] They were killed by the sword. They
> went about in sheepskins and goatskins. They were deprived, oppressed,
> badly treated, **38** these people of whom the world is not worthy. They wan-
> dered over desert places and mountains and caves and holes in the ground.
> **39** Now even though all of these were witnessed to by faith, they did not
> receive the promise[d] **40** because God had prepared[e] something better for us,
> so that they would not be brought to perfection apart from us.

a. A number of MSS insert "and also" (*te kai*) after the name of Barak, as appears also between David and Samuel, in order to relieve the asyndetic character of four names in sequence. The shorter and harder reading is to be preferred.

b. P^{46} alters "kingdoms" (*basileias*) to "kings" (*basileis*), possibly because the biblical account concerning Joshua emphasizes the conquering of kings rather than kingdoms (see Josh 12:24).

c. Many Christian scribes were startled by the rare *epristhēsan* ("they were sawed in half"), especially since no such act or verb was found in Scripture; so they tried to correct it by altering to "were tested" (*epeirasthēsan*). P46 and a few other witnesses have the reading accepted here, which demands to be accepted because it is surely the harder to explain as a scribal emendation.

d. A few witnesses, the most important being A, change "the promise" (*tēn epangelian*) to "the promises" (*tas epangelias*), even though it sets up a direct opposition to 11:33.

e. A handful of witnesses have *prosblepsamenou* ("looking at") instead of *problepsamenou* ("looking ahead" or "preparing"). More striking, P46 puts the participle in the nominative case, which destroys the genitive absolute construction, and, more significant, shifts the "looking forward" from God to humans! The resulting translation would be, "they did not receive the promise of God because they were looking toward something better for us."

[11:32–34] The author's rhetorical art is never more obvious than in these final verses of chapter 11. He begins with an oratorical throat clearing like that in 5:11; the sentiment that time would fail the speaker if he tried to develop his point more extensively is standard (see, e.g., Isocrates, *Oration* 1.11; Philo, *Special Laws* 4.238; *Sacrifice of Abel and Cain* 27). As throughout the New Testament, the participle of *diēgeomai* means here "narrating" (see Mark 5:16; 9:9; Luke 8:39; 9:10; Acts 8:33; 9:27; 12:17).

The stories of the judges (Gideon, Barak, Samson, Jephthah, and Samuel), as well as those concerning King David and the prophets, would indeed take up even more space than he has devoted to the patriarchs and Moses. The author does not say why he selects these names, or why he arranges them in this sequence. The biblical order would be Barak (Judg 4–5), Gideon (Judg 6–8), Jephthah (Judg 11–12), Samson (Judg 13–16), Samuel (1 Sam 1), and David (1 Sam 16). No single aspect of their stories is singled out, because they are meant to stand as representative of the faith that moved and directed all those who spoke and acted for God and through whom also God spoke and acted.

Their deeds are summarized by a series of three triads. The first describes positive accomplishments, the second astonishing escapes, and the third the power to overcome. The first triad best fits the story of the conquest of the land and the tumultuous period of the judges. Joshua promised the people when they had entered the land that "the living God is among you" and that he would "drive out from before you the Canaanites, the Hittites, the Hivites, the Perrizites, the Girgashites, the Amorites, and the Jebusites" (Josh 3:10), and indeed those kingdoms fled before the militant people of Israel (Josh 5:1; 8:18–23; 9:1–27; 10:1–43; 11:1–23), a story of unrelenting victory summarized and celebrated in Josh 12:1–24. The phrase "accomplished justice" (*eirgasanto dikaiosynēn*) is a translator's judgment call. It could equally be rendered "acted justly." Since the focus seems to be on the time of the judges, however, the more political version is preferable (see Deut 16:18), for the great accomplishment of the major judges was to establish some sort of stability after periods of chaos among the tribes, beginning with Joshua's righteous division of the land (Josh 13:1–22), and extending through the deeds of other judges (see Judg 2:18–19; 5:31; 8:28; 12:7–15). In the broadest sense, they also "obtained promises" (*epetykon epangeliōn*): the phrase can refer to the conquest of the land itself, which certainly fulfilled the promise made first to Abraham (Gen 15:12–16; 17:8), and remembered by Moses (Deut 11:8–17) and Joshua (Josh 1:1–6).

The next triad summarizes the escapes from danger by heroes of faith. The phrase "shut the mouths of lions" may have specific reference to Daniel, whom God saved from the den of lions (Dan 6:19–23), an incident that became emblematic for God's rescuing care (see 1 Macc 2:60; 4 Macc 16:3; 18:13), although both Samson and David also achieved victory over the frightening animals, Samson by tearing one apart with his hands (Judg 14:6) and David by catching the lion by the jaw (1 Sam 17:34–35). The quenching of powerful fire is also associated with Daniel. The three young men Shadrach, Meshach, and Abednego were thrown into a blazing fire and emerged unharmed (Dan 3:13–26). In the LXX addition to the scene, the three young men praise God for their escape (Dan 3:50, 88). This rescue also is celebrated in other Jewish literature (1 Macc 2:59; 3 Macc 6:6; 4 Macc 16:3, 21; 18:12). The "edge of the sword," in turn, appears frequently as an image of violent death at human hands (see Sir 28:18; Josh 19:48), and can stand for the escapes from death by David (1 Sam 19:10–18; 2 Sam 15:14) and the prophets Elijah (1 Kgs 19:1–18) and Elisha (2 Kgs 6:1–33).

Although the final triad shifts to the passive voice, the three phrases focus on aggressive capacities. The passive voice of the verb in the first two phrases indicates that it is God who gives the "empowerment from weakness" and enables them to become "mighty in war." The author may well be thinking again of the judges who did great deeds when seized by God's Spirit, such as Deborah (Judg 4:4–5:31), Gideon (7:9–25), and Samson (15:1–20). Such figures became "mighty in war" (see Sir 46:1; 47:5) because the God who empowered them was also "mighty in war" (Ps 23:9). And because they were powerful in battle, they were able to "turn back foreign armies." The verb *klinein* ("to lean") is here used in its military sense of turning back an attack (see Josephus, *J.W.* 5.94; 6.79). The noun *parembolē* often refers to the "camp" of soldiers (Polybius, *History* 3.75.5; Exod 14:19) as it will in Heb 13:11. But it can also refer to a company of soldiers, or an "army" (see Gen 32:2; 1 Macc 3:15; 10:49). Although any number of exploits may have been in the author's mind, the most natural allusion would be to the conquests won by the Maccabees (see, e.g., 1 Macc 3:23–26; 4:6–25; 5:3, 21–36).

[35–38] Sarah and Rahab were women mentioned by name earlier in the encomium (Heb 11:11, 31). Now anonymous women of faith are celebrated, who "received back their dead by resurrection (*ex anastaseōs*). The obvious reference is to the women whose children were raised from the dead by the prophets Elijah and Elisha. They are unnamed here because they go unnamed in the biblical account as well. In 1 Kgs 17:8–24 Elijah befriends a widow of Zarephath; when her son dies, the prophet extends his body on that of the boy and resuscitates him. In 2 Kgs 4:11–37 the prophet Elisha befriends a Shunnamite woman, and stretches himself on the body of the woman's son when he dies, until his breath returns. Such stories reaffirm a powerful theme running throughout the entire composition: God can and does give life to the dead (see Heb 11:12, 18).

But the author wants to argue that such resuscitations, in which mortality is deferred but not transcended, are, like the rescue of Isaac from death, a "parable" for a more profound sort of resurrection, by which God not only returns people to their empirical existence but elevates them to a share in God's own life. This is the "better resurrection" (*kreittonos anastaseōs*) for which those who were being tortured held out, refusing the offer of "release" (*apolytrōsis*). The reference is again undoubtedly to the stories of the Maccabean martyrs. The aged scribe Eleazar was offered the chance of life if he renounced the law of God, but he refused and willingly went on "the rack" (2 Macc 6:28). The noun translated "rack" is *tympanon*, literally "a drum," because the victim was stretched out on it like the skin of a drum. From this arose the verb used here, *tympanizein,* "to torture" (see Plutarch, *How to Tell a Flatterer* 17 [*Mor.* 60A]; Josephus, *Ag. Ap.* 1.149). Eleazar thus became "an example of nobility and a memorial of courage" (2 Macc 6:31). And when the seven brothers were tortured, they made clear that they expected from God a greater gift of life through resurrection: "You dismiss us from the present life, but the King of the universe will raise us to an everlasting reward of life, because we have died for his laws" (2 Macc 7:9; see also 7:14, 23).

This last part of the encomium began with all positive achievements, showing the power of God at work in the world. Now, in Heb 11:36, the author's list both accelerates its pace and focuses entirely on the hard conditions those who in the past were faithful had to endure. The author speaks of their "experience" (for *peiran labein* see Deut 28:56; Josephus, *Ant.* 5.150) in entirely negative terms. The stories about the Maccabees continue to provide a backdrop to these characterizations, but allusions to earlier prophets are also likely. The "taunts" (*empaigmōn*) picks up from 2 Macc 7:7, 10, and the "whips" (*mastigōn*) echoes 2 Macc 7:1, 37; 9:11. The mention of "chains and prison," however, applies less to the Maccabees than it does to the several incarcerations of the prophet Jeremiah (Jer 20:2, 7; 29:26; 37:15; 1 Kgs 32:27; 2 Chr 16:10). The combination of "mockery" and "prison," in turn, has its most obvious point of reference in the author's mention of his hearers' earlier days when they were willing to undergo such treatment and be associated with those who also were experiencing it

(Heb 10:32–34). They too were "oppressed" (*thliboumenoi*, 10:33) and "badly treated" (*kakouchoumenoi*; see 11:25).

Those treated this way, though regarded dismissively by others, were honored by God. Indeed, the "world is not worthy (*axios*)" of them. The implication is clear. Like the author's audience, the forebears in faith looked to God as their source of approval, rather than the court of human reputation. The contrast between the two measures of value (and honor) is made even sharper by the final phrases in this recital: those of whom the world was not worthy could find no permanent place in this world: they wandered about (*planōmenoi*) in the physical sense, even though in the spiritual sense their direction was true. They were forced to live in deserts and mountains and caves and "holes in the ground." Although this list of temporary shelters might allude to any number of figures, such as David, Elijah, Elisha, or the Maccabees, the main reference must surely be to the hearers, whose property has been expropriated (10:34) and in truth have no permanent city here (13:14), and who are called to follow their leader Jesus "outside the camp" (13:13), sharing the suffering and shame of the pioneer and perfecter of faith.

[39–40] The author concludes the encomium by drawing together once more his hearers and their forebears in the faith. His carefully balanced statement includes "all these" (the ones he has been describing) and "us" (the author and his hearers). He begins with something of a restatement of 10:36. There he had declared to the hearers, "for you have need of endurance in order that, by doing the will of God, you might receive the promise (*komisēsthe tēn epangelian*)." Now he states of the ancient heroes, "they did not receive the promise (*ouk ekomisanto tēn epangelian*)." The promise, in short, remains to be received by both the ancient and the present people of faith. The heroes of old did not receive it "even though" (the participle is concessive) they were "witnessed to by [of, through] faith." This, in fact, has been the theme of the encomium: the phrase *dia pisteōs* continues the drumbeat that has sounded throughout the chapter, and the participle *martyrēthentes* provides a bracket corresponding to the statements in 11:2, 3, and 5.

Even though they did not attain the promise, God's providential design includes the faithful of the past with those of the present. God has prepared (*problepsamenou*) something better (*kreitton ti*) for us: that is why the promise remains for the hearers. The "something better" corresponds, as throughout the composition, to the life in the presence of God made available through the faithful death and triumphant resurrection of Jesus. This has been, the author asserts, in God's plan all along; this is what the ancients looked toward and for the sake of which they endured. The promise, therefore, is not simply for "us"; it is for "all these" as well: "so that they would not be brought to perfection (*teleiōthōsin*) apart from us (*chōris hēmōn*)." We have seen that "perfection" means precisely that access to God's presence made possible through the great high priest

Jesus (2:10; 5:9; 7:19, 28; 9:9; 10:1, 14). The clear implication of this statement is that the faithful from Abel to the Maccabean martyrs will share in this same access to God.

Excursus 7: In Praise of Israel's Heroes

In excursus 2 on "the wilderness as paradigm," we saw how Hebrews can be located among a variety of ancient Jewish compositions that in one manner or another retell the biblical story, usually from a definite ideological perspective or with a definite hortatory aim. Chapter 11 reveals another way that Hebrews shares in this rich tradition of scriptural interpretation: through shorter recitals of the story within longer compositions, recitals that select features of the long biblical story, or certain figures from that story, to stand as examples.

Simply in terms of form, a striking parallel appears in Philo's *Rewards and Punishments* 11–14, which forms a miniature encomium on hope (*elpis*). In the manner of Heb 11, Philo begins with a twofold characterization of hope as "the first seed, the fountain of our lives," and follows with three clauses beginning with the same phrase "in hope" (*elpidi*). Also parallel to Heb 11 is the way Philo speaks of those lacking hope as condemned by God and those having it as being "worthy of approval" (12) from the one who gives rewards. Also like Heb 12, Philo closes his encomium with an athletic image of "the winner of the crown in this athletic contest." The only connection to the biblical story is slight, however, through reference to the name of Enosh (see Gen 4:26).

We find examples of short summaries of the story already in the book of Joshua. Joshua summons all the tribes of Israel and in the name of the Lord retells the story from Abraham, through Isaac, Jacob, and Esau, to Moses and Aaron, and their own generation, asking the people for a renewed commitment to the covenant (Josh 24:1–15). Similar short recitals are found in other biblical books, but without mentioning specific names. The prophet Ezekiel, again speaking in the name of the Lord, rehearses the story from the exodus to the exile (Ezek 20:2–38). No names are mentioned, and it is not a heroic tale; the emphasis is on repeated apostasies. Similar in tone is the retelling of the people's story—this time naming only Abraham and Moses—by the scribe Ezra, when the people are gathered after the exile to hear the reading of the law and renew their commitment to it; once more there is a contrast between the wonderful blessings bestowed on Abraham's descendants and their repeated disobedience and rebellion (Neh 9:6–38). More positive in tone are the celebrations of God's wonders for the people in Pss 135:1–26 and 77:1–72, the last of which climaxes in the blessings shown toward David, but with no other figure mentioned by name. A final example is the report given by Achior, leader of the Ammonites during the time of the heroine Judith, which gains its impressiveness from the fact that it is an enemy of the people who witnesses to the special protection God gives this people when they obey him. This recital mentions no Israelite by name (see Jdt 5:5–21).

Two versions are extant from Hellenistic Judaism that do not name figures explicitly, but the characters are easily recognizable from the descriptions provided. In the book of Wisdom, the recital is part of the praise of Wisdom (*Sophia*) for her work among the people. We recognize Adam in "the first-formed father of the world" (10:1) and Noah as "the righteous man" who is saved from a flood (10:5). The author works through the story, attaching specific attributes to the unnamed characters: Adam, Cain and Abel, Noah, Abraham, Lot, Jacob, Joseph, and most extensively, Moses (10:16–11:14). The thread running through it is the punishment of the wicked and the protection provided to the righteous, with the story moving toward the ransom of the Israelite people from Egypt and the punishment of the Egyptians for their idolatry (Wis 12–14).

Similarly, in *On the Virtues*, Philo provides no names, but clearly alludes to Adam and Eve, Cain and Abel, Noah, Ham, Shem, and Japheth, in a short essay devoted to the thesis that nobility derives from virtue rather than from high birth. The point is demonstrated above all by Adam, who had more nobility of origin than any other human, since he was shaped directly by God, but who nevertheless suffered the punishment that was due his lack of virtue (*On the Virtues* 198–205). In these Hellenistic Jewish writings, we see a shift from recitations that focus on the people as a whole—either to celebrate God's goodness or mercy, or to warn against a heritage of rebellion—to a focus on individuals as moral exemplars (both positive and negative) for the readers.

The tendency is obvious in the recitations concerning the past found in the Maccabean books. In 1 Macc 2:51–59 we find an extremely compressed list that includes Abraham, Joseph, Phinehas, Joshua, Caleb, David, Elijah, and then more recent heroes: Hananiah, Azariah, and Mishael (the LXX version of the Three Young Men of the book of Daniel), and Daniel himself. Short as the list is, it contains short characterizations of each figure that makes them deserve "great honor and an everlasting name" (2:51). Abraham was tested, Joseph met distress, Phinehas was zealous, and so on. The point? "Observe from generation to generation, that none of those who put their trust in him will lack strength" (2:61).

Likewise, 4 Macc 16:2–25 lists those who demonstrated that "devout reason is sovereign over the emotions" (16:1): Daniel, Mishael, the mother of the seven brothers, Eleazar, Hananiah, Azariah, Abraham, Isaac, and Jacob. A more elaborate version appears in 4 Macc 18:1–19, again with the purpose of showing that "devout reason is master of all emotions" (18:2). The list includes those who suffered for the sake of the law and "were not only admired by men but were also deemed worthy to share in a divine inheritance" (18:3). The list includes Abraham, Cain and Abel, Joseph, Phinehas, Hananiah, Azariah and Mishael, Daniel, Isaiah, David, Solomon, Ezekiel, and Moses. Distinctive to this list is the inclusion of quotations concerning affliction drawn from Isaiah, David, Solomon, and Moses.

The most elaborate example of an encomiastic list drawn from Scripture is surely that found in Sirach, which begins, "Now let us praise famous men" (Sir 44:1). The list starts with Enoch (44:16), and includes Noah (44:17–18), Abraham (44:19–21), Isaac (44:22), Jacob (44:23–45), Moses (45:1–5), Aaron (45:6–22), Phinehas (45:23–24), David (45:25–26), Joshua (46:1–7), Caleb (46:8–10), the judges (46:11–12), Samuel (46:13–20), Nathan (47:1), David again (47:2–11), Solomon (47:12–23), Rehoboam and Jeroboam (47:23–25), Elijah (48:1–11), Elisha (48:12–16), Hezekiah (48:17–29), Josiah (49:1–3), Jeremiah (49:6–7), Ezekiel (49:8–10), Zerubbabel (49:11), Jeshua (49:12), Nehemiah (49:13), Enoch (49:14), Joseph (49:15), Shem and Seth (49:16), and Adam (49:16). The climax is reached with the high priest Simon son of Onias (50:1–21).

Not only is the roll call extensive, it is notable for its selections—note the absence of Isaiah and the inclusion of Shem and Seth!—and for its sometimes lengthy characterizations. The list is also distinctive for its obvious focus on the priesthood (see the extensive treatment of Aaron and Simon). Some of the characterizations, as we have seen, correspond to ones we have observed in Heb 11, and like the author of Hebrews, Sirach is not terribly concerned with putting the figures in strict chronological sequence. Sirach does not, however, have the same strong thematic pulse as we have seen in Hebrews' repeated "in faith."

The distinctiveness of Heb 11 is clear also when it is compared to other New Testament recitals, both of which name certain figures in Israel's history, but with a purpose other than providing moral exemplars. In Stephen's speech before the Sanhedrin, the recital begins with Abraham, and includes Isaac, Jacob, Joseph (and his brothers), Moses, Aaron, David, and Solomon. The emphasis falls on the twofold appearance of Joseph and especially Moses, and the people's rejection of God's prophets (Acts 7:2–50). In his Letter to the Romans, Paul tells the story in a different way, in terms of a distinction between natural descent and descent according to the spirit, and in terms of a dialectic of acceptance and rejection involving Jews and Gentiles. Paul names Abraham, Sarah, Isaac, Rebecca, Jacob, Esau, Moses, Hosea, Isaiah, David, Elijah, and Isaiah, not as exemplars of virtue, but as figures who are caught up in God's working out of his plan in history (Rom 9:6–11:36). In comparison to these other New Testament renderings, Hebrews is far more positive, not only with respect to the faith demonstrated by humans from Abel to the Maccabees, but also with respect to their sharing in the inheritance with those who now follow Jesus as the pioneer and perfecter of faith (12:1–3).

12:1–17 Exhortation to Join the Pilgrimage of Faith

The author of Hebrews has masterfully alternated exposition and exhortation throughout the composition. Having led his hearers through the exposition on the faith demonstrated by the heroes of Israel's past, he now shifts almost entirely to exhortation as he brings his composition to its conclusion. He seeks to draw his hearers, who are, we have learned, weary and disheartened because of very real sufferings (10:32–34), into an enthusiastic participation in the pilgrimage of the people of faith toward the living God.

The intricacy of the author's argument can be shown by the recurrence of the image of Christ as the "pioneer and perfecter of faith" (12:2), which was presented first in 2:10. The author then elaborated a picture of the people "on the way" in 3:1–4:13 through recalling the wilderness generation that failed in faith. Next he developed the long argument concerning Jesus the priest, who was perfected through his obedient suffering and made it possible for others to enter God's presence as well. Then he returned to a depiction of the people Israel, making its pilgrimage toward a heavenly city through the ages and still poised to receive the promised rest that is found only in God. These themes are now pulled together, as he summons his hearers to look to Jesus as they, with the author, run the race that is set before them (12:1–2).

Even as he calls them to a renewed commitment to the pilgrimage of faith, however, the author needs to provide a final vital instruction. The image of "following Jesus," after all, is only an image. They require a deeper understanding of the essential link between their experience of suffering and shame, and the very process by which Jesus himself was brought to full perfection as son. Thus 12:4–11, which can easily be regarded as a digression, is actually one of the essential keys to the entire composition, as the author shows how suffering is to be regarded as an education in sonship. That point made, the author continues with his exhortation, characteristically emphasizing the danger of apostasy through the presentation of Esau as an example not to be imitated.

12:1 For this very reason, since we also have so great[a] a cloud of witnesses,
let us put aside every impediment and inhibiting[b] sin, and let us run with
endurance the race that is set before us. **2** Let us keep our eyes on Jesus,
the pioneer and perfecter of faith. He endured a cross,[c] despising its shame
for the sake of the joy that was set before him. He has taken a seat[d] at
the right hand of the throne of God. **3** Consider the one[e] who endured
such great opposition[f] directed toward him by sinners, so that you do not
become discouraged or dispirited.

4 In[g] your struggle against[h] sin, you have not yet resisted to the point
of blood. **5** And have you completely forgotten the exhortation that is
addressed to you as sons? "My[i] son, do not neglect the Lord's instruc-
tion, nor grow dispirited when you are rebuked by him. **6** The Lord
instructs the one he loves. And to every son he accepts, he applies the
whip." **7** You are enduring for the sake of[j] an education. God is treating
you as sons. Now to what son[k] does a father not provide education? **8** And
if you are left out of an instruction in which all have participated, then
you are not sons, you are bastards. **9** Moreover, we have had human
fathers as instructors and we showed them respect; shall we not even[l]
more subject ourselves to the Father of spirits,[m] and live? **10** They
instructed us for a few days according to their own view of things. But
he does it for our benefit, so that we can participate in his holiness. **11**
Now[n] all instruction, while it is going on, seems more a matter of grief
than of joy. But for those who have been fully trained, it yields in the end
the peaceful fruit that is righteousness.

12 Therefore, strengthen your drooping hands and wobbly knees, **13**
and make straight[o] paths for your feet, so that what is lame may not
become dislocated, but rather be healed. **14** Pursue peace with all people,
and the holiness apart from which no one will see the Lord. **15** Take care
that no one be excluded from God's gift. "Let no bitter root grow and
cause trouble,"[p] and through it[q] many[r] become defiled. **16** Let none of you
be a fornicator or profane person like Esau. He exchanged his[s] right[t] as a

firstborn for a single meal. 17 For you also know that afterward, he wanted to inherit the blessing. Even though he sought it with tears, he was rejected, for he found no opportunity to repent.

a. The original hand of א has *tēlikauton* rather than *tosouton*, but the meaning is the same in either case.

b. The diction is obscure: *euperistaton* is read by the best and most MSS; it means something like "easily ensnaring." P^{46} has *euperispaston*, which means "easily distracting." Neither term is widely attested.

c. Two early papyri (P^{13} and P^{46}) and the original hand of D add the definite article, to form "the cross," but the anarthrous version is both harder and better attested, therefore to be preferred.

d. P^{46} has the aorist tense, *ekathisen,* which would denote a discrete action, but the perfect tense *kekathiken*, which has the sense of a continuing effect, is found in all other MSS.

e. Several MSS, including P^{13} and P^{46}, omit the definite article as redundant. It is sufficiently well attested to retain. The omission also better fits the plural pronouns that follow.

f. A substantial number of witnesses (including P^{13} and P^{46}, as well as—with slight variations—the original hands of א and D) have *autous* or *heautous* ("them/themselves"), rather than the *heauton* ("himself"), read by A and a smaller set of MSS. The meaning would be quite different, making the object of their consideration not Jesus but the cloud of witnesses. Here the rhetorical logic must decide the issue against the bulk of the evidence.

g. The original hand of D and a few other MSS insert the inferential *gar* ("for"), which would have been expected and would make for a smoother transition.

h. P^{13} and P^{46} have *agōnizomenoi* ("your struggle") rather than *antagōnizomenoi* ("your struggle against"), but the variant does not affect the meaning.

i. The LXX does not contain the personal pronoun *mou* ("my"), which is also omitted from the citation by the original hand of D and a cluster of other witnesses.

j. Some few witnesses have *ei* ("if") rather than *eis* ("for"), which would dramatically change the meaning of the sentence: rather than "you are enduring for the sake of an education (*paideia*)," it would be, "if you are enduring instruction (*paideia*)."

k. The majority of MSS—including D and the corrector of א—supply the verb *estin* ("is") that seems to be demanded here. The shorter and harder reading is found in P^{13}, the original hand of א, and A.

l. The textual evidence for including or excluding the particle *de* is substantial on both sides. No great interpretive consequence results from either option.

m. The great majority of MSS read "of spirits" here. One MS has "of spiritual realities (*pneumatikōn*)" and a few others "of fathers (*paterōn*)."

n. Thinking that the particle *de* is redundant and wrongly placed (especially since its correlative *men* follows rather than precedes it, as normal), a number of scribes chose to omit it, but the *de* enjoys considerable and early MS support.

o. Perhaps considering the present imperative *poieite* (which implies continuing action) inappropriate, some witnesses—the second hand of א, as well as D and A—have the aorist imperative *poiēsate*, while another (048) has the simple future tense. The present tense is found in P^{46} and the original hand of א.

p. Although the verb *enochlē* seems to deviate from LXX *en cholē*, it is massively supported by the textual evidence, and could come from an alternative reading in the LXX tradition.

q. Many witnesses—א and D among them—have "through this" (*dia tautēs*) rather than "through it" (*di' autēs*). Both P[46] and A have the reading "through it," found in Nestle-Aland[27].

r. The evidence is evenly split between the MSS reading "the many" (*hoi polloi*) and those reading simply "many" (*polloi*). The temptation to supply the customary article may explain those including it.

s.The reflexive pronoun *heautou* ("his own") is found in P[46], א, A, and C, but is corrected to "his" (*autou*) by a later hand in א and is found in the original hand of D. The reflexive is the harder reading and therefore accepted as more likely being the original.

t. P[46] has the feminine plural *tas prōtotokeias* ("birthrights") rather than the neuter plural (*ta prōtotokia*) found in Nestle-Aland[27] and in the LXX.

[12:1–4] The entire section is dominated by a single complex metaphor whose basic structure must be grasped if we are to appreciate the flow of the author's exhortation. We saw in 10:32 that the author introduced an athletic image, when he recalled to his hearers the "great contest of sufferings" (*pollēn athlēsin*) that they had endured in their earlier days. Now that athletic image takes over, most obviously in the opening verses of chapter 12. Those who have been "wandering" and "moving about," we learn, are actually engaged in a journey with a goal and a reward. The image is that of the marathon run at the Olympic Games. The runners begin far away from the city in some remote place with few observers, move through growing crowds and greater fatigue, and finally emerge in the stadium before a massed assembly of spectators who watch and applaud as the runners complete their final lap. In these opening verses, the author makes that crowd of witnesses to be the earlier heroes of faith who have preceded the hearers in the pilgrimage of faith, but cannot finish the race without the present generation (11:40). So vivid is the metaphor (life = Olympic contest) that present-day readers might forget that this spatial and social imagery intends to communicate something about the moral life of believers: it has a start, it has difficulties and discouragements, there is a time lapse between start and finish, it requires endurance, and most of all there is a reward when the goal is reached. For the moral life depicted in terms of participation in athletic games, above all at Olympia, see Epictetus, *Discourses* 1.24.1–3; 3.22.51–52; 3.25.2–5; Cicero, *De officiis* 3.10.12.[1]

To speak of a "cloud" of witnesses simply adds another metaphorical layer. This is the only use of *nephos* in the New Testament, which prefers the term

1. For full discussion see N. C. Croy, *Endurance in Suffering: Hebrews 12:1–13 in Its Rhetorical, Religious, and Philosophical Context* (SNTSMS 98; Cambridge: Cambridge University Press, 1998).

nephelē (see Matt 17:5; Mark 13:26; Acts 1:9). The noun suggests a cluster that is at once dense and opaque, even dark, and is used in other literature for a crowd of people (see Herodotus 8.109; Diogenes Laertius, *Lives* 8.16). The noun "witness" (*martyr*) in this description certainly means something more than "spectator." These are the heroes of faith who have themselves been "witnessed to" through faith and by God (see Heb 11:2, 3, 5, 39). They are not simply onlookers; they are fellow pilgrims who have run the same course to which this generation of believers is committed. It is small wonder that this image of a "cloud of witnesses" lends itself so well to the belief in a communion of saints, bound together by the same life and effort. Indeed, the author has suggested that these witnesses themselves need the present generation to complete the race if they are themselves to be perfected (11:40). From the start of his discourse, the author has exhorted his hearers to pay attention to the all-seeing eyes of God as their judge rather than human opinion (4:11–13). Now the eyes of those who have struggled for the faith are added to this alternative court of opinion for the measuring of what is honorable and what is shameful.

Making the athletic imagery explicit, the author exhorts his hearers to "run the race that is set before us," once more identifying himself with his audience by using the first person plural. The term *agōna* can apply to any athletic contest from racing to wrestling. But here it must be translated as "race" because of the verb *trechein* ("to run"; cf. Euripides, *Orestes* 847; Herodotus 8.102; 9.60.1; 7.11.3; Plato, *Phaedrus* 247B; Lucian, *Gymnosophists* 15; Philo, *Allegorical Laws* 3.48). This race—the movement of their lives of faith toward God—will require of them that they endure (*di' hypomonēs*), a virtue that the hearers had demonstrated earlier when experiencing tribulations (10:32), and to which the author again summoned them (10:36).

Even before enduring the rigors of a long race, however, they must prepare by divesting themselves of anything that might hold them back. The participle *apothemenoi* ("putting aside") is used in other New Testament compositions for the taking off of qualities as though they were clothes (Rom 13:12; Eph 4:22, 25; Col 3:8; Jas 1:21; 1 Pet 2:1). Here it is a matter of eliminating the "weight" that holds them back—we find the same concern among present-day runners who wear aerodynamic running suits and swimmers who shave their bodies. The noun *onchos* is otherwise unattested in the New Testament and LXX, but occurs in Hellenistic Jewish writings (e.g., Josephus, *J.W.* 4.319; 7.443). The weight is once more metaphorical, standing for moral qualities that might impede their growth in faith. What could count as such an "impediment" (as I have translated)? If we are to take seriously the entire preceding argument, we would have to list all the possessions that could tempt them to avoid the sort of suffering that following in the path of Jesus involves, including property, safety, and honor (see 10:32–34). It is possible that "inhibiting sin" is simply a way of making "impediment" more specific, but it more likely refers to the spirit of rebellion that the author in 3:13 associated with *hamartia* ("sin"), or the way in which *hamartia* can offer a temporary advantage that draws one away from the oppressed people, as in the case of Moses (11:25). As the textual notes indicate, we cannot achieve much more precision than this, since both of the terms offered by the textual witnesses are obscure.

As they set out on the race laid before them, they are above all to "keep their eyes" (*aphorōntes*; see Phil 2:23) on Jesus, the one who runs ahead of them and has already finished the race that is the life of faith. It is, to be sure, a striking statement, notable first for its use of the simple name Jesus, emphasizing in a manner characteristic of Hebrews the shared humanity of Jesus and those who follow after him (Heb 2:9; 3:1; 6:20; 7:22; 10:19; 12:24; 13:12). Second, it is notable for having them visually imagine Jesus running ahead of them on the same course. Third, the epithet "pioneer (*archēgos*) and perfecter (*teleiōtēs*) of faith" echoes two earlier statements concerning Jesus. In 2:10 the author had stated that it was fitting for the God who was leading many sons to glory to "perfect the pioneer of their salvation through suffering." And in 10:14 he declared that "through one offering he has perfected forever those who are being sanctified." By attaching the terms "pioneer" and "perfecter" specifically to the noun "faith" (*pistis*), the author not only brings to a climax the exposition that began in 11:1 (or more properly, 10:36), but also makes clear that this "race" is a matter of moral and religious transformation in which the "faithful" Jesus (3:1) and believers are intimately linked.

This climactic presentation of Jesus as the hearer's moral exemplar also echoes the very beginning of the composition, where the author stated of the Son, "having made purification for sins, he took a seat at the right hand of the majesty on high" (1:3). That same pattern is now traced in terms of Jesus' human disposition of faith. He also "endured a cross" (*hypemeinen stauron*). Remarkably, for all the references to Jesus' suffering and death earlier in this discourse (2:10, 14, 18; 4:15; 5:2, 7–8; 9:12, 14; 10:19), this is the only time Hebrews mentions the actual instrument of Jesus' execution. Equally remarkable, he says nothing here about the physical dimensions of Jesus' death on the cross. The author focuses instead on crucifixion's being the most shameful of all deaths in antiquity.[2] Jesus' obedient faith is expressed by his "despising the shame" (*aischynēs kataphronēsas*) of the cross.

Such a reversal of perception—despising that which was antiquity's greatest source of shame—was possible because Jesus looked to God as the source of his honor and glory, rather than to the court of human opinion. By the mystery of God's will, the shameful cross is the instrument of entry into the authentic glory and honor with which God crowns Jesus (see 2:7, 9; 3:3; 5:4). That

2. See M. Hengel, *Crucifixion in the Ancient World and the Folly of the Message of the Cross*, trans. J. Bowden (Philadelphia: Fortress Press, 1977).

Jesus could "despise the shame" of the cross also made him the model for those who have experienced shame and affliction because of their allegiance to him (10:33). The phrase that I have translated "for the sake (*anti*) of the joy (*chara*) that was set before him" represents an exegetical as well as a translation decision. This sense of *anti* is well attested in the positive sense of "for," as when the author says in 12:16 that Esau exchanged his birthright for the sake of a single meal. Aristotle says that people can even endure pain and disgrace "for (*anti*) some great and noble object" (*Nicomachean Ethics* 1165A). But *anti* can also be read as "instead of." Here the example of Moses might be adduced: he considered the reproach of the Messiah as "greater wealth" than the riches of Egypt (11:26). Yet, even in the case of Moses, he chose to associate himself with the oppressed people of God because he "looked to the reward."[3]

That Jesus endured for the sake of the reward would not appear morally problematic in the least for ancient readers, certainly not within the context of the athletic metaphor for moral endeavor. And it once more reveals Jesus as the model for those who have endured and do endure with an eye to the reward that God gives to those who seek him (10:34, 35, 36, 39), and who can observe among the crowd of witnesses those who have looked to God as the one who rewards (11:6, 10, 14–16, 26). The reward for Jesus was his exaltation to the right hand of God. The echo of 1:3 reminds us again of the pervasive presence of Ps 109:1–4 throughout this composition.

The author now turns his hearers' attention from the reward that was Christ's exaltation to the enormity of his suffering. He does not focus on the physical suffering that was inevitable in crucifixion, but on the experience of opposition from others. He tells them to "consider (*analogisasthe*) the one who endured such great opposition (*antilogian*) directed toward him by sinners." The verb *analogizomai* suggests not simply the fixing of mental attention (see Plato, *Republic* 330E; Xenophon, *Memorabilia* 2.1.4), or even the making of a comparison (Plato, *Theaetetus* 186A; Aristotle, *Politics* 1320B). By considering "how great" (*toiautēn*) was the opposition directed against Jesus by sinners (*hamartōloi*), they are better to assess their own. The term "sinners" here can refer only to those who opposed Jesus during his human ministry and were responsible for his shameful death. Despite this great opposition, Jesus "endured," and thus provides the model for the community addressed by the author. And calculating the difference between the shame they have experienced from their neighbors and that experienced by Jesus, they should not grow "discouraged" (*kamēte tais psychais*) or "dispirited" (*eklyomenoi*).

The diction again suggests the metaphor underlying this section of exhortation. The verb *kamnein* means to be weary or fatigued (see 4 Macc 3:8), and one would be that way at the end of a race or after a long wrestling contest.

3. For discussion see P. E. Bonnard, "La traduction de Hébreux 12,2: 'C'est en vue de la joie que Jesus endura la croix,'" *NRT* 97 (1975): 415–23; and P. Andriessen, "Renonçant à la joie qui lui revenait," *NRT* 97 (1975): 424–38.

Here, however, it is not physical exhaustion but that affecting the spirit (*tais psychais*; see Philo, *Posterity of Cain* 31; Josephus, *Ant.* 2.290). Similarly, the participle *eklyomenoi* signifies physical weariness (Josephus, *Ant.* 5.134), but also appears figuratively for psychological dispiritedness (see Polybius, *History* 20.4.7). The choice of the verb *eklyein* itself may have been influenced by its appearance in Prov 3:11, which the author is about to cite.

The author reminds the hearers of the conclusion they should reach by means of their reckoning. Jesus shed his blood, but they "have not yet resisted to the point of blood." The verb *antagōnizomai* fits within the language of the games, suggesting in particular the struggles involved in wrestling with opponents, rather than racing on a track. Jesus was opposed by "sinners" and was put to death. The hearers are resisting "sin" in a moral battle, and although they have indeed suffered taunts and even the loss of their property, they need a sense of "proportion" (*analogia*): they are not yet in the position of Jesus or even in the position of those heroes of faith who experienced such chilling forms of torture and execution (11:36–38).

[5–13] These verses are critical to understanding both the Christology of Hebrews and its vision of discipleship. Yet, because the metaphorical field within which they work is often missed, the following section can be regarded as the intrusion of an offensively banal bit of advice. We are, in fact, within the same metaphor as in 12:1–4, where the moral life was sketched in terms of participation in athletic games. The first clue is the use of the verb *gymnazomai* in 12:11, and the second is the consistent use of *paideia* throughout the passage.

These verbal clues point us in the direction of the ancient gymnasium as the locus both of sports and education, where the "training" (*gymnazein*) of body and mind went together, where the exercising of physical muscles and the exercising of moral faculties (see 5:4) were learned through instruction and practice and discipline. The gymnasium was the place of preparation for participation in a great athletic contest (10:32) before a great cloud of witnesses (12:1), and it was the place as well for the preparation of the mind and will of young men who were to take up full participation as citizens in the life of the Greek *polis*.[4] The main point here is that the physical and mental activities were so intertwined that the term *paideia* could be used for the entire process of instruction, as well as for the "instruction" that addressed the mind and the "discipline" that addressed the body.

So central was this institution and its practices to Greek life that it is no wonder that the term *paideia* can mean "education" and also "culture" in the broadest sense, for the entire point of the process of education/training was to socialize young men into the mores and values of Greek culture.[5] What is of importance in all this for the passage in Hebrews is that we understand the same subject

4. See E. N. Gardiner, *Athletics of the Ancient World* (Chicago: Ares, 1980).

5. See, e.g., the classic study of W. Jaeger, *Paideia: The Ideals of Greek Culture*, trans. G. Highet, 3 vols. (New York: Oxford University Press, 1939–45).

matter to be running through the entire discussion: the hearers' transformation into "sons" who are "perfected" through the suffering ingredient to obedient faith, as was their pioneer, Jesus.

Although the first part of verse 5 is often punctuated as a statement (see NRSV), I think it works better as a question. As a good rhetorician, the author reminds his readers of what they appear to have "completely forgotten" (*eklelēsthe*), just as in 10:32 he tells them to "remember" (*anamimnēskesthe*) their earlier enthusiasm. In this case it is a passage of Scripture (Prov 3:11–12) that the author introduces in two ways. First, he calls the passage a *paraklēsis*, the same term he uses for his own composition (13:22), and which can bear the sense of "comfort" as well as of "exhortation." The Scripture passage contains both. Second, the author contemporizes the passage: it does not simply speak to ancient students of the sages. It speaks for God, who now addresses the author and his hearers as "sons" (*hymin hōs huiois*). It is, therefore, about their present education as "sons" that Scripture is understood to speak.

The citation from the LXX is precise, except that many manuscripts add the personal pronoun "my" (*mou*), to form "my son." Otherwise, the text of Scripture is thought to speak clearly and directly to the author's own day. What is God telling them in these words? The two sentences go together, with the connective *gar* in verse 6 indicating that it explains the previous statement. The son is not to "neglect" (*oligōrei*) the Lord's instruction (*paideia*). The verb means to "treat as little or lesser" and tilts the response in the direction of "despise" (see Josephus, *Ant.* 5.132; *Ag. Ap.* 2.172). And although *paideia* is often translated as "discipline" (NRSV, NAB), it must here bear the broader meaning of "instruction," which includes but is not limited to forms of discipline. The son is not to treat the instruction of the father lightly or dismissively, but neither is he to "shrink away" or "grow dispirited" by being rebuked or corrected (*elenchomenos*). The text of Proverbs here provides one of the verbs (*eklyein*) that the author used for his hearers in 12:3. If the son treats the instruction too lightly, he cannot be educated; but if he cowers before correction, he cannot be educated either. How, then, does verse 6 provide the proper understanding? First, the son must grasp that instruction is an expression of love from father to son. Second, the son must understand that the son who is fully accepted by the father will indeed be disciplined—the application of the whip (*mastigoi*) prevents the son from self-destruction through failure to recognize the dangers in certain behaviors.

The next statement in verse 7, then, should be read within this broad educational/cultural/athletic metaphor-field. Translations of *eis paideian hypomenete* as a command ("endure for the sake of discipline") do not actually make sense: it is the instruction that makes endurance necessary; one would not endure in order to bring about discipline. I think that it is far better to read the verb as the present indicative, namely as the author's clarification of their experience in light of the scriptural citation: "you are enduring for the sake of an education."

What sort of education is God providing them? It is not simply that God is treating them in the manner that fathers treat their sons; rather, God is treating them "as sons," that is, as God's own sons.

Here is the essential link between Christology and discipleship. From 2:10 we learned that God intended not only to perfect Jesus as Son through his suffering, but that Jesus was to be the pioneer of "many sons" whom God would lead to glory, that is, to God's own presence. By now designating his hearers as "sons" whom God is educating, the author picks up from that earlier statement, and from the characterization of Jesus as "pioneer and perfecter of faith" in 12:2. We remember also how the author spoke of Jesus' own process of perfecting in 5:7–10: "although he was a son, he learned (*emathen*) obedience from the things he suffered (*epathen*)." In commenting on that passage, I noted the use of the Hellenistic educational maxim, *mathein pathein*, "to learn is to suffer" or "to suffer is to learn."

The suffering experienced by Jesus was integral to his obedient and faithful response to God. In just the same manner, the author here insists, the sufferings experienced by these discouraged and dispirited Christians are the very means by which they are now to be educated into the status of "sons" like the Son of God, Jesus. When the author declares in 12:7 that "God is treating you as sons," he means also that "God is treating you as God treated his own beloved Son."

Once the link between education and the father-son relationship is established, the author can elaborate four dimensions of that relationship. Each sentence exploits the analogy between the human parental role and the divine. The first statement begins with a rhetorical question, "What father does not educate his son?" The intended answer must be, "There is none." It is unthinkable. The elaboration in the next sentence reveals two cultural assumptions built into the question. The first is that within the Hellenistic household, it was the father's responsibility to oversee the education of sons once they had passed from the care of mothers and pedagogues (see Plutarch, *Education of Children* 7–9; *Mor.* 4B–7C). This assumption underlies a number of other New Testament passages (see 1 Cor 4:15–20; Gal 4:19; 1 Thess 2:11; 2 Tim 2:1). The second Greco-Roman cultural assumption is that such education was restricted to "freeborn," that is, legitimate, children. Bastard offspring were not regarded as having a moral claim for such education in citizenship. The corollary of receiving education, therefore, is that God regards them as his true sons, children who are, as Scripture attests, "loved" and "accepted."

The next elaboration of the analogy, in verse 9, takes the form of a "lesser to greater" argument, so characteristic of this composition. If the hearers show respect (*enetrepometha*) to the "fathers in the flesh" (*tēs sarkos hēmon pateras*), should they "not even more (*ou poly de mallon*)" submit themselves to the Father of spirits and live? Three aspects of this rhetorical question deserve particular attention. The first is that this is the only time Hebrews uses the designation "father" for God in respect to others than Jesus (see 1:5). Such reticence is the more surprising in light of other New Testament compositions that call God "Father" with great frequency (see only Matt 26:39; Mark 11:25; Luke 9:26; John 1:14; Rom 1:7; 1 Cor 8:6; 2 Cor 1:3; Gal 4:6; Eph 1:7; Phil 2:11; Col 3:17; 1 Thess 1:1; 2 Thess 2:16; 1 Tim 1:2; 2 Tim 1:2; Titus 1:4; Phlm 3; Jas 1:17; 1 Pet 1:2; 2 Pet 1:17; 1 John 1:2; 2 John 3; Jude 1; Rev 1:6). Second, God is called the Father "of spirits" (*tōn pneumatōn*), which is unusual though not entirely unattested (see Num 16:22; 27:16; *Jub.* 10.3).

We will see later in the chapter that the pilgrims approach the "city of the living God" where "spirits of righteous people . . . have been brought to perfection" (12:22–23). The designation might, then, mean simply, "Father of all living beings," that is, who live with authentic life. This is in fact the implication of the third aspect of the statement: submission to the Father of spirits means "we will live" (*kai zēsomen*). We have seen earlier in the composition that "life" (*zōē*) and "living" (*zēn*) are understood in this composition above all in terms of sharing in God's own existence (2:15; 3:12; 4:12; 7:3, 8, 16, 25; 9:14, 17; 10:20, 31). Indeed, that is the promise expressed by the prophet Habakkuk, "my righteous one will live from faith" (Hab 2:4), the citation of which headed up the author's long encomium on faith (10:38). We are therefore to see our "submission" to the Father in terms of the obedience of faith demonstrated by Jesus, and our "living" as a share in God's life that is the reward for those who have such faith, a reward secured for all who follow by Jesus, who has gone there first through his exaltation to the right hand of God's throne (12:2).

The third elaboration of the analogy (in v. 10) provides a twofold contrast between God's instruction and that carried out by human fathers. The first is that human fathers can only instruct according to their own perceptions and often their own prejudices (*kata to dokoun autois*). God's instruction, however, is always *epi to sympheron* ("for our benefit"). The term *sympheron* is used widely in moral discourse for what is to one's advantage or benefit (see Plato, *Republic* 341E; Epictetus, *Discourses* 2.22.20; Josephus, *Ant.* 1.162; *J.W.* 1.158; *Life* 48, 370; 4 Macc 5:11). God's instruction leads us to what is truly our advantage. The second contrast is similar to the one Hebrews has consistently drawn with respect to the earthly cult and the eternal priesthood of Jesus. Human fathers instruct "for a few days"—their influence is temporary and transitory. But God's instruction prepares us for God's own presence, so that we can participate (*metalabein*) in his holiness (*tēs hagiotētos autou*). In short, the instruction as sons that is being given to these followers of Jesus is to prepare them for a share in God's own power and presence, the holiness that Jesus himself has entered before them (see 2:11; 6:4; 8:2; 9:12, 24; 10:10, 14, 19, 29).

The final elaboration of the analogy in 12:11 contrasts the pain of the experience with the joy of the result. As long as any instruction or discipline is ongoing (*to paron*) it causes *lypē* ("sorrow" or "grief") rather than *chara* ("joy"). We see here precisely the structure of the exhortation of the letter as a whole, and the example of Jesus, who endured the cross "for the joy (*chara*) that was set before him" (12:2). No student of any art or craft would disagree, nor would the practitioner of any sport: the practice involved in any training is most often painful, a stretching of muscles and emotions and ideas. It is the result that brings joy. Those who are "thoroughly trained" (the nuance of the perfect tense, *gegymnasmenois*) receive back as their reward "a peaceful fruit of righteousness." This conclusion echoes the statement in 5:13–14, where the author contrasted an infant "untested by a word of righteousness" to a mature person, who is able to eat solid food (cf. *karpos*, "fruit," here), those who have their moral habits thoroughly trained for the discrimination between good and evil. The struggle of learning gives way to the peace given by a maturity measured by "the righteous one" who truly lives out of faith (10:36).

Having clarified what is happening to them in their afflictions, the author closes this paragraph with a return to the physical imagery of the race or athletic competition, which stands for their pilgrimage toward God. They are to "straighten up," that is, strengthen, their drooping hands and wobbly knees—corresponding to their discouragement and dispiritedness—and make straight paths for their feet. If they do not become healed, then their disability will grow even greater. Many of the Greek terms in verses 12–13 are obscure, but the thrust of the argument is clear enough. The language about hands and knees stands for dispositions of fidelity and endurance. The call to make straight paths for the feet is a call to continued progress in their moral transformation, their education in sonship, the participation in the great pilgrimage of faith toward the living God.

[14–17] The author now shifts from his extended sports/education metaphor to some straightforward exhortation. As always, the focus is on fidelity to their commitment, now spelled out in terms of their relationship to God and to other humans. On one side, they are to "pursue peace with all people" (*eirēnēn diōkete meta pantōn*). The theme of peace was initiated in 7:2, where Melchizedek's rule over Salem was interpreted as his being "king of peace." In 11:32 we learned that Rahab received Israelite spies "in peace." And in 13:20 the author will pray to "the God of peace" for his hearers. Most pertinently, we have just read in 12:11 that the fully educated person will receive "the peaceful fruit that is righteousness." The pursuit of peace, then, is a natural expression of righteousness. There is no reason to think that this pursuit of peace should include only members of the community. Indeed, pursuing peace "with all people" seems particularly important—and particularly difficult—in conditions of oppression. The author asks them both to remain constant to their confession and to seek peace even with those who mock them and do them harm.

They are also to pursue "the holiness apart from which no one will see the Lord." As with the pursuit of peace, the present imperative can suggest the continuation of efforts already begun: "go on seeking." Throughout this composition, the term "holiness" (*hagiasmos*) means much more than the ritual demarcation of times and places as dedicated to God (the sacred as opposed to the profane). It means the transformation of life dedicated to God. Sanctification as something that can be pursued is the human search for full entry into the presence of the one who, through Christ's spirit, is already present to them. Understanding "holiness" as shorthand for God's presence and power enables us to understand as well that "seeing God" is not physical sight (as in the vision of Moses and the elders of the people in Exod 24:10), but rather full participation in God's life, or, as the author stated in Heb 12:10, "to share in his holiness" (*metalabein tēs hagiotētos autou*).

Corresponding to "seeking peace with all people" is the author's warning in 12:15 about falling short of God's gift and allowing a "root of bitterness" to grow. The use of the verb *hysteroun* ("to fall short, to lack") recalls the warning in 4:1 that follows the display of the negative example provided by the wilderness generation. They fell short by their faithlessness and disobedience, and did not enter the land. The odd expression concerning the root of bitterness or "bitter root" (*rhiza pikrias*) returns us to that desert context and to the warnings delivered by Moses to the people while still in the wilderness. In Deut 29:17 Moses speaks of the bitter root as a member of the covenant people who thinks he is safe because he belongs to this people, even if he walks "in the stubbornness of his heart."

Deuteronomy 29:19 declares that the result of such double-mindedness would be the "sweeping away of dry and moist alike." The implication is that each member of the community must authentically live out the demands of covenant not only for their own sake but for the sake of the community as a whole. Their apostasy threatens the safety and integrity of all. This is made clear by the next clause, "and through it [the bitter root] many become defiled (*mianthōsin*)." Defilement stands over against the holiness that is to characterize the community (see 1 Macc 1:63; *Let. Aris.* 166; Josephus, *J.W.* 4.323; *T. Benj.* 8.3; Titus 1:15).

Corresponding to seeking God's holiness, in turn, is the warning against becoming like Esau, Jacob's brother (Heb 12:16–17). The thought remains consistent, for the designation of Esau as a *pornos* ("fornicator") means he is a covenant breaker. In the dominant biblical tradition, just as marriage served to symbolize the covenant relationship between the Lord and the people, so fornication symbolized apostasy through the practice of idolatry (see, e.g., Deut 31:16; Num 14:33; Hos 1:2; Jer 2:20). Similarly, to be *bebēlos* ("profane") means precisely to be unconcerned with the demands of God's holiness (Lev 10:10; 21:9; Ezek 4:14; 21:25; 22:36; 3 Macc 2:14, 17; Philo, *Moses* 2.158; *Allegorical Laws* 1.62; Josephus, *J.W.* 6.271; *Ant.* 15.20; 1 Tim 1:9; 4:7; 6:20; 2 Tim 2:16).

Scripture itself, to be sure, calls Esau neither of these things. The author of Hebrews is here relying, as in other places, on the sort of traditions that Jewish interpreters had developed on the basis of clues provided by Scripture's silences as well as its statements. Genesis 25:27–28 calls Esau a skillful hunter, a man of the open air, whom his father Isaac loved because of the game he provided. Rebekah, in contrast, preferred the quiet Jacob who lived in tents. The incident to which Hebrews alludes occurs in Gen 25:29–34. Coming in hungry from the field, Esau asks Jacob for some of the red pottage he had prepared. Jacob responds, *apodou moi sēmeron ta prōtotokia sou emoi* ("Give in return to me this day your birthright"), words that Hebrews faithfully echoes in its statement. The exchange is made, and Esau's appetite is satisfied. But Gen 25:34 comments, *kai ephaulisen Esau ta prōtotokia* ("and Esau despised his birthright").

The next time we see Esau in Scripture is in Gen 26:34–35, when he marries two Hittite women, who caused conflict with Rebekah and Isaac. The marrying of two foreign women could easily, in light of later standards, be regarded by Jews as the equivalent of "fornication/idolatry," especially since Esau is also identified as Edom (Gen 25:30), which in later Jewish lore becomes the code word for the Roman Empire, and therefore the chief example of an idolatrous, sexually promiscuous people. For ancient moral logic generally, incontinence with respect to food is integrally linked to incontinence with respect to sex, and that may be the basis for the harsh characterization of Esau here and in other Jewish texts (see Philo, *Virtues* 208; *Allegorical Laws* 3.139–40; *Jub.* 25.1–8; *Gen. Rab.* 65; *Exod. Rab.* 116a; *b. Baba Batra* 16b).

The author assumes that the hearers know all this, so he concludes this section by stating "for you know that" (*iste gar hoti*), which serves both to remind and slightly to rebuke those who are in danger of forgetting fundamental truths (cf. Rom 11:2; 1 Cor 3:16; 5:6; 6:2–3; Jas 1:19; 4:4). The lesson drawn from Esau's behavior is that he was excluded from the blessing that would give him the inheritance. We note the use here of *klēronomia* ("inheritance"), which plays such a strong thematic role throughout the letter (1:2, 14; 6:17; 9:15; 11:7). Moreover, he could not get it back once he had abandoned it, even though he "sought it with tears." The author alludes to Gen 27:30–40: Esau seeks the blessing from Isaac and is told that his brother Jacob had been blessed instead. Esau "cried out with a loud cry and great bitterness (*pikran sphodra*)" (Gen 27:34). He does finally receive a secondary blessing from his father, but he is not able to "inherit" as he should have as firstborn, because of his impulsive action.

The mention of "tears" is particularly interesting precisely because it is absent from the LXX. Does the author want us to be reminded of the "great cry and tears" attributed to Jesus in the days of his flesh, when he prayed to the God who was able to save him from death? Jesus, the author told us, was heard because of his *eulabeia* (5:7). He did not need to repent, because he was without sin (4:15) and had sought his father's will from the moment of his entrance into the world

(10:5–10). It was, indeed, his unfailing obedient faith that gave him entrance into his eternal inheritance (1:2, 4). From Esau the hearers are to draw the opposite lesson, which the author has been emphasizing from the start of the composition, for Esau "found no opportunity to repent." The expression *topos metanoias* ("place for repentance") is attested elsewhere (see Wis 12:10; *4 Ezra* 9.12; *2 Bar.* 85.12; *1 Clem.* 7.5). For our author, Esau's rejection of his birthright was a form of apostasy. Esau stands as an example to the hearers of this discourse, that repentance from such a fundamental turning away, such a "despising" of God's gift, is not an option (see Heb 2:3; 4:1–2; 6:4–8; 10:26–31).

12:18–29 Approaching the Living God

Here at the end of the author's long discourse comes the final use of the argument *a minore ad maius* ("from the lesser to the greater") that has structured so much of the composition. Using the same verb "you have come" at the beginning of verses 18 and 22, he contrasts the experience of fearsome power by the Israelites when their pilgrimage from Egypt brought them to Mount Sinai, where they received the law from Moses, to the experience of his hearers who have come, at the end of their pilgrimage of faith, to the presence of the living God through Jesus (12:18–24). The contrast is spelled out on one side by a set of terms that describe all the physical phenomena accompanying the giving of the law, and on the other side by a set of terms describing the spiritual realities experienced through Christ. No matter how great and fear-inspiring the events accompanying the covenant under Moses, the realities of the new covenant mediated by the blood of Jesus are greater, for they have to do with the actual experience of the living God.

That comparison made, the author turns to a final warning (12:19–29). If the gift given now is so much greater, then the peril facing those who reject or abuse it is greater as well. Once again, the argument is from the lesser to the greater. Those who rejected the one who spoke from earth could not escape. What chance do those have who reject the one who now speaks from heaven? The composition returns to its starting point: the God who spoke in the past speaks "better" and more powerfully now through his Son (see 1:1). In response to the presence of God, who is a "devouring fire," dispositions of reverence and awe are demanded; in response to the gift of an "unshakeable kingdom," the acceptable worship of thanksgiving is appropriate.

> **12:18** For you have not come to something that can be touched[a] and a blaz-
> ing fire and darkness and gloom[b] and whirlwind, **19** a blast of trumpet and
> sound of words. Those hearing it asked that no more[c] word be spoken to
> them,[d] **20** for they could not bear what was being commanded. If even an

animal touched the mountain, it was stoned. 21 And so fearful was the
sight that Moses said, "I am terrified and trembling."[e] 22 Rather, you have
come to Mount Zion and[f] a city of the living God, a heavenly Jerusalem,
and to multitudes[g] of angels in festal gathering, 23 and to an assembly of
firstborn enrolled in heaven, and to God, judge of all, and to spirits[h] of
righteous people who have been brought to perfection,[i] 24 and to Jesus,
the mediator of a new covenant, and to a sprinkling of blood that is speak-
ing better[j] than Abel.[k]

25 Watch that you do not reject the one who is speaking. For if those
people did not escape[l] when they had rejected the one[m] who warned them
on earth, how much less shall we, if we turn away from the one from
heaven,[n] 26 whose voice then shook the earth, but now makes a promise
that says, "Once more I will shake[o] not only the earth but also the heaven."
27 Now the "once more" indicates the removal of what was being shak-
en[p] as things that have been made, so that the things not shaken might
remain. 28 Therefore, since we have received an unshakeable kingdom,
let us[q] give thanks. Through it let us offer acceptable worship[r] to God with
reverence and awe.[s] 29 For[t] indeed our God is a consuming fire.

a. The majority of MSS, including D, supplies the expected noun "mountain" (*orei*) here, but the shorter and harder reading that omits it (thereby making *psēlaphōmenō* a substantive) is sufficiently well attested to make it the preferred reading.

b. A substantial number of witnesses, among them P[46] and the second corrector of ℵ, have the more common noun *skotō* ("darkness") rather than the rare *zophō* ("gloom"), but it is attested by the original hand of ℵ and D, as well as by A and C.

c. The original version of ℵ and a few other MSS drop the negative particle *mē*, probably because the verb *paraitēomai* was understood as "refuse" (as in 12:5) rather than as "ask," in which case the negative would be redundant.

d. A replaces the aorist passive infinitive *prostethēnai* with the active voice, *prostheinai*, which would require taking God as the implied subject.

e. ℵ and the original hand of D have *ektromos* rather than *entromos*, read by the majority of witnesses. There is no difference in meaning.

f. The original hand of D omits the *kai* ("and"), which would make the asyndeton between "Mount Zion" and "city of God" severe. It is the shorter and harder reading, to be sure, but undoubtedly arose mechanically because of the frequent recurrence of *kai* in these lines.

g. The original hand of D again has a unique reading, replacing "a multitude of angels" (*myriasin angelōn*) with "many holy ones" (*myriōn hagiōn*).

h. The original hand of D and several Latin witnesses have *pneumati* ("a spirit") rather than *pneumasi* ("spirits"), clearly a misreading of the version found in all other witnesses.

i. The original version of ℵ has *teleiōn dedikiōmenois* ("righteous ones from among the perfect") and the original hand of D has "of the righteous who have been established (as a foundation)." Neither has a strong claim to be considered original.

j. P[46] has a distinctive reading, making a plural noun *kreittona* ("better things") rather than the neuter singular *kreitton* used as a comparative with *para*.

k. P[46] and some Latin versions have *to Abel* rather than *ton Abel*, making *Abel* a genitive and *to* referring back to "the blood" (*to haima*). The blood of Jesus would then be speaking better than the blood of Abel (see 11:4).

l. The majority of witnesses (including P[46], D, and the second corrector of א) have the simpler form *ephygon* rather than the compound *exephygon*, which is read by the original hand of א, A, and others. For *ekphygein* see also 2:3.

m. Some witnesses rearrange the sequence of words here, since the present arrangement could yield the translation "did not escape upon earth the one warning them," rather than "did not escape the one warning them upon the earth," but the sequence in Nestle-Aland[27] is attested by P[46] and the best uncials.

n. Some MSS prefer the singular *ouranou* to the plural *ouranōn* for "from heaven," but the plural enjoys overwhelming support.

o. The present tense of *seiō* ("I shake") is found in many MSS, probably under the influence of the LXX of Hag 2:21, where the present tense appears. The future is the harder reading and is well attested (see, e.g., P[46], א, A).

p. There is considerable uncertainty concerning the presence of the definite article *tēn* preceding the participle "of what was being shaken." If the article is dropped, then we must translate "a removal" rather than "the removal."

q. Some MSS (P[46], א, and others) have the present indicative of *echomen* rather than the subjunctive, which would demand "we are giving thanks" rather than "let us give thanks" (found in the correction of P[46] and in A). Here and in the following case, the subjunctive makes better sense of the sentence in context.

r. The present indicative *latreuomen* ("we are offering worship") is found in the same MSS that have "we give thanks" in the preceding phrase. Once more, the subjunctive is both well attested and logical in context.

s. Some witnesses reverse the sequence of the two nouns, and others replace *deous* ("awe") with *aidous* ("respect"). The version here translated is supported by P[46], the original hand of א, A, C, and D.

t. D replaces the *kai* ("and") with *kyrios* ("lord"), creating, "for the Lord our God," rather than "for indeed our God." This singular reading is overwhelmed by a consensus among other witnesses.

[12:18–24] With the statement "you have come" (*proselēlythate*) in 12:18 and 22, the author solemnly affirms that they have, in principle and in their imagination, if not yet fully with respect to their mortal lives, reached the goal of their pilgrimage. The vision he presents, to be sure, is proleptic. If they had literally "arrived" then there would have been no need for the exhortation to endurance, no need for warnings against falling away. But as a stirring conclusion to his exhortation, the author provides his hearers with an imaginative sense of what their inheritance, what their reward, might be. Those hearing the discourse in Greek would recognize in the very words "you have arrived/approached" (*proserchein*) the climax to the series of statements concerning "approaching the throne of grace" (4:6) that is God's presence (see 7:25; 10:1, 22; 11:6).

As so often in this composition, the author develops the image by means of *synkrisis* (comparison). In this case, the comparison is drawn on one side from the accounts of the giving of the law at Mount Sinai, drawn from Exodus and Deuteronomy, and on the other side, from a cluster of images concerning the goal of this pilgrimage—some already anticipated within the earlier discourse, some appearing here for the first time. The author's goal is to heighten the greatness of the present reality, and he does this effectively by reminding his hearers just how powerful and frightening the event at Sinai was.

We get an immediate sense of the author's direction when he states that they have not come to something that can be touched (*psēlaphōmenō*). The Platonic worldview of the author appears here once more in the contrast between the material realm—however impressive—and the spiritual realm. All the pyrotechnics of revelation at Sinai are simply that, a feast of sound and sight, but not bearing within them the deepest reality. The substantive "something that can be touched" emphasizes the sheer physicality of the Sinai covenant; for the verb *psēlaphaō* see Gen 27:12, 21; Judg 16:26; Pss 113:15; 134:17; Nah 3:1; Isa 59:10; Luke 24:39; 1 John 1:1). The palpable experiences are enumerated from the descriptions in Scripture of the people of Israel's arrival at Sinai. The "burning fire" (see Herodotus 1.86; Isa 4:5) comes from the descriptions in Deut 4:11, 5:22–23, and 9:15. The "darkness" (*gnophos*) and the "whirlwind" or storm (*thyella*) likewise are drawn from Deut 4:11 and 5:22. The only distinctive term is the one I translate as "gloom" (*zophos*), which in other literature is particularly associated with darkness of the nether regions (see Homer *Od.* 20.356; *Il.* 15.191; 2 Pet 2:4, 17; Jude 6, 13). The "blast of trumpet" (*salpingos ēchō*) and "sound of words" (*phōnē rhēmatōn*) come from the scene described in Exod 19:16, 19.

So fearful was the Sinai kratophany that the people asked that nothing more be spoken to them. The verb *paraiteomai* here has its meaning of "request" (see Herodotus 1.24.90; Xenophon, *Memorabilia* 2.2.14; Mark 15:6). The reference is to Exod 20:19: when the people saw all the powerful display, they told Moses, "You speak to us, and we will listen; but do not let God speak to us or we will die" (see also Deut 5:25). Hebrews adds as an explanation, "for they could not bear (*ouk epheron*) what was being commanded (*to diastellomenon*)." It is not clear whether the author intends his hearers to understand by this expression Moses' warning that they would die if they broke through to the Lord's presence (see Exod 19:21), or the stipulation that whoever broke through would be stoned (Exod 19:12–13), or simply that the people could not "bear" (see Rom 9:22; 2 John 10; Heb 13:13) the words of the Decalogue that God had just spoken in their hearing (Exod 20:2–17). The verb *diastellomai* means simply "to command," and it appears in the sense of ordinance in 2 Macc 14:28.

Most probably, it is the threat of being killed if they come too close that the author means, for he follows immediately with an allusion to Exod 19:12–13.

I translate *kan* as "If even," for Hebrews focuses on the stoning of an animal that broke the barrier, while in fact the prohibition called for the killing of humans who broke through as well. Note the effect of this gathering of specific details: although the people approached the mountain, they did not enter into the actual presence of God; indeed, they were kept at a safe distance because of the dangerous power that was on display on the mountain.

The fearsomeness of the experience is given expression by Moses' own words. We have learned earlier in the composition that Moses was *pistos* ("faithful") as a servant in God's house (3:2, 5), and that he anticipated the faith of Jesus by his choice of identifying with an oppressed people ("the reproach of the Messiah") rather than take advantage of the privileges that were his in Egypt (11:24–26). So we have been schooled to regard Moses in entirely positive terms. Yet "so fearful was the sight" that the Moses who had faced down Pharaoh exclaimed, "I am terrified (*ekphobos eimi*)." For *phoberos* ("fearsome") see Herodotus 7.139; *Let. Aris.* 194; *T. Jos.* 6.2. Our author has used it twice earlier, once to describe the punishment coming upon God's foes (10:27) and once to describe "falling into the hands of the living God" (10:31).

The allusion here is not to the Sinai event as described in Exodus but rather to Moses' own account of it in Deut 9:19. He says that he lay prostrate before the Lord for forty days, neither eating nor drinking, because of the sin of the people: "For I was afraid that the anger that the Lord bore against you was so fierce that he would destroy you." By ascribing to Moses the term *ekphobos* and by adding to it the term *entromos* ("trembling"; see Ps 17:8; Acts 7:32; 16:29), Hebrews signals that Moses indeed confronts the living God and that he shared the fear of the people. Such fear is not, indeed, to Moses' discredit. It is precisely such fear of God that recognizes the truth about reality and enables people of faith to resist in the face of human threats.

When the author turns to the realities that his hearers have "come to," he seeks to emphasize two things. First, in contrast to the Sinai covenant, they have to do not with palpable things that can be touched, and are therefore temporary, but with spiritual things, that are, because they are spiritual, eternal (remember again the Platonic worldview). Second, in contrast to the Sinai kratophany that generated fear and the threat of death, they have come to a celebration of life. He begins with the threefold characterization of the "place," and continues with a fivefold characterization of those inhabiting the "place" to which they have come. I put quotation marks around the word "place" as a reminder that this is entirely an imaginative evocation. If the author is truly speaking about entry into God's life, as I think he is, then there is no more *place* with God than there is *time*. Spiritual realities are by definition not local. Imagination is therefore also required of the reader.

The destination of the pilgrims, then, is suggested by a set of deeply evocative images. The first is "Mount Zion." The choice of a "mountain" to correspond to

Mount Sinai is obvious, especially since mountains in general are so much associated with revelation. The term "Zion" is connected above all with the Davidic dynasty (see 2 Sam 5:7; 1 Kgs 8:1; Pss 2:6; 9:12; 47:3), most notably in the psalm that has played such a thematic role in this composition. Immediately after the declaration of the Lord that the Lord should sit at his right hand, Ps 109:2 says, "The LORD sends out from Zion your mighty scepter. Rule in the midst of your foes." Those who have followed the argument of Hebrews to this point will surely understand that the Mount Zion spoken of here is not the seat of temporal rule over Israel, but of God's eschatological rule through Christ, just as in Rev 14:1–5.

The second image is "city of the living God." As we have seen throughout the composition, the expression "living God" (found in Deut 4:33; 5:26; Ps 83:2, etc.) is a favorite of Hebrews (3:12; 9:14), finding especially powerful expression in 10:31, "Falling into the hands of the living God is a fearful thing." The image of a city (*polis*) has equally been well prepared by the author. In 11:10 he spoke of the patriarchs as designating themselves as sojourners and aliens because they were seeking a city with foundations, and in 11:16 he asserted that God had indeed prepared a city for them. The contrast between this eternal city and the transitory ones of earth is struck once more in 13:14. The image is distinctive but not unique. Although he does not actually use the word *polis*, Paul's language strongly suggests that he shared the same imaginative vision of God's realm, when he tells the Philippians that their *politeuma* is in heaven (Phil 3:20), and tells them to exercise their citizenship (*politeuesthe*) in a manner worthy of the gospel of Christ (Phil 1:27). The book of Revelation also uses this image for God's presence, when it speaks of a "holy city" (Rev 21:2; 22:19).

The third image, of a "heavenly Jerusalem" (*Ierousalēm epouraniō*), is also found in both Revelation and Paul. In Rev 3:12 the seer speaks of "the city of my God, the new Jerusalem which comes down out of heaven from my God." In Rev 21:2 we find "new Jerusalem," and in 21:10 the "holy city Jerusalem." Finally, we read again in 21:2 of "the holy city, a new Jerusalem, coming down out of heaven from God." Similarly, in Gal 4:26 Paul contrasts the "now Jerusalem"—by which he means the physical city—and the *anō Ierousalēm*, "the Jerusalem that is above." The three images are, in a sense, one: they all evoke the political and cultic center of Israel, the place where the human king ruled and where the temple cult was practiced, but transposed to a transcendent realization "in heaven." For *epouranios* ("heavenly") elsewhere in this composition, see Heb 3:1, "heavenly call"; 6:4, "heavenly gift"; 8:5, "heavenly tent"; and 9:13, "heavenly sacrifices." As always in the Platonism of Hebrews, the contrast is not simply between matter and spirit, but above all between what is merely human and what is of God (cf., in Paul, 1 Cor 15:40; Eph 1:3, 20; 2:6; 3:10).

The most impressive aspect of the city of God is that it is filled with life, and life of a more powerful sort than is available on earth. Here are countless numbers of angels (for *myrias* in this sense, see Luke 12:1; Acts 21:20; Jude 14; Rev

5:11; 19:16). At the very start of the composition, the author had been concerned to put the *angeloi* in their place beneath the Son (1:4–5, 6, 7; 2:2, 5, 7, 9, 16), and there designated them as "ministering spirits" (*leitourgika pneumata*), whose mission was to serve those who were to inherit salvation (1:14). Now, as the pilgrims approach God's throne (see 4:16), the angels are present as part of the welcoming and celebratory throng. The noun *panyrgis* is frequently used for a festival day in wider Greek literature (see Herodotus 2.59.58; Xenophon, *Cyropaedia* 6.1.10) and in Scripture as well (see Hos 2:11; 9:5; Amos 5:21; Ezek 46:11).

The pilgrims approach as well another common feature of Greek civic life, namely the *ekklēsia*, the official gathering of the citizens or their representatives. The term here undoubtedly has that ordinary sense (see Josephus, *Ant.* 12.164; 19.332; 1 Macc 3:13; Sir 26:5; Acts 19:32, 40), rather than the narrower meaning of "church" as made up of the assembly of believers (see also Heb 2:12). As we have seen, the author uses *episynagōgoē* for the gathering of the community on earth (10:25). The assembly in this instance is made up of another part of the heavenly population, "the firstborn enrolled in heaven." The image suggests something like the Book of Life in *1 En.* 98.7, in which the names of the righteous are registered (for *apographein* in this sense, see Luke 2:1, 3, 5), as when Jesus tells his disciples, "Do not rejoice at this, that the spirits submit to you, but rejoice that your names are written in heaven" (Luke 10:20).

But who are the "firstborn" (*prōtotokoi*)? The author earlier has referred only to the firstborn children of Israel whom the destroyer did not touch (11:28), and to Jesus as the firstborn coming into the world (1:6). But he has also connected the rights of the firstborn (*prōtotokia*) to the inheritance in his account of Jacob and Esau in the passage immediately preceding this one (12:16–17). We are undoubtedly to think of the firstborn here in terms of all those "sons" whom God is leading into glory together with Jesus (2:10).

If this is the case, then the "spirits of righteous people brought to perfection" (*pneumasi dikaiōn teteleiōmenōn*) must be another way of characterizing the same participants in the true inheritance, which is a share in God's holiness (12:10). The use of "spirits" simply reminds that the way they now live is as God lives, not in their former mortal bodies but in the dimension of spirit. The author has used *dikaios* ("righteous person") twice earlier. In 10:38 it appears in the citation from Hab 2:4, "My righteous one will live from faith," and in 11:4 it is used with reference to Abel: it was through faith that Abel was testified to as righteous. It cannot be by accident that in both occurrences of the term there is the intimation of a life beyond mortality. In the case of Abel, as we have seen, the author states that, although he died, he continues to speak (11:4). It is precisely in their sharing in God's eternal life that the righteous find their fullest "perfection." This is the final use of *teleioō* in the composition, and it is appropriate that it echoes the first usage in 2:10, which declared God's intention to bring many sons to glory through the perfecting of their pioneer through suffering (see also 5:9; 7:19, 28; 9:9; 10:1, 14; 11:40). This final occurrence appears in the context of the contest won, the pilgrimage accomplished, the goal reached, that is, in the context of God's existence that is glory (for *doxa* see 1:3; 2:7, 9, 10; 3:3; 13:21).

The city of God is therefore filled with angels and saints. We might be surprised at the order in which the author presents "God" and "Jesus" in his imaginative display. Theologically, God deserves the climactic position as the source and goal of all beings. In this instance, Hebrews designates God as the eschatological judge of all creatures (*kritē pantōn;* see Pss 7:11; 49:6; 67:5; 74:7; Sir 32:12; Isa 30:18; 33:22; 63:7; 2 Tim 4:8; Jas 4:11); it is as judge that God can testify to the righteousness of humans. Rhetorically, however, the climactic position held by Jesus is appropriate, since it serves at once to assert Jesus' full humanity (note the simple name *Iēsous*) and his role as mediator (*mesitēs*), while also placing him definitively at God's side, a place that was his from the beginning (see 1:1–4).

The description of Jesus is a brilliant summation of the author's argument concerning him. He is a mediator (see 8:6; 9:15) of a covenant between God and humans that is both new (see 8:8; 9:15) and better (7:22; 8:6), because it is not temporary but eternal (13:20). His mediation is accomplished through his death, which is here, as earlier, expressed in terms of a ritual "sprinkling" (*rhantismos*; see 9:13, 19, 21; 10:22) of his own blood (2:14; 9:13, 19, 22, 25; 10:4, 19, 29). The description of Jesus is rounded off impressively by the statement that his blood "is speaking" (*lalounti*) better than Abel (12:24). The allusion to Abel, we recognize, echoes the statement in 11:4 that although he died he still speaks. In Abel's case, his speaking was a form of witness that reached God's ears.

In the case of the blood of Christ, the speaking is "better" (*kreitton*) on at least three counts. First, it speaks more clearly than any word expressed in the story of Scripture. Second, it speaks more powerfully, for it reaches all humans. Third, it speaks from and of a greater reality: Abel's blood crying out for justice is only a symbol of the victory over death and sin achieved by the death and exaltation of Christ. Once more, by the use of *lalein*, the author reminds his hearers of the way in which God, who spoke through the prophets (1:1) and angels (2:2) and law (9:19), speaks most fully and effectively through his Son (1:2; 2:3; 3:5; 4:8; 5:5; 11:18).

[25–29] After affirming the greatness of the "place" to which they have come in their journey of faith—through an act of imagination that anticipates that toward which they are still striving—the author now issues his final solemn warning. The form of the warning, *Blepete mē* ("Watch that"), reminds us of the caution issued in 3:12 (*Blepete mēpote*), and has much the same point. In 3:12 the hearers were warned against any one of them having an evil heart of faithlessness that would turn them away (*apostēnai*) from the living God. Here they are warned not to reject (*paraiteomai*) the one who is speaking (*ton* *lalounta*). The "one speaking" must refer back to the line immediately preceding this one. It is God who speaks to them through the blood of Jesus. And the verb "reject" (*paraiteomai*) is clearly meant to echo the use of the same verb in the description of the Sinai event in 12:19. The request of the people not to have anything more said to them is therefore understood as a refusal of the one who was speaking to them. Now the argument *a minore ad maius* takes on its most potent moral force: the greater the gift, the greater the peril involved in its rejection.

The author quickly fills in the logic. The Israelites who refused the one warning them on earth did not escape. The translation of *chrēmatizein* as "warned" depends on the context. The verb can mean, as in 8:5, simply "to reveal" (see Luke 2:26; Acts 16:22), and could theoretically refer to the content of God's revelation of the Decalogue. But Hebrews also uses the verb for the warning God gave to Noah before the flood (11:7). If we understand it, then, as "warning," to what does it refer? The obvious candidate is the prohibition of touching the mountain on penalty of death (see 12:20). The mention of "escape" (*ekphygein*) also reminds us of the rhetorical question posed by the author in 2:2: he asks "how shall we escape" when we neglect so great a salvation, when those who transgressed the word delivered by angels (the law) were punished for every transgression.

In the present case, the phrase "how much more" (*poly mallon*) must be translated "how much less" since it is cast in the negative rather than the positive. There is no chance to escape for those "who turn away" (*apostrephomenoi*; see *apostenai* in 3:12), because they are addressed by the one who "speaks from heaven" (*ton ap' ouranōn*). It is God who speaks both then and now (see 1:1). As always in this composition, the difference is the agent through whom God speaks. Now God addresses them through Jesus Christ, and the blood he has shed on their behalf. The consequences of turning away from this voice are much greater; for the force of *apostrephein*, see Xenophon, *Cyropaedia* 5.5.36; Josephus, *Ant.* 4.135; 6.340; Hos 8:3; Jer 15:6; Luke 23:14; Acts 3:26; Rom 11:26; 2 Tim 1:15; 4:4; Titus 1:14).

The author moves to his final comparison in verses 26–27. In Scripture we hear of God's presence "shaking the earth" (*saleuein tēn gēn*). In the Song of Deborah, we read that "the mountains quaked before the LORD, the one of Sinai, before the LORD, the God of Israel" (Judg 5:5). Likewise, in Ps 67:8, "the earth quaked, the heavens poured down at the presence of God, the God of Sinai" (see also Pss 9:27; 17:7; 76:18; 81:5; 96:4; 97:7). Such palpable evidence for God's power and presence is indeed awesome. But Scripture also contains a "promise" (*epēngeltai*) concerning the present. The voice (*phōnē*) continues to address them today (see Heb 3:7, 15; 4:7). As God made promises in the past (6:13; 10:23; 11:11), so does Scripture bear witness to promises yet to be fulfilled.

With slight modification, the author cites Hag 2:6 and 21. The postexilic prophet had exhorted the returning exiles to rebuild the temple. In 2:6 he had told them this statement of the Lord: "I am with you, says the LORD of hosts, according to the promise that I made you when you came out of Egypt. My spirit abides among you. Fear not." In other words, God is with them now, after the exile, precisely as he was with them at Sinai. Building on the traditional language used for that theophany, the prophet continues, "once again, in a little while, I will shake the heavens and the earth and the sea and the dry land." God will do this to accomplish the rebuilding of the temple that had been destroyed (Hag 2:6). Then in 2:21 Haggai declares, "I am about to strike the heavens and the earth, and to overthrow the throne of kingdoms; I am about to destroy the strength of the kingdoms of the nations." I have quoted this passage more fully for two reasons: to show more clearly how Hebrews excerpts and modifies, and also to suggest that the Scripture's mention of "promise" at the start and "kingdoms" at the end may have had real influence on the flow of our author's thought.

As always in this composition, the citation is from the LXX. The verb *seiō* (shake) has much the same meaning as *saleuō* (see Josephus, *Ant.* 4.44; Matt 21:10; 27:51) and can be used to describe earthquakes (Herodotus 7.129; Thucydides, *Peloponnesian War* 4.52). In the future tense (*seisō*, "I will shake"), it forms a promise of what God will do in the future. Hebrews ignores the prophet's language about the sea and dry land, and focuses only on the heaven and earth. As it happens, the LXX reverses the word sequence found in the MT, "heavens and earth," having instead, "earth and heaven." The author of Hebrews emphasizes the contrast between the two by inserting the words "not only" (*ou monon*) and "but" (*alla*). In his interpretation of the citation, in verse 27, the author focuses on the LXX phrase *eti hapax*, which I have translated as "once more." The term *hapax* echoes earlier uses (see 6:4; 9:7, 26, 27, 28; 10:2), but here may bear also some of the nuance of *ephapax* ("once for all"), as in 7:27; 9:12; and 10:10. The author insists that this phrase makes something "clear" (*dēloi*; see 9:5; 12:27), namely, that his "shaking" will have a definitive, eschatological character. It is not, as it was in the prophet, a matter of God acting once more as God did in the past. It is, rather, a matter of a radical and final change. There is a "removal" (*metathesis*) like that involving the law and the cult under the covenant of Sinai (7:12), and that involving Enoch's disappearance from among humans (11:5).

The things shaken are to be removed, by which, the author clarifies, he means "things that have been made" (see 1:2). This phrase helps us understand how the Platonic worldview of Hebrews is placed within the frame of biblical symbolism. For Platonic cosmology, that which is material and of the body is transitory and corrupt, always coming into being and always going out of being, while that which is not material, the soul, remains steady, for it is eternal. We find the same contrast between the transitory and the permanent in Hebrews. But for our author, the distinction is not between matter and spirit as such, but between that which is created and that which participates in God. What "remains" (*meinē*) therefore is not the mental as opposed to the physical, but what "receives a share in God's holiness" (12:10), as opposed to things that do not enter into the "city of the living God." These are "not shaken" (*mē saleuomena*).[1]

The author states conclusively that he and his hearers alike have been given such participation in what remains forever, "since we have received (*paralambanontes*) an unshakeable kingdom (*basileian asaleuton*)." The appearance of "kingdom" at this point in the composition may at first seem surprising, especially after the presentation of God's place as a heavenly city (12:22). But we quickly remember that in antiquity *basileia* is very much connected to *polis*; even the Roman Empire extended the power of a single city across the known world (*oikoumenē*). We have also noted above how the context of the Haggai citation speaks of God overthrowing other kingdoms—with the implication that God will establish his own rule.

More than anything else, however, the term *basileia* finally provides the framework for all the language previously used about the Son's royal status and power. In 1:8 we read as addressed to the Son, "your throne, O God, is forever and ever, and the scepter of righteousness is the scepter of your kingdom (*basileias sou*)." Indeed, the image of kingship has been inextricably linked to the image of priesthood throughout the composition through the use of Ps 109:1–4. Melchizedek is both priest and king, and in this manner is likened to the eternal Son of God (Heb 7:1–2). Psalm 109:1 asserts that the Son has taken a seat at the right hand of the throne of God to exercise rule (Heb 1:3, 13; 8:1), and believers are exhorted to approach the throne of God (1:8; 4:16), at whose right hand Christ now sits (8:1; 12:2).

All of this imagery confirms that Hebrews shares the common Christian understanding of the "rule of God" (*basieleia tou theou*) established through Jesus (Matt 4:17; 26:29; Mark 1:15; 14:25; Luke 4:43; 22:16; John 18:63; Acts 14:22; Rom 14:17; 1 Cor 6:9; Gal 5:21; Eph 5:5; Col 4:11; 1 Thess 2:12; 2 Thess 1:5; 2 Tim 4:1; Jas 2:5; 2 Pet 1:11; Rev 1:9), even if this composition elaborates that conviction in a distinctively complex fashion.

13:1–17 Exhortation to Faithful Living in Community

In this penultimate section of Hebrews above all it is important to resist the temptation to forget the powerful rhetorical character of the composition. The

1. For discussion see R. A. Stewart, "Creation and Matter in the Epistle to the Hebrews," *NTS* 12 (1965–66): 284–93; and W. Eisele, *Ein unerschütterliches Reich: Die mittelplatonische Umformung des Parusiegedankens im Hebräerbrief* (BZNW 116; New York: de Gruyter, 2003).

section 13:1–17 is far from an afterthought. It brings the hearers to a direct engagement with the behaviors that are consistent with the dispositions of faith, hope, and love that the author has consistently encouraged among them.[1]

Around a set of statements concerning their understanding of Jesus—in contrast to various and strange teachings and practices alien to their convictions (13:8–14)—we find two other sets of statements of a most practical character (13:1–7, 15–17). Virtually everything said here echoes earlier passages in which the author praises what his hearers are doing or exhorts them to do. Indeed, the several references to memory in this section suggest that the hearers are already well aware of their obligations (13:2, 3, 7, 16). We are not surprised, given the emphasis earlier on the loss of property (see 10:32–34), to find that the hearers are encouraged, in both sets of statements, to share possessions. What does appear explicitly for the first time is the call to imitate the faith (13:7) and to show trust and obedience to the human leaders of the community (13:17), although even these exhortations have some precedent earlier in the composition (see 6:12).

13:1 Let mutual love continue. **2** Do not neglect hospitality, for through this
some have unknowingly provided a welcome to angels. **3** Be mindful of
prisoners, as though you also were imprisoned, and of those being
afflicted as though you were in their bodies. **4** Let marriage be honored
by all, and let the marriage bed be without defilement, for[a] God will judge
fornicators and adulterers. **5** Let your manner of living be without greed.
Be content[b] with what you have. For he himself said, "I will surely never
abandon you, nor will I ever leave you desolate,"[c] **6** so that we can boldly
declare, "The Lord is my help, and[d] I will not be afraid. What will a
human do to me?"

7 Remember your leaders,[e] who spoke the word of God to you; as you
carefully consider the outcome of their manner of life, imitate their faith.
8 Jesus Christ is the same yesterday and today and forever.[f] **9** Do not be
drawn away[g] by various and strange teachings. For it is good that the heart
be made secure by a gift, not by dietary laws that offer nothing useful to
those who practice them.[h] **10** We have an altar from which those who wor-
ship in the tent have no right[i] to eat. **11** Through a high priest they bring
into the sanctuary the blood of animals for sin. The bodies of these ani-
mals are burned outside the camp. **12** For this reason, Jesus also suffered
outside the gate[j] in order to sanctify the people through his own blood. **13**
Therefore, let us go to him outside the camp, bearing his reproach. **14** For
we do not have a permanent city here. We are seeking the city to come.

1. See esp. F. V. Filson, *'Yesterday': A Study of Hebrews in the Light of Chapter 13* (SBT 2/4; Naperville, IL: Allenson, 1967).

15 Let us therefore[k] through him continually offer up a sacrifice of praise to God, one that is the fruit of lips confessing his name. 16 Do not neglect beneficence and[l] sharing possessions, because God is pleased by such sacrifices. 17 Since your leaders are tireless in your behalf as people who must give an account of themselves,[m] trust them and obey them, so that they might do this with joy and without complaint. This would do you no good.

a. The majority of MSS, including C and the second corrector of D, have *de* here rather than *gar* (found in P^{46}, ℵ, A, and the original hand of D). Perhaps such scribes considered the second clause to be adversative rather than explanatory.

b. P^{46} and a few other witnesses have the singular *arkoumenos* here, thinking that it modifies the noun *tropos*, but the plural participle can stand alone as an imperative and was so understood by other witnesses.

c. The future tense *enkatalipō* ("I will leave desolate") is read by the original hand of D and a scattering of other witnesses, and is found in Deut 31:6. It is included as the best reading by Nestle-Aland[27], despite the massive evidence for the present tense (see P^{46}, ℵ, A, C, etc.), which would also be the harder reading.

d. The original hand of ℵ as well as C and some other versions lack the conjunction *kai*, which is absent also from Ps 117:6. It is included by P^{46}, A, D, and the second corrector of ℵ.

e. The original version of D has a singular reading here; instead of *hēgoumenōn* ("leaders"), it has *proēgoumenōn*, perhaps influenced—since so much else in the first verses of Heb 13 resembles Rom 12—by the presence of *proēgoumenoi* in Rom 12:10.

f. Again, the original hand of D has the singular reading of *amēn* at the end of this sentence. The scribe was apparently impressed by the liturgical sound of "forever" (*eis tous aiōnas*) and added the appropriate response!

g. Rather than *parapheresthe* ("be drawn or carried away") a small number of MSS have the verb *peripheresthe* ("be carried around"), possibly under the influence of Eph 5:4.

h. The majority of witnesses, including such important MSS as the second correctors of ℵ and A, as well as C, have the aorist tense of the participle (*peripatēsantes*), which would place the following of food laws in the past. The decision to follow P^{46}, the original hand of ℵ, A, and D in reading the present participle could have real consequences in the matter of dating the composition.

i. The original hand of D and 0243 omit *exousian* ("right"), probably because of its similarity to *echousin*, which appears immediately before it in the sentence.

j. P^{46} and a few other witnesses have "camp" (*parembolēs*) rather than "gate" (*pylēs*), undoubtedly under the influence of *parembolēs* appearing immediately before and after it (vv. 11, 13).

k. The ninth-century MS K and a few others have *dia touto oun* ("on this account therefore") rather than *di' autou oun* ("through him therefore"); the variant undoubtedly arose mechanically.

l. P^{46} and the original hand of D add the definite article *tēs* before *koinōnias*, which would change the meaning from "sharing" (as in possessions) to "the sharing" or fellowship.

m. The original hand of D adds a clarifying phrase, *peri hymōn* ("concerning you"), so that the phrase reads, "as people who must give an account of themselves concerning you."

[13:1–7] These instructions about life in the community flow immediately from 12:28, which called for a giving of thanks that is a worship pleasing to God. It is striking that the service of God is expressed by moral dispositions and behaviors in common. The first practice is *philadelphia*, which I have translated as "mutual love," but which is literally "brotherly love." By using the third person imperative *menetō* the author suggests that such mutual love is among the "things not shaken" that "remain" in God's eternal rule (see 12:27). The ideal of brotherly love is well attested in the Greek world (see Plutarch's tractate, *On Brotherly Love* [*Mor.* 478B–492D]; Lucian, *Dialogues of the Dead* 26) and in Judaism (4 Macc 13:23, 26; 14:1; Philo, *Embassy* 87; Josephus, *Ant.* 4.26). Elsewhere in the New Testament, we find *philadelphia* as a Christian ideal in Rom 12:10; 1 Thess 4:9; 1 Pet 1:22; 2 Pet 1:7. As Plutarch's discourse on the subject makes clear, brotherly love is not merely a matter of sentiment, but involves a complex set of dispositions and practices. Above all, it involves mutual sharing of possessions and activities. That is why some of the New Testament passages calling for brotherly love modify it with language about feelings. Thus in Rom 12:10 brotherly love is to be accompanied by "affection" (*philostorgoi*), and in 1 Pet 1:22 with "sincerity" (*anypokriton*).

For the same reason, the author of Hebrews moves immediately to the specific practice of hospitality, which is a concrete expression of mutual love, but one that extends the same sort of concern to the outsider. Hospitality is connected to brotherly love by an obvious linguistic link: love among brothers (*philadelphia*) extends itself to love for strangers (*philoxenia*). Hospitality—making place for strangers in one's own place—is at once one of the simplest and most transparent, yet also most complex and culturally embedded, of human interactions. Making room for another is a form of sharing possessions. It also demands the sort of "stretching" and "suffering" that characterizes obedient faith.

The term *philoxenia* does not appear in the LXX, but is attested frequently in Hellenistic literature (Plato, *Laws* 953A; Epictetus, *Discourses* 1.28.23) and in Hellenistic Judaism (Philo, *On Abraham* 114; Josephus, *Life* 142). It appears as an ideal in early Christian compositions (Rom 12:13; 1 Tim 3:2; Titus 1:8; 1 Pet 4:9), and even when the term is not used, the practice is obviously esteemed among a rapidly spreading, itinerant movement (see Luke 10:16; Acts 10:24; 16:15; 21:4; 28:1–2; Rom 16:1–2; 1 Cor 16:5–12; Gal 4:14; Phil 2:19–30; Col 4:10; Phlm 8–20; Jas 2:1–4, 25; 2 John 10–11; 3 John 5–12). The exhortation "Do not neglect" (*mē epilanthenesthe*) sharpens the basic sense of *epilanthanomai* ("to forget"; see 1 Macc 1:49; 2 Macc 2:2; Mark 9:14; Jas 1:24) in the direction of a willful neglect or lack of care (see Pss 9:13; 73:19). The author earlier used the verb with respect to God's "forgetting/overlooking" their dedication and effort (Heb 6:16).

The author explains the command to practice hospitality by noting how some have given welcome (*xenizontes*) to angels (*angelous*) without knowing it. The construction translated as the adverb "unknowingly"—the verb *lanthanein* plus the accusative—is attested elsewhere (see Herodotus 1.44; Xenophon, *Memorabilia* 4.3.9) and is actually the main verb in this clause, with "giving welcome" appearing as an aorist participle. But the English sentence works better by arranging the syntax the way it is in the translation. The phrase *dia tautēs* ("through this") reminds us of similar constructions in this section (see Heb 11:4, 7; 12:15, 28).

The mention of "some" (*tines*) welcoming angels in this fashion makes the reference general rather than particular. In Gen 19:1–14 angels visit the city of Sodom and are refused hospitality; in Judg 6:11–14 an angel of the Lord announces the birth of Samson; in Tob 12:1–20 the angel Raphael visits Tobit's household. The term *angelos* ("angel") is used in all these visitations. A passage where the term "angel" does not appear, however, probably best captures the "unknowing" character of hospitality: the visit of the three men to Abraham and Sarah in Gen 18:12–15 to announce the birth of Isaac. In traditional Jewish interpretation of this passage, the three men were understood to be angels (Philo, *Abraham* 107, 113; Josephus, *Ant.* 1.196). The point for the hearers of this discourse is clear: they must be willing to extend hospitality to all strangers, for they can never know what manner of visitation from God the strangers might bring. For those whose own property has been taken away, to be sure, such openness and trust toward the other demands a generous ability to act on the basis of what cannot be seen as though it was seen, that is, in faith.

The opposite of being "neglectful" is to "be mindful" (*mimnēskesthe*) in a manner stronger than simply calling to mind, namely, to care for, or be concerned about (see Epictetus, *Discourses* 3.24.100; Josephus, *J.W.* 4.340; Gen 30:22; Luke 23:42). The author tells his hearers that they are to have this disposition toward those in prison (*tōn desmiōn*). This reminds us—and was meant to remind the first hearers—of the "earlier days" spoken of in 10:32, when they "suffered with prisoners." As in the earlier passage, the hearers of this discourse are not themselves pictured as being in prison. But they are tempted to ignore and neglect their colleagues who are in chains because of the shame associated with that condition. Earlier, the author had commended their "suffering with" (*synepathēsate*, 10:34). Now he urges them to the closest possible identification, caring for those in prison "as though fellow prisoners" (*hōs syndedemenoi*). Mutual love means sharing in the unfortunate circumstances experienced by the brethren, rather than removing oneself in disdain or fear.

In exactly the same way, they are to remember, or care for, those who are being badly treated. The verb *kakouchein* echoes the earlier story of Moses, who chose to suffer hardship with the people of God rather than enjoy the temporary advantage given by sin—that is, by associating with the privileges of the oppressors. Our author expects the same choice of his hearers. They are not to avoid a share in such suffering but are to act as though they themselves were in the bodies of those undergoing such hardship. The phrase *hōs autoi ontes en sōmati* is a bit odd but is paralleled almost exactly by a passage in Philo (*Special Laws* 3.161), and is clearly intended to express an intense identification with those who are suffering.

The author shifts in verses 4–5 from expressions of mutual love to a classic consideration of moral concerns in antiquity, both involving the disposition of the body: sexuality and the use of material possessions. It is the mystery (and complexity) of somatic existence that links these themes. Ancient moralists, indeed, grasped the moral connection between sexual incontinence and greed. Both pointed to disordered or excessive desires. Both led to reckless behavior destructive of proper human relationships. We are not surprised, therefore, to see statements on sexual and economic behavior standing side by side as they do in Heb 13:4–5, because the same combination occurs in other New Testament texts (Luke 16:9–18; 1 Cor 5:1–6:11; Eph 5:3–5; Col 3:5; 1 Thess 4:3–7), as it is also in a number of Hellenistic moral discourses (see Epictetus, *Discourses* 3.7.21; Lucian, *Nigrinus* 115–16; *T. Jud.* 18.2; Philo, *Abraham* 133–34; *Posterity of Cain* 116).

Both exhortations in verses 4–5 have the imperative *estō* understood; thus "Let marriage be honored by all" (*timios ho gamos en pasin*). The phrase *en pasin* could equally be translated as "among all," or even "in all respects." The use of honor/shame language is fascinating, for it is an odd paradox of human psychology that those experiencing shame in the public realm will sometimes find compensation through shameful acts in the private sphere. Cheating in marriage can be rationalized as a form of payback for larger humiliations. If marriage itself is viewed in terms of honor, however, such shameful acts of cheating are revealed in their true nature. The second phrase, "and let the marriage bed (*koitē*) be without defilement (*amiantos*)," does not add to but rather clarifies the first statement, by focusing on the sexual rather than the legal or relational aspects of marriage. The noun *koitē* ("bed") means, first, a place for sleeping (Josephus, *Ant.* 6.52), is often used as metonymy for marriage (Aeschylus, *Suppliants* 804; Euripides, *Medea* 152), and can be used as well simply for sexual intercourse (Lev 15:21–26; Wis 3:13, 16). The Greek term for "defiling" the marriage bed suggests, in another way, the honorable and holy character of the marriage relationship (for *miainein* see 12:15), and the combination *koitēn miainein* is found in Gen 49:4; *T. Reu.* 1.6; and Josephus, *Ant.* 2.55.

Marriage is not held in honor when people practice fornication. A *pornos* in the narrower sense is a male prostitute, just as a *pornē* is a female prostitute (see Xenophon, *Memorabilia* 1.6.13), but in the LXX the term *porneia* is used generally for sexual activity outside marriage (Hos 1:2; 2:2; Isa 47:10), and *pornos* is used in Sir 23:16–18 for the man who "dishonors the marriage bed," because he says, "Who can see me?" forgetting that God sees everything and that he will be punished (Sir 23:19–21). The New Testament uses the term *pornos* (as it does *porneia*) for every form of sexual immorality (see 1 Cor 5:9–11; 6:9; Eph 5:5; 1 Tim 1:10; Rev 21:8; 22:15). The *pornos* in this passage defiles the marriage bed/relationship by despising it and seeking pleasure where he will. We remember that the gluttonous and heedless Esau, who exchanged his birthright for a momentary pleasure, earlier provided the author with the opportunity to warn his hearers: "Do not become a fornicator or profane person like Esau" (Heb 12:16).

The adulterer (*moichos*) defiles the bed by breaking the bond of fidelity with the spouse. In Israel marriage was a natural symbol for covenantal loyalty between God and humans, quite literally as well, since obedience to the commandment not to serve other gods and not to commit adultery are both fundamental expressions of the covenant (see Exod 20:2–17; Deut 5:6–21). Adultery therefore becomes an equally natural sign of the rupture of covenant through disloyalty and idolatry (see Isa 54:4–8; 57:3; Ps 72:27; Jer 3:6–10; 13:27; Hos 3:1; 9:1; Ezek 16:38; 23:45). When Hebrews asserts that "God will judge" both fornicators and adulterers, he is only confirming the universal opinion of Scripture, as indicated already by the text from Sir 23:16–21 (see also Ezek 18:30; 23:36; 23:45; 24:14), and as affirmed earlier by the author, "the Lord will judge his people" (Heb 10:30; see Deut 32:36).

It is always hazardous to make arguments from silence, but the conservative and conventional character of these comments concerning sexuality allows us to draw two cautious conclusions concerning those addressed by the author. Notable is the simplicity of the command and its focus on marriage. In this respect, it resembles 1 Thess 4:3–6 more than 1 Cor 6–7. This suggests that the author saw, or assumed, that his hearers were not troubled by specific problems having to do with sexuality, as the Corinthians were. The author also mentions no alternative to marriage, such as virginity or widowhood (see 1 Cor 7:1–40; 1 Tim 5:3–16). We cannot conclude that the readers of Hebrews did not have or honor other expressions of sexuality beside marriage, but we can state that there is no evidence for them in this discourse.

The hearers are also told to be "without greed" (*aphilargyros*) in the conduct of their life (*tropos*; see Xenophon, *Cyropaedia* 8.3.49; 2 Macc 5:22; Josephus, *Ant.* 12.252). The vice of *philargyria*, literally "love of money," is one of the classic categories of vice in the Greco-Roman moral glossary, and gives rise to a number of statements like that attributed to Bion, "Love of money is the mother city of all evils" (Diogenes Laertius, *Lives* 6.50; see also Diodorus Siculus, *Library of History* 21.1.4; *Sib. Or.* 8.17; *Sentences of Pseudo-Phocylides* 42; Philo, *Special Laws* 4.65), and is a staple of attacks against avaricious false philosophers (Dio Chrysostom, *Oration* 32.9; Julian, *Oration* 6.181C; Lucian, *Runaways* 14; *Timon* 56). Not surprisingly, we find the vice ascribed to opponents in New Testament compositions (Luke 16:14; 2 Tim 3:2).

The most impressive parallel to the present passage is provided by 1 Tim 6:10. Paul states a version of the truism similar to Bion's: "Love of money (*philargyria*) is a root for every kind of wickedness." More impressively, Paul combines this to a call for *autarkeia* or self-sufficiency (1 Tim 6:6; see also 2 Cor 9:8; Phil 4:11–12). Hebrews also opposes "being content (*arkoumenoi*) with what you have (*tois parousin*)" to greed. The phrase is found also in Xenophon, *Symposium* 4.42 (see also Xenophon, *Cyropaedia* 8.4.6; Luke 3:14; John 14:8; 2 Cor 12:9; 1 Tim 6:8). Such "contentment" is the prerequisite for the ability to share possessions, which the author will enjoin on the hearers in Heb 13:16. Although the warning against greed and the call to contentment are indeed conventional in ancient moral discourse, they also represent a heroic ideal for hearers whose possessions had been taken away by force (10:34). The anxiety provoked by such loss is exactly what can generate the compulsive need to acquire and hoard possessions.[2]

The contentment of the hearers is not to be based simply on a philosophical outlook, but on their relationship with a God who has gifted them with an unshakeable kingdom. They understand that the things that cannot be shaken are greater than the things that can be shaken (12:27–28). What cannot be shaken above all is the God in whom they put their trust. The author therefore frames their ability to accept shame and hardship, to commit themselves to sexual fidelity, and to abstain from greed by reminding them of the basis of their confidence (*parrēsia*) in the face of hard circumstances. For the final time in this Scripture-laden composition, the author uses a citation to make his point. Distinctive to this double citation, however, is that it bears both upon the loyalty of the God who speaks and upon the human response that follows from taking God's declaration as true.

God's statement, "I will surely never abandon you, nor will I ever leave you desolate," resembles two passages in the LXX but does not agree completely with either. In Gen 28:15 the Lord appears to Jacob and promises him *hoti ou mē se enkatalipō* ("that I will surely not leave you desolate") until he accomplishes everything he had promised. Although this agrees with Hebrews in having the first person future tense of the verb, it also matches only the last part of the statement. The use of *enkataleipein* is nevertheless fascinating. It is the verb used by

2. See L. T. Johnson, *Sharing Possessions: Mandate and Symbol of Faith* (Overtures to Biblical Theology; Philadelphia: Fortress Press, 1981).

Ps 21:2 and cited by Matthew and Mark for Jesus' cry of desolation on the cross (Matt 27:46; Mark 15:34). It is also found in Ps 15:10, cited in Acts 2:27 for God's not "abandoning" Jesus in death. More particularly, it used by Paul for his "abandonment" by his followers (2 Tim 4:10, 16), and Hebrews has used the same verb in 10:25 for some among the believers' "abandoning" their assemblies.

A fuller antecedent is provided by Deut 31:6 and 8, where Moses assures the people (and Joshua) concerning "the LORD who goes before you," that "he will surely not leave you nor will he leave you desolate." The terms here correspond exactly to those in Hebrews, except that they are in the third person singular future, rather than the first person singular. Did Hebrews adapt this citation and place it as a direct address from God? Note the introduction, "For he himself said" (*autos gar eirēken*). This is certainly possible, for we have seen the author adapt other passages (see Heb 10:17 and 12:26). Another possibility is that the author had before him an alternative version of the LXX in which God's words are reported in direct rather than in indirect discourse. In fact, Philo quotes the same citation in the same form as in Hebrews (*Confusion of Tongues* 166). More important, to be sure, is the content of God's declaration. He will not leave his people abandoned and he will not "leave" (*aniēmi*) them in the sense of neglect or forsake them (see Euripides, *Suppliants* 1042; Xenophon, *Cyropaedia* 7.5.70). This is a powerful statement of absolute loyalty, from the God who is a "consuming fire" (Heb 12:29). It is, indeed, a terrible thing to fall into the hands of the living God (10:31), but it is also, paradoxically, the safest of all places to be.

Just as God's pledge of fidelity is in the first person, so is the response of the believers, who have been "emboldened" (*tharrountas*) by God's declaration. This is the "confidence" and "boldness" (*parrēsia*) they have as they approach God (3:6; 4:16; 10:19, 35). This time the citation is drawn from Ps 117:6, except for the addition of the word "and": "The LORD is my helper (*boēthos*) and I will not be afraid (*ou phobēthēsomai*), what will a human (*anthrōpos*) do to me?" The LXX version, lacking the "and," reads as follows: "The LORD is my help. I will not fear what a human will do to me." The verse brings together two important themes of the composition. The first is that true "help" is to be found with God, even though he is himself fearsome. It is at God's throne of grace that help (*boētheia*) can be found (4:16), and it was in order to provide help (*boētheia*) to humans that Jesus was tested in every way that they are (2:18). The second is that true fear of the Lord, and the confidence that it gives, enables the faithful to overcome fear of other humans. On this basis, the parents of Moses did not fear the dictates of Pharaoh (11:23), and Moses himself did not fear the wrath of the king (11:27).

The actual verse cited is certainly pertinent to the point the author wants to make: it is trust in the Lord's help that enables believers to be generous and faithful in their lives with each other. As is the case in some other citations, moreover, the single verse quoted may also carry with it nuances from the context of the original psalm. This is, we recognize, the psalm quoted by the Gospels with reference to Jesus as the stone rejected by the builders but made the cornerstone by God (Ps 117:22; see Matt 21:42; Luke 20:17; Acts 4:11). In light of the way Hebrews so closely joins Jesus and his brothers whom he leads to God's glory, we can see how other parts of this same psalm may well have resonated with our author, lines such as "it is good to hope in the LORD rather than to hope in rulers" (117:9); "the LORD has taken hold of me; the LORD is my strength and my song" (117:113–114); "with discipline the LORD has disciplined me, and to death he has not handed me over" (117:18); and, "This is the gate of the LORD, the righteous go in through it" (117:20).

Like other early Christian communities—even those that had been in existence only a short time—those to whom Hebrews is addressed would have had some form of local leadership. The author mentions them three times in this final chapter (13:7, 17, 24), using the same term, *hēgoumenoi*, in each case. The term refers to leaders of any sort (Sophocles, *Philoctetes* 386; *T. Zeb.* 10.2) and to leaders among the disciples of Jesus (Luke 22:46; Acts 14:12; 15:22) without identification of specific function. The same can be said, to be sure, of other descriptions of leaders among early Christian communities (cf. Rom 12:6–8; 1 Cor 16:15–18; 1 Thess 5:12–13).

Here the leaders are identified as the ones who "spoke the word of God to you" (*elalēsan hymin ton logon tou theou*). Within the lexicon of Hebrews, this is an exalted function indeed, since both "word of God" (2:12; 4:2, 12; 6:1) and "speaking" (1:1, 2; 2:2, 3; 3:5; 4:8; 5:5; 11:4, 18; 12:24–25) carry powerful resonances. This description helps distinguish this mention of leaders from that in 13:17. There the hearers are to trust and obey their leaders—suggesting that they are still present—but the language here points to a former role of preaching or teaching, perhaps even at the start of the community (see 2:3; 6:1).

We notice that it is with respect to these leaders of the past that the present-day hearers are to "remember" (*mnēmoneuete*), to "consider (*anatheōrountes*) the outcome of their manner of life (*tēn ekbasin tēs anastrophēs*)," and to "imitate their faith" (*mimeisthe tēn pistin*). In effect, then, these leaders of the past offer to the hearers a continuation of the roll call of faith they had heard in chapter 11. They not only "spoke the word of God" but enacted it through their faithful way of life. As in other hortatory literature from antiquity, we find here a combination of memory and imitation, enabled by a "gazing" at the model to be imitated (see Epictetus, *Discourses* 2.14.17–23; Seneca, *Natural Questions* 1.17.4; *On Anger* 36.1–3; Plutarch, *On Listening to Lectures* 8 [*Mor.* 42A-B]; Jas 1:22–25). Here they are to "consider/gaze on" those leaders of the past, just as the author had told them to "look to" Jesus (12:2); and, as in the case of Jesus (and of earlier heroes), it is the "outcome" of their manner of life that is of particular importance, meaning: how they suffered, how they died, and how they found a place in the city of the living God (12:2; see also 11:4, 5, 7, 21, 22). Precisely such "remembering" through "gazing" enables them to imitate their faith. The hearers are privileged to have had in their own experience leaders from whom they could learn how faith works and to what it leads (see also 6:12).

[8–14] The author now turns to the present circumstances in which the readers find themselves. The combination of specific detail (at the level of imagery) and vague reference (at the level of history) makes this section maddening to those who want to pin down the precise situation to which this discourse was addressed. Themes concerning priesthood reappear for the first time since 10:19–25, now in terms of options available to the present-day hearers. As in the earlier argument, the central point is clear enough: the followers of Jesus are in touch with what is eternal, while the tempting alternatives are merely temporary. Thus the statement concerning the eternal status of Jesus in 13:8 and that concerning the permanent city to come in 13:14 provide a frame around the warning against going astray after alternatives. Within this frame, verses 9–13 assert the *exousia* ("right") pertaining to membership in the people of the crucified Messiah, and the consequences for discipleship that follow from having Jesus as the pioneer and perfecter of faith.

The declaration concerning "Jesus Christ" is certainly solemn—only here and in 10:10 and 13:21 is the combination found—but its function, as Attridge correctly notes (392), is to reassure the hearers that, although their leaders may pass away, the basis of their faith and hope remains the same. The phrase *ho autos* ("the same") echoes the very beginning of the composition. In contrast to the changes in the created order, the Son is declared to be "the same, and [your] years will not cease" (1:12). The phrase "yesterday and today" (*echthes kai sēmeron*) in turn echoes the biblical idiom (1 Sam 20:27; 2 Sam 15:20; Sir 38:22), as well as the theme of God's word speaking both in the past and every day as long as it can be called "today" (3:7, 13, 15; 4:7). The affirmation that Jesus Christ is the same "forever" (*eis tous aiōnas*) confirms his eternal being (1:8) and priesthood (5:6; 6:20; 7:17, 21, 28) as well as the salvation he has accomplished (5:9; 9:12), which they are to inherit (9:15).

The hearers are therefore warned "not to be drawn away by various and strange teachings." Instead, their hearts are to be "made secure" by the gift they have already been given: God's work among them through Christ (6:1–12; 10:21–39). The verb *parapheresthai* means literally "to flow away," like a river (see Plutarch, *Obsolescence of Oracles* 39, *Mor*. 432B; Jude 12) and can be used for being misled by error (Plato, *Philebus* 38D; *Phaedrus* 265D). The contrast between wandering among alien teaching and standing firm in the tradition reminds us of the spatial imagery used in 2 Tim 2:14–3:17: error consists in movement, truth in constancy. Similarly, putting "teachings" in the plural and calling them "various" (*poikilais*) emphasizes the contrast to the implied singleness of the truth upheld by the hearers and speaker, just as the adjective "strange" (*xenais*) emphasizes their difference from "the basic teaching about the Messiah" (6:1) and the deeper instruction concerning the Messiah given by our author.

The statement that this alternative lore has not profited those who have walked in it is standard criticism of opposing doctrines in antiquity, for it is the usefulness of teaching—its usefulness, that is, for shaping the moral life—that measures its value (see Plato, *Gorgias* 504E; Epictetus, *Discourses* 1.4.16; 3.24.51; Josephus, *Ant.* 17.154; Philo, *Migration of Abraham* 55; *Posterity and Exile of Cain* 86; Rom 2:25; 1 Cor 15:32; Jas 2:14–19; 1 Tim 4:8; 2 Tim 3:16; Titus 3:3). Our author had, indeed, stated earlier that even the Word of God did not profit some who had heard it because it was not received by faith (Heb 4:2).

But what sort of teachings are these, and who is propagating them? This historical judgment is made difficult by the multitude of possibilities. The only specific detail provided is the noun *brōma* in the plural ("foods"), which I have translated as "dietary laws" because of the context of "teaching" and because the author speaks of some "walking" (*peripatein*) in them. A concern for dietary rules—together with mention of those who worship in the tent (*skēnē*)—suggests that some form of contemporary Jewish practice and ideology is enticing some of the hearers.[3]

Can we be more specific? Does concern for dietary regulations here stand as synecdoche for a commitment to the covenant of law? We know that disputes over the eating of certain foods divided some early Christian communities with Jewish membership (see Mark 7:1–8; Acts 10:1–11:30; 1 Cor 8–10; Rom 14:1–23; Rev 2:14, 20). Or does "foods" here have specific reference to the sharing of food offered in sacrifice (see Lev 3:1–17; 7:11–21; Ezek 44:30–31)? Paul uses language similar to this in 1 Cor 9:13: "Do you not know that those who perform the temple service eat what belongs to the temple, and those who minister at the altar share in the sacrificial offerings?" Our author also continues, "We have an altar from which those who worship in the tent have no right to eat" (Heb 13:10).

Paul uses the practice as an analogy for the financial support of ministers of the gospel. Does Hebrews intend a similar metaphorical use? The answer hinges on how literally we take the subsequent comparison between the disposal of bodies outside the camp and the suffering of Jesus outside the gate (13:11–12). Although the use of the present tense to describe the practice could suggest contemporary usage, the reference here, as in earlier descriptions of the cult, is more likely to the ritual of the Day of Atonement as laid out in Leviticus. The author does not speak of carcasses brought from the Jerusalem temple outside the city to be burned, but of carcasses brought "outside the camp." In the same way, "dietary regulations" may stand for the whole complex of laws

3. For discussion see H. Koester, "'Outside the Camp': Hebrews 13:9–14," *HTR* 55 (1963): 299–315; N. H. Young, "'Bearing His Reproach' (Heb 13.9–14)," *NTS* 48 (2002): 243–61; M. E. Isaacs, "Hebrews 13.9–16 revisited," *NTS* 43 (1997): 268–84.

dealing with material things that the author regards as ineffective for the perfection of persons (see 9:9–10; 10:1–4). That this is likely is shown also by contrast. When the author asserts that he and his hearers "have an altar," he cannot—in light of everything that has gone before this—mean an actual physical altar or place of cult.

He refers, rather, to the "heart" (*kardia*), the seat of human disposition. It was the heart that led people astray under the earlier covenant (3:8, 10), and was to be renewed under the new covenant (8:10). It is on the heart that God was to inscribe his laws (10:16). And it is with true hearts full of faith and cleansed of an evil conscience that people now can approach god (10:22). The author therefore affirms that it is this internal "place" that is the altar from which they "eat," that is, share in the worship consisting in praise and thanksgiving to God (12:28).

They are able to give thanks because they have been "made secure" (*bebaiousthai*) by a "gift" (*charis*), namely God's unshakeable kingdom (12:28). For "gift/grace" as thematic in the composition, see 2:9; 4:16; 10:29; 12:15, and for "secure" (*bebaios*), see 2:2, 3; 3:6, 14; 6:16, 19; 9:17. It is because God has secured them by his gift that they have no need to stray into teachings that are unprofitable since they concern only external matters and do not accomplish the moral transformation of those who practice them.

The author's next words, however, serve not to comfort but to challenge his hearers, as he moves into a further and final comparison between the cult of the tent and the sacrifice of Christ. Leviticus 6:23 specifies that any sacrifice whose blood has been used for atonement cannot be eaten but must be consumed by fire. And in the specific instructions for the Day of Atonement, Lev 16:27 says, "The sin offering of bull and goat, whose blood was brought into the sanctuary to make atonement, shall be taken outside the camp (*exō tēs parembolēs*), where the hides and flesh and offal shall be burned up (*katakausousin*) in the fire." Only when the one who has so disposed the carcasses has been cleansed with water can he reenter the camp (*eis tēn parembolēn*, Lev 16:28). Hebrews sharpens the comparison by specifying that it is "through a high priest" that the offering was made, so we know the reference is to the Day of Atonement.

Then, in a stunning turn, the author declares, "For this reason (*dio*), Jesus also (*kai Iēsous*) suffered outside the gate in order to sanctify (*hagiasē*) the people through his own blood." It is a stunning turn because here, at last, the author merges literary and historical horizons. Although there is evidence that public execution regularly took place outside the walls of a city (see Lev 24:14, 23; Num 15:35–36; 1 Kgs 21:13; Acts 7:58), this statement can also reflect specific knowledge concerning the crucifixion of Jesus. John 19:17–20 says that Jesus "went out to Golgotha, a place near the city." This historical allusion intersects the symbolism drawn from Scripture concerning the Day of Atonement. If Jesus had acted out a ritual imitation of the ancient cult, his blood would have been spilled in the temple and his body burned outside the gate. But here it is all one act: his despised rejection and death outside the gate is itself an entering into the heavenly sanctuary (through the veil of his flesh), and an eternal offering for the sanctification of the people.

The author's conclusion—that the listeners should go to meet him outside the camp—is equally stunning but not surprising. Indeed, this has been the point toward which all his exhortation has been leading: that believers are to follow in the path already traveled by Jesus, the pioneer and perfecter of faith. The link between Jesus' obedient suffering and theirs is made even stronger by the exhortation's finale. Jesus' death had been one in which he "despised the shame of the cross" (12:2). Like Moses, who chose to bear "the reproach of the Messiah" (*oneidismon Christou*, 11:26), his followers also are to "bear his reproach" (*ton oneidismon autou pherontes*) as they go out to meet him at his place of execution. There could hardly be a more complete fit between the understanding of Christology and discipleship. They have been "gifted" precisely so that they might share in the process of perfecting that God worked in Jesus, suffering if not to the point of physically shedding blood (12:4), yet to the point of enduring shame and reproach caused by their commitment.

Then, making an explicit link between himself, his hearers, and the heroes of faith that he had praised in chapter 11, the author reminds them, "we do not have a permanent city here. We are seeking the city to come" (13:14; see 11:14–16). In his imaginative evocation of their approach to God in 12:18–24, the author spoke of the city of the living God. It is real. But the author and his hearers are not yet there in their mortal bodies. For now, they must live light on the earth, willingly embracing their diaspora condition, the marginality and ostracism that comes to them for the confession of a crucified Messiah.

[15–17] The intimate link between Christ and the hearers of this discourse—and the speaker—is indicated once more by the exhortation, "let us offer (*anapherōmen*) a sacrifice of praise continually (*dia pantos*) to God through him (*di' autou*)." Since Jesus "lives always to make intercession for them" (7:25), believers can continue in every circumstance to praise God through him. The choice of "offering up" (*anapherein*) and "sacrifice" (*thysia*) deliberately echoes the language of sacrifice used earlier in the composition (see 7:25; 8:3; 9:9, 23, 28).

By identifying their sacrifice as one consisting in praise, "the fruit of lips confessing his name," Hebrews joins a broad stream of Greco-Roman and Jewish piety that regarded moral virtue and verbal praise as more appropriate offerings to the Divine than animal sacrifices (see Epictetus, *Enchiridion* 31.5; Apollonius of Tyana, *Letter* 26; Sir 34:18–35:11; *Pss. Sol.* 15.3; *T. Levi* 3.5–6; 1QS 9:4–5), a perspective found in other New Testament writings as well (Rom 12:1–2; Phil 2:17; 4:18; 1 Pet 2:5; John 4:24). For the specific use of "lips" as synecdoche for speech to God, see Pss 50:15; 62:3, 5; 70:23; 118:171; for "confession" earlier in Hebrews, see 3:1; 4:14; 10:23; and for "name," see 1:4; 2:12;

6:10. Just as the result of training/discipline is a "peaceful fruit (*karpos*) of righteousness," so does the confession of God's name in the robust sense meant by Hebrews yield the "fruit" (*karpos*) that is a sacrifice of praise.

What is that robust sense of confession? It includes the specific practices of sharing among those having the same commitment. As in 13:2 the hearers were told "not to neglect" hospitality, here they are instructed "do not neglect" (*mē epilanthanesthe*) other forms of sharing material possessions. The term *eupoiia* can be used for a "good act" in general (Philo, *Change of Names* 24; Josephus, *Ant.* 2.261) or, more particularly, for an act of beneficence (Diogenes Laertius, *Lives* 10.10). If we take it in the latter sense, then we must suppose that the hearers are in a position to show beneficence to others. They may have had their property seized (Heb 10:34), but the other instructions given by the author suggest they are still in a position to help others (as through hospitality). That such help extends to the sharing of material possessions is made more likely by the addition of the term *koinōnia*. Once more, the noun can be used for a variety of ways of sharing (see 2:14; Titus 1:4; Jude 3; 1 Tim 5:22), but the context here supports taking this as making material things available to others (see Acts 2:44; 4:32; Rom 12:13; Gal 6:6; Phil 4:15). Whether we take these terms in a wider or a narrower sense, it is clear that actions contributing to the welfare of others are essential to the sacrifice of praise that is "pleasing to God" (see Heb 11:5, 6; 12:28; and esp. 13:21 below).

Another expression of mutual love (13:1) is the relationship among community members and their leaders. In 13:17 the *hēgoumenois hymōn* ("your leaders") must refer to those presently in authority, in contrast to those who formerly spoke the word of God to them, and whose faith they are to imitate. These current leaders are characterized by their diligence: they are "tireless." The verb *agrypnein* means literally to go sleepless (see 2 Sam 12:21; Pss 101:7; 126:1; Prov 8:34), and from that literal meaning takes on the sense of being alert or watchful (Mark 13:33; Luke 21:36; Eph 6:18). In this case, it also has the sense of keeping watch over or caring for something (Plutarch, *Alex. fort.* 4; *Mor.* 337B), specifically the lives or souls in their charge (*hyper tōn psychōn hymōn*; cf. 6:19; 10:39; 12:3). Their diligence is spurred by their awareness of God's judgment. They are themselves under authority, and must "give an account" of themselves (*hōs logon apodōsontes*; see Luke 16:2; Acts 19:40) to the Judge of all (12:23), who is a consuming fire (12:29). The realization that leaders must render an account not only for their own lives but for the care they have shown for the lives of those under their authority should be a powerful check against the natural tendency toward arrogance among those placed in such positions.

The author's concern is that the community "trust" (*peithesthe*) and "obey" (*hypeikete*) their leaders. I take the verb *peithō* in the passive imperative to mean "depend on" or "put trust" in someone (see also Heb 2:13; 6:9), in order to relieve what otherwise would be a redundancy, since *hypeikō*—found only here in the New Testament—means to give way or submit to someone (Homer, *Od.* 12.117; Plato, *Laws* 717D; Philo, *Life of Moses* 1.156; 4 Macc 6:35). We can determine nothing about the place or date of the composition from this straightforward command to obey leaders. Such attitudes were commonplace in the stratified world of antiquity in which everyone was "a person under authority" (Luke 7:8) and required to pay obedience to someone of higher rank. Directions like these are also found in the earliest Christian writings, not only with respect to apostolic figures like Paul (see 1 Cor 4:18–21; 2 Cor 13:5–10; Phlm 21–22), but also with respect to leaders of local assemblies (1 Cor 16:15–18; 1 Thess 5:12–13).

In the present case, the author advises such trust and obedience so that the leaders can carry out their obligations "joyfully" (*meta charas*) and not "complaining" (*mē stenazontes*). The term "joy" is always a positive quality (see 1 Chr 28:12; Tob 7:18; Pss 20:6; 29:11; Wis 8:16; Isa 66:10; Luke 1:14; John 15:11; Rom 15:13; 1 Thess 1:6) and here recalls the attitude with which the hearers accepted the expropriation of their property (Heb 10:34), the reason for which Jesus despised the shame of the cross (12:2), and what is not experienced during discipline but only afterward (12:11). The onerous work of leadership is made joyful when carried out in an atmosphere of trust and cooperation. In contrast, when such dispositions are lacking, leaders "groan" as though under a heavy burden (for *stenazein* see Tob 3:1; Job 9:27; 23:2; Wis 5:3; Isa 19:8; Ezek 21:6; Rom 8:23; 2 Cor 5:2–4; Jas 5:9).

The author concludes laconically: This (*touto*)—meaning acting in a way that would make leaders groan—is "unprofitable" or "harmful" to the hearers. The adjective *alysiteles* is not found elsewhere in Scripture, but is well attested in Hellenistic literature (Plato, *Cratylus* 417D; Xenophon, *Oecumenicus* 14.5; Philo, *Special Laws* 1.100). Just as dietary laws are "without profit" to those who practice them because they do not touch interior dispositions (Heb 13:9), so is mechanical or reluctant obedience "without profit" if not carried out with interior dispositions of trust and obedience.

13:18–25 Final Prayers and Greeting

The conclusion of the discourse provides its only truly epistolary elements, even though they are rudimentary and for the most part conventional. After a request that prayer be extended also to "us"—presumably the author (and possibly his companions)—especially that they quickly rejoin the hearers (13:18–19), we find a solemn prayer directed to the hearers (13:20–21), then a brief set of statements concerning the composition (13:22), the movements of Timothy and the author (13:23), and mutual greetings (13:24). In a manner reminiscent of Paul's letters, the composition closes with a final greeting that is also a benediction (13:25).

Such elements do not make Hebrews a genuine letter, but since letters in earliest Christianity were read aloud to the gathered assembly, the distinction between letter and speech is not great. These conventional epistolary elements could, indeed, have been added to the discourse as it was being prepared for delivery through an emissary. Despite being teased endlessly by curious scholars, the few details provided here do not satisfactorily identify author or readers, the time or place of composition. They do serve to remind us of the remarkable way in which early Christian communities joined themselves together through networks of personal and written communication, even in circumstances that made such communication difficult.

> **13:18** Pray for us,[a] for we are convinced that we have a good conscience.
> We want to conduct ourselves well in every respect. **19** I ask you to do this
> above all, so that I might be restored to you more quickly. **20** Now may the
> God of peace, who raised from the dead by the blood of a new covenant
> the great shepherd of the sheep our Lord Jesus,[b] **21** equip you to do his will
> in every good thing,[c] accomplishing among us[d] what is pleasing to him[e]
> through Jesus Christ, to whom be glory for ever and ever.[f] Amen. **22** I beg
> you, brothers, to put up with[g] the word of exhortation that, however briefly,
> I have written to you. **23** Know that our[h] brother Timothy has been released.
> If he comes quickly, I will see you with him. **24** Greet all[i] your leaders and
> all the saints. Those from Italy greet you. **25** Grace be with all of you.[j]

a. The original hand of D has *kai* ("and"), which would make a closer connection to the prayer of praise in 13:15.

b. The original hand of D and a variety of other MSS add *Christon* ("Christ") to the name *Iēsoun* ("Jesus"), a natural expansion, especially in light of the full *Iēsou Christou* following immediately in 13:21.

c. Some witnesses add to "good thing" (the neuter adjective *agathō* used as a substantive) the clarification "deed" (*ergō*) or "deed and word" (*ergō kai logō*).

d. It is easy to confuse *hymin* ("you") with *hēmin* ("us"), and some witnesses—among them C—have the second person plural personal pronoun rather than the first person. The effect would be to direct the prayer exclusively to the hearers.

e. Some important witnesses, including A, C, and the original hand of א, supply the dative pronoun *autō* to make the phrase "pleasing to him" explicit.

f. Nestle-Aland^{27} includes—as a very doubtful reading—the phrase "and ever" (Gk. *tōn aiōnōn*, "of the ages"). The MS evidence is evenly split. That P^{46} (our earliest witness) lacks it and that it is a natural liturgical addition make the inclusion rather than exclusion more logical.

g. Some MSS, including the original hand of D, have the infinitive *anechesthai* (following *parakalō de hymas*) rather than the imperative *anechesthe*. The meaning is the same in either case.

h. A substantial number of witnesses (including P[46] and the original hand of א) include the personal pronoun *hēmōn* ("our"). The pronoun is omitted by the second corrector of א and of D, as well as the majority of MSS.

i. P[46] omits *pantas* ("all") from the phrase "all your leaders." If it did not arise mechanically, the intention behind the alteration is obscure.

j. The original hand of D has "the saints" (*tōn hagiōn*) rather than "you" (*hymōn*) in the final blessing. The majority of MSS add "amen" at the end. Some MSS also add a *subscriptio* to the letter. P[46] and D have none. Those MSS that add one range from the simple *Pros Hebraious* ("to the Hebrews") in א and C, to the much more elaborate "To the Hebrews written in Hebrew from Italy anonymously through Timothy" in the MS designated 104.

[13:18–19] Throughout the composition, the author has used the plural when speaking of himself (see 4:13; 5:11; 6:9), and does so again in a request for prayer, such as we find also in Rom 15:30; Col 4:3; 1 Thess 5:25; and 2 Thess 3:1. The "us" could include companions of the author, but the immediate shift to the first person singular suggests that the request is for the author himself.

The request has two statements following. The first provides a reason or motivation (*gar*), and the second a specific intention. It is not at all clear how the author's declaration of a good conscience should serve as a reason for their praying. But the present tense of the imperative could be taken as an indication that they are already praying and are being asked to continue in their prayer. In this case, the profession of a good conscience could be a witness to the author's participation in fellowship (*koinōnia*) that he has encouraged among them. We note that the author expresses confidence concerning himself (*peithometha . . . hoti . . . echomen*) just as earlier he had expressed confidence about the hearers' own commitment (*pepeismetha peri hymōn*, 6:9).

This suggestion appears more probable when we remember that the author shares with his readers in the work of Christ, which is to purify the human conscience (9:9, 14; 10:2, 22), enabling them to live a holiness defined in terms of moral dispositions. The conviction of having a "good" conscience that testifies to one's manner of life is found in Paul (see 2 Cor 1:12; Rom 9:1), who also speaks of people having a "good" (*agathos*) or "pure" (*katharos*) conscience (1 Tim 1:5, 19; 3:9; 2 Tim 1:3). The statement that "we want (*thelontes*) to conduct ourselves well (*kalōs anastrephesthai*) in every respect (*en pasin*)" stands in loose apposition to "have a good conscience," with the participle capable of being read as "as we want," or "since we want," or even as "so that we want." In any rendering, the verb *thelein* should be understood as stronger than a mere velleity; it is cognate to *thelēma*, used for the "will" of God in 10:7, "I have come to do your will, O God," and in the prayer that will follow shortly, "to do his will in every good thing."

The verb *anastrephesthai* echoes the noun *anastrophē* that was used with reference to the former leaders of the community in 13:7. Together with the modifier "in every respect," the term points to the entire conduct of life rather than a particular set of actions. Everything should be carried out "well" or even "nobly" (*kalōs*). For a similar use of the verb *anastrephesthai*, see 2 Cor 1:12; Eph 2:3; 1 Tim 3:15; 1 Pet 1:17; for the noun *anastrophē*, see Gal 1:13; Eph 4:22; 1 Tim 4:12; Jas 3:13; 1 Pet 1:15, 18; 2:12; 3:1, 2, 16. The author here declares that he "wants" or "wills" to be the sort of leader whom they can imitate, as they do their earlier leaders (13:7).

The author also provides a particular focus for their prayer. He especially (*perissoterōs*; see 2:1; 6:17; 7:15) wants them to do this thing, in order that he might be restored to them (*apokatastathō hymin*) the more quickly (*tachion*). Sharing in the fellowship of their life, he hopes to share in the fellowship of their hospitality (13:2) as well. But he will not come as a stranger. The verb *apokathistēmi* means returning to a former condition (see 2 Sam 9:7; Job 8:6; 2 Macc 11:25; Josephus, *Ant.* 15.195; Matt 12:13; 17:11; Mark 3:5; Luke 6:10; Acts 1:6). Here it clearly implies that the author was formerly part of their community life; thus he was able to recall for them their own earlier experiences and efforts (2:3–4; 6:9–12; 10:32–34). The adverb *tachion* is the comparative of *tacheōs* ("quickly, at once") but can be used absolutely (Josephus, *Life* 310; John 13:27; 1 Tim 3:14), as it is below in 13:23. In the present case, however, the comparative sense ("more quickly") is appropriate because the author suggests that their prayer will speed him to them faster than if they did not pray.

[20–21] The author's own prayer begins with a wish (in the optative mood) for his hearers (*hymas*) and extends to include himself as well (*hēmōn*). The description of God as *ho theos tēs eirēnēs* ("the God of peace") is attested elsewhere (see *T. Dan* 5.2), especially in Paul's letters (Rom 15:33; 16:20; 2 Cor 13:11; Phil 4:9; 1 Thess 5:23; and 2 Thess 3:16, "Lord of peace"). That God is the source of peace is even more frequently stated in Paul's letters (Rom 1:7; 5:1; 1 Cor 1:3; 7:17; 14:33; 2 Cor 1:2; Gal 1:3; Eph 1:2; 2:14, 15, 17; Phil 1:2; 4:7; Col 1:2; 1 Thess 1:1; 2 Thess 1:2; 3:16; 1 Tim 1:2; Titus 1:4; Phlm 3). This is one among many small touches in the conclusion to this composition that have reminded readers, ancient and modern, of Paul and have suggested close association with the Pauline circle. For peace as thematic in Hebrews, see also 7:2; 11:31; 12:11, 14.

God's identity is elaborated through a statement concerning his work. One extended participial clause states, in a highly abbreviated fashion, the experiential and confessional premise underlying the author's complex argument. First and foremost, he is the God who raised Jesus from among the dead. Once more, we are reminded of similar statements in Paul (see Rom 4:24; 10:9). The verb used here, however, is not *egeirein* ("raise") but *anagagōn*, which means literally to lead up from a lower to a higher place (see Luke 2:22; 4:5; 12:4). It is used elsewhere for "leading up" someone from among the dead as from a subterranean realm (see Lucian, *Dialogues of the Dead* 23; 1 Sam 2:6, 28; Ps 29:4), and Paul uses it also for the resurrection of Jesus in Rom 10:7. Hebrews uses *egeirein* for resurrection only in the general principle stated in 11:19, and this is the composition's only direct reference to the resurrection of Jesus as such. It is not perhaps by accident that the author chooses to use a term that fits well within the theme of royal exaltation (see Plutarch, *Numa* 16; Plato, *Republic* 529A, 533D).

Second, the one whom God has raised is designated as *kyrios* ("Lord"), a term used in the earliest Christian confession concerning the resurrection (1 Cor 12:3; Rom 10:9), and implicitly thematic in Hebrews through the use of Ps 109:1 (see Heb 1:10; 2:3; 7:14, 21). Jesus also receives here a designation not found in the rest of the composition, "great shepherd of the sheep" (*ton poimena tōn probatōn ton megan*). The image of the shepherd appears as a revealer in the Hermetic literature (see *Poimandres* 1.1), and Philo uses the image for the divine word (*Change of Names* 116; *Noah the Planter* 51). In Scripture Abel was designated as a *poimēn probatōn* (Gen 4:2; see Heb 11:4), as was David (1 Sam 16:11), who gave rise to the expectation for a messiah who would shepherd the people (Mic 5:2–4; Zech 11:4–17; Isa 40:11; 63:11; Ezek 34:1–31; *Pss. Sol.* 17.40).

In the New Testament, the image is connected to Jesus in the Synoptic Gospels through his parables (Matt 18:12–14; Luke 15:3–7) and through literary characterization (Mark 6:34; 14:27), and is made explicit by Jesus' self-designation in the Gospel of John (10:11, 14). The most striking parallel to the use in Hebrews, though, is found in 1 Peter. After describing the suffering of Christ as an example for believers, 1 Pet 2:25 declares, "You were going astray like sheep, but you have been returned to the shepherd (*poimena*) and guardian (*episkopon*) of your souls." And in 5:4 the author of 1 Peter promises his readers that "when the chief shepherd (*archipoimenos*) appears, you will receive the unfading crown of glory." By calling Jesus the "great" (*mega*) shepherd, the author of Hebrews echoes the description of him as great high priest (4:14; 10:21).

Third, God has also established an "eternal covenant in blood." All these terms are thematic in the composition: "covenant" (*diathēkē*; 7:22; 8:6, 8, 10; 9:20; 10:16, 29; 12:24), "eternal" (*aiōnion*; 5:9; 6:2; 9:12, 14, 15), and "blood" (*haima*; 9:14; 10:4, 19, 29; 12:24; 13:12). What is impressive here is the intricate way in which the author linked the sacrificial death of Jesus to his being "led up," so that death and exaltation appear as a single movement toward God (cf. 10:19–21).

Up to this point, the passage has simply identified the God to whom the prayer is addressed, with an emphasis on what God did to Jesus. Now the prayer shifts its focus to what God might do for the hearers through Jesus. The prayer thus subtly asserts Jesus' status as the Lord through whom God now accomplishes his will among humans. God is asked to "equip you" (*katartisai hymas*).

The verb *katartizein* is not haphazardly selected; the author uses it for the fashioning of the world through God's word in 11:3, and, even more pertinently, for the "fitting" of the Son with a body through which he can do God's will in 10:5. The connection between Jesus and the hearers is thereby once more affirmed, and is reinforced by the phrase "to do his will in every good thing," for it was said of Jesus that he was given a body precisely "to do your will, O God" (10:7). The author also made clear in 10:36 that the people of faith needed to have endurance in order to receive the inheritance "by having done the will of God." The human response of Jesus to God in obedient faith is now to be the response of those "many sons" whom God is "leading (*agagonta*) to glory" through the same path of perfection (2:10).

The prayer characteristically joins this moral/religious response of "doing God's will" (the obedience of faith) to the ritual language of sacrifice. Such worship as this is "pleasing to him" (*euareston enōpion autou*). In 11:5–6 the author spoke of faith as necessary for pleasing God, and in 12:28 declared that a disposition of thanksgiving is worship "pleasing to God." Finally, he said that beneficence and sharing possessions were "sacrifices pleasing to God" (13:16). Once more, it is Paul whose language most clearly approaches that of Hebrews in this regard (see Rom 14:18; 2 Cor 5:9; Eph 5:10; Titus 2:9; Phil 4:18). Romans 12:1–2 provides an especially close parallel: Paul tells his readers to offer their "bodies as a living sacrifice, holy and acceptable to God, your spiritual worship," and spells this out in terms of a renewal of the mind that enables them to do "what is good (*agathon*) and acceptable (*euareston*) and perfect (*teleion*)."

Here the human response of doing God's will is also accomplished (*poiōn*) by God through Jesus Christ (*dia Iēsou Christou*), so that the final phrase "to whom be glory forever" (*hō hē doxa eis tous aiōnas*) has a definitely ambiguous character. Its most obvious referent is Jesus Christ, who shared God's *doxa* from the first (1:3) and to whom God gave honor (*timē*) and glory (*doxa*) at his exaltation to the right hand (2:7, 9; 3:3), but it can equally be directed to God the source of all things, and the one working through Jesus Christ to bring many sons to glory (*doxa*; 2:10).

[22–25] It is not uncharacteristic of some early Christian letters, especially those attributed to Paul, to end with personal comments concerning the author and his readers (see especially Rom 15:15–16:23; 1 Cor 16:1–21; Phil 4:21–23; Col 4:7–18; 1 Thess 5:26–28; 2 Thess 3:17–18; 2 Tim 4:9–22; Titus 3:12–15; Phlm 22–24; 1 Pet 5:12–14). Those made at the end of Hebrews are tantalizing but not ultimately informative. They consist in four discrete statements: (a) a plea for the acceptance of the letter; (b) a scrap of personal news about Timothy; (c) mutual greetings; (d) a final prayer/greeting.

The author begins with a conventional request for the readers/hearers to accept his composition. As we have seen throughout, Hebrews is clearly a discourse prepared for oral delivery. But that scarcely precludes its being sent, and read, as a "letter," as the use of the verb *epistellein* ("to write to someone") suggests (see Plato, *Epistles* 363B; Josephus, *Ant.* 4.13; 14.52; Acts 15:20; 21:25). Although the verb *parakalein* has consistently had the meaning "exhort" up to this point (3:13; 10:25; 13:19), in the present case it has the more deferential sense of "beg" or "request" (cf. Matt 8:5; 14:36; Acts 16:9; 24:4; Phlm 9–10). In contrast, the characterization of what was sent as *logou tēs paraklēseōs* must almost certainly be understood as "word of exhortation" or "hortatory speech" (see 12:5; cf. Paul's speech in Antioch of Pisidia in Acts 13:15). The translation "word of exhortation" also captures something of the character of the speech (see Heb 6:18): the discourse has, after all, provided encouragement and comfort through its message of what God has done in Christ; but even more markedly, it has provided strong exhortation concerning what that gift requires of its recipients in terms of faithful obedience.

Like his earlier self-consciously rhetorical turns (see 5:11; 11:32), the author's request that his hearers "put up with" (*anechesthe*) his composition is a delicate way of acknowledging the imposition that it represents. The sense, then, is that they be willing to listen (see Philo, *Every Good Man Is Free* 36; Josephus, *Ag. Ap.* 2.126); the verb is used in 2 Tim 4:3 for those unwilling to listen to healthy teaching (see also Hermas, *Mand.* 4.2.1). Equally conventional is the mitigating phrase that he has written as briefly as possible (*dia bracheōn*). Brevity was much admired in ancient rhetoric (see, e.g., Plato, *Gorgias* 449C; *Protagoras* 336A; *Let. Aris.* 128), and a claim to have written briefly has the additional benefit of suggesting a capacity for even greater amplitude of argument and adornment. The closest parallel in the New Testament is once more found in 1 Peter, which speaks of being written *di' oligōn* ("through a few words") by way of exhortation (*parakalōn*, 1 Pet 5:12).

The author's addressing them as "brothers" (*adelphoi*) reminds them—and us—of the (fictive) kinship that binds them together. We remember that God's work is "bringing many sons to glory" (2:10), which involved Christ's "not being ashamed to call them brothers" (2:11) and becoming like his brothers in every way (2:17). Those who belong to Christ, therefore, rightly call one another brothers (and sisters), as we see in the author's own previous use of the vocative (3:1, 12; 10:19).

This usage also provides a neat transition to the news about "our brother" (*adelphon hēmōn*) Timothy. The verb *ginōskete* can be taken as indicative ("you know") or as imperative "be informed," and each makes sense in this context. If we read the indicative, the author builds his future hope (expressed in the next clause) on what they already know; if we read the imperative, then the author is informing them of the basis of his future hope.

The simple use of the name Timothy—the only contemporary named personally in the composition—suggests someone well known to the readers. Among scholars, it generates the hope of being able to locate the composition's date and authorship. The most obvious and likely connection is to Paul. Timothy was a companion of Paul in his missionary work (Acts 16:1–3; 17:14–15; 18:5; 19:22; 20:4), a trusted delegate (1 Cor 4:17; 16:10; Phil 2:19; 1 Thess 3:2, 6), who was Paul's "fellow worker" (Rom 16:21) and "brother" (2 Cor 1:1; Col 1:1). He was involved in the writing of six of Paul's letters (see 2 Cor 1:1; Phil 1:1; 1 Thess 1:1; Phlm 1; Col 1:1; 2 Thess 1:1), and he received two letters from Paul, one as his delegate in Ephesus (1 Tim 1:1–3), and one serving to encourage him when Paul was in prison (2 Tim 1:1–2, 8). The greeting of Philemon, furthermore, suggests that Timothy shared Paul's imprisonment at the time he wrote that letter (Phlm 1).

The close association of Timothy with Paul undoubtedly led some early readers to assume Pauline authorship of Hebrews, despite its many points of stylistic and conceptual distinctiveness. But it must also be recognized that the Pauline circle was extensive, and others within his mission team could also have used the same designation of "brother" with respect to Timothy that Paul did. As pointed out in the section on "Author" in the Introduction, Apollos could also serve nicely as a candidate for authorship. But absolutely nothing definitive on this point can be established. Still less can be said about Timothy's "release" (see Matt 27:15–26; Acts 3:13; 5:40) or "being sent away" (Matt 14:15, 22; Acts 19:40), possible translations of the passive participle *apolelymenon*. All we can say is that it provides the basis for the author's hope that—if Timothy arrives quickly (*tachion*)—he might see the hearers in the author's company (*meth' hou . . . opsomai hymas*).

Similar frustration faces efforts to derive specific historical knowledge from the final greetings in 13:24. It is striking that "leaders" (*hēgoumenous*) are mentioned for the third time; as in 13:17, the current rather than former leaders of the community are obviously meant. They are greeted together with "all the saints" (*pantas tous hagious*). The designation "saints" is frequent for members of Pauline communities (Rom 1:7; 16:15; 1 Cor 1:2; 6:1–2; 14:33; 16:15; 2 Cor 1:1; 13:12; Eph 1:1; 6:18; Phil 1:1; 4:22; Col 1:2; 1 Thess 5:27; Phlm 7) and for the community in Jerusalem (Rom 15:25–26, 31; 1 Cor 16:1; 2 Cor 8:4; 9:1, 12). The "greeting of the saints" appears at the end of several of Paul's letters (Rom 16:15; Eph 6:18; Phil 4:22).

The designation is particularly apt in this composition, in which the sanctification worked by God through Christ plays a central thematic role (2:11; 10:10, 14, 29; 13:12), and in which the striving of the hearers can be described as pursuing holiness (12:14). The author refers to the hearers earlier as "holy brethren" (*hagioi adelphoi*, 3:1) and praises them for their service of "the saints" in the community (6:10).

Can anything concrete be derived from the phrase "those from Italy" (*hoi apo tēs Italias*) who send greetings? Not really. The designation "Italy" refers to the territory generally rather than the city of Rome (see Herodotus 1.24; Josephus, *Ant.* 16.7; Acts 27:1, 6). The phrase "from Italy" is used in Acts 18:2 of Priscilla and Aquila, who came to Corinth and joined Paul's circle, after they had left Rome because of Claudius's edict. Precisely this reference, however, points to the difficulty inherent in the phrase. It could be used here of those who were presently in Italy with the author and sent their greetings. But it could equally refer to those who had originally been from Italy and were now with the author, wherever he was.

The composition closes with another greeting typical of Pauline letters (with several variations): "Grace (*charis*) be with all of you" (see Rom 16:20; Phil 4:23; 1 Cor 16:23; Gal 6:18; Eph 6:24; 2 Cor 13:13; Col 4:18; 1 Thess 5:28; 2 Thess 3:18; 1 Tim 6:21; 2 Tim 4:22; Titus 3:15; Phlm 25), a greeting that in the case of Hebrews has special weight because of the specific emphasis given to the divine gift (*charis*) that shapes their present life and future hope (see 2:9; 4:16; 10:29; 12:15, 28; 13:9).

INDEX OF ANCIENT SOURCES

OLD TESTAMENT

Genesis

1:3 70, 132
1:6 70
1:9 70
1:11 70
1:14 70
1:18 209
1:26–27 19
1:28 90
2:2 24, 123, 127, 128, 129
2:4 73
2:7 19
2:19–20 73
2:25 135
3:7 135
3:8 243
3:10 135
3:11 135
3:12–18 164
3:24 133
4:2–7 280
4:2 355
4:5 281
4:10 281
4:16 243
4:26 310
5:1–32 176
5:21–24 282
5:22 282
5:24 282
6:2 76, 83
6:4 76, 83
6:9–7:5 284
6:9–10 176
6:9 96, 284
6:13 284
6:14 284
6:18 192, 252
6:22 285
7:1 284
7:5 284
8:1 90, 165
8:20–21 284
9:8–27 176
9:9–17 192
9:15–16 165
9:15 90, 209
10:1–32 176
11:10–32 176
11:10–26 182
12:2–4 289
12:2–3 169
12:4 289
12:7 289
12:8 289
12:10 290
12:12 289
12:22 289
13:15–16 289
13:16 289
14:16 175
14:17–20 174, 175
14:18 24
14:19 179
14:20 179
15:1 70
15:4 64
15:5 169, 289
15:6 169
15:8 289
15:9 133
15:10–11 134
15:12–16 307
15:13–15 296
15:13–14 289
15:16 289
15:18–21 289
15:18 192
16:1–6 291
16:7 83
17:2–21 192
17:2–8 289
17:7 212, 252
17:8 290, 307
17:10–21 291
17:16 289
17:22–27 176
18:1 289
18:10 289
18:9–12 291
18:11 292
18:12–14 340
18:13 209
18:19 156
19:1–14 340
19:9 290
19:20 171
19:29 90
20:1 290
21:1–10 295
21:1 90
21:8–13 291
21:11 295
21:12 24, 289, 295
21:17 83
21:23 290
22:1 289, 294
22:1–19 294
22:2 294
22:11 83, 294
22:15 289
22:16–17 169, 171, 191, 289
22:16 116, 169, 170
22:17 168, 169, 289, 292
23:4 289, 292
24:12 142
24:36 209
25:13 78
25:27–28 325
25:29–34 296, 325
25:30 325
25:34 325
26:25 199
26:34–35 325

Genesis (*continued*)
27:1 209
27:5–17 296
27:12 329
27:19 78
27:21 329
27:27–29 296
27:39–40 296
27:30–40 325
27:34 325
28:13 293
28:15 343
28:17 262
30:22 340
30:27 142
31:11 83
31:25 199
32:2 307
32:5 142
35:3 269
35:23 78
35:27 290
37:1 290
37:15 115
42:21 269
47:29–31 296
47:31 24, 289, 296
48:15–20 296
48:21 296
49:1–28 296
49:4 341
49:10 187
49:25 104
50:24 90
50:25 296
50:28 116

Exodus
1:8 298
1:15–22 298
2:1 178
2:2 298
2:6 298
2:11–15 200
2:11 298, 299
2:14–15 301
2:14 301
2:24 90, 165, 192, 209
3:2 83
3:4 289, 302
3:6 293
3:10 129
3:13–15 73
3:16 90
3:21 142
4:10 109
4:14 116
4:22–23 79
4:27 178
4:31 90, 269
5:1 129
6:3 223
6:4 290
6:5 90, 165, 209
6:6 236
6:7 129, 208
7:4 266
7:17 208
10:2 208
10:23 69
12:5 96
12:7 303
12:12 266
12:21–36 301
12:21 302
12:23–27 303
12:23 303
12:25 303
12:29–30 303
13:5 116, 169
13:15 236
13:17–15:24 301
13:19 297
14:13 301
14:19 83, 307
14:21 303
14:27 303
15:8 302
15:13 236
15:17–18 75
16:7 69
16:10 69
16:30 129
16:31 220
16:32–34 220
16:33 220
17:1–7 119
17:1 70
17:2 115
17:7 115
17:18:19–23 142
18:19 142
18:21 142
19–31 87
19:3–23 201
19:3 109, 289
19:5 114
19:6 70
19:8 114
19:12–13 329
19:12 242
19:15 192
19:16 329
19:19 329
19:20 302
19:21 329
20:2–17 329, 342
20:6 208
20:10–11 129
20:10 290
20:22 109
21:4 171
21:20–21 242
22:7 104
22:10–13 170
23:20 83
23:22 192
24:3–8 241
24:3 241
24:4–18 201
24:4 241
24:5 235, 241
24:6 241, 289, 302
24:7–8 214, 241
24:7 241
24:8 23, 241
24:9–11 302
24:10 324
24:16 69
25:1–31:11 220
25:8 199
25:16–22 103
25:16 220
25:17–22 220
25:21 221
25:22 221
25:23–30 219
25:29 222
25:30 219
25:40 19, 200
26:1–36 199
26:30 201
26:31 172
26:33–34 217
26:37 257
27:9 199
27:20 222
27:21 173, 199
28:1–3 178
28:11 144
28:35 198
28:41–43 178
29:1–46 97, 178
29:1 238
29:4 225
29:9–34 17, 96
29:21 302
29:22–34 185

29:28–42 195
29:30 198
29:46 208
30:1 220
30:6 220
30:7 178
30:8 222
30:10 71, 178
31:2 201
31:12 302
31:13 208
32:14 104
32:19 302
33:11 302
33:12 142, 223
33:17–34:7 108
33:18 109
33:21 116
34:1–4 201
34:5 73
34:6–7 192
34:6 104, 263
34:7 208
34:10 192
34:14 73
34:21 116, 126, 129
34:27–35 302
35:2 116, 126
35:11 199
35:31–40 219
36:2–39 220
36:3 219
36:18 257
37:5 173
37:19 198
37:17–24 219
38:6 199
38:7–9 220
39:36 219
40:2–38 199, 220
40:3 173
40:15 178, 179
40:4 219
40:9–10 242
40:23 219
40:26–27 220
40:34 221
40:44 219

Leviticus
1:2 143
1:3 238
1:10 179
2:1–3:7 143
2:1 143
2:3 179, 225
2:8 143
2:10 179, 225
2:13 192
3:1–17 347
3:2 179
3:5 179
3:8 179
3:12 179
4:1–5:19 143
4:1–35 143
4:2–17 223
4:3 103, 139
4:5 17, 96
4:6 173
4:7 242
4:17 173
4:18 242
4:20 242
4:23 143
4:25 242
4:30 242
5:11 242
5:13 225
5:20–24 169
6:1–7 143
6:18 225
6:23 348
6:24–30 225
6:24 179
7:11–21 347
7:19 143
7:27 96, 185
8:1–34 97
8:6 225
8:15 242
8:19 242
8:21–33 17, 96, 185
9:6 69
9:9 143
9:12 302
10:6 109
10:10 324
11:1–42 225
11:32–38 225
12:1–15:33 225
14:4 241
14:6–7 242
14:14 242
15:1–33 242
15:21–26 341
16:1–34 25, 143
16:2–28 103
16:2 173, 221, 222
16:3 222
16:3–5 223
16:4 225
16:6–10 223
16:6 144
16:7–33 199
16:11–14 223
16:12 173
16:14–27 237
16:14–16 26
16:14 179, 221
16:15–19 242
16:15–17 223
16:15 173, 221
16:16 199, 223
16:18–19 223
16:20–28 217
16:20–22 223
16:20 199
16:23–28 223
16:26 242
16:27 348
16:28 225, 348
16:30 71, 223
16:32 96
16:33 199
17:4 242
17:11 26, 237, 242
17:13 242
17:14 237
18:25 266
19:2 97
19:12 169
19:22 242
20:17 253
21:1–22 179
21:6 143
21:9 324
21:10 96, 139
22:6 242
23:9–21 143
23:32 129
23:38 262
24:5–9 219
24:8 192
24:14 348
24:23 348
25:29 236
25:48 236
26:1 199
26:9 192
26:12 208
26:17 243
26:25 171
26:30 199
26:35 129

Numbers
1:47–54 178

Numbers (*continued*)
2:33 178
3:3 96
3:10 142
3:14–40 178
3:26 257
3:38 178, 219
3:44–51 178
3:44 178
4:18 303
5:1–7 97
6:14 238
7:10–11 241
7:84 241
8:22 198
9:7 143
11:1 116
11:12 116
12:1 108
12:2 108
12:3 108
12:6–8 108
12:7 105, 107
12:8 108
12:9 116, 302
14:10 69
14:16 169
14:29 119
14:21–22 116
14:21 117, 132
14:22 119
14:28 117, 132
14:32 119
14:33 324
15:3 262
15:4 143
15:5 225
15:7 225
15:10 225
15:20 262
15:22–31 262
15:22–30 223
15:25–26 242
15:35–36 348
16:22 322
16:27 322
16:46 242
17:16–26 220
17:25 220
18:8–9 97
18:10 178
18:21 178, 179
18:24 179
18:26 179
18:29 97
19:2 238
19:6 241
19:9–17 237
19:11–22 225
19:7 225
20:22–20 179
21:24 133
22:3 116
22:22 83
23:3–8 195
24:6 199
24:15–17 75
24:16 155, 176
24:17 187
25:4 161
25:12 192
25:26 171
27:57–62 178
28:7–10 225
28:15 225
29:39 262
30:3 169
31:2 266
31:21–24 242
31:48 142
31:50 242
33:4 266
35:25 139
35:28 139
35:30 263
35:32 139
35:33 242

Deuteronomy
1:8 67, 16
1:12 277
1:13 142
1:14 163
1:17 115
1:19 262
1:26–27 119
1:26 120
1:32–34 120
1:43 146
2:7 262
3:24 109
4:6 120
4:1 114
4:2 114
4:5 208
4:9–10 208
4:10 67
4:11 329
4:13 192
4:23 192
4:26 114, 117
4:29 269, 284
4:30 158
4:31 192, 264
4:33 117, 132, 331
4:34 114, 115
4:42 171
5:1 114
5:2 192
5:3 114
5:5 70
5:6–21 342
5:10 208
5:12 97
5:14 290
5:15 72, 97
5:22–23 329
5:22 329
5:24 69
5:25 329
5:26 133, 331
6:2 114
6:3–4 114
6:4–5 73, 192
6:6–9 192
6:6 207
6:7–9 208
6:16 115
7:2 210
7:4 302
7:6 129
7:8 236
7:9 208
7:19 115
7:26 116
8:2 115
8:17 262
9:1 114
9:5 116
9:9–10 220
9:15 329
9:19 330
9:22 115
9:23 119, 146
9:26 236
10:1–5 220
11:6 277
11:8–17 307
11:17 116
11:18–19 116
11:19–20 208
12:6–8 262
12:9 116, 126
13:3 115
13:5 236
13:6–10 264
14:3–21 225
15:18 115

16:18 307
16:20 117
17:2–6 264
17:6 263
17:12–13 262
17:18 252
18:6 290
18:18–19 75
19:1 210, 264
19:15 88, 263
20:5 241, 256
20:20 303
21:14 263
23:22 169
26:5 272, 290
26:15 129
26:17–19 208
27:15 290
28:29 252
28:53 269
28:56 308
28:65 224
29:1 192
29:3 114, 115
29:17 324
29:19 324
29:20 263
29:27 259
29:39 262
30:1 164
30:2–16 164
30:2 158
30:17 164
31:6 338, 344
31:8 344
31:16 324
31:24 115
31:27 115
32:3 72
32:4 195
32:6 266
32:8 176
32:35–36 266
32:35 256
32:36 266, 342
32:41 266
32:43 74, 78, 266
33:8–11 75
33:8 115
33:9–10 155
33:10 223
33:21 156
33:29 111, 129
34:10–12 108
34:10 108, 302
34:11 108, 114

Joshua
1:1–6 307
1:1 198
1:2 109, 128
1:6 116
2:1 304
2:6–7 128
2:11 304
2:12–13 304
2:14 304
3:10 303, 306
4:7 224
5:1 306
5:8 300
6:2 304
6:14–26 303
6:20 133
6:25 304
6:26 75
8:18–23 306
8:24 133
9:1–27 306
10:1–43 306
10:13 224
11:1–23 306
12:1–24 306
12:24 305
13:1–22 307
18:1 199
19:48 307
22:13 103, 139
23:2 209
24:1–15 120, 310
24:25 192
24:27 114
24:32 297
24:33 103

Judges
1:7 266
1:25 133
1:35 109
2:1 83, 116
2:10 208
2:18–19 307
3:17 298
3:20 132
4–5 306
4:4–5:31 307
4:15 133
5:5 334
5:31 307
6–8 306
6:4 277
6:11–14 340
6:11 83
7:9–25 307
8:18 199
8:28 307
9:4 263
9:23 263
10:14 269
11–12 306
11:34 294
11:36 266
12:7–15 307
13:6 262
13–16 306
13:8 162
14:6 307
15:1–20 307
15:18 266
16:26 329
20:2 129

Ruth
1:12 209, 278
1:16 90
2:10 292

1 Samuel
1:18 142
2:6 355
2:10 208
2:17 189, 263
2:28 355
3:21 223
4:4 221
8:1 209
8:5 209
11:14 241
12:2 209
13:14 284
14:24 92
14:48 264
15:24 132
16 306
16:11 355
17:12 187
17:26 300
17:34–35 307
17:53 264
19:10–18 307
19:24 135
20:27 346
21:4–6 219
25:3 115
29:6 256
29:9 83

2 Samuel
3:39 142
4:8 266

2 Samuel (*continued*)
4:9 269
4:13 129
5:7 331
6:2 221
7:1–8 227
7:9–16 77
7:9 78
7:10 75
7:11–14 75, 77
7:12–16 227
7:13 78
7:14 74, 75, 76, 77
9:7 354
12:9 132
12:21 350
13:18 198
14:17 83
14:22 180
15:4 142
15:14 307
15:20 346
21:5 210
24:14 266

1 Kings
1:47 180
6:1–7:51 227
6:12–13 227
8:1 331
8:6 227
8:9 220
8:11 227
8:56 116, 126
8:63 256
9:7 210
10:5 223
12:3 115
12:24 132
13:21 115
13:26 115
15:3 96
17:8–24 308
19:1–18 307
21:13 348
32:27 308

2 Kings
2:11–12 283
4:11–37 308
6:1–33 307
9:36 132
10:3 149
19:31 263

1 Chronicles
9:32 219
10:13 132
12:18 104
15:5 132
16:15–18 212
16:25 262
17:13 74, 76
21:13 266
28:2 224
24:12 351
29:11 72
29:22 185

2 Chronicles
2:7 241
3:10–12 219
5:10 220
7:5 240, 256
9:4 224
11:2 132
15:8 161, 240
16:10 308
20:18 161
24:13 224
28:19 161
29:6 161
30:7 161
30:16 224
35:10 224
35:15 224
36:21 129

Ezra
3:12–13 228

Nehemiah
1:5 262
4:14 262
5:9 300
8:7 224
9:3 224
9:6–38 310
9:7 224
9:8–23 120
13:4–29 228
13:11 224

Esther
3:13 243
8:13 210
10:10 129

Job
1:6 76
1:21 135
2:1 76, 87
2:3 195
2:9 302
6:11 167
8:6 354
9:4 167
9:27 351
9:33 203
23:2 351
26:6 135
31:20 180
34:3 92
36:5 195
38:7 76

Psalms (LXX numbering)
2:1 75, 77
2:5 116, 302
2:6 77, 97, 142, 331
2:7 74, 75, 76, 77, 82, 114, 144
2:8 77
2:11 77
2:12 302
4:3 195
4:4 115
4:6 69, 243
5:7 97, 208
5:8 156
5:9 115
5:10 115
6:4 142, 208
7:4 266
7:5 264
7:11 333
7:66 116
8:5–7 22, 51, 85, 89
8:6 144
8:7 89
9:1 115
9:3 243
9:8 81
9:9 269
9:12 331
9:13 340
9:20 142
9:27 334
10:5 97
11:1 195
11:2 115
11:4 19
12:5 142, 208
12:7 210
14:2 238
14:11 210
15:10 344
15:11 243
16:3 115
16:7 208
16:13 123

17:6 97
17:7 334
17:8 330
17:23 238
17:30 238
17:47 266
18:1–2 66
18:1 69
19:2 97
19:4 170
29:6 351
21:1 98
21:2 344
21:3 97
21:11 269
21:14 98
21:19 98
21:20 294
21:23 22, 98, 99, 250
22:5 293
22:6 208
23:4 169
23:6 243, 284
23:9 307
24:3 167
24:4 116
24:6–7 209
24:6 142, 209
24:7 165
24:10 116, 208
24:11 103
24:16 294
24:22 269
26:8 243, 284
26:11 116
27:8–9 129
28:1 73, 83
28:2 97
28:11 129
29:4 195, 355
29:11 351
30:16 142, 208
30:23 266
32:6 70, 280
32:9 132
32:11 171
33:6 162
33:7 83
33:8 92
34:17 294
35:2 115
35:9 69
36:18 238
36:25 209
36:40 104
37:9 135
38:12 292
39:1 251
39:2 251
39:3 251
39:6–8 246, 250
39:6 253
39:7 252, 278
39:8 242
39:9 125
39:10–11 208, 251
39:11–17 250
40:3 104
40:7–9 24, 52
40:8 22
40:10 266
41:2 243
43:26 104
44:3 80
44:7–8 49, 50, 74, 79, 80
44:7 81, 140
44:8 80, 176
45:5 104, 243
45:10 208
46:2 262
46:8 97
47:3 331
47:9 129
48:8 236
49:6 333
49:21 243
50:1 208
50:6 223
50:15 349
55:11 132
56:2 176
56:4 133
62:3 349
62:5 349
62:10 133
64:3 103
64:5 97
64:9 293
65:10 115
66:4 81
67:5 97, 333
67:8 334
67:11 125
68:9 263
68:10 301
69:4 284
70:22 97
70:23 349
72:27 342
73:2 209
73:16 280
73:18 209
73:19 340
74:2 82
74:7 333
75:7 262
76:18 334
77:1–72 310
77:5–67 121
77:17–18 121
77:33–37 121
77:59 121
77:8 115
77:14 69
77:17 115
77:20 293
77:38 103, 264
77:40 115
77:41 115
77:43 114
77:56 115, 176
77:64 133
78:1 97
78:5 263
78:8 209
78:9 103
78:11 72
79:2 221
80:7 115
80:10 257
81:5 334
81:6 83
82:16 284
83:2 117, 132, 331
85:15 104
85:17 104
88:3–4 301
88:4 293
88:6 83
88:7 76
88:15 69
88:19–21 301
88:27 72
88:27–37 301
88:28 79
88:37 280
88:39 301
88:42 301
88:50 209
88:51–52 301
88:51 301
92:4 76
93:1 266
94 46, 47, 116
94:1–3 114
94:4–5 114

Psalms (*continued*)
94:7–11 110, 112, 114, 119, 121, 126, 128, 169, 186
94:7 77, 114, 123, 128, 183
94:8 45
94:9 115
94:10 115
94:11 24, 122, 123, 126, 128
95:2 125
95:4 262
95:10 81
96:1 78
96:2 78
96:4 334
96:7 74, 78
97:7 334
97:9 81
98:1 221
98:2 72
98:3 262
98:9 97
99:3 208
101:7 350
101:12 81
101:13 81
101:26–28 50, 74, 79, 80, 81, 88
102:5 161
102:8 104
103:4 74, 79, 82, 198
103:27 142
103:30 161
104 120, 121
104:3 284
104:4 284
104:10 212
104:28 115
105:4 90, 209
105:6–33 121
105:7 115
105:14 115
105:26 121
105:33 115
105:43 115
108:12 264
109 21, 99, 183, 190, 197, 251, 253
109:1–4 49, 191, 318, 336
109:1 71, 72, 73, 74, 77, 81, 82, 88, 90, 140, 144, 145, 171, 197, 262, 336, 355
109:2 331
109:3 81
109:4 22, 24, 81, 116, 138, 140, 144, 145, 149, 169, 171, 173, 175, 176, 183, 186, 188, 191, 196, 263
110 (MT) 21, 29, 72, 183
110:1 (MT) 81
110:4 (MT) 104
110:9 (LXX) 236, 262
111:4 104
112:5 72
113:15 329
113:17 109
113:20 109, 209
114:5 104
117:2 109
117:9 345
117:6 262, 345
117:9 345
117:18 345
117:20 345
117:22 345
117:113–114 345
118:10–11 155
118:15 116
118:25 133
118:33 116
118:50 133
118:73 293
118:105 69
118:130 162
118:151 116
118:171 349
118:176 115
120:8 256
126:1 350
129:7 236
131:1 209
131:17 293
134 120
134:9 114
134:14 266
134:17 329
135 120
135:1–26 310
135:12 72
136:7 90
137:2 97
137:6 72
138:1 115
139:1–18 135
144:3 72
145:17 195
146:15 132
147:9 223
148:5 73
150:2 72

Proverbs
1:4 195
3:11–12 58, 320
3:11 320
3:21 86
4:27 115
6:24 163
8:1–9:6 132
8:5 195
8:22–31 67
8:34 350
11:5 238
12:1 278
13:8 278
13:10 278
16:5 284
17:6 111
18:10 72
19:21 171
22:29 154
27:21 140
28:5 284

Qoheleth
1:9 257
5:2 19
5:14 135
9:4–5 100
10:11 226

Isaiah
1:2 263
1:3 208
1:10 66, 132
1:11–31 253
2:12–21 260
2:18 199
3:25 133
4:5 329
5:1–7 164
6:3 229
6:10 158
8 98
8:11 75
8:12–13 99
8:17–18 98, 99, 250
8:17 22
8:18 22
9:6–9 177
9:13 158
10:11 199
11:1 187
12:6 97
16:12 199

16:13 70
19:8 351
20:2 135
21:9 199
22:19 224
26:11 263
26:20 273
28 98
28:4 132
30:18 333
31:1 284
32:17 177
33:22 333
37:4 117, 132
37:17 132
38:7 70
40:8 66
40:11 355
40:9 125
42:6 289
42:14 302
43:1 289
43:19 206
44:10 189
45:3 208, 289
46:3 158
47:10 342
48:4 115
48:6 206
49:2 133
49:8 104, 117
49:15 132
49:23 208
51:2 289
52:7 125
53:12 245
54:4–8 342
55:6 284
57:3 342
59:10 329
59:20–21 214
59:27 214
60:1 162
60:6 125
60:16 208
61:1 125
61:6 198
62:2 206
63:7 333
63:11 355
65:15 206
65:17 206
66:1 19
66:5 66
66:10 351
66:15 263
66:22 206

Jeremiah

1:1 66
1:4 66, 132
2:20 324
2:1–3:5 120
2:8 189
3:6–10 342
4:10 133
4:17 207
4:22 208
5:1 208
6:26 294
6:10 300
7:1–4 227
7:5–6 227
7:13 289
7:14–15 228
7:23 208
8:7 208
9:3 208
9:11 210
9:24 208
11:4 208
11:19 195
11:20 135
13:27 342
15:6 334
15:15 167
20:2 308
20:7 308
21:14 263
22:24 117, 132
23:5 187
23:40 300
27:4 284
27:45 170
29:20 170
29:26 308
30:1 205
30:3 205
31:1–6 205
31:3–5 207
31:19–20 205
31:23–29 205
31:27 205
31:31–34 203, 246, 250, 252, 254
31:31–32 27
31:31 205
31:32 102, 206
31:33 113, 206, 254
31:34 21, 254
31:38 205
37:1 (LXX) 205
37:15 308
38:31–34 (LXX) 203
38:31 (LXX) 205
38:22 (LXX) 206
38:34 (LXX) 21
39:37 259

Ezekiel

1:3 90
1:26–28 221
2:1 90
2:9 252
3:1–3 252
3:12 229
5:11 228
4:14 324
6:2 90
6:13 208
6:14 210
7:17 208
8:1–9:10 228
9:30 221
10:1–22 221
11:16 228
11:17–19 228
11:19 206
11:22–23 228
12:3 90
13:23 208
14:13 161
15:8 161
16:7 135
16:27 135
16:38 342
18:24 161
18:30 342
18:31 206
19:5 278
19:10–14 164
20:1–31 120
20:2–38 310
20:4 121
20:13 121
20:14 121
20:27 121, 161
20:30 121
21:6 351
21:25 324
22:36 324
23:29 135
23:36 342
23:45 342
24:14 342
28:17 161
34:1–31 355
36:5–6 228

Ezekiel (*continued*)
36:26 206
37:26–27 208
40:3–47:12 228
43:1–5 228
43:11 277
44:10 75
44:30–31 347
45:4 219
46:11 332
48:35 228

Daniel
2:5–47 223
3:13–26 307
4:10 83
4:13 83
4:20 83
6:13 194
6:19–23 307
6:27 199
7:10 83
7:26–27 160
7:26 245
8:17 224
9:26–27 244
11:35 244
12:2 159
12:13 244

Hosea
1:1 66
1:2 324, 342
1:9–10 129
1:10 117, 132
2:2 342
2:3 135
2:11 332
3:1 342
3:14–23 120
4:15 169
8:3 334
9:1 342
9:5 332
12:18 300
13:14 100

Joel
1:1 132
1:15 260
2:13 104
2:19 300
2:32 125
3:14 260

Amos
4:10 133
5:1 66, 132
5:18–20 260
5:21 332
7:9 133
8:9–14 260
8:10 294
9:11 75

Jonah
4:2 104

Micah
1:1 66, 132
1:7 210
5:2–4 355
5:5 177
5:14 210
7:13 210

Nahum
1:15 125
2:7 277
3:1 329

Habakkuk
2:3 268
2:4 273, 274, 279, 281, 322, 332

Zephaniah
1:14–18 260
1:18 263
3:8 263

Haggai
1:1 139
1:11 133
1:12 139
1:14 139
2:3 139
2:6 21, 334, 335
2:20 132
2:21 334, 335

Zechariah
1:1 66
1:7 132
1:9 83
1:12 83
1:13 163, 210
2:9 117, 132
3:1 83, 103, 139
3:8 187
3:9 103, 139
6:11 103, 139
6:12 187
9:10 177
11:4–17 355
12:10 294
14:1 260

Malachi
1:3 210

OLD TESTAMENT APOCRYPHA

1 Esdras
5:38 185

2 Esdras
3:15 212

Tobit
3:1 351
3:3 223
5:4 83
5:17 83
5:20 83
7:18 351
12:1–20 340
14:3 209

Judith
4:1 210
4:6 103
4:12 199
4:14 103
5:5–21 310
5:20 223
11:23 298
16:20 199

Wisdom of Solomon
1:2 243
1:11 189
2:14 278
2:24 100
3:6 210
3:10 207
3:13 341
3:16 341
4:10 283
5:3 351
6:9 161
7:18 155
7:22–24 135
7:25–26 50
7:26 19, 68, 69, 70
7:27 70
8:1 70
8:3–6 67
8:16 351
8:20 194, 195
9:1 70, 132, 280
9:6 96
10:1 310

10:5 294, 310
10:16–11:14 311
10:16 109
10:17 284
11:6 278
12–14 311
12:10 326
13:6 284
14:8 199
14:22 149
14:29–30 169
16:28 194
17:4 243
17:20 226
18:14–16 133
18:24 72
18:25 83, 303
19:13 269

Sirach
2:2 302
2:15 284
2:18 266
3:6 146
4:29 154
6:21 113, 115
7:30 198
8:1 266
10:2 198
11:2 154
12:15 302
14:18 99
17:12 212
18:11 167
19:15 193
23:2 223
23:11 169
23:16–21 342
23:16–18 342
23:19–21 342
24:1–12 67
26:5 332
27:2 134
28:18 133, 307
32:12 333
34:18–35:11 349
34:26 146
35:19 167
38:22 346
39:13 146
41:1–4 100
41:3 146
42:15 70, 280
42:18 226
44:1 311
44:16 202, 283, 311
44:17 96
44:17–18 311
44:18 212
44:19–21 311
44:20 294
44:22 311
44:23–45 311
45:1–5 311
45:5 302
45:6–22 311
45:7 212
45:15 212
45:23–24 311
45:23 120
45:24 185
46:1–10 120
46:1 307
46:13–20 311
47:1 311
47:2–11 311
47:5 307
47:12–23 311
47:23–25 311
48:1–11 311
48:12–16 311
48:17–29 311
48:22 83
49:1–3 311
49:6–7 311
49:8–10 311
49:11 311
49:12 311
49:13 311
49:14 311
49:15 297, 311
49:16 311
50:1–21 311
50:1 103

Epistle of Jeremiah
63 177
70 177

Song of the Three Young Men
3:54–55 221
3:50 307
3:88 307

Susanna
7 298
23 266

1 Maccabees
1:21–28 228
1:49 339
1:54–61 228
1:63 324
2:1 186
2:51–59 311
2:51 311
2:54 185
2:59 307
2:60 307
2:61 311
3:5 307
3:13 332
3:23–26 307
3:43 199
3:49 185
3:59 199
4:6–25 307
4:36–58 228
4:36 241
4:54–56 241
4:57–59 241
5:1 241
5:3 307
5:21–36 307
6:28 308
6:31 308
7:9 185, 308
7:14 308
7:21 185
7:23 308
8:32 194
10:20 103, 139
10:49 307
10:61 194
10:63 194
10:64 194
11:25 194
12:3 103
13:39 223
14:30–48 228
14:41 186, 228
16:3 209

2 Maccabees
1:36 149
2:2 339
2:7 260, 261
2:9 241
2:19 241
2:28–32 219
2:52 294
3:1 139
3:4 103
4:1 290
4:7–10 228
4:13 103
4:14 207
4:36 194

2 Maccabees (*continued*)
5:22 342
6:1–6 228
6:6 129
6:12 264
6:14 167
6:26 245
7:1 308
7:7 308
7:9 159
7:10 308
7:11 159
7:14 159
7:17 245, 302
7:19 245
7:23 159
7:37 308
8:21 293
9:11 308
10:3–8 228
10:29 83
11:6 83
11:25 354
13:14 293
14:28 329
14:30 279
14:31–36 228
14:36 195
15:1 116, 126
15:34 195
16:28 193
18:11 281

3 Maccabees
1:11 103, 139
2:14 324
5:5 198
6:6 307
6:77 194
7:14 161
7:16 300

4 Maccabees
2–6 127
2:22 143
3:8 318
4:1 111
4:10 83
4:13 103, 139
4:16 103
4:24 264
5:11 322
5:18 127
5:35 185
6:7 259
6:35 351
7:6 185
7:11 83
7:13 127
8:7 300
8:11 245
9:9 302
9:28 302
10:1 302
10:5 134
12:2 143
13:23 140, 270, 339
13:26 339
14:1 339
16:1 311
16:2–25 311
16:3 307
16:21 307
17:3 259
18:1–19 311
18:2 311
18:3 311
18:12 307
18:13 307

NEW TESTAMENT

Matthew
1:1–3 187
1:1 187
1:6 187
1:20–24 84
2:1 187, 235
2:5 22
2:12 201, 284
2:17 74
2:22 201, 284
3:2 260
3:7 159
3:8 158
3:10–12 164, 263
3:11 158
3:21 273
4:1 100
4:6 84
4:11 84
4:16 187
4:17 260, 336
4:21 280
5:1 209
5:5 67
5:7 104
5:12 284
5:22 263
5:34–37 170
5:34 170
6:1–16 284
6:4 135
6:6 135
6:7 146
7:3 259
7:19 263
8:5 357
8:20 90
9:4 135
9:18 159
9:27 187
10:2 107
10:41–42 284
10:23 300
11:12 271
11:19 90
12:1–8 219
12:5 135
12:13 354
13:1–9 164
13:2 269
13:9 271
13:18 114
13:24–30 164
13:29 84
13:30 164
13:39 244
13:40 244
13:41 84, 90
13:42 263
13:49 84, 244
14:15 358
14:22 358
14:31 102
14:36 357
15:6 132
15:7 279
15:22 187
15:25 104
16:5 165
16:9 279
16:11 279
16:17–18 176
16:17 99
16:28 92
17:5 316
17:9 187
17:11 354
17:25 264
18:8 160
18:10 84
18:12–14 355
18:12 264
18:16 88, 263
18:35 106
19:8 115
19:28 90
19:29 67

20:8 284
20:19 187
20:22 92
21:10 335
21:12–13 232
21:18 125
21:28 264
21:30 191
21:32 191
21:38 67
21:42 345
22:30 84
22:37 165
22:44 71
23:25 271
24:1–2 232
24:3 244
24:9 269
24:15 279
24:27 90
24:29 269
24:31 84
24:37–38 286
25:4 115
25:21 271
25:23 271
25:25–30 100
25:31–46 29, 245
25:31 84
25:34 67, 293
25:36 270
25:41 84, 100, 160, 263
25:43 270
25:44 270
25:46 160
26:13 84
26:19 302
26:24 71
26:27 49, 92
26:28 192, 214, 237, 241, 242, 245
26:29 92, 336
26:36–46 51, 145
26:38 145
26:39 322
26:61 232
26:63 117, 133
27:1 103
27:3 191
27:15–26 358
27:24–25 237
27:35 98
27:44 269
27:46 98, 261, 344
27:51 232, 335
28:2 84
28:8 271
28:19 163
28:20 244

Mark
1:2 22
1:4 159, 242
1:11 77
1:13 84
1:15 260, 336
2:23–28 219
3:5 354
3:14 107
3:17 176
4:3–9 164
5:16 306
5:23 159
6:21 142
6:25 166
6:26 263
6:34 355
7:1–8 347
7:2 265
7:4 159
7:9 263
7:14 114
7:15–23 237
8:31 90
8:32 111
8:38 84
9:1 92
9:9 306
9:14 339
9:24 104
10:5 115
10:13 159
10:17 67
10:21 125
10:38–39 92
10:45 90, 92, 95, 245
10:47 187
10:50 272
11:11 232
11:25 322
12:7 67
12:26 159
12:30 165
12:36 72
13:1–2 232
13:26 316
13:27 84
13:33 350
14:1 130
14:11 142
14:16 302
14:23–25 92
14:24 92, 192, 214, 237, 241, 245
14:25 336
14:27 355
14:32–42 145
14:33–34 145
14:36 145
14:58 199, 232
14:62 72
15:6 329
15:14 98
15:32 269
15:34 98, 261, 344
15:37 232
16:14 115

Luke
1:1 65
1:2 28
1:4 172
1:11 84
1:14 271, 351
1:27 187
1:32–33 77
1:32 187
1:54 209
1:55 102
1:68 236
1:72 192, 209
1:77 242
1:78 187
2:1 332
2:3 332
2:4 187
2:5 146, 332
2:7 79
2:9 84
2:10 271
2:22 354
2:23 22
2:26 201, 284, 334
2:32 332
2:38 236
3:3 159, 242
3:14 343
3:22 77
3:23–33 187
3:23 187
4:5 354
4:10 84
4:28 302
4:43 336
5:1 132
5:7 118
5:32 158
6:1–5 219

Luke (*continued*)
6:10 354
6:13 107
6:22 269
6:23 284
7:8 351
7:12 294
7:19 273
7:30 170, 189, 263
8:2 141
8:3 270
8:12 100
8:21 132
8:39 306
8:42 294
9:10 306
9:23 300
9:26 84, 322
9:27 92
9:38 294
9:40 100
9:47 102
9:52 84
10:16 114, 189, 263, 339
10:18 100
10:20 332
10:25 67
10:27 166
11:21 270
11:39 271
11:45 265
11:47–48 65
12:1 331
12:4 354
12:6 165
12:15 270
12:33 270
12:44 270
12:24 106
12:27 106
12:42 142
12:51 125, 235
13:6–9 164
13:11 193, 194
14:4 102
14:21 235
15:2 271
15:3–7 355
15:7 271
15:10 84, 271
15:20 135
16:1 270
16:2 136, 137, 350
16:9–18 341
16:9 160
16:14 343
17:3 86
17:22 166
17:33 274
17:26–27 286
18:6 114
18:7–8 266
18:18 67
18:33 187
18:38 187
19:3 146
19:11 125
19:20 245
19:45–46 232
20:14 67
20:17 345
20:35 159
20:42 72
21:5 232
21:27 95
21:36 350
22:2 103, 214
22:12 146
22:13 302
22:15 166
22:16 336
22:20 92, 192, 237, 241
22:39–46 145
22:43 84
22:46 345
22:48 264
22:69 72
23:14 334
23:34 98
23:42 340
23:45 232
24:5 133
24:18 290
24:21 236
24:26 97
24:27 242
24:39 329
24:41 146
24:52 271
24:53 222

John
1:1–18 30
1:1–2 132
1:1 50, 80
1:3 68
1:4–14 69
1:9 198, 273
1:10 68
1:13–14 30
1:13 99
1:14 294, 322
1:18 50, 80, 294
1:38 176
1:42 176
1:51 84
2:13–22 232
3:6 30
3:8 163
3:12 106
3:15 148
3:16 148, 165, 294
3:31 273
4:24 349
5:4 84
5:24 148
5:25–29 245
5:29 159
5:39 125
6:14 273
6:15 271
6:31 121
6:32 121
6:33 199
6:48–50 121
6:51 92
6:60 115
6:70 100
7:4 111
7:18 141
7:32 103
8:15 30
8:33 102
8:46 141
8:52 92
9:7 176
10:11 355
10:12 271
10:14 355
10:35 132
11:50–51 92
12:27–43 145
12:27 51, 145
12:29 84
12:31 100
12:48 263
13:2 100
13:15 131, 202
13:27 354
13:38 300
14:8 343
14:30 100
15:1 199
15:6 164, 263
15:9 165
15:11 271, 351
15:12 166
15:17 166

16:20 271
16:33 269
17:2 148
17:23 165
18:11 92
18:20 111
18:63 336
19:17–20 348
19:14 302
19:24 98
19:34 237
20:12 84
20:28 50, 80

Acts
1:2 107
1:6 354
1:9 316
1:20 22
1:24 135
2:1–4 28
2:19 89
2:21 166
2:22 89
2:23 170
2:25 222
2:27 344
2:30–31 187
2:34 72
2:36 73
2:38 163, 166, 242
2:39 289
2:43 28, 89
2:44 350
2:45 271
3:6 166
3:13–14 300
3:13 358
3:16 166
3:25 192, 214
3:26 334
4:1 103
4:2 159
4:11 345
4:13 111, 140
4:28 170
4:29 111, 140
4:30 89
4:31 132, 140
4:32 270, 350
4:36 41
5:2 125
5:12 28, 89
5:15 100
5:19 84
5:31 96, 158, 242
5:37–38 117
5:40 166, 358
6:2 132
6:6 159
6:7 132
6:8 89
7:2–50 312
7:2 95
7:5 102
7:6 240
7:8 192, 214
7:11 65
7:16 297
7:18 186
7:17 289
7:20 298, 299
7:22 299
7:23–29 121
7:24–27 299
7:24 266, 298
7:30–39 121
7:30 84, 87
7:32 320
7:34 129
7:35 84
7:38 87, 155
7:39–43 122
7:39 65, 122
7:44 65
7:48 199
7:51 122
7:52 65
7:53 84, 87
7:55 95
7:56 90
7:58 348
8:3 270
8:12–17 29
8:12 166
8:17–18 159
8:18 163
8:26 84
8:33 306
9:2 270
9:12 159
9:13 166
9:27 42, 102, 306
9:32 166
10:1–11:30 347
10:3 84
10:14 265
10:15 237
10:22 201, 284
10:24 339
10:28 265
10:31 146
10:36 125
10:38 100
10:43 242
10:44–47 163
11:1 132
11:9 237
11:19–30 42
11:19 269
11:26 201
12:3–5 270
12:4 302
12:7 84
12:17 306
13:1–15:35 42
13:3 159
13:5 132
13:7 132
13:13 77
13:15 10, 357
13:23 77, 102, 289
13:36 170
13:22–23 187
13:38 242
13:44–48 132
13:46 160
13:52 271
14:11 102
14:12 345
14:13 89
14:14 107
14:15 102, 117, 133, 159
14:17 127
14:22 269, 336
15:3 271
15:8 135
15:9 71
15:12 89
15:14 129
15:16–17 75
15:20 357
15:22 345
15:38 117
15:40–18:5 41
16:1–3 358
16:9 357
16:15 339
16:22 334
16:24–34 270
16:29 330
17:3 97, 187
17:10 259
17:14–17 358
17:18 125
17:24 199
17:29 135

Acts (*continued*)
17:31 29
17:32 160
18:2–3 41
18:2 40, 358
18:5–17 44
18:5 358
18:11 132
18:12 257
18:13 89
18:18 41
18:21 160
18:24–28 42, 88
18:26 41
19:1 42
19:3 159
19:6 159, 163
19:11 89
19:12 100
19:22 166, 358
19:24 290
19:28 302
19:32 332
19:38 290
19:40 332, 350, 358
20:4 358
20:23 269
20:27 170
20:28 237, 274
21:4 339
21:20 331
21:25 357
21:29 165, 269
21:34 172
22:24–29 270
22:30 172
22:31 269
23:1 226
23:8 84, 159
24:1 293
24:4 357
24:16 226
24:21 160
24:24–27 270
25:24 194
26:6 289
26:18 242
27:1 358
27:6 358
27:3 84
27:29 172
27:30 172
27:40 172
28:1–2 339
28:20 143
28:30–31 270

Romans
1:1–15 63
1:1–5 65
1:1 107
1:3 187
1:5 148, 166
1:7 166, 322, 354, 358
1:15 125
1:16 98, 165, 293
1:17 156, 273
1:18–32 118
1:23 95
1:26 86
2:3 87
2:4 158, 167
2:7 148, 160
2:8 119, 302
2:15 165, 226
2:16 245
2:23 87
2:24 166
2:25 125, 347
3:2 155
3:3 117
3:5 156, 165
3:6 244
3:8 87
3:10–18 75
3:21–26 214, 256
3:21 244
3:24–26 239
3:24–25 232
3:25 49, 103, 235, 237, 253
4:1–25 30, 268
4:2 111
4:4 284
4:13 67, 102
4:13–20 289
4:15 87
4:16 86
4:17 268
4:19 106
4:19–24 292
4:20 117
4:24 354
5:1 30, 256, 354
5:3 269
5:5 165
5:6 189
5:8 92, 165
5:9 237, 238
5:10 238
5:12–21 30, 31, 180, 248
5:12 86
5:14 87
5:15 31, 238
5:17 238
5:19 87
5:21 148
6:1 187
6:4 159
6:5–11 68
6:19 141
6:20–23 68
6:21–22 164
7:1–8:11 215
7:14 188
8:3 102, 189
8:17 67
8:18 97
8:19 245
8:22 294
8:23 245, 351
8:25 245
8:26 141
8:27 135, 194
8:28 166
8:29 79, 98, 249
8:34 72, 92
8:35 165
8:38 84
8:39 165
9–11 75
9:1 226, 353
9:4 192
9:5 50, 80
9:6–11:36 312
9:6–13 288
9:7 102
9:8–9 289
9:22 167, 329
9:25–26 129
9:26 117, 133
9:32–33 99
10:7 355
10:9 73, 354, 355
10:13 166
10:14 114
10:15 125
10:16–17 126
10:21 119
11:1–2 129
11:1 288
11:2 194, 325
11:6 244
11:12 238

11:20 117
11:23 117
11:26 334
11:27 214
11:29 106
11:32 119
11:36 95
12:1–2 232, 349, 356
12:6–8 345
12:7 155
12:8 166
12:9 166
12:10 338, 339
12:11 166
12:13 339, 350
12:19 256, 266
13:2 162
13:5 226
13:6 198
13:10 166
13:12 260, 316
14:1–23 35, 347
14:1 157
14:10–12 245
14:12 136
14:14 265
14:15 166
14:17 336
14:18 356
15:3 269, 300
15:13 271, 351
15:14 164
15:15–16 356
15:16 198
15:17 188
15:19 89
15:25–26 358
15:29 167
15:30 353
15:39 259
15:31 166, 358
15:33 354
16:1–2 339
16:2 166, 271
16:3–4 41
16:4 135
16:15 166, 358
16:16 166
16:18 195
16:20 354, 359
16:21 358
16:22 11
16:25–26 65
16:27 95
16:26 148, 244

1 Corinthians
1:1–9 63
1:2 166, 358
1:3 354
1:7 125, 245
1:8 260
1:10 22, 166
1:11 42, 223
1:13 92
1:17–18 42
1:17 128
1:20 67
1:26 106
1:27 189
2:4 89
2:6 156
2:9 166, 293
3:1–3 29, 43
3:1–2 156
3:1 188
3:3 29, 188
3:5–22 42
3:8 284
3:9 232
3:10–11 158
3:13 223, 260, 263
3:16–17 232
3:16 325
4:1–6 42
4:5 135
4:9 84, 107, 269
4:15–20 321
4:15 42
4:17 86, 358
4:18–21 351
4:19 160
4:20 89
5:1–6:11 341
5:5 260
5:6 325
5:7 49, 232, 302
5:9–11 342
5:10 244
6:1–2 166, 358
6–7 342
6:2–3 325
6:3 84
6:9–10 67
6:9 336, 342
6:16 166
7:1–40 342
7:17 354
8:1–13 35, 43
8:1–3 135
8:3 166
8:4–6 95
8:6 68, 322
8:7–10 141
8:7 226
8:10 226
8:12 226
9:6 42
9:11 188
9:13 347
9:16 111
9:24–27 16
10:1–13 43, 122
10:1–4 122, 161
10:1 65
10:5 119, 122, 162
10:6–11 131
10:6 65
10:7 122
10:8 122
10:9–10 122
10:11 122, 171
10:16 237
10:25–29 226
11:7 249
11:10 84
11:13 95
11:24 92
11:25 173, 214, 237, 241
11:27 237
12:3 68, 73, 355
12:6 133
12:10 89, 157
12:11 28, 89, 133
12:13 29
12:22 238
12:24 126
12:28–29 155
12:28 89, 107
13:1–13 166
13:3 125, 270
13:4 167
13:5 167
13:10 17
13:13 261
14:6 125
14:24 278
14:33 354, 358
15:1 125
15:3 92, 138, 173
15:12–13 160
15:20–23 160
15:24–26 100
15:25–27 91
15:25 72
15:26 100

1 Corinthians (*continued*)
15:32 125, 347
15:40 106, 331
15:43 95, 141
15:45 68, 215
15:48 106
15:49 249
15:50 67, 99
15:55 100
16:1–21 356
16:1 358
16:5–12 339
16:7 160
16:9 133
16:10 358
16:12 42
16:15–18 345, 351
16:15 358
16:19 41
16:23 359

2 Corinthians
1:1 166, 358
1:2 354
1:3 322
1:4 269
1:12 188, 226, 353, 354
1:14 111, 260
1:19 41
2:17 132
3:3 117, 133, 188
3:6 215
3:7–18 34, 69
3:9 238
3:14 215
3:18 95, 249
4–5 40
4:2 132, 226
4:4–6 162
4:4 67
4:6 162, 249
4:17 148
5:1 148, 199, 235
5:2–4 351
5:9 356
5:11 226
5:14 165
5:15 68
5:21 141
6:2 104
6:6–18 232
6:16 117, 129, 133
6:18 77
7:1 71
7:4 271
7:8 192
7:11 166
7:15 268
8:2 271
8:4 358
8:7 166
8:19–20 166
8:24 165
9:1 358
9:3 111
9:4 69, 278
9:7 166
9:8 343
9:12 343
10:4 188
10:6 87
10:10 42, 189
10:16 125
11:17 69, 278
11:22 102, 270
11:30 141
12:1–5 139
12:9 343
12:12 28, 89
13:1 88
13:5–10 351
13:11 165, 354
13:12 358
13:13 359

Galatians
1:3 354
1:4 92, 173
1:9 125
1:13 354
2:3 126
2:5 126
2:8 133
2:10 131
2:13 42
2:20 92, 173
2:21 156, 189, 263
3:2 133
3:5 89, 133
3:6–18 288
3:10 22
3:11 273
3:14–29 289
3:14–18 192
3:15 189, 192, 240, 263
3:15–17 215
3:16–18 30
3:16 102
3:19–20 203
3:19 34, 84, 87
3:29 102
4:6 163, 322
4:7 67
4:9 34, 135
4:13 141
4:14 339
4:19 321
4:21–31 215, 288
4:23 289
4:26 215, 331
4:28 215, 289
4:29 215
5:2 125
5:5 245
5:6 166
5:12 37
5:13–14 37
5:13 166
5:14 166
5:21 67, 336
5:22 167, 271
6:4 111
6:6 350
6:8 148
6:15 68
6:18 359

Ephesians
1:1 166, 358
1:2 354
1:3 106, 331
1:7 237, 242, 322
1:11 133, 170
1:13 163
1:14 274
1:18 106, 162
1:19 133
1:20 72, 107, 133, 331
2:2 119
2:3 254
2:4 165
2:6 106, 331
2:11 199
2:12 192, 214, 289
2:13 237
2:14 354
2:15 354
2:17 354
2:18 30
2:19–22 232
2:19 290
3:4 279
3:10–14 80
3:10–11 84
3:10 331
3:12 111, 140
3:13 269
3:19 29, 165

4:2–7 28, 29
4:2 166, 167
4:3 131
4:5 159
4:11 155
4:22 118, 316, 354
4:27 100
5:2 166, 173
5:3–5 341
5:3 95
5:4 338
5:5 67, 336, 342
5:10 356
5:12–14 268
5:14 162
5:15 29
5:26 258
6:11 100
6:12 84, 99
6:17 133
6:18 166, 350, 358
6:24 359

Philippians
1:1 166, 358
1:2 354
1:9 166
1:14 132
1:22 300
1:23 238
1:27 331
2:1 166
2:2 271
2:3 265
2:6–11 92
2:6 265, 271
2:7 102
2:8 149
2:9–11 73
2:9–10 166
2:9 93
2:10 106
2:11 322
2:13 133
2:14 111
2:17 349
2:19–30 339
2:19 358
2:23 317
2:25 198, 265
2:29 271
3:4 147
3:7 265
3:10 97
3:11 160
3:13 165
3:14 106
3:19 164
3:20 245, 331
4:7 354
4:9 354
4:11–12 343
4:12 125
4:14 269
4:15 350
4:18 349, 356
4:21–23 356
4:22 358
4:23 359

Colossians
1:1 358
1:2 166, 354, 358
1:6 114
1:11 167, 271
1:13 165
1:14 237, 242
1:15 79, 245, 249
1:16 34, 68, 84
1:8 79, 223
1:20 237
1:24 269
1:28 132
1:29 133
2:2 167
2:8 118
2:11 199
2:12 133, 159
2:17 202, 248
2:18 34, 84
2:20–22 35
3:1 72
3:5 341
3:8 316
3:10 249
3:12 166, 167
3:17 322
3:22–4:1 135
4:3 353
4:7–18 356
4:10 339
4:11 336
4:16 11
4:18 359

1 Thessalonians
1:1 41, 322, 354, 358
1:3 260
1:4 165
1:5 89
1:6 271, 351
1:9 29, 98, 117, 133, 159, 234, 256
1:10 245
2:1 256, 261
2:4 135
2:11 321
2:12 336
2:13 125, 132, 133
2:17 131
2:19 271
3:2 358
3:6 358
3:12 166
4:3–7 341, 342
4:8 263
4:9 166, 339
4:14 187
5:1 117
5:2 260
5:4 260
5:10 92
5:12–13 345, 351
5:23 134, 354
5:25 353
5:26–28 356
5:27 11, 166, 358
5:28 359

2 Thessalonians
1:1 41, 358
1:2 354
1:5 336
1:7 84
1:8 263
1:9 160
2:1 261
2:2 260
2:12 245
2:13 300
2:16 322
3:1 353
3:5 165
3:16 354
3:17–18 356
3:18 359

1 Timothy
1:1–3 358
1:2 322, 354
1:4 86, 117
1:5 226, 353
1:6 155
1:14 165
1:9 324
1:10 342
1:16 164, 165
1:19 226, 353
2:4 261
2:5 203

1 Timothy (*continued*)
2:8 195
2:10 95
3:1 166, 293
3:2 339
3:6 100
3:9 266, 353
3:10 166
3:13 166, 274
3:14 354
3:15 117, 133, 354
4:1–4 159
4:2 226
4:7 324
4:8 347
4:10 177, 133
4:12 354
5:3–16 342
5:10 260
5:12 263
5:19 88, 263
5:20 278
5:22 350
5:23 141
5:25 260
6:6 343
6:8 343
6:10 293, 343
6:12 102
6:18 260
6:17 300
6:20 324
6:21 359

2 Timothy
1:1–2 358
1:2 322
1:3 226, 353
1:5 164
1:6 159, 268
1:8 300, 358
1:9–10 65
1:10 100
1:13 165
2:1 321
2:3 300
2:7 279
2:8 187
2:9 132
2:10 160
2:14–3:17 346
2:16 324
2:17 131
2:18 160
2:19 166
2:25 158, 261
2:26 100
3:2 343
3:7 261
3:10 167
3:16 347
4:1 336
4:2 142, 278
4:3 357
4:4 334
4:5 167
4:8 166, 245, 333
4:9 131
4:9–22 356
4:10 344
4:16 344
4:18 106
4:19 41
4:22 359

Titus
1:1 261
1:4 322, 350, 354
1:5 143
1:8 195, 339
1:14 334
1:15 266, 324
2:4 92
2:5 132
2:7 260
2:9 356
2:12 219
2:13 50
2:14 71, 236, 260
3:3 347
3:4 80
3:5 258
3:7 67
3:8 260
3:9 189
3:12–15 356
3:12 131
3:13 42
3:14 260
3:15 359

Philemon
1 358
3 322, 354
5 166
6 133
7 166, 358
8–20 339
9–10 357
14 262
16 238
21–22 351
22–24 356
25 359

Hebrews
1:1–2:18 11
1:1–2:4 13
1:1–14 32
1:1–4 8, 10, 11, 12, 63, 75, 86, 146, 333
1:1–3 50, 193
1:1–2 20, 31, 50, 64
1:1 22, 45, 74, 76, 86, 89, 98, 109, 114, 205, 206, 211, 326, 333, 334, 345
1:2–4 68
1:2–3 72
1:2–5 30
1:2 29, 46, 49, 67, 73, 81, 82, 107, 109, 139, 147, 177, 235, 240, 279, 285, 325, 326, 333, 335, 345
1:3–4 30, 37, 144
1:3 6, 17, 29, 49, 50, 64, 69, 70, 72, 78, 81, 91, 94, 95, 103, 109, 118, 135, 139, 109, 118, 135, 139, 140, 141, 143, 188, 189, 193, 197, 221, 239, 253, 277, 280, 317, 318, 333, 336, 356
1:4–2:9 178
1:4–5 332
1:4 32, 67, 72, 74, 82, 86, 90, 166, 167, 172, 189, 240, 243, 293, 326, 349
1:5–2:8 12, 24
1:5–14 11, 34, 50, 68, 74, 84, 89, 250
1:5 22, 49, 63, 72, 114, 139, 147, 177, 266, 322
1:6 22, 45, 49, 50, 72, 78, 90, 189, 250, 280, 296, 332
1:7–8 22
1:7 45, 72, 107, 134, 198, 236, 332
1:8 49, 50, 79, 114, 139, 147, 221, 279, 336, 346
1:9 37, 80, 86, 176, 260
1:10 49, 88, 109, 355
1:11 171

1:12–13 250
1:12 346
1:13 30, 49, 72, 79, 88, 91, 95, 139, 336
1:14 45, 74, 82, 84, 86, 87, 89, 101, 138, 147, 165, 167, 209, 240, 245, 325, 332
2–3 6
2:1–18 79
2:1–8 51, 84
2:1–4 8, 10, 11, 31, 46, 56, 85, 89, 95, 106, 139, 152, 155, 263, 264
2:1 9, 22, 110, 114, 117, 119, 244, 354
2:2–4 86, 87
2:2–3 240
2:2 14, 32, 34, 72, 86, 118, 132, 156, 170, 172, 239, 272, 284, 332, 333, 334, 345, 348
2:3–4 9, 85, 88, 158, 267, 354
2:3 15, 28, 36, 49, 65, 82, 86, 87, 88, 96, 99, 110, 114, 147, 163, 165, 170, 172, 245, 251, 255, 326, 328, 333, 345, 348, 355
2:4 70, 89, 114, 134, 163, 171, 235, 236, 279
2:5–18 10
2:5–9 11, 13, 14, 85
2:5–8 50
2:5 10, 49, 72, 79, 85, 88, 96, 332
2:6–8 45
2:6 8, 49, 139
2:7 17, 49, 69, 72, 144, 317, 332, 333, 356
2:8 91
2:9–10 139
2:9 9, 17, 21, 29, 48, 49, 51, 63, 69,72, 73, 79, 85, 90, 92, 94, 95, 98, 100, 101, 106, 109, 144, 146, 162, 244, 265, 317, 332, 333, 348, 356, 359
2:10–12:27 13
2:10–6:20 13
2:10–5:10 13
2:10–18 11, 45, 51, 93, 104, 107, 110, 140
2:10–13 95
2:10 9,17, 37, 49, 52, 53, 58, 82, 88, 90, 91, 93, 100, 102, 103, 104, 118, 119, 130, 139, 147, 148, 165, 171, 173, 185, 190, 194, 226, 236, 240, 245, 310, 312, 317, 321, 332, 333, 356, 357
2:11–17 93
2:11 49, 51, 93, 94, 97, 102, 106, 240, 265, 293, 322, 357, 358
2:12–13 22, 51, 93, 98
2:12 22, 166, 251, 258, 332, 349
2:13–14 95
2:13 103, 266, 350
2:14–18 10, 29, 150
2:14–15 93, 99
2:14 9, 30, 35, 51, 92, 94, 102, 145, 193, 236, 237, 270, 317, 333, 350
2:15 51, 105, 111, 124, 146, 262, 322
2:16–18 205
2:16 51, 72, 78, 82, 93, 97, 101, 110, 168, 206, 211, 288, 332
2:17–18 51, 152, 137
2:17 20, 49, 51, 94, 99, 102, 106, 107, 129,137, 139, 140, 141, 142, 147, 148, 150, 357
2:18 8, 36, 51, 91, 93, 102, 104, 106, 140, 142, 170, 294, 317, 344
3:1–5:10 12
3–4 290
3:1–4:13 11, 137, 312,105
3:1–4:11 25, 256
3:1–4:6 7
3:1–6 10, 104, 105, 122, 167, 297
3:1–5 178, 240, 246
3:1 9, 10, 35, 48, 49, 57, 80, 103, 106, 109, 110, 118, 122, 124, 130, 136, 137, 139, 148, 151, 152, 162, 171, 240, 258, 259, 317, 331, 349, 357, 358
3:2–6 10, 34
3:2–5 169
3:2 107, 108, 114, 128, 148, 150, 169, 287, 330
3:3 17, 49, 78, 108, 109, 220, 264, 317, 333, 356
3:4 109
3:5–7 31
3:5–6 32
3:5 297, 301, 330, 333, 345
3:6 14, 15, 29, 48, 49, 87, 108, 112, 114, 118, 139, 140, 144, 147, 148, 150, 167, 169, 172, 240, 256, 257, 258, 259, 272, 276, 344, 348
3:7–4:11 10, 43, 77, 105, 110, 111, 175, 212
3:7–19 108, 111, 122, 147, 161, 206
3:7–13 10
3:7–11 22, 112, 113, 117, 126
3:7 9, 23, 127, 134, 223, 236, 250, 254, 265, 334, 346
3:8–10 115
3:8 115, 134, 147, 148, 258, 348
3:10 114, 119, 134, 148, 250, 348
3:11 115, 122, 169
3:12–4:4 139
3:12–4:1 36
3:12–19 262
3:12–15 117, 155
3:12–14 152
3:12–13 123, 124, 143, 148
3:12 9, 106, 112, 117, 118, 133, 134, 141, 150, 238, 257, 259, 266, 322, 331, 333, 334, 357
3:13–15 128
3:13 117, 119, 141, 150, 260, 300, 317, 346, 357
3:14–19 10
3:14 48, 69, 80, 87, 103, 106, 110, 118, 124, 144, 162, 172, 258, 277, 348
3:15 22, 103, 112, 114, 118, 135, 334, 346
3:16–18 8, 12, 128
3:16 141, 240
3:17–18 124, 274

Hebrews (*continued*)
3:17 22, 113, 116, 117, 118, 119, 131, 141, 148, 261
3:18–19 128
3:18 113, 119, 150, 298, 304
3:19 8, 112, 126, 131, 141, 148, 150
4:1–10 32, 207, 253, 274
4:1–2 32, 56, 326
4:1 10, 15, 116, 123, 126, 131, 139, 152, 260, 262, 272, 299, 324
4:2–10 10
4:2–3 123
4:2 29, 114, 132, 141, 156, 258, 347
4:3–11 186
4:3 9, 22, 79, 112, 126, 127, 244, 279
4:4–5 123, 127
4:4 45
4:5 127
4:6 128, 129, 131, 272, 298, 328
4:7–8 183
4:7 9, 23, 24, 46, 112, 114, 135, 258, 334, 346
4:8–14 25
4:8–10 128
4:8–9 8, 123
4:8 303, 333, 345
4:9 130
4:10 123, 130
4:11–16 10, 56
4:11–13 130, 139, 316
4:11–12 32
4:11 9, 20, 36, 123, 130, 132, 152, 202, 255
4:12–13 8, 31, 45, 46, 123, 131
4:12 23, 46, 114, 125, 128, 132, 136, 156, 257, 258, 274, 322
4:13 13, 46, 132, 135, 152, 154, 353
4:14–6:20 11
4:14–5:10 137, 152
4:14–16 137, 152
4:14 10, 30, 32, 36, 48, 49, 91, 107, 137, 142, 146, 147, 148, 171, 177, 195, 198, 258, 264, 349, 355
4:15–16 150
4:15 30, 45, 51, 71, 103, 139, 141, 143, 147, 148, 150, 195, 239, 270, 317, 325
4:16 8, 9, 30, 49, 92, 111, 189, 221, 256, 257, 265, 283, 332, 336, 344, 348, 359
5–10 32, 35, 274
5:1–10 10, 30
5:1–4 137, 142, 222
5:1 52, 97, 103, 107, 137, 141, 142, 173, 197, 200, 225, 244, 248
5:2 51, 115, 143, 147, 317
5:3 64, 129, 141, 145, 195
5:4–5 178
5:4 143, 149, 289, 317, 319
5:5–10 144, 149
5:5–9 142
5:5–6 137
5:5 17, 22, 48, 49, 77, 103, 110, 144, 145, 147, 149, 154, 158, 333, 345
5:6 30, 72, 81, 174, 175, 178, 190, 279
5:7–10 137, 168, 186, 196, 238, 246, 321
5:7–9 53, 54
5:7–8 167, 317
5:7 30, 51, 54, 143, 145, 146, 237, 251, 285, 325
5:8–10 169
5:8–9 53, 97
5:8 8, 49, 54, 58, 91, 126, 141, 145, 147, 148, 149, 155, 250, 285, 289
5:9 14, 17, 49, 51, 52, 54, 82, 88, 140, 141, 148, 150, 160, 165, 185, 186, 193, 226, 236, 245, 303, 310, 333, 346, 355
5:10 49, 72, 103, 139, 149, 154, 155, 173, 178
5:11–10:39 12
5:11–6:20 13, 138
5:11–6:12 152, 154, 168
5:11–6:3 14, 43, 152
5:11–14 16, 29, 152
5:11–12 157
5:11 9, 10, 16, 22, 36, 48, 132, 136, 152, 158, 165, 166, 172, 353, 357
5:12–14 9
5:12 16, 29, 36, 38, 158
5:13–14 156, 166, 323
5:13 16, 81, 132, 176
5:14 9, 16, 17, 53, 57, 185, 226
5:15 294
6:1–13 196
6:1–12 346
6:1–6 4
6:1–5 235
6:1–3 34, 152, 157
6:1–2 29, 162
6:1 9, 17, 29, 48, 53, 70, 110, 132, 155, 157, 161, 226, 250, 345, 347
6:2 129, 148, 236, 238, 260, 355
6:3 110, 165
6:4–12 56, 152
6:4–8 36, 98, 152, 160, 255, 261, 262, 326
6:4–6 223
6:4–5 92, 161, 267
6:4 80, 106, 118, 134, 236, 261, 265, 268, 322, 331, 335
6:5 9, 17, 70, 160, 260, 279
6:6–8 32, 157
6:6 9, 29, 37, 49, 51, 139, 158, 159, 177, 264
6:7–8 9
6:8 260
6:9–12 152, 157, 164, 354
6:9–11 353
6:9 10, 22, 32, 72, 82, 88, 147, 189, 243, 245, 293, 350, 353
6:10 29, 56, 170, 260, 350, 358
6:11–12 166
6:11 9, 15, 29, 111, 131, 165, 189, 258, 259, 276
6:12 29, 67, 124, 166, 168, 169, 240, 258, 272, 275, 277, 288, 289, 337, 246
6:13–20 167, 205
6:13–18 9, 30, 35, 190, 191, 211, 259
6:13–17 171
6:13–15 168
6:13–14 22, 67
6:13 152, 169, 171, 175, 235, 254, 288, 334

6:14–18 240
6:14 159
6:15–19 189
6:15 124, 167, 169, 272
6:16–18 169
6:16 9, 235, 240, 340, 348
6:17 67, 82, 86, 124, 240, 272, 285, 325, 354
6:18 15, 29, 111, 171, 249, 258, 260, 277, 357
6:19–20 37, 139, 171, 172
6:19 9, 32, 86, 87, 134, 172, 198, 219, 240, 257, 274, 348, 350
6:20 8, 9, 48, 49, 552, 72, 91, 96, 103, 139, 189, 198, 244, 317, 346
7:1–10:39 13, 144, 173, 256
7:1–10:25 13, 25
7:1–9:28 10
7:1–28 11, 168
7:1–3 175
7:1–2 22, 174, 336
7:1 49, 154, 174
7:2 21, 24, 49, 81, 323, 354
7:3 24, 49, 72, 174, 264, 322
7:4–10 9, 174, 178, 180
7:4 9, 180
7:5 23, 129, 147, 183
7:1–3 8
7:3 139, 198
7:4–10 25, 35
7:4 288
7:5 179
7:6 272, 288, 289
7:7 32, 72, 189, 243, 293
7:8 180, 188, 190, 254, 257, 279, 322
7:9 8, 29
7:10 174
7:11–19 183, 190, 202
7:11–14 25, 27
7:11–12 8
7:11 52, 72, 129, 184, 185, 186, 203, 226, 239
7:12 9, 184, 185, 187, 189, 215, 239, 242, 335
7:13–19 200
7:13–14 187
7:14 49, 184, 188, 355
7:15–19 188
7:15–16 188
7:15 72, 86, 184, 186, 193, 354
7:16 23, 70, 194, 225, 322
7:17 72, 143, 183, 190, 279, 346
7:18 23, 184, 209, 245, 253, 263
7:19 15, 17, 32, 53, 72, 111, 184, 185, 193, 236, 243, 258, 277, 293, 310, 333
7:20–28 190
7:20–22 190, 191
7:20–21 191
7:20 103
7:21 73, 103, 116, 279, 346, 355
7:22 25, 32, 48, 49, 72, 91, 189, 192, 203, 243, 293, 317, 333, 355
7:23–25 65, 190, 193, 200
7:23–24 8
7:23 103
7:24 178, 185, 198, 279
7:25 51, 147, 193, 194, 198, 243, 257, 283, 322, 328, 349
7:26–27 190, 197
7:26 30, 49, 72, 95, 63, 139, 194, 195, 197, 219
7:27–28 39
7:27 29, 103, 129, 139, 141, 143, 162, 194, 195, 198, 242, 245, 335
7:28 17, 31, 49, 103, 132, 139, 143, 156, 185, 209, 226, 236, 279, 310, 333, 346
8:1–10:18 11, 172
8:1–13 45, 216
8:1–6 196
8:1–2 37, 139, 197, 219
8:1 10, 22, 30, 49, 72, 103, 139, 195, 221, 336
8:2 20, 49, 198, 199, 202, 235, 243, 258, 261, 322
8:3–6 199
8:3–4 25, 39, 196, 225
8:3 103, 143, 200, 216, 233, 248, 349
8:4–6 215
8:4 103, 200
8:5 17, 19, 106, 131, 200, 218, 223, 243, 284, 331, 334
8:6–13 25, 45, 192
8:6 32, 49, 72, 107, 125, 171, 189, 192, 198, 200, 202, 203, 239, 243, 244, 272, 293, 333, 355
8:7–13 196, 200, 203, 215, 239
8:7–9 205
8:7 206
8:8–12 27, 246, 254
8:8–10 192
8:8 22, 205, 333, 355
8:9–13 186
8:9 102, 206, 207, 209
8:10–13 207
8:10 129, 135, 206, 258, 355
8:11 206, 239
8:12 141
8:13 210
9:1–10:18 25, 196
9:1–10 25, 200, 215, 218, 232, 235
9:1–5 9, 199, 215, 217
9:1 217, 218, 225, 235
9:2–5 219
9:2–3 218
9:3 199, 257
9:4 192, 203, 219
9:5 17, 69, 103, 220, 335
9:6–10 222
9:6–7 216, 219, 222
9:6 17, 103, 218
9:7–8 39
9:7 103, 129, 143, 162, 195, 218, 262, 335
9:8–14 71
9:8–10 223
9:8 134, 236, 243, 244, 256, 265
9:9–10 216, 235, 348
9:9 17, 52, 185, 218, 225, 236, 238, 249, 258, 295, 310, 333, 349, 353
9:10 35, 42, 43, 129, 159, 239
9:11–10:18 200, 216
9:11–28 232
9:11–12 235

Hebrews (*continued*)
9:11 17, 48, 49, 52, 103, 110, 130, 185, 218, 226, 235, 242, 249
9:12–14 52
9:12 148, 160, 162, 195, 199, 234, 235, 237, 239, 243, 244, 317, 322, 335, 346, 355
9:13–14 237, 265
9:14 48, 71, 110, 117, 133, 134, 148, 159, 160, 218, 226, 235, 237, 249, 257, 258, 265, 266, 317, 322, 331, 353, 355
9:15–17 239
9:15 27, 66, 67, 82, 86, 87, 107 , 125, 148, 160, 167, 171, 180, 192, 203, 236, 237, 240, 258, 265, 272, 285, 289, 325, 331, 333, 346, 355
9:16–22 9, 35, 45
9:16 8, 192, 203, 240, 242
9:17 32, 87, 170, 192, 203, 239, 240, 322, 348
9:18–22 241
9:18 237, 256
9:19 23, 129, 237, 258, 333
9:20 23, 71, 192, 203, 237, 241, 265, 355
9:21 198, 237, 258, 333
9:22–23 179
9:22 237, 242, 333
9:23–26 242
9:23 20, 32, 71, 72, 106, 131, 189, 202, 242, 245, 248, 249, 293, 349
9:24 20, 48, 91, 110, 139, 198, 199, 235, 243, 244, 258, 261, 322, 349
9:25–26 244
9:25 103, 199, 237, 243, 333
9:26 20, 67, 79, 91, 141, 161, 245, 263, 279, 335
9:27–28 244, 245
9:27 162, 185, 245, 262, 335
9:28 21, 22, 29, 48, 51, 52, 79, 82, 88, 110, 141, 147,162, 165, 223, 245, 250, 260, 273, 303, 335
10–12 149
10:1–22 267
10:1–18 246
10:1–10 244
10:1–4 248, 348
10:1–3 39
10:1–2 246
10:1 17, 20, 33, 53, 65, 143, 178, 185, 226, 234, 235, 248, 249, 253, 277, 283, 310, 328, 333
10:2–3 250
10:2 8, 71, 103, 141, 162, 218, 223, 226, 249, 250, 258, 261, 335, 353
10:3–4 159
10:3 141, 249
10:4 141, 185, 237, 333, 355
10:5–10 238, 240, 246, 295, 325
10:5–7 22, 24, 29, 52
10:5 20, 29, 45, 79, 250, 258, 279, 280, 356
10:7 22, 52, 242, 252, 272, 282, 284, 353, 356
10:8 254
10:9 52, 141, 146, 148, 150, 254, 272
10:10–14 246
10:10 48, 52, 56, 91, 110, 141, 162, 186, 195, 251, 258, 265, 272, 322, 335, 346, 358
10:11–14 253, 258
10:11 141, 244
10:12 30, 49, 72, 141, 178, 223
10:13 260, 262
10:14 7, 53, 178, 185, 186, 226, 236, 265, 310, 317, 322, 333, 358
10:15–18 246, 254
10:15 22, 23, 113, 134, 223, 236, 254, 265, 279
10:16–22 115
10:16–17 22, 27
10:16 135, 192, 203, 251, 254, 258, 287, 348, 355
10:17–18 242
10:17 21, 141, 204, 223, 250, 344
10:18 141, 209, 246, 254, 261, 333
10:19–12:29 11
10:19–39 56, 275
10:19–31 56, 246, 254
10:19–25 8, 254, 346
10:19–22 30
10:19–21 256, 355
10:19 48, 52, 91, 106, 111, 140, 152, 199, 237, 265, 272, 317, 322, 333, 344, 355, 357
10:20 20, 30, 139, 322
10:21–39 346
10:21 49, 139, 355
10:22 9, 29, 30, 135, 167, 198, 226, 256, 257, 261, 283, 287, 328, 333, 348, 353
10:23–25 258, 267
10:23 15, 29, 107, 110, 111, 292, 334, 349
10:24–29 36
10:24 29
10:25 9, 29, 36, 39, 117, 164, 256, 267, 271, 272, 273, 300, 332, 344, 357
10:26–39 13
10:26–31 254, 267, 326
10:26–29 163
10:26 141, 223, 258, 263, 268, 272
10:27 15, 264, 265, 266, 330
10:28–31 263
10:28 23, 88
10:29 49, 92, 134, 139, 192, 203, 237, 292, 322, 348, 355, 358, 359
10:30–31 45, 272
10:30 129, 265, 272, 342
10:31 15, 117, 133, 136, 137, 239, 257, 262, 322, 330, 331, 344
10:32–12:17 6
10:32–39 98, 267

10:32–35 35, 36, 41, 56, 58, 166, 167, 309, 312, 316, 337, 354
10:32–33 301
10:32 29, 38, 91, 162, 277, 315, 316, 319, 320, 340
10:33 17, 35, 37, 268, 271, 300, 309, 318
10:34 5, 9, 29, 32, 35, 56, 72, 170, 178, 189, 268, 278, 309, 318, 340, 343, 350, 351
10:35–39 37, 267, 272, 274
10:35 111, 140, 278, 284, 318, 344
10:36–39 302
10:36 125, 309, 316, 317, 318, 323
10:37–38 22
10:37 260
10:38 29, 134, 267, 274, 281, 285, 322, 332
10:39 29, 36, 56, 134, 150, 209, 275, 278, 318, 350
11 8, 13, 23, 25, 29, 56, 75, 241, 258, 270, 310, 312, 349
11:1–12:29 10
11:1–12:27 13
11:1–12:24 14
11:1–12:13 12
11:1–40 255, 267, 272
11:1–7 274
11:1–4 63
11:1 249, 259, 274, 275, 278, 279, 283, 285, 289, 292, 302, 317
11:2 275, 279, 309, 316
11:3–31 24
11:3 45, 66, 67, 70, 275, 283, 309, 316, 356
11:4 45, 46, 273, 275, 279, 303, 328, 332, 333, 328, 332, 333, 340, 345, 346, 355
11:5–13 319
11:5–7 282
11:5–6 356
11:5 45, 275, 279, 309, 316, 335, 346, 350
11:6 45, 150, 244, 257, 272, 275, 282, 283, 293, 301, 328, 350
11:7–8 67, 82, 285
11:7 45, 79, 81, 82, 88, 146, 147, 176, 201, 209, 240, 275, 279, 325, 334, 340, 346
11:8–22 286
11:8–19 25
11:8–16 9, 30, 56, 240
11:8–12 30, 171, 288
11:8–11 292
11:8–10 271
11:8 45, 147, 167, 240, 286, 289
11:9–11 170
11:9–10 286, 289
11:9 124, 272, 275, 286, 289, 292
11:10 6, 9, 36. 262, 286, 291, 293, 331
11:11 45, 70, 78, 102, 259, 275, 286, 289, 291, 295, 307, 334
11:12 98, 102, 275, 287, 289, 292, 308
11:13–16 24, 36, 286, 292
11:13–14 305
11:13 107, 124, 272, 275, 286, 291
11:14–16 278, 349
11:14 349
11:15–16 7
11:15 293
11:16 32, 45, 72, 91, 98, 106, 189, 272, 287, 290, 331
11:17–20 45
11:17–19 169, 286, 294, 305
11:17 8, 124, 272, 275, 286, 289
11:18 24, 78, 102, 289, 308, 345
11:19 224, 275, 286, 287, 354
11:20–22 286
11:20–21 287, 289, 295
11:21 24, 275, 286, 289, 346
11:22 275, 286, 291, 346
11:23–31 297
11:23–28 105, 110
11:23–26 298
11:23 15, 124, 262, 297, 298, 302, 344
11:24–26 330
11:25–26 298
11:25 129, 309, 317
11:26 17, 110, 235, 269, 272, 275, 284, 292, 297, 318, 349
11:27 15, 124, 262, 297, 298, 299, 344
11:28 79, 237, 280, 297, 303, 332
11:29 297
11:30–31 303
11:30 297
11:31 275, 297, 298, 307, 354
11:32–40 304
11:32–34 306
11:32–38 24
11:32 10, 23, 65, 275, 304, 323, 357
11:33–34 305
11:33 81, 124, 176, 272, 275, 305
11:34–35 8
11:35 32, 72, 160, 189, 236, 271, 275, 305
11:36–37 305
11:36 308
11:37–38 305
11:38 79, 115, 271, 275, 279, 305
11:39–12:1 91
11:39–40 309
11:39 45, 125, 272, 275, 281, 305, 316
11:40 17, 32, 53, 72, 185, 189, 226, 236, 284, 315, 316, 333
12:1–28 56
12:1–11 268
12:1–4 315, 319
12:1–3 9, 10, 16, 24, 269, 275, 312
12:1–2 186, 240, 312
12:1 9, 57, 88, 167, 263, 319
12:2–3 272
12:2 9, 17, 29, 37, 49, 51, 52, 57, 91, 96, 104, 106, 110, 152, 161, 172, 173, 185, 221, 236, 246, 271, 312, 321, 322, 323, 336, 345, 346, 349, 351

Hebrews (*continued*)
12:3 9, 58, 134, 274, 300, 320, 350
12:4–11 147, 149, 313
12:4 35, 58, 237, 349
12:5–11 57, 58
12:5–6 22, 58
12:5 320, 357
12:6 4, 260, 320
12:7–12 16
12:7–11 9, 264
12:7–8 58
12:7 58, 59, 272, 321
12:8 80
12:9 81, 134, 236, 321
12:10–11 58
12:10 16, 322, 324, 332, 336
12:11–13 9
12:11 9, 57, 156, 176, 177, 271, 319, 322, 323, 351, 354
12:12–13 131, 323
12:12 9, 16, 36, 57, 141
12:13 35
12:14–13:19 12
12:14–17 323
12:14 304, 354, 358
12:15 92, 125, 265, 324, 340, 341, 348, 359
12:16–17 36, 296, 324, 332
12:16 56, 318, 342
12:17 32, 67, 147, 158, 161, 164
12:18–24 8, 9, 326, 328, 349
12:18 9, 257, 283, 326, 328
12:19–29 326
12:19 9, 132, 334
12:20 9, 70, 334
12:21 9, 15, 262
12:22–24 7, 32
12:22–23 322
12:22 9, 24, 30, 72, 101, 106, 117, 133, 239, 257, 266, 286, 290, 293, 294, 326, 328, 336
12:23 17, 53, 79, 134, 185, 226, 236, 273, 281, 350
12:24–25 345
12:24 30, 32, 46, 48, 49, 72, 91, 107, 171, 189, 192, 203, 237, 281, 317, 333, 355
12:25–29 333
12:25–27 14
12:25–26 46
12:25 87, 201, 259
12:26–28 260
12:26–27 260, 334
12:26 21, 22, 91, 344
12:27–28 343
12:27 99, 178, 223, 335, 339
12:28–13:21 13
12:28 49, 91, 92, 146, 218, 265, 339, 340, 348, 350, 356, 359
12:29 344, 350
13:1–21 11
13:1–17 336, 337
13:1–7 337
13:1 8, 29, 56, 350
13:2 29, 35, 56, 72, 101, 337, 354
13:3 29, 56, 59, 98, 270, 337
13:4–5 341
13:4 4, 8, 29, 39, 56
13:5–6 56
13:5 29, 35
13:6 15, 124, 165, 262, 299
13:7 29, 38, 39, 48, 56, 132, 136, 156, 167, 337, 345, 353, 354
13:8–16 257
13:8–14 337, 346
13:8 6, 8, 48, 81, 91, 110, 279, 346
13:9–13 346
13:9–10 227
13:9 9, 32, 35, 36, 42, 43, 56, 87, 92, 125, 135, 172, 226, 240, 265, 351, 359
13:10–11 39
13:10 218, 347
13:11–12 347
13:11 36, 103, 141, 165, 199, 237, 307
13:12–13 51, 57
13:12 48, 91, 129, 237, 265, 317, 355, 358
13:13–14 35, 36
13:13 9, 17, 37, 59, 70, 98, 110, 269, 301, 309, 329
13:14 9, 30, 178, 290, 309, 331, 346, 349
13:15–17 337, 349
13:15 29, 56, 107, 146, 166, 222, 352
13:16 29, 35, 56, 166, 337, 343, 356
13:17 29, 39, 56, 132, 134, 274, 337, 345, 350, 358
13:18–25 351
13:18–19 56, 351, 353
13:18 14, 226
13:19 10, 86, 117, 260, 357
13:20–21 12, 56, 251, 254
13:20 30, 48, 49, 91, 139, 160, 177, 184, 192, 203, 237, 333
13:21 17, 91, 95, 110, 279, 333, 346, 350, 352
13:22–25 11, 13, 63, 356
13:22 10, 46, 106, 117, 132, 136, 154, 171, 260, 320, 351
13:23–24 41
13:23 10, 14, 40, 351, 354
13:24 10, 14, 38, 39, 166, 345, 351, 358
13:25 10, 92, 265, 352

James
1:2 265, 271
1:23–24 259
1:12 166
1:17 322
1:19 325
1:21 316
1:22–25 345
1:24 165, 339
1:27 195
2:1–4 339
2:5 67, 336
2:7 163, 166
2:8 166
2:14–19 347
2:14 125
2:16 125
2:21–24 294
2:25 298, 304, 339
3:13 354
4:4 325
4:7 100

4:8 71
4:11 333
4:12 87
4:15 160
5:3 263
5:8 260
5:9 351
5:10 131, 166, 202
5:12 170
5:14 141
5:17 102

1 Peter
1:1–10 65
1:1 30
1:2 30, 237, 322
1:4 67, 195
1:7 263
1:8 166
1:9 237, 238
1:11 97, 223
1:12 125, 166
1:15 354
1:16 22
1:17 354
1:18 236, 354
1:19 30, 141, 232
1:21 49
1:22 339
1:23 132, 133
1:25 125
2:1 316
2:3 29
2:5 232, 349
2:6–10 75
2:8 99
2:9–10 129
2:9 162, 232, 274
2:11 30, 188, 290
2:12 226, 260, 354
2:22 30, 141
2:24 245
2:25 30, 355
3:1 119, 354
3:2 354
3:14–15 99
3:16 226, 354
3:18 30, 141
3:20–22 286
3:20 119, 167
3:21–22 30
3:21 159, 226, 243
3:22 84
4:1 135
4:9 339
4:11 155
4:13 97
4:14 166, 269
5:2 262
5:4 30, 355
5:8 98, 100
5:10 148
5:12–14 356
5:12 41, 357

2 Peter
1:1 80
1:7 322, 339
1:9 71
1:10 131
1:11 148, 336
1:12 147
1:14 223
2:4 84, 329
2:5 286
2:9 286
2:6 131, 202
2:17 329
3:5 70, 280
3:7 263
3:9 167
3:10 260
3:14 131
3:15 167

1 John
1:1 329
1:2 98, 148, 322
1:5 98
1:7–9 71
1:7 49, 237
2:2 103
2:5 165
2:14 132
2:20 166
3:1 165
3:5–7 141
3:8 100
3:11 166
3:17 165
4:7 166
4:9 165, 294
4:10 103
4:16 165

2 John
3 322
8 284
10–11 339
10 329

3 John
5–12 339
6 166

Jude
1 322
3 350
6 84, 329
12 346
13 329
14 331

Revelation
1:1 84
1:2 132
1:5 79, 237
1:6 322
1:9 132, 336
1:13 84, 90
1:19 133
1:20 84
2:1 84
2:12 133
2:14 347
2:20 347
3:12 232, 331
4:1–11 139, 232
5:2 84
5:5 187
5:6–10 232
5:9 237
5:11 332
5:12 49
7:1 84
7:11 84
7:14 237
12:6 293
12:7–9 84, 100
12:9 100
12:11 237
14:1–5 331
14:14 90
14:17–18 84
15:4 195
16:5 195
17:16 263
18:4 129
18:8 263
19:7 293
19:13 132, 237
19:16 332
20:1 84
20:2 100
20:4–15 160
20:4 132
20:11–15 160
20:12 245
20:14 100, 263
21:1 232

Revelation (*continued*)
21:2 293, 331
21:4 100
21:7 77
21:8 342
21:10 331
21:17 265
21:22 232
22:8 84
22:12 284
22:15 342
22:16 84, 187
22:19 331

GRECO-ROMAN LITERATURE

Aelius Aristides

Orations
40.14 96

Aeschylus

Agamemnon
177 147

Suppliants
804 341

Aesop

Fables
134.1–3 147
223.2–3 147

Apollonius of Tyana

Letters
26 349

Aristotle

Athenian Constitution
29.4 252

Eudaemonian Ethics
1149A 156

Metaphysics
1009B 101
1021B 96

Nicomachean Ethics
1098B 157
1109B 262
1123B 298
1133A 266
1162A 115
1165A 318

Parts of Animals
432A 134

Politics
1262B 290
1291A 156, 198
1307A 269
1314B 300
1320B 318

Rhetoric
1 13
1369B 264
1355A 265
1375B 257
1410A 278

Artemidorus

Oneirocritica
2.23 172
3.14 277
3.67 154

Cicero

Atticus
6.9.3 189

de Oficiis
3.10.12 315

Demosthenes

Orations
28.5 252

Dio Chrysostom

Orations 10
6.42 100
12.35 134
17.39 272
32.9 343
32.10 111, 140
76.2 252
77/78.45 140

Diodorus Siculus

Library of History
1.86.3 177
4.46.4 203
4.54.7 203
15.48 210
21.1.4 343

Diogenes Laertius

Lives
6.50 343
7.56 155
7.85 226
7.128 96
8.16 316
8.22 170
10.10 350

Epictetus

Discourses 10
1.1.17 160
1.4.16 125
1.7.30 155
1.13.3 291
1.14.16 347
1.24.1–3 315
1.25.4 299
1.28.23 339
2.1.14 146
2.2.20 156
2.10.15 272
2.14.11 135
2.14.17–23 345
2.15.1 193
2.16.39 156
2,18.28 268
2.21.3 104
2.22.20 322
3.2.2 144, 145
3.7.21 341
3.20.10 280
3.21.12 160
3.22.59 268
3.22.51–52 315
3.24.51 125, 347
3.24.100 340
3.24.113 87
3.25.1–4 268
3.25.2–5 315
4.7.15–17 100

Enchiridion
31.5 349
33.5 170
51.1 155
51.2 193

Fragment
286 140

Euripides

Andromache
609 284

Hippolytus
255 134

Ion
104 256

Medea
152 341

Orestes
400 264

425 264

Suppliants
1042 344

Heliodorus

Ethiopians
5.1.5 155

Herodotus

Persian War
1.24 329, 358
1.44 340
1.86 329
1.171 143
1.196 236
1.207 147
1.208 156
2.14 264
2.23 254
2.36 269
2.37 103
2.59 332
2.63 222
3.1 300
3.118 256
4.26 222
4.121 173
5.77 236
6.67 269
6.95 235
7.11 316
7.31 290
7.129 335
7.139 330
7.203 173
8.100 136
8.101 316
8.109 316
9.60 316
9.71 269

Homer

Iliad
2.149 302
2.196 302
4.157 264
6.129 106
15.191 329
15.371 293
24.757 257

Odyssey
4.23 109
5.191 104
10.78 302
10.461 302
12.117 351
17.366 293
17.784 106
20.356 329
21.329 278
21.345 300

Isocrates

Oration
1.11 306

Nicocles
10 157

Julian

Oration
2.61C 194

Lucian

Demonax
3.11 140

Dialogues of the Dead
2 245
11 272
15 189
22 355
25 339

Gymnosophists
15 316

Nigrinus
115–116 341

Runaways
13 343

Timon
56 343

Lucretius

On the Nature of Things
1.102–26 100

Marcus Aurelius

Meditations
12.2 135

Orphic Hymn
77.2 194, 195

Ovid

Metamorphoses 82
8.611–724 102

Papyri

BGU
4.1020.9 193
1113.5 192

Elaphantine
15.3 277

London
1.113.1.26 203

OGIS
753.8 192

Oxyrhynchus
82.3 198
237.viii.26 277
489.13 192
490.4 192
1088.56 133
1298.19 203
1470.6 243

Tebtunis
61 [b].184 277
311.27 170

Philostratus

Life of Apollonius
1.17 155

Plato

Alcibiades
135d 160

Apology
39C 278

Charmides
154A 173

Cratylus
391B 249
401D 96
407E 83
417D 351
420D 243
439A 249

Epistles
363B 357

Eryx
401C 100

Gorgias
449C 357
481B 131
484A 264
504E 347

Laws
650B 157
653A 96
663B 195

Laws *(continued)*
714A 264
717D 351
759D 115
869B 101
876E 201
947A 103
953A 339
961C 172
966B 165

Phaedo
80D 160
90C 87
95B 197

Phaedrus
109A 259
247B 316
249C 17, 96
265D 346
268E 157
276A 278

Philebus
38D 346

Protagoras
336A 357

Republic
330E 318
341E 322
379A 201
380C 201
393D 236
396C 201
402D 201
403E 201
433A 156
439B 293
509D–521B 17
517B 177
529A 354
529D 156
529E 290
533D 354
556B 261
564B 177
575D 189
590C 269
614B–621D 245

Statesman
260C 134

Symposium
174D 86
179A 261
203C 109

Theaetetus
157D 302
171E 201
177B 167
186A 318

Timaeus
21C 96
27C–29D 17
43A–45E 134
69A–90E 134
83A 300

Plutarch

Antony
32 136

Brotherly Love 339

Consolation to Apollonius
2 143
12 210

Curiosity
10 161

Demosthenes
20.4 134

Divine Vengeance
23–26 245

Education of Children
7–9 321
14 271

Fortune of Alexander
4 350

How to Tell a Flatterer
17 308

Isis and Osiris
46 203
78 95

Listening to Lectures
8 345

Marcellus
9 280

Obsolescence of Oracles
23 158
39 346
45 284

Pompey
6 299

Sayings of Kings and Commanders: Alcibiades
4 136
5.4 192

Superstition
3 129

Table-Talk
6.14 257

Polybius

History
3.75.5 307
4.50.10 278
4.766.9 194
5.11.5 210
8.11.8 161
8.36.5 189
9.36.10 263
10.26.3 265
12.12.2 161
20.4.7 319
27.6.3 292
32.6.4 292

Pseudo-Aristotle

On the World
395A 69, 277

Pseudo-Isocrates

Demonicus
21 157

Seneca

Anger
36.1–3 345

Moral Epistles
24 100
83.1–2 135
88.20 156

Natural Questions
1.17.4 345

Providence
2.1–6 140

Sophocles

Philoctetes
342 265
386 345

Trachiniae
143 147

Theophrastus

Characters
15.4 236
27.5 135

Thucydides

Peloponnesian War
1.222 87
1.135 278
2.2.2 262
4.51 335
4.104.2 271
6.8 284
7.79 134

Xenophon

Anabasis
2.3.15 245
3.4.44 279
4.4.11 86
6.1.19 165
18.16 189

Cyropaedia
1.6.38 262
3.1.19 245
5.5.36 334
6.1.10 332
6.2.5 259
6.3.18 197
7.5.70 344
8.3.49 342
8.4.6 343
8.8.4 261

Memorabilia
1.6.13 342
2.1.1 155
2.1.4 318
2.1.18 262
2.1.33 300
2.2.14 329
2.3.14 271
2.5.5 236
2.7.6 198
3.2.1 149
3.3.13 259
4.2.32 141
4.3.9 340

Oecumenicos
6.6 290
9.1 130
14.5 351

Symposium
4.42 343
8.26 110

JEWISH LITERATURE

Aboth de Rabbi Nathan
2 183
33 294

Apocalypse of Abraham
24.5 281

Apocalypse of Ezra
5.12 291

Apocalypse of Elijah
4.7–19 283
5.32 283

Aristeas

Letter
69 145
99 228
121 157
125 140
128 225, 226, 357
132–133 135
141–171 27
142 226
158 226
162 226
166 324
176–177 155
194 330
257 271
315 265

Aristobolos 17

Artapanus

On the Jews
3 299
3.19 302
3.37 303

Ascension of Isaiah
6.8 281

Assumption of Moses
10.1 100

Babylonian Talmud
Bab.Bat. 16b 325
Meg. 14b–15a 304
Men. 93b 242
Ned. 32b 183
Yom. 9b 231
Yom. 21b 230
Zeb. 6a 242

2 Baruch
4.3–7 230
77.15 212
85.12 326

Deuteronomy Rabbah
6.14 231
7.2 231

1 Enoch
1.7 245
5.5 245
9.3 83
9.5 135
10.13 100
12.2 83
14–19 139
14.8–25 229
14.19 229
15.5 99
20.5 83
22.5–7 282
50.1–5 245
53–56 245
70–71 139
70.1–3 283
71.1 83
71.8 229
71.14–17 229
85–90 229
89.40–41 229
89.51–54 229
89.73–74 229
90.35 229
90.36 229
98.7 332

2 Enoch 283
22.5 283
22.6 83
29.1 83
67 139
70–72 285
71–72 183

3 Enoch 283
1 229
6–7 139

Eupolemus

Fragments
2.1 120
3.26 120

Exodus Rabbah
2.26–27 304
35.4 231

Exodus Rabbah (*continued*)
116a 325

4 Ezra 122
3.11 285
7.33–34 160
9.12 326
9.36–37 212
10.19–24 230
10.38–54 230
13.1 100
14.29–30 121

Genesis Rabbah
25.1 283
26.3 183
43.6–8 183
65 325

Josephus

Antiquities
1.14 172
1.38 189
1.52 302
1.53 281
1.54 280
1.162 322
1.179–181 182
1.180 177
1.196 340
1.222–236 294
1.267 194
2.55 341
2.100 297
2.200 297
2.218 299
2.223–253 299
2.254–256 299, 302
2.261 350
2.290 319
2.338–344 303
3.11 120
3.33 120
3.139–150 219
3.147 220
3.198 220
3.296 120
3.299 120
4.13 357
4.26 339
4.43 335
4.102–150 39
4.123 222
4.135 334
4.224–257 39
5.1–120 303
5.8 304
5.42 201, 284
5.132 320
5.134 319
5.150 308
6.52 341
6.340 334
7.223 166
8.202 131
8.208 172
8.319 235
9.273 222
11.159 292
11.196 189
11.270 100
11.387 180
12.112 265
12.128 143
12.164 332
12.252 342
13.96 134
13.245 166
13.363 100
14.52 357
15.20 324
15.195 354
15.370–372 170
16.7 358
16.103 226
16.120 136
16.149 178
16.212 226
16.404 270
17.154 347
17.203 131
18.4 278
18.14–17 159
18.177 159
19.332 332
20.214 271
20.267 160

Apion
1.65 187
1.149 308
1.284 185
2.126 357
2.172 320
2.178 157
2.193–198 228

Life
48 322
142 339
205 261
298 279
310 354
334 143
370 322

Jewish War
1.246 293
1.152 219
1.158 322
2.4 252
2.135 170
2.341 199
2.455 228
2.539 228
4.149 144
4.164 144
4.319 316
4.340 228, 324
4.340 340
5.94 307
5.184–237 228
5.216 219
5.217 220
5.369 228
5.412 228
5.419 228
6.79 307
6.99 195
6.103 131, 202
6.110 228
6.250 228
6.271 324
6.438 176, 177, 182
7.69 157
7.443 316

Jubilees
1.17–18 229
1.23 229
1.25 229
1.26 229
1.27–28 229
2.2 83
4.7–8 281
4.26 229
4.22–24 283
4.31–34 281
5.1–2 87
5.2 285
5.5–6 84, 87
5.13 87
5.19 285
6.22 87
10.3 322
10.17 283
13.22–25 181
13.26–27 181
18.1–19 294
21.16–23 120

24–27 296
25.1–8 325
35.17 83
46.9 297
47.3 299
47.9 299
47.11–12 299
47.12 301
48.14 303
50.1–2 87
50.4 120

Lamentations Rabbah
246 230

Leviticus Rabbah
25.6 183

Life of Adam and Eve
24.2 281

Martyrdom of Isaiah 24

Mekilta on Exodus
5 [38b] 286
15.17 230
18.1 304

Mishnah

Aboth
3.3 231
3.7 231
5.3 294

Tamid
1.4 220
3.1 220
3.6 220
3.9 220
6.1 220

Yoma
8.9 223

Numbers Rabbah
11.2 231
12.4 230
13.6 230

Pesikta Rabbati
16a 230

Philo

Abraham
16 283
27–34 284
31 177
104 135
107 340
113 340
114 339
121 149
133–134 341
167–207 294
177 295
194–197 295
235 182, 271
257 143
273 170

Allegorical Laws
1.10 157
1.31 19
1.62 324
2.55 177
2.102 197
3.14 302
3.48 316
3.79–82 182
3.79 176
3.96 201
3.97–99 202
3.100 302
3.101 243
3.102 19, 202
3.128–137 27
3.139–140 325
3.203 170
3.204 170

Change of Names
24 350
61–82 176
86 83
116 355
192 70

Cherubim
13 172
27 133
29 146, 235
31 133
49 291
78 135
98 230
120 290

Confusion of Tongues
92–98 96
166 344

Creation of the World
13 180
132 291

Decalogue
2–7 120
36 155
85–95 169
85 170

Dreams
1.12 170
1.62 238
1.90 135
1.149 230
1.188 202
1.206 201, 202
1.214–215 222
1.215 182
1.239 83
1.188 154
2.107 147

Drunkeness
51 180

Embassy
86 339
144 194

Eternity of the World
112 193

Every Good Man Is Free
22 100
37 357
160 156

Flight and Finding
93 199
108 182
138 147

Giants
6 83
17 83
52 182

God's Immutability
57 280

Joseph
107 140

Life of Moses
1.8 299
1.23–31 299
1.29 259
1.43–46 299
1.49–50 302
1.156 351
1.58 302
1.176–180 303
1.181–185 120
1.235–236 120
2.9 185

Life of Moses *(continued)*
2.14–15 212
2.55 147
2.56 155
2.94 220
2.97–104 219
2.101 220
2.149 96
2.158 324
2.188 155
2.224 144
2.238 201, 284
2.280 147

Migration of Abraham
18 297
54 125
55 347
91 185

Noah the Planter
9 156
17–19 164
18 69
51 355
90 89
160 156

Posterity and Exile
31 319
48 223
86 125, 347
109 292
116 341

Preliminary Studies
18 156
44–45 176
99 182
100 220
149–150 155

Questions on Exodus
25.22 219
82 19

Questions on Genesis
1.4 19
1.60 280
1.61 281
1.70 281
1.83 283
1.97 284
3.12 291

Rewards and Punishments
4 278
11–14 310
12 310
28 302

Sacrifice of Abel and Cain
24–26 306
91 172

Sobriety
62 230
68 230

Special Laws
1.42 144
1.100 351
1.145–50 27
1.167 27
1.188 27
1.202–211 27
1.205 242
1.246 164
1.261 159
1.321 111
2.2–38 169
2.196 223
3.161 341
3.187 187
4.29 147
4.65 343
4.238 306

Virtues
158 259
198–205 311
208 325

Who Is the Heir?
22 146
36 70
73 147
130–131 134
133 154
204 164
221 154, 219
226 219, 220
256 202

Worse Attacks Better
13 136
83 69

Psalms of Solomon
15.3 349
17.40 355

Pseudo-Philo

Biblical Antiquities
2.1 281
3.4 285
8.4 212
9.12 299
9:16–10.1 299
9.19 299
10.6 303
10.7 120
11.2 212
12.4 120
16.1–7 120
19.5 120
19.6–7 120
20.1–3 303

Pseudo-Phocylides

Sentences
42 343

Qoheleth Rabbah
V, 6, 1 304

Qumran Writings

1QS
1.5 213
1.7 213
1.8 213
1.11–12 213
1.15 213
1.16–18 27
1.18 213
1.19 213
2.10 213
2.12 213
2.18–24 231
2.19–20 213
2.18 213
1.25–26 213
3.2 28
3.4–9 159
3.11 213
3.13–4.26 28
4.22 213
5.1–3 213
5.2–3 28, 213
5.5–7 231
5.6 213
5.7–9 231
5.8 213
5.9 213
5.13–14 159
5.18 213
5.19 213
5.20 213
6.15 213
6.17–27 28
6.17–22 213
6.19 213
6.24–7.27 213
7.24–25 213

8.3–9 231
8.6–8 28, 213
8.10 213
8.13–16 213
8.16 213
8.19 213
8.22–24 213
9.3–11 28, 213
9.3–7 231
9.4–5 349
10.10 213

CD
1.4 213
1.17–20 213
2.2 213
3.3 121
3.4 213
4.9 213
3.12–13 121
3.12 213
3.13 121
6.2 213
6.10 213
6.19 213
8.21 213
12.11 213
13.14 213
14.2 213
15.5–6 213
19.3 213
19.13 213
19.24 213
20.1 213
20.12 213
20.25 213

1Qsa
1.2–3 213
1.19–26 213
2.1–21 28
2.15 213

1QapGen
22.12–17 181

4QFlor
1.1–7 231
1.6 28, 75, 213

4QpHab
1.11–14 231
2.12 213
5.10–14 231
8.7–15 231
8.9 27, 213
9.9–10 213, 231
9.9 27, 213
11.12 231
12.1–10 271

4QshirShab 83
1.20 231
11.1–3 192
22.1–3 182

4QTest 75

4QTemple 231

11QMelch 28, 231
2.6–25 182

Ruth Rabbah
2.1 304

Sibylline Oracles
1.125–135 285
1.128–129 285
1.147 285, 286
1.150–198 286
1.268 285
1.280 285
8.17 343

Sifre on Deuteronomy
343 176

Sifre on Numbers
6.25 231
12.5 230
43 285

Song Rabbah
I, 3, 3 304
I, 15, 2 304
IV, 1, 2 304
VI, 2, 3 304

Tanchuma
35a 231

Targums

Onqelos
Gen 14:18–20 181

Pseudo-Jonathan
Gen 14:18–20 182
Gen 14:18 176
Gen 31:45–50 176

Neofiti
Gen 14:18–19 181

Targum on Joshua
2.1 304

Testament of Abraham
13.2 282

Testaments of 12 Patriarchs

TBenj
2.5 118
7.3 281
8.3 324
9.2 229
12.2 297

TDan
5.2 354

TIssa
5.4 281

TJos
4.6 195
6.3 330

TJud
18.2 341
23.3 271, 300
26.1 110

TLevi 231
3.4–6 229
3.5–6 349
5.1–3 229
5.1 229
8.14 187
18.3 100
18.5 83

TNaph
2.7 145

TReub
1.5 341
4.3 226
4.7 300

TSim
3.6 270
8.2–7 297

TZab
10.2 345

CHRISTIAN LITERATURE

Alexander of Alexandria

Epistles on Arian Heresy
1.12 5, 6
2.3 6

Ambrose of Milan

On Christian Faith
1.7.49 4

***On Christian Faith* (*continued*)**
1.13–79 4
3.2.84–91 4, 6

On the Holy Spirit
1.4.47 4
2.128 4
3.140 4

On Penance 163

The Apostolic Constitutions
7.37.1–5 285
7.37.2 281
7.39.2–4 285
8.5.1–4 285
8.5.11 281
8.12.53–54 281

Athanasius

Defense of His Flight
16 6
21 6

Defense of Nicene Definition
12 6

Four Discourses against Arius
1.12 6
1.36 6
2.48 6
2.8.9 6
3.65 6

Paschal Letter
39 5

Augustine 21, 34

City of God
18.50 4

Enchiridion
58 4

Epistles of John
8.7 6

Harmony of the Gospels
2.4 6

On Forgiveness of Sins
1.50 4

On Nature and Grace
14 4, 5

On the Trinity
3.11 4

Barnabas

Letter
16.4 39

Basil the Great

Hexaemeron
9.6 6

On the Spirit
6 6
19 6

Benedict of Nursia

Rule for Monks
Prologue 7

1 Clement
7.5 326
7.6 286
36:1–5 3, 38
47 3

Clement of Alexandria

Stromata
1.2.1 286
1.4 4
2.4 6
4.16 6
4.161.3 183
7.10 4

Cyprian of Carthage

Against the Jews 75

Letter
51 163

Cyril of Jerusalem

Catechetical Lectures
5 6
10.11 6
10.14 6
12.17 6

Dionysius of Alexandria

Epistle
3.2 5

Epiphanius

Panarion
59.1.1–3.5 163

Eusebius

Historia Ecclesiastica
3.3.5 5
3.25.2 5
3.38.1–3 3
5.26 4
6.20.3 4
6.25.11–14 4, 41
6.41.6 5

Preparation for the Gospel
9.17.5–6 182
9.17.9 282

Gregory of Nazianzus

Orations
29.17 6
38.1 6

Gregory of Nyssa

Against Eunomius
1.39 6
2.11 6
8.5 6

Life of Moses 7

Gregory Thaumaturgus

Homily on Christ's Baptism 5

Hilary of Poitiers

On the Trinity
4.11 4

Hugh of St. Victor

Didascalion
4.2–6 5

Ignatius of Antioch

Eph. 5.1 126

Mag. 3.1 145

Jerome

Letters
22.39 4
46.2 4
63.2 4
129 4
130.12 4

John Chrysostom

Homilies on Hebrews ***5***
Argument 2 5
1.3 6

John of Damascus

Orthodox Faith
10 6
11 6
15 6

Martin Luther

Commentary on Genesis 42

Methodius of Olympus

Banquet of the Ten Virgins
5.7 5
9.5 5

Discourse on Resurrection
1.5 5

Oration on Simeon and Anna
8 5, 6

Origen

Against Celsus
7.7 6

Commentary on John
6 4
20 4

First Principles
2.6.4 4
4.1.21 4

Homilies on Joshua
1.7–2.3 7

Homilies on Numbers
7.5 7
9.7 7
12.3 7
17.4 7
23.11 7
27.2–12 7

Letter to Africanus
9 4

Pseudo-Macarius

Spiritual Homilies
46.4 7

Rufinus of Aquila

Commentary on the Apostles' Creed
3.5.29 4
30 4

SHEPHERD OF HERMAS

Mand.
4.2.1 357
4.3.1–7 4, 163

Sim.
9.2.2 163
9.26.5–6 163

Vis.
2.2.4–5 163

Tertullian

Against the Jews 183

On Modesty 4, 41, 163

Thomas à Kempis

Imitation of Christ
1.23 7
2.1 7
4.11 7

OTHER

Melchizedek 183

Poimandres
1.1 355

Sentences of Sextus
79 140

INDEX OF MODERN AUTHORS

Aland, B., xiii, 3
Aland, K., xiii, 3
Allen, D. L., xviii, 41
Anderson, C. P., xviii, 30, 34
Anderson, G., xviii, 25
Anderson, H., xviii, 48
Andriessen, P., xix, 318
Attridge, H., ix, xvii, xix, 8, 13, 30, 38, 70, 89, 122, 124, 137, 146, 171, 191, 199, 216, 234, 237, 248, 254, 270, 278, 301, 346

Barrett, C. K., xix, 20
Barth, M., xix, 22
Bateman, H. W., xix, 24, 75
Becker, E.-M., xix, 136
Bénétrau, S., xix, 280
Betz, O., xix, 276
Bonnard, P. E., xix, 318
Bonnardière, A. M., xix, 5
Braun, H., xvii
Brawley, R. L., xix, 91
Bruce, F. F., xvii, xix, 11, 49
Buchanan, G. W., xvii, 34, 72, 140

Charlesworth, J. H., xi
Cockerill, G. E., xix, 295
Cody, A., xix, 142, 218
Cosby, M. R., xix, 275
Coste, J., xix
Craddock, F. B., xvii
Croy, N. C., xx, 315

Dahl, N. A., xx, 256
D'Angelo, M. R., xx, 107, 297
Darnell, D. R., xx, 116
Davidson, R. M., xx, 173
Delcor, M., xx, 181
Delling, G., xx, 17
Demarest, B. A., xx, 177
DeSilva, D., ix, xvii, xx, 16, 20, 37, 104, 144
Dey, L. K. K., xx, 20, 83
Dodd, C. H., xx, 77
Dolfe, K.-G. E., xx, 102
Dunnill, J., xx, 33

Eisele, W., xx, 336
Eisenbaum, P. M., xx, 23, 50, 275
Ellingworth, P., xvii, xx, 3, 8, 30, 89, 236

Fensham, F. C., xxi, 27
Filson, F. V., xxi, 56, 337
Fitzmyer, J. A., xxi, 181
Flusser, D., xxi
Fritsch, Ch. T., xxi, 236

Gardiner, E. N., xxi, 16, 319
Gheorghita, R., xxi, 21, 273
Gleason, R. C., xxi, 116
Goppelt, L., xxi, 200
Grässer, E., xvii
Gray, P., xxi, 14, 51, 124
Greenlee, J. H., xxi, 291
Greer, R. A., xxi, 5
Grelot, P., xvii
Gudorf, M. C., xxi, 101
Guthrie, D., xvii
Guthrie, G. H., xxi, 12, 22

Hagner, D. A., xvii
Hahnemann, G. M. xxi, 4
Hamm, D., xxi, 51
Hanson, A. T., xxi
Hay, D. M., xxii, 73
Hays, R. B., xxii, 77
Hegermann, H., xvii
Hengel, M., xxii, 317
Héring, J., xvii
Hofius, O., xxii, 127, 257
Hoppins, R., xxii, 41
Horbury, W., xxii, 142, 179
Horst, P. W. van der, xxii, 291
Horton, F. C., xxii, 181
Hughes, G., xxii, 23
Hughes, J. J., xxii, 240

Hughes, P. E., xvii
Hunt, B. P., xxii, 33
Hurst, L. D., xxii, 15, 44, 49

Irwin, J., xxii, 291
Isaacs, M. E., xxii, 33, 347

Jaeger, W., 319
Jewett, R., xviii
Jobes, K. H., xxiii, 251
Johnson, L. T., xxiii, 2, 15, 17, 21, 26, 39, 40, 47, 48, 53, 55, 77, 152, 343
Johnson, M., xxiii, 15
Johnson, R. W., xxiii, 33
Johnsson, W. G., xxiii, 9, 25, 71
Johnston, G., xxiv, 96

Karavidopoulos, J., xiii
Käsemann, E., xxiv, 9, 19
Kennedy, G. A., xxiv, 12
Kiley, M., xxiv, 157
Koester, C. R., xviii, xxiv, 5, 12, 13, 14, 19, 89, 146, 148, 156, 164, 199, 209, 216, 217, 224, 237
Koester, H., xxiv, 347

Lakoff, G., xxiii, xxiv, 15
Lane, W. L., xviii, 12, 64, 89
Lee, J. A. L., xxiv, 157
Lehne, S., xxiv, 211
Leithart, P. J., xxiv, 258
Lewis, J. P., xxiv, 284
Lewis, T. W., xxiv, 274
Lightfoot, N. R., xxiv, 146
Lindars, B., xxiv, 12, 33
Loader, W. R. G., xxiv, 48
Long, T. G., xviii
Longenecker, R., xxiv, 288

MacRae, G. W., xxv, 20
Malone, F. A., xxv, 205
Manson, T. W., xxiv, 34
Manson, W., xxv
Marmion, C., ix
Marrou, H., xxv, 16
Marrow, S. B., xxv, 111
Martin, D. B., xxv, 109
Martinez, F. G., xi
Martini, C. M., xiii
März, C. P., xviii
Mathewson, D., xxv, 161
McCown, W., xxiv, 10
McNamara, M., xxv, 181
McNichol, L., xxv, 83
Meier, J. P., xxv, 68, 75
Melbourne, B. L., xxv, 57
Metzger, B. M., xiii
Michel, O., xviii
Minear, P. S., xxv, 2
Mitchell, A. C., xxv, 95
Moffatt, J. A., xviii
Montefiore, H., xviii, 34, 44

Nardoni, E., xxv, 118
Nash, R. H., xxv, 20
Nelson, R. D., xxv, 25
Neusner, J., xxv, 225
Newsom, C., xxv, 28, 83
Neyrey, J. H., xxv, 177

Olbricht, T. H., xxvi, 12
Owen, H. P., xxvi, 156

Peterson, D., xxvi, 17
Pfitzner, V. C., xviii, xxvi, 16

Rahner, K., xxvi, 54
Rhee, V., xxvi, 56
Rose, C., xxvi, 275
Royster, G., xviii, 96

Sabourin, L., xxvi, 161
Salevao, I., xxvi, 33
Schein, B., xxv, 288
Schenck, K. L., xxv, 67, 74
Scholer, J. M., xxv, 190
Schröger, F., xxvi
Schunack, G., xviii
Seid, T. W., xxvi, 174
Silberman, L. H., xxvi, 87
Smyth, H. W., 237
Solari, J. K., xxvi, 158
Sowers, S. G., xxvi, 20, 24
Spicq, C., ix, xviii. xxvii, 8, 17, 30, 34
Stanley, S., xxvii, 224
Sterling, G., xxvii, 18
Stevenson, G., xxvii, 227
Stevenson-Moessner, J., xxvii, 26
Stewart, R. A., xxvii, 336
Sundberg, A. C., xxvii, 4
Swetnam, J., xxvi, 236, 266, 294

Talbert, C. H., xxvii, 16
Thompson, J. W., xxvii, 17, 27
Thornton, T. C. G., xxvii, 242
Timo, E., xxvii, 139
Trompf, G. W., xxvii, 132

Vaganay, L., xxvii, 12
Vanhoye, A., xxvii, 12, 49, 190

Van Vliet, H., xxviii, 88, 263

Weinfeld, M., xxviii, 205
Weiss, H. F., xviii
Westcott, B. F., xviii, 301
Westfall, C. L., xxvii, 107
Wiid, J., xxviii, 240
Wilcox, M., xxviii, 200
Williamson, C. M., xxviii, 34
Williamson, R., xxviii, 18, 28
Wilson, R. McL., xviii
Witherington, B., xxviii, 30
Worley, D. R., xxviii, 36, 168
Wray, J. H., xxviii, 127

Yadin, Y., xxviii, 27
Young, F. M., xxviii, 5, 25
Young, N. H., xxviii, 173, 242, 257, 347

INDEX OF SUBJECTS

Aaron, 144, 178–179, 183, 184
Abel, 332, 355
Abraham, 102, 110, 116, 124, 167, 168–173, 174–181, 240, 259, 286, 288, 292, 295
allegory, 19
angels, 32, 34, 72–84, 87
athletic imagery, 16, 57, 268, 315, 316, 318, 319, 323
atonement, 102–103, 237, 348

body, 20–21, 51, 91, 98, 251, 257, 258, 356

Christology, 2, 6, 7, 29, 39, 48–56, 321, 346, 349
city of God, 290, 293, 322, 331, 336, 346, 349
confidence, 111, 256, 272, 277, 299, 343, 344
conscience, 238, 249, 348, 353
covenant, 25–26, 45, 171, 186, 192, 203–215, 239, 240, 265, 333, 348, 355
crucifixion, 37, 46, 161, 317

death, 92, 100–101, 117, 146, 233, 237–239, 245, 275, 303, 317, 330, 333
discipleship, 1, 6, 29, 56–60, 147, 321, 331–332, 334, 340, 349

education, 16, 54, 57–58, 147, 150, 155–158, 313, 319, 320–321
Enoch, 282–283, 289
Esau, 313, 324, 342
eschatology, 20, 39, 91, 164, 244–245, 260, 268, 273, 331, 335

faith, 23, 29, 46, 51, 53, 56, 103, 107, 112, 114, 122, 126, 141, 148, 149–152, 169, 208, 246, 259, 272, 274, 275, 277, 283, 289, 295, 302, 303, 304, 306, 312, 313, 322, 337, 339, 340, 356
faithlessness, 117, 119, 122, 126, 131, 148, 161, 304, 324
fear, 100–101, 124, 146, 262, 299, 302, 330, 344

God's life, 130, 147, 164, 184, 186, 188, 189, 194, 230, 322
grace, 130, 141–142, 256, 265, 348, 359

heart, 134–135
high priest (Jesus as), 2, 11, 20, 25, 35, 49, 103, 137, 149, 173, 188, 190–196, 198, 233, 254, 279, 309–310, 312, 346
historical criticism, 1
holiness, 97, 322, 324, 335, 353, 358
hospitality, 339–340
holy place, 189, 198, 217
honor (glory) and shame, 16–17, 37, 46, 51, 69, 95, 98, 108–109, 111, 144, 161, 221, 269, 293, 298, 200–301, 308–309, 317–318, 333, 341, 349, 356
hope, 111, 128, 167, 168–173, 189, 193, 240, 255, 259, 276, 277, 337, 359

inheritance, 67, 167–173, 240, 275, 325–326, 328, 356
Isaac, 294, 295, 325

Joshua, 126–131, 303, 306
joy, 271, 318, 323, 351
judgment, 266, 316, 333, 342, 350

king (enthronement), 71, 77, 90, 139–140, 145, 331, 335, 336

law, 22, 25, 36–37, 84, 87, 179, 183–189, 191, 242, 252, 333, 334
leaders of community, 345–346, 350–351
letter, 9–11, 351–359
Levi, 178
living God (the), 45–48, 117, 128, 132–133, 164, 180, 239, 274, 322, 326, 331, 336, 346
love, 260, 337, 339, 350

marriage, 341–342
mediator (Christ as), 49, 171, 192, 196, 203, 239, 333

Melchizedek, 136, 144, 149, 154, 168, 173, 174–181, 181–183, 186, 187, 203, 282, 283, 285, 336
metaphor, 9, 15, 21, 69, 109, 155, 156, 172, 223–224, 315
moral transformation, 131, 186, 211, 226, 253, 283, 315, 317, 320, 323
Moses, 32, 104–105, 108, 110, 169, 178, 269, 297–303, 318, 330

Noah, 284–286, 289, 310

oath, 116, 167, 168–173
obedience, 56, 114, 126, 131, 141, 147, 148, 149–152, 186, 208, 246, 250, 251, 285, 205, 302, 322, 349, 350–351, 356
Origen, 3, 5, 21, 34, 40, 41

patristic interpretation, 3–7, 163
peace, 177, 323, 354
people of God (Israel), 129, 130, 257, 299, 318
perfection, 17, 26, 51–55, 96, 101, 141, 151, 185–186, 189, 226, 235–236, 240, 305, 309–310, 313, 316, 320–321, 332, 356
Philo, 7, 17, 18, 20, 21, 24, 27
pilgrimage, 7, 9, 10, 131, 161, 256, 258, 262, 274, 290, 312, 313, 323, 328, 333
Platonic worldview, 17–21, 40, 45, 47, 65–66, 120, 131, 134, 173, 186, 188, 193, 201–202, 218, 224, 226, 235, 243–244, 277, 280, 329, 330, 331, 335
priesthood, 139–144, 173–181, 183–189, 191–196, 252, 311
promise, 124–125, 128, 167, 168–173, 240, 255, 272, 275, 289, 305, 306, 309, 168–173, 240, 255
purification, 71, 225, 237–238, 241, 258

Rahab, 275, 297, 298, 303, 304, 307
redemption, 236–237, 239
repentance, 158–159, 163–164
rest (Sabbath), 122, 125, 126–131, 274, 290, 303
resurrection/exaltation, 20, 29, 52, 71, 81, 90, 139–140, 146, 148, 160, 187, 188, 221–222, 232, 271, 305, 308, 333, 354–355
rhetoric, 8, 12–15, 31, 33, 88, 89, 124, 131, 139, 165, 167, 174–175, 194, 219, 306, 357

sacrifice, 25–27, 30, 39, 49, 146, 169, 185, 195, 214, 222, 238, 279, 302, 30–3, 348–349, 356
salvation, 88, 102, 104, 145, 147, 148, 149, 165, 245
sanctification, 186, 237, 253, 165, 348–349, 358
sanctuary, 198, 199, 216–224, 227–232
Sarah, 275, 286, 291, 292, 295, 307
Scripture, 21–25, 45, 47–48, 77, 176–177, 187, 265
Septuagint, xiii, 21, 185, 217, 289, 344
sermon, 10, 258, 333, 352
sharing possessions, 342–344, 350
sin, 25, 71, 92, 117–119, 148, 254, 261, 316–317, 319
Son (Son of God), 49, 50, 56, 64–68, 69, 70, 74, 75, 77, 80, 97, 108–109, 132, 139, 147, 151, 177, 246, 264, 313, 320, 321, 332, 333
structure (of composition), 11–14
suffering, 16, 35, 37, 51, 52–54, 58, 60, 91–92, 95, 100, 104, 145, 147, 149–152, 236, 268, 270, 300, 313, 320, 321, 339, 349

tent/temple, 38–39, 52, 103, 198, 199, 216–222, 227–232
text-criticism, xiii, 3, 64, 76, 86, 94, 112–113, 118, 123–124, 126, 138, 153–154, 174–175, 197, 216–217, 219, 234–235, 247–248, 255–256, 267–268, 276, 287–288, 298, 305–306, 313–315, 327–328, 338–339, 352–353

wilderness, 112, 119–122, 125, 128, 130, 141, 147, 161, 199, 274, 290, 293, 310, 324
word of God, 131–135, 345